GEORGE BOWEN

of

BOMBAY

"It came into my mind that there was needed such a life of Paul as could not by any means be issued from any printing press. We wanted Paul himself, embodied, breathing, moving and repeating before our eyes the life described in the New Testament. One of us must become Paul himself." (Bowen's Journal, March 30, 1848).

"I want to have Christ walking about the streets of Bombay as He did about those of Jerusalem and living among this people as He did among the Jews. He was emphatically the friend of the people. They were His family, His home. . . . I want to have Jesus the missionary in my mind's eye continually. By the grace of God I may at length learn to love. Love overcometh everything. It will be a blessed day when I feel at home in these streets, and can linger in them without any desire save to continue preaching the Word." (Journal, June 29, 1848).

"Probably the holiest man in this world is he who retains keenly and abidingly the sense of his liability to sin. I desire to be that man." (Journal, May 7, 1849).

"I can never do too much for Him, that hath done so much for me as to make me a Christian. And I will labor to be like my Savior, by making humility lovely in the eyes of all men, and by following the merciful and meek example of my dear Jesus." (George Herbert, 1626).

GEORGE BOWEN

of

BOMBAY

MISSIONARY † SCHOLAR † MYSTIC † SAINT

by
ROBERT E. SPEER

Harvey Christian Publishers Inc.
449 Hackett Pike, Richmond, KY 40475
423-768-2297
HarveycpBooks@gmail.com
www.Harveycp.com

Copyright © 2021 Harvey Christian Publishers Inc.

ISBN: 978-1-932774-85-6

Cover design by R. Barry Tait
rbctait@gmail.com

Printed by
Lightning Source
La Vergne, TN 37086

Preface

In the sketch of Bowen's Life which appeared in the *Bombay Guardian* of February 11, 1888, six days after his death, Dr. J. E. Robinson, later Bishop Robinson of the Methodist Episcopal Church, wrote: "It is hoped that, later, a worthy biography of this great missionary will be duly furnished to the world. The only available, and in any sense complete, material for such a biography is in possession of the writer. It may therefore be stated that all productions or publications professing to be a life of Rev. George Bowen are entirely unauthorized and not to be regarded as reliable, however they may in general approximate the truth."

Bishop Robinson was never able to carry out his purpose and when fifteen years later he learned of my interest in Bowen he generously passed on to me his bound volumes of the *Bombay Guardian* from 1866, when Bowen revived it, to 1886, and also a copy of *Oluph,* the Scandinavian tragedy which Bowen wrote in his boyhood and which was published by Osborn and Buckingham of New York in 1836. Under date of July 24, 1902, Dr. Robinson wrote from Calcutta:

> Your letter of May 15th, inquiring about material for a biography of the late Rev. George Bowen, reached me in due course, and ought to have been answered sooner, but the death of a missionary colleague of our Mission in this city threw extra work on me, which has crowded me somewhat of late.
>
> I have always regarded it as a great pity that a biography of Mr. Bowen was not undertaken soon after his death. When in America in 1888, the year he died, I made some overtures in that direction to members of his family, and consulted with one or two old friends of his about it, but the way seemed blocked. It was made plain to me at the time that his correspondence in the hands of members of his family would not be available. I then let the matter drop. Now I am glad to learn that the idea of preparing a biography has come to you. There is no man whom I should be more pleased to cooperate with in any possible way than yourself, and anything I can do to help you I shall be pleased to do.
>
> The material belonging to George Bowen which came to me after his death was very meager. There were a great many very brief outlines of sermons and addresses that he had delivered, written on

the backs of envelopes, wrappers of newspapers and small pieces of paper. These were mixed up in an amazing fashion, and most of them are in my possession still. Two or three years ago I published a number of them in a few successive numbers of the *Indian Witness.*

Then there were two old MS. Journals, in tattered binding, written with poor ink, which had spread into the dampish paper, and was much faded. Out of these had been cut many pages which he had used in the "Reminiscences" which he published in successive volumes of the *Bombay Guardian* in the eighties. From these journals had been made many extracts which appeared in the same "Reminiscences." . . .

Then, I have some twenty annual volumes of the *Bombay Guardian* which I prize as a personal treasure, and these I would be quite willing to loan you for the purpose in view, if you desire. I presume you have access to the volumes of the *Bombay Guardian* in one or other of the New York libraries, but you are welcome to these in my possession at any time. I will box them up carefully and send them to you, if you wish to have them.

Besides the foregoing there is absolutely nothing else left by George Bowen in my possession. When proceeding to America in 1888 I took home with me and handed over to Mr. Bowen's sisters a packet of their letters which I had found among the papers he left. A number of other letters of a purely business character and of no importance in any way, some of them partly destroyed by white ants, I myself burned. They would have been of no use whatever for biographical purposes.

Bishop Robinson also gave every encouragement in suggesting sources of information. Many of those who knew Bowen had already died but I followed up all the living and gathered reminiscences from their affectionate memories. The work was undertaken none too soon as all of these have now passed on.

Among them all, the most helpful was the Rev. W. W. Atterbury, D. D., who had known the Bowen family from his early boyhood and who wrote a sketch of George for *The Church at Home and Abroad,* August, 1888, which was later published as a leaflet by the American Tract Society. Dr. Atterbury not only wrote out his own recollections but offered invaluable advice and gave me a volume of 433 pages in which, in a beautiful hand, Bowen's letters to his family, from July 28, 1847 to April 5, 1858, had been transcribed by one of his sisters. In addition Dr. Atterbury passed on to me 145 letters of Bowen to his father, mother and sisters, beginning with a letter of August 12, 1846, from Milford, Pa., to his mother, and ending with a letter of Jan. 19, 1883, from Bombay to his sister Catherine.

Others who are now almost all gone who supplied letters or their own recollections of Bowen were Lieut.-Col. G. W. Oldham, Bishop E. G. Andrews, Bishop J. M. Thoburn, the Rev. E. S. Hume, D. D., the Rev. J. Murray Mitchell, D. D., the Rev. E. A. B. Hallam, the Rev. L. B. Tedford, the Rev. and Mrs. Samuel J. Barrows, Mrs. W. R. Williams, Mr. S. E. Bridgman, the Rev. Theodore L. Cuyler, D. D., the Rev. Richard Burges, the Rev. J. S. Stone, D. D., Mr. Rutlonj, Mrs. William G. Greenwood, the Rev. H. W. Ballentine, D. D., Mrs. S. C. Dean, Mrs. Anna Ballantine Park, Mrs. L. D. Osborn, the Rev. Alfred S. L. Baker, the Rev. H. de St. Dalmas, the Rev. C. P. Hard, the Rev. Isaac F. Row, the Rev. J. G. Potter, Mrs. L. D. Hanscom. The American Board of Commissioners for Foreign Missions has kindly furnished copies of all of Bowen's letters to the Board, beginning with his letter of Dec. 12, 1846, offering himself for service as a foreign missionary, and ending with his letter of Dec. 13, 1865.

All of Bowen's classmates of the Class of 1847 at Union Theological Seminary, New York City, have long since passed away, but I had letters from two of them, Dr. Edwin A. Bulkley and Dr. Alfred H. Dashiell, and recollections of him from the Rev. Stephen Strong and the Rev. S. P. Leeds who were in the Seminary with him. But I learned most about his Seminary career from the Rev. William Aikman, D. D., of Bowen's Class of 1847, who also wrote one of the best memorial sketches, which appeared in *The Missionary Review of the World* for June, 1888.

While no life of Bowen has ever been issued, many references, some brief and some extensive, have appeared in missionary magazines and books. The following list embraces those which are of consequence: New York *Christian advocate,* 1888, p. 120, an estimate by Bishop Thoburn; *The Gospel in All Lands,* 1888, p. 135; Bishop William Taylor, *Four Years Campaign in India,* pp. 237, 389; Bishop William Taylor, *Story of My Life,* pp. 524 ff; Bishop William Taylor, *Ten Years of Self-Supporting Missions in India,* pp. 338, 433; Bliss, *Encyclopedia of Missions,* art. George Bowen; *Methodist Record,* 1888, Vol. 1; Bishop J. W. Thoburn, *India and Malaysia,* p. 429; *Missionary Review of the World,* 1889, pp 299, 300, art, "What is Success?", p. 520 f., art, by Dr. Robert Aikman, pp. 416-419; *Central Christian Advocate,* April 4, 1888, pp. 299, 300; *Central Christian Advocate,* April 4, 1888, art. By B. H. Badley, "A Saintly Worker Crowned"; *Indian Witness,* Feb. 18, 1888, art. By D. Osborne; *Forward,* Dec. 23, 1899, art, by the Rev. J. Sumner Stone, M. D., "George Bowen, 'the White Yogi.'"

Beyond every other indebtedness, however, I must acknowledge my obligation to an old friend, Mr. Henry W. Rankin of Northfield, Mass., step-son of Dr. Aikman. Mr. Rankin for many years was associated with Mr. D. L. Moody in his relation to the Northfield Schools and Conferences. No one else had made such a study of Bowen and his writings as Mr. Rankin had made, and he gave me letters of Bowen's to him, the only existent copy of Bowen's romance *The Pupil of Raphael* published by Wiley and Putnam, New York, in 1843, and copies of Bowen's *Life of Mohammed,* published in Bombay in 1856, of his various tracts and pamphlets and a sumptuously bound set of the files of the *Bombay Guardian* from 1879 to 1894, which contain in the years 1879 to 1883 the autobiography of Bowen from childhood through the year 1850, narrated in the third person, in 237 installments. It is to be regretted that Mr. Rankin was prevented by ill health from undertaking this biography himself and also from publishing those studies in metaphysics and philosophy which he had made through many years and which if published would have given him a high place in American scholarship. I cannot be too grateful for the stimulus and inspiration of Mr. Rankin's friendship over nearly half a century.

Bowen was not consistent in capitalizing pronouns referring to God or Christ but such capitalization has been used throughout this book. His Bible references have been kept, some in Arabic and some in Roman numerals.

The form of this volume has been chosen deliberately. It is a memoir of Bowen, comprising selections from his own diaries, letters, personal reminiscences and his writings in his paper, and from the testimonies and estimates of the men and women who knew him; so that the reader can make up his own opinion of the man and his views, and of his methods of life and work in India. It is not an attempt to appraise Bowen and his thoughts and ways. I conceive that the true business of a biographer is not to set forth his interpretation of the life with which he is dealing, whether it be in the way of approval or disapproval, but to present the material in such form and fullness as will enable each one who reads to form his own judgment for himself.

It is to be regretted that this memoir could not have been published many years ago while Bowen's name was still remembered. That was not possible, however, and it is appropriate that it should appear now on the fiftieth anniversary of Bowen's death.

Robert E. Speer.

Published writings of George Bowen:
Daily Meditations
Love Revealed
The Amens of Christ

Contents

   Preface 5
1. Family 10
2. Boyhood and Youth 19
3. Three Years Abroad 39
4. In New York City, 1840-1844 60
5. The Illumination of a Hopeless Love 92
6. His Conversion to Christianity 104
7. At Union Theological Seminary 114
8. Missionary Appointment 153
9. Voyage to India, 1847 165
10. Beginning Work in India 178
11. A Decisive Year, 1849 209
12. From 1850 to 1855 273
13. Ten Years of Independent Work, 1855—1865 306
14. The Bombay Guardian 340
15. Re-establishment of Relations with American Board,
    1865-1871 349
16. Association with the Methodist Church in India 361
17. Bowen as a Writer 406
18. Bowen's Correspondence with Henry W. Rankin 461
19. Closing Testimony 471
    Index 503

1. Family

Of George Bowen's ancestry beyond his father and mother he left no record and it has not been possible to trace any. He begins his autobiography with his birth in Middlebury, Vermont, on April 30, 1816. Who his grandparents were, where the family stock came from, how his parents came to be living in Middlebury, are questions regarding which even his intimate friends were able to supply no information. The Rev. John E. Bowen of Westport, New York, was believed to have prepared a very complete Bowen genealogy but every effort to trace this has failed. It is worth while mentioning that Mr. Charles W. Bowen, who was living in Providence, R. I., in 1909, supposed that George "was descended from the common ancestor of the family, Richard Bowen, who emigrated with his wife and seven children from Glammorganshire in Wales in 1640, settled first in Roxbury, Mass., and then with thirty-nine other families under the leadership of the Rev. Samuel Newman, in 1643, founded a new settlement in Massachusetts which they named 'Rehoboth': 'The Lord hath made room for us.' Richard had four sons, William, Obadiah, Richard and Thomas." Mr. Charles Bowen was descended from Obadiah but which of the four was George Bowen's ancestor he did not know.

Of Bowen's boyhood in New England we are likewise ignorant. Our full knowledge of him and of his remarkable life and of his extraordinary mind begins at the age of twelve after the removal of the family to New York City. His autobiography which appeared in installments in the *Bombay Guardian* in the years 1879-1883 begins, however, with one interesting reference to his father which relates to his childhood home. The "Reminiscences" open with an explanation of their publication:

> At different times, by different parties, the writer has been asked to put on record the principal facts in his life. The parties who have suggested this are persons in whose judgment he has a good deal of confidence. It was their belief that such an account would be to the honor of Him Whose grace has been so conspicuously shown in the life of the writer. He has always felt an almost insuperable repugnance to a compliance with this request. At the same time he had the feeling that it might be due to the Savior to show what he had been saved from, and by what process he had been brought to God. Under this conviction and at the same time influenced by the restraint to which reference has been made, he published in the *Bombay Guardian* in 1861, in blank verses, some thoughts on Isa. 42:4 in which were embodied the leading facts of

his life. But there was so much more buried than there was expressed in the lines, that we doubt if anybody penetrated their meaning. Under renewed solicitation we are trying to screw our courage up to the point of attempting an autobiographical sketch, and it may be that we shall take some of those lines as a basis of exposition. An excessive dislike of being made the subject of attention, is moderated by the thought that there is that in every life which, rightly stated, will serve to show forth the glory of Him Who leads and bears with His blind children in this world. For the sake of convenience the writer sometimes will drop the personal pronoun I, we, he, and will speak of himself as Homunculus or simply as H.

Some time ago there came into the hands of H. a tract entitled "The Two Fortunes," written by Cheyne Brady, some of the things mentioned in which could only apply to H. while the other particulars of the narrative were very wide indeed of the truth. Among other things the subject was said to have died a number of years ago in Bombay. How such a narrative came to be written, it would be difficult to say. Facts and romance are very prettily blended: but the existence of such a tract may perhaps furnish an additional reason for writing the proposed reminiscences. . . .

Homunculus was twenty-eight years of age when there came into his hand a letter that gave him some information about the first year of his life that surprised him greatly. It was a letter written a few months after his birth by his father to *his* father. The writer of this letter told how he had been recently led to give himself to the Lord and how happy he was in the consciousness of reconciliation with God, and he most earnestly and affectionately urged upon his father to seek the Lord and to lay hold on eternal life. Nothing in the world could have more surprised Homunculus than to read such a letter, he never having known his father as a religious man, having indeed known him for many years as an irreligious man. He subsequently ascertained that there had been a revival of religion in Middlebury the very year that he was born, that his father had been converted, was received to the church, but not having the sympathy of my mother in it, he had gradually grown cold and finally laid aside his profession of religion. But in the fervor of his first love he wrote this earnest letter to his aged father. That the letter was not received amiss appears from the fact of its preservation.

The father of H. had a literary turn and collected a very good library, which his children found the benefit of as they grew up. He was engaged in business, and gradually became more and more absorbed in it. He was more than once unfortunate in business but the effect of this seems to have been to stir him up to more thorough devotion to business pursuits. He was much attached to his family and for their sakes he was desirous of making a fortune. He had two sons and two daughters, all still living (in Jan. 1879), and none of them ever married. He was his eldest son, and he was particularly desirous that he should have the training necessary to make him a successful merchant.

Bowen's comment on his father as an irreligious man refers to the period of Bowen's young manhood before he went to India. Shortly after George left America the father returned fully and heartily to his Christian faith but lived only a few months in his recovered happiness and peace. On hearing of his death, George writes to Harriet from Bombay on May 7, 1848:

> I feel thankful that you had time to write me so fully as you have done, and that I have so many precious words and facts on which to feed my mind. Sorrow has its appetites and becomes worse than sorrow when there is no aliment for them. I have been deeply moved by these tidings. Christians are not made unhappy by the death of Christian friends; but I think they are more affected than impenitent persons are when these friends die. For the love of Christ develops in us one to another a strength of affection that is not common with the unrenewed. . . .I am led to praise God as often as I come to the throne of grace. Grace has so abounded towards our father, first in sparing him during 57 years of impenitence and ungodliness; next in accomplishing what is perhaps one of the rarest of God's works of mercy, namely the *genuine, unequivocal* conversion of a heart frosted by so many of this world's winters; and finally in giving him such a beautiful and happy exit from the world. . . .I love to look upon the scenes you describe and doubt not that we will all treasure them while life lasts.
>
> One prayer I have many times and with much fervor offered when at home to God, namely that there might be the destruction of all reserve in our family, and a fusion of all our hearts in Christ. Perhaps this prayer was in a measure fulfilled during my father's sickness; and that it was a season of greatly augmented love one to another. So I should judge from your letter. For this I thank God and shall thank Him. One of the first things to come into my mind was this, that if Frank had been home and if tidings had been received of my arrival, the trial might have been less to him. But it seemed so manifestly ordered that I could not but be reconciled. And there is not a word in your letter that exhibits anxiety as to my safety so that I feel rebuked for doubting your faith and his. Among his sayings repeated by you there is none that has any reference to myself. Of this I am rather glad. His affection for me seemed of old to be inordinate and I rejoice to see the evidence that Christ had become all in all to him. Of Christ he could speak, you say, but concerning everything else was apathetic. I praise God for giving him not only grace but opportunity to exhibit in his dying hours to others the spirit

that had been put in him. Might not many in our church of his age who have been spending nearly all their days in the courts of the Lord and who do yet seem to be groping in darkness, might not many such profit by considering the faith and joy of this believer brought between the 11 and 12 hours into the Kingdom. . . . Oh, why should Frank have gone away on another long voyage without having come to a knowledge of Christ! . . . Bro. Dodd wrote that Frank had gone on a six months' voyage to Demerara and Amsterdam. You wrote that he had gone on a 16 months' voyage to South Africa. I suppose he has sailed for South Africa via Demerara.

The next day, May 8, 1848, he wrote a long letter of affectionate comfort to his mother, sending her a draft for $60 saved from his modest salary of $40 a month, and expressing his conviction that it was his father's new found faith which had prolonged his life: "Dear Mother, what a cause of lifelong gratitude to the Savior we have for the grace bestowed upon him. I am overpowered when I think of it. Contrast him as he was on that sick bed and what he was during any portion of the long, long period preceding his conversion. His soul seems to have been feeding on Christ, satisfied with Christ, absorbed in Christ. This is the essential mark of true religion. What conceivable legacy of gold or silver could be so precious as the words and looks that gave index of the Redeemer's presence with him?"

There will be later references to Bowen's father but it may be well to summarize here what is known of the rest of the family. No one is living now who remembers them, but the late W. W. Atterbury, a greatly beloved minister of the Presbyterian Church who was secretary for some years of the American Tract Society, wrote out some years ago his boyhood recollections:

> My acquaintance with the Bowen family began when I was a boy of ten or twelve. They were near neighbors, in the city, of our family. The Bowen family consisted of the father, a wholesale merchant in comfortable circumstances; his wife, George, two daughters, Harriet and Catherine, and the youngest, Frank, a boy of my own age. George was especially intimate with one of my older brothers, John G. Atterbury, a graduate of Yale, practicing as a young lawyer in New York City. As I recollect, they were not at all a religious family, although the mother, a very kind and motherly lady, occasionally attended an Episcopal church in the neighborhood. After a year or two our acquaintance with the family was somewhat interrupted by our removal to another part of the city, and by my going to college at New Haven as well as by the removal of my brother, J. G. Atterbury, to Detroit where he established himself in the practice of law.

During this interval George Bowen spent three or four years in foreign travel, much of the time in Italy, and making a trip if I remember right, up the Nile, unusual in those days. The father met with business reverses and when George Bowen returned to this country, he lived rather a recluse life, devoting himself to literature, music, etc. The younger son, Frank, proving wild and unmanageable, they sent him to sea and little or nothing was heard of him for a long time.

In April, 1844, having finished my college studies, I was in the city, and as my father's family had just moved over to Paterson, N. J., I boarded for a short time in the same house in which the Bowen family boarded at that time. It was in West Washington Place.

In a conversation with Dr. Atterbury, in October, 1905, he gave a narration of Frank's adventurous career. "He was the renegade of the family," Dr. Atterbury said:

He was shipped off on a vessel by George before the great change came in George's life, and went to the Eastern seas. The family did not hear from him for six or eight years and then he turned up a true and handsome sailor. He had been engaged in navigating in the East Indies. When he returned, George had gone to India and all the family had been converted. It was a different atmosphere and Frank went off to the East again. George would hear from him occasionally. He was a gentleman and a gentleman's son, smooth-tongued and bright. Now and then a check would come from him anonymously through Bloodgood. Some years later Frank turned up again in New York. He had been commander of a coolie ship. In a mutiny he had hanged a number of the coolies on a yard arm. Then he was a slaver (the "Nightingale"?) during the Civil War. His vessel was seized on the coast of Africa by a U. S. cruiser. The captain (Gordon) and crew were taken off and brought to America and hanged. A man named Bowen was among these men, but it was not Frank. Frank had been on the vessel as First officer and had been left on board. One day word came that he was to be taken off his ship and removed to the frigate. That night a little boat drifted along under his window and he dropped in and got ashore. Some one had connived at his escape. He returned to the U. S. and attempted without avail to collect some money owed to him in Cuba as a result of his participation in the Patriot War.

Mr. B. B. Atterbury, the father of Mrs Kilaen Van Rensellaer, of Dr. B. C. Atterbury for twenty years a devoted medical missionary in Peking, China, and of the Rev. Anson P. Atterbury, D. D., for fifty-one years a useful minister in the Presbyterian Church, gave Frank a set of nautical instruments and he went out to the East again. He was next heard of on a ship of filibusters in Mexico in Walker's time. The ship was blockaded but Frank escaped, declaring that he knew all about those harbors and could not be caught. He returned to America again and hung about his sisters, who helped him.

One day Frank wrote to his sisters that he was going to kill himself. At their request Dr. Atterbury went to see him and candidly told Frank that this was the best thing he could do with himself. Dr. Atterbury took him to live with him for a time in Westchester County. On November 22, 1894, the gambler and adventurer died a decent death and was buried in Woodlawn.

Under date of Nov. 7, 1846, Bowen, then in Union Theological Seminary, wrote in his diary: "Last night, I dreamed of F. B. that he came into a room where I was with others, and announced that he had experienced a change of heart. I sat down today and wrote him about it." To this Bowen added in July, 1881, "This person died some years after, with a hope in Christ."

All of Frank's letters to the family in New York and to George in Bombay have disappeared except one brief note without date to his mother as he was sailing on the ship "Washington" from New York to San Francisco, a long letter to the family from San Francisco, July 29, 1850, and one to his sisters, who had been living at 235 West 38th Street, dated Rio de Janeiro, June 4, 1878, in handwriting much like George's.

The two sisters, younger than George and older than Frank, were Harriet and Catherine. The father died in the Spring of 1848 shortly after George's departure for India and the mother and sisters lived together until the mother's death in 1867. Harriet was engaged in teaching private pupils, among them Miss Anthony, who became Mrs. Frederick Vanderbilt. Mrs. W. R. Williams, whose husband was one of the ablest Baptist ministers in New York City, and who was the mother of Mr. Mornay Williams and the Rev. Leighton Williams, told me that Harriet was "small and slight and Frenchy, very bright and vivacious, a teacher in good families in New York and also in the Industrial School of Dr. Williams' Olivet Church." "Kate," according to Mrs. Williams, "was an ordinary awkward working woman." But she was for a time on the clerical staff of the Presbyterian Board of Foreign Missions, then located at 23 Centre Street. At the end of her life Mrs. Williams said Kate was working in a book-binding room. When Harriet's failing health prevented her from teaching, "the use of a house in Forsham," Dr. Atterbury wrote, "was given her by a friend where she and her sister passed their last days. A circle of her former pupils and friends raised a small sum annually for the support of the sisters by which they were enabled to live in comparative comfort."

The only letters from the sisters which it has been possible to find are a packet of letters to Mr. Rankin about Bowen's books, and two, one without date from Harriet to George, and the other dated August 3, 1888, from Catherine to Dr. John Gillespie of the Presbyterian Board of Foreign Missions, thanking him for some copies of the articles on Bowen by Dr. W. W. Atterbury in *The Church at Home and Abroad* for August, 1888. Bowen printed from time to time in the *Bombay Guardian* extracts from letters from "Theophila," who, I suspect, must have been Harriet. In her letter Harriet wrote:

> Dear George:
>
> I write now in answer to your astonishing communications. I have been deeply and variously affected by them. I am not quite certain of their divine truth. Holy men have sometimes been misled by their own imagination. It is possible (though judging from your character, not probable) that you are mistaken and that the fulfillment of those prophecies will not take place in our day. I greatly long to know your view now, a day, presented to your mind as the epoch of certain accomplished predictions (Matt. 24), having passed. I have sorrowed at the thought of what you must have suffered if disappointed in such sanguine hopes, of the blow which your faith must have received. I am daily hoping for a letter which may relieve my doubts.
>
> On the other hand I say to myself that there is nothing in Scripture which positively forbids the supposition that the last times are near. I recall to my mind that as the time was approaching for the fulfillment of prophecies about Christ's coming, revelations were made to holy persons such as Simeon, etc. At any rate, since I received your note I have been endeavoring to live and act as if its declarations were strictly true. I persuade myself that my time of probation, labor, prayer is confined to this summer. I began immediately to read the Apocalypse and spend some hours every day on this study. I ask God to reveal to me all that He is willing to reveal, and above all to make this part of Scripture available to my sanctification. I learned much concerning my own state and the state of Christians in the addresses to the Churches, and the sublime and awful scenes which follow have greatly interested and impressed me, without being accompanied by any persuasion of a particular time, yet as they pass before my mind I say to myself: My eyes shall shortly behold these things, perhaps this year—let me be ready.
>
> Since the receipt of your note I have felt that the Lord was teaching me and guiding me with more distinctness than for some time before, yet not with the distinctness which I desire. The day after reading your startling disclosures, Mr. Dickinson brought me the *Life of Mde. Guyon of Upham*. I have always had a prejudice against her character and a fear of this book, yet I now feel persuaded that I was providentially made acquainted with both at this time.

Harriet seems to have been living at this time at 296 Fourth Street. Kate's letter to Dr. Gillespie was dated, "Fordham, N. Y., Aug. 3 (1888)":

Family

Dear Dr. Gillespie:

Your note arrived (sic) in advance of the package. I thank you very much for your thoughtfulness in procuring these for me. Some of our friends and relatives will have an opportunity of seeing this article who would not otherwise do so. We are greatly pleased with the sketch itself and with the cut also. I am indebted to somebody for their numbers of *The Church*. Is it you? (I always use that name under protest. It is a misnomer. We do not propose to be *The* Church.) One interesting fact has not been mentioned so far in any of the accounts. George has always kept up his music. As a young man at home he was fond of sitting down to the piano improvising as he played. A letter recently received from India written by one of his friends and former pupils, says that he was accustomed to dine at her house one day in the week. If he came in before they were quite ready he would sit down to the piano and improvise in his old way and the sounds would be their greeting as they came up stairs.

A writer in an India paper—which I have not at hand to quote from—speaks of his social qualities. How in visiting a family he would interest himself in each member, in the cares of the parents, in their joys, in the games and plays of the children. I remember years ago hearing some one speak of the narrative he would compose for the entertainment of her children. As a young man before his conversion he was exceedingly reserved at home, these social characteristics not being natural to him.

I am feeling much better than I did. Somewhat like myself, which I have not for the last six months. As I become stronger I feel that I would like some object for my days. When I was feeling so miserable I was content to do whatever the fancy of the moment dictated. Now I begin to feel that I want something that must be done.

Yours very truly,
C. Bowen.

Catherine died on June 3, 1894 and Harriet in Fordham in January, 1905. The two sisters were buried in the same grave with Frank in grave number 49, Range 126, Lot A, Woodlawn Cemetery.

Of his mother and father, Bowen writes in his notebook:

May 16, 1849. My mother's birthday, 65 years. How much of my mother there is in me. A troublesome volatility of mind, erratic, incontrollable, a flightiness, that must give the Spirit of God more to do to accomplish any end in my mind, I think than in the mind of any other. I never go through with one idea without going half over the universe in a hundred different directions. It is like taking a serpent for a walking stick; a new miracle is needed every moment. I have inherited this from my mother; and we both have reason to adore the patience of our Lord, Who has contrived to write His laws somewhat in the shifting sands, the rippling water of our hearts. The use of the pen and habits of study have been a great advantage to me, aiding me to resist this dispersive tendency of my mind. Perhaps the Spirit of God will make the remainder of this to praise Him in some way. My mother, it is not to be denied, was naturally endowed by God with some singularly good qualities. The best is: a keen sense of responsibility. The idea of a duty would never let her rest. What contributed to the preservation of this was perhaps her ignorance of duty. If she had had any proper notion of what she ought to do, her conscience would probably have refused to perform its office; but with the meager view she had thereof, her sense of obligation was enabled to retain its edge. I think that my sisters and myself have inherited much of this. I think that before my conversion I had a singularly keen sense of duty, though accompanied with utter blindness as to what constituted duty. My mother possessed naturally also a very remarkable disposition to think of the wants of others, and alleviate them. There was nothing in it of genuine Christian love; for no person was so much irritated by ingratitude; there was no reference to God in it all, but she was continually seeking to please others. If their own tastes differed from hers, she made no difference; but gave what pleased herself, so that her kindnesses were often but little appreciated. She never could find enjoyment in anything, while she thought that others were wanting it.

May 17. Today my father's birthday. My father's influence upon me, was far less than my mother's, I think. I cannot remember a time when my mother seemed to have affection for him; she seemed to be unwilling that he should have the affection and confidence of his children. She had great sensitiveness, continually imagining that she was slighted. The natural consequence was that she was slighted. No language can tell the distress caused by this temper of hers. Oh, the unhappiness of that family for the last fifteen years of our natural state. What combative and repulsive elements! Glory to the cross by which we were made one.

Bowen's diary for Dec. 16, 1866, speaks of four cousins, children of a brother of his father: "My cousin, Eugenia Bowen, is a nun in a convent at Pittsburgh and has been there many years. West Bowen, it is supposed, died in the war. Seymour Bowen is studying for priest's orders, Roman Catholic. Blanche and her husband, all the family, I believe, are R. C., the fruit of the father's infidelity. What a contrast between the dealing of God with that family and with our family!"

2. Boyhood and Youth

In the second installment of his *"Reminiscences"* published in the *Bombay Guardian* of Jan.18, 1879, Bowen gives an account of his boyhood from twelve to seventeen, as remembered and interpreted after half a century. He is speaking of himself as "Homunculus" or more simply, as "H":

> When H. was twelve years of age his father gave him a dispensation from school life and took him into his own counting room. He had then recently gone into business with his step-son for the importation of English dry-goods. The only schooling H. had was before that time. H. was disposed to think in after years that he should have been left at school for some years more; but possibly it was for the best. It often happens in this world that the very abundance of our opportunities hinders us from valuing them and improving them. H. carried with him the feeling that he had much to learn, and a desire to improve such time as he could command in studying.
>
> He was very fond of reading and as he got time devoured the books that were in his father's library. Though so many years have gone by, he has a distinct recollection of most of those books. There was Plutarch in eight volumes and he can remember a particular place in the upper back stairs of the house, 171 Green St., where in the summer evenings he would pore over the fascinating sketches of illustrious Romans and Greeks making each his idol as he read about him. There was Rollin's *Ancient History* and Xenophon's *Cyropedia.* This last book exercised a great influence over him and deeply impressed his youthful mind with the conviction that a man who wanted to be distinguished among men should practice a rigid discipline like that of the youthful Cyrus, learning to endure hardness and keeping his appetites in good subjection. There was Hume's history and he remembers that when he was still a schoolboy, the colored cook, a stout woman, Roxana Worthington, by name, who was for many years in the family and regarded herself as a corporate member of the same, who did not know how to read but was very desirous of finding out what had been going on in the world before she made her appearance, used to bribe him to come to read to her out of Rollin or out of Hume, at night, when her work was done.
>
> H's reading was by no means confined to history; his appetite was somewhat omnivorous; the *Arabian Nights* had a charm for him; so had

Scott's novels, but above all Shakespeare. Shakespeare was a passion with him for many years. For several years after he had been made a clerk, he would in the daytime be running to the Exchange or Post Office or Custom House or perhaps be in the hold of a Liverpool ship hunting up the boxes and bales consigned to the house and expediting their landing, or at the store attending to them, or in the office copying letters, or keeping books or, in slack times, up in the garret reading some favorite book; in the evening he would be at Signor Da Ponte's learning French, Italian or Spanish, or at home reading Shakespeare or some other book.

When about fourteen he took lessons on the piano from a burly Englishman but not fancying his strictness he left off taking lessons and went on by himself. A great passion for music took possession of him when about sixteen, when the Italian Opera Company came to New York, and for a dozen years there was hardly anything he more cared for than Italian Operatic music.

The following books are still remembered as in the home library, all of which in turn occupied the attention of H. and of his elder sister, between whom a great attachment existed, with great similarity of tastes: Nicolson's Cyclopedia, *Memoir of Duc de Sully,* Washington Irving, Good's *Book of Nature,* Locke *On the Understanding,* Dugald Stewart, Walter Scott, *Memoirs of Las Casas* (St. Helena), Miss Edgeworth, Telemachus, Saurin's *Sermons,* Henry's Commentary, Lemprieve, Lavoisne's Atlas, *Scottish Chiefs,* Goldsmith, etc, to which were added many books in the French, Italian and German as these languages were successively studied. He also had the privilege of getting books from the Clinton Hall Library, afterwards the Mercantile Library.

Homunculus does not remember that he was ever in those days or at any time, spoken to on the subject of religion by his parents. There was no family prayer and perhaps not any in private. Still the family had a pew in St. Thomas' Church (Episcopal) and doubtless thought itself as religious as its neighbors. H. can vaguely recall that once from Saturday night to Monday morning he had some uneasiness on the subject of religion; but it passed away.

At the age of seventeen H. fancied that he was intended by nature to shine in the world as an author. He thought it was his mission to write some tragedies that would astonish the world by their marks of genius. In the course of a year or two he wrote three or four. One of these was entitled *Henry IV of Germany,* another was Scandinavian in its name and characters, another was founded on something in Sismondi's *History of the Italian Republics.* Two at least were published, but received no attention from the critics, a thing that was at the time very surprising to the author and terribly galling. Instead of profiting by this rebuke, H. determined that he would yet conquer the attention of men. H. was in those days a great dreamer but his dreams were of a kind that stimulated him to exertion. He was intoxicated with conceit but knew how to veil this self-admiration so as to appear to his acquaintances a modest, sober-minded youth, with better tastes than the generality of young men. He was thought to be exceptionally moral, but yet would not for all the world have consented that certain facts should be divulged to man. We do not divulge them, and that for the reason that we do not think it would be to the glory of God or the good of any. H. had from his mother, however, a deep sense of obligation and an inability to tolerate any neglect of it, a horror of everything mean, at the same time his conceptions of the true standard were vague enough.

An entry in his journal in Switzerland in 1836 reveals the work which he had been doing in his ambition to produce a great drama: "I have written one miserable indiction, shocking in taste, nothing to plot, nineteen months ago; 2d, another, verbiage, verbiage, but speaking an ardent passion for liberty; 3d, another, where thoughts were spun out into lines, thirteen months ago. 4th, another, where thoughts were concentrated into adjectives, every line was laborious to read as to write, ten months ago. 5th, another, good seven months ago. These are the labor of a year, but what a year!"

The tragedies to which Bowen refers have disappeared save for the Scandinavian tragedy, *Oluph,* which was published in New York in 1836 when Bowen was twenty, although he says it was written when he was a year or two younger. It is a remarkable production for a boy in his teens. The scenes with one exception are in Nadaros, the ancient capital of Norway and the seat of the Earls of Drontheim. The exceptional scene is laid upon an island not distant. The time is the tenth century. The personae are Oluph and Hakon, princes of Norway, Sigurd, Earl of Drontheim, and his three sons, Asgilda, Queen of Norway, Alsifa, daughter of Sigurd, nobles and others. Hakon tricks Oluph into the unwitting murder of their father. Oluph vows to slay the murderer. When he discovers the truth he carries out his vow by suicide, after Hakon's perfidy has been discovered and punished. The tragedy is interwoven by the love of Oluph and Alsifa and the jealous hate of Guldhardt for Oluph and his conspiracy with Hakon. The play is conceived with extraordinary skill and wrought out in feeling and in language with real power. The author had worked himself fully into the Norse atmosphere of the time which he is depicting and his tragedy is superior to much of the American literature of his day.

In the section of his "Reminiscences 56", published in the *Bombay Guardian,* Jan. 21, 1880, Bowen wrote of *Oluph* as follows:

> Writing these reminiscences of years gone by, we thought we would like to see again some of those things which Homunculus wrote and published in youth. A friend in America to whom this desire was expressed, having a copy of *Oluph, a tragedy,* published in 1836, lately forwarded it and we have thus had an opportunity of reading it again after an interval of thirty-five years. It is a book of 105 pp., 12mo. The title page has only the title of the book, and even if the book had more merit than it has it would have been a wonder if it had not fallen stillborn from the press. The writer had the idea that if it could not of itself arrest the attention of the public, it mattered little what became of it. If it had borne his name, a considerable circle of his friends would probably have interested themselves in it. We are not aware that it ever received the slightest notice from critics or anybody else. People are not disposed to lay siege to 105 pages of blank verse, without some prior assurance that their pains will be rewarded. We cannot conscientiously say that there is anything here to reward the pains of the reader. The versification is elaborate rather than flowing, and often stiff and strained if not pedantic. The plot exhibits some ingenuity.
>
> The scene is in Norway before the old Scandinavian religion had passed away. Oluph, the principal person, heir to the throne, is away fighting an enemy who had invaded the land. He is victorious. Returning, he obeys a command given by his father, and extirpates some bands of robbers who have been infesting the land. Reaching the capital he is surprised to learn that the king had gone forth to meet him, and is unable to account for the fact that he did not fall in with him. Soon the murdered body of the king is found lying upon the most conspicuous altar of the capital. His death is a mystery upon which all the interest of the tragedy turns. Oluph succeeds to the throne; but he has a step-mother and a step-brother, who spread a rumor that Oluph caused the death of his father. It is unnecessary to trace the plot through the various details of the five acts. Oluph had bound himself by a solemn oath to take the life of the one who had caused the death of his father. It turns out at length that it was really Oluph who had taken the life of his father without knowing it. The old man had been taken captive by the robbers and was with them in their hiding-place when Oluph and his troops fell upon them and put them to the sword. In fulfillment of his vow Oluph immolates himself. We give one scene from this play, asking pardon of our readers, if any of them grudge the space thus taken up.

Act 4, Scene 3. *An island; rugged and obscure spot thereon; in the back ground a huge rock, covered with strange characters. A fire. Thunder.*

Thorstein.
Not vainly have I toiled. There goeth abroad
The soul of slaughter and disease and crime;
Peace is effrayed, and in the quietest house
Starts out the brother's word; in still repose
His sire the son doth stifle; noiseless creeps
The wife with horrid steel, while fondled youth
Drops poison in the cup; unconsciously
With villainy hand in hand virtue conspires.
These things fore-doomed, foreknown, come now to pass.
Thrones tremble; kings, more wretched than the worst,
Who pitiably buy life, cry out on death.
'Tis awful, but 'tis gladsome to that spirit
Which is beyond the nature of these base.
What moves this way? The step of royalty;
She comes; a nature like mine own, not boasting
A kindred feeling with the multitudes.

Enter *Asgilda.*
High-born, all hail!
Asgilda. O prince of mysteries,
Who thriddest these dark narrows of dread fate,
Whose darkness only we behold and shake—
Give me the knowledge that I crave.
Thorstein. I know
The longing that hath led thee; thy desire
Shall meet my smile. But hither comes another
Bent to the same demand. Once to the twain
Answer shall spoken be.
Asgilda. Who is that other?
Thorstein. Wait silently.
Asgilda. Tell me; your might is great,
But I have aided potently ere now
The power whose speech I pant for; say.
Thorstein. Behold! (*Asgilda* retires).

Enter *Oluph*
Oluph. I know thee to be Thorstein; chieftaincy
And high attainment in the art, is writ
On the bold brow of thee. 'Tis whom I seek.

Thorstein. Welcome, thou sovereign of an hour, and hail!
Oluph. By mysteries and darkness, by yon sky
That the wild thunder troubles, by the hour
That aids you in your searchings, by all things
Which minister the power that ye do vaunt
And by the light within you, and the Heaven
To which that light belongs to quench or nourish,
Tell me what hand unhallowed murdered him
From whom I sprung.
Thorstein. And when you hear his name—
Oluph. Instruct me where he dwelleth.
Thorstein. Would ye slay?
Oluph. Swift as the wind, more eager than the flame I'd be upon him.
Thorstein. Then avoid this place,
Get to some cave and crouch from treacherous day
And man's discovering mind; forego all joys
That wait on motion and companionship;
E'en in the tomb impenetrable seek
The ignorance of death; for this to know
Which ye demand of us is poison's worst.
Oluph. Answer to me, else may your dangerous craft,
Your sorcerous arts be ruin on your head.
Thorstein. Be wise, O Prince.
Oluph. Reply to me, O wizard.
Else I put forth mine own supremacy
And sweep thee and thy partners from the land;
Ay, every vestige of the art uproot
In these dominions, and with foul disgrace
Pursue your name.
Thorstein. Beware mine ire, rash prince.
Oluph. I dare it and defy thee to make known
This murderer of a king.
Thorstein. Brave not your fate.
Oluph. Thine own is sorely periled.
Thorstein. Hearken, tremble.
It was your hand that slew your royal parent.
Oluph. Miscreant, is this thy art?
Thorstein. Hence with thy sword!
One word of mine can hurl thee in the waters,
Never to appear.

Oluph. Time is misspent.
But I once more thy boasted knowledge task.
Where is the old companion of my sire
Who journeyed with him in his last outgoing?
Thorstein. E'en in your place Einstein with you dwells;
Hourly he meets your eye and from his tongue
Drops ever in your ear his wisest knowledge.
Oluph. I leave thee; bootless is all question held
With arrogating ignorance like thine.
Fool, do my subjects deign to give thee fame,
By thy unmeaning accents to be swayed,
Before thee as a prophet to bow down?
Imposter, I depart from thee, but shall
These thy revilings well remember.
Thorstein. Prince,
Arrest thee; thou shalt hear truth unbesought
Detested by thy subjects, on the field
Betrayed, o'erthrown by foreign foemen, driven
From company of goodness, most debased,
Thy only death-hour shall be happiness.
Oluph. False prophet, hast thou ended?
Thorstein. Ay, (*Exit Oluph*)
Lady, thou hast been answered.
Asgilda. His the deed?
Terrible gods, how may this be believed?
Thorstein. It shall not be gainsaid. He is the doer.
Asgilda. I'd sell the afterworld to know this true.
Thorstein. Why suffer doubt? Our part partakes thy faith.
If still uncertain, Einstein will approve.
Asgilda. It is the dearest, best beloved word
Dropped ever on mine ear. Farewell! My guards
Wait for me restless. Thanks for your impartments.

At the age of eighteen Bowen withdrew from his father's business. His journal written at the time explains his course:

Oct. 15, 1834. I began to conceive a dislike for business upon my return to the city. And very good reasons conspired to produce this dislike. I had been seven years in a store at the age when boys are usually at school improving their minds. At twelve years of age I entered the store, knowing nothing, literally nothing. I had but few opportunities to improve myself while in business, but by these few I believe I profited. I studied French and Italian and read considerable history. But when I found myself at the age of eighteen unacquainted with Latin and a hundred other things, I began to perceive the injustice done me by taking me from school at so early an age, and to experience a distaste for business and a desire for study. Unable to satisfy this, I felt very miserable, became morose in my temper when in company, and pensive and melancholy when alone. I knew that my father's chief desire was to see me a merchant but I resolved to satisfy in some way my taste for study, and accordingly on Monday, Oct. 13, about 12 o'clock, perceiving that my father was alone in his counting room, I followed the bent of a sudden resolution and addressed him thus: "Sir, I am going to make a proposition to you which I hope you will consider favorably. I have been in the store constantly for seven years at an age when boys are at school. I consequently find myself without the knowledge essential to a young man, and moreover I have not the taste for business I ought to have. Therefore I wish you to let me devote a year to study. At the end of that time I will have much improved myself, and moreover I will have a zeal for business."

"Well now, George," he replied, a pause succeeding each word, "if you shall leave the store for any length of time, you will never be fit for business, and will never be willing to return to it." He added something about the manner in which he first got along in the world, by perseverance and assiduous attention to business, and by devoting his leisure moments to study.

"But I have no time to read and can only pursue one study at a time. And as for losing a taste for business, my taste will certainly not be increased by my continuing here. I shall conceive an utter disgust for it and will not think myself obliged to pay any attention to it. Besides, Sir, think how young I was when I left school. Boys usually. . . ." Here I checked myself luckily; I should have certainly provoked him, had I spoken my sense of the injustice. He would probably have answered in a severe manner, and I should not have gained my point.

He continued, "This interferes with all my intended arrangements; it was my intention to retire from business in a couple of years and to have given you a capital wherewith to begin business. But now your place will be occupied by some other person and at the end of a year you will be much less fit for business than you now are. Now you are not so good a clerk as you were in 1829."

"I know it and that is my argument for leaving the store, but if I leave I will come back with the intention of making myself a good merchant, and certainly I have no desire to follow any profession. I feel that I must make my living by this means."

Boyhood and Youth

"Well," he replied, "I am willing that you should leave but not to return again. You must enter some other counting room when you get through your studies." I replied that I would willingly do that. He then told me that I might leave.

"I am much obliged to you," I answered.

"No, you are not," he said, "I do not wish to control you in your desires." And then ended this conversation and with it my mercantile life.

There followed in his journal this memorandum:

> Today I become a student. To learn and do the following things I will devote a year: the Latin language, Greek, German, Spanish, Mathematics, Chemistry, Astronomy, Philosophy, a perfect knowledge of history from the birth of Noah to the death of Napoleon. To improve myself in French and Italian, acquire a perfect knowledge of English grammar, and read all the celebrated writers on natural and mental philosophy.

Forty-five years later Bowen wrote in comment on this period of his life and on these entries in his boyhood journal:

> How superlatively ridiculous were these resolutions. To H's inexperience it seemed as though a year all to oneself was sufficient to master all these branches. He gradually came to see that it was neither necessary nor desirable that a man should be a proficient in all departments of knowledge, and that the part of wisdom was to find out what would be of special use in the line of life likely to be followed by him, and give himself to the acquisition of these. Desultoriness continued, however, for some years to be a serious impediment to his progress. The love of study was also counterbalanced by the love of composition.
>
> Homunculus thinks it proper to say that while he cannot justify the reproach cast by the youth upon his father, and while he is convinced that in the case of multitudes who enjoy collegiate advantages, the gain is not in proportion to the cost, yet he is conscious that in all probability his mind would at this day be greatly better in many respects if it had had the drilling and disciplining available in schools. It is not good for a young man, even when there is a taste for study and for the appreciation of the value of time, to have unrestricted liberty as regards the occupation of his time. To this day the writer is troubled with an imaginativeness and flightiness that allow the mind in reading a single sentence, or hearing one, to go with a hop, skip and a jump from the earth to Jupiter, to the sun and to Sirius, and get back before the sentence is finished. Like an ant or a dog, that, in going from one point to another makes a diversion at every step to the right or to the left, but manages to reach the terminus none the less.

Mention has been made of a sister between whom and H. existed a great similarity of tastes. She was a person of remarkable mental endowments, without anything of H.'s self-sufficiency. Naturally shrinking and retiring, or made so by her extreme sensitiveness, she yet had a wonderful power of characterizing others and after making the acquaintance of anybody could not rest until she had made a pen sketch of the individual. If she paid a visit in another city, her letters would furnish a portrait gallery of the people she met there. She had probably a greater influence on H. than any other person and had mainly to do with the formation of his tastes though without any such aim on her part. Remembering his attachment to her, H. is constrained to notice also his failures with regard to other members of the family. His manner towards them was marked by reserve and want of confidence, especially towards his father, though he himself was always treated with kindness. This must have caused pain much more than he allowed himself to inquire. To this day the bitterness of self-reproach is awakened by the recollection of it. If anything H. was treated with too great indulgence and forbearance. Happy the family when there is entire freedom of intercourse between all the members, and perfect freedom from reserve; where love and not self-attention is in the ascendant.

Something more of Bowen's boyhood mind in this eighteenth year of his age is indicated in his journal of August, 1834, where he indulges in a vehement protest against anything like a restraint upon liberty of thought and action:

In what country would they dare to impede a man traveling on Sunday, and imprison him till the succeeding day? Such has been done in Connecticut. I cannot express the indignation I feel for such bigots. They have their (Bible) societies in almost every place in the United States. They have done some good to the people in a moral respect; in temperance; but does this privilege them to revile and insult every respectable man who is not totally abstemious? I have heard them express such sentiments as these: "O for a life whose only occupations should be prayer and praise to Thee O God!" Now I consider it an insult to the divine Creator to contemn all the powers and capabilities, intellectual and physical, that He has given us, wherewith to enjoy or employ ourselves in this world. I am reading Volney's *Ruines,* by which I am completely fascinated. During the last three or four months Reason has been assiduously at work in my mind and has thrown out a considerable quantity of rubbish formerly existing there. A pretty large space having been cleared, Volney comes to occupy it. This is just the work I desired to read and what pleasure do I experience in reading his wonderful and profound reasoning.

Two incidents will suffice to indicate the high strung emotionalism of Bowen's youthful period. Bowen related these in the eighth installment of his "Reminiscences" in the *Bombay Guardian* of March 1, 1879:

> At one time there was a great deal of excitement in the United States and certain acts of the president (Andrew Jackson) appeared to some to indicate a desire on his part to make himself independent of the constitutional checks. H., then about sixteen, embraced this conviction and did not know what to do to relieve his bosom of the perilous stuff with which it was surcharged. He wrote an anonymous letter to the President, warning him that if he persisted in his course, there were those who deemed it their duty to save the country by shooting him (or something to that effect). A few days after he had committed his letter to the post, what was his astonishment to see it in print, on one of the bulletins in Wall Street. The President had had it published. Before posting the letter, he had shown the superscription to a friend, and this friend now suspected him of having written the letter that the President had made public. It was a good thing for H. that this friend did not communicate his suspicions to others. . . . Some time after, a young man, a mere lad, the son of the Secretary of the Navy, a midshipman on board a man-of-war, was hung at the yard arm judicially, for having written some foolish memoranda breathing a spirit of mutiny towards the commander of the vessel.

Bowen said this experience of his communication to the President cured him "forever of the desire to write anonymous letters. So far as he can remember it was the first and last that he ever wrote."

The other incident was the contemplation of a possible murder. For a time he carried "about with him a loaded pistol. He had a feeling of intense vindictiveness towards a certain person and persuaded himself that it would be a service rendered to society, if he were put out of the way. But then it would be a very unpleasant thing and very unbecoming to be accused of homicide. If the thing could have been brought about without compromising himself or his friends in any way, very well. But how could that be? H. did not know; but thought that it was as well to be prepared if such an opportunity should be thrown in his way."

In his "Reminiscences" Bowen recorded two other experiences of his youth, one of which cut deeper in his inner life than any he had as yet known, while the other was illustrative of his type of acquaintanceships and of his mental attitude. His literary efforts had met with disappointment from which he had suffered keenly. He was now still more deeply wounded by "an impeachment of his father's integrity. A consignment of goods of a new fabric had been received from England and there was a question with regard to one of the materials that entered into the composition of it whether (if we remember rightly) it was cotton or worsted. Upon this depended the amount of duty payable. It was the custom to order one package of every sort of goods to be sent to the Custom-House to be examined; the appraiser then came to the store and satisfied himself with respect to the rest. Beforehand, H's father had shown a sample of the goods to the appraiser and had been guided by him in making out the entry, at the lower rate of duty. Some other merchant received a similar consignment, and upon that the higher duty was paid. This discrepancy was afterwards discovered, and the Customs authorities, unwilling perhaps to let it appear that there had been any mistake on their part, accused the importer who had paid the lower duty of having used deception.

"Representations which H. at the time attributed to the malice of an individual were made that had the effect of causing the Collector of Customs to seize all the goods in the establishment and remove them to the Custom-House to be anew appraised. They were proved to have been correctly entered and were restored; only the particular consignment that was wrong, was seized." This transaction caused Bowen "the profoundest grief he had even known, for it touched him where he was most acutely sensitive."

The other experience illustrated Bowen's interests and associations. He was devoted to Italy and the opera. Among his acquaintances was the actor Pietro Maroncelli, a friend of Silvio Pellico, the author of *I misi frigioni*. Maroncelli and Pellico were condemned "to imprisonment for life for conspiring to liberate Italy from the Austrian yoke. Maroncelli was imprisoned for many years in the fortress of Spielburg, and there underwent the amputation of his leg. After suffering for a term of years, he was pardoned and liberated, married a German lady who connected herself with an Italian operatic company and then came to New York. . . . H's sister and himself thought the world of Maroncelli, who was an enthusiast in the cause of Italian liberty, music and literature. Sga. Maroncelli left the stage and supported herself by teaching music. Maroncelli taught languages. A little girl was born to them whom they called Sylvia, and H. was asked to act as the representative of Sylvia Pellico as godfather for the child, baptized by a Roman Catholic priest. H. complied for the oddity of the thing, though his skeptical sentiments were known."

Bowen's skepticism began at the age of seventeen and lasted until his conversion at the age of twenty-eight in 1844. In the fifth installment of his "Reminiscences" in the *Bombay Guardian* of Feb. 8, 1879, he gives an account of his early religious attitudes:

> When seventeen years of age, H. became a skeptic, or rather a disbeliever. A skeptic is one who doubts the truth of revealed religion. H. had scarcely begun to doubt, before he made up his mind that there

was no such thing as revealed religion, and that it was absurd to imagine that there was such a thing. He became charmed by the idea that he was making a discovery hidden from the common people, and the making of which was evidence of an understanding emancipated from the shackles of prejudice. It was evident to him that the mass of Christians received the Bible traditionally, without any enquiry as to its real claims, and he willingly adopted the opinion that it was unsustained by evidence. One of the authors that he delighted in was Gibbon. He was charmed with the dignity and suggestiveness of his style. The chapter in which that author undertakes to account for the spread of Christianity powerfully arrested his attention. He easily persuaded himself that the causes assigned by Gibbon were really adequate to explain its wonderful success. Did H. refer the matter to some one better acquainted than himself with the claims of the Gospel? Did he turn to those authors who exhibit the grounds on which its claim to be accepted as from God rests? Nothing of the kind. He did not mention his doubts to an experienced Christian. He ventilated them to youthful companions who would think his skeptical remarks to be a proof of his superior discernment. He paid a visit that same year to an uncle living in another town. What the influence of this uncle was, may be gathered from the following extract from a journal kept at the time:

"Uncle R. is a great man. He, with me, or rather I, with him, make reason my God. He is superior to the common prejudices and predilections of the day. He is no sectarian. We have no knowledge other than this world, except the innate consciousness of a God and a future existence. This consciousness may be perhaps the hope of immortality which man finds necessary to his happiness. The Bible is but tradition and I do not think it inspired. The first part of the Bible is entitled to no consideration, then, on the point of fact. And the Testaments, too, that treats of the man Christ Jesus whose religion cost more blood than any or perhaps every other religion in the world.

"Look at the Spaniards at their first landing in this country. They rushed into the capital of the Indians; they went into the temples and when they saw men kneeling to the image of the sun, they exclaimed, 'Horrible idolatry,' seized a couple of pieces of wood, placed them crossways, and commenced the work of massacre and destruction of the poor and defenseless Indians crying out, 'Kneel to the image of the All-merciful religion of Jesus Christ.' Hundreds of thousands died for their idolatry. And their religion was infinitely more plausible and reasonable than that of the worshippers of the cross. And this is but a unit in the immense destruction committed by them. The horrible calamities of the dark ages may all be attributed to this religion. The bigotry which destroyed the valuable writings of profane authors and only handed down their own obscure traditions, written by the priests for their own emolument, still pervades this religion in this enlightened age.

"My uncle Richard has thought upon all this and he observes, nature has implanted in our breasts the great moral principle of reason. This tells us that this world must have had a creator; and moreover that morality is the greatest perfection to which man can arrive; and that moral perfection is sufficient for our happiness in this world and the next. You may believe in one God or a dozen; in a true God or a fictitious one; the perfection of morality is all-requisite and all-sufficient. For it is ridiculous to suppose that God whom reason tells us to be a great and good being, should judge us by the rectitude or incorrectness of our creed. If there is such a thing as a true creed, it cannot possibly bear the comparative ratio of one to a thousand others. Therefore to say that a thousand to one of us will be punished, for disbelief in the true God, is preposterous. Reason and morality should be the foundation and the substance of our life and happiness." July 1834.

This will suffice to show where H. was at the time in question, and where he continued for many years. We are sorry to say that many whose name and intellectuality should have saved them from such crudities, have expressed themselves very much after the same fashion. It did not come into the mind of H. to search the Scriptures, to find out how far the religion which had wrought such desolations in the earth, was really the religion of the Bible.

A very cursory examination would have shown him that the religion of Christ condemns nothing more emphatically than the use of violence in its propagation, and that no one should really embrace it except from conviction and cordial reception. H. was an ardent republican and would have been very much disgusted if any one had brought forward the horrors of the Reign of Terror to show that republicanism tended to the destruction of society. In the early days of his unbelief he sometimes used this argument to show that the existence of a Creator could not be affirmed, a posteriori: If we say that a world so wonderful and glorious as this is, must have had a creator, the difficulty is only removed one step back; for the Creator must be more wonderful than his works and by the same reasoning himself demands a Creator and this one another. But although this argument was not answered by others, he soon saw that it was fallacious. For the Being demanded by a world like this is One who is omnipotent, omniscient, and self-existent; in such a Being there is nothing to indicate an outside Designer and an argument founded on the evidences of design in creation could have no application to him. He is sufficient unto Himself which the world of our senses is certainly not.

So H. ceased to speak against the existence of a God, but denied that God had given any revelation of Himself. In the course of the following year or two, he read the works of Volney, Voltaire, Shelley, Hume, Bayle and became thoroughly settled in his unbelief. He cannot remember that at any time for a period of eleven years his mind was once shaken in its conviction that there was no such thing as a revelation, and that a belief in the possibility of the supernatural was ridiculous. It was more or less of a mystery to him how Christians could be so simple as to cling, in an enlightened age like this, to the idea of an inspired revelation. He rather pitied them for their simplicity, but at the same time thought that as they derived a certain measure of peace from their religion, and had not sufficient strength of mind to get along without it, it was not worth while to make war upon their convictions.

In the *Bombay Guardian* in 1861, in the issues Oct. 26 to Dec. 28, Bowen printed a metrical account of his religious experience. No copy survives, but the character of this production and its interpretation of his youthful skepticism are sufficiently indicated in the quotation from it and comment on it in "Reminiscences 6" in the *Guardian* of Feb. 15, 1879:

> In unsuspected silence of the heart.
> This creed wrought wondrously, all other faiths
> Contemningly dismissing; most of all
> The faith that draws the sinner to the blood
> Once shed on Calvary. Was it not enough
> That Jews and Gentiles slew with wicked hands
> The Prince of Life, that men should dare, with spears,
> Aim from the grave uprising to waylay,
> And strive to murder thus the hopes of man
> Ascending with him? Gibbon, Hume, Voltaire,
> With Volney and like-minded many, thus
> Conspiring, recognition glad from him
> —The youth whose course we trace—experienced.
> Spurning the limits of their blasphemies,
> In limitless defiance of the Name
> Breathed in all winds and murmuring streams, and woven
> Into the very fibers of all things,
> His voice was heard, not heartily nor long.

Many who declaim against a creed, and refuse to believe in any religion claiming to be of divine origin, do so for the simple reason that their minds are already preoccupied with another creed, faith in themselves. It is just the preference of self to God, the desire to be supreme over the powers and opportunities that belong to one's individuality. As with Homunculus so with many others, the spirit of skepticism is more awakened by the Gospel which requires us to trust in Him Who died on Calvary to give man access to God, than by other systems professedly revealed. It is in Christian lands, not in Mohammedan or heathen, that Deism, Infidelity and Secularism have been specially manifest. Strauss and others, who have exerted themselves so much to persuade men that Christ rose not from the dead, have waged a more cruel war against the interests of humanity than was waged by those who put him to death. Yet H. professing to be animated by the highest regard for the interests of mankind, was delighted to drink in the teachings of these writers and suffered them to detain him captive in their own dark region for eleven years. As we have said, he for a while went beyond them in denying the existence of God, or at least the proof of such existence. A man cannot make a piece of mechanism but what it will testify to him and show forth in some respects what manner of man he is; the product tells more about the producer than about itself; and the works of God cannot but testify of Him, and it is especially to man that their testimony is addressed, not to the inferior creation. Men, even the most degraded, the most savage, perceive this testimony; and if we have people in these days denying it, it is not from want of capacity, but from indisposition to contemplate any power in whose presence they can but shrivel to insignificance. The dethronization of God is for the sake of the enthronization of man.

> Enough at length the Bible fabulous
> To know, and from all claims emancipated
> To walk in conscious freedom. Liberty
> To call the falsehoods of his fancy truth,
> And on the face of things created write
> —Over the name of God obliterate—
> A vain wild dream, and stately to the skies
> The self-perfecting image of himself
> Ideally to rear, such liberty
> Forsaking all to find, he found, and with it
> Unutterable barrenness of good.

Liberty and self are two things that are irreconcilably opposed. Liberty and love, such is the blissful union ordained by heaven. Liberty is only liberty when it is consecrated to love; liberty swayed by self can only be a curse.

> Who deem the Gospel glorious, them he deemed
> Ignoble, and deplored the dwarfed conceptions
> That in the poverty of Nazareth
> Saw strength and beauty; yet what best in him
> Challenged complacency, had been bestowed
> —Little he thought it—by the Nazarene
> Who from the tree of life in shaking fruit
> To satisfy his people, all around
> Shed paradisal odors.

While H. looked with disdain upon Christians as the victims of a strange delusion, he little thought that he was indebted for the very things upon which he prided himself, to the religion of the Bible. It is indeed true that Christ, in blessing His people, blessed those among whom their lot is cast. The American republic had its origin in the intense desire of Christians to find a place where they should be free to worship God according to the dictate of their own hearts. What was it but the desire for religious liberty that brought about the English Revolution, that grand event that has had so much to do with the pathway of progress in which the nineteenth century is moving? In thousands of ways the world is influenced to its own profit by the very Christianity that it pretends to look down upon. Hereafter it will be seen that not in vain the Lord Jesus has taught His people to pray for those among whom their lot is cast.

> That faith should have embellished, their report
> To Jesus bore in tears, and thrice not merely,
> Not merely three times thrice, told how all goodness
> Around the roots of this unconquered tree
> Inveterately fruitless, had been poured.
> Why cumbers it the ground? Lay at its roots
> The axe, and bring its hated branches low.
> Thus earth and Heaven, and thousand ministries
> Angelic, in the interests of man
> Prayed fervently and ever. Yet the Lamb.
> One respite and another granting, bore
> The accumulation of outrageous wrongs.

The whole creation, made subject to vanity, not willingly, but by reason of Him Who hath subjected the same in hope, groaneth and travaileth in pain together until now. Nature, with its myriad ministries, exists for the same purpose for which God reigns, viz., for the revelation of God's loving law to His creatures, and the apostle seems to hear a wild protest ascending from sun, moon and earth to the throne on the awful waste of God's goodness thus lavished on mankind. Designed to lead him to repentance it only seems to have the effect of intensifying his pride and self-sufficiency. Men speak of mysteries. But the greatest of all mysteries is the long-suffering goodness of God towards an ungodly race and it is only Christianity that can give any adequate explanation of this mystery.

> Methinks that sin had never in this world
> A stronghold so impregnable; for sin
> Is strongest where suspicion least finds place.
> Never discountenanced by doubt, his faith
> A frozen ocean, certainty itself
> Was his conviction that no prayer of man
> Was ever heard in Heaven, no call of Heaven
> Heard ever on this earth. He battled not.
> With happy credulousness; common minds
> Could not the icy pinnacles of truth
> Climb without sorrow; leave them to their dream.

We have known a great many unbelievers, but never one whose deliverance from this habit of mind seemed so unlikely as that of H. During eleven years he cannot remember a moment when there crossed his mind the idea that possibly he was mistaken in his conclusions. If he had had more proselytizing zeal, he would have come more in contact with the truth, and thus possibly might have discovered the inadequacy of his own reasonings. He lived in a world of his own, and when he mingled in society accommodated himself to the ideas and prejudices of men, so far as he could do it conscientiously, thinking it a pity to disturb them in beliefs which they considered essential to their peace of mind and which perhaps were so.

His assured conviction was "that man has such an opportunity for goodness that he does not need the interposition of any higher power to be guided into the best paths." Or as he expressed it in his poem:

> The human heart and goodness
> Seek ardently each other . . .
> Religion has no fruits
> That liberty insuppliant may not match.

3. Three Years Abroad

In June, 1836, when Bowen was twenty, accompanied by the other members of his father's family, he went abroad and was gone for more than three years, returning to New York in January, 1840. Twenty-eight installments of his "Reminiscences" are devoted to these years in Europe and the Near East. In his journal he records a love affair on the voyage to Havre in which he and two friends, unknown to one another, became involved with the same girl. At this period there was a good deal of melodrama in Bowen. Both this and his ambition and the germs of characteristics which later had full development appear in his contemporary journal:

> I want to be alone. I long to take the pen dramatic in my hand. The intervals between my tragedies are always tedious. I shall not cease to write them until I acquire some reputation as a basis whereon ambition can construct. Hours, days, months slip away. I feel myself growing old and the goal not reached.
>
> Yes, one stage of my race I have gained. I am satisfied that my last, *Oluph*, indicates a mind above mediocrity. That only of all that I have written, can I read. And I will declare to these pages what shall not fall from my lips, that be the manner in which I have treated the subject good or bad, yet the subject is one of the finest that I have ever seen treated.
>
> Then wherefore should I despond? I never have, never will. From my infancy I have never doubted that I should attain eminence; it has been my determination, nor day or night have I forgotten it. I have seen no American newspapers since I left, and of course, have seen no criticism on *Oluph*. I have just learnt, however, that the N. Y. American, speaking of it, says: The paper and print are very good, but the matter unreadable. Eh bien!
>
> I wonder if any one else indulges in the same kind of day-visions that I always have. I believe that not a day has passed over my head for years that I have not in a reverie dreamed a dream which described a whole existence. It is not mere castle building, for though I sometimes scale the world with its obstacles even to the loftiest pitch that ever man attained, yet oftener and indeed generally they are of a mournful tenor. I love to picture forth myself in the most melancholy, most unhappy situation. Loss of friends, relatives, property, aye, of limbs; alone with my gloom on some desolate rock, I long to taste misery, even the bitterest, to have the face of the world bent against me. Why is this? Of what stuff am I

made that situations which would make life a curse to another become dear to me? I remember indulging in that sort of aspiration in my twelfth year. Is it that I feel powers within me that can only develop themselves in their strength when desolation is around? It is simply this, that I am of a tragic temperament. Give me some hut built upon a rugged shore with man behind me and the sea before me, the dashing of waves, the roaring wind and storm my inspiration, and I can live my life away in writing tragedies, careless of the judgment of the world and bodying forth my own society in the characters of my own creation. Yet I am very far from being devoid of human sympathies.

After a stay in Paris the family went to Switzerland, then on for leisurely visits in Italy and Germany, five weeks in Milan, a month in Venice, two months in Rome, two long visits in Florence, then a visit to Antwerp and Brussels and then return to Paris in July, 1837. A few quotations from Bowen's ample journal must suffice, passing over his account of scenery and picking out only a few of his self-revealing entries:

> Music is my divinity and Bellini her high priest before whom I bow. I esteem him a genius as great as ever illumined the world, a poet if ever there was one; every bar of his music is a poetical image and speaks a language independent of those that separate men. I owe all to him, all that I ever shall become.
>
> I bought this morning Sterne's *Sentimental Journal*, and in spite of my intention to prolong the pleasure, read it through immediately. It is a dear book and one I delight in as well as *The Man of Feeling*. It puts one in a confessional disposition. I believe men are less disposed to grieve for crimes than for lesser wrongs, such as the letting of opportunity to do good pass by unprofited. I know that when memory wants to strike a blow at me, she reminds me of times when my hand obeyed not the impulse of a benevolent humor, when to give was a duty.
>
> At Vreyburgh I heard delightful music issuing from the most powerful organ I ever listened to. I could have listened a whole day, but rather a whole night; such sublime tones are better fitted for the midnight hour. A German piece was played, representing a nun, praying during a thunder-storm. I think she is a lover whom the fates have afflicted with a lot worse than that of death. Memory without life. Just as we were starting I had the miserable fortune to see a being such as I have seen but two others. One whose person is my idea of perfection, and whose soul beams in her face, like sunlight on the tops of a melancholy forest. Sadness, sentiment, passion. Is it my curse to see such beings as in a dream, to be whirled past them in the world's

giddy dance, and never again meet? If a happy chance ever favors me again, it shall be my fault if it prove the adventure of a moment.

Oct. 14, 1836. Arrived at Milan. Austrian soldiers in a diversity of pleasing uniforms, first strike the eye and awake indignation. The Roman columns (Colonne di San Lorenzo) visited today, believed to be of the 4th century.

Six months have rolled away, on wheels whose every revolution has been a torture to me impelled by a destiny cruel because idle, over a waste to which no bound appears, in a twilight atmosphere, without sun, without darkness. O God, better than an abyss opening before me free me from unproductive negative existence, when all my faculties corrode in my mind unused, a mind where hope is pale and where resignation is banished. Not a step nearer that for which alone I live, than I was six months ago. O, the spells of mental agony which I of late experience.

How am I happy when composing, or was rather. It was like walking abroad upon a mountain at sunrise, the rapid rush and glow of thought accelerated as my action proceeded. A commonplace existence, an existence with which many are content, is to me a curse worse than life in solitary imprisonment. Then in moments when the mind is battling among itself with contending fires, I have the additional torture of being visited with self-blame. Why—(I cry to my energies) should I not renew myself, and hew me out from the opposition of circumstances, a cell for my faculties to inhabit? What? is my thread broken there where it was wrought the most strongly? Can I not remount to the trunk whence I have branched? O! but I need the chastening of solitude, the purging power of meditation. In my other days I was alone among a multitude of things. Having channeled in my mind a bed for the chosen train of thought to flow along, nothing could interrupt its course. I saw everything that passed around me, heard everything, but all was converted to useful ore by the alchemy of that *idea* and were (!) borne along in its current.

Why should society, habits and the requisition of circumstances be obstacles at the present time? O but solitude is the whetting-stone of thought. A magnet with whose virtue when the mind is coated, it can lightly bear this oppression of society.

"Questo santo legame della schielta amicizia era ed e tuttavia nel mio modo di pensare e di vivre, un bisogno de primo necessita, ma la mia ritrosa e difficile e severa natura, me rende e rendera finche io vivo, poco atto ad inspirala in altrui, e altro modo ritenuto nel porre in altri la mia." This, from Alfieri's life of himself, describes me also and I may add *dell' amore* with the greater reason that I have always had dear inestimable friends.

> I have an idea that I shall some day write a drama on the subject of and entitled *Christ.* I never could, with all the aid of reason or imagination, realize the efficacy of the sacrifice which, according to the Scriptures, He made for man's salvation. What suffering was crucifixion for a God? Surely much less than the like would have been for a man who must want that confidence which He possessed. It was but an episode in His life, His descent to earth, and any physical pain that He experienced, could not be commensurate with the immensity of the consequences, redemption for all mankind. I know it is difficult to imagine anything that could be; unless it were the descent of a God into hell. But something between the two. I would then make a Christ susceptible to the charms of mortal woman. I would paint Him with all that amiable modesty, that sweetness of character which seem rather the perfections of man than of God, that soft and gentle melancholy which seems ever to have waited upon Him. And I would make Him experience such love for a beautiful being, not a Christian, as should set all the finer elements of His materialized character at war. To treat this subject were a task worthy of the greatest energies, highest faculties; let me prepare.

He returns to this idea again and again:

> If ever I write that *Christ* on which my thoughts dwell lately, I will endeavor to make my mind the fountain of the great spirit of the Greeks as transmitted to us in their great creations, and infuse it into the drama.
>
> *March 7, 1837.* Have been in Rome fifty days. In no city that we have visited have I more enjoyed myself; no city pleases me more. This is the more surprising as there was no Opera. We have found acquaintances here and though when I am at home anywhere and have my books I am independent of society, yet when voyaging, scudding before the wind, or becalmed, now in a fair gulf, now in a foul one, companions are decidedly agreeable and useful.
>
> The last week was the Holy one. Three times I heard the famous *Miserere* of Allegri, some of the harmony of which is most beautiful, the opening sublime. Such a magnificent sight as St. Peter's has presented Thursday, Friday and Saturday, is well worth coming from the other continent to behold. The contrasts were most striking; soldiers and priests, nobility and a mob, two thousand fair ladies and as many fine gentlemen, brass bands and lugubrious chori. Well, adieu to Rome, the most noble, most ignoble of names. Here you see ignorance more degrading than a Hottentot's standing on the tomb of genius.
>
> *April 16.* By the by, I've almost forgotten my poor old journal. Behold us at Naples. Left Rome *March 28.* Lovely weather. Saw the

sea at Terracina and ruminated on the beach, cigar in mouth, over the vicissitudes of human events and the nothingness and nonsense of my own existence. It is a great bore that God should have taken it into His head to put this spirit, soul, essence of mine into a human body and make a creature of me.

The extraordinary effect wrought by a girl in a book, shall not be passing but lasting; a dwarf shall grow a giant, before I forget the resolutions which I am silently making. Could we be known to each other, could I find the chords of her heart responsive to mine, I am prescient that I should be radiant with a new existence. I should prepare myself for the great task, for the *Christ*. She alone could give me the ideal of that one whom I am to body forth as the temptress of the Son of God, making the heir of heaven's throne hesitate between her and heaven.

Aug. 30, 1837. Paris. I have now a copy of the New Testament, and am about to read this work. It is perhaps ten years since I read it. I shall now determine whether I shall undertake the task I have sometimes proposed to myself, viz., the dramatizing of Christ; not the vulgar Christ, but the God of my own imagination, who was fearfully tempted, but who triumphed in sorrow. . . . About this time there was a preacher called John. He attired himself in a goat-skin and lived on sauterelles and wild honey, preached in the deserts and prognosticated a change and consequently became popular. Crowds came to him from all quarters, and were freed from the penalty of their sins by being immersed in water, an easy way to purchase proselytes. Jesus came to him to be baptized. John, either fanatic or politic, acknowledged Him for his Lord and baptized Him. . . . I have finished the evangelists and find that they will be of no use to me. Luckily the life of Christ is involved in utter obscurity until He reached His 30th year when He commenced preaching. It is probable that he followed His trade as carpenter until that time. However, my Christ shall be no carpenter.

There is no character more admirable to my mind than that of Mirabeau. He was a great man; a genius; and when I use the word genius, I mean something more than the world understands by it. I knew nothing of him until lately. I first read his *Correspondence of Vincennes,* portions of which have rather an equivocal reputation, but all of which has inspired me with the greatest interest for this youth. I felt an exceeding desire to know something of the after career of this character, and reading Thiers I find him in the French Revolution sublime. I did not think a Frenchman could be so great. I am now reading his *Memoires* by himself, father, uncle and adopted son, and they furnish me with the details of his history with which I was unacquainted.

Can I explain the singular idea that has just sprung up in my mind? That the earth has a spirit; that every great globe, world, planet, star, is inhabited by a great mind or thought or guardian which is to it what the mind of man is to man's body. That it grows with it, is inseparable from it, died with it. For geology tells us that the world has grown and grows. For the mind of man has grown up in him. Who shall deny it? When the matter of man was in its most imperfect and inchoate state, then was the mind corresponding; and the clash of minds produced by the social state, has bred up the mind. Who shall ask for a first great cause, and reject an inherent impulse to improvement throughout all essence? Mankind does. Then tell, me, mankind, what you think of that first great cause? Must it not possess all the greatness and more, of its creations? Must not all wonder and admiration and query turn from His superb work to Him? Is not His Creation more wonderful than His Creations? Why multiply difficulties? Why not be contented with the mystery of existence without adding another and greater in seeking a Creator for it? Existence cannot be created. Tell me how? Ask a child how God became; likely he will tell you that God grew. All we see about us is growth. Then it is a speculation no more foolish than others to suppose matter to have been before mind. For mind to be born of matter is no more incomprehensible and unreasonable than for matter to have become. Quite as probable as for a spirit to have existed from all eternity, which has no example in nature, which the faculties of man are not able to conceive, and which accordingly we must not be asked to believe. It is but a simple speculation. If a man finds pleasure in dreaming it a truth, let him; it won't hurt him. If we wish anything which is beyond the pale of our senses and reason we must forbid reason to trouble herself with our creed. For of what we know nothing, we can believe nothing.

Here no disappointment. This is happiness, the pride of happiness. Under such a beautiful sky, the atmosphere so pure, the weather so agreeable, to go from one monument to another, where time has obliterated the names of the great of old to inscribe his own, yet could not banish the spirits of those great ones which still here, there and everywhere around us fill us with that inspiration which is to the few congenial minds the influx of power. This is life. Here would I live, here stop and give up time to create out of these materials something that in the judgment of the few, might stand up beside these glorious structures, if such be given me. The *Christ* is the daily food of my mind.

When the family was back in Paris in July, 1837, after the year in Italy, Switzerland and Germany, the question of Bowen's financial relations to his father arose again:

My mind is sometimes unworthily occupied; with longings too, which I would once have contemned. The desire of money. Money! I sometimes imagine that as a means it is the most necessary thing to happiness. But this does not come from my nature, and only from momentary, though often recurring despondency, occasioned by the sense of my dependence. But I will cease to despond and I will cease to curse.

Have obtained information respecting my father's designs towards me. He said to my mother, "George is now of age; I will give him half my fortune." My mother opposed it saying, "He will dissipate it. Give him half his portion now; if he spends that, the other will remain for him, and with his acquired experience he will preserve it better." Where is this half or quarter of the kingdom? When shall it be forthcoming? Never! He never can part with his money. Anything but that. And then he complained of my want of confidence towards him. An old complaint. Is it natural for a child to repose confidence in a parent who is unconfiding? Confidence begets confidence.

I can but say that my mother's advice was shrewd. But my father's proposition was all talk. I know him. (It would not have been so if H. had conducted himself differently).

Read Bulwer's *La Valliers*. Trashy in general. Some poetical ideas but not happily expressed. The diction is inelegant, some of it coarse and vulgar. As a drama it is nothing. He has a good opinion of himself; d . . . the critics and their virulent abuse. Oh how important it is for an author not to let the world see his egotism.

Aug. 7. Established in winter quarters in the Rue Castiglione. I have a delightful little room in the corner of the house with a balcony which commands the Place Vendome and the Tuilleries. A fine place to smoke cigars and cogitate of a moonlight night. Have been to the Louvre. What a magnificent gallery! Nothing like it in the world. I was actually giddy with delight when I got in the midst of the Italian school. I could not move my eyes without seeing a Raphael, a da Vinci, a Domenichino, a Murillo, a Titan, a Guido. . . . I must form some plan for my studies this winter. . . . Oh the inconsistencies of human nature, specially of my father's. Even after all that he and his family have gone through, he still has the desire of accumulating money. He this morning proposed to me to go into business in New York with his cousin, putting in on his own account a capital of $ . . . and on mine one of $ . . . I refused it on the spot, saying that I would live a beggar all my life, rather than go into business in New York. No words can express my indignation.

Bowen's later comment on this last entry was, "It was the father that had the right to be indignant."

The next two years Bowen spent in Paris, with a visit to England in the spring of 1839. His diaries refer cryptically to various "Lethean" experiences which he deplores, but they leave the depth and gravity of these experiences to the imagination. "Over much that occupied him," he says, "he is compelled to draw a veil." A few notes of "Reminiscences," quoting his journal of this period must suffice:

> I propose to myself to take notes of the things I read but I am too indolent to begin. (There is a list of about 90 volumes in different languages, read during the last year.) Mirabeau in his *Prussian Monarchy*, has this remark on the character of Frederic the Great: "If he was not born valiant, he has nevertheless shown himself valiant even to rashness; it is to his great mind and not to the natural disposition of his blood, that his heroic energy is due. Here the rivalry between genius and nature contributed altogether to the glory of the genius." This is fine and true. I do not think that I am physically or rather constitutionally brave; I would not wish to be. There is no merit in this animal valor, at least little compared with that which is produced by sentiments of honor, duty and ambition. *Oct. 11.* I have heard Grisi, Tamburini, Lablache and Ivanhoff. Grisi is sublime, Lablache wonderful, Tamburini excellent. *29.* Have heard Rubini. What pathos in his voice. Voice and style perfection. Grisi is always divine.

Some of the succeeding pages are covered with extracts in French from Mad. De Stael's *L'Allemagne:*

> Mad. De Stael has considerable erudition united to a powerful imagination. But her erudition is not, it seems to me, acquired from much study, but rather from the erudition of others. She has not drawn from the fountainhead, but from the basin into which many streams have flowed—reading her observations on the English, French and German philosophers. I infer that the benevolence native to her heart, inclines her to accept that which these writers let believe rather than what they wish to conceal. I believe that until the last half of the last century, the philosophers paid deference to the opinions or prejudices of the world, so far as to conceal certain tenets which might shock them. She judges Locke by the apparent spirit of the work. Some who would wish to believe themselves the initiated (like myself perhaps,) think they discover in his book, that his pretended deductions from the principles he started from, are not very sincere.
> (The above remark simply shows that H. had a habit of projecting his own mind into the books that he read, and found it easier to believe that when they spoke respectfully of religion, they spoke insincerely than that they had any real respect for it. In other words, if he did not find his

own views in the obvious tenor of the book, he would conclude that they were there in a veiled form).

The recent French philosophers, having rejected God &c. have based morality on mundane interests. Kant combats this doctrine founding it upon duty, at the same time that he attributes to religion an interested motive.

Feb. 1838. I am reading Voltaire's *Melanges Historiques* and *Philosophical Works.* I am compelled to entertain a higher estimate of his genius than was my wont. To form a correct opinion of any history whatever, one should study his *Melanges.* His skepticism is of the greatest utility in profane history at all events. I must give him more credit for impartiality. He is almost converting me to the opinion that there is a supreme being.

I am firmly persuaded that nature or providence or what you may call it, is a mind which inhabits, penetrates, encompasses this globe; that every globe is inhabited by something similar; that these are among themselves in their individuality as individuals among the human species; that the sun is the master-spirit, the nature of all these subordinate powers. That the mind or intelligence is the result of the five senses; that these senses are as wonderful a witness of the divine genius as a mind embodied in man at his birth would be. That this intelligence perishes with man and his senses. I do not believe in a little being called the soul, distinct and independent of the mind, responsible for actions prompted by the mind or understanding. If the mind and soul are one, and it becomes crazed or imbecile so that all the understanding is out of joint and deformed, is this insane essence to mount the skies with the healthiest and best?

In June and July, 1838, he was in London:

June 14. I write this in London where I hope to pass a month agreeably. Have here found my friend F. who has introduced me to his family circle from whom I experience much politeness. Rode out yesterday with him and his sister in Hyde Park, a delightful promenade. The regiments of ladies on horseback were a singular and pretty sight; at the approach of a thunderstorm they made a fine charge at the gate. Dined with them. Later in the evening, we went to a cigar divan and at midnight to Evans' where glees and songs were sung, and drank gin and water. Went to bed at 2:30.

3rd. Have spent many similar evenings to the above, though more frequently at the Opera. Have been to the National Gallery, which boasts a fine gallery of ancient pictures. The Murillo, the Claude on each side, the Correggio and da Vinci on the same wall, are my favorites.

The collection is small but includes some admirable paintings. The Exhibition of works of modern artists is, I think, rather better than the one at Paris this year. *23rd*. Have been to see St. Paul's and admire the exterior of it very much. Seen from the river, especially, it is very imposing. *29th*. The Coronation is just over. I saw the procession, which satisfied me. The spectators were by hundreds of thousands. Have seen an oratorio, the *Judas Maccabeus* of Handel, chorus of 500, truly grand. But time is necessary before one can appreciate a school of music such as this belongs to.

I left London for H . . . Park, the seat of the Earl of . . . and the residence of friend F. Spent one of the happiest weeks of my life there. Delightful concerts were got up every evening.

About fifty pages of his journal in the winter of 1838-1839 are covered with notes of books, mostly German and French:

October, 1838. Have begun Herder's *Philosophy of History*. Have read the first volume, the *Vorwelt,* with but little interest. It consists of speculations upon the veriest minutiae, of importance to some students doubtless but what is it to me if the palace of temple of Dshemshid at Persepolis was of two stories or one? There is a poem of Dshemshid translated, which I like.

From Herder: "Though commonly no epitaph or enconium tells us how long a man survived himself, yet is this, alas! one of the greatest and least rare curiosities in human existence. The earlier the play of our faculties and passions begins, the more rapidly it is continued and through foreign occurrences in various ways assaulted, so much the more frequently do we perceive instances of that weariness of the soul, of that overthrow of the combatant without death or visible wound, of old age in our prime, aye, in our youth. Long may a man move about his own tombstatue, his spirit already departed; the shadow and memorial of his former self!"

A good many pages are devoted to the translation, in blank verse, of a melodrama by Herder, entitled *Ariadne Libera.*

With the dramas of Goethe that I have read, I am dissatisfied. I cannot say I think he has made much out of Egmont. The history acquires no additional interest in the drama. The conclusion bad. What does Torque to Tasso amount to? An interminable long play about nothing. There is absolutely not the slightest action, and nothing to indemnify us for its absence. The same thing may be said of *The Natural Daughter.* Iphigenia pleases but little more. Faust is alone among his dramas. I like better Schiller's, especially *Don Carlos.* But *Wallenstein* might very well, I think, have been made into a five act tragedy. Each part of a trilogy should be itself a drama. The *Piccolomini* is but a first act.

Have been delighted with Wieland's *Agathon.* Many portions of it trace what I have experienced. Voila a list of the German works I have read since the commencement of this year. (We give only the names of the authors): Chamisso, Vol. 1, Goethe, 17, Heine, 4; Herder, 5; E. T. W. Hoffman, 10, Klopstock, 2; Lessing, 1; Musaeus, 1; Jean Paul, 2; Schiller, 2; Wieland, 6.

Klopstock's *Messias* is truly a poem; the first six books are to me very beautiful. Twenty years he devoted to the creation of this work. Mad. de Stael's critiques upon him and it are very just. Wieland's *Oberon* has also afforded me much pleasure. I do not repugn the peu de sévérité exhibited in the love plot. It is very well in a profane epic.

Winter has come round again and brought the opera, source of my most refined and exalted pleasures. Only recently I have learned—not to admire, I always did it—but to feel Mozart. What a chef d'oeuvre is *Don Giovanni*; perhaps the greatest in music. I would wish to hear it for a month.

Dec. 31st. The German Library being broken up, I am interrupted in the progress I was making towards a knowledge of German literature. Have read eighty volumes, however, in six months. (After this we have long extracts from Winkelman's history of Art, French translation. The descriptions of the master-pieces of ancient sculpture are given in full).

Am reading some *Essais sur la Peinture* by Diderot, and his ideas generally on Design, Color, Light and Shade, Conception, Composition, Contrast, Expression, so accord with mine that I would wish to note them all, were it practicable. (Works by the Duchess D'Abrantes, Geo. Sand, Balzac, Spindler, James, Cousin, the life of Voltaire, the Margrave de Bayreuth, are noticed). Letters and memoirs of Ganganelli, Clement XIV., please me much, especially the early letters, when he was a simple Franciscan. But they are said by Dr. Johnson to be spurious.

In the spring of 1839 he suddenly conceived the idea of going to the Near East. On March 1, he writes:

Thinking of the countries that border the East of the Mediterranean, which I have so long desired to see, I suddenly proposed to myself an immediate journey to those parts, and at dinner proposed it to my father who consented. So I shall be off the latter part of this month for Greece, Turkey, Syria, Palestine, Egypt and Sicily. It will be an era in my life. I anticipate much pleasure and am resolved to derive all the instruction from it in my power. I must travel rapidly and economically, but will endeavor to see to every thing remarkable in my route.

Bowen left Paris alone, accordingly, on March 29, 1839, going down the Rhone to Avignon, from Aix to Marseilles by carriage, and thence by sea to Genoa, and by way of Leghorn, Naples, Messina, Syracuse and Malta, to Alexandria. He traveled with but little luggage but could not dispense with Shakespeare's complete works in one volume, Byron's in another and Shelley. Three months were spent in Egypt, including a trip up the Nile to Edfon, Philae, and Karnack, ancient Thebes, returning to Cairo in July. Traveling up the Nile a hundred years ago was very different from today, but Bowen made friends wherever he went, and the diary is full of the happy and helpful acquaintances, and of shrewd insights and reflections:

> Sicily is an abandoned country. A local government would do wonders in regenerating this beautiful island. Misery stares you in the face and hangs upon your footsteps, constantly. Messina is full of convents. Entering a church which was entirely deserted and looking through a gilt grille, espied a number of nuns in an adjoining cloister, at prayers. One of them with beautiful Sicilian eyes, coquetted with us the whole time. Delightful, but tantalizing.
>
> Mounted donkeys and rode to Karnak. Thebes not what I had anticipated. I had not anticipated that I could ride a mile or two without seeing any object of antiquity, and was consequently rather out of humor. This endured till I had passed under the western propylon of the great temple of Karnak, into the dromos. I seated myself on the ground and gazed long at this wonderful spectacle. Such columns, such capitals! The wonder is not that these edifices have endured so long but that the hand of man has been able to injure them as it has. Were this temple perfect, I believe it would be the greatest monument in the world. Climbed to the top and sat there a long time. No words can express the feelings with which one regards these stupendous pillars surmounted by capitals twenty feet in diameter. We spent the day in wandering among these ruins. We returned by the avenues of sphinxes which are all decapitated.
>
> Yesterday visited Heliopolis. A tall obelisk, in the midst of a field, is all that remains of the famous city of the sun. Saw the sycamore where the Virgin rested with the infant Jesus, when she came from Bethlehem! I can't deny that it looks old enough; to look at, it might have been planted by Cain in his wanderings. Saw the ruins of a beautiful mosque said to have been the original of that of Cordova. Went this morning to Boulac, to see a collection of stuffed birds belonging to the Italian I had seen at Assouan. He spent two years in Senaar &c., making it. I have spent several pleasant evenings with Dr. A., an Englishman in the Pasha's service and a clever man. Met at his house a French gentlemen

who has been a long time with the army in Syria, and with whom I was much pleased.

It is long since Luigi and I agreed to see the sun rise from the top of the great pyramid. . . . The corner by which we ascended was in the shade, but I went up without any assistance. It is much steeper than I had supposed; the angle is 50 degrees. When half way up we stopped for a few minutes, and then pushing on reached the summit in perhaps 20 minutes from the time we started. The top is a quadrangle of about 30 ft. and here we passed the night. After supping and smoking, my companions lay down to sleep. It would be difficult to analyze the sensations I experienced here, on the summit of this the grandest and perhaps the most ancient monument existing, in this silence of midnight only interrupted by the dismal howling of the jackal in the distance, a dozen Bedouins lying around enveloped in their long cloaks, the dim light of the waning moon faintly disclosing the expanded plain and the majestic Nile. At one I lay down on the stone floor, taking the provision bag for a pillow. I slept a couple of hours, and awoke somewhat chilled by the dew. It was a beautiful spectacle to see the day break, and the first beams of the sun fall on the surrounding objects, discovered to my view the sphinx, the tombs, the numerous small pyramids which seem there to do honor to those they surround. It was now that I felt all their grandeur, and that my eye could first conceive their gigantic proportions. "The watch-towers of Time, from whose summit, when about to expire, he will take his last look."

July 27. Passing by a sycamore, a Turk sitting in the shade of it, hailed us and invited us to stop. We did so, and after some refreshment, all three started off together. Pleased with our companion, Mr. J. and I invited him to accompany us to Alexandria. Found all right aboard our beautiful boat, but a strong head wind was blowing. Just as the full disc of the moon was visible above the bank, we pushed off. Our new friend, a native of Carvallo, (the birthplace of Mohammed Ali), was an ex-Governor of the portion of the delta through which we were passing. He had spent a year in El Yemen, and seven years in the Hedjaz. He was polite and very communicative and we did not repent having invited him to accompany us. We had many long conversations in Arabic and we understood all he said. He also taught us a little Turkish.

On August 2, 1839, Bowen left Alexandria for Syria:

Arrived at Beirut early on the morning of the 4th. At dinner the previous evening I had drunk a good deal of wine, and had insisted

on lying on deck all night, against all remonstrance, and it was under
these circumstances that I opened my eyes on Lebanon. Agreeably
disappointed by being allowed to land without quarantine. Beirut is a
detestable little town, charmingly situated; we spent two days there. We
hired a servant, Giuseppe, a Maltese, arranged with a muleteer to take
us to Baalbek and thence to Damascus, for 300 piastres, (four mules),
and got off Aug. 6 at 7 a.m. I had been quite ill at Beirut and a little
dispirited, but when I had ridden a few hours on the mule, I felt as well
and as gay as ever. Stopped about noon at a fountain on the mountains,
commanding a fine view of Beirut and the sea. Afterwards for several
hours we were completely environed by heavy mists that hid everything
from view. The thermometer which the preceding day had been at 28
centigrade now stood at 13. The house where we stopped for the night,
afforded a beautiful view of Coelo-Syria and the Anti-Lebanon.

Among the amazing ruins of Baalbek he wept over the wreckage which the Saracens had wrought. He describes the great temples with singular accuracy, but the gigantic measurements impressed him less than the historical associations: "I never experienced so strong an impression in the presence of any other ruins as I did in the presence of these." From Baalbek he passed on to Damascus, lodging with the Cupachin friars at their Convent:

A Padre Tommaso, Franciscan, a singular personage, loquacious,
inquisitive, who has resided 30 years in Damascus, knows everything
and is au courant of everything which is going on, showed us the way
hither. (He was murdered in 1840). We were exceedingly well received
by the friars, and have every reason to be pleased with their kindness
and attention. They were only three in number and all Spaniards. The
superior, Father Valentine, flattered me by always seeking my society. I
had many agreeable conversations with him.

In Damascus and from Damascus to the Sea of Galilee and Tiberias and Nazareth, Bowen moved among the tragedies and perils and disorder which characterized Syria a hundred years ago. In Nazareth, with an English companion, he visited the scenes of Jesus' boyhood, including the Virgin's Fountain, where a number of women "were waiting their turn, some of them pretty," and then went on to Mount Tabor, Sebaste, Nablus, Beeroth, where the roads from Damascus and Caesarea meet, and then to Jerusalem. He spoke without feeling or special interest of the sites associated with Jesus' life and death. He was not at all well and suffered from rheumatism and from the exposure and hardship of his travel, but he rose from his sick bed to go on to

Jericho and the Dead Sea, the Convent of San Saba, to Bethlehem and back to Jerusalem: "I was always prepared to find Jerusalem an uninteresting place, but the reality was worse than my expectations."

He left Jerusalem, August 31, for Jaffa (Joppa). Looking back on this visit to the Holy Land forty years later, Bowen wrote in his "Reminiscences 34":

> The following is from the metrical account of H's experience from which we quoted in the earlier numbers of these reminiscences:
>
>> "In many lands
>> Wandering, at length, where once the lowly feet
>> Of Jesus to and fro with healing sped,
>> Where mountains, rivers, plains, trees, habitations,
>> Fountains and brooks, the rocks, the land, the herb,
>> The rose, the lily, thorns and figs, the vine,
>> The sycamore, the olive, shepherds' flocks
>> The fishers' barques, hewn sepulchers and forts,
>> And goodly stones from one another thrown,
>> And the great void made by the land's own children
>> In strangest exile absent, to all eyes
>> By unbelief not sealed hermetically,
>> Unfold expressively the Gospel, thither came
>> The Gospel-scorner. In his armor now
>> Some joint to find, the arrow of conviction
>> Surely shall fail not? None. He lays his head
>> Where the unsheltered head of Christ was lain,
>> Sits where He sat, stands where He stood and knelt
>> And was in agony, and moves just where,
>> Mayhap, the dying glance of Jesus fell:
>> Yet the conviction of his mind by doubt
>> Was shaken, no, not once. Ah, who may tell
>> The secret scandal of that time, or who
>> Its deep opprobrium may hear? What tongue
>> The ever crucified forbearance speak
>> That gave the winds, the sun, the dews, the waves,
>> Commission to watch, tenderly the steps
>> Of one whose adamantine rule it was
>> No tributary grateful thought to send
>> Heavenward?"

Like an unlettered man in the midst of an ample library, this unbeliever journeyed through the land that men call the Holy Land, unaided and unaffected by its eloquent testimonies. He found his way from Lebanon to Hermon, from Hermon to Mount Tabor; thence to Ebal and Gerizim, and thence to the Mount of Olives and Mt. Moriah and the hills of Judea, and then to Mt. Carmel; wandered on the shores of the Sea of Galilee and saw the sites of the cities where Christ spent so large a portion of His time; visited Jericho and the Dead Sea, Joppa and Tyre and Sidon, and found no reason to change the opinion vaguely held by him to the effect that Jesus of Nazareth doubtless lived and journeyed according to the itinerary given in the New Testament, but without any commission from Heaven, and without special claim on the regard of men. He little dreamed that he himself had much in the way of intellectual and moral light and many privileges that he would not have had, if Christ had not lived, thought, prayed and fulfilled the Scriptures on the cross. He believed in Jesus as he believed in Herod or any other historical character, only he thought that the real history of Jesus was harder to be got at because of the obscuring myths in which it had become enveloped. It will be observed that Homunculus did not seek to proselytize; he did not think that common minds would be any the better for his skepticism. It was on the whole pleasanter for them to believe in Jesus of Nazareth; if they felt the need of salvation, His Name and the ideas connected with it would do as well as any. He fancied that it was only a superior mind, as he imagined his own to be, that could get along happily without any recognition of Providence and without the hope of a future life. So he for the most part kept his views to himself, speaking of them only when his associates seemed to be in harmony with himself. He was naturally averse to controversy. It is probable that the missionaries met by him in his travels got the idea that he was a Christian, because of the unaggressive character of his infidelity. The facts of the case, were they fully portrayed, would show in an extraordinary degree the power of the self-deception residing in the human heart.

Part of September Bowen spent in Stamboul (Constantinople).

September 20. The doctor accompanied me to Stamboul to see the Sultan pass on his way to the mosque, it being Friday. The streets were lined with guards keeping back an enormous crowd, composed principally of women. Bands of music were playing at certain stations. Laborers were busily engaged covering the pavement with earth, for the hoof of the Sultan's horse must not touch anything with a hard surface. Had a very good view of the Sultan Abdul Medjid. He appears older than he really is, twenty-three rather than seventeen. He is ruining his health, everyone says. His aunt presented him with a beautiful Circassian the day he girded the sword, and she is but one of many. Saw him afterwards embarking in his caique. At his approach a band of music with a chorus of voices commenced an air and continued it till he left the shore. The moment he sat down under the rich canopy in the stern, an officer knelt at the bow facing him, and remained in that position; thirty-two gilded oars stuck the water, the golden prow shot forward, the cortege in various caiques, some of them hardly less splendid, followed, and in a very few minutes, they were out of sight. In the afternoon made an excursion to the "sweet waters" in a caique. Happy they who have the opportunity of making daily such agreeable excursions. The Golden Horn gradually diminishes in width until it has only the width of a canal; fine elms and plane trees grow along its borders. Here and there were hundreds of Turkish or Armenian ladies spending the afternoon. (One is reminded of the place near Philippi, where Paul found a company of women and addressed them). I passed a very stupid evening at the house of a missionary.

The missionary proved less uninteresting on closer acquaintance:

I pass an hour every evening at the house of Mr. Robertson, missionary, who is a gentleman of considerable literary attainments and of a refined and cultivated taste in several of the fine arts.

September 27. Visited the whirling dervishes. We found ourselves in a very pretty circular building, about 50 ft. in diameter. An inner space of about 30 ft. in diameter was partitioned from the rest by a low railing. The outer space was soon filled by Turks and a few Europeans. The orchestra and chorus were in a gallery over our heads. The dervishes entered one by one, and made a low inclination before the place occupied by the superior; it was in the direction of Mecca; they then sat down on the floor close to the railing. They had cone-shaped hats and cloaks of different colors. After a long recitation by the superior, the music commenced. The instruments were quite new to me, and the plaintive notes of the flute were rather pleasing. The music was all in the minor mode. A long chant from a man with a stentorian voice succeeded. The dervishes then arose and made the tour of the place three times, in slow measured steps, always bending their bodies when they passed the keblah. They laid aside their cloaks and commenced turning. Their rotary motion caused their white frocks, heavy at the borders, to stand out; their hands were stretched out one a little higher than the shoulder, the other a little lower. They were about sixteen in number, and considerable address was necessary not to touch each other. At first they changed places very slowly, turning very rapidly, but nearly on the same spot. Their eyes appeared closed or fixed on the ground. Their motions were graceful and I felt not in the least inclined to ridicule. Not a Turk there felt more solemnly disposed than myself. When a pause occurred, we left to go aboard the steamer. It was after sundown when the steamer left. I was loth to bid adieu to Stamboul.

From Stamboul Bowen returned to Paris. He had a thirty-day quarantine at Malta where he came near to a duel over some insulting remarks about America which he resented, and where he wrote in his journal:

> Thought is a terrible burden to me just now, and I abandon myself to gaiety. I have a presentiment that misfortunes are lowering upon our house, and that I shall receive tidings of accumulated ills. I have made up my mind to receive them manfully, and not to think of my own share when others more in need of consolation have an equally heavy one. Meanwhile I will not let these forebodings prevent my enjoying the calm, unclouded present.

Bowen's "Reminiscences" 37 and 38 deal with his return to Paris and New York, with one of his "Lethean" experiences and with his state of mind on taking up his life again at home:

> We have seen that Homunculus completed his oriental tour, reaching Paris November 7, 1839. No thanks were rendered to God for his preservation during his absence. It was taken as a matter of course, or as a thing for which his own sagacity and prudence were to be commended, that he should have returned safe, and sound. His parents, sisters and brother had returned to America some months previously, and he found letters from them expressing their expectation that he would soon join them. He could not, however, tear himself immediately away from Paris. He spent a month there, thus briefly noticed in his journal:
>
> The Opera, the Louvre, some choice friends; the days flew unnoted away. Halcyon days! A month of unalloyed happiness, except for the thought of approaching separation.
>
> A letter from dear friend F. contained the assurance of his continued friendship, and an invitation from his amiable family to spend some time at Hurstbourne Park before my return to America. But Parisian chains did not permit.
>
> Under the head of Dec. 7 the journal speaks of his departure from Paris. It speaks particularly of the parting with one with whom he had been intimate for two years, but says nothing of the promises then untruthfully made and without which the parting would have been different. H. prided himself greatly on his regard for honor and truthfulness, and really imagined that he abhorred all manner of falsehood; and yet persuaded

himself that it was sometimes right to deceive another rather than cause pain to that other.

Eugene and Colin embraced me with the greatest effusion when the diligence was ready to start for Havre, and the grief of parting with these friends served to assuage—by making me partially forget—that of the previous parting.

December 8. I arrived about 10.30 a.m. at Havre, and was informed that the ship *Iowa* had weighed anchor and was passing out of the basin, and that I had not a moment to lose if I wished to get on board. At the latest moment I succeeded in getting on board with my baggage.

There were thirteen passengers on board. The passage was not altogether uneventful, but the events are not mentioned in the journal, and so far as memory serves, were not such as deserve a place in memory except for the sake of humiliation.

January, 1840. We arrived the evening of the 7th, and reaching home (3 Albion Place, New York) about 11 p.m. I found my eldest sister sitting up for me and all well.

I am gradually resuming my old habits, and my existence is of an even tenor. I feel the want of excitement of some kind or other, and unfortunately I cannot bring myself to seek for it within myself and in my literary occupations. Some years of wandering have not made me so appreciative of tranquility as I would need to be; satiety comes sooner to me now than ever. My friends, Patience, a firm Resolution, and a something which I never yet found, will set all right.

From this time on H.'s note-book abounds with extracts from books, thoughts suggested in reading, comments, &c. We shall produce—or leave—these as may seem desirable.

> Compute the chances
> And deem there's ne'er a one in dangerous times
> Who wins the race of glory, but than him
> A thousand men more gloriously endowed
> Have fallen upon the course; a thousand others
> Have had their fortunes foundered by a chance
> Whilst lighter barques pushed by them; to whom add
> A smaller tally of the singular few
> Who, gifted with predominating powers
> Bear yet a temperate will and keep the peace;
> The world knows nothing of its greatest men.

Il n'y a rein de tel qu'un accès de folie pour render raisonnable.

To obtain an audience of us, Wisdom is sometimes obliged to resort to such means as the poor ecclesiastic who, having words of severe truth to say to Leo X, and being repeatedly denied access, at last disguised himself as a buffoon and so, obtaining ready admittance, enjoyed the long desired opportunity of pouring into the ears of the Pope, complaint and reproof.

I have lately thought much of the *Christ*. I have in imagination drawn the first scene. Upon a desolate mountain top overlooking the sea of Tiberias, of a starlight night, a youth enters who has received his death-blow. He lies down beneath a blasted tree and dies. His sister enters and while she is kneeling by his body, a flash of lightning descends from the cloudless sky, runs down the tree, and the spirit of an archangel enters the dead body of the youth. The surprised angel rises from the earth, listens to the terrified, joyous girl, and receives from the invisible lips of deity his instructions. The girl screams with horror at the supernatural voice and rushes out. Christ, a youth of twenty arrives with a stranger, a messenger from Satan who has seduced him to desert his home and wander with him over the earth. This envoy from hell must be an Abaddon, a hater yet slave of Satan, ever thinking upon the blissful state from which he fell, of melancholy temperament, susceptible of admiration for what is good and beautiful, yet compelled by his destiny to obey in all things the mandates of Satan. The three depart together.

I was wild for commencing this task immediately, till I happened to read in the *Foreign Quarterly Review* some remarks upon the general propriety of the great and imposing subjects which modern poets are more apt to attempt than to complete; if we were to signalize half the errors and failings and dangers to which these lofty themes expose the inadequate powers of the author, and consequent distortion and vulgar familiarity which they are apt to reflect upon the reader's mind, we should be led far away from the work (Quinet's *Ahasuerus*) before us, and we should have to expose what in our opinion is one of the sorest maladies and worst ambitions of our time.

But unless something else presents itself to my mind as food for immediate leisure, I will embrace this daring idea.

We go on with the extracts from the note-book kept by H. after his return to America.

June 1, 1840. Have been at home five months, and in what manner have I occupied myself? In the beginning of March, I was persuaded by my friend Frank Brown to commence the study of law. During about two months I persevered in the reading of Blackstone, &c. and then abandoned the avocation. Difficulties arose through my being unable to produce the required affidavits, and I had become disinclined to the study. The late period at which I was beginning these wearisome studies, my predilection for other pursuits, the instability of my tastes which require a wide and varied field to disport upon, and which loathe compulsory toil in any undivided path, all conspired to make the studies repugnant.

Have been reading a great number of books in diverse languages on a variety of subjects, in a very promiscuous manner. I am now resolved to devote the summer to the composition of a work of fiction, the scene of which shall be Rome, the epoch the commencement of the 16th century and the principal personae the distinguished artists and literati of that day. For the plan of the work I take the Serapions Bruder of Hoffman as a model.

Memoirs of Las Casas. Said Napoleon at St. Helena. In the character and conduct of Mohamet, Voltaire has departed both from nature and from history. He has degraded Mohamet by making him descend to the lowest intrigues. He has represented a great man who changed the face of the world as acting like a scoundrel worthy of the gallows. He has no less absurdly travestied the character of Omar, which has been drawn like that of a cut-throat in a melodrama. Voltaire committed a fundamental error in attributing to intrigue what was solely the result of opinion. Those who have wrought great changes in the world never succeeded by gaining over chiefs; but always by exciting the multitude. The first is the resource of intrigue, and produces only secondary results; the second is the resort of genius and changes the face of the universe.

Sincerity compels us to transcribe here a copy of a letter written by a young American gentleman in Paris, a medical student, to a friend of his in New York. The only explanation needed is that H. had written to the party referred to in the letter, to the effect that he was expecting to leave America for some distant country. This was not the truth; yet there was scarcely anything on which H. prided himself more than on his truthfulness, imagining that he had a much higher standard of honor in this regard than common people had. He justified himself in this particular untruth, by the plea that it was better for the party to whom he was writing that she should be saved from doing what she proposed.

"Your friend, Mr. B. (Homunculus) need not fear that our mutual acquaintance of the Rue—, M. M., will cross the Atlantic to join him. She would have been glad to do so until the receipt of his letter to the contrary, but poor woman, she would have been equally unable, whatever had been the tenor of his letter. She is now in the last stage of Phthisis Pulmonalis, and a few days or at most weeks will terminate her existence.

"I found her on my return in January, living alone, depressed with care, despondency, and in want of many of the necessary conveniences against the severity of the season. I soon found that she was ill with Phthisis, and begged her to have a physician. She refused on account of the expense, and contented herself with such trifling advice as I could give her, until, finding her getting worse, I refused (from prudential motives, as she was utterly without a friend or relative in Paris, and I was a stranger and too young to take the responsibility of what I foresaw would prove an incurable case) to prescribe. After a month or more, necessity compelled her to consent, but she knew no physician and was indisposed to pay one. I therefore induced M. Chassaignac to visit her which he did with great kindness and generosity. In the midst of this the necessity of changing her lodgings for cheaper ones, with the efforts necessary in so doing, rendered her worse. As M. C. could not visit her often enough, she has now a good physician who sees her every other day, but notwithstanding poor M. will in a few days cease to feel her troubles and misfortunes.

"When I first saw her sickness and situation, I could not refuse her the trifling care, and it has thus eventuated that I am the only one to advise her, and relieve the ennui of solitude during the most of her sickness. In the house she now lives in there are, however, kind people who attend to her, and for the last six weeks I have persuaded her to hire a servant. The circumstances of my being so often with her among all her troubles, has naturally drawn forth her confidence, and it is thus that I am acquainted with her relations with Mr. B. since his departure. But you would be sadly struck to see how her beauty has faded."

After this, many pages of the note book are covered with extracts from Calderon's plays in Spanish and with comments on them. We pass these over.

Necessity, cause penultimate of all things, to save herself the trouble of attending to the minutiae of human affairs, gave man his free will that he might attend to them himself. With our free-will we are agents of necessity, and have the responsibility of agents.

"Il n'est pas assez d' avoir de grandes qualités, il en faut avoir l' économie."—Rouchefoucauld. Those who have the most must economize the most. The majority of men get along very well without talents; the possession of them is mortal to some.

Passions enfeeble each other; a single power acquires force from the suppression and negation of the others.

Have been reading *The Voice from St. Helena.* Most of Napoleon's prophecies will probably eventually be realized; but he does not seem to have foreseen the prolonged term of repose into which Europe would sink when his career was ended. He fancied that the impetus which he had given to human affairs would take a long time to spend itself. He said: "An Englishman should consider that man England's worst enemy who advised a war with China. She would in the end be beaten, and perhaps a revolution in India would follow."

Have re-read Lamartine's *Pilgrimage to the East*. It is interesting as it is a poet who writes, one who appreciates and feels the beauties of nature and art, though I think that sensibility predominates over judgment. He does not think so himself, but has, on the contrary, a very lofty idea of his own profundity and penetration. On every page almost is a prophecy, many of which have been already belied.

The next pages are covered with extracts from Andre Chenier, including the poem which he was writing when the executioner came to summon him to the guillotine. One of the extracts is the following:

"Il est si doux, si beau, de s'être fait soi-mème, De devoir tout à soi, tout aux beaux arts qu'on aime."

This was quite the idea of H. in those days—that it is an honorable and an excellent thing to be self-made and owe all to one's own efforts and to the fine arts that one has lovingly cultivated. Another extract from a French author, translated, would read thus: "Good at heart, I have not always taken the trouble to let it be seen; this is my greatest fault." Homunculus adds: "And mine. But may not every man thus excuse himself? What merit is there in active virtue?" How many deceive themselves in this way, looking at their aspirations instead of at what they do, and imagining their character is more shown by the former than by the latter.

4. In New York City, 1840-1844

For the four years, 1840-1844, Bowen lived at home in New York the life of a dilettante, spending his time in reading, music, the opera, art and emotional and intellectual self-indulgence. In spite of his critical attitude toward his father in the matter of money, he seems to have continued to depend upon his father's support, his own literary ambitions producing nothing. In his "Reminiscences" in the *Guardian* of Apr. 24, 1880 he describes his life during these years:

> Homunculus was living all the time a most selfish life. His room was the back third story of 3 Albion Place. He would get up when all the rest of the family were at breakfast, and come down when all the rest were through. Then during the time required by the servants to clean his room and light the fire, he would occupy himself in playing on the piano in the parlor by himself, very much annoyed if anybody else lingered there. As soon as his room was ready, he would ascend to his room fill his narghile and smoke it, or smoke a chibouque, or a cigar. This room opened on the library. Almost every day, the whole day, he would continue smoking, reading, writing, dreaming. In the latter part of the day an acquaintance might come in and have a smoke and a chat, and he would generally spend his evenings out visiting somewhere, finishing off in some place of entertainment. When was he ever known to seek out any poor family, or try to be helpful in any way to the needy? It was much more convenient to write disguised eulogies on himself, and dream that he was soon to surprise mankind with the evidence of his goodness and greatness. We read lately of a lady in Boston who had a lion shut up in her drawing-room. If it had been a bear that occupied that third story backroom of Albion Place, Fourth St., New York, H's parents, sisters and brother would have been as much benefited socially. We would have our readers take note that the admiration of the good, means very little so long as a man has nothing more sovereign than this to enable him to do the good. Meliora video proboque, deteriora sequor.

George's egoism, his alternations of mood, his attitude to his father and to business, his literary activity, his melodramatic ambition are illustrated in his journal entry of Sept. 28, 1841:

> *September 28, 1841.* It was galling to hear reproaches from one on whom I was dependent, so, resolved to make the odious sacrifice. I

entered May 19 a counting-room and during three months and three days endured the pains of purgatory. When I revolted August 23, I resolved to give myself some weeks of recreation and immediately resumed the *Agathon* with an ardor I had never before known. In one week I had written the second act, in another the third; the next, I idealized without my pen in the country; the fourth I composed the lyrics, and recomposed the prologue and first act. September 23, it was completed. Since, I have been occupied in copying it off. I pronounce this month the happiest of my life, an uninterrupted state of enjoyment. It is succeeded by one of despondence, doubt, hopelessness. Desperate thoughts pass through me, as I see it cast in imagination upon the reckless waters of the world to sink. I am convinced there is some virtue in it; shall I confess? I am convinced that a work which has for so many years been nurtured by my most profound thoughts, observations, felicitous inspirations, (every man has some) which has been such a source of unequalled pleasure to myself, which is of such a bold flight and lofty inspiration, I am convinced that such a work is of no ordinary worth. Yet I have almost the certainty that it will meet at best with neglect, if indeed depreciation, condemnation were not better. Someone considers me, I believe, almost as an enemy, one to whom the rites of hospitality and the paternal hearth have been too long accessible. Oh! if I were but the guest of a Bedouin sheik, or in the ultra-Missouri wilds gaining my sustenance with the sweat of my brow. There at least I could enjoy my inner world unmolested. Life must be worth something. Nature must have some receptacle for me, better than the tomb. Hamlet shall not be the proplasm in which my character will fit; ambition without strength, strength of aspiration without endeavor.

Bowen's later comment is, "We need not say that the reflections of H. upon his father were unjust. The marvel is that the latter should have so long borne with one who gave no evidence that he was anything but a selfish, unsociable dreamer."

This is a just judgment of his father but a harsh judgment of himself. George's journals for these four years are amazing. They represent a breadth and thoroughness of reading, a richness and penetration of philosophical reflection, a courage of intellectual skepticism, a wealth of culture and a maturity of mind which, with all their vagaries, their sophomoric and melodramatic and egoistic qualities, give them rank with any of the analytic autobiographies of history. Both they and the "Reminiscences" ought long ago to have been published. In lieu of such publication some representative selections may be made available here:

Yesterday was the *30th April, 1841,* and I completed my 25th year. A year utterly null and sterile, not to be remembered. Omissions as ten to one to performances. Ennui of late has had me in his demon clutches. The tempter su ... has beckoned me at times, but has not found me weak enough. He never will, if I know myself. The mental torture which I have experienced for some months is equal to that I underwent and recorded in Milan, 1836; its causes nearly the same. Yet, under different circumstances, the life I now lead would make me happy and would be productive. Independence, the only God essential, shall I never know? With literature I am blasé, at the same time that my ambition to distinguish myself in it is paramount. Ambition without an incentive. I have much less confidence in my powers than I had six years ago. It is only lately, however, that I have cleared my mind of all respect for its former achievements, and acknowledged their worthlessness. It is a good omen perhaps. I am no longer in that desperate hurry for reputation "which o'er leapt its self and fell on the other side." Another good token perhaps. But timidity prevents me from improving my moments.

My *Agathon* (Christ) progresses slowly, but feeling that I must publish much before I can venture to give that to the public, I do not bring all my energies to bear upon it. My father has shared in the financial ruin that has come upon almost everybody in this country, and my maintenance irks him, if maintenance it can be called. Under these circumstances I cannot enjoy nor improve my leisure. I am endeavoring to procure an occupation, and here I meet with difficulties. Disgust grows upon me; disgust for everything and everybody. Desultory reading and the mobility of my mind are great hindrances. If I could divide myself into two persons, and make one absolute master of the other, I could do great things. But as it is, more anarchy and civil strife, or alternate reign and unprofitable truce.

I have been for how many years trying to get at my own character; I don't know what good it has done me. Two culminating influences in a man's mind impede each other. It is music which has hindered my literary performances. Perhaps for the former I have more capability than for the latter; I often regret that I did not obey a veleité almost a volonté which for some time inclined me in Italy, in 1836, to stop at the Conservatory of Naples and give myself up to musical composition. I might have been something—but who knows?

Rasselas. "He spent four months in resolving to lose no more time in idle resolves. Discovering at length that what is not to be repaired is not to be regretted, he for a few moments regretted his regrets," &c. So Jean Jacques says: "Toute la vigueur de sa volonté s'épuisé à résoudre; il n'en a plus pour executer."

A short biography of Kleist by Tieck impresses me. He committed suicide while still young. He appears to have been always like myself wrestling with a mysterious nature. There is to me in Jean Paul a sweet melancholy in the gravity and repose of the style even when relating the most humorous things; wherein the style seems to heighten the humor. As in Mozart's *Don Giovanni* the buffic portions of the drama are allied with sublimest music, which seems to be expressing one of the deepest secrets of existence.

January 2nd, 1842. Another year has come round. It is sickening to think of and I will not think much about it. However, I have had time to sculpture some of the spokes in the wheel of time during this last rotation; not perhaps, not indeed let me say, with Phidias' immortalizing chisel, but with imaginative arabesques wrought with all the craft that was in me. Three purgatorial spokes are wrapt about with mourning weeds, but weeds of martyrdom for which I give myself glory; they taught me that between working and starving, the choice is decidedly in favor of the latter. Of course I mean uncongenial working. The first spoke I garlanded with love-flowers, but they soon faded, (the whirl of time killed them) and have not been since renewed. The last has been unsightly, armed with the tongue of base duns, and I sought unconsciousness in translating Hauff's *Wine-Phantasies.*

It has been a scheming experimental year; a year of waiting for a phantasmal non so che. Will I never be able to furrow it into my mind that man lives from moment to moment, not from year to year, that human affairs are not of themselves mutable, and their changes must proceed from the will of man, that this waiting is making clay of oneself for the sun of eternity to harden into a useless statue, and that one might as well be a denizen of the petrified city of Eshmounein as to count time instead of letting time count him and his developing faculties. What a destiny! To be born, and eat and get breath and pamper imagination merely for the purpose of saying bitter things to oneself!

There must be something disjointed in one's mental cottage when he looks with semi-philosophical disdain upon the world's great agent, resolution; when he delays to scale the mountains of his horizon, because his imagination has stood occasionally upon their summit, and tells him the outlook is humbug, that the matutinal mists which give a charm to the landscape, are dissolved and replaced by common sunshine, nothing better than what is around him. But no worse, remember that; action and movement are the angel wings of the mind. When one ceases to contemplate the progress of something beneath his labors, he ceases to live; life is progress. The happiest days are when one is growing to physical maturity. When he has attained this his mind must continue the progress; though but a shadow it is the only vestige and remembrancer of earlier enjoyment.

In his sketch of modern astronomy, Chalmers gives a magnificent outline of the imaginable universe. My mind never before took in such a wide conception of creation, never before expanded so comprehensively. But it was the expansion of a desert, desolating. Meditating on abstract things for the first time in my life, induced a sensation of positive misery. I read it deep in the past night; a terrific storm was raging without; I was predisposed from some unknown physical cause to a gloomy train of thought, and thence the desolating effect of the reading. Of a fine sunshine morning, it would have produced an elevation of the mind; engendered the self-gratulating thoughts of that power in man to raise himself to the comprehension of the infinite, to take in not only all the visible creation, but the vastly more which his fancy suggests, and so to make himself the equal of the universal Spirit; and awakened the conviction that the mind of a creator could only differ from mine own in degree.

Humiliation would not have been my sentiment. Yet I almost felt last night the necessity of circumscribing my sphere of observation, and resolutely to ignore that bourn where the precipices of knowledge plunge in the ocean of mystery. Happy the man who can venture thither under the governance of a fixed idea, which makes everything even the boundless unknown administer congenial nutriment. Such I am fully convinced will never make its way into my brain. The organs of thought are differently combined in every man. Each mind is of its own individual and single architecture. It chooses its own ideas. All the essential material itself supplies. It may gradually submit to have niches placed in and about it, its cornices to be molded in arabesques, its spires to be set off with foreign contributions, but will never lose its own peculiar character, rather assimilate to it these additions. Its tone is one. There is such a thing as idiosyncrasy. The mind is no more plastic than the body, but like the body obeys in its development its own particular laws. Growth is but a magnification, not an alteration.

Immortality implies transmigration. I would sooner believe in the deathlessness of spirit, if it were offered me to believe its existence confined to this earth. No doctrine is better calculated to deter men from crime than the Pythagorean. How little the fears and hopes of a future life influence the world in their daily actions.

How much more fearlessly, or with how much more indifference, did the men of the last century enounce their convictions in matters religious than they of this century do. Probably because books were then read by the few, the enlightened, now by the mass, unsusceptible of more than a partial enlightenment.

It was Lessing who said that there was no pleasure in the discovery of truths, but many and great in the pursuit of them. Thus for an illustration, in a work of fiction which represents an action, the interest ceases there where the unravelment of the plot, the explanation of the mysteries, begins. It may be otherwise in a state where one truth is a stepping stone to another, and where the matter of knowledge being infinite the progress would be endless. But this I doubt, for in an infinity of cognizable things, acquisition would be no progress. We would ascend with very little interest a mountain which we knew to be without a summit. We must see or imagine the possibility of a term to all that claims our attention. Unless indeed in the future state there would be the same inequality of powers that here distinguishes men; then competition would be an incentive.

In a state of perfection there is no glory, and no delight; when prayer ceases and the aim is attained, annihilation might as well come, or reconstruction.

In the notes of 1842 there are copious extracts with remarks from Borne's *Criticisms*, Goethe's *Theater* and *Deutsche Literatur*, Bayle, Dumas, Gautier, Soulie, Carlyle, Bulwer, Heine, Bacon, etc., with occasional outbursts of poetry:

I will not believe that earth can ever behold the annihilation of evil. This is to be deemed an eternal necessity; necessary to the good of reverberation to sound, reflection to light. Absence of evil implies the ignorance of good. But though it be not extinguished, it may cease to be the triumphant antagonist of the better part of humanity. It may be made to spend its malevolence on itself, like a captive demon; and the sight of its misery teach virtue to know itself to be happiness. Supposing that this orb is yet to endure some myriads of years, what are we that now dwell upon it but the infants of time? And shall we lift our eyes and our aspirations already to other spheres and forget the glorious futurities of our own? No, if I am to be born again, let it be in successive earthly lives; let me grow with earth; and be myself the minister of my own excellence, and construct myself the mount of paradise; for I am yet to know that man deserves any other than such as he can himself work out.

The most successful tempter is he who aiming no shaft at virtue, exhibiting no scorn for goodness, is solely engrossed by the endeavor to beautify and elevate Vice.

I cannot consider Bulwer a man of genius. He is often brilliant, rarely does he give evidence of a profundity that results from inward research, though sometimes he seems profound with the thoughts of others. He is more keenly susceptible to the wonderful than to the genuinely beautiful. His egotism is never concealed.... How different, how much more pleasing the modest tone of Carlyle's enthusiasm, adoring genius as something sought and found within himself.

Read with intense delight Goethe's *Helena,* and at the same time Carlyle's critique on it and occasional translations. What a creature! I feel the same passionate desire to see and obtain her which actuated Faust to have her recreated. This dramatic personification begets in me the identical effect which of all statues the Venus Callypige alone could induce, in the Museo Borbonico.

I fancy that mankind are held in restraint by the fear, 1st, of opinion; 2nd, of the laws; 3rd, of self-reproach; 4th, of Heaven. After much consideration this is the order in which I conceive these restraints from evil-doing to rank.

Carlyle: "Heine is another of the proofs which minds like his from time to time are sent hither to give, that the man is not the product of his circumstances, but that, in a far higher degree, the circumstances are the product of the man." With what intensity did I cherish, some seven years ago, this belief, how fervently and wholly cling to it! What gloomy years followed the moment when I doubted it. Years of bitterness made more bitter by reluctance to yield to this doubt altogether and surrender myself to circumstances, with eyes opened to the fallacy of my youthful creed. Yes, the proof that I never entirely resigned faith in the power of the human will, is the periodical return of this inward strife and self-inflicted torment. But the material constitution of man may be even more hostile to successful battle than the external circumstances themselves. But Will that is worthy of the name should quell even this obstacle.

The delineation of character (in dramas) is frequently nothing but the delineation of paroxysm. A phase is well-represented, but that phase ill represents the life. What we want to see is such demeanor as will show us not merely the momentary bearing of the individual, but in what manner he must have lived his whole life.

A single sane disbeliever suffices to demonstrate the non-existence of innate religious ideas. It is contrary to the universal economy of Nature, and argues an unexampled penury on her part, thus to forestall the efforts of her creatures, when these efforts are evidently equal to the attainment of the knowledge.

A great aid to truth is no doubt to make our words always subservient to it; but this general rule admits exceptions. There may be cases in which truth on the lips is treachery. Truth, in its highest sense, includes all virtues, and he has a weak conception of it who deems it only resident in language.

Is the Holy Ghost anything but the Demiourgos of Plato?

Life-weariness is usually but weariness of too much freedom.

A high wind, sweeping over a rich and beautiful region, bears off merely straw, chaff and sand.

The elephant may be killed by the infusion of a drop of milk in his veins.

As the herbalist, to investigate the structure of a flower, first plucks it and then lets it wither, so the man must die before his character be rightly studied.

There was no misery in the world till the word happiness was invented.

Nothing seems to me more impertinent than speculation about a Supreme. What business has man with him? The last syllable of a Mystery of which we cannot read the first letter?

Tieck, describing Sophie von K., the loved of Novalis, says:

"All persons that have known this wondrous loved one, agree in testifying that no description can express in what grace and celestial harmony the fair being moved, what beauty shone in her, what softness and majesty encircled her." I revel in such descriptions; would ascend Caucasus to see the incarnations of them.

Yesterday, the *30th of April, 1842,* I attained my 26th year, and I can regard another birthday, another flea-hop through eternity, with somewhat better satisfaction than the few preceding awakened. I am conscious of mental growth, of a more sane way of life, of resolution having come to stand and become productive. I have read much, not as heretofore, desultorily, but rightly, with meditation and advantage. I feel there is hope for the future; though unsymboled from without. I see my aurora dawning within me. I know there is something else to do besides waiting, that external circumstances need have no influence upon my life, that I have but to utter, and can utter; the words are within me.

O life! O thou imprisoned soul of mine! A mystery, you may be a fallacy, but I will do something with you. Though but a bubble in space, I will feast while I can my moral vision with whatever celestial hues may dance over its evanescent sphere. A mystery; it may bring to my eyes tears, but to my spirit no womanly softness. What is it now subdues me at this long past midnight hour? Subdues me outwardly, but the strength within not that. By force of arm, I will uplift my horizon and plant it further and further, and then work freely.

Time! If there should be no such thing, and some god taking his siesta in his paradise and dreaming us! But I look on another universe than in the year gone by. I see that there is a universe, and one not easily explained either; not a household affair, but a something altogether cryptic, insoluble, wonderful. There is thaumaturgy in it. Awake my soul, and be thou thaumaturgic. Not a living boor, but could he pluck up his soul by the roots and cast it into the world, but would outdo all Platos, Homers, Shakespeares. Thus much is in every man. The greatest is but the deepest and longest breathed self-diver who can bring up the most of those secret treasures which are nowhere unexistent. The right mind-pump is yet to be invented. But some eductive strength is to each, and mine is to be tasked, and there is no need of despair even at the doom-second. To be remerged into the whole, that is the law of matter; and spirit can but have an equal privilege. The past is our enemy, so is the future; let me know no friend but the present, and heartily work with it.

I must endeavor to stay the enormous waste of imagination, the indulgence of which is always a waste when the subject is oneself. The quantity which goes to make up any one of my day visions of a nonsensical future, would suffice to carry a common novel hero through at least one volume. Could I control my imagination so that it should only subserve the literary creation upon which I am engaged, it would be profitable but worse than profitless are its results when allowed to play with my own future. There is a recoil that submerges and devastates the rock of the present where a man should stand, intent rather on seeking to spread a layer of healthful glebe, a grassy sod, and, if practicable, a pleasant flower bed; not as a couch to tempt his indolence, but as a garden where the generations may come and gather grateful bouquets, or better still, medicinal herbs.

The generations take charge of poetry as of the quintessence and portable spirit of the age, and posterity esteems it accordingly. The more concentrated it is the longer will it bear transportation, and the higher will be its value, provided only that the concentration destroy not its native quality.

Looking just now at the picture of Dives and Lazarus which overhangs my mantel, I saw for the first time that the naked figure of Lazarus degrades all the remaining twenty in costume. Though occupying a small corner of the picture, yet he seems to be himself the picture, and all the rest accessorial. He alone is significant, all the rest insignificant. Looking in his nudity like a man he makes the others look like effigies. So nature revenges herself on pomp, poverty, and pride.

The owl is called the bird of wisdom, as it sees in the dark. But to see in the light is more difficult. Dante lived in the dark and saw much. The sun shuts out from us the universe; only when we are turned from him, do we see it; even the bodies of our own system we see only by night. In the dark ages a little light went far and told much. In the days of light, it is hard to detain the manifest more than one's neighbors. I believe in man's progress but I am forced to believe that its rate diminishes.

In the summer of 1842 he had two sharp experiences. Another of his love affairs proved futile. On July 26 he writes:

11 p.m. L'axe a tournée. Je suis heureux. Je n'ose pas confier mon bonheur à des pages qui pourraient un jour recontrer un regard etranger. Dorenavant tout le monde m'est étranger, hors une seule personne, la plus admirable, la plus aimante, &c., &c.

Bowen's later comment is: "H. had happened that evening to find himself in the society of a person who made him believe that she had a great liking for him and who forgot all about it the next day."

The other pang was the rejection of a prose fiction manuscript. He had composed it in six weeks and spent a similar time in transcribing it. What it was we do not know. He said that he was satisfied with it and hoped by its success to extricate himself from some undescribed difficulties and to prepare the way for his greater work, the *Agathon,* the humanistic Christ story on which he had been working. The mss. was declined and he had a dark day:

It is difficult not to despair. By the foolish indulgence of a most inordinate imagination I have filled life with so many necessities that to live in sheer privation is an impossibility. Every beautiful contribution that is among nature's rarest, I have regarded as among the primary inalienable goods without which life is a state of galley servitude. All the invisible choirs that chant the praises of Resignation are gone with the unavailing melodies. I hear them not.

But he remembered Jean Paul, sepulchral silence, grinding poverty, and "then faint applause, becoming louder and more distinct till it became universal." The next day all was serene: "If there is anything celestial in man's mind, it is its elasticity, its voluntary revolution from a clouded firmament to another more serene. It almost seems as though our griefs were like the discharges of artillery which fill the scene for a moment with smoke and obscurity but which break up and scatter the heavy nebulous masses that shut out our sky. The same wind that brings us darkness will expel it beyond our neighboring horizon. We need but wait. Adventitious occurrences bring us our misfortunes; but the heart does not require any adventitious aid to repulse them again; it has itself the strength. Before midnight yesterday, I was restored to perfect tranquility and all that had oppressed me during the day was entirely forgotten."

He found some comfort in a humanistic reading of à Kempis in French which a friend of kindred Parisian ideas of life had commended to him.

It is lamentable that the mightiest effort of the mind is incompetent to give that serenity and courage which is sometimes inspired by the merest accident, and change in the external world, a riven cloud in the sky opening a path for the sunbeam, the grinding of the hand-organ, a tumbler of champagne, a jeu d'esprit from your neighbor, the laugh of a child, the song of a bird.

Jean Paul. "Keep constantly in view the fact that sorrow for a minute-old occurrence is just as unreasonable as sorrow for a thirty-year old one." Surely Jean Paul must know that the heart is not like an exhausted air pump where sounds are unreverberated; that it is not, like Time, existent only in the present. It is rather like the surface of a lake, which the calmer it is the more troubled is it by the stone you throw into it, like a valley, the stiller it is, the more are the echoes protracted. But it is good to remember that the circles die away, and that the echoes die away, and that calmness will come again. It would profit us little if our emotions were instantaneous, dying in their fall; their true value consists in the vibrations.

I don't trouble myself much about the Supreme Being, but I have long inclined to the opinion that I find to be the basis of Spinoza's theory, namely that God was natura naturata and natura naturans at once.

I fear that this is a poorly-conditioned world. I am sometimes inclined to think that, in the creation of humanity, some essential element was left out, by the absence of which everything stands awry, and ignoble, and forlorn. And if man do not despair, if he hold his peace and do his best, why, the Gods, who work with their ample and faultless machinery, may look on and admire him.

Quand, j'aurai oublié ce que j'ai ressenti pour—il me faundra seulement lire l'Hesperus de Jean Paul; le jour que je ne pourrai me rappeler quelle idée je me suis fait d'elle, le portrait de Clotilde me le rappelera. Si c'est dans mon destin d'eprouver encore des sentimens pareils, ce sera pour une femme qui ressemble et qui approche de ce portrait, à moins que je ne sois encore la victime, d'une aussi funeste illusion.

I do not know any writings more difficult to pass judgment upon, or more difficult not to admire, than those of Jean Paul. This Hesperus has wrought my feeling up to enthusiasm. A class of emotions the most spiritualized and the most indeterminable, which no man beside him has thought of giving words to, he clothes in an apt, beautiful, extraordinary language, obscure only to those who know nothing of the feelings expressed therein.

Given the immortality of the spirit, any period in the future, save the 100th year, is nearer to us than yesterday. Brood then over a past evil!

What a multitude of sins have their chrysalids in our hearts; but we mind them not till they have got wings and changed their aurelia for a nest. The dormant virtues within us pass for very virtues and have our best regard; but the sins that nestle in our thoughts and have not yet become visible to others, we do not in the least notice. Conscience seems mirror-like, reflecting from the upper surface only; a hell may be beneath, it yet smiles in ignorance.

The greater our physical needs, the less are we ashamed to ask for relief; the greater our moral, the more are we ashamed to beg. The most ignorant man is the one least willing to acknowledge his deficiencies; and the offer of knowledge he regards as an insult.

I did not know before that there had been a genius of the name of Blake. A genius run mad, but of a high order. I know no Englishman of a similar idiosyncrasy. His is one of those characters I cannot meet with without emotion. A genuine enthusiasm is something with which my best feelings always stir in sympathy. The son of a hosier, a passion for painting and poetry showed itself in his earliest youth; he was apprenticed to a graver. Specimens of his poetry exhibit a mind acted upon by a strong, worthy impulse, and possessed of a right sense of whatever in our nature is worthy of being sung. Cunningham, in his *Eminent Painters* gives his life.

In female beauty, those very persons who, with their standard, their ideal, make war upon all dissimilar art, would they consult their own experiences, would discover that each in the course of his life has felt an equally passionate admiration for women totally dissimilar. Try their best they cannot enforce their heart to enslave itself in this manner. Their judgment only.

Men love their moral independence so much that they will not allow their own experience to be binding upon them, even for their own good. Were not this so, I would note down that this day, October 8, I am harassed by cares and would hope that in looking back upon it from some undisturbed day I could make it an argument for rejoicing. But I know that I will not; for why should I not, by a similar retrospection contrast my present annoyance with the greater griefs of my past?

Do you wish to avenge yourself of an injury? Abstain religiously from all retaliation. If you examine yourself you will find that any revenge taken upon you by another has only embittered your feelings toward him. The greatest villain when subjected to torture, forgets his crimes in proportion to the greatness of his suffering. The severer the punishment inflicted, the more will he compassionate himself. Do you want to make a man feel sorry for the injury he has done you? Intensify the harm he has done you; make him guiltier of a greater crime than he has conscience for.

Young men whose desire of knowledge is exceeded by the desire to show the world what knowledge they have, may profit by the example of Herschel, who spent the greater part of his life in inventing and perfecting instruments for astronomical observations, and only in his old age effected his great discoveries with them. Too great eagerness for fame is the greatest hindrance to its attainment. If you can do anything better than your contemporaries, it is rash to imagine that they can immediately appreciate it.

How I envy those, a Jean Paul for instance, who have in their memory a bright particular spot, namely, their childhood. I have had no childhood. I have no recollection of such a state. I can revive no sensation then experienced; there are no facts of that period standing historically in my memory. I can only account for this by supposing that I was so much given to reflection that objects of perception affected me slightly.

Matter and Spirit are primarily simple essences. Life is the agent by which they come together. By the agency of life they assume an infinity of forms. As the forms of matter are numberless, so are the forms of spirit. But the primary simple essence runs through all matter and through all spirit. What is material in us belongs to the matter of the universe; what is spiritual to the universal spirit. The extinction of life under one form is merely a preparation for life under another form. Matter is resolved to its primary simple particles, to enter subsequently new combinations; spirit returns to the universal spirit, to re-emerge thence in some new conjunction with matter. In these conjunctions spirit takes nothing from matter; life does not administer knowledge, it merely develops it. In leaving matter, spirit parts with no knowledge, for this primarily belonged to it. This now may be a solution of the mystery or it may not. To our question nature gives 10,000 answers. One of these is the true, but which of them? And how to know it?

Oct. 17th. In reconsidering yesterday's thoughts on Matter and Spirit, I become aware that it is both difficult and rash to carry through the analogy, and from the destinies of the first to deduce an argument to demonstrate those of the latter. From the suggestion that life administers no knowledge to the spiritual conjux, I now shrink back with repugnance. For I would rather believe that there are no Gods, than believe that there is no progress. Under the operation of life matter puts on beauty. The beauty did not originally belong to the monads, but merely the capacity for beautiful combinations and forms. So must I perforce believe of mind that at the period of its conjunction with matter, it is not perfect but possesses merely an aptitude for greater perfection. Still, I am reasoning by analogy. But here I cease; many differences, each of them essential, present themselves.

Eckerman's *Conversations with Goethe.* "I have ever been esteemed one of fortune's chief favorites; nor can I complain of the course my life has taken. Yet truly there has been nothing but toil and care; and in my 75th year, I may say that I have never had four weeks of genuine pleasure." Thus say the majority of old men. But genial toil is genuine pleasure. A man's notion of happiness varies with his varying moods.

"In the end we retain from our studies only that part which we can practically apply." This fact has rendered me submissive to my natural inclinations. I no longer attempt to thwart them. I study only what I believe may be of practical utility in forming my mind. Knowledge of which I do not perceive that I can make any use, however valuable it be, I let it alone.

The comparison of man with plants is generally made in an opprobrious sense. To my mind it greatly flatters the former. A plant develops all its powers. From the moment of its germination, it works incessantly, silently, successfully. It shoots up to its due height; it darts its branches in every direction; it evolves everywhere the nourishment which suits it and aids it best, it clothes itself in beauty, it arms itself against storms, it is pliable yet abates not of its strength and finally it gives all the fruit for which it hath means. Does man do this?

My first work, what shall it be? Let your first work be to fashion your mind and render it as complete as may be; then all your other works will be easy.

When I consider that the life and health of Goethe were just sufficiently protracted for him to finish the second part of Faust, the most magnificent poem of modern times, it almost seems credible that he was in the hands of a special spirit of providence. But why not believe that a genuine intellectual will is itself a providence, with power over the material man?

New York, Oct. 24, 1842. We have more encouragement from the world for the exhibition of what is bad in our character, than for the manifestation of our virtues. Men do not so much make war upon each other, as upon each other's virtues. The reflection that every man has in him something better than he allows to appear, tends to justify the leniency with which I love to regard my race.

It is laughable how much, in the progress of years, we abate from the first demands which, on entering the second hall of life, we confidently addressed to Fate; but we in vain discount our anticipations; we just have to renounce them. Happiness now is a thing I should never dream of soliciting; but I cannot help soliciting a change of cares. This seems modest enough in my own judgment; but in that of Fate (a convenient word for a blind mortal) quite too inordinate to be gratified. We have doubtless powers of our own, not altogether contemptible; but if we repose with them for a brief season, we find ourselves on awakening bound down by a thousand Lilliputian threads of circumstance, separately nothing, but collectively overpowering. Indeed, I think that the pettiest impediments are those we are least capable of conquering; the sword will sunder a strong cord, that fails to sever a suspended hair.

Rousseau: "L' ingratitude serait plus rare, si les bienfaits a usure étaient moins communs." Usurious benefits; kindnesses placed out of interest; I like the expression; it well characterizes the detestable selfishness by which most men are influenced even in their kindnesses.

There is no more pernicious habit than that of thinking, at the close of every day, that Chance may render the morrow a different one. Rather reproach yourself that you have not made the lost day a different one, and go to bed with the resolution to utilize the reproach on the morrow. Or still better—for nothing is more futile than a resolution between the taking and the accomplishing of which you put an interval of rest—make the day a different one before you retire to rest. Make it a rule always to deserve sleep; otherwise you will enjoy neither it nor your waking state. Sleep, to many, is but the continuance of their day-lethargy; and its only good is that the mind cannot then upbraid itself with its listlessness. When insensibility is a blessing to a healthy man, a curse is implied in consciousness; not the malediction of fate, but well-merited, self-malediction. O the moments that we waste! Time, enriched by them, would deserve to be called an eternity; what is more, an eternity of usefulness, which is, happiness. Time, to each of us, is a fountain of golden waters unceasing till we, exhausted, lie down beneath it in sleep and are deaf to its murmurs.

When I hear one speak much of a particular virtue, I generally conclude that the most vicious part of his character is just there. Aristotle places every virtue between two vices, of which one is the excess, the other the defect. Now when a man plumes himself much upon one virtue, *e.g.,* firmness, it is reasonable to conclude that he carries it to its excess, obstinacy. The excess of a virtue is worse than its deficiency; for it is very difficult to fall back to the juste milieu, less so to attain to it. It is hard to convince a man that a habit is vicious which under any aspect it is virtuous. The spendthrift is much nearer virtue than the miser; yet the conscience of the latter will trouble him little.

It would be a great thing indeed if language, which is man's own invention, were equal to all the contemplations of his immortal part. There is an incommunicable poetry in the soul.

The principal cause of my present discontent is that I do not hear voices from the Trophonian recesses of my mind. I know well enough how they are to be heard; how I am to acquire the consciousness of the poetry within me. Let me but resolutely rid myself of the prosaic, habitual thoughts that are as sties and cataracts to the inner eye divine, and I will have the consciousness of what is best in me, and the ability to use it. Our acquisitions are of little use except in supplying us with forms and fitting outward embodiments for the creations of the deep afflatus which alone assures us that we have a soul, and not merely a higher order of instinct than the bestial world.

In the infinite there is but starlight. Dost thou glorify, above all, the beams of the sun? Lo, the incommensurable is the undisputed ground of night. Thy sun with its satellites is but a star like the rest; a tiny gem on the robe of night.

Time is a flame that we feed with all our treasures and fan with all our sighs. The puff of destiny may at any moment extinguish it, and leave us in irremediable darkness. And if we sit slothful and unmindful of the light, what will it matter if darkness surprise us? We can do no less in the grave; there we can lie slothful.

I remember a time when my mind would ruminate for a month upon some truth it has got hold of; and that single truth would avail me more for all social purposes than all my present acquisitions do. Is it not for this that we love the conversation of women? Is it not because their moral nature exhibits that beautiful superficies that is now inextricably at the base of our own? Is it not because she preserves the love and admiration of her own ideas? Does not weary of them? Turns their light here and there upon surrounding objects? In a word, is it not because she has enthusiasm? Can you conceive of an enthusiastic Job or Minerva? Does Job or Minerva interest us or lay hold upon our affections? What were more tiresome to himself or others than a wise mortal? Sir Charles Grandison does not engage our sympathies. But this is a sad conclusion to come to, that we can gain no treasure in this world without losing a greater. We would care very little for any immortality except an immortality of youth. Truly we must be born again to enjoy eternity.

I made these reflections on awakening this morning. How remarkable is the fact that while in all our day-dreams Fancy brings us into no situation where our self-love is not flattered, and does not manifest at every step her Armida-like solicitude for our pleasure, we should be led in our dreams by night, by a guide so very unamiable as not to consider in the least degree whether our vanity be caressed or wounded. To what insults are we not forced to listen in our dreams? To what ignominies are we not obliged to submit. How little account is made of our likes and dislikes! As much regard is paid to the person we hate and as much respect to the thing despised, as to our sovereign self. The feeling of identity is the slightest possible. In our waking moments, all things else are objects and ourselves the beholder; in our dreams we are fused into the mass and are one of the objects, one for which, very often, the deputy of Sommus, the dream-potentate scruples not to exhibit the most supreme disdain. Was I not last night most ingloriously kicked by a creature that looked not worthy to be my shoe-black, and instead of being allowed to exhibit any resentment, was I not hurried to a new scene where new indignities awaited me? What if it should be that exile, Nature, whom we rejoice to have driven out among us, and whose place of refuge we reck not to know, if she it were, hiding deep within us and revenging herself for the diurnal banishment, by committing nightly murder upon our individual and proud identity, and drowning us in the fluid, indifferent universe.

I am seldom so much interested in a book as I have been in H. Jung Stilling's life, without finding some thought worthy to be noted; but in this I have found nothing to extract. What constitutes its charm is the account of his peculiar personal experiences. A truly remarkable character. A life checkered indeed and visited with the severest trials, but exhibiting a steady progress from a most humble condition, that of tailor's apprentice, to very high honors. A mystic, too much inclined to believe in preternatural interpositions, in presentiments, in signal and miraculous responses to his prayer, firmly convinced that he was under the special guidance of providence, his early taste for intellectual pursuits was the real cause that he emerged from his obscurity.

The character of a man is simple at the moment, but complex in the sum of moments that make up a period of his life. It is subjected to a law of movement as imperative as that which causes the planets to revolve. I speak of the involuntary man, of what you may call his mere consciousness. His individual, ever present identity, I allow myself to compare to a peregrinating ant doomed to wander for ever and ever over the vast world of his mental nature, never stationary, occupying but the minutest portion of the ground at any one moment, now among arid sands where there is too much sunshine and no enjoyment, now upon the snow-banks of misfortune, destined to impart a new energy to the soil, now among the marshes stagnant and unprofiting as self-contempt, and now haply among perishable flower-gardens of joy.

It has always been a great objection to the pleasing theory of the perfectibility of man, that during what we call the dark ages, the light of knowledge is dimmed, obscured and nearly extinct. Madame de Stael offers some hints that serve to refute this objection. How small a portion of the human race were the enlightened Greeks and Romans. How likely it seems that the decline and fall of the Roman Empire operated not to bury this acquired knowledge, but to disseminate it among an immense population. It seems to be the design of Nature that a single nation which far outstrips all contemporary nations in civilization shall pay the penalty by a bankruptcy which impoverishing her and enriching all her sisters restores the equilibrium of the moral universe. Formerly, when reflecting on the vicissitudes of art, on the long era of languishment which succeeds an epoch of special vigor, it appeared to me that man was destined to advance as waves that reach an acme break, and recede for a new impetus and a further advance. I believe it now; but I perceive what I did not then, that intellect, though enfeebled in individuals in such recessive periods, is strengthened in the mass. For instance: There is no Raphael in our day, exercising his God-like influence, but the Raphael who died three centuries ago is exercising a far wider and better influence at the present day than he did in his own. The number of those who appreciate and profit by his works has been increasing with every generation. Many imagine that they adduce an unanswerable argument against the perfectibility of man whom they refer to Homer who, as the very dawn of civilization, gave to the world a work that has not been surpassed. But is not that work exercising this day an incomparably greater influence than it did in the days of its author?

It seems essential to the cultivation of the fine arts that they should be pursued where the largest number of constant spectators is to be found.

The example of suicide never can become contagious. This is perhaps an error. There is contagion in every example in this world.

As soon as we eradicate an ancient prejudice, we stand in need of a new virtue. If there is an interim, it witnesses the rise of a new vice.

What dead letters, to most men, are those in which they embody the most important rules of moral conduct! They seem to set great store by them, and speak as though it would be a most serious thing to lose them from their memory; and think it an imperative duty to communicate them to children. It often chances that the young perceive the real life and soul and beauty that dwell in them, and see that this duty is absolutely connected with their utilization and exhibition in generous conduct. Then, noting the strange contrast between these much admired precepts and the actual conduct of their elders, their earnest expression of noble maxims and equally earnest practice of a quite opposite code, they lift up their voices and ask for an explanation. Then the elders laugh. What? Imagine that we would degrade these holy maxims by subjecting them to the drudgery of our daily life? Oh, no; these golden maxims are the divinest things we have; they were sent to us all the way from Heaven by special messengers, and we take good care not to contaminate them by bringing them into contact with the base things of this world. And so they refer the foolish enthusiasts to a later period of life when they will understand how to treat rightly these glorious principles.

Love is the short, delightsome path to the same heaven to which the circuitous, rugged path of genuine ambition leads. Against the illusions of the first there is less help than against those of the second.

In 1842 Bowen made notes on 105 volumes, having read probably 150. "In some previous years he had read more volumes but had never read so much." He annotated especially Lessing's *Laocoon,* and *Limits of Poetry and Painting,* Stewarts' *Elements of the Philosophy of the Human Mind,* and Guizot's *Lectures on European Civilization:*

> *1st of January, 1843.* I have seen with reluctance the departure of a year to which I owe perhaps more than to any of its predecessors. Perhaps it is the first time in my life that in reviewing the experiences and performances of the past year, I can congratulate myself upon the former, and consider with unmixed approbation the latter. Yet it would be most difficult to render this intelligible to another. My outward circumstances have gone peggiorando; the things I have attempted out of my chamber have fallen through, until I could not but admire the constancy and consistency of the sors that manages or rather mismanages the external events of my life; my material prospects are precisely what they have always been when at the worst. Yet I am contented in the best sense of the word. I remember none of my mishaps with regret; they none of them affected me longer than was absolutely necessary for producing the good results for which they were fitted.
>
> The fact is, my present glad state of mind is explicable with a word. I am sensible of very considerable mental progress. I have formed the best habits possible, and have so fitted and involved myself in them that I will not easily be stripped again. I have brought my imagination under a certain degree of control and will no longer owe to it the great but inane and unfruitful pleasures which I was daily wont to draw from its exhaustless resources. I no longer employ myself in opening fanciful vistas into the future, but occupy myself simply with the place I stand on. As one who makes a path through a dense forest, having chosen my path I pursue it by line and compass, and do not listen to the suggestions of child-eyed imagination and follow here and there, right and left, a visionary and unprogressive route.
>
> A man has a multitude of judgments whose truth he sees but will not grasp; this is my state, but in the last year I have laid hold of most of these truths and begun to utilize them. I have not improved the theory of my character, but have commenced reducing it to practice. I was accustomed to languish for independence, even when I saw it well within my reach; I cajoled myself into the belief that there were kinds of

independence and only one of them the boon I desired. But I perceive that real independence is one, though the means of its attainment differ; and that the most practical means are the best. I made up my mind to this effect: The things that I have reluctantly dispensed with, I can dispense with and may as well joyfully dispense with. I have always possessed in an eminent degree the faculty of removing my thoughts from a displeasing object, to those that please. I made another and greater effort, and taking them from those that simply please and do not profit, I directed them to those that profit and therefore conduce to pleasure. I have made some progress toward the acquisition of a good prose style, an acquisition whose immense importance only dawned upon me as I advanced upon the attainment of it. I perceive that until this last year, the most essential means of improvement was neglected. It is like a new sense.

Poetry only developed a fragment of my mind; a development that was injurious to the whole. All partial culture has an inevitable tendency to enfeeble and exhaust the soil. When the faculties are equally cultivated the mind will yield Egyptian harvests. . . . I have been thrice humanized; once, through the imagination, once, upon compulsion, and once through admiration. The last endures. I have had one, the most fortunate escape of my life. To conclude: that which I always sighed for I now deprecate, change.

Goethe (on Laocoon) pretends that in works of art, independent of the beauty of representation, there should exist a certain beauty in the general outline, a symmetrical figure that would please the eye at a distance where the character of the whole would be imperceptible; in fact, an architectural ornament. I cannot agree with him. Some most indifferent artists attend to this. A line connecting the heads in Bassano's pieces describes usually some pretty figure, when there is no other beauty to be discovered. Because the pyramidal form of the Laocoon group pleases the eye, it does not follow that it should be a rule of art to obtain this effect.

With more justice he insists that when an action is represented, the complement of the action should be exhibited. That is, when an object is delineated in some relation to another object, that other must not be omitted. And he mentions a few examples of works that fulfill this demand. He does not, however, refer to the Apollo Belvedere. It would not be possible, however, to give the complement of this. The eye of Apollo follows his arrows into impenetrable space, the object of his vision is as far from him as earth from Heaven. He, the God, could penetrate this infinitude with a glance; but it would take humanity long to traverse it. If we saw the Python, the Apollo would lose greatly; the proximity would rob him of his divinity, and like Admetus, we would not know the God.

January 10. I no longer take delight in history; to tell the truth I find it most wearisome, even the best. The changes in its chime are so few, the repetitions, with merely adventitious difference, so endless, that my mind grows obtuse under the great monotony. There is so much that is stereotype that I look long in vain for a novelty upon which to fasten a train of thought. Until the age of nineteen I had a passion for this kind of literature; and for some years later I continued to read much of it, rather from a notion of its value than from a pure taste for it. How has it benefited me? Not at all, if its permanency in memory be a test. The whole mass is swept as completely from my grasp as though it had never been within it. Of the 1,000 volumes that I have probably read, all would now be new to me and all superlatively dull. The very titles of many have escaped me; how completely dead then must their contents be to me. Fortunately I know that such is not a sure test. For whatever is read con amore is not profitless. The histories that I studied with interest, undoubtedly exercised my judgment and have perhaps contributed to the education of my mind more by their suggestions than by their communications. History, as it is often written, is more removed from nature, from the sphere of ordinary life, than even the censured extravagances of romance; and in fact, when the historian dashes his page with a tint of romance, the interest this inspires is an evidence of an approximation to the nature that makes us all kin. The great error of many historians is the assumption of dignity. They overlook the generality of mankind and refuse to look a poor child of nature honestly and affectionately in the face.

Perhaps almost every man's opinion of himself is founded upon certain dispositions which are incidental to him, rather than upon the general disposition of his mind. To those chance moods in which some nobler faculties stir within him, he complacently refers himself for the justification of pride of self. The heart has its Sabbaths; and in the act of self-judgment it looks to these alone. But the world makes no distinction between these Sabbaths and the week-days of our nature, and thinks of us by the aggregate of what it sees.

A man is perhaps justifiable in taking these exceptional moods as the measure of his capabilities. How many a common life has opened and expanded into one of nobleness and magnanimous well-doing and honorable luster, simply from a casual mood retained and elevated and devotedly followed as a soldier follows the consecrated standard of his faith. The invisible Genius that summons to high deeds does not, like a pertinacious beggar, beset the door of our heart, but returns, at intervals, to repeat the gentle knock. The door half open, a brief communion takes place and he departs; we make this fragmentary communion the measure of our moral worth and are foolishly indignant at the contrast offered by the world's admeasurement. For capabilities, even the highest, only acquire significance by their fruits. They are as a fine Cremona without the bow; the bow, the practice will alone avail to bring out the sublime tones. Let a man resolve to judge himself solely by those incontestable evidences that the world possesses of his abilities. Let him range himself with the mass until, by his works, he has gained a title to promotion. Let him resent no reproach to which an unexercised faculty within him can alone give a response.

Alas, what bitterness of heart, what cruel, piercing acerbity, what alliances of pride and hate, of self-worship and misanthropy, what antagonism of confidence and despair, of humiliation and lofty aspiration, result from these well-remembered but disobeyed premonitions of a nobler way of life! The evil principle of humanity is incarnate in Indolence, and impartial nature sees throughout her expanded realm, no such enemy as Passivity. It may be said that all crimes stand upon the delusive road of ease, and point to a phantasmal castle of Indolence.

Perhaps the more a religion is involved in hulls of superstition, the longer will be its career. As often as the popular greed of novelty awakes, the religion will but have to throw off one of the gross superstitions that obscure it, and it will appear new-bright and altogether admirable. A pure and spotless creed, one whose celestial, immaterial outline tolerates none of the vile adjuncts of error and wild belief, could hardly become popular. But there never has been a creed which artful superstition was impotent to set off and degrade. The Christian dogma owes much perhaps to the immense mass of superstitions beneath which in its very infancy, it was almost extinguished, and athwart which it sent so feeble a heavenly light. Slowly with the centuries one and another have fallen away and ever with the increase of illumination, or rather diminution of darkness, the people have shouted in jubilee as for a new Messiah. But there is danger always that as a religion becomes refined and spiritualized its subtle and unconfined essence will evaporate and return to heaven.

A religion without symbols soon ceases to be a religion for the masses. The common mind must have the object of its worship brought down to death or it will give over worshipping. It has not the power or the will to elevate itself into the vague expanse of a heaven. And herein consists the great utility of temples and periodical worship. Men consider their churches to be the habitation of a God, "at home" there once a week for their reception. It seems to be an inevitable law that worship creates for itself symbols; and perhaps the fervency of prayer is proportioned to the proximity of the subject addressed. There may be a creed without idols, but I suspect there has never been a religion. An idol need not be a material, tangible object in nature or in art; it may equally as well be an image of the brain, and the effusion of a contrite spirit, when not addressed to a substantial presence, is always offered up to a deity clothed by strong imagination in some shadowy likeness of matter.

It follows that the force of the religious sentiment is always in a corresponding ratio with the impurity of the creed which elicits it; and that in ages of grossest superstition and in idolatrous lands, there is more fervency of worship than where a purified belief abstracts itself from earthly paraphernalia and disdains to interfere with the laws of nature.

Jacobi said that Nature concealed God from him; it conceals God from most men when they are taught not to seek Him there. When they surmise that God is on the other side of nature, they get in the habit of relying upon nature to defend them from Him. But men of much veneration always feel the necessity of creating him in nature; for thought must cease to be impassioned before it can (if it can) abstract itself entirely from material forms; and this is not the less true, that they obey this necessity without being conscious of it.

Let the most religious man, however, cast a retrospective glance upon his devotional hours, and he will become aware that the intensity of his worship was in proportion to the distinctness and materiality of the vision he beheld. No people are more devout than the Mohammedans, and I believe one reason to consist in the fact that they have given their God a place in Nature; from Bucharest, from Morocco, from Ispahan, their eyes and their prayers are addressed to Mecca.

Christianity never glowed with such enthusiastic fire as in the era of the Crusades when men stood with their faces and their burning thoughts turned to the Holy Land, the fore-court of heaven, the favorite dwelling-place of their deity; and they rushed with mad devotion towards it as though they heard wafted from that violated region the lamentations of the Supreme Being tortured by the presence of infidels in that sacred land.

Why is it that the popular mind is so adverse to Pantheism? If men find it beyond their power to be religious with a purely abstract, unsymbolized creed, a creed that relegates the divinity beyond material nature, why are they reluctant to give Him all nature? They seem to think that they have given Him enough in giving Him churches and chapels and one of their seven days, and they are outrageous at the agrarian proposition to divide with Him all time, matter and spirit. What brutal notions of an eternal, spiritual essence must they have who suppose that it can prefer one particle of matter to another and that it can be susceptible to the emotions of disgust which certain qualities thereof arouse in a sensual being.

A pregnant word is that of the scoffing Heine: "Catholicism reversed the Pantheism she found in Europe, and in place of deifying nature, she diabolized it." But whenever a right reverence for the dignity of the human mind shall be prevalent with men, the tendency will be again to Pantheism, but to a far other and more perfect Pantheism than was known to the martial Greeks and ancient Germans. When will that be? When will mankind entertain this right reverence? When it ceases to be merely retrospective, when it ceases to justify its evil propensities by the example of history, when it listens to the better pulsations of its nature and presses earnestly forward to a goal at length apprehended as real.

Bowen's later comment is, "All that is true in Pantheism is found in Christianity and there alone."

January 26, 1843. Commenced *Erythreus* about Feb. 10; finished 1st book about March 20; 2nd book, April 14; began 3rd, July 30; finished Oct. 16; began 4th, Dec. 5; finished Jan. 5, 1844, and wrote five chapters of 5th book in January.

A bold, bad man may bring many virtues into disrepute, and a hero of mixed composition scarcely ever fails of bringing some vices into fashion.

The romancer distils life; out of a hundred grains of corn he extracts the drop of spirit.

The nature of things is not even constant in inconstancy. When we expect to be disappointed we are sure to be disappointed of our disappointment.

February 3, 1843. It is surprising what respect intemperate passion claims for itself. The man who is accustomed to yield to it, almost invariably regards it as something ennobling. Instead of blushing for the tyranny it exercises over his better self, and endeavoring to resist it as the worst inheritance of childhood, he avows the tyranny on every occasion and accompanies the avowal with regrets that are merely hypocritical. The explanation of the vain-glory with which some men confess an indomitable temper, is to be found in the fact that they confound it with courage. It is a bastard of courage. A distinguishing feature in courage is calmness.

Rousseau says that "when men are corrupt it is better that they should be learned than ignorant; but if they are good it is to be feared that science will corrupt them." Corruption seems an inevitable chasm in the progress of civilization; but will not regenerate man discover a more glorious civilization beyond? From the muddy Styx a man came forth a demigod.

The true destiny of knowledge is to perfect thought by tasking it.

The mental progress of men may be compared to the ancient torch races; too rapid a movement will extinguish the flambeau as effectually as a fall. It has been observed that arts and sciences owe their decline generally to men of genius.

Feb. 6, 1843. Nature, like Napoleon her audacious imitator, envisages her end regardless of sacrifices. She inundates Europe with a fatal flux of Barbarians that their descendants may live under social institutions of an ameliorative character; she depopulates a hemisphere that it may serve as a vast cradle to civilization; she leads man through a long array of dismal centuries to a brighter yet to come.

Men lock up their God in magnificent churches and visit Him once a week to keep Him docile.

Almost every great resurrection of a people has been preceded by a slight relaxation of the severity of oppression. That men may apprehend the nature of the injustice done them by an oppressive rule, it seems to be necessary that they should first be led one step from its profoundest gloom. As men accustom themselves to darkness in the long duration of an Arctic night, so they familiarize themselves with servitude, lose the right apprehension of cruelty, and regard the eclipse of liberty not only as something natural, but as something luminous. They come at last to think that to grope is the natural action of man. But the first gleam of dawning light that reveals to them the darkness in which they stand, renews the sense of a better and truer condition, and infuses into them the spirit to accomplish their own exodus. A tyrant needs to be not more wily in usurping than in restoring liberty. He has but to keep the treasure from the sight of the people. Once lulled to oblivion of the theft, give them but a glimpse of it, through impolicy, temerity or remorse, and he stands in imminent peril.

Sometimes, standing in Night, I please myself in releasing my spirit from the particular laws of matter to which it is subject; expelling for a time the foolish notion of an above and a beneath, I look abroad in infinitude with a purely spiritual eye. I take up the sun with its attendant planets, earth among the rest, and compress them into a little star, as they are in truth, and put this star along with the others in the far night where it really is. I then see that the great all is starlit gloom, and sunlight the mere accident of proximity. I then rush down on the pinions of disembodied thought through infinitude till all that starry heaven, that wonderful dome with its millions of suns each as far apart from the other as all from our earth, till all is shrunken into one little star, one in a new night-world of stars. I go no further, for infinity is the despair of all thought, save the Master-thought.

A man should be careful not to surrender himself too habitually or frequently to the seductions of an enthusiasm that embraces the interests of all his race. It is an emotion too powerful to be available in every daily life. He should, however, welcome it from time to time and regard it as a luxury to be economized. The expansion it gives the heart is not otherwise than beneficent when its visits are separated by ceremonial intervals. But its constant presence is dangerous to the mind by the continual incense of flattery which it offers up deluding a man thereby into the belief that his life is holy because his contemplations are beautiful. In these days men fancy that the great idea of nature has been discovered, and all start up with the paltry tools of their various handicrafts to aid her in completing it. How she must wish them all at the d.... I give myself a little lash here; but it does not hurt.

He writes out an extended analysis of Schiller's *Sendung Moses* (Legation of Moses). Its rejection of the supernatural and its conjecture of the natural causes of those effects which are attributed to the supernatural, he found wholly agreeable to his mind.

> He (Schiller) even attributes, I think with not much propriety, a great degree of our present culture to the theosophy of Moses. True, we owe it to the doctrine of a single God; but, as Schiller afterwards shows, Moses got this doctrine from the Egyptian priests, and it is not impossible that it would have eventually become esoteric and disseminated, though it had not been betrayed by him in the natural course of events.
>
> The Spartans, the most sober, the Sybarites, the most voluptuous, were equally idle people living by the labor of their slaves; they were the idlest races mentioned in history.
>
> How was it that inactivity nourished the virtues of the one nation and engendered the vices of the other? It was doubtless by the operation of their different laws, the different moral principles which spoke through their legislative codes. In Sparta there were no individual interests; all were merged in the nation. The citizen's pride was that he was a member of the state; not that he was a man, but a Spartan. The patriotic sentiment overrode the common impulses of personal vanity. He was free only in this sense that he belonged to a free community. The freedom of the Spartan was the shade of a broad tree that over-canopied the entire nation; not a garment which invested and which isolated the man. Among the Sybarites on the contrary, the interest of the mass so far from merging in itself the interest of the individual was rather regarded as

hostile to it. The Sybarites had no country; each was his own secret king and demigod, not the less zealously worshipped that he was enforced in some measure to exhibit a show of deference to the nominal sovereign, the community.

There is a dynamic force in death as in life, and corruption implies quite as imperatively the presence of an active agency as growth itself. The cessation of life is simply inanimation, and without the development of new powers an inanimate body would remain forever inalterable. But how startling, how wonderful is this new, this strange vitality that springs up at the departure of that to which we appropriate the name of life! It is as though a million of living, breathing, sentient and willful beings were upon the instant enfranchised from the thralldom which had held them powerless and subject to one superior, tyrannical life. They cast off the bonds which united them one to another; each revels in the consciousness of its restored individuality; the appetites of its restored individuality; the appetites of each are now recovered to itself, its life is its own, the peculiar wants of its being are felt once more: it has powers and the freedom to gratify its wants, or to fight for their gratification; and a fearful strife immediately begins. Each atom is its own sovereign now and arms itself for spoil; its own despotic will controls its movements; it goes about in the glow of autocratic energy to glut its awakened powers, to devour, to spoil, to enjoy. Horrible spectacle! Yet wherefore horrible? Man, pausing in the contemplation of an ideal world created by his own noble aspirations and peopled by his glorious faculties with sublime images of the godhead, shivers to behold this other spectacle. But his spirit, though allied with life, is not essentially life. And between the animated atom and the animated world of atoms which constitute the beautiful presence of an Antinous, immaterial nature knows no distinction. Rigorous and few are the esthetic demands of man; but universal and without law (for they include all law) are those of nature.

Shall I believe that of the Supreme Being which conflicts with my most exalted conception of supreme justice? No, though I saw it in the Bible; No, though I saw it written in the heavens themselves in letters of fire; No, though I heard it in the voice of omnipotence at the footstool of the final Judge. I would arise and thus would I say: The soul by which I live eternally is stamped with a glorious image of infallible virtue, a visible impress glowing in undimmed brightness as often as that soul escapes from the oppression and obscurity of earth to bathe in the empyrean of truth; by that impress I know my Creator, and that Creator is my only God. Be thou Jehovah, be Thou the God of all mankind beside, disown Thou this my conception of the beneficent and I disown Thee, I deny Thee, I defy Thee. There is another greater than Thou, who, as He forbids me to adore Thee, gives me the courage to oppose Thee.

Man perplexes the woof of his own destinies and then attributes to nature the perplexity, and expects from her the restoration. I consider that man has yet got something to do with his passions and here upon this earth too. Men are in the habit of looking upon their own century as the ultimatum of time; but wherefore, since they can look backward through 60 centuries, should they not look forward as many? And since man can look back upon such a mass of evil of his own accomplishment, should he not look forward upon as much of good?

Was not the mission of Luther successful hereby, that he told every man something known by that man before; and that in the voice of the reformer the unspoken thought of each individual found utterance?

It has often seemed to me that we were without any strong grounds for believing the beams of the sun to contain in themselves heat. In my eclectic philosophy stands the system of those who maintain the immateriality of Light, regarding it as simply the pulsations of a very subtle fluid. Heat is evolved in our atmosphere; but may not this be the result of the commingling of light with our atmosphere so that the sun's rays are unacquainted with heat until they approach the planets and their satellites?

Unjust and foolish is the contempt which some at the present day testify for the great originals; they do not consider how much of their own knowledge is derived from the ancients by imperceptible transfusion. The wisdom of the ancients is our common sense.

Madame de Stael considers M. Necker and M. Mirabeau, like Cicero and Catiline, types of the good and bad principle. She considers the genius of Mirabeau which demanded rather the conflict and the conquest than peaceful acquisition by concession, to have been fatal to France. All which I in no wise accept. What was fatal to France was his premature death. She disserts upon his immoralities. His moeurs had undoubtedly been bad, but they were the consequences of a deplorable education and of a state of things against which he lifted up his voice and at last his avenging hand. "La petite morale tue la grande," was his frequent exclamation and one full of the essence of truth.

Bonaparte, in making peace with the Pope in 1797, stipulated for the delivery of two antique busts, those of Junius and Marcus Brutus. How many will have clambered to a throne upon the shoulders of the Bruti.

Adversity is to the heart what the bee to the flower; robbing it at the moment, but preparing it for a more beautiful efflorescence.

The hypocrite reposes upon virtues as upon a bed of flowers, crushing them.

We all admire candor when somebody else is to get the benefit of it. Who shall say that we are not disinterested?

There are some kinds of seed that need to be trodden well under foot before they will germinate; and there are not wanting husbandmen willing to do this business. The French revolution saw many of these seeds well-trodden down. The enemies of France rejoiced; but the germs were not the less living that they were lost to sight.

We are like Habakkuk when good actions are to be done, and need that the angel of the Lord should take us by the hair of the head.

Schlegel here cannot let pass an occasion to speak slightingly of Plutarch. Now, if there be an ancient of them all who has contributed more than Plutarch to modern instruction if not culture, I know him not. He has had three centuries of unbounded popularity. Schlegel laughs at him for mentioning such minutiae as that Philip Antigonus, Hannibal and Sertorius were all one-eyed. It is a poor philosophy that rejects such trifles as unimportant. I believe that deformities oftentimes affect the development of the intellectual faculties. Napoleon was the child of antiquity; he owed more to Plutarch than to all besides; his impulses urged him constantly to square his actions rather by the morality of the ancients than of the moderns. How much Shakespeare owed to Plutarch is obvious.

The passions which belong to an individual in a civilized state are doubtless very different from those which pertain to a man in a state of nature Where the mental faculties have had some development, the imagination imparts to the passions an unnatural intensity. Sensuality kills many more Europeans than Africans. Nature has given us passions, but she has likewise given us an intellect; we must take our choice between these. A loose rein given to our passions, we will never discover that we have a plastic mind.

Demosthenes was fined 50,000 dollars once for being silent. A fact to be pondered. Query, what would Athens have given had he spoken? A queer world, this. Paganini sustained a suit brought against him when I was in Paris, to make him play; he was condemned and had to pay high for exemption. It is rather a dangerous thing to do the world a benefit; the world condemns you to repeat it while you live, or else become the subject of obloquy and persecution. The world is right. It does well to rate highly the privilege of working for it. The incessant labor it imposes is the laborer's best blessing. A noble mind could not ask anything better than the imposition of such a task. The fault with regard to Demosthenes was that Athens would have him speak so and not so; wished him to speak its thought.

During these same months he made many annotations on Hallam's *Europe in the Middle Ages;* Arnold's *Lectures on Modern History;* Schlegel's

Philosophy of History; Gliddon's *Egypt;* Hume's *Essays and Treatises; Review of Spinoza;* Ockley's *History of the Saracens;* Coleridge's *Table Talk;* Hazlitt on Human Action; Koch's *Revolutions of Europe;* Emerson's *Essays;* D'Israeli's *Miscellanies;* Channing's *Essays;* Lamb's *Letters;* Hazlitt's *Spirit of the Age;* Scott's *Diary;* Priestley; Voltaire's *Mélanges Historiques:*

> "Voltaire, ce singe de genie, chez l'homme en mission par le diable envoyé," says Victor Hugo, and I am almost willing to allow that in Voltaire we see the parody of genius, so disgusting to me are these two volumes of *Mélanges Historiques.* And yet I once read them with satisfaction. My tastes have certainly been greatly purified since then. I have got back to my earlier, better nature.
>
> Hide fire in a napkin and misdeeds in time.
>
> Every man possesses in an astonishing degree one talent and one virtue; sophistry for the vindication of his faults; charity for their palliation.

It is not known what became of Bowen's great literary project, *Agathon,* the tragedy with Christ as the central figure, and other works to which there are references in his journal:

> *Aug. 6.* Have been a week writing the 2nd chapter of the 3rd book of *Erythreus,* and consider that I have tolerably improved the time. I have been an eclectic with my thoughts, and could have filled with the refuse three times as much paper as I used. I am delighted at the recovery of my long-lost diligent habits; I owe it to the absence and equally to the influence of Apollonia Naturata. This was a fictitious name given to a woman friend, who under medical advice, had gone to try some sulfur springs in Virginia.
>
> *Aug. 19.* Have read in the last two weeks D'Israeli's *Miscellanies* and Channing's *Essays.* Have read them merely as a recreation, say rather, relaxation, passively, not very profitably. But when I write with assiduity, when my thoughts are absorbed by the conduct of a plot, I cannot read with much profit. Among the best weeks of my life, the two last, Chs. 3, 4, 5. Ye Gods! When I think of the wasted time of this summer. Channing's works I must read again some day. They are a mine of inestimable thought. I find in them the source of much that has been since written by others. The day before yesterday, parted with my brother, gone a long and dubious journey. These partings are detestable things. There is a constriction of the heart produced by parting with a dear friend, that is very different from any other painful sensation. We feel at

such moments how much more important than any other interests, than pecuniary interests, then intellectual interests, than the interests of our ambition, or of our social position are those of our natural affections.

Aug. 26th. Chs. 5 and 6. Encore des adieux.

Sept. 9th. Chs. 7-12. Have been writing six weeks without intermission. Feel today a disposition to relax. Have been so occupied as scarcely to pay attention to some things that would at another moment have afflicted me much.

Oct. 7. E. ritornata l'infelice e adorata. *14.* Week of tears, of admiration and compassion. Next week must witness the completion of the 3rd book. What else?

The only work of these years which appears to have been published, but of which, so far as is known, only one copy survives, was the romance entitled *The Pupil of Raphael* written in 1842 or 1843. Bowen did not remember the date. It was published anonymously at his own expense by Wiley and Putnam in 1843 in two small volumes of 210 and 217 pages. It shows how thoroughly his mind was saturated with Italy and it is a book of real philosophical insight, but it is melodramatic and theatrical and full of extraordinary words, such as manducated, celsitude, insunderable, indompted, inexorcisable, etc. Thirty-seven years later Bowen printed in the *Bombay Guardian* a letter from a friend in America with no comment of his own, criticizing the romance:

> *The Pupil*, certainly, was thrust into the world in a form little likely to attract; badly printed in close lines, on poor paper, and without binding. I felt sad, the other day, after reading some pages if it, sad, through pity of your old self. There seems such a waste of mental product. The reader, the ordinary reader, is allured by the incidents of a romance, and suddenly finds himself in the midst of a dissertation on Art, or on some point in philosophy or morals for which he finds in himself no preparedness of mind. It would have been better for you as an author if you had put these really original and valuable thoughts in a purely didactic form. An essay, published in some review of intellectual pretensions, would have found some receptive readers, and the fruits of your reflections would not have been quite lost. There is too much of a good thing in *The Pupil of Raphael,* too much compressed thought. Then, the compressed and ill-printed lines weary the eyes and crowd the attention. If your early works had not been printed at the expense of the author, they would at least have had the publisher's patronage, and the benefit of his efforts to gain that of the public.

The romance, however, both in its plot, its moralizing, its philosophy and its art, while deserving no immortality, was superior to much contemporary literature of the first half of the nineteenth century in America. Long afterwards Bowen, who had no copy of the book, wrote to Mr. Rankin under date of Bombay, August 11, 1885:

> You must not suppose that my literary appetite is at all what it was in early days. The greater part of modern literature is to me Vanity of vanities. I am none the less very thankful for the kind interest you show in me. But you and your friend might have left that *Pupil of Raphael* to its well deserved oblivion. I have not the slightest recollection of it, of the plot, the characters, the sentiments, *not a solitary recollection*, so that I cannot appreciate your friend's critique. One thing ever troubles me, viz., that you should not be experiencing the faith that God expects of you. Let God be true, though every man a liar. Instead of trying to justify this, that and the other man, justify God. Do Him justice. The same you would expect for yourself. As you would wish your own word to be honored, so honor His. Salvation is in that very thing. I was just on the border of despair in 1845, till on the 4th of December, I saw that all I had been seeking in myself, I had in Christ. I had been tormenting myself to looking hourly to my own heart for the dawn of a brighter day, looking, (if you please) for Christ in my heart rather than for Christ in the Word, and I found life, joy and peace when I let go my own heart and looked to Christ alone. As the Israelites looked to the brazen serpent.

5. The Illumination of a Hopeless Love

Bowen's old life now came to an end. The ephemeral love affairs of past years were transcended in a great devotion which completely changed the man and his mind and sent him out on a radically new and different career. The first reference to the new influence is under date of Nov. 15, 1842, in his journal:

> This day ends the episode of twenty-five days. Episode! A more odious word is not to be found in the dialects of men. It is the scoffing exponent of life itself. Either we stand on a bleak rock and see glorious arks of safety passing at a distance or, drifting on some fragment down the stream of time, we see along the banks diversified spots of beauty. It truly appears that whatever is lovely is episodical in life. Is it not different in eternity? But . . . eternity. What is it to me? The existing second is all in which man has an estate, and even in that his will has the feeblest influence. But I believe the recollection of this last transitory period will be more purely complacent and of more enduring freshness than others have been. Such a delicious sensation is that of unmixed admiration, and at the same time so rare, that it were unpardonable not to indulge it as long as heart is capable of shining with a light fed only by memory.

A few days later he writes:

> Schiller. "Religion penetrates a man's whole nature and searches out what is peculiar in him to ennoble it entirely." Any genuine, complete love does this. It unweaves the character, rejects the rotting and the coarsest threads and constructs a new and better woof.

His beloved's name was Emma Morris. He calls her in one entry "Apollonia Naturata." There is no account of their relations until July 24, 1843. Bowen's later "Reminiscences" say that she had been in the south and that on her return he had accompanied her and some of her friends on an excursion to Long Island and that the sections of his journal which were not preserved were full of "rhapsody and idolatry."

Of his first and last meetings with her Bowen wrote in his private diary of May 22, 1870:

> Very sad news of Mrs. Augustus Stebbins, the sister of Emma Morris, at whose marriage with my friend Aug. S. I first met Emma, she who was destined to change my life for time and eternity. . . . I remember once

going with these two sisters to Jersey City to see them off in the train for Virginia and that was the last time I ever saw Emma.

July 24th, 1843. 20th to the 24th. Bonheur sans mélange, les plus beaux jours de ma vie.

July 25th. O that every act of my life could henceforward be a testimonial that I live for her. My past life merges in the present, and my future dates from it. The stars, the suns that throng infinitude all reflect to me no more than my thought of her. She is all these, all that was ever created beautiful. The word belongs to her, to her every thought, every word, every movement.

Ill health sent her south to some sulfur springs in Virginia and on Oct. 20, 1843 he writes:

Perhaps the dreariest week in my life. The year that is completed this night was opened by the most memorable moment in my existence. A year ago tonight this very moment it may be, I saw her for the first time. As I look back on the past I can see nothing anterior to that moment worth remembering. Had I then any presentiment of what prolonged strange influences would flow from it? No. I had nothing but a sense of inexpressible happiness. It was a bridal evening, but I was the happy one.

I have no courage now to dwell upon the blessedness of that hour, now that my mind is a prey to wretchedness. But I remember that when parting from her in the open, moonlit air at midnight some voice remonstrated with her for exposing herself; I hastily asked if she had not health, and she as hastily answered that she had. I then recollected what I had before been told that she was ill of a mortal malady. But I would not believe it, have always refused to believe it and will not believe it. When I must believe it let me be spared the horror of living a waste remainder of life on an earth from which all glory will have departed. I shake resolutely from my mind these awful prognostics, and surrender myself to the benignities of imagination, and see her standing in the future, not too distant, in the next spring, in perfect health. And yet I cannot deny that these prognostics scare me from all peace. Though I know them untruthful, yet the mere sound of the lugubrious words fills me with distress. Would that a life could purchase something, purchase from the future an inviolable assurance that she shall yet live many years. She shall. Let me not doubt it. If she is to die some day, I will become religious even to superstition, and create heaven in my belief that she may dwell there, in her sublime identity, and be worshipped there, to be rejoined by me in some other day. (This very idea was afterwards carried out by Comte).

> With all solemnity I here declare that I would give up my immortal soul to be flung by the Creator into chaos so that she might have eternal life, so that her individual soul be compassed by a heaven of immortality. But the thought of her death makes hideous all life. She will not die. If restoration be from a Providence, it will come to her; and I shall behold her some time clad in rejuvenescent health, and give voice to that which now holds my soul in its theurgic embrace. She is divine in suffering. Would that I could see her and give her one reason more why she should live; for it has always seemed to me that the volition has power over death.
>
> I cannot hear of a young angelic being going down the steps of death one by one, without thinking that there is some horrible mistake at work, and that a passionate invocation may awaken the suffering one to life. But why do I write these things? I know well enough that there is nothing to fear and that she will recover soon. But of these sufferings! My soul is wrung with compassion and idolatry, when I hear of them. She smiles no more, they tell me. This alone darkens for me the face of all things. And so changed! They who enter her room go hastily but overcome. And yet she considers everybody rather than herself, studying always to cheer her friends and persuade them that she will soon be well and free from suffering. Being asked if I should not be sent for, she said, "No, for what pleasure would it give him to see such a sickly creature as I now am." She thought it would pain me to see how changed she is since I last saw her, July 29th. It is the moral beauty that I adore, and this is of everlasting inviolability, beyond all scathe.

Again he writes on Nov. 2, 1843:

> I do not know whether the predominant power of hope in my mind be the cause of greater solace or misery. It often has the evil effect of postponing and making more difficult the turning point of resignation. But, as in the present instance resignation will be impossible, (yes criminal, cowardly, vile,) and so to be regarded as a devout person would consider resignation to the loss of Heaven, I think that the indefeasible hope within me is a blessing. Yet there are moments in which I pay fearfully for its long consolations.
>
> The other night, Oct. 31, at the dead of night, the moonlight streaming into my chamber, all the false, the horrid death-notes that have been forced into my ear, resounded within me like the dread enunciations of an inevitable doom. Hope for the time was spent; not a ray. She would surely die. I was nearly wild with agony. A dreadful night. But the beams of the next day's sun quickened once more the fervor of hope. I hope now. But my heart is always full with repressed tears. What a faculty of gladdening myself I possess in my imagination.

The Illumination of a Hopeless Love

Every day some new dream takes me from the real world and gives me many hours of delight. This morning, for instance, what happiness was mine for nearly an hour! My fantasy was: the physicians had said, blood of a healthy subject would restore her and I gave mine; they were bound to eternal secrecy; day by day, pound after pound I gave of my blood and every day I was cheered with tidings of her convalescence; as I descended to the grave she returned to life; and I died blessed for she at last stood clothed in pristine health and she would never know that her new life was my gift. Beautiful dream! Would that it could be realized! But alas, but oh the awful thought! Her restoration depends on an invisible, inexorable agency over which the entire population of the earth, leagued and animated by my own hope, all mankind, the entire race of human beings, have not more influence than the tiniest mote that trembles in the sunbeam. All the most sacred places of the earth might stream with sacrifices and not forward by one pulsation her recovery. The martyrdom of all good men were of no more avail than one of my tears. And all the tears of all the most godlike of earth would bring her less succor than a momentary spring shower.

Oh, the dread mystery that marches before time! Oh, for some assurance that there is indeed something that marches before time, that time is directed, that time is not a senseless, arbitrary, supreme nonentity. That a Will is cognizant of her malady and provident of her end! That the hours that come to her receive their instructions from a supreme intelligence. I have a faint, unnecessary belief that there is a providence for the race, the genus; but unfortunately I have not the beneficent belief which recognizes a providence for the individual. What is the race to me? I would offer up the whole earth for her.

Oh, for something to pray to! Oh, that there were no ills but such as sacrifices might remove! I never thought that I should regret the dissipated illusions which left me in utter immedicable doubt of all beyond nature. For myself alone, I never should. If I walk in the eye of a God or not, if my soul is perishable or immortal, is a question that never troubled me, though often asked; would never trouble me; but if her soul shall re-exist or not is one that agonizes me. It shall, it must; hers, if no other. Folly! Can we believe in such eclecticism? Hers and all then. Oh, if I had never contemplated any soul but hers, had never morbidly gazed on my own mind, the doubt would never have been. But why speak of annihilation? Is there not anguish enough in the thought of death for her? The thought were intolerable, and I write about it because it is not truly, visibly in my mind. A distinct, undivided conception of such a thing has never come there. For I yet know that she shall live. But the necessity of hoping is sadness enough. Oh, that I were vilely superstitious and had before me some symbol in whose divine efficacy I had rooted faith, and could kneel before it and pour out day and night my misery and hope in prayer. Prayer! Beautiful invention!

There is such a solace in weakness, such pain in the involuntary, unavailing fortitude of isolation. No, I can never taste the sweet relief of prayer, the thought that by burning words I had obtained relief for her. For I can see nothing to pray to, and my words would be as hypocritical as cold. Admidable being! Apollonia (the name of the chief character in the work that Homunculus was then writing, and to which he gave the name *Erythreus,*) is but a faint, faint portrait of her. All of her own sex that approach her, even for a few minutes only, are forced to forget themselves, their own enthroned interests, their merits, their pettinesses, forget the woman in themselves and recognize only her excellence. Did I not see the other day an elderly lady whose eyes glistened with a peculiar sensibility as she spoke of having known her as a child of singular fascinations? Oh, my wasted life! The wasted years when I did not know of her existence, when she was only dimly seen in imagination and hope. And to think that I cannot see her; everybody except myself; menials, marble-hearted physicians, nurses, everybody.

November 9. Better, beautiful word! But no, an ugly cacophonous word, not worthy of its sense. Mieux is hardly better. There is no articulate token of goodness in the sound of it. Mejor, a rude masculine word. Besser is still worse. Meglio is best, is excellent and fitly expressive. Sta meglio, meglio, meglio.

17th. Have had a week's remission of tears, a week of assured and patient hopefulness, a week of comparative consolation. But it is cruelly terminated. I have just received information that the evening before last her physician declared to her that she had but two months to live. Her friends, wishing her to see another physician, disclosed to her that the doctor was dealing insincerely with her, encouraging her while he discouraged them. She declined, however, unwilling to pain the physician in attendance, and asked him to tell her what he really thought of her case, and then told her that she had but two months to live. I regard his proceeding as most unjustifiable and only calculated to accelerate the event.

18th. Meglio, meglio, meglio, and my mind is again a serviceable thing. She is too good for earth, says one to me. Why for earth? Earth wants all the good souls it can have; wants them more than Heaven, I think.

Already deep changes were taking place in him. A little real experience of life and love was doing for him in a few weeks what years of introspection and speculation had not done. His atheism was fast slipping off him:

The Illumination of a Hopeless Love

Every man in the course of 24 hours passes through as many mysteries as the Eleusinian, Egyptian, Samothracian, Cabirian, Isiac, Mithraic and Bacchic put together. Dreaming; waking; thinking; unthinking, and every operation indeed of the man material or immaterial.

To the doctrine of predestination which Godwin seems to approve, I am irreconcilably opposed. We are God's workmen; God creates man to be His assistant. He calls him into existence, puts him in the field, fully equipped for labor and conscious of his duties, and leaves him in absolute option to work or not, ill or well as he listeth; but so cunning is the equipment of man, that according as his labor is is his fare. Every man is his own sufficient monitor, castigator, recompenser.

If we say that God had in the beginning foreknowledge of all eternity, then the existence of God through eternity must be simply a stale and profitless contemplation of what He has already seen. With Him there is no difference between the thing seen in thought and the thing seen in corporate form. God works in time, even as every man. It is a bold thing to invent attributes for God; it is not more bold to dispute them. There is one writing in my mind, one ineffaceable scripture, the beneficence of God. I assert not God to be omnipotent or omniscient or immutable. Perfection with me is highest merit; merit involves option; option supposes the possibility of change. There is no meaning in the word omnipotent; *e.g.,* God is not omnipotent if He cannot know the future; He is not omnipotent if He cannot ignore the future. Who shall say what He has chosen? I for one will not believe that He is eternally engaged in repetition, working out exteriorly just the things that He has been conversant with from all eternity and that it is impossible for Him to have a new thought.

Love absorbs individualities; blots out the idiosyncrasy which all foregoing time and circumstances had been laboriously forming; and abruptly imposes an aspect, demeanor, mode of thought, phraseology, and principle of action of its own. This is not the virtue but the error of the passion. For though the metamorphosis is generally an elevation, a transition into a worthier state of existence, yet a man's individuality is quite too important a thing to be thus unceremoniously blotted out. It is in fact what outline is in art; obliterate it anywhere and there life ceases; and love is generally a breaking up of the continuity of life and principle of identity. At the best, there is between his present and past a tenuous, airy Bridge of Sighs. The passion is only respectable when it allies itself with the individuality, limiting its destructive influence to the weaknesses and imperfections of the character.

Dec. 2. How great is the accumulation of sorrow that awaits me. It will be of that kind which has to be thoroughly endured, which knows no commutation, and the only alleviation of which is to be disclosed from the bosom of itself, from its own very center. The only consolation will be the apotheosis of the sorrow. In absolute self-surrenderment I must go with it to the end. The fulfillment of its own law will be the regeneration of peace. I have a dim presentiment of what will be revealed to me in the very depth of it.... The belief in the soul's immortality is not instinctive in humanity, but every mind is so constituted that it may attain to the apprehension of it. This seems to me reasonable. I think that if no mention of such a destiny had ever been made to me, I still would have conjectured it, after looking a few times on death. I doubt now if there have been communities without the belief. Individuals, yes; so there have been individuals who have immured themselves in places where it was impossible for their muscles to be of the slightest use, and yet continued to live. Indeed I never yet questioned that the spiritual principle might live for ever; my only question was if our identity resides in that. My impulse of late is to say, yes. Is the mind material or not? Material? if so, how could we ever have consciousness of it? We could only perceive it; nothing more. Our consciousness must itself be a spiritual principle, self-evidently and without demonstration. Our consciousness, (to define by analogy), must be a sentient being in the midst of a gallery of art, the spectator of the mind.

The ideal hypothesis rests upon these premises: that it is impossible to show that the soul can know anything out of itself or that we can be conscious of anything but the modification of our consciousness. It gives unimpeachable evidence that our knowledge of the existence of matter must be prior to any intellectual process. But if the mind be material how do we know it? It is all folly. Our mind is simply our consciousness modified; as the modifications in the material world perpetuate themselves, so in spirit, and it is impossible that the soul should at a certain point shake off for ever all past modifications and return at a leap to its original essence. The sovereign Spirit, with infinity for a treasury, has no need of such miserable economy; it can afford an eternity and a universe to every individual spirituality; nobody ever dared to deny it to the power to bestow immortality and if it had not predestined it, it would I believe have conferred it, in answer to the unanimous supplications of men.

December 13, 1843. Night. The utter dissolution of hope took place in me this evening. I learn from her sister that her death is momently impending. She partakes of the Communion tomorrow morning. She is conscious and resigned. The final and infallible symptoms have begun. And yet she said today that she felt better, and asked if it was very, very certain that she must die. And I will never see her again upon this earth.

Though I do not wholly apprehend it, though the idea of her death is a dim and half-unmeaning thing in my mind, yet I feel as though we were now within a few hours of doomsday. Does not the very troop of agonies that escorts death to humanity, intimate the higher life beyond? My mind bears against the mystery passionately.

14th. Brute things show no anguish when they see one another die. There must be something more than a merely terrestrial providence. It cannot be that death seizes on lives so beautiful merely that the hearts of the surviving may be bettered. Comparing the means with the end it seems to me like plucking a magnificent flower to hide a dunghill; like grinding the most precious and resplendent stones into mortar for a building. Often, during the last year I have been without the thought of her; many an hour has gone by in mental occupation in which there was no reference to her, and gone by not uncomfortably; true, the expectation of seeing her again was in my mind, and I might at any moment have recurred to it, though I did not; yet in my occupation I was wholly unconscious of any such expectation, and for the time it might be considered unexistent; may there not be hours in my future during which in the like occupation the death of that hope may be unperceived? In those past hours she was for the time dead to me, yet my thoughts were serene. Soon she will be irrecoverably dead to me. But oh how much more easy to lose the sentiment of a living hope, than to lose the consciousness of the extinction of that hope. I am weaning myself back to egotism, and those thoughts of consolation that once seemed to me culpable, and now at times seem so, I invite to my mind. For the fullness of sympathy is death. Yet I loathe myself for listening to any argument for its repression.

I see now the reason of the great difficulty experienced in attaining as I have the conception of the truth. For ten years intellectual skepticism was the law of my being. I had implacably resolved that in it was the utmost possible human truth, that anything beyond an interrogation point was a mistake. I sought in every impression that which was conformable to this idea; what appeared unconformable, I determined was not so and, if rightly comprehended, would prove not to be so. Consequently that original conception became augmented by the tremendous force of uninterrupted habit, a force that in its effects is precisely as a momentum in physics, which at every second diminishes the resisting energy. And even when my suffering heart spoke at length and bore testimony to the divine truth, still the habit of the intellect swayed me; I persisted in believing that there was nothing beyond it. Now, I commune with my heart and I feel the assurance that the two will at last mingle in harmony.

15th. She yesterday partook of her last Communion. She exerted her feeble and fast vanishing power of articulation to express her deep sense of her great unworthiness to partake of it. The clergyman assured her that she would certainly be among the blessed. With that exceeding reverence for sacred things that she has always exhibited, she insisted, notwithstanding her weakness, upon arising and receiving the sacrament upon her knees. The effort was made but it was in vain. Placed in a chair, the brightness of her eyes triumphing over death, that faint sweet smile upon her features, her prayer-book in her hand, she witnessed the solemn ministration. Afterwards, in reply to a question, she said that she sometimes prayed; it was not often she could command her thoughts, dispersed as they were by suffering, but when she succeeded and could give her mind to prayer, she experienced a rapturous pleasure, greater than anything remembered. She did not speak again during the day. Now, beyond a doubt, her thoughts recur no more to earthly things. I will never again be in her thoughts in this life; a stranger to her; as one who is not. Terrestrial existences are now the shadows; what is dawning upon her is the reality. Perhaps, before losing me utterly from her mind, she breathed a prayer for me. Perhaps, in the other world, her spirit may be intelligent of mine. Let my life be one endeavor, one unceasing, supreme endeavor to render itself worthy of her contemplation in the invisible world to which she will presently be hieing. And may I not protract her life in this material world by appropriating her virtues, and enduing something of her divine character, and giving it perpetual expression in my conduct? According as I do this, I may indulge the hope of meeting her in the world beyond.

16th. My mind is almost emboldened to look again at hope. To allay her sufferings powerful opiates have been administered to her; this may account for the turn her thoughts have taken. She fancies that her decease is not at hand; that she will live a little while; and asks that preparations be immediately made for a voyage to a warmer climate. Her absolute weakness is too plainly visible. Still, a ray of hope visits me.

December 21. I have sent her this letter: "I write . . . not to express to you the state of my mind since the extinction of all hope, for I would not add one pang to what you suffer, . . . but rather to speak of the chastening and exalting influences that have accompanied this affliction. Surely, it will be a satisfaction to you to know that you have been in your last earthly hours the means of rescuing me from a state of lamentable doubt and uncertainty to a blissful belief in the soul's high and everlasting destinies. And that the despair caused by the announcement that I should never more see you on earth was soon visited by a divine intimation that a blissful paradise would be the abode of your enfranchised spirit.

With one hope I survive then; the hope that by a constant recollection and intimation of your virtues, by diligently striving to make my life more worthy of your contemplation, and perhaps by the mediation of a prayer that you may breathe for me, I may at some future day arrive at the same sphere of unfading joy. With unspeakable happiness would I have preserved your life at the price of my own; but I knew not what I wished; and my changed heart knows that there is a peculiar benediction in your lot, and that the misfortune is theirs alone who lose for a while the consolations of your presence and the example of your virtues."

Have I done wrong in sending this? I felt an intense desire to send my voice to her soul before it winged its way from the material universe and I chose words that might fortify her resignation.

She died on Jan. 26, 1844 and Bowen found his rationalism a poor rag in the midst of a real and tragic experience:

January 30. The reaction has come, and I feel now every hour more keenly that I am alone the tenant of a vast desolate solitude. In vain does transcendental and illuminated Reason endeavor—like the braver and loftier of two sisters treading a sacrificial path by chidings or solicitations to embolden the childlike and weak Nature within me; in vain are all the indications of the blessedness beyond the altar. My recollection of the joys and beautiful imaginings of the past triumphs over the spiritual dim perceptions of the celestial blessedness. Nature triumphs in me; cries mutinously against the doom; the dispensation seems exquisite and unjustifiable cruelty. The mystery is so absolute; our speculations so guideless and fallible; though we know that something is true, we know not what that something is. And withal, the soul's wish is single and explicit; it demands a particular happiness, one and no other, and shrinks from all that is diverse, however magnificent and divine; and therefore it sickens and droops and will not be comforted.

Her dying bequest to Bowen was a copy of the Bible, and for her sake he read it for the two months that followed, with a sympathetic attitude to religion but without prayer, nor any faith in its claim to be a revelation from God nor any abandonment consciously of his skepticism, but his journal shows the radical shifting of his thought:

Sunday, Feb. 4th. I have this day received a gift bequeathed by her to me, a Holy Bible, with words of benediction on the clasp, with an injunction from her to read it daily and also to attend the house of God. Holy it is, holy it shall ever be to me, if for no other reason than that this book has been to her so abundant with beautiful influences, pacifying her with most cruel destiny and imparting to her so distinct a perception of the future bliss, or if for no other reason than that she hoped the legacy would be a bond between us linking our souls and a gracious mean of effecting our union in the world to come. It will be to me a phylactery of incomparable virtue. I shall commune with it as with an angel dispatched from the sphere of her present abode with kindly messages.

Feb. 16. Have read Berkeley's *Theory of Vision, Principles of Human Knowledge,* and the three amplificatory dialogues. These works have been to me an intellectual Gospel, and given all my vacillating opinions a steadying key-stone. Through Fichte I was acquainted with this doctrine before; and before I began to read Berkeley, had embraced heart and mind the great creed. The arguments by which I reached conviction were supplied by my own searching thoughts, and I read Berkeley to see what arguments he relied upon. They are quite different; better fitted to popularize the doctrine. A doctrine carries most powerful conviction to that mind whose pre-existing convictions are least offended by it. I find on looking back, that as long ago as Nov. 9, I was fairly on the way towards that goal which I have lately reached. I knew that if this world existed only in the thought of God it would exist in as much reality as men now impute to it. Had I but clung a little to that thought I would have arrived where Fichte and Berkeley have brought me, without their aid. I am displeased with Berkeley for having omitted to deduce one important fact from his discoveries, this, namely, that there can be no possible truth in the doctrine of Predestination. Nay, he seems to admit this doctrine in full force.

He says in the 3rd dialogue: "All objects are eternally known by God, or, which is the same thing, have an eternal existence in His mind; but when things before imperceptible to creatures are, by a decree of God, perceptible to them, then they are said to begin a relative existence with respect to created minds." And again: "Things, with regard to us, may properly be said to begin their existence or be created, when God decreed that they should become perceptible to intelligent creatures, in that order and manner which He then established and which we now call the laws of nature."

Now a child, it seems to me, might confute this. God had foreknowledge of this world, just as it is, in all its relations, of every day, minute, second of its career, of every atom and every modification of every atom; in a word must have looked upon this very world, just as it is; for if the foreknowledge and the knowledge differed in the least particular, it could not have been this world of which He had foreknowledge, but some other; consequently the archetypal thought in His mind, must have been peopled by percipient things just as now. Wherein let me ask, would that foreseen world have been distinguishable from this repetition of it, save in the succession? For each percipient being in it must have been identical with a corresponding percipient being in this. For instance he who reads these words must have been represented in that preconceived world by a percipient being exactly similar and in exactly similar circumstances, having the same belief in the reality of the things about him, having the same conscience, the same merits and demerits and what is more, the same well founded hope of immortality. Now I aver that one of these two worlds was absolutely unnecessary and consequently impossible. It surprises me much that Berkeley—maintaining as he does that this world has no existence save in perception, that is, has no existence but such a one as the Predestinarian assigns to its archetype in the thought of God—should yet have consented to that doctrine.

Were it the practice of God to look forth from the rising and the setting sun, and cry out in words audible and intelligible to every man "I am," were this an ancient, constant, eternal practice with Him, I say that in process of time the merest observation of a philosopher touching a blade of grass would give to men a more confirmatory demonstration of the existence of God than that morning and evening proclamation.

Seven years later in India he wrote in his diary of March 25, 1850:

> In a dream last night I was seeking the image of Emma Morris in a living member of her family. Presently it was told me to wait and she herself should be restored to me My soul is this day quite melted down by the goodness of God manifested in her instance, plucking her so wonderfully at the last moment, as a brand from the burning, and bringing her into that fold into which by means of her death I was myself to be brought. Shall I see her again? On this earth? And Christ in her? God will show us great and wondrous things which we know not of. The last week had embraced in her a delightful revival of intercessory prayer. I long since covenanted with the Lord to live to pray.

In his diary of Jan. 28, 1866, he writes: "Sunday. Twenty-two years since E. M. was buried. An hour never to be forgotten." Feb. 4, 1866: "Twenty-two years since I received the Bible left me by Emma Morris which now is before me and is daily read. How marvelous Thy ways, oh, Thou Dweller of my heart, and utterly baffling to finite wisdom. Two months I read it without seeing the stamp of God. Then I knew it as the gift of God, the angel of my future life. I consecrated myself absolutely to the guidance of this angel."

6. His Conversion to Christianity

In the 75-80 sections of the "Reminiscences" Bowen takes up the story at this point and gives a full account of his transition from his egoistic and speculative skepticism to a full and abiding Christian faith. The Freudian or compensatory psychologist may make what he pleases out of the change. Bowen knew that something real had occurred in his full personality. This was his own later story based on his journal:

> We now come to the great turning point in the life-story we have been so long tracing. During February and March, 1844, H. spent a portion of every day in reading the Bible that had been bequeathed to him, without for a moment entertaining the idea that it was a revelation. He also on Sunday put in an appearance at some church (Episcopal) because of the injunction to that effect left by the deceased.
>
> One night towards the end of March, perhaps about the 25th, before going to bed, something led him to say aloud what was in his mind, to this effect. "If there is One above all who notices the desires of men, I wish that He would take note of this fact, that if it please Him to make known His will concerning me, I shall think it my highest privilege to do that will, whatever it may be and whatever it may involve." Immediately there came a feeling into my mind that it was foolish to make such a proposition as that, for it could not be expected that God would take knowledge of my wishes. The thoughts that had been occupying my mind were these. If I, with all my faculties, have been brought into existence by God, no one, in the nature of things, can be so competent to instruct me as to the best kind of life to lead, as He. The maker of an engine knows best what the engine is fitted to accomplish and the conditions under which it must be worked in order to get these results. Still, the long habit of unbelief made it impossible to entertain a decided faith that God would attend to any prayer of man.
>
> On the 28th of the same month H. went to the Mercantile Library, situated in Beekman St., New York, from whence he had been for years in the habit of getting out books. He asked for Paley's *Natural Theology*, a work that seeks to establish the existence of God by the evidences of design in nature. H. had been reading Lord Brougham on the same subject, and thought he would like to see what Paley had to say upon it.

The librarian took down a book and handed it to him, and, perhaps for the first time in his life, he put it under his arm without looking at it and returned home. His father had some time before removed to No. 50 West Washington Place and H. occupied the front room on the third story. When he got home he looked at the book and to his surprise and disgust found that a mistake had been made and that Paley's *Evidences of Christianity* had been given him. It was two miles from the Library, and he could not think of retracing his steps that day. So there was no help for it; he must go without a book to read until he had another opportunity of going to the library. He said to himself, I cannot waste my time on a book that tries to show that the Bible is from God, for I know well enough that it is not. However, before laying it aside he glanced at the first sentence, which runs thus:

"I deem it unnecessary to prove that mankind stood in need of a revelation, because I have met with no serious person who thinks that even under the Christian revelation we have too much light, or any degree of assurance that is superfluous. Let it be remembered too, that the question lies betwixt this religion and none; for if the Christian religion be not credible, no one with whom we have to do will support the pretensions of any other."

H. was much struck with this remark, as he had just a little before been thinking on the subject himself, and he felt some curiosity to see what the writer had more to say on that subject. So he quoted that remark in his note-book, adding this comment: "This, the first sentence of the book, strikes me forcibly." He read the first page and the second and the third, meaning every moment to lay the book aside, but getting interested he read a good deal. On the same day, occurs this entry:

Paley. "Now in what way can a revelation be made but by miracles? In none which we are able to conceive." Let is not be insisted that miracles, if performed at all, would have been performed in such a manner that no spectator could continue a disbeliever. I believe that even in the performance of miracles there would have been observed a respect for the free-will of man; that some play-room would have been left for the heart and reason, to the end that belief might be accompanied by some degree of merit.

Then follow these remarks:

"*March 28.* It is only the small minority of mankind, the most intellectual of every generation, who are able to attain to an elevated conception of God, by the mere light of nature. But the struggles made by men in all ages and in all climes to attain to a knowledge of and belief in God, attest the necessity of such knowledge and such faith to the well-being of the species; and as it is but rational to think that our well-being is a consideration with God, it is well to believe, by consequence, that the inspiration of such knowledge and faith was a part of His determinate scheme.

"Now had human reason been an unerring guide in extramundane things, and been so from the beginning or from early ages, had the thinking few of each generation been accordant in their metaphysics and unanimous in inculcating one particular system, it is probable that the mass of men would have been content to adopt this system, human reason would have been a sufficient authority, sufficient for God and man. But the very contrary is true, and the philosophic gods are as different as they are numerous; and the happiness of the unthinking many demanding a conviction such as mutable and incompatible and unintelligible philosophies (unintelligible to the unlearned masses) could not inspire, it became necessary that religion should be imparted by heaven or by men falsely pretending to be ambassadors of heaven.

"Before going further, however, let us ask if it be true that religion is necessary to the well-being of man? And true that humanity was so constituted as to render it impossible by the mere light of nature to obtain that religion? Impossible, I mean, not for the few but for all and under all circumstances? The necessity of it may go undisputed, since it is of universal acknowledgment; and it is more reasonable to defer to the concurrent voices of all in every age and clime, as to the knowledge of what they want, than to the opinions of individual theorists. And as, with one exception, there has never been a popular religion that did not claim for itself a divine sanction, and as the rational religion of the revolutionary French was glaringly inconducive to their well-being, it follows that the religion wanted was one purporting to be of extranatural origin. And it is again reasonable to conclude from this universal avowal of the insufficiency of reason or nature that such insufficiency exists.

"The question that now arises is this: Shall we believe that God is satisfied to let the human race be governed by religions whose sanctions are delusive, or shall we believe that He has given to one a virtual sanction? In other words, human reason, being incapable of inspiring that entire conviction regarding the unseen world which is necessary to man's well-being, it follows that the religion wanted was one purporting to be of extranatural origin. And it is again reasonable to conclude from this universal avowal of the insufficiency of reason or nature that such insufficiency exists. The question that now arises is this: Shall we believe that God is satisfied to let the human race be governed by religions whose sanctions are delusive, or shall we believe that He has given to one a virtual sanction? In other words, human reason, being incapable of inspiring that entire conviction regarding the unseen world which is necessary to man's well-being here, was it more agreeable to God that imposture and credulity should be the substituted agents than that He Himself should impart the truth? Though reason be unable to scale the heavens and bring truth from thence, or, having brought it, to show that it has brought it thence, yet there is no hindrance to its operations in things purely natural; and consequently wherever there is a continuous intellectual development, there must the inventions of imposture be detected, sooner of later.

"Now, in the creation of humanity, the Creator must have been aware that this necessity of religion would be felt, and that, if a religion were not given, a fraudulent one would be contrived, and He accordingly must have resolved upon one of two things, viz., either to give a religion or to let an impostor give it. Now, whether does it more derogate from our idea of a just God—and no sane mind ever admitted the idea of a God who was not just—that He should directly impart that amount of divine truth which is necessary to man's well-being here, and to which by his mere reason he cannot attain, or that He should commission imposture to substitute shows of divine truth?

"The right answer to this is so obvious as to be superfluous. Be it allowed then that a revelation was imposed, they were offered; for we are bound to believe that regard was always had to the free-will of man upon the exercise of which depended his merits and demerits; and every generation was free to receive or reject the divine inheritance, and to display herein a virtue or a sin, reason or unreason. Say that in time men lapsed utterly from the divine knowledge and gave themselves to false religions; it being admitted that the ability to find the true one was not in them, and that they must therefore forever either be subject to the false or receive from heaven a new revelation, the question now arises, is it more consonant to our idea of God that He should permit them to remain forever under the domination of false beliefs, or that He should try them anew and give then once more a revelation?"

We have seen some of the reflections that passed through the mind and pen of Homunculus on the 28th March, 1844, after reading a portion of Paley's *Evidences of Christianity*. He then called himself to account for disregarding the convictions and enquiries of so many years by entertaining for a moment the idea that this religion could possibly be what it claimed to be. He had promised to visit a friend in the country. It was Saturday. So, leaving his books he went away and stopped with his friend till the beginning of the following week. He remembers seeing there a volume of Doddridge's *Rise and Progress of Religion in the Soul,* and read it with interest because of its devotional character. He came back to the city with a determination to find out the truth regarding Christianity and have it definitely settled whether it could be regarded as from God or not. He sat down to read Paley's *Evidences* with a determination not to be hoodwinked by any sophistries or pretences of logic, but to scrutinize narrowly every argument.

April 2, 1844. Paley's *Evidences*: "If it be said that men easily believe what they anxiously desire, I answer that in my opinion the very contrary of this is nearer the truth." Questionable. However, it cannot be said that men are only prone to believe promises of good fortune, favorable prophecies, and their own hopes, for they are scarcely less ready to believe denunciations of evil; indeed the imagination has never devised anything so awful and so repugnant to human hopes as did not find believers. I think it must be conceded that there is in the mind an equal readiness to admit what responds to its most passionate hopes and to its intensest fears. It is a cause of wonder that in any age and country so enlightened as this, Miller's prophecies should have had any vogue. These prophecies were opposed to the hopes of men and those believed them whose minds had not the strength to bear up against the terrors they excited.

Miller has just been predicting (in February) at Washington that Christ would appear that year and destroy the world.

Paley: This contempt prior to examination is an intellectual vice from which the greatest faculties of mind are not free. I know not, indeed, whether the men of the greatest faculties of mind are not the most subject to it.

April 3. In answer to those who contend that the disputability of the miracles is a sufficient evidence of their falsity, he refers to the order of nature which is not one of unmixed good. We recognize Beneficence but cannot demonstrate Optimism in the system; yet we do not doubt that it is the workmanship of a perfect Being. It is obvious to me that the Deity would not forestall the exercise of man's powers by his manifestations. There is scarcely an opinion, not one that depends upon a process of reasoning, which has not found a dissenter.

A man once wrote a book to prove the impossibility of God; I think that man and his book may be adduced as evidence of the divine origin of Christianity. For he lived in a world where it was not absolutely forbidden him to indulge any opinion whatever; and it is remarkable of what is called the Christian revelation that it does not impinge upon this freedom. Not all who saw the miracles believed. That they had seen miracles they allowed but that they had been wrought by God they did not allow; they professed to ascribe them to diabolic agency. Irresistible proof, says Paley, would restrain the voluntary powers too much, would not answer the purpose of probation, would call for no exercise of candor, seriousness, humility, inquiry, no submission of passions, interests and prejudices, to moral evidences and to probable truth, no habits of reflection, none of that previous desire to learn and to obey the will of God which forms perhaps the test of the virtuous principles, and which induces men to attend with care and reverence to every credible intimation of that will, and to resign present advantages and present pleasures to every reasonable expectation of propitiating His favor.

Same date. Perhaps there was no conviction in my mind more undisputed and more inveterate than one whose decease these days have witnessed; it was of this import: belief and disbelief are independent of the volition, they are purely intellectual operations and consequently are not the subject of commendation or censure. There is truth in the tenet; that truth engrossed my perception; and the falsehood with which it was combined was unsuspected. My argument was this: Belief is a mental determination, either immediate or reached by some reasoning process, to the effect that a certain thing is true. It may not be true, but it is true for him; he conscientiously receives it as such. He was not free to choose between it and something else; it seemed to him true and he had to receive it. There is injustice in all punishment inflicted on account of belief; and there is but one way of changing it, viz., by causing that which seemed true to seem not true. I am not answerable for the obliquities of my moral vision, for I am not aware of them; make me aware of them and they will be straightway amended, for conscience allows no man to love falsehood better than truth. I say that I have become sensible of the fallacy of this reasoning.

There is a virtue exercised or infringed in the adoption of almost any belief. The impulse of the mind is to consider first—not if such a thing be true or false—but how our decision will affect what we have regarded as our interests. Self-love leads us to esteem our opinions more than those of others, not so much because we know them worthier, as because they are ours; and when any testimony is offered the tendency of which is to overthrow them there is a disposition to take for granted its falsehood, rather than show disrespect to ourselves by impartial enquiry.

It is scarcely possible for any mind whatever to free itself from all bias, without a great and continuous effort. Let an enlightened Chinese read the Koran and the New Testament and he will not fail to attribute superior sanctity to the latter were it only on account of its superior morality; yet it would be too much to expect that a Mohametan, whose mind has been from his earliest years accustomed to treat the Koran as his standard, should enter impartially and honestly upon the consideration of the Bible.

Take the instance of those who witnessed the raising of Lazarus, and who yet believed not on Christ. They did not deny that he had been raised from the dead; miraculously raised; through the mediation of Christ; still they denied that Jesus was what He professed to be. Had they really believed, it is impossible that they should have had the hardihood to set themselves against Him. Are they then to be condemned? I answer at once in the affirmative. Had they not counteracted the evidence of their reason and stifled the voice of their conscience, they would have reflected that the end for which this miracle was wrought, the doctrines it was meant to corroborate, were not such as attested diabolic origin; and the beauty of Christ's character would have appealed to their kindliest feelings. It was their repugnance to Christ and His doctrines which determined their unbelief. Few, very few, I incline to think, arrive at their conclusions by legitimate deductions; the majority of men are in the habit of adopting only those opinions which correspond with and strengthen those that are already in their minds, and perhaps it would not be going too far to say that a man's belief is generally an index to his character.

As regards myself, nothing ever came to pass more utterly removed from all my expectations than the condemnation I am at this time enforced to pronounce upon my past beliefs. Had an angel from Heaven blamed me for entertaining them I know not if I would have listened patiently. If I had been called upon, any time during the first three months of this year, to state my religious views, what would they have been? As follows: I believe the religious sentiment inborn in the mind of man, reminding him from time to time of the unseen God; I believe the soul to be immortal and that the nature of its immortality is determined by the good or evil predominating in this life; I believe in an ever active providence; in the unity of God. I do not believe in a revelation, either as necessary or possible; for it is not consonant with my notions of a God that He should interfere with a system that He has once established; or that He should create the human mind without power to achieve for itself all necessary knowledge. I consequently do not believe in the divinity of Christ or that He wrought miracles. But I believe that this earth has never seen a man more after God's image than Christ; and that the sincere worship of Christians is peculiarly acceptable to God, being the adoration of virtue; and that upon their arrival in the other world they are congratulated upon their belief rather than reproached for it.

I revere the Bible above all other books, for it alone teaches a doctrine in obedience to which consists the happiness not only of the individual but of the species, the doctrine of self-denial. I do not think myself justified in speaking with disrespect of the doctrines of Christianity or of the facts which they suppose; though if positively required to speak the truth, I would have to speak it. Such is the account which I would have rendered of myself previous to the 28th of March, dating from December. Now, if I condemn myself for that frame of mind, I cannot help but condemn those whose minds are in a similar frame, and I am exceeding loath to do this.

April 3rd, 1844, was Good Friday. Homunculus was thoroughly convinced by the reading of Paley's *Evidences* that the Gospels were a faithful record of events that had really taken place, in accordance with predictions that had been given to the Jews centuries before. The Bible then was a revelation from God. These reflections passed through the mind of H. The Christianity of the Bible is true; it does not follow that the Christianity of the churches is true. A religion that is from God must be fitted to elevate and ennoble the lives of those who truly embrace it; but most of the Christians that one comes in contact with give no evidence of being under the influence of any very lofty principles.

Let me, however, note well the lesson that is set before me this day, the lesson of my great fallibility of judgment. God has given a revelation and I have been hearing about it all my days, yet was never able to recognize the divine origin of it till now. If I could make a mistake with regard to a matter of such supreme importance, I have no reason to think highly of my judgments regarding other matters. But it certainly does seem probable that most Christians have missed the true teaching of the Bible. My impression is that many of the doctrines for which Christians exhibit so much zeal are not taught in the Bible. Let me examine it for myself, and see what it really teaches. But O! how important it is that I should do this without any bias; but a readiness to receive what is really taught therein.

Christ says that if any man will do His will, is willing to do His will whatever it may be, he shall know of the doctrine. It is evident that God has been leading me without my knowing it; I cannot doubt that He will continue to lead me, now that I wait upon Him for the needed light. Accordingly H. from this time forward gave considerable time to the reading of the New Testament. He did not open his mind to anybody else; and none of the family knew, for some time, of the change that had taken place in his views. Day by day, he got light with regard to many points. He soon found that it would not do for him to allow his mind to be occupied with the thoughts of a friend who had been taken away, and whose departure had been made such a blessing to him. It was of highest importance that he should give his thoughts to God and become acquainted with his Maker and Redeemer.

It was not long before he came to see the divinity of Christ and the propitiatory nature of His death. He did not at this time experience any very deep conviction of sinfulness. Recognizing the hand of God in what had come to pass, he had a deep persuasion that God wanted to save him, and he was led to believe that He would do it, by the consciousness of his willingness to be taught and led of Christ. The Bible taught that all men needed salvation. So he must need it, though he did not understand much about this need. The Bible also taught that Christ was provided and offered to sinners as their Savior. Just how He would save, H. did not know; but he could not doubt that Christ was equal to the work that He had taken in hand; accordingly he made himself over to Him to be saved.

H. may be said to have passed from death unto life in this month of April, 1844, though he is unable to specify the day. In Paley's *Evidences* the attention of the reader is concentrated on the testimony to Christ's mission furnished by the lives and teaching of the apostles. On the 3rd of April, H. consented to that testimony and placed himself under the teaching of Christ, and perhaps that may be regarded as the day that determined his future destiny.

Immediately after reading Paley, H. turned to Gibbon to read again the 15th chapter, which had been the means eleven years before of making him a disbeliever in Christianity. He now was able to see the poverty and inadequacy of the arguments there paraded in explanation of the spread of Christianity.

On the 1st of May, the house in which we lived was taken as a boarding-house, and we continued to live there as boarders. The Rev. John Atterbury, belonging to a family with which he had been acquainted for many years, came to live there. It was to him that H. first announced the fact of his conversion to Christianity. He was helpful in many ways. H. told him that he purposed becoming a foreign missionary. This purpose was formed as early as April 26th.

Mr. A. lent to H. some books that gave him information concerning missions. Also Gaussen's book on Inspiration. As Paley makes a great deal of the dissimilarities of the four Gospels, showing that there was no concert among the writers as to what they should write, H. was rather unwilling to receive Gaussen's arguments for plenary inspiration, but found that they were perfectly valid, and has ever since been thankful for the high appreciation of the text of Scripture thus obtained. Mr. A. took H. to the Mercer St. Presbyterian Church, Dr. Skinner, pastor, and H. found so much spiritual benefit from the discourses there heard that he continued to go there. It was only on the 23rd of May that H. took an opportunity of giving his sister H. his testimony to the truth of the

Bible. It should be stated that there was no Christian in the family. H.'s mother was in the habit of going to the Episcopal church sometimes, but was quite ignorant of the need of being born again. H., the sister, was Unitarian rather than anything else, having a great admiration for Channing, but without any personal faith in Christ. Both she and her sister and their father became believers this same year; the mother somewhat later. On the 9th of June, H. was baptized upon a profession of his faith in Christ, in the Mercer St. Church, by Dr. Skinner and on the same day partook of the Lord's Supper. His brother Frank, the only other member of the family, had left on the 1st of May for a three years' voyage and since that day the two brothers have never met.

He had come himself into the Christian faith. All that he had consciously or unconsciously sought for years he had now found. Should he keep it to himself or share it with others whose opportunities had been less than his? In the last lines of his metrical autobiography quoted in the *Bombay Guardian* of Aug. 7, 1880 he gives the answer. He had resolved to go out as a foreign missionary:

> Thy hand the helm
> Guided, oh Christ, and dangers day by day
> Confounded, saw a barque so frangible
> Elude their touch of death. Line upon line,
> Instructive, day by day build strangely up
> The renovated temple of the mind,
> (Like Herod's when each worthless stone gave way
> To one its opposite in chiseled strength).
> Too long the secret slumbers; and believers
> Abide in unbelief of mercy gone
> To be the guest of such an enemy.
> Must Providence do all? The Savior knows
> What sinner He hath found and slowly lets
> The unused feet with ruggedness make
>   Acquaintance.
>   But the time recedes when love
> Her lessons in seclusion is content
> To give. Surprised, the world beholds one more
> And such! A witness from the ranks of sin
> Stand up for Christ, and in his hand Christ's word
> Grasping, turning heathenward his steadfast face.

7. At Union Theological Seminary

Bowen entered Union Seminary in New York city in the fall of 1844. In his "Reminiscences" he writes:

> Homunculus had conceived a desire to spend his days as a foreign missionary, even before he had informed a single soul of the change that had been wrought in him. He supposed that there would be nothing to hinder him from going abroad in this capacity at once, just as he was, with his Bible under his arm. When he came to mention this purpose to his friends Mr. Atterbury and Dr. Skinner, he was strongly advised by them to prosecute a course of study in the Union Theological Seminary, before going abroad. Dr. S. thought a two years' course would suffice. Perhaps H. would have been frightened at the idea of spending three years in preparation; he consented to study two years; eventually he came to see that the three years were needed. But he had never been to college and would he be admitted to the seminary? He called upon the professors and was encouraged by them to believe that if he gave the summer to the study of Greek, he could enter at the beginning of the term in the autumn. So he began to apply himself diligently to the study of Greek.
>
> He was soon led to consider that, in consequence of the sedentary way in which he had for so many ears been accustomed to pass his time, seeking in himself and in his books the means of passing it agreeably, he was singularly ill-fitted to speak to men about religion, and that if he was to be a missionary it was high time he began to cultivate the necessary aptitude. He took a class in the Sunday-school, and then got the missionary of the Tract Society to assign him to a district, which he could visit and labor in. This district consisted of a block of houses, mostly tenements, with different families in each room. He tried to visit all these once a week, speaking to those who were willing to be spoken to, distributing tracts and caring for them as he best could. Eventually a meeting was established among them. Some of them were Romanists, some were infidels. H. became acquainted with an infidel shoemaker, who had generally the Bible opened before him as he worked at his trade, searching for matter for his lectures, for he was an infidel lecturer. He was a man of about 75 years old, and H. often went to see him, hoping that he would be led by his testimony and arguments to read the Bible in a different spirit. But the old man was most bitter in his opposition to the Bible, and delighted to impute the worst of motives to all who had had to do with the writing of the Scriptures. His imagination was fully

employed in conceiving a bad cause for everything that is narrated in the Bible. He detested the Jews as a nation, but was charmed with them when they put Christ and His followers to death. His name was Offen and he wrote a book of which he presented me with a copy, breathing throughout the spirit of Tom Paine. He died before H. left America, and unhappily died as he had lived. H. had anticipated that it would be enough for him to tell his story and infidels would at once abandon their infidelity; but he found that this was far from being the case.

Homunculus had been for many years very much addicted to smoking. He cared much more for it than for eating. As soon as he became a follower of Christ, it struck him as unseemly that he should be the slave of this or any other appetite, and he made up his mind that he would break it off. He did this not at all in a heroic way. He made up his mind that he would purchase only the poorest and cheapest tobacco; in this way, he soon lost his pleasure in it and easily renounced it and has never since had any desire for it. He of course made it the subject of prayer that he might get the victory in this Parthian way. Another detestable habit was that of using profane language. He saw the evil of this as soon as he came to know Christ, and found it necessary to maintain an attitude of continual watchfulness lest he should give way to the old habit. He remembers that the braced habit of mind by which he sought to save himself from this vice, went over with him even into his dreams. He gave up the use of wine and all intoxicants at the same time, without solicitation or suggestion, believing that the spirit of the New Testament favored total abstinence.

Some time in the course of this summer H. had a dream that impressed him and encouraged him. It is related in the *Daily Meditations* under the passage "Thou shalt compass me about with songs of deliverance." Psa. 32:7.

The dream is narrated in the section of *Daily Meditations,* (English edition) one of Bowen's later books, for June 2:

A person known to us once had a dream, which may help to illustrate the text. He had been very recently brought to the knowledge of Christ's saving truth. He dreamt that he found himself in an open plain, when suddenly a terrible being appeared, from whom he felt that he must escape, if he would not for ever perish. The only object that his eye could discern was a small and rather mean-looking house. To this he fled; entered it; and feeling that he was pursued, passed through it, and through a yard that was attached to it. Presently he found himself at the foot of a mighty precipice that rose as perpendicularly as a wall, and towered above the skies. The enemy was upon him. He felt that he must go up this wall-like precipice, or be lost; so he attempted the ascent. His hands were here of no use; for there was nothing for them to seize; and he had to plant his feet, in defiance of all laws of gravitation, horizontally against the wall. Yet he was actually enabled to mount up in this way. A prodigious effort was needed at first; (yet, if there had been no invisible aid, what could even a prodigious effort have accomplished under such circumstances?) but as he held on his way, and mounted higher and higher, even into the skies, the task became less difficult; and though new heights, not anticipated, remained to be climbed, yet he found a heart to climb them cheerfully and hopefully. At length he reached the summit, and a vision, glorious beyond description, burst upon his view. A multitude of the heavenly host were there, scattered over the plain, and crowded upon gentle hills that overlooked the scene; their eyes were all on him; and they all burst forth with songs of deliverance on his account; while a being glorious enough to be the Lord of all this enraptured host came to him who had there arrived, and received him as he fainted through the force of unspeakable emotions, and bore him away not altogether insensible, for the songs of the jubilant host still sounded in his ears.

Bowen's "Reminiscences" continue:

A copy of a letter written by the father of H. to his own father, twenty-eight years before, in the year when H. was born, came into the hands of the latter. To his great astonishment he found his father writing in an earnest Christian strain, entreating his father to give his heart to the Lord, and telling him that he had recently come to know Christ as his Savior. He showed the letter to his father and had some talk with him about religion. The father acknowledged that he had at the time when he wrote the letter, felt the power of religion and had afterwards fallen back; he added that for many years he had been supremely unhappy and had often gone to bed with the wish that he might never open his eyes again in this world. It gave me great joy (this was before my baptism) to tell him of the change that had been wrought in me, and to urge him to give himself anew to Christ. This he was not long in doing, and the last years of his life were passed in the peace and joy that come from believing.

He had a sister, married to Daniel Ostrander, a well-known minister and presiding elder in the Methodist Church. These two persons had died in the latter part of 1843 in the city of New York. All that H. knew about them was that there were some relatives of the family on the father's side who were Methodists, with whom, because they were such, the family had shunned all intercourse, only mentioning them in terms of ridicule. Thirty years after, H., reading Stevens' *History of the Methodist Episcopal Church,* was surprised to find very interesting notices of Mr. and Mrs. O. who were spoken of in the highest terms as devoted and useful Christians, adorning the Gospel in their lives and in their death. Little thought H. in the day when he and his sister used to make merry over the supposed bigotry and want of polish in these relatives, that a day would come when he would have rejoiced exceedingly if he could have looked back upon some real acquaintanceship with these good people. It is reasonable to believe that they had often made the city relatives that gave them the cold shoulder, the subject of prayer, and that the Lord had regard unto these prayers. They had scarcely passed away when the Lord began to work powerfully among us.

About the beginning of October, H. began his attendance at Union Theological Seminary in New York. Dr. E. Robinson, author of *Researches in the Holy Land,* and well known for his hermeneutical attainments, was one of our professors and Dr. White was professor of Systematic Theology. These were halcyon days. H. felt strangely at first in this crowd of young men who had been all their days in contact with sacred things, and looked with a sort of awe upon many so much younger than himself handling religious topics with a familiarity that seemed almost miraculous.

Fifty-seven installments of the "Reminiscences," in the issues of the *Bombay Guardian* from Aug. 14, 1880 to Sept. 17, 1881, deal with Bowen's course at Union Seminary, for the three years 1844-1847, and are filled with quotations from his journal for these years. One volume of the diary had been devoured by white ants but the substance of it had appeared in the *Guardian* in 1860 and 1861 and was reproduced in the account in the "Reminiscences" of the Union Seminary days. In this reproduction Bowen says in the *Guardian* of Feb. 26, 1881:

> We take this opportunity of submitting to our readers the following rule to be observed not merely in reading the *Bombay Guardian* but in reading anything that has truth in it, anything that is worth reading, viz., To read as though we were never to have another opportunity of reading it, seeking to get from it, into our own experience, the truth contained in it. What we eat only benefits us as it becomes a part of our own system; and what we read must become a component part of ourselves, or else it will profit us nothing.

Bowen began his seminary course with the same excessive introspective subjectivism in which he had lived ever since his boyhood. He never lost his faculty and habit of relentless self-scrutiny, but the recluse aspects of his life began to be replaced now by ever widening human fellowships, and his intellectual and emotional self-indulgence yielded to the passion of spiritual service and practical ministry. His naturalistic mysticism deepened into religious experience. He was an extraordinary intellectual and spiritual force in the Seminary, as the testimonies of his classmates will reveal, and his journal is not unworthy of being ranked with Augustine's *Confessions,* the *Thoughts* of Pascal and the letters and writings of Madame Guyon and Fénelon. The quotations which can be made from it will only very inadequately represent it and his mental and spiritual growth:

> *July 11, 1844.* It is now upward of three months since the Gospel truth was revealed to me; more than two since I dedicated myself to Him; and more than one since I made a public profession of Christianity; and yet, when I consider what I am, I am constrained to confess that I have sadly abused the mercies of God. I have been shamefully passive; the Spirit of God will not work without my cooperation; I am not to be saved in my own despite, but by the fullest and most incessant activity of all my powers in coalition with the divine Spirit. It is by my imagination that I am so cruelly withheld from the divine presence. This is my great rock of offence; this it is that so harasses me, manifesting itself whenever I would take a step forward, and sleeping only when I sleep.
>
> "Lovest thou me?" Alas, that I cannot answer Thee, oh Jesus, in the words of Peter, Lord, Thou knowest that I love Thee: for Thou knowest, oh my Redeemer, that I love Thee not. That which I feel is not what Thou callest love. In all my devotional exercises, I have been seemingly separated by a partition from the object addressed; conscious that I was heard by Him, I yet beheld Him not. It is for me to break down this wall.
>
> *July 20.* When I remember what I was a year ago this day, in whose society, and with what idolatrous and engrossing passion I was filled, and contrast with that my present state, I am filled, no, I am not but should be filled with amazement that that adorable Being to whom I belong, should receive from me such cold and passionless tributes of affection. How does that retrospective glance condemn me! Everything tells me that I am imperfectly acquainted with myself. Until I become better acquainted with myself, it were futile to expect any real augmentation of spiritual religion. I do not attach sufficient importance, nor give sufficient time to self-examination. My studies absorb too much of my time and attention.
>
> *October 13, 1844.* A most interesting day; for today my two sisters, recently brought out of the shadow of death, will enter the visible church and partake of the Lord's Supper. I, too, am to commemorate the death of my Savior. But how unfit I am! How altogether unworthy! Were my heart but broken by a sense of my sins it would be well. But what can break such adamant? I thank God that the Holy Spirit has the power and much besides. . . . I am the most unaccountable being; I know that I am not living the divine life, yet go on, day after day, with as much complacency and unconcern, as though everything were achieved. I

know that my theological studies are a great hindrance to me, and leave me not much time to attend to my spiritual necessities; but I cannot excuse myself thus; for I find time abundantly to minister to the calls of my vanity.

During this Christmas vacation his friend, W. W. Atterbury, who had gone to the Divinity School in New Haven, saw something of Bowen and writes:

His conversation was quiet, thoughtful, with no excitement or exaggeration and ended with prayer whenever circumstances permitted. I remember how simple, childlike, with quiet, gentle voice, his prayers were. On New Year's Day, following the custom then prevalent, he made a call upon the family of a friend with whom I was staying, and I remember their speaking of that interview as so unusual, as his conversation was almost wholly on the one theme which occupied his heart. About that time I remember the pain with which I was told that a pastor in the city (himself an earnest Christian) had said of Bowen, "Is he not a little out of his mind?" or words to that effect, simply because he talked and acted as if religion were a reality.

The diary continues:

March 24, 1845. Alexander was a sedulous imitator of Achilles. He never traveled without *Homer*; never slept without it; and thought it incumbent on him not to come short in any respect. It was sufficient that Achilles had done anything, to make it necessary that he should do it; going so far as even to drag at his chariot-wheels the body of an enemy. Is it not surprising that these miserable heroes should find such steady, consistent and determined imitators, and Jesus Christ be so feebly and idly followed even by those who profess to find Him altogether admirable and the chiefest among ten thousand?

March 28. I feel prompted to begin again my diary. We are too much in the habit of forgetting what manner of person we are, and some daily record may help us to see the sort of life we are leading. A year ago today I received from the library Paley's *Evidences.* A prodigious change must take place in me. I want now to be doing all the good I can, and not let a day go by without benefiting somebody. He that watereth others shall himself be watered.

Some of the prominent characteristics of Harlan Page's efforts for the salvation of men. It was the burden of his heart and the purpose of his life. Always had a list of persons to be prayed and labored for. It was not the great object of his life to be himself happy; but rather by persevering labor and self-denial to glorify God in winning souls to Him.

It was that glorious sense of divine things, that love to souls, and that heavenly unction which were at once the spring of his fidelity and causes of his success.

Perfect obligation on the part of man, and perfect dependence in his relations to God, did not jar in his mind. His sense of dependence threw him on his knees, his sense of duty summoned him to effort; and prayer and effort, effort and prayer were the business of his life.

He was fruitful in devising expedients for doing good.

March 30. I suppose this heart of mine is one of the greatest problems in the universe. It would seem to be trying how much goodness it could experience without being broken. His mercies have followed me all this Sabbath, although I have been in my usual dead state. There is more and more of the semblance of godliness in my life, and less and less of the reality, I fear. Oh, for the heart of some Christians! What a heaven on earth! If I could but hate myself rightly, it would be something.

We may go further, and say that students of theology and ministers, instead of coming for their every day standard to the Bible, take it from the conduct of one another. And no man thinks he falls much short of his duty, when he does not fall below the average of practice. This is wrong unquestionably. God speaks to us in the Bible, and not in the defective consciences of those around us. And we must come to the Bible and there learn what God thinks of our conduct and what He would have us to do.

April 1. Seeing these words, "And He" Jesus, "went into the house," this thought sprang up in my mind: Here is God, the fashioner of the universe, the mighty Father, the Wonderful, the Counselor, the Prince of Peace, living our common life, opening doors, entering houses, sitting down, eating, drinking, talking, sleeping, dressing, and undressing Himself, in all things conforming to the daily usages of men. Now who knows but what the remembrance of all these usages is to be sanctified to us by the fact of His participation? Are they not redeemed from commonness by this fact? Sin has degraded everything so that the daily exigencies of life appear contemptible to us, but the holiness of Christ may have a converse effect and redeem them from this commonness. At all events, it is evident that we may have communion with Christ in the doing of all these things. When we see the King in His glory on His throne, we shall not forget that He became man for us and entered into all the details of human life.

We have some authority over our inner being, but it is limited to the acquisition of knowledge. Our efforts must be intellectual, not sensitive. Love is the fruit of knowledge. Love is spontaneous and follows of its own accord upon a right acquaintance with the object. I must not immediately seek an augmentation of love. It would soon wear me out and at the same time the difficulty would go on increasing. I desire to glory in Christ; well, I must go on studying His character in Scripture, limiting my views simply to this, the becoming acquainted with Him, without any reference to my feelings. I have been studying parts of Scripture with a mind made up of self-condemnation for coldness, and pantings after more fervor. It is certainly a good ground for humiliation that I am so little affected by motives worthy to induce in reasonable beings absorbing love. But the evil is deep-seated and cannot be removed by any struggles. Love seeks a peaceful bosom for its haven.

May 23. I feel that as I am I can do nothing, can never glorify my Redeemer, can never feel deeply for souls, never do anything for their salvation. I feel that I am unfit for anything, life, death or eternity. What I want is—if I may so express it—a personal acquaintance with Jesus: by faith to have such a view of Him as shall make me as much acquainted with Him as I am with material things.

What motives for virtuous conduct exist! The way of sin is unspeakably harder. The inducements to virtue unspeakably greater. Surrounded by vice and misery, one would think it would be difficult to restrain men from good deeds. God has given to every creature ability and permission to do good. What opportunities and what motives have I had. My deeds were voluntary and they were not good. What sins of omission. Let me consider the value of a life, all the worth of J. B. Taylor's twenty-eight years, all the blessings communicated by such a life not only upon one's own generation but for all time, upon a number continually augmenting, and finally, through all eternity, and then remember that I have thrown such a life away, thrown it voluntarily and deliberately away with contempt and scorn.

July 11. Perhaps the happiest day of my life. I may say, the happiest. I have enjoyed such views of Christ as never before. Four precious seasons of prayer and praise. I saw Him for the first time as the bridegroom, mine. My texts were Isa. 61:10; Song 2:16. Some of the moments were rapturous. Let the memory of this day never perish. His love is mingled with pity, the love of the weak for the strong. It is as though a gate were suddenly opened before me. My great encouragements were the garments of salvation, the robe of His righteousness. I see now that the great love expressed by the figures of the text must be a truth; consider Calvary. O may this love of Christ be shed abroad more fully in my heart.

The summer vacations of 1845 and 1846 were spent by Bowen and his friend and fellow student, Joshua Edwards Ford (who later went to Syria and worked there from 1848 to 1865 and was followed by his saintly son, George A. Ford of Sidon,) as unpaid agents of the American Bible Society and the

American Tract Society in Pike County, Pennsylvania, then a much wilder section even than today. Bowen's later "Reminiscences" describe their work together:

> We engaged a horse and wagon (without a driver); had it laden with the books of the Tract Society and of the Bible Society; and started for the principal town, Milford. We became acquainted with the ministers and were taken charge of by a very good man whose house became our headquarters while in that neighborhood. We were provided with knapsacks in which we could pack away a considerable supply of good reading. Filling these, we started out in the morning, one in one direction, one in another. We sought to gain admission for ourselves and pack in every house, and where we had an opportunity we talked to the people of the grace of God and prayed with them. Most of the inhabitants of the country were living on clearings in the woods, half a dozen families to the square mile, or less. Most of them were very poor and many of them very degraded. Infidelity was in some parts very rife. Almost the whole of every day was spent on foot ascertaining from one house the bearings of the next. In the evening we could sometimes come together again and encourage one another.

He wrote to his mother from Milford, Pa., on Aug. 12, 1846: "I wish you may all have the same heavenly peace that dwells in my own soul. . . . I am favored with an abiding consciousness of my Savior's presence. It is this which will make Heaven to be Heaven and why should it not make earth Heaven? . . . I have never enjoyed any time more than I have these few weeks past. I have been wandering amid beautiful scenery, and since my own nature is in more harmony with the divine, I appreciate and enjoy God's works more. I am lost in contemplating the boundless love that encompasses man, speaking to him from sky and field, mountain and stream." He wrote to Harriet from Honesdale, on Aug. 24, of the immoderate supply of food on the country dinner tables, "eighteen different sorts of food." His piety seems to have been unequal to the control of his appetite and he longed for some of his mother's remedies. On Sept. 4 he wrote to Kate from a remote section—"no place nearer than twelve or fifteen miles"—with irreligion or bad religion all about him, but with a hospitable welcome at "the home of my excellent friend, Mr. Joseph Brown, one of the salt of the earth," an Irish Calvinist at peace with his Arminian neighbors.

In September, after seven weeks in Pike County, he was back in the Seminary:

> *Sept. 1, 1845.* What I want is one thing; to know more of Christ and Him crucified. This is the great difficulty. I must be freed from all the stupidity of my mind on this subject. The life that I live in the flesh I

want to live it by faith in the Son of God. And is He not made unto us sanctification, as well as righteousness?

Sept. 12. Is it not the truth that He, Christ Jesus, is at this time far more solicitous that I should have the knowledge I seek, than I myself am? . . . The great pernicious error is that we are continually judging Christ by ourselves, and ascribing to Him our own variableness—fervent love when we experience it, and indifference when we are indifferent, as though He loved us in return for our love, whereas it is just the other way; He loved us when we hated Him and were most unworthy of His regard. He knew what He did when He set His love on us; He knew our character, but He gave us His love to raise us from sin. His love works love in us, and every other grace, and is indispensable to every part of our Christian course, and when we are most cold and stupid, then we most need the persuasion of His love toward us. Without this there would be no deliverance.

Sept. 16. Am I near to Christ? Is not this the first thing? Is not the most direct and brief the best way to Him? If I have need to study any doctrines, is it not better to study them with Him than without Him? The subject mentioned above is important, more so than is there represented; but first in importance is Jesus. I am far from Him, lamentably far. How utterly careful should we be never to let a precious thought of Him escape from the mind. How leaky the mind for everything good.

They that follow on hard to attain anything feel the necessity of concentrating their attention upon one specific line. They feel that they are wasting their time if they go now a little in one direction and now in another. Though other paths be good and desirable yet they fix upon the one that seems best, and adhere to that, turning neither to the right nor left. Now what I want is the knowledge of our Lord Jesus Christ. There is no propriety in using any circuitous routes. Let me go right to the Gospel and pursue that unremittingly without any deviation until I have made the progress I need. Let me study every passage in His life, and keep my mind to it until I see, first the glory of God in it; second, its relation to myself. May the Lord help. I will read the Gospels of Mark and John. This day resolved, September 27, 1845, and my name subscribed.

Oct. 10. I think I am now at my worst estate. Have been for a week most deeply exercised. It has seemed to me that I had but one thing to do; to go to the mercy-seat and hold on until I had attained the blessing I covet, even sanctification. Last Saturday night a young man and myself agreed to pray until Monday night. I prayed till then and have been praying ever since. Strange to say, I have been getting worse and worse. The more I pray the more devilish I get, if I mistake not. I have already lost all pleasure in tract-visiting, Sabbath school instruction, and efforts for the good of others generally. I have lost all pleasure in reading the Word of God. I am a miserable being. I am famishing in the midst of abundance. What now shall I do? To whom shall I go? Is there another Calvary? God forbid. The sun shines brightly for everybody; but clouds and darkness are around me. It is awful that the Word of God should be distasteful to me. It is so because of the pain excited by my insensibility. If I were more alarmed it might be better with me; but I cannot renounce my hope. It is my misery that I attained a hope without attaining a sense of the preciousness of Christ. God deliver me from a false peace. O man, proud man, what a helpless creature art thou when thou wouldst put on holiness.

Oct. 11. Last night a book came providentially into my hand, which I trust is to be the means of a blessing to my soul. If I can read providences, it is clear what God would have me strive for, even sanctification. Upham's *Interior Life.* It has opened my eyes in one respect. I see where my faith fails. The faith I want is an appropriative faith, one by which I can regard God as my God, Christ as my own Savior, the Holy Spirit as in the world for my sanctification. And the reason that the Word of God has not been more operative on me is that I have not read it with this particular faith. The Bible addresses men individually. Love individualizes its objects. It is not God's love for the race that is going to affect us, but His love for me and me.

Oct. 28. I was impressed the other day on hearing the 1st and 2nd Peter read, with the apostle's earnestness in recommending the cultivation of a religious memory in verses 12-15. By forgetfulness I frustrate the work of the Spirit, and greatly multiply the hindrances to a work of grace. How disgraceful to be ever learning anew the same lesson! Better, I believe, to retain an old truth than to get a new one. Let me adopt other habits with reference to this miserable failing of my mind. The leak must be stopped.

Oct. 30. "Come to Christ." . . . To come is an individual act; the man who comes separates himself from the crowd that he may draw near to Christ and enter into personal relations with Him. He ceases for the moment to remember that Christ is the Savior of all; the engrossing thought is that Christ is his Savior.

What a barren and joyless life the Christian will have of it who shrinks from beholding his Father's smile! Must not this be highly displeasing to God? This modesty is only another form of selfishness and unbelief. Is not the unsophisticated spirit of a child, free from everything like artificial and labored modesty, that which best pleases Him?

Have at length discharged that great duty which has been weighing upon me so long, and to the non-fulfillment of which I ascribed much of the discomfort of my soul. One month ago I was praying with tears that

I might have strength for it, and yet I did not seem to think that I could have it without some change of circumstances. And now when I seem to myself to be in a declining and low state, I do it with very little of an effort. May God bless it.

"This duty," Bowen added later, "had reference to his father. He thought that his father was not as devoted and self-denying as he should be, and felt that he ought to speak to him, but shrunk from it. His father received very well what he had to say to him."

December 4, 1845, as Bowen felt in his later life, was "the beginning of a new era." The entry for the day in his diary records:

> Thanksgiving. I look back upon a year crowded with mercies. Amazing is the goodness of God to this house. Goodness, moreover, is exalted by the unworthiness of its object; so that we must multiply the blessings of God by our sins to have a right view of them. And now, have I not been long enough in this cold, dying state? Am I doing myself any good, the church any good, the world any good, God any good, by thus living? I feel this day like beginning anew and setting my face like a flint in the direction of the heavenly Jerusalem. Heard an excellent discourse this morning on Hosea 9:12, "Woe unto them if I depart from them." There is but one way of escaping this woe, the greatest of all imaginable, and this is by each one's resolving that let others live in coldness, worldliness, selfishness, barrenness, insensibility, he, for his part, will die unto these and live unto the Lord. Blessed Spirit, I have so often grieved Thee by breaking my solemn vows, that I fear, in my present cold state, to make a new promise. But can I refuse to make it? Let me have faith in Thee. Lord I make it. . . . This is indeed a day to be remembered and may well stand as the beginning of a new era. Visited an old man, upwards of seventy, this afternoon, for whom I sometime ago procured a Bible, and to whom I had lent Doddridge. He has been a hard character, an infidel, but God has had mercy upon him. I found him this afternoon a penitent. What an argument for me to keep the promises! After reading Luke 8:22-36 with sanctifying meditation on the glorious power of Christ over the physical and over the moral world, I enjoyed a sweet and long-protracted season of prayer. I had never had so much faith. I felt that I was heard. O may the blessed God forbid any retrogression upon my part. Onward, onward, into the fullness of God's love.
>
> *Dec. 9.* My peace flows like a river. It is impossible to record all the thoughts of God that are precious towards me. I awoke before daylight and had an enrapturing view of the believer's privileges. It seemed to me that there was nothing in Heaven more valuable than the New Testament. For the glory of God is the excellence of Heaven; but in

redemption this glory preeminently shines. I am sure the angels desire to look into these things. It may be that the most blessed moments in the existence of Moses and Elias, were those on the Mt. of Transfiguration, when they spake of His decease. I no more envy those disciples of our Lord who lived and journeyed with Him. He is as much, nay, more with the believer now than He was then. We have more for faith to feed upon; the glories of His complex nature were but feebly revealed to them in comparison. They that saw the miracles could not understand them as well as I can, the blessed Spirit helping me.

11th. Goodness and mercy follow me unceasingly. This is life. In what state have I been? In one of unbelief, shutting my eyes to the blessings of the Gospel, and yet miserable in my darkness and privation. Last evening, my peace was interrupted; and though I felt that I was not deserted, I lost in some degree the prevalency of faith. I was troubled to know what could be the reason and sought it in an act of self-indulgence. But this morning on awakening, the Comforter revealed it to me. I had been seeking unconsciously for objects out of the Bible. I was not satisfied to see my God in His holy Word, to see His glory spiritually, and looked, as I so long and ignorantly had done, for some immediate illumination. I must very carefully avoid this rock. My recent blessings have all come to me through simple faith in the Word. There will I seek my Redeemer and there only. There only I find God manifest in the flesh. . . . Our Lord was a man of sorrows and acquainted with grief; despised and rejected of men; He endured the continual contradiction of sinners. But it is said that He once rejoiced in spirit. O what was it that banished for a little His sorrows? Was it the coming of Moses and Elias in glory to speak to Him? Was it the coming of angels to minister unto Him? Was it the descent of the Holy Spirit? Was it the voice of the Father proclaiming Him well-beloved? No, the circumstance that cheered and irradiated His mind was this: His Heavenly Father had given some gifts of His love to His disciples. The seventy had received an abundant measure of faith and joy, and the heart of Jesus was made glad, and He burst out into thanksgiving to God. Blessed Jesus! Let this word be precious unto me and full of best encouragement. In asking for myself I am asking for Jesus.

Dec. 31. Day before yesterday I took two resolutions which I consider important. The first is this: I will do every duty, so far as may be consistent with the well-doing of it, as soon as possible. In this resolution I have special reference to those duties which my involve something of unpleasantness. The habit of procrastination has been one of the worst of all my bad habits. For the carrying out of this resolution I need the special aid of my heavenly Father, and shall have it. The other is this, one of Pres. Edwards': Resolved, to exercise myself in this all my life long, viz., with the greatest openness to declare my ways to God, and to lay open my soul to Him—all my sins, temptations, difficulties, sorrows, fears, hopes, desires and everything and every circumstance. I have already found this productive of good. Yesterday was a day of indescribable happiness. My Savior was sensibly near to me all day, and on retiring at night I felt that I had as much as I could bear; my cup ran over. A third resolution I have taken is to have God a party in all my studies. In all my studies to seek constantly a sense of His eye upon me, and to have reference in all simply to His approbation. To make Him the daily judge of my progress.

Jan. 12, 1846. If yesterday was a day to be remembered, what shall I say of today? I have this day been introduced into a new state of existence. Eye hath not seen, ear hath not heard, nor hath the heart of man conceived the things that God hath prepared for them that love Him. If I had not been supported, I could not have survived the experiences of this day. I feel that Heaven has come down into my soul, and God is enthroned there. Oh, the astonishing revelations of the love of God this day made me. I cannot conceive that the raptures of dying saints have ever exceeded what I have this day known. And all arises from new views of the character of God. In an instant, the meaning, never suspected, of half the Scripture started into the full view of my mind. It is a new life, because, as I said, all arises out of new views of His holy and adorable character, which by His grace, never shall be taken away from me.

15th. If He was ever present on this earth, if He was present that night of the last Passover, He was with us in this little upper chamber, (third story of my father's house in 13th St., New York). As Brother H. remarked afterwards, it was all like a dream. Heaven-like indeed! We sat together in a heavenly place in Christ. The prayers offered have prevailed already. A wonderful work has gone forward in all our souls. Last evening was similar, we could have sat and sung our souls away. The Savior is furnishing us with work to do, and enabling us to do it. This is altogether the most fruitful week of my life. Have just been to see one of the brethren of the seminary, whom God has been leading and who now thirsts for the higher life. Savior, bless that interview. On the 12th I was lifted up from the Heaven in which I had been walking five weeks, for the great kingdom of Heaven is a succession ascending up the Heaven of heavens. But today my wild and extravagant faith asked to go still higher, and lo, I was presently removed, and am now in a sphere of indescribable, undreamt-of love. I think there was never any paradise till this.

Jan. 16. I feel the infinite heart of God beating against my heart. I cannot work; I cannot think; I can but love. My soul is in Heaven, Heaven in my soul; abide in me and I in Thee. Never knew before the delight of song. God is love. Thinking on this, I wondered how He found time to evince wisdom, truth and His other attributes; when it came into my mind that love was not an attribute in the sense these were; but God Himself was love, and the exercise of His attributes was always the exercise and manifestation of love.

Jan. 19. A word that I heard lately in a sermon, illustrates the erroneousness of the prevailing notions of holiness. It was said that a man possessed of holiness would be happy, even if—were such a case supposable—he were driven from the presence of God. The idea seems to be that holiness is something pertaining to the man himself; it belongs to him; and is such a good that the possession of it must always involve a feeling of self-complacency. Now the holy man is the only man in the world who is without a feeling of self-complacency. For holiness is not a property of the individual, something belonging to him; but simply this, God working in him both to do and to will of His good pleasure. He of whom this is true has indeed complacency, but it is complacency in God. He cannot forget that the river flowing through his soul, proceeds from the throne of God; so that if God should cease for a moment to work in him, he would cease to be holy.

The change which Bowen believed was now taking place in his Christian life was described in a letter which he wrote on Jan. 26, 1846, to John G. Atterbury, then in Flint, Michigan:

Dear Brother in Christ:

I have been a long while desirous of making time to write you, and especially since the occurrence of an event which I know you will be pleased to hear of; so I hasten to improve a few minutes leisure. The event is this: You remember you gave me a copy of Doddridge, which was to me no doubt of unspeakable benefit. It is of very great importance what books we read in Christian infancy. Well, God has been pleased to bless this book recently. There was an old Englishman in my tract district, seventy years old, very deaf, very skeptical, very wicked. I thought him about the most unpromising case. I for a long time in vain endeavored to get him to buy a Bible. He moved away; and after a while, became impressed that it was proper for him to have a Bible in the home, and came to me for one. I supplied him; and then took him your Doddridge, and made him promise to read it. After some weeks I called, and asked him how he progressed in the book. "It's a dangerous book," said he. "A dangerous book," I replied, somewhat startled, and not knowing what mischief I could have done. "Yes," said he, "it's dangerous. It makes a man's case out to be very bad. It shows him there's no hope for him at all. But," he continued, "it begins to grow a little better. I've come to a chapter that shows there is hope after all." I was rejoiced and cheered to hear him talk so; and was led to pray with more faith for him. In the beginning of December I went again, and found him, as I have reason to believe, a true convert. Rheumatism had confined him to the house, and he had read Doddridge twice, looking out all the texts in the Bible. I have seen him many times since, and am confident that he is one of Christ's own. So I have looked on Doddridge with new veneration, and introduced him to other sinners.

I write now, my dear John, to tell you of the wonderful things that God has done for me lately, and I trust that what I have to say may make you see new beauty and new glory in the face of our Immanuel. We are one in Him; and what He does for me, He does for all. Christian blessings are common property. Oh if we lived in that perfect fellowship meditated by our Savior, a Christian in the center of India could not receive a blessing in which a fellow Christian in this country would not participate.

Since last Spring I have had the impression on my mind that it was not only my privilege, but my calling to live a higher life than that which I had known either in myself or others—a life of faith. Faith that is the substance of things hoped for, the evidence and realization of things unseen; which makes Christ more intimately ours than He was Peter's or John's in the days of His flesh; and whose fruits appear in love, joy and peace. The life of faith such as I saw portrayed in the Scriptures, seemed to me the most blessed life; and one that would make any spot in the universe, any labor, any tribulation, pleasant and even glorious. I began soon to seek it with all diligence; and during nearly all the year I was in a continued succession of conflicts—protracted periods of striving, weeping, lamenting, despondency, in a word, seasons of great unhappiness. For I found I made no progress whatever; my endeavors instead of developing faith only served to show me how little I had. I never doubted about my being a Christian; but it was misery to me to be such a Christian. I think some of these were the most distressing days I have ever known. All this was over-ruled for good; as the tendency of these experiences was to show me my utter weakness, and helplessness morally, and to abate in me that faith in myself which was the great hindrance to faith in God.

About the beginning of October, God put it into my heart to commence the study of the Scriptures after a new plan. I concluded that the Word had not sanctified me, because I had not received it as truth. I had not exercised individual and appropriating faith. So I took one of the Gospels, and proceeded to meditate in it, verse by verse, three hours a day, with rigid long-protracted meditation, prayer and self-applications, viewing each verse in all possible relations to myself, and extracting the sanctifying juices assiduously. This soon became the most delightful employment I had ever engaged in, and the most profitable. Every day

I became more convinced that the great thing our Lord came to see was faith; and His greatest pain and disappointment arose from the unbelief of His disciples. Faith, the whole Gospel; and according as He addressed the two classes of self-righteous and publicans, His two-fold aim was to destroy faith in self and inspire faith in Himself. I came along to Luke 8:22-36, and on the 4th of Dec. was meditating on these two illustrious displays of Christ and power, when by the grace of God, my eyes were opened to see His all-sufficiency as my Redeemer, and I began to lead the life of faith. Since then the assurance of faith has been mine.

During the first ten days I walked totteringly. My plan was several times interrupted, and most happily; for I was thus led to see where my safety and where my danger lay. For I found that exactly as I ceased to be satisfied with the bare Word of God, and looked for forms and exercises to minister to my faith, unbelief came upon me and darkness. Thus the Scriptures became a lamp to my feet. Ever since I have had uninterrupted peace, peace which passeth understanding, flowing like a river, and ever broader and deeper. The conditions I found to be, the bare Word of God, and entire consecration. I find it necessary to keep my conscience unspotted in all things great and small. A most important revelation God put into my heart at the beginning—to increase my demands upon the exception of my blessing, to make each the stepping stone to another, to try and see what I could do towards emptying the wells of salvation. Another was this: to make my Jesus the most intimate and confidential of friends; my bosom companion; and every folly, failing, sin, fear, hope, desire, everything, to take to Him at once, confident that He could no more repulse me than He would the apple of His eye, and that to wash away sin was the joy set before Him for the sake of which He endured the cross, despising the shame.

I feel that a sense of the love of God in Christ Jesus is the only motive of sufficient strength to break the power of any sin; that the whole united powers of the universe are weak in comparison with the love of Calvary, that this draws the sinner in the first instance, and this alone ever enables us to take a step in holiness. This is a new and wondrous view to me: during all my Christian course I have gone upon the assumption that the tendency of sin was to make me forfeit the favor of God, as that of good resolutions, exercises and consecrations was to procure me it. In other words, I proceeded in the theory of all grace, but in practice on a mixture of law. My great gain now is a realizing and practical sense of this truth that "God worketh in us both to will and to do every good thing," and without Him we can do nothing. I supposed I had known all of joy that a Christian in this world could know during the month of December; but a fortnight ago today, my blessed Father took me up into another heaven of this great kingdom of Heaven, and all since then has been happiness beyond expression, if indeed it has entered into the hearts of many to conceive. I feel like crying to my Christian brother, Up, up, an immeasurable region of God's own peace is here, and room for all. Honor God by having unbounded desire after holiness and usefulness. Let the world go, all of it. Be emptied of self. Trust to God.

I have some confidence now that God will glorify Himself by me. As I was before, I could only have been an obstacle in His way. But having put self down, and taken possession of my soul, He can do with me what He lists. He can create me to be what He will, just as in my original creation. He obeyed His own sovereign wisdom. Whatever work He has for me to do, He will enable me to do it. He is answering prayer gloriously. His spirit is moving upon the minds of the brethren, and they are gathering in little clusters to ask for a baptism of the Spirit. I would rather see one candidate for the ministry converted, than fifty impenitent. I incline to think that is what God is waiting for. This letter is all about myself but do not believe but that I always take a deep and tender interest in your welfare, and bless the God and Father of our Lord Jesus Christ, for the unspeakable good He did my soul through you. I ask not, if you are happy, comfortable, praised. Are you glorifying God? Let us be the meekest of men, and the weakest; we will be the usefullest and the strongest of Christians. I pray for you and yours. Remember us all at a throne of Grace,
    Your brother,
        Geo. Bowen, Jr.

Resuming selections from his journal:

Feb. 7. Have neglected my diary a whole week. Many seasons of wondrous blessedness to my soul, of strange and ravishing intimacy with Christ. But I find that manifestations which lifted me above the earth, and filled me with emotions of great intensity a few weeks ago, have now become almost as matters of course.

In February, 1881, Bowen reviewed these entries in this journal of his Seminary days and his memories of the experiences which they recorded and set down his judgment of them, after more than thirty years of life and work in India:

In *May, 1845,* H. had a very bright and joyful day, caused by the recognition of the love of God in Christ, which stood out from the ordinary experience of that time most conspicuously. It was a little bit broken off from the life of faith and given him to taste, that he might realize how far below his privilege he was living. He made up his mind that if God would ever give him another blessing like that, he would make any and every sacrifice that might be necessary to retain it. He would make the retention of it, a matter of life and death.

The two months spent in Pike County, Penn., going from house to house with books and Bibles, and talking and praying in every house, made him bitterly sensible of the need of some better experience than he had. There was ever a painful sense of obligation. He went through the work unflinchingly, but without realizing that Christ's yoke is easy and His burden is light. There was a shrinking from the unpleasantness of encountering a chilling reception. When people were interested, he could cheerfully talk to them of Christ; but when they were not, he did it as a duty.

He was persuaded that the standard of Christian living pictured in the New Testament was altogether higher than Christians generally supposed; and believed it to be his privilege to seek and attain this.

The reading of Upham's *Interior Life,* confirmed him in this idea, and encouraged him by the evidence that there were others who saw it.

The resolution that he came to, to read the Bible with the belief that there was something sanctifying in every verse and passage would help the mind to lay hold of it; especially the habit of thus meditating on Scripture formed in consequence of this resolution, was of the highest importance in preparing him to enter in at length, to the desired experience.

The delay that took place, the long-protracted season of watching and waiting and weeping and praying and searching, was like a complete turning of himself inside out, so that he was delivered for ever from the disposition to look for anything good in himself.

The great hindrance was the idea that emancipation was to come through some change of his feelings and affections. "Just as I am" was a good song to sing when the question related to forgiveness of sin; but he could not discern how it could have any pertinency when the question related to sanctification. For holiness implies a prodigious change of heart.

Nothing in Heaven or earth astonished him more than the discovery made on the 4th of December, 1845, that Jesus was his sanctification, and that all he had to do was to abide in Him as the branch in the vine, and the goodness of Christ would sway him moment by moment, and it would always be Christ's goodness not his own; for there is none good save one, that is God.

When the discovery was made, he was filled with wonder, love and praise, but also with a sense of the need of perpetual vigilance, lest, at any time, he should forget his absolute dependence on Christ. He felt that he must watch against everything, even in matters lawful, which could in any way weaken his sense of dependence. He felt he was under law to Christ, in eating, drinking and sleeping, and study and conversation; that he must habitually stand ready to cut off a right hand, to secure the continued realization of Christ's love. All self-denial now became easy; the sense of God's love filled him with joy unspeakable, and he valued nothing more than the opportunity of expressing his own love in return.

In his journals of the Spring of 1846 are entries such as these:

> Last evening it seemed as though the barriers were breaking down between the invisible world where God is, and myself. My frame was shaken by the nearness of the divine essence.
>
> The heaven of those who love God, is the place where they can best serve Him.
>
> After considering His mighty power in creation, and yet the perfect ease with which He did all, making a blade of grass with not more ease than a solar system, I considered that there was one work that was not easy. I looked at Gethsemane and saw Him agonize as no creature could. Redemption was a hard work. The forgiveness of my sins cost God more than the creation of many suns.
>
> Communing with Jesus this morning it was impressed upon my mind that the thing to which I should give almost my whole attention, is preparation for future usefulness. God, blessed be His Name, will never encourage me in self-indulgence; will not supply me by immediate revelation with the treasures of gracious knowledge I required. No, I must study, study, study. My meat and drink must be the acquisition of divine knowledge. Let me get more of the Bible than any other man, into my heart. God's truth must pass through the alembic of the living soul, before it will be extensively blessed. One man, mighty in the Scriptures, will be mightier than a thousand silently distributed copies of the Bible. God, as a general rule, will not put so much honor on mere soulless matter, as to save souls with it alone. Human self-denial is the grand condition of the progress of God's work.
>
> I want to have an intense realization of the presence of Jesus in this world, overflowing with interest in its concerns, and vainly seeking among His own some to be the mouthpieces of His love. I feel that He is straitened in us. His feelings can receive no expansion, no expression. It is true His everlasting Word speaks gloriously. But He is not satisfied with past expressions. He is a living Savior, and has a heart full of unquenchable enthusiasm, and He has constituted us, His mortal friends upon this earth, the exponents of this. I have a more vivid idea than I can put on paper: Jesus was remarkably social and is. Let me realize, as the

companion of all my walks and pursuits, the New Testament Jesus. Oh that His whole soul might find its exhibition through mine.

May 2. A week of wonders to my soul. Christ has come with an undreamt-of fullness; and the best is, I feel I have but just begun to receive of His fullness. Every meeting for social prayer has become to me a place of indescribable blessedness. Were Christ bodily present, I could not more truly take the petitions offered and present them to Him. Others think that He is present; I know it, by most remarkable attestations.

May 16. I hear a voice saying unto me daily: "Ask no more; I have fully answered your petitions; the blessings are accumulated around you; and Heaven is waiting to see you appropriate them and give them to a dying world." Mark 9:22-23. The laws of my activity are not changed, because I have Christ to strengthen me; to do is the same thing it always was; and if there is anything to be done I must do it. The fact is, I must introduce the element of determination into my daily and hourly life. I must go about resolving that glorious things shall come to pass. Men must be converted, Christians must be sanctified. I must move with desperate energy; for death is busy everywhere and the night cometh. How have I been living? I have not been living, only talking.

May 21. A day of blessing. Hours of sweet meditation on the 6th of John, and of precious communion with Him Whose words are contained therein, and Who dwelleth in me and I in Him. Altogether a calm, sweet day. Offered a prayer tonight for new discoveries of the glory of God in Christ, and new experience of the power of His sufferings. I mention it here to show Thee that I am in earnest, and look for its fulfillment. I am not sure but that I have the beginning of it. I feel weak from the physical effects of my Savior's nearness. I should be lost in amazement; whereas I live as though all were in the course of nature. Think I am making some little advances to a spirit of lovingness. But oh what remains!

May 28. It is not new truth I want, so much as the improvement of what I have. Would it not be best to let all go that keeps me back from understanding this great truth, that Thou, O God of infinitude, Thou in Whom are hid all treasures, Who art from everlasting to everlasting, rich in unimaginable blessedness, the native fount of all holiness, that Thou art my God? Mine, mine, mine. All mine. As altogether and absolutely mine as though there were not another creature to share Thee with me. I find that nothing gives me so vast an idea of Thine infinitude, as the thought that Thou art an infinite God to each of Thy creatures. Each one may come to Thee, and ask with as large desires as though he were himself Thy whole universe, and all the faculties and affections of Thy mighty being, concentrated upon him. This God is mine, and He is dwelling in my soul. And my highest obligation is to live upon

Him, instead of on myself. To use Him, to draw from His resources continually, to consider myself the almoner of the world and He my treasurer. Oh, it is base in me to want for anything! I must follow hard on. I must give expansion and amplitude to my desires.

June 4. We depend on faith for our knowledge of one another. My friend is not that body which I see, that voice which I hear, those looks that meet me, that conduct which interests me; but he is something of which these are evidences. His body, voice, looks, motions, may die and be no more; but he will still be himself, still have his present character, still be what I love and admire. Faith is admission upon testimony. Upon testimony only we found our belief of another's character. How unembarrassed is the operation of this faith, as regards our friends. It is as though we actually saw their spirits and characters; we are satisfied with the evidence. Now evidence may be of different kinds, while it is equally perfect. Jesus Christ, when in the flesh, could only be known by faith; now that He is in His Word, He must be so known; and His Word is no doubt a more abundant testimony and revelation than His person itself was.

Let me read the New Testament through twenty pages a day, with one aim prominently in view, the ascertaining of God's way of presenting the Gospel. And I want to make this a season of Calvary fellowship, till I shall have imbibed the mighty compassion of the Savior for dying souls. I want to make these weeks of self-denial; I suspect that there is much yet to be crucified within me. I need to study minutely human character. I never can cope successfully unless I look my particular enemy in the face. Merely to take the sword and go into the battle and slash right and left without ever fixing the eye on an individual is no way to be victorious. Wise as serpents. God's truths are few; but they assume under the direction of the Spirit thousand-fold phase and form, according to the individual and the experience.

July 7. I have talked very freely about my need of humility, without feeling my need of it. The general silent unconscious sentiment of my heart is, that I am more in the favor of Christ than others; that I am somebody—something! I want to show the world what good terms I am on with the Savior. I want to take the sublimest, costliest, sacredest thing in God's universe, and procure with it the admiration of my fellow-Christians. Is any sin more to be abhorred? Yet how little sensibility I show at the recognition of it. Without humility I can never be useful; nor do I desire to be useful without it. It would ill become a God of purity to reward self-complacency in this way. I must be dead, as Christ was dead, to the opinions o men. I must not take my motives part of them from the throne of God and part from the pit of corruption. There is a great deal of room yet to be made in my heart, for God. There is a large unconquered region. It is useless to think of foreign conquests first. I am immeasurably far from perfection, and am glad to see it. I rejoice to learn that I may have so much more of the life of God in the soul. And now let me realize the full power of prayer this week, for myself and for others.

Some of the summer jottings were these:

> Rebellion: unwillingness to receive all from God.
> Faith: voluntary reception of all from Him.
> Of Him, through Him, to Him, all. Receive everything from Him, retain it through Him, use it for Him; this is the life of faith.
> Independence is death.
> We are unwilling to receive from God and retain through God, because we are unwilling to use for God. To do as we will, we must be sole proprietors.
> So far as men feel that they receive from God, they must feel their obligation to use for God.
> Imperfect consecration arises from the imperfect sense of our dependence for all on God.
> Pray without ceasing; not because God does not answer prayer, but because He does. Our wants are renewed every moment, and so must our supplies be. God's government consists in giving. He is love; and it is the life of love to give. It is rebellion for us to be satisfied. In ceasing to receive we cease to be united to God.
> All created excellence is the excellence of the Creator. Instead of contrasting finite wisdom with infinite, learn to view all true wisdom as God's wisdom, all the love there is as His, all holiness as His. Of Him are all things. All loveliness is God's loveliness. All true happiness is His.
> It is only in our hearts that Satan can harm us.
> The highest kind of knowledge is the knowledge of God's love: for He is love. We must use the knowledge of His various attributes as a means; this knowledge as an end. We must know His wisdom, power, greatness, in order to know the excellency of His love. We are apt to think that we honor God more by recognition of His wisdom, majesty, holiness, power; but we honor Him most by recognition of His love. Among men every other attribute confers glory before this. In Heaven none confers such glory. It is the aim of love to bestow happiness; of divine love, the utmost happiness. Not the greatest number of happy beings, but the utmost happiness.

The last year in the Seminary carried forward the rich and deepening experience of the year preceding:

Oct 1. The cross was the manifestation of an immutable nature. What is there exhibited is something that is, was, and shall be everlastingly. Christ did not love more, when suspended betwixt Heaven and earth, than always before and always since. It was a perfect expression of the divine character, and therefore sufficient to all eternity. If we should see a cross erected, and Christ crucified every day anew, we would have no more evidence of divine love than we have. Such repeated demonstrations may be of value among men, whose dispositions are liable to change; but cannot be needed from an unchangeable God. Christ is at this moment for me what He was for me on the cross. That is, One Whose desire for my happiness knoweth no bounds.

Faith is not intended to deprive the will of power, but greatly to increase its power by transferring it from self to God. The kingdom of God is within you. If I could but have faith in the presence and dominion of God within me, all the time, I would enjoy that presence and that determining power all the time, and my life would be characterized by energy and liberty.

Oct. 13. A blessed day this. I have resolved, from this time forward, to live upon love. I am going to live a life of supreme selfishness, and know nothing but Christ and Him crucified, nothing but that God Who is love. Of this I am sure, that the world, if it knew its own interests, and if any of them were dependent on me, would to a man drive me to the bosom of God. Let this henceforth be my only virtue, to know the love of God. I call it selfishness, by a liberty of speech. But indeed to be heartily willing to live thus, is the death of self. It is to abandon the fatal position of wishing to owe something to oneself. It is to have felicity in the heart, striking outward. My own natural heart is repugnant to this felicity; it wants to be doing something. This happiness in the heart extinguishes self. We want to have happiness the other side of service; God wants us to have it this side. Knowledge of His love is union to Him. Our union is perfected as we by faith discover the length, breadth, height, depth. All our usefulness is as our union to God. The closer the intimacy in which we live with Him, the more productive will be our lives. Therefore I am actually showing more love to a dying world when feasting on the love of God than at any other time. The happiness of the world is dependent on the amount of faith in the world; everyone that has faith must regard it as his highest obligation to have more. Faith is the knowledge of the love of God.

Oct. 26. Let all my senses be avenues of the glory of God, consecrated to the reception of Him. What was my eye made for but to discover His loveliness, to answer His glance of love? What was my ear made for but to hear His voice? What was my palate made for but to taste the bread of life? What were my lips made for but to be kissed with the kisses of His mouth? And every sense, what for, but to apprehend the Creator of all, Who made all things for His own pleasure? Now, when I hear music, let me hear the music of God and be ravished; when I see beauty, let me see the beauty of God; let all fragrance, all sweetness, everything to apprehend which with pleasure there exists a provision in my physical, spiritual or intellectual nature, be a vehicle of God to my soul. Let me seek for worth everywhere; for beauty, for whatever is admirable, persuaded that it all belongs to God and is the exponent of Himself. In a word not only my powers but my susceptibilities must be engaged for God.

Oct. 27. Returning from the evening meeting, my father related a delightful incident concerning himself. He was dreaming the night before that he, in course of conversation with someone, said, "You must learn that to live by faith, it is necessary to live by faith every hour." And immediately on saying that he seemed to hear a voice of singular melody, beauty, gentleness, winningness, saying these words, "Why don't you do it?" A voice full of tender reproach and gentle upbraiding, like the voice of a child. Whose could it be but the voice of Jesus? And the circumstance appeared to have made a profound impression upon him. May it be greatly blessed to him. No message could be more opportune.

In regard to public speaking, all experience teaches me this, that grace is given me at the moment needed and not before. In vain I try to overcome my nervousness and palpitation of heart before the moment arrives; faith is not given me for this; but when I am actually on my feet before the audience, then I am strengthened. Let this very consideration tend to banish that preliminary conflict. This truth is general, and of continual application.

I become more and more convinced that the essential thing in Christianity is progress; an ocean of sins and errors in a man who is making progress is less displeasing to God, than a lakelet in one who is stationary. For this is the great truth, that every minute of a life not characterized by strugglings after holiness, is a minute in which all the sins of the individual are repeated. For the sin of standing still is not one sin but all sin. A struggling for holiness is a protestation against all the sin of the individual; a respite in the Christian's life is a toleration of all that sin.

Jan. 14, 1847. I find in the Epistles a good deal of language in connection with the subject of the cross, that indicates an experience far beyond my own, "That I may know the fellowship of His sufferings and be made conformable to His death." "For I am crucified with Christ." "How shall we that are dead to sin, live any longer therein?" and all that chapter. "For I bear about in my body" the dying of the Lord Jesus that the life also, &c., "For I am crucified to the world." "That we being dead to sin, should live unto righteousness." "He that hath suffered in the flesh hath ceased from sin." I am a babe in the knowledge of the cross. There is something here that the church knows nothing about. It is implied that the believer may be brought to a wonderful fellowship with the Savior in His sufferings; and that, in this fellowship, sin is tortured to death. There is some undreamt-of knowledge here in which all our interests are bound up. I begin to feel new attractions to the cross. My union to Christ is to be effected not so much in my life as in His death. I want to know how to preach the cross; and am shamefully ignorant. Let me determine to know nothing but Christ and Him crucified.

Apr. 19. Yesterday my first Sabbath in the pulpit. Preached three times. Was sustained; but disappointed in the results. Have everything to learn in the matter of getting men's attention and making impressions upon them. It is a great work; and God will task all of one's energy, all of one's faith. I was somewhat favored in one respect—freedom from reflex acts. . . . I want to bear about in my body the dying of the Lord Jesus; so that when I stand up to preach I may be in sympathy with His death, having the same mind that was in Him on Calvary. I shall never have a congregation more out of sympathy with its preacher, than that which Christ had on Calvary. I shall be crucified with Him, when willing to be as much despised, hated and maltreated as He was there; and animated at the same time by His love and self-forgetting compassion. Another thought: progress must be made every time I preach; I must have more of Christ in every sermon. The question arises, What has become of the prayers I offered last week for a distinguishing blessing on my preaching? Answer: God knows my chief desire to be for usefulness, on the whole, during my life, and not for great success on any one particular occasion; and He saw that this desire would be best promoted by such a measure of influence as I had yesterday to begin with.

I suppose that one of the greatest of all triumphs for Satan would be to have my body become transparent while I was preaching, so that men could see the inner man. I do not know how I am to be remedied. In regard to anyone else, I might hope in God's means; but these means have been so lavished on me, I have seen so much of Christ crucified, that it seems to me I am beyond restoration. If God knows of any way by which I may be made an honest, open man, with a mind flowing spontaneously out at every avenue, so that every fellowman may have the freedom of my nature, and handle the hidden things of my soul better than I myself could now do, I beg of Him to bring it to pass.

May 5. The sunshine of God fills my soul, I have but one thing to do—to love Christ and trust in Him, and all will be well. The unsearchable riches of Christ are my riches. Despondency is guilt; especially in me.

May 12. David's hardest battle (preliminary to his encounter with Goliath) was with his brethren and Saul and the soldiers of Saul's army; his courage received its most violent shocks from them. There is much instruction in this. David was conqueror from the moment he had forced his way through the army of temptations, with his trust in God unshaken. I need to feel that God will not work mightily save through the mighty working of my soul; that my enemies will treat me as chaff, unless I treat them as gigantic; that there will be lions in my path if it be the path to Heaven; that unless my days are filled with stern and well-directed energy, I am not benefiting the world; that whatever is less than this is destruction to souls. I have waited long enough to see my soul strengthened in inaction; I must act, in reckless disregard of all the weakness of my moral nature.

I want to feel on rising in the morning, like a soldier on the plains of Marengo and Austerlitz; it is to be a day of battle. There is no need of faint-heartedness; a cheerful courage is the best; but the armor, the whole armor of God must be put on.

June 3. To know the love of God is to obtain it. Love is given by one creature to another, simply by making it known; it may be by deeds or by declarations; the revelation of it is the giving of it. I need but to know God, and His love is mine.... We must learn to sift away the finery of prayer. It must be tested by its products.... If I cannot bring the Spirit of God into the heart of those I am now with, what madness to think I can do the heathen any good.... I feel that God in these eighteen months has given me much that might be given to the church and the world, and ought to be; but which I am wholly unable to give. I have no faculty of self-delivery. I need that another should enter into me, having this faculty, to energize my nature and use me for God. I need Christ. Christ living in me.

Bowen's three years in the Seminary were completed in the early summer of 1847. For the latter half of his course his longing that Christ should live in him and through him was fulfilled in a measure that profoundly influenced the Seminary and the lives of his fellow-students. Of the few classmates or fellow-students who were living nearly fifty years after their graduation (in 1905) the following wrote out reminiscences for this memorial:

> The Rev. Robert Gray, Dublin, Virginia: "Bowen always impressed me as one of the most consecrated Christians I ever knew and this, I think, was the sentiment concerning him with all of the students at the

Seminary.... We had in that class, 1847, many very devoted servants of the Master, some seven or eight who became foreign missionaries, but none more devoted and more beloved by his fellow-students than George Bowen."

The Rev. Alfred H. Dashiell, Livingston, Staten Island: "No one could be in communion with him and not be impressed with his eminently spiritual life. No one can fail to remember his devout walking with God. You could not be in his presence for the shortest time without receiving from his conversation earnest promptings to a consecration of life."

The Rev. Edwin A. Bulkley, Rutherford, N. J.: "The immediate impression of acquaintance with him and his life plan was very decided and made itself apparent in every direction. So absorbed was he in the ordinary and special studies of his profession, and in the fulfillment of his consecration to Christ that he at times seemed absent-minded and to depreciate the opportunities for sacred learning which were greatly important in preparation for the ministry. Yet he knew that it would evidently be a mistake not to give as much to the class-room as to the chapel. The recollection of his life previous to conversion made him distant and possibly morose to some but soon all saw that there was a sad sweetness in his character which was but the token of his happy devotion to his Master and of his eager desire to have many equally enlisted. In consequence he became very influential in a revival in the Seminary and particularly in the missionary service. Not one of his fellows of that period failed to receive its impulse and it has not been lost after many succeeding years. This intentness in chosen work doubtless had much to do with the unique and independent work as undertaken in India and will long make the name of Bowen a remembered name. Our characterization of him always seems weak by reason of his peculiarity and ardor. Methods as employed by him may seem insufficient and mistaken but his word and work will continue to live."

The Rev. S. P. Leeds, Hanover, N. H.: "In the autumn of 1844 I observed in the Seminary a man of dark complexion. We were members of the same church (Mercer St. Presbyterian). Before long I heard him deliver one of the usual addresses before the Seminary and was impressed with the fact that he could never become a preacher—certainly not without a radical change. The only man that I ever knew in the pulpit that at all reminded me of him was my friend, Dr. G. H. Houghton of the Episcopal Church. I was glad when I heard that he was to be a foreign missionary.

"Modest and reticent, somewhat older than most, he soon made a deep impression on his fellow-students. His conversation and his occasional exhortations in religious meetings continued with the fervor of our gifted pastor, Dr. Thomas H. Skinner, Sr., to impress me with a type of piety, at once thoughtful and fervent, whose claim upon Christians I have never abandoned in the sixty years since. The 'eccentricities' and 'weaknesses' of George Bowen's life I am not so sure of as I might be. I am by no means certain that it is not occasionally wise for a missionary, especially if unmarried, to work independently of a missionary organization. (Pretty certain *Daily Meditations* would not have been written otherwise, I surmise). As for his going into the Methodist Church, one of the old Presbyterian-Congregational discipline and order, like myself, can understand what may have been his reasons. There is a vast deal of impedimenta—as the Romans called their army baggage, you remember—about the Congregationalists and Presbyterians in my judgment, and not a little among the Baptists. Very likely the Methodists have accumulated a fair share of other kinds since Bowen joined them. But, past fourscore, and as my family seem to think 'of sound and disposing mind' as yet, I do heartily wish one could have more of 'go' among us—less of the McClellan type (excellence in defense) and more of the Grant—'The army that stays in its trenches is beaten,' said the great general. Oh, to move on.

"One season Bowen and I with four others united in a daily half-hour prayer meeting at six in the morning. It interests me to recall that, expressing to him afterwards my dissatisfaction with myself in connection with these meetings, I was surprised to hear the same confession from him. Perhaps our zeal was greater than our wisdom. One or two of the six turned out—well, very poorly, I have understood.

"Nevertheless I used to say that he seemed to me in those years one who could be compared to a fire even were it kindled in an iceberg. He burst directly from Christ. Holy he was indeed. He started a fire in the Seminary that was a genuine 'revival' in the strictest sense. I think that at its close, one-quarter, say twenty-five out of 100 of our students, had devoted themselves to the missionary work. I like to recall our affectionate intimacy and the good he did me."

Bowen's diary makes frequent mention of his Seminary friends with whom and for whom he prayed, and of his longing and strivings for a revival in the Seminary, in the Mercer Street Church and throughout the entire Christian Church:

Jan. 19, 1846. Yesterday was a delightful and profitable Sabbath. Things from which I should formerly have anticipated no result, I now feel must redound to the glory of God through the prayer of faith which He permits me to offer up. The meeting of young men in the afternoon was unspeakably solemn. Trust that Jesus will bring these other three out into that broad place where we stand. God is at work and it is pleasant to see all our expectations concerning the manner confounded, while fulfilled concerning the result. He doubtless means that the leaven shall go through the church as it is going through the Seminary, privately and from individual to individual. This is doubtless to be a great week; the last was but introductory. My prayer is that I may be the meekest man that ever lived, meeker than Moses, as meek as Christ; the most loving of all God's creatures, and the most useful of all the Lamb's company.

Jan. 20. Faithful and ever-adorable Friend. What happiness in communion with Him! If I begin to think that there is any abatement, presently He comes with more tenderness and affection than ever. What joy I had this morning in hearing Isaiah 41 read! I can do all through Christ. He has blessed young Lockwood in answer to our prayers of Sabbath afternoon. Father, glorify Thyself in this youth, let him be a man after Thine own heart and Thy messenger for the heathen. He has blessed brother Leeds too, but more is needed, and there is more in the wells of salvation. Had a long talk this morning with Bro. Durnett, and pray that immeasurable good may result. We have engaged to pray without ceasing for the descent of the Holy Spirit upon the Seminary. He thinks that I shall be tried by imputations of perfectionism. I believe I am made willing to be tried in any way that God pleases.

Jan. 21. Had another interview last evening with Bro. Aikman. Oh, how hard to let everything go and drop into the arms of God! Because some things are in themselves good and authorized, he thinks he may retain them, even though he admits that their operation is adverse to him. Sought to show him that entire consecration implies a total surrender of everything into the hand of God, father, mother, all affections, all expectations, no matter how sacred they might seem. There must be a moment when all shall be in the hand of God, and we ourselves standing naked in the midst of a great desert. After that, God will restore us what He will, but we may take, but as of free grace and tender love. Have this morning had a season of extraordinary faith. I arose from my knees nothing doubting that the petitions I had offered for my mother, Dr. Skinner, our church, the Seminary, the University, were heard, "and an affirmative decree issued by the divine mind." I prayed also to be the holiest and most useful of men. Two or three instances have occurred of brethren who seemed to have had a great blessing, but after a day or two, darkness supervened. Self-righteousness, imagining that there was something in the act of consecration that elicited an extraordinary measure of God's love, and losing the sense of this when the sense of sin returned; or else thinking that God had done all He could be expected to do, and the blessing received was the measure and limit of His grace. The great thing to bear in mind is that sin, repented of, is not to separate us from God, but to bring us to Him. Allowed sin, of course, will separate us from Him.

Jan. 24. Have had this morning two of the meetings, and precious ones they were. The last especially was a heavenly place in Christ. We spent an hour on our knees and then had a profitable interchange of thought on the subject of faith. . . . Jesus was in the third meeting. We were six; and I trust He glorified Himself. I feel that the exercises of this day have awakened a new feeling in the Seminary. . . . The Holy Ghost is never in a hurry. It is of supreme importance for us not to use precipitation in our words or acts. Haste implies weakness, and the Spirit of God is all-powerful, and holds subject every heart of man; and when He has anything for me to say, He will make time and place for me to say it. My custom is to sit still when others talk, and to talk when others are silent.

Jan. 28. It was a precious time, full of power and invigoration. A heaven on earth. Oh, for larger capacities to comprehend all the blessings God is giving us. A dying world was uppermost in our thoughts and prayers. I have had the persuasion all along that God was doing all this good to souls because I had prayed in faith; but I begin now to see that He gave me the prayer of faith because He was desirous of doing good to souls. Had an interview with Bro. Zivley. The work goes forward in his soul. He wants to give up everything and give himself wholly to this one matter. The spirit of prayer and the love of God's Word abound more and more. Have just had a most powerful blessing in prayer. The atmosphere about me was intense and warm with divine love. God is doubtless ready to carry me up; let me only put away every impediment. In meetings, since my spiritual baptism, I have taken this course: to sit still and let the providences of my Savior move me, giving myself no manner of anxiety. A suspicion has come into my mind that perhaps my natural repugnance to public speaking indulged itself here somewhat, and the question arises if my course should not be this: to go forward for Christ and do everything with all my might, leaving to His providence to hinder and repress me. With regard to eating, drinking and sleeping I thus proceed; I look for intimations when to stop. Now it should be my meat to do my Father's will in spreading His kingdom. I will leave this matter open till I have studied it a little more.

June 10, 1846. Since Monday, I have been excluding myself almost entirely from my prayers, and filling them with the wants of others. I never had such views of Christ's love for His people, and His intense willingness to heal their backslidings and crown them with loving-kindness; nor have ever been more conscious of sympathy with Him that in thus giving Himself up to their concerns. Look not every man upon his own things, but every man on the things of others. I have asked God to answer upon others all the prayers I have been offering up for myself hitherto. What is sanctification? What but love? Surely this is the way to make progress in holiness: to be forgetting self and remembering others. Paul seems to have had little to do with prayer for himself; but was ever entreating the churches to pray for him that his mouth might be opened. While he prays that the Ephesians may know the love of Christ, he adds, with all saints, directing their desires to the interests of others. There is exquisite happiness in praying for the saints, when we realize the love of Christ for them.

Among the young men whom Bowen influenced in the Mercer Street Church was Ralph Wells, one of the most useful and beloved lay workers of the last half of the century; while of his Seminary group seventeen went to the foreign field: Mills and Dwight and Taylor to the Sandwich Islands, Richards to China, Cochran and Coan to Persia, Wood and Dulles to India, Dodd and Crane and Parsons and Marsh to Turkey, Ford to Syria, Abraham, Livingstone and Best to Africa.

Bowen's comments on the two teachers at Union Seminary who most deeply impressed him are worth recording. They were written more than thirty years later and printed in the *Bombay Guardian* of September 24, 1881:

> In our day, the chief burden of instruction in the Seminary was modestly, patiently borne by Dr. Henry White—nomen venerabile! Though not eminent for brilliant genius or profound learning, or commanding eloquence, or polished manner, I shall ever hold him in highest honor and esteem, as a most excellent teacher of the science of God. He had a clear head, discriminating judgment, sound common-sense, wise tact, and a warm heart—all pervaded with a child-like faith in Christ and His salvation.
>
> I see him now in his lecture room, not standing in majestic authority to stamp upon his pupils' mind his own system of theology, but sitting familiarly among them to guide their studies. First, he names a list of topics, and sends them to their Bibles and a few standard authors to settle and define views for themselves; then, in the way of recitation, he calls each to tell his views, and put his questions. With quick perception and ready wit, he notes errors, exposes crudities, and clears up difficulties. Then, at last, he reads his lecture, without pretension or rhetorical display, yet with limpid clearness and terse compactness; presents the truth as he understands it, confirmed by arguments that cannot well be gainsaid. He brings us up fully to the line of that which God's Word makes plain,

but cares not to lead us over into the open field of vague speculation, where human conceits, miscalled the dicta of pure reason, keep false lights blazing and shadows dancing only to deceive. His students thus retained their own individuality, unconstrained by any overshadowing greatness of their teacher. Each mind was trained to work in the way most true to itself, and made to grow in knowledge of divine things by inward digestion of proper food, rather than by outward accretion. Each took the armor of divine truth, and fitted it to himself, so as to have it best at command for the service before him.

As with passing years I have studied in theory and by observation of manifest results, different methods of instruction, I grow strong in the conviction that his was the true method for such a school as this. In a remarkable degree, I think those whom he thus taught have remained steadfast in the evangelical faith, and have ministered to the edification, and not to the defection of other souls with respect to that faith. Better this, certainly, than to have made himself the father of an ism, with no matter how large and devoted a following; or in the attempt to be wise beyond what is written, to have left minds bewildered in the wild vagaries of speculation, however fair and fascinating. How far his successors have adopted his method, I am not able to say; but I am happy to believe that the theology of our Alma Mater has been kept free from any distinctive peculiarity that implies distortion, balanced in the grand simplicity and profound depth of Christ's own teaching. So, for the good of men and the glory of God, may it ever remain true to the thought and aim of its first Professor of Systematic Theology!

We were much favored also by the instructions of that world-renowned scholar, Dr. Edward Robinson. He came to us in the midst of our course of study, fresh from his researches in Palestine, and his exegesis of the Greek of the Gospels was enriched with illustrations drawn from his recent observations, which so defined places and customs as to give vivid reality to the scenes of our Savior's life. His own standard of ministerial scholarship was set high. He was intolerant of shams. Hence more than any of our instructors, he strove to hold those whom he taught to honest and faithful work in study. There was thus, in his bearing as a teacher, a look and tone of severity which chafed some. But it proceeded from the kindest intent, and there was a warm side to his heart, and a personal interest for every earnest student. To all such, he offered kind words of encouragement with willing and effective help. Some can never forget the fatherly affection with which he visited them in sickness and cheered them in despondency. And blessed to all was the stern discipline he gave to tone up the intellectual activities—a kind of discipline needed no less in the Theological Seminary than in the College, to counteract lazy shiftlessness; a phase of human depravity to which students everywhere are peculiarly exposed. From Dr. Robinson's labors both as teacher and as author, there came to his pupils and to the world a timely and helpful impulse to thorough investigation of the exact meaning of the sacred Scriptures. With the balanced judgment characteristic of his mind, he resisted alike the tendency of German rationalism, and of easy English evangelicalism, and stood earnestly for the true meaning of God's Word as it comes to us, a message of divine truth. Acknowledging its supreme authority, he would know, and have us know, simply and fully what is written.

On Bowen's death in 1888 Dr. Robert Aikman of Madison, N. J., one of his dear friends, named in his journal, wrote in *The Missionary Review of the World,* June, 1888, an account of Bowen's influence in the Seminary with which this chapter can best be concluded:

> I do not propose even to sketch the life of this saintly man and eminent missionary; but having been his classmate and familiar friend during this theological course in Union Seminary, I would like to speak of some of those early experiences which gave tone and color to his unique spiritual life and career.
>
> Of the class which entered the Seminary in 1844 Bowen was almost the oldest man, having been born April 13, 1816. There was nothing striking in his countenance or personal appearance—of slight frame, quiet demeanor, unimpassioned utterance, and no magnetism of manner—a man who could hardly ever be an orator, and indeed who never came to be one—a most unpretentious man, and courteous as was to be expected of one who had been much in the world of men.
>
> Within the few months during which classmates learn to place each other, we all came to know that Bowen was different from most men, and better than most of us. He had never been to college, yet his Greek and Hebrew recitations were among the finest, and his thoughts at our missionary and prayer meetings, expressed with choice simplicity, were original and quickening beyond the common run. He looked at Bible truth in a novel way, which yet was evidently his natural way. He was not communicative of himself, but we learned that he was newly born into the Christian life, and almost up to his entrance upon ministerial studies had been a skeptic, utterly unacquainted with religious truth, and as ignorant of the Bible as a man of his general intelligence and cultivation could well be. The remarkable and pathetic manner in which his mind was turned to the Bible and his striking conversion have been well told and will never lose their interest. Up to that period he was an

infidel of the French school, and although never a mocker, he told me that he had always regarded the Bible very much as he had regarded Aesop's Fables.

Out of this darkness Bowen came into sudden light, and the light was strange and wonderful and sweet. He probably never had a doubt of Bible truth, of the way of life through Christ, and of his own acceptance with God, from the beginning to the end of his Christian life; and it was at first matter of surprise to him that any believer should have doubts as to his spiritual estate. His expressions were the least hackneyed of any man I ever knew, which, no doubt, was because he had read almost nothing upon religious subjects and was so unacquainted with the views of other Christians. He drew water directly from the wells of salvation, and it is both interesting and profitable to know that he became an evangelical believer; without bigotry, caring little for denominational peculiarities, but evangelical through and through.

About the middle of our junior year, Bowen passed into a spiritual experience which I find it difficult to describe, although I was somewhat familiar with the process and results. He had been giving himself more and more to protracted and intense study of the Bible, and particularly the Gospel of St. John, and more especially still, to those deep portions of it which comprise the Savior's last discourses with His disciples in the Passover room. He discovered that there was an experience to which he had not attained, and in which it was possible permanently to abide—a state of absolute certainty as to spiritual truths, of entire devotement to the glory of God, and of rest in God. This, of course, was nothing else than the "abiding" of which our Lord speaks, and it was not different in its nature from that of Bowen's first experience; but it came to him as almost new, and so it came to his classmates. I shall never forget an evening prayer meeting in the Seminary and the impression which his testimony made upon his classmates, although nothing could be less ostentatious than his words and manner. One of our most intelligent men arose and said, "Is this something new in the Christian life, or is it a deepening of the currents which flow in all our hearts?" No doubt it was the latter, but it made the impression almost of newness.

At that time Bowen began to come under the power of a mental habit, not peculiar to him indeed except as to its completeness and permanence. He made a distinct effort to realize the actual and personal presence of the Savior with him, to become intimately and at all times conscious of the nearness of Jesus as one to be spoken and walked with. This grew by cultivation to be a great life power with him. One day, Bowen, J. Edwards Ford (afterwards of the Syrian Mission) and myself were together in the room of Thomas A. Weed. The last named was a genial and even jovial man, and a great favorite of us all. He led the conversation into the line of the nearness of Christ to His own, in order, I suppose, to draw remarks from Bowen, who, after a while, said in his quiet way, "I have at this moment a more vivid sense that Jesus is in the room here than I have that either of you three are."

Quite a singular illustration of the power of this mental habit, occurred with him in Bombay. In the fall of 1848, when he had been less than a year on missionary ground, he was seized with what seemed to be a fatal attack of ulceration of the larynx. This was long before the days of telegraphs, and on the day when the India packet sailed Bowen was supposed to be dying. Obituaries appeared in the papers and in one of our religious journals a tribute to his memory and a chastened lament over his "early sickness and death." The very night the ship sailed the ulceration was arrested and his recovery began. During this illness he began to be troubled with the not uncommon hallucination of groups of persons apparently visible in his room. He said to himself, "I will arrest this delusion by the realized presence of Jesus; of that I am sure," and as these forms began to appear he succeeded in banishing them simply by the power of this fixed habit of his mind. I have always believed that this habit was almost the greatest force in his life, and it is certain that he endeavored to make it such.

In the complete surrender of himself to Christ, George Bowen has had many equals, but few I think who became at once and so utterly dead to all former things. Just as absolutely as Paul, did he say, What things were gain to me those I counted loss for Christ; yea, doubtless, and I count all things but loss for the excellency of the knowledge of Christ Jesus my Lord. All his literary ambitions and pursuits, all his linguistic attainments, all his social reputation, he not only laid upon the altar, but he seemed to forget that he had ever had such attainments of objects. I was often with him in his room and in the family circle, yet I never heard him speak of Italian or French art, although he was master of both languages and had looked with appreciative eye on most of the galleries of Europe, in this resembling the great apostle, who saw the temples, statuary, and altars of Athens, yet spake of the one altar only, and made that the text for a sermon. I am not characterizing this, but simply making the statement. He had entered upon a literary career. From others I knew that the Putmans had published a graceful volume from his pen; he never alluded to it in my hearing. One of the family told me that he had nearly completed a much larger work, of which all I ever saw was some manuscript pages which he was putting to some common use; it never saw the light, except perhaps as kindling material. I think he underestimated the influence of his early literary habits, and his study of the modern languages; they were of greater service to him all through his life than he seemed to recognize. His facility in acquiring languages was such that he commenced preaching in the difficult Marathi tongue before he had been nine months in Bombay. The ease with which he accomplished his varied literary and editorial work was due to the practice of those early years, when he was building better than he knew and preparing for future work divinely planned for him.

When he gave himself to foreign missions he made two resolves—never to marry and never to return to his native land. So he lived alone, and died where he had labored. It may be questioned whether his choice to live so near the low plane of Hindu life in food and expenditure was a wise choice; it would not have been possible had he been a married man, as most missionaries will be and ought to be, but his course was prayerfully and deliberately taken, and he had the right to be his own judge. That most devoted Scotsman, William C. Burns, adopted the Chinese mode of living, and went so far as to adopt the Chinese dress. In later life he expressed doubts as to the wisdom of this course, and said that he would probably not do the same if his missionary life were to begin over again. When Bowen withdrew from the American Board and adopted his new mode of life, Dr. Rufus Anderson said it was well to have one man make such an experiment and to mark the result. Christian Frederick Schwartz and George Bowen were men of great ability, entire consecration, and of wide Christian influence; each was unselfish and generous to the last degree, and the work of each abides and will ever abide. That Schwartz hindered his influence because he lived in European modes, or Bowen helped his by living in the Hindu mode, who shall say?

A remarkable feature of Bowen's work has awakened thought among his friends. It is not known that many conversions can be traced to his personal efforts. That he himself ever mourned this or even regarded it as strange does not appear. The Head of the church gives to every man his own work, and Bowen's work seems to have been as nearly perfect as is often given to man to do. When Bishop Randolph Foster returned from India he said to me, Bowen is called the Saint of India. To be thought of as such by the many missionaries of the great peninsula is proof of an influence for good greater than is often given to men to exert. He said once to his classmates, "Our aim must be to bear the greatest possible amount of the best possible fruit." It is enough to say of him that for more than forty years he endeavored to fulfill the purpose thus tersely expressed.

The last time I saw him we were standing at the parting of Broadway and one of the avenues. He said quietly, "It is as if you took this road and I took that, to meet soon where the streets join again."

The class that entered Union Theological Seminary in 1844 had this distinction, that eleven of those who were its members became foreign missionaries. Bowen was the last who remained in the foreign field, and was the latest of them all to be taken Home.

In the *Missionary Review* of July, 1888, Dr. Aikman added a note entitled, "What is Success?" in which he said:

> Since writing this brief article on George Bowen for the June number of this *Review*, I have been made acquainted with his own thoughts in regard to his lack of direct success in winning souls, during his long missionary ministry. It was a great sorrow to him. It weighed heavily upon his heart all through his life in India. In a letter written not long before his death and shortly after the fall which fractured his thigh, alluding to this apparent failure, he said: "Compared to the great trial which has followed me for forty years, this physical disability is a very small thing to bear."
>
> This is certainly suggestive. The Lord measures success in a different way from man. The greatest of the prophets threw himself under the juniper tree, bewailing the utter failure of his life, and requesting for himself only that he might die. How pathetic was the career of Jeremiah! When a mere youth, called to confront the desperate depravity of a whole generation, king, priest and people against him, with never a ray of hope thrown upon the future of his ministry. Dying in Egypt without a convert! Yet the influence of these two old heroes will never die out of the world. Many a man is never so influential as after he is dead; dying prematurely, perhaps, like Abel, but like him, though dead, still speaking.
>
> Foreign missions afford many illustrations of such ways of God. Samuel A. Mills was buried in the ocean when his work for the heathen was only in anticipation. Harriet Newell, at nineteen years of age, died when her lips had hardly taught a heathen syllable. Yet their brief lives are still great living forces in the work of foreign missions. David Brainerd's brief and marvelous work among the Indians won perhaps seventy heathen souls to Christ. Of the subsequent lives of these converted Indians, or their descendants, who can speak? But the short life of Brainerd is among the richest treasures of the Church. When he was dead he became at once a greater power than when he was alive. So he continues to be, and so will be so long as his memoirs live in missionary annals. Good and great men and women are usually greater powers after death than during life. They wait for the last of earth before the men of the earth know how great and good they were; then they begin really to live.

Among such as these, undoubtedly, Bowen will have his place. Filled with the Holy Spirit, dwelling in the mount of God, while yet among men, exerting a widening influence for Christ and holiness through India, his name will not die out of mission records; and he, too, will henceforth be greater after death than he was during life.

Compare Bowen's sense of failure with Lord Kelvin's as Sir J. J. Thomson described it in his delightful *Recollections and Reflections:*

Any notice about the progress of physics in the latter part of last century would be like the play of *Hamlet* without the Prince of Denmark if it did not deal with the part played in it by Lord Kelvin, who for more than forty years before his death in 1907 had been the most potent influence in British physics.

His first paper appeared in 1841, and from then until his death in 1907 there was no year without a paper, and few without many. They cover all branches of physics and record some of the greatest discoveries made in his generation. He himself, was not satisfied, for at his jubilee in 1896 he said, "One word characterizes the most strenuous of the efforts for the advancement of science that I have made perseveringly during fifty-five years, and that word is FAILURE. I know no more of electric and magnetic forces or of the relation between ether, electricity and ponderable matter, or of chemical affinity than I knew and tried to teach to my students of natural philosophy fifty years ago in my first session as Professor." Science never had a more enthusiastic, stimulating or indefatigable leader.

8. Missionary Appointment

On Dec. 12, 1836 Bowen wrote to the American Board of Commissioners for Foreign Missions in Boston, offering himself for foreign missionary service, as follows:

New York, Dec. 12, 1846.

Dear Sirs,

I write for the purpose of offering my services as Missionary of the American Board. I am a member of the Senior Class in the Union Th. Seminary. Enclosed please find certain testimonials.

In compliance with the directions given in your Manual, I will now endeavor to give you some account of my history, character and circumstances.

I was 30 years old the 30th of last April. Have been brought up in this city. My father has been generally in a situation to give his children educational advantages, though I was never sent to college. I was in his counting room for some years previous to my 18th, when I withdrew and gave myself to study which had become my preference; and my vocation since, as far as it has been anything, has been that of a student. At 20 I accompanied the family abroad. We traveled on the Continent, lived in Paris a couple of years, and then I visited the East, spending three months in Egypt, a month or so in Palestine, and a little time in Constantinople. I then returned to this country whither they had preceded me. Since 1840 my life has been stationary here, and my habits sedentary. All this time I was a thorough infidel. I became a skeptic when about 18 years old, and during ten years was as confirmed in unbelief as any man I ever saw, and I have seen some of the worst exhibitions of infidelity.

During that period the opinion that there was no revelation had as much the force of a demonstration in my mind as any other whatever. My reading lay much in the Italian Works and German Literature, with which languages I was acquainted, and I became pretty well imbued with the sentiments and arguments of the anti-Christian portion of that literature. Perhaps Satan never had anyone he was so sure of. In the Spring of 1844 God, by a succession of striking providences, came and made me know Himself, myself, His Son as reconciling us. I then consecrated myself to the service of His Son, Christ Jesus, and almost simultaneously to the work of a foreign missionary. I was permitted to enter the Seminary in the fall of that year, and have seen no reason to doubt, up to this time, that He approved my determination.

During my impenitent life, I had scarcely any intercourse with Christians, and my life was almost as little influenced, directly, by Christianity, as though there were no such system in the world. On being brought to the truth, I became a great student of the Bible; and continuing for some time without much Christian intercourse, my notions of the Christian standard were formed from the N. T. and not from the church. And accordingly I have felt myself constrained to seek a higher life than many seem to aim at. It is now more than a year that I have been permitted to live a life characterized by conscious union to the Savior, by unbroken peace, and by a conviction of the all-sufficiency of Christ. I feel that there is everything in our religion to excite a high degree of enthusiasm, and everything in Christ to render the Christian mighty in word and deed. I believe that whatever truly good and great is to be done in this world is to be done by faith in the Son of God. I find great reason for profound humiliation in view of the little fruit which these convictions and enjoyment have yielded to the cause of Christ, in view of disgraceful unprofitableness, and uncrucified selfishness.

Whatever fitness I may have for the missionary work, has been all given me since my conversion. My former life had been utterly wasted and worse than wasted, and I reached the beach of the church as a shipwrecked man, naked, and with nothing but my skin. I don't see that my knowledge of modern languages can be turned to any account at all. On the other hand my deficiencies are countless. I believe that God has quickened and ameliorated my intellectual powers since my conversion.

My health has always been excellent. Though my body is spare and unpromising, yet my constitution is strong and rugged, I think. I can bear extremes of heat and cold tolerably well. I don't remember to have ever been confined a whole day to bed by sickness.

In conversation with Dr. Armstrong last year, he directed my attention to the Maratha field; I became interested in it, and have been accustomed to regard it since, as my field. My desire is to go to the *heathen*, to the hardest field, the field of greatest exigency. Perhaps the principal bias in my mind, is to a field where the population is larger. At the same time I am timid about expressing any predilection. I should consider it as the greatest of calamities to go to any other than the very field which God in His wisdom may have selected. My age I have been in the habit of regarding as a reason why I should not undertake a language as difficult as the Chinese. Wherever I am, I desire to be a preacher. I expect to go unmarried.

I place great confidence in the prayerfulness of the Committee. I trust that they will be guided from on High, both in the matter of my acceptance or rejection, and in that of my destination.

I don't see that the fact of my having visited the Levant should have any weight with you. I am not aware that it has given me any special fitness for that field.

I remain with great esteem and Christian affection,
Yours Truly,
Geo. Bowen, Jr.
88 W. Thirteenth St.

The Board received the following testimonials regarding the applicant:

Flint, Mich., Nov. 17, 1846.

To the Secretary of the A. B. C. F. M.,
Gentlemen,

Mr. Geo. Bowen requests me to furnish you with some testimonial respecting him, as he stands a candidate for an appointment under your board.

I have known him for many years and previous to the summer of 1831, when he left for Europe and I came west, was in habit of daily intercourse with him. From that time I had only occasional interviews until the Spring of '44, when I was providentially for a few weeks an inmate of the same house, and at the time his mind was led thro' those exercises and inquiries that emancipated him from a most profound ignorance of the Gospel, and contempt for its professions, and conducted him to a deep conviction and cordial embrace of the truth as it is in Jesus. At this crisis indeed of his history I was an intimate and constant witness of the nature and progress of his experience, but since then have been separated from him and had opportunity to enjoy only occasional intercourse, and some correspondence which exhibited the character of his mind and heart.

Respecting his religious character I may remark that in my limited experience I have not met with an individual, in whom the change of a conversion was so conspicuous in clearly indicating the transforming energy of the Divine Spirit; and his piety since has seemed to be marked with more than a common measure of simplicity and adherence to the testimony of God. He seems to me to have been led by the Spirit to an experimental discovery of the nature of a life by faith in the Son of God in measure beyond the most of Christians with whom it is my happiness to have intercourse. And all that I am able to learn of his habits and employments corresponds with this judgment.

Previous to his conversion, his education, which I believe was left much to haphazard and his own humor, had led him into an acquaintance with French, German and Italian literature rather than to those studies which we are agreed to be necessary for the best development and discipline of the mental powers. Immediately upon his conversion, I believe, he changed entirely his habits and subjected his mind to those exercises and studies which might better fit him for usefulness. Of his success I cannot speak so well as his instructor in the Seminary and his classmate, who have been the witnesses of his daily performances. His natural capacities I esteem good. I have always noticed him to possess a good judgment and a ready and just observation of both men and things Under a quiet and reserved exterior he has more than ordinary fervor of spirit and sameness of purpose. He has manifested great facility in acquiring languages which I have attributed mainly to the tenacity with which he pursues the study in hand to its consummation. He is much practiced and very successful in communicating his thoughts by writing; but formerly was not so happy in oral communication. His deficiency here, however, was not marked, nor was it owing to any constitutional impediment of mind or body, but solely I think to habits of reserve and diffidence which he suffered to grow upon him. In this particular the experience of the past two years must have wrought, I presume, a change in him

A series of events acting upon a sensitive frame, had induced in him, years before his conversion, habits of seclusion from society, and great reserve even from his own family, so that he seems to have been in a measure providentially prepared for the peculiar trials of the Missionary in being cut off from the support of social sympathy. Part of his time while abroad in his travels in the coasts of the Mediterranean, he had some experience of the impressions suffered by dwelling *alone* among strangers speaking a strange tongue.

His physical constitution, tho' bearing no appearance of robustness, I should think fitted to endure privations. I do not recollect, in my acquaintance with him, ever to have heard him complain of indisposition, or to have known him sick.

I have diffidence in giving my testimonial in this method both as being myself a stranger to your Board, and because of the responsibility of the trust to the filling of which it is designed to guide you. But being called upon, I must speak. I have thought from the time of his conversion, from his peculiar temperament, the divorce which was wrought in his mind from the old circles at home, this familiarity with foreign habits, and his mental conditions, etc., that the Lord was preparing him as a chosen vessel to carry the Gospel abroad. His own thoughts early connected his adhesion to Christ with a missionary life; but being myself suspicious that there might be something attractive to him in the adventures of such a life, and that there might be thence an unconscious influence in the determination of the first great issue before his mind, I cautioned him against complicating the two, as it might prove to be the Lord's will for him to stay and preach the Gospel to his own countrymen, or to not preach at all. I am free to say that I believe him fitted for usefulness in any part of the missionary field. I believe he will serve the Master judiciously, industriously, meekly, wherever he may be sent. And I pray God that you may be guided from above in your decision concerning this brother, and that if he shall go out under your auspices, his labor may be blest to the great extension of the Redeemer's Kingdom.

With the greatest respect for you gentlemen, individually, and with lively sympathy in the cause of your Board, I am,

Your fellow servant under the most Gracious of Masters,
John G. Atterbury.

New York, Dec. 10, 1846.

My Dear Sirs,

I am happy to give my testimony to the excellent Christian character of Mr. George Bowen of the Union Theological Seminary in this city, who informs me that he is about to offer himself to the A. B. C. F. M. as a Missionary. I have been acquainted with him for nearly two years. He appears to be a devotedly pious young man, and anxious to labor for the spiritual benefit of his fellowmen. He was appointed in colporteur labors in Pike Co., Pa.. with Mr. Ford, of whom I wrote you a few weeks ago. So far as we have been able to learn, his labors were very acceptable and useful. His work was arduous and fatiguing. He traveled over most of the county on foot carrying his books in a knapsack, visiting families wherever he could find them. My impression is that he will make a devoted and useful missionary, and that he is worthy the confidence of the committee.

Were my opinion asked I should say that I think him better adapted to labor with other missionaries of experience than to take the lead at a new Station.

With my sincere sympathies in the recent affliction of the Board, in which all our benevolent Institutions participate and their officers especially, I am,

Yours Truly,
O. Eastman.

Theological Seminary, N. Y. Oct.

I am requested to furnish a testimonial in behalf of Mr. George Bowen, a member of the Senior Class in this Seminary in good standing.

Mr. Bowen is a remarkable man; he is now about 30 years of age. Until within three or four years, he was a confirmed infidel. He was a man of fine intellectual tastes, traveled extremely in Europe, especially in Italy; made himself familiar in the modern languages; and published a book on the state of the Church in Italy, which is highly spoken of. His conversion took place under God in consequence of the accidental and unwilling perusal of Paley's *Evidences*. He afterwards connected himself with the Seminary where he has maintained a high rank as a scholar and a Christian. Having felt the gloom of infidelity, he now rejoices the more in the light of the Gospel. He has a higher influence in the Seminary than any other student, and all for good. I regard him as one of the most promising young men who have ever directed themselves to the Seminary work.

The particulars of his conversion and Christian character will, I presume, be made known to you by the Rev. Dr. Skinner, his pastor.

E. Robinson,
Prof. in the Th. Seminary, N. Y.

P. S. During the vacations of the last two years, Mr. Bowen and Mr. Ford have gone out together as colporteurs in one of the western counties of Pa. (Pike County, however, is the north-eastern County of the state. Dr. Robinson knew far more of the geography of Palestine than of Pennsylvania).

Mr. George Bowen, Jr. is a member of the Mercer Street Presbyterian Church in New York, in good and regular standing. He has been connected with that Church about two years and a half, during which time he has been in all respects a most exemplary church member; and, as his pastor and brethren believe, growing in grace and in the knowledge of our Lord and Savior, Jesus Christ. His removal from us will be a great loss to us; but, I am sure I express the conviction of the Church, when I declare my own, that we have no member so well fitted as he is, by the knowledge of the truth, by deep experience of it in the heart, and by sanctification of the Spirit, for the missionary work; and under this conviction we rejoice that his heart induces him, to seek a connection with the A. B. C. F. M. that he may be sent as a messenger of the grace of God to the heathen; of his intellectual and literary qualifications for this work, the Professors of the Theological Seminary of which he is a member will bear witness.

Thomas H. Skinner,
Pastor of the Mercer St. Ch.

Missionary Appointment

New York, Dec. 15, '46.

My dear Brothers,

What I have said concerning Mr. Bowen, in the certificate of his membership and standing in the Church is very far below what I might have said without going beyond the truth. I will say to you that he is one of the holiest and most spiritual, and lovely Christians I have known during my whole ministry. I say this, in view of evidences which have been steadily multiplying since I first became acquainted with him. On my own account, I cannot but grieve that Mr. B. desires to be sent to the heathen. He has so helped me, by his prayers, and his holy life; by his bright and consistent example in all respects; that I hardly know how I can dispense with him; but God can supply his place; and in their confidence, I surrender him to you.

He is a convert from infidelity; but even when he was an unbeliever his morals were pure and his life blameless and lovely to the eye of man. His conversion was very remarkable; and his growth in religion, has been, so far as I know, unparalleled. His piety is of the deepest tone, having the same type, in general, as Brainerd's and Edwards'.

I do not say these things of him, hastily, but under the most sober sense of my responsibility. If the Board receive him, I am confident that they will have received one whom the Lord hath sent to them

Mr. B. has been abroad and is acquainted with several modern languages.

Yours very affectionately,
T. H. Skinner.

Bowen's offer was accepted by the American Board and he was appointed by the Prudential Committee on December 29, 1846, and assigned to the Maratha Mission in India.

Bowen's journal for the six months preceding his sailing for India contains frequent reference to his missionary purpose:

Dec. 31, 1846. On the 24th I left for Boston with Bros. W. & C. Bros. H., R. and C. were also with us and the Lord Jesus gave us a heavenly, never-to-be-forgotten night. Christian communion never seemed so precious. Bro. J. of Andover, took us down there, and there (at the Seminary) we passed three or four days full of blessedness. One long prayer meeting. They seemed to receive our suggestions and exhortations with open mouth. We were permitted to see quite a movement in favor of higher attainments, and consecration to the missionary work. I highly prize the attachments formed there, in the Spirit, never to be broken I trust. Yesterday received my nomination as a missionary. One thing calls for special thankfulness, that I have such evidence of my designation's being according to the will of God.

I feel that this is a solemn time. I have made this a day of thanksgiving for the immense goodness of God to me during the past year, 365 days of surpassing goodness, 365 days of such happiness as all the accumulated happiness of the impenitent world would not equal. Unbelief is the great sin. According to my faith it has been unto me; and according to my unbelief it has been unto me. If I had 'let God be true' my existence in the earth would have been a source of great blessing, far and near.

I wish to begin the new year with a firm, unflinching hold of this assertion, "All things are possible to him that believeth." Let me believe as though there were none besides me to believe in this world.

Feb. 3, 1847. In going to the heathen, I must go to live the life of Jesus. That is, to make myself one of the people, and one with them: and win the reputation of being the friend of publicans and sinners. It is said of Jesus, "the common people heard Him gladly"; and again, "this man receiveth sinners and eateth with them." There was such a manifestation of love in His walk and conversation, and such a concealment of whatever might intimidate and repel, that all, even the lowest and vilest, were inspired with confidence towards Him. Even the leper, afraid of every other man, was not afraid of Christ. Now, the missionary must inspire the heathen about Him with the same confidence. He must throw himself right in among them. Find his friends among them. Not have a little detached world of his own, for himself, family, friends, from which to emerge for the purpose of visiting and talking to the heathen. The people must be convinced that he has set his love upon them; that he desires their affections; has no desire to be better off than they. "The common people heard Him gladly." At many stations, it is most difficult to get men to hear. The preaching of the Gospel has nothing in it to interest them. The truth that Christ preached was just as repugnant to His hearers, as it is to ours. But He was full of grace as well as of truth.

There are some peculiar difficulties arising out of caste. The missionary may not live, I believe, among the natives, in their houses and at their tables, because of the rules of caste. The degradation, the low moral and mental condition of the people, is a difficulty to some, I fear. Another is that missionaries have already marked out, trodden and beaten a path; and that there will be risk in innovation. Again, nothing makes consecration so difficult as intercourse with the rich and refined. The attractions of cultivated society I shall need to regard as enemies to me and my vocation. For what Christ aimed at was to be thought the friend of publicans and sinners. This was His greatest attainment; pursued by Him as earnestly as the ambitious man pursues his aims. He

Missionary Appointment

gloried in it, putting it in the list of His greatest works, making it one of the strong evidences of His Messiahship, that the Gospel was preached to the poor.

I want to feel that this is a radical matter. Without it there is no preparation at all. Nothing can take the place of it.

Feb. 20. A man may go to heathen shores, get a perfect knowledge of the language, preach the Gospel in that language, preach it long, preach it ably, and yet be ten thousand miles away from the heathen. Without the Spirit of God one is just as near the heathen in New York as in Bombay. It is not physical nearness that will ensure the influence they need. The great fact with regard to India is that God is there, even this Jesus in Whom all the promises are yea and amen. The missionary goes to India to see God rather than the heathen, to preach to Him rather than them. His business is with God. We might as well carry so much earth as carry the mere Gospel with us. (Tarry, said Christ, until endued with power from on high). The truth hurts, it kills, when separate from the Spirit. Unmixed with faith, it is a dangerous thing to handle. Hence the necessity of always seeking immediate results. The apostles seemed to expect final success or final non-success, as they went from place to place. Long time abode they wherever they were prospered. We are disposed to be satisfied with mere inklings of success at the outset; such as, a willingness to hear, to receive books, to enter schools. We ought never to seek such large success as when the Gospel is first preached.

June 23. How little I appreciate the many tokens of Christian love that come flowing in upon me from all quarters. God values nothing so much. In order to obtain this love He became a servant, suffered and died; and yet how little am I affected by it. Let me appreciate it as God does; every word, look or act of love, let it be to me more than thousands of gold and silver. Let me meditate upon it, and seek to feel the full power of it. . . . No language can speak the goodness of Jesus. I would gird up the loins of my mind and press forward into the fullness of His love, until I shall be thoroughly rooted in love. Last Saturday received word of a vessel to sail in a few weeks for India. May God fill these weeks with fruitfulness.

24. Have had some most precious thoughts today. I have been sometimes exceedingly pained by the reflection that God should have committed Himself to me, revealed His love so marvelously, and yet to so little profit. I have almost been ashamed for God; that He should have come so near to one whose life is so little influenced by His love. But it has seemed to me today that nothing of all the love shown to me will ever be lost, but that it shall serve to enkindle the piety of Heaven. It is an admirable way of showing love to the inhabitants of Heaven and to all the holy universe, to take a wretch of such unmitigated vileness, and make him the object of unsurpassable kindness. For, in fact, the proofs of love given him concern them as much as him; they make known not only his God but theirs. If our God, they say, loves this abominable sinner, so as even to wash him from his sins in His own blood, what must be His love to those who have never transgressed? God thus makes known to them more of His heart than He could have otherwise possibly have done. It is probable that a new flame of love has been kindled in the hearts of many angels by the marks of love God has given me.

He records the closing meetings at the Seminary and the circumstances of his ordination:

> *June 27.* This evening should be remembered. The members of the Seminary partook of the Lord's Supper, preparatory to our dispersion through the earth—to China, Ceylon, Madura, Bombay, Syria, Sandwich Islands, &c. I thought of the first times, when the disciples walked with Jesus three years, receiving His instructions, occasionally going out for a month or two to labor by themselves; and then parted with Him, after having seen His body broken and blood shed for them. I had a delightful sense of the Savior, the King of kings and Lord of lords, upon His throne, dismissing us on an embassy of love to a dying world. He was looking at those to whom we go; the love He gave us was love for them; all the instructions received by us during these years, all His longsuffering shown towards us, sprang from His love to them. I want to be lost in the Savior's love to the sinners we are sent to. All the Father's love to the Son became simply a means of expressing His love to us; and so His love to us should be used to signify His love to the world we now enter. I was much occupied by Paul's language: "Who now rejoice in my sufferings for you, and fill up that which is behind of the afflictions of Christ in my flesh for His body's sake, which is the church." God grant that I may do this; and that Christ may be magnified in my body.
>
> *July 2nd.* Have had some trials. Ministers here think I do wrong in going to the heathen. I ought to stay here, and let others go. Such sentiments as these from men of experience and reputation are hard to bear. They do but show me still more clearly what is the path of duty. If everybody else forsakes the heathen, let me only give myself more thoroughly to them. This evening had a trying conversation with my half-brother. He was altogether opposed to my going. The missionary enterprise was the perfection of folly in his eyes. This I was prepared for. But he considered it wrong in me to go, as well as foolish. My father might die, (this contingency came actually to pass before many

months), and his family be left without means of support; and I would be relieved of the burden of supporting them by my residence abroad, which burden would fall elsewhere. (This prophecy was not fulfilled). This was exceedingly painful to bear. Nothing is harder than to be numbered among the transgressors. I have been unfaithful to this dear, misguided relative; let me pray for him in faith.

July 4th. Ordained this evening, (Sabbath) to the ministry of the Gospel.

Bowen's later "Reminiscences" remark regarding his diary of these days:

This is the only notice that occurs of the ordination of this individual. It was on the fourth of July, the day observed throughout the United States in celebration of the Declaration of Independence; but as it fell this year on Sunday, the celebration took place on Monday. The ordination took place in the Mercer St. Church, a little more than three years after the baptism of the same party in the same church. A considerable number of the leading Presbyterian and Congregational ministers took part in the ordination. The sermon was preached by the Rev. Dr. Skinner, on the text (Eccl. 7:10) "Say not thou, What is the cause that the former days are better than these? for thou doest not enquire wisely concerning this." In this discourse the preacher sought to show that it was a great privilege to be living at this day when the whole world is being made so rapidly accessible to the Gospel, when the nations that are most concerned for the Gospel are at the summit of political power and commercial interest, when the knowledge that was once reserved for the specially-favored, now percolates all through the community. The charge to the candidate was given by Rev. Dr. Anderson of the Am. Board. The right hand of fellowship by the Rev. Dr. Thompson, of the Broadway Tabernacle. The Rev. Dr. Wm. Patton, the Rev. Dr. Cheevers, perhaps others, took part. The sensations experienced when these good men laid their hands upon the head of the candidate, set him apart for the work of preaching Christ to the dwellers in India, and invoked the blessing of God upon him and his work, are still vividly remembered. The church was crowded, and there were many there who had known the candidate in the days of his worldliness and infidelity, and who glorified God for the grace bestowed upon him.

In the *Bombay Guardian* of Sept. 17, 1881, Bowen summarized his missionary experience at Union Seminary:

H. had spent three years in the Union Theological Seminary, University Place, New York. (Residing at his father's house, he daily attended the recitations and meetings in the Seminary). He never can cease to praise God for the blessed days spent here, especially after the 4th of December, 1845, when the Master introduced him into the life of faith. Enraptured with the discoveries then made of the all-sufficiency and perfect availableness of the grace of Christ, he felt impelled to speak to one and another of his fellow-students of these discoveries, and tried to persuade them all that it was their privilege to have the habitual fullness of the Spirit's presence. Very many sought and found the blessing, and it was not long before there was a glorious revival of a character almost unknown until then. There was a good deal of opposition, a good deal of suspicion; people talked of Oberlinism and Perfectionism; but God gave grace to those who had entered into this life of special faith so to conduct themselves as to live down the opposition. The Theology taught in the Seminary was known as that of the New School, being a modified form of Calvinism.

One of the results of the revival spoken of, was a readiness on the part of the students to offer themselves for the foreign mission work. In the nine classes that had graduated previous to 1847 there were but five altogether who went to the foreign field; out of the class that graduated in 1847, there were eight foreign missionaries, and others would have gone had their health permitted; out of the class that graduated in 1848, six became foreign missionaries; in 1849, three; in 1850, four. A memoir of a missionary who died in Persia in 1865 has been published, in which mention is made of his having entered Union Theological Seminary in 1847, and the writer of the book, referring to it, says: "He there joined a band of young men consecrated to the noblest work that can summon the energies of the human heart. At that date these consecrated walls were like cedar and spice and sandalwood, redolent with the blessed graces of living saints just gone in Christ's Name to Christ's work." Of the eight that left in 1847, two went to Western India, three to the Sandwich Islands, one to Syria, one to Persia and one to China.

9. Voyage to India, 1847

Bowen left New York by boat for Boston, July 27, 1847. Long afterwards he wrote: "Never can he forget the hour when for the last time he knelt amid the loved ones at home commending them to God in prayer, or the form of his father on the wharf as the vessel receded. When this was no longer visible he returned to the saloon and, finding a Bible there, read the 49th chapter of Isaiah, a chapter that seemed especially for him." "The last time" was not a figure of speech. Bowen never returned to America. Like William Carey he spent his whole life in India, without vacations or furloughs, and he never saw again any member of his family after that farewell of July 27.

He wrote to all the members of the family, except Frank, who was abroad on the "Silas Richards," during the four days in Boston before he sailed on July 31 on the "Goodwin" for Bombay. It was an ice ship carrying ice to India both as cargo and as ballast. To his mother he wrote: "There cannot by any possibility be too much earnestness in religion. . . . Dear mother, I bless God over and over again for what He has done for you. But, oh, much remains to be done. I want to have you exert a positively Christian influence, an influence that will have the effect of drawing souls to Christ. A person may exert a moral influence without honoring religion. It must be evident to all that we love Christ and despise everything that does not tend to His glory." To his father, "I believe that this trial is very great for you. It is possible that you will be more affected by it than any other. If so, I hope you may derive the greatest blessing from it. God is infinitely rich and wants nothing; and if He takes anything from us, it is for the purpose of giving something a great deal better. I hope that both you and I may learn at this time, and better and better the longer we live, the all-sufficiency of Christ, and see that intimacy with Him that shall make us independent of all other sources of happiness." In the same tenor he wrote to Harriet and Kate, with last words to all just as the ship sailed.

There were but three passengers, Bowen and Mr. and Mrs. Wood, all assigned to Western India. Wood had been Bowen's classmate in the Seminary. They undertook at once on the voyage the study of Marathi and his thought and occupations during these six months at sea are recorded in his journal. A few extracts must suffice:

Rules for reading the Bible.
1. Read with unbroken attention.
2. Get something new from every verse before you leave it.

3. Exercise faith in all you read, promises, commands, threatenings.
4. Self-examination.
5. Seek to have your affections stirred up by it.
6. Keep Jesus in view.
7. Read the Bible more than any other book—more than all others.
8. Neglect no part of Scripture.
9. See the scene.
10. Read the text abundantly.
11. Examine yourself in what you have read.
12. Converse about what you have read.
13. Turn it into prayer.
14. Obey it, at once. Obey the commands, plead the promises.

Aug. 12. Began the Marathi. (H. had found a Grammar, Dictionary and New Testament at the Mission's Rooms in Boston, and had obtained permission to take them with him, to be used on the voyage in getting some knowledge of the language).

19th. My mind is much occupied with respect to this crew. I feel as though I might as well be thrown overboard, as reach Bombay without the conversion of some of these souls. One thing astonishes me and that is the degree of love I sometimes feel for them. And some things have appeared to strengthen our faith. One of the worst of them expressed to me the other night, his desire to become a Christian. And the steward is sensible of his need of Christ. In addition to our other exercises, I expect to begin a Bible-class next Sabbath.

Aug. 27. What is it to walk worthy of the Lord? To be looking unto Jesus incessantly, exercising faith and feeling dependence all the time. Constant vigilance to know and do His will. Seeking His glory as a famishing man seeks bread. Making much of moments and opportunities. It consists in loving the Gospel, carrying on the Gospel in one's life. So to live as to impress men with the excellence of Christ, and have His approbation continually. What would the Savior do in a four or five months' voyage at sea? Would He be all the time preaching, judging, censuring? One thing He would do: He would clothe Himself in love. There would be a wonderful manifestation of love, expressed in ways they could recognize. He healed men of their bodily diseases in order that He might display His benevolent disposition in ways they could understand. For me to converse with them about these things that exclusively interest them is not in itself condemnable, I think. I want to exhibit friendliness in a way they can recognize, and thus my Gospel will come to them with more power. But I doubt not that I overshoot the mark.

Sept. 16. Butler's *Analogy*: "Practical habits are formed and strengthened by repeated acts, and passive impressions grow weaker by repetition." A truth that cannot be too much borne in mind. Hence we see the necessity of constantly growing in the knowledge of God. In God alone have we a compensation for the loss thus sustained. If what we see of God today affects us more today than it probably will tomorrow, new discoveries of His character may be made, tomorrow, and so on to all eternity. So that the loss of emotion stimulates to action thus we are kept under the law of progress. Why am I less affected by the character of Jesus and His love than once I was? To the end that I may be stimulated to seek new discoveries of love. At the same time a habit of obedience formed requires less emotional incitement than a habit in its inception. So that I gain both ways. The great habit I want to form is the habit of faith. It can only be formed by daily, hourly, minutely exercise. Habit, this blessed law of our nature, is my friend if I am in the path of Jesus.

Sept. 29. This then is the great point to be conquered. I want to find my highest joy in doing good and my next highest in efforts to do good. It never requires an effort to please myself, and I want to go about these labors in just the spirit and with more than the enjoyment of self-indulgence. If I have love to Christ then here is a foundation for such enjoyment. I have only to cultivate the faith by which the wants of my neighbor will be seen to be the pressing wants of the Lamb of God, wants expressed in agonies and blood.

Oct. 2. Have read since I came on board, Memoirs of Grant, (Nestorian missionary), Cheever's *Lectures on Pilgrim's Progress,* Hopkins' *Lectures on the Evidences,* Butler's *Analogy,* Chalmer's Bridgewater Treatise, Dibble's *Sandwich Islands,* Moffat's *Southern Africa,* Jenyns, Leslie, Littleton and Watson on the Evidences, *Philosophy of the Plan of Salvation,* Bogue's *Evidences,* Jenkyns' *Union of the Spirit and the Church, Elijah the Tishbite, Thy Kingdom come.*

Oct. 14. My true interest is to dam up the sensual sources of gratification in order that I may be driven absolutely to Christ and His kingdom for enjoyment. I want to find my whole happiness in the advancement of Christ's cause, and I need to be wonderfully jealous of everything that offers to please me in any way. We are a vast deal more sensual than we suspect.

The severest element in the sufferings of Christ was doubtless the unloveliness of the objects He came to die for. Then let me with all energy and assiduity link Christ to every human being and love him not in a way of my own choosing but in the way of His appointment. He commanded His disciples to watch and pray in Gethsemane and they went to sleep; He commanded them not to draw the sword and they drew it. Love does not choose its own way of doing good to its object; the lover fixes on those things that he knows will please the loved one, not on those which will merely please himself. This is perfectly understood among mortals. But we are prone to obey God as we call it, by following certain courses that are most convenient to ourselves.

Dec. 21. Have read since Oct. 3rd, *Memoirs* of Martyn, Brainerd, Swartz, Buchanan, Venn's *Duty of Man,* Paley's *Horae Paulinae,* a good deal of Lardner's work on Art and Science, Offen's *Legacy,* Finney's *Sermons,* half of Newton on the Prophecies, Martyr Lamb, Peabody's Sermons.

The voyage was a time of continued excessive introspection. In later years Bowen recognized this, and also his morbid self-examinations and appraisals. But he was learning lessons. He prayed for favoring winds and good progress for the ship, and on one occasion did so publicly to demonstrate his power in prayer, and learned a wholesome lesson in humility from the experience. (See *Bombay Guardian,* Dec 10, 1881, p. 645).

On Dec. 23, 1847 there is one entry of which Bowen long afterwards emphasized one sentence:

Some kinds of seed spring up incontinently; others remain long buried, but none the less yield abundant fruit. In the Christian church it is a creditable thing to accomplish great immediate results, and to go through life clothed in the halo of one's own influence. There is in the church a very marked tendency to notice and admire anyone that seems to be wielding power. It may be that God will mature fruit rapidly, according to the faithfulness of His servants. This has been my opinion and I may yet see it to be correct. But *it appears to me now that the highest style of Christian in God's sight is one who lives in the wise exercise of all his powers, sparing himself not at all, doing all to produce great and immediate results, yet esteeming that in God's favor is his life, repining not when there is no appearance of fruit, and willing to be thought unprofitable by the church.* Am I willing to forego the honor that cometh from man? God grant me such faith in Him and such love to souls that I shall strive according to His working that worketh in me mightily, doing all to save them, and yet entertaining such confidence in the greater love of God as to believe that He doeth all well even when I see no sign of vegetation above the surface. The great thing is to have a conscience void of offence, a heart full of love. And the love to man and the love to God must never impinge on one another. Full of love to the Savior manifesting itself in the greatest efforts for the good of man. Am I willing that God should answer the prayers offered for the good of those on board this vessel years hence so that my part in it shall not be known? It is God that giveth the increase; and every man shall receive his own reward according to his own labors, not according to his successes.

Dec. 30. Have been reading this diary and have found much to humble me; many precious intimations of the Scriptures received but to be lost. Let me here gather up some of these.
1. Prayer as a means of faith in the condition of sinners.
2. To have faith must first desire to have it. Look at the reasons.
3. The only genuine earnestness is that which will not let God go.
4. Maintained faith is true faith. A good start and perseverance.
5. Past faith aggravates the sin of present unbelief.
6. The Cross is the Power of God; not a visit to hell or Heaven.
7. What is sanctification? Love.
8. Exquisite happiness is praying for others, when God's love to them is realized.
9. The importance of right public prayer; more than preaching.
10. We seek not to create but to recognize divine love.
11. I want to be lost in the Savior's love to the sinners we are sent to.
12. Why has God shown me His love for men but that I may exercise the faith they fail to?
13. Remember past answers to prayer. They came slowly but they came.
14. The great thing in preaching—to get out of one's self; be wrapt up in others.
15. The Holy Ghost is God's love now, as the crucifixion was then.
16. And as this love passeth knowledge, an unlimited measure of the Spirit.
17. Practical habits strengthened by repeated acts; the habit of unbelief has had a life to grow in.
18. Prayer is promise.
19. He could better part with the universe than with the reputation of a prayer-answerer.
20. The sins of every sinner are the woes of Christ; let them be mine.
21. Find my highest enjoyment in doing, next highest in efforts to do good.
22. It requires no effort to please one's self. Love finds its pleasure in doing good, and so needs no effort to do it.
23. To forget my prayers is to lose their answers.
24. God cannot believe for me. (The highest faith is simply letting God be true). Cease expecting greater motives to faith.

25. The Holy Spirit God's parakletos (Advocate) with me; Christ mine with God.
26. The same effort (faith) needed to keep truth in the mind as to bring it there.
27. Important every morning to bring the mind under the influence of old truths as to discover new ones.
28. When it is hard to love, we may infer that it is easy to hate.
29. In vain I call Christ glorious if I relax in prayer. True prayer is the same as saying, Holy, Holy, Holy, Lord God of Hosts.
30. Strong faith is a strong persuasion of God's glory.
31. Is it not possible to be so filled with the Spirit as to do more than *all others* are doing? What crowns are offered.
32. How much can be done in a day.
33. Energetic bracing of the mind, (faith in the indwelling Spirit?).
34. Remember the lake of fire where I properly belong, and a crust of bread will awaken unknown gratitude.
35. Just so far as we are planted in the likeness of His death we shall be of His resurrection.
36. There should be a peculiar element in the sinner's love to Christ.
37. If it is wrong to expect a mighty manifestation of the Spirit, Christ's cross is wrong.
38. Experiment on the cross.
39. A dead man becomes the property of the living; so Christ.
40. Worlds of mercy emptied for my sanctification.
41. Scourge the mind if you will have it work. (On the contrary, cease from doing it, and look to Christ, on the principle of the expulsive power of a new affection).
42. Never utter a word of a man that will make it more difficult to love him.
43. How some men seek Heaven! But conformity to the will of God is my Heaven.
44. To realize Christ's abhorrence of my sin. But not without realizing His readiness to save from it.
45. In my formation, body and soul, God had reference to the communication of Himself.
46. What is absolutely necessary to my content? How much of Christ?
47. Are any vanities contributing to my content?
48. Christ knows how. Has power in me that I have not (believe only).
49. True humility appears in hungering and thirsting after righteousness. (And in recognizing the work of the Spirit within).

50. It is consistent with God's love to let us fall into sin just so far as we do not watch.
51. Strange that after 10,000 experiences the Christian should be without a constant sense of danger. (Perfect love casts our fear. God seeks to bring His children to a life characterized by love rather than fear).
52. Unwatchfulness is sin. Watch thou in all things.
53. The true testimony of conscience not obtained without cross-examination. See 1 Kings 22, for an example.
54. The Holy Ghost is with us not merely to show us truth but to bring us under the power of it.
55. Satan chiefly aims to hide men's souls from me.
56. In preaching, see the mark you want to hit and aim at it.
57. Beware lest ye fall from steadfastness.
58. Christ liveth in me while His word liveth in me.

What a shame in such a world as this, that prayer should ever be offered in vain! I look back over these pages and how many unanswered prayers meet my eye. Unanswered because unmaintained. Instead of being a rock, a wave of the sea; and I was not there to receive the answer.

Dec. 31. In public preaching I may discover my measure of faith, and thus ascertain pretty nearly whether the preaching will be of use or not. I have utterly failed as a preacher; not failed in all respects, in minor respects, but in this great respect that self has not been lost in interest for others.

Jan. 8, 1848. I was in tears most of the night at the thought of my perfect uselessness on board here or in the church of Christ at all. The rivers of living waters are not even rills. Has God sent upon me strong delusion that I should believe a lie—viz., that the Savior is mine and my wants are His, while nothing in my influence shows that Christ has any connection with me? There is not enough of the Spirit of God with me to hinder the captain from stretching himself out on the sofa and going to sleep at evening prayers. How many an indication of good has appeared and hastened to be gone faster than it came. As well send a bale of cotton to the Marathas as send me. I feel sick of sterile happiness. What sort of spiritual enjoyment is that which yields nothing to mankind? If I cannot be useful let me be miserable. It is only an insult to the miseries of my fellow-men to be feasting on angels' food and have nothing to give them.

Jan. 11. Christ has drawn me to the cross and shown me His love for sinners, that I may go to them and unfold it to them in their own language. The love of Christ for men is to constrain me in preaching to them. What is required of me then is an extraordinary sense of the greatness of that love and the power to describe it. I must have my soul fired with the fire of Christ, and be animated with the zeal of true interpretation....

I have derived my chief enjoyment in social prayer from the habit of losing myself and my wants, and praying exclusively for others. I have been sensibly blest and conscious of the approbation of God. At such times God has seemed to say, Love is sanctification, you will obtain what you ask for yourself by losing yourself and employing yourself only about others. Why not give myself entirely up to the wants of others, praying only for them, thinking only for them, studying them, reading the Bible for them, in a word, living immediately for them? I have imagined that to live for them, I must be mainly occupied with my own heart and work away at that, pray ever for that, &c. But I do believe that this is an error. As I occupy myself about others my own heart will grow in grace. This is grace, this is the blessing, to have no wants but the wants of others. This enormous contemplation tends to egotism. Long experience shows that there may be abundance of spiritual exercise without any progress towards the death of self. Self is killed by being lost sight of. In honor preferring one another. Look not every man on his own things but on those of others. The health of the eye is in living out of itself, in conversing unceasingly with everything save with the eye itself; and so it is with the soul. Look at Jesus; we find His gaze always directed to others. Look at Paul. God helping me, I will begin now in earnest. Ostracizing myself. Coming to the throne of grace, only as a proxy.

Only two letters survive of any which Bowen may have written on the "Goodwin"; doubtless there were many to his Seminary friends. The Rev. Stephen C. Strong, Wellesley, Mass., wrote to me through his sister, Mrs. J. N. Harris of New London, Conn., "I knew him very slightly, but met him, I presume, in some classmate's room once or twice and had a little conversation with him. When he went to India, in the service of the American Board, he wrote several letters to some of the Seminary students and named several to whom he would like to have them loaned, and I felt quite honored when I learned that I was one of the group." This was the letter which Mr. Strong had copied into his "commonplace book":

The face of nature—the more I study it, the more evangelical does it become. We have an unction from the Holy One—know all things. The fear of the Lord is the beginning of wisdom. Our eyes must first be opened by Him Who is the Truth—the Sun of Righteousness—and only after that can we take our first, right look at anything in nature, or in art, history or fiction, Heaven, earth or Hell. In the visible creation there is that love that was manifest in the flesh; love whose length and breadth, height and depth are immeasurable. I am continually stumbling upon the promises of the Bible when I roam among the works o God: and the ray of light that comes tearing down to me at the rate of two hundred thousand miles a second, seems to have just breath enough to exclaim for Him that sent it: "I am the good Shepherd, that giveth His life for the sheep," and then expire. I find this Calvary love breathing through every sluice and crevice in nature; but I find also the threatenings of the Gospel. Jesus Christ came not to condemn the world. His errand was love; but it was a love that dealt both in promises and threatenings. The word of God revealed in the Gospels is not retributive and decisive, but premonitory; as it were, the forecasted shadow of itself, intended like His goodness, to lead men to repentance.

And so with the wrath of God revealed in nature. It is not retributive, for it is carnal, fugitive and undistinguishing. It forbids all men to look upon this world as a place of punishment, for all men know that the worse they become the more they love a residence in this world. But it is premonitory, and tells all who have ears to hear, that there is a greater one to come, for those who fail to understand the loving kindness of the Lord. What I admire is, the particular amount of this element of evil, blended with the good of this world. The benevolence of God remains intact, and for their lives men cannot escape the conviction of it. And yet it is revealed from Heaven that He is something more than benevolent.

My habitual impression is that to create the new heavens and the new earth of prophecy, it will not be necessary to change the material world we live in, but simply the eyes with which we look upon it. Enough to bind the earthquakes, and bury back the volcanoes, and tame down the lightning; to throw out the few foreign elements introduced because of sin. Then, with our souls all alive with love to God, life would be a heaven indeed.

There is nothing truer than that man is dead in sin—his whole nature. I was not aware until this voyage how extensive was the empire of this death in me. For I have seen that the least of the ends for which the beautiful works of God were given, is that material end which men consider the great one. Take an encyclopedia and read an article on Light, and then be assured that the man knows nothing about it. He has found out some of its material properties and purposes; but though he had found out all, yet is he still a hundred of millions of miles from the intention of God in bestowing it. I believe that in all His works God addresses the soul; and this body of ours is simply the instrument for apprehending these external signs and symbols by which He addresses us. And I have felt that my senses are steeped in death.

The Bible, and every word of it, is sealed up, until God be heard in it; and everything in nature I conceive to be under the same seal. It gloriously exalts God, I think, to view Him as singly intent upon addressing our spiritual natures. The tree has some higher mission than simply to give shade, fruit, fuel for the good of the bodies of men. Every leaf and fiber of it exists primarily to make known the perfections of our God, to repeat in new strains the promises of the Gospel, and to do something towards the elevation of our moral natures. And it is only because man is without the Spirit that these effects are not produced.

I assure you that as I was one day sitting in the mizzen top, I was really frightened by the discovery of the awful dearth in which my senses had hitherto been bound. I was shocked at the thought of going out of the world, and leaving my body for the worms, before I had ever discovered, or dreamed of, the end for which that body was given me. All other ends were mediate: the great end was the enjoyment of God. My sense of feeling, taste, sight, hearing, smell, were all given as so many sources by which God should communicate to me the knowledge of Himself. And how had I been degrading them every hour and every minute of my life! Just as though all the gold in the world should be taken to make spades and hods for day-laborers; and all the diamonds in the world to give light to those that toil in coal mines. Were I filled with the Holy Ghost, I could not eat a crust of bread without some new enjoyment of God. In connection with these thoughts consider the passage: "I have formed thee for myself."

Later he adds:

In regard to what I wrote you about yesterday, the true way to enjoy God in external creation is to mix up His words and His works together. Practice this and you will find the combination precious.

Consider the Sun as preaching to you with intense zeal and burning eloquence from the words: "I am the light of the world"—or from these:—"In him was life and the life was the light of men." Or, the Moon (shining by reflected light) from these: "Ye are the light of the world." "Because I live, ye shall live also." "Beholding the glory of the Lord, changed into the same image from glory to glory." "Looking unto Jesus." "As the Father hath sent me into the world, even so send I you into the world." "Without me ye can do nothing." "Of his fulness have we all received."

The other letter that is preserved is a long serial letter to the family of sixteen pages in Bowen's exceedingly fine and close handwriting. Harriet copied it in her own beautiful penmanship in the volume of 433 pages, containing

Voyage to India 1847

Bowen's letters to the family from July 28, 1847 to April 5, 1858. Harriet's copy fills 58 crowded pages. The letter is dated Dec. 20, 1847 with sections of later dates and a postscript written on Jan. 25, after reaching Bombay. It is made up largely of his religious meditations and appeals but tells also of the experiences of the long voyage, his relations, both religious and social, with the crew, the vessels sighted, the adverse winds, and currents:

> Unless we get a breeze we shall in a day or two be carried back over the line or else carried ashore on some of these coral islands (the Maldives) that we passed west of us. Nothing can be more insidious than these currents. We get a little breeze and seem to be making a good course, and going on our way and all the time we are carried in the direction most repugnant to us. And without a wind we are utterly at their mercy. An island might be distinctly in sight, and a serene noontide sky above us, and every discernible thing wearing a friendly and benign aspect and yet this invisible current, so secret that none of our senses can discover it, might carry us right upon the reef that surrounds that island. So true is it that the dangers we find it impossible to dread are the only ones to be dreaded. We saw an English barque, the "King William," bound for New South Wales and sailed in company with her for a thousand miles. Parted company and after another thousand miles sailing, came together again and then parted for good.
>
> We had about 70 days of uninterrupted sunshine from Boston to the Cape of Good Hope. . . . I must tell you that I am a great sailor. . . . I have often been bending and reefing sails. . . . I can go up thirty feet of a rope by my hands alone. . . . We took several albatrosses with a hook and line, not dreading what Coleridge warns against in his *Ancient Mariner.* (The sailors knew nothing of this superstition). The albatross is a very handsome bird, often of spotless white, measuring from ten to twelve feet from tip to top. . . . One day as I was seated on the far-top gallant yard, meditating on the day's text, and thinking of those at home, I saw a whale approaching from a distance in grand style. He bore right down upon us and I apprehended for a moment or two that he would dash right into the boat and break through (for they have their strength), but he sheered off and lay alongside, exhibiting his vast proportions to our astonished gaze. He was 80 or 100 feet long. What is amazing is that the food of the monstrous creatures consists entirely of animalcule, too fine almost for sight. . . . We caught three sharks. This was the way. The noose of a rope was let down into the water and a piece of pork at the end of another rope to attract the shark. When within the noose, he was quickly made fast in it, and all hands pulled him on deck. One thing

took my attention as I saw them swimming under our stern. Every shark (every male one) is guided by a pilot fish, a handsome ring-streaked fish, eight or ten inches in length, which swims just before the mouth of the shark and marshals him the way that he should go. The shark has not to see for himself, think for himself or smell for himself; the pilot fish is his intellect and his senses at once. . . .

In the January 1st section of the letter he sends greetings to all the family and to his long-time friend, Roxy, the cook, and to his step-brother, Nat, and his family.

They landed in Bombay on Jan. 19, 1848, 172 days after sailing from Boston. Of the voyage and his arrival Bowen wrote long afterwards in his "Reminiscences, 146":

Early in the voyage, Homunculus overcame a feeling of trepidation, and made his way to the mizzen top-gallant and after that continued to spend some time very day aloft, with a book and his own thoughts. He gradually came to lend a hand whenever the sailors were employed on the rigging; learned to take part in bending sails and even in reefing them; and finally became so much at home in these matters that he would go up at night with the men to take in a reef, when it was blowing a gale. Somewhere in the region of Mauritius we encountered a hurricane, but came safely out of it. It was, if we remember rightly, the Captain's first voyage as Captain and he had never been to Bombay; he was very careful; we thought him timid, sometimes. It was doubtless a trial to him to be shut up with two missionaries and a missionary's wife as his only passengers for nearly six months, but he submitted to it with a tolerably good grace.

Homunculus spent most of his time in studying Marathi. Dr. Stevenson's grammar taught him the letters and how to pronounce them, after a fashion, and other things, and before the end of the voyage he had read the Gospels The ship had been provisioned in hope of a much shorter passage and for the last month or so we had an opportunity of preparing ourselves for supposed missionary hardships by eating and drinking what was sometimes not altogether palatable. . . .

Shortly after anchoring, Mr. Allen, the missionary, who had been in the country twenty years, came on board and took us ashore. Landing at the Apollo Bunder, we drove to the American Mission House. . . . The evening of the day I arrived, I had a conversation with Mr. A. in which reference was made (by him) to the mode of living of the missionaries, its stylishness and expensiveness. It was very difficult for them at home to pronounce a correct judgment or for anyone who had not resided here long enough to inform himself of the peculiar genius of the people, the nature of the climate, the customs of Europeans.

Perhaps there is no country where the distinction of classes is more regarded, and where influence is so much dependent upon the particular class or rank assigned to an individual in the common estimation. Many things that would be creditable in other countries, as plainness of living, voluntary poverty, renunciation of the goods of this world, do only here demean the person and strip him of influence in the eyes of the Natives.

If a man does not live as Europeans live, if he conforms to the customs of the Natives, that is, if he walks, waits upon himself, eats what they eat, observes no etiquette, &c., &c., he will be ranked by them with the lowest, and be treated with contempt and indifference. The influence of a different style of living I could see for myself; servants, teachers, Natives generally exhibited the excess of deference, bowing down to the ground, and uttering abundant protestations. Further, no constitution from our climate could bear exposure to the sun of this, or go through anything like its previous measure of exercise or effort. All experience showed, sooner or later, that habits of self-indulgence were, in a sense, absolutely and religiously required. The question was whether it was necessary to live in a manner that should please Christians at home, or in a mode that would tend to give influence here. There might be an error as to the particular degree to which conformity to the customs of Europeans should be carried; while human nature, even in Christians, is what it is, errors would probably be committed. I did not dissent; admitted the force of the reasons; agreed that an error might easily be made; and said that if we failed to please them at home, it mattered little provided we pleased Christ.

10. Beginning Work in India

Bowen's first letter after his arrival in Bombay appears to have been written to Dr. Rufus Anderson, the extraordinarily able and resolute secretary of the American Board. In the letter dated Jan. 30, 1848, Bowen refers to his voyage and to his first impressions:

> I sometimes during the voyage regretted not having shipped before the mast. I should then have been more among the men. It is true, that during the latter portion of the voyage, I spent some portion of every day among them. The passage money would have been economized; and when I consider how the funds of the Board are chiefly contributed, I feel that these funds are sacred to the positive necessities of missionaries and missions. . . . I should rather be in favor of unmarried missionaries coming out before the mast, when they felt so inclined; and if I should, which God forbid, be obliged to take a similar voyage, I would so take it. God forbid, I say; for I feel myself in my haven, anchored in India. I desire of God simply the privilege of living and dying in this land the life and death of a true follower of Christ. I deplore the many years of my life that have been spent away from the heathen, and feel that I must not deprive them of any more of my time. . . .
>
> Mr. Allen has given me a great deal of information with regard to India; and I incline to believe that in regard to many things relating to this land, we are under an illusion at home. But my notions of things are yet crude and immature, and I will not venture to express them, till justified by further observation. One thing I must say, that the difficulties in the way of the Gospel seem to me unsurpassably great in this place. And this also, that there is surprisingly little direct preaching of the Gospel to the Natives. Again the Europeans here have as many ministers in proportion to numbers, as any part of our population at home, yet as a whole their influence in whatever relates to the Gospel is nil. How the Natives, from what they see of Christianity, can form an idea in the remotest degree approximating to the true, I cannot conceive.
>
> Being requested to preach last night before the Scotch Free Church, I could not but preach a regular missionary sermon, setting forth their obligations to the heathens around them. Perhaps their obligations are less felt by the church of Christ in this heathen land, than by the church at home. But I must check myself, for I have no right yet to entertain opinions. . . . I never have felt more than I now do the importance of

missionaries being consecrated on your side of the Atlantic, and setting out with right evangelic views of what is required of them. India is a place not a bit better than America to acquire such graces as humility, self-denial, renunciation of the world. And I do still think that a change in the condition of things, must begin in the heart of your seminaries.

I hope that I shall enjoy, throughout our future correspondence, the free communication of your sentiments in all that relates to me and my doings, and that I shall show myself worthy of it, by a becoming teachableness.

His first family letter was to his father, dated Jan. 31, 1848. He is living alone with Mr. Allen:

I am most pleasantly domiciliated in a room on the first floor, nearly twice the size of my little room at home, with two windows, about as dark as I used to make mine at home; in a word I do not know how anything could be pleasanter. I feel grateful to the Savior for having provided me such a nice place to learn Marathi in. . . . While in some respects the English government here has seemed to facilitate the introduction of the Gospel, in other respects, it seems to one only to have reared up new barriers. I ask myself, would my vocation here be more difficult, if mine were the first white face ever seen; and I am answered by the recollection of many aids and facilities that have been provided in grammar, dictionaries, translation, dissemination of the Scriptures, &c. But after all, how little has been accomplished, how few souls saved and sanctified. But oh, it is a blessed thing to be here. I feel as though I had reached my haven. My desire is that Christ may teach me to love these heathen, and do them good till my last breath. God be with you and bless you abundantly.

His first letter to Harriet, who was his most constant and intimate correspondent, was dated Feb. 27 and was full of spiritual admonition, with bits of news about the Mission and an account of a visit to the island of Elephantina, five or six miles from Bombay, with its cave full of sculptures of mythological figures. He closes the letter:

Detested (!) by the opinion of some that we are to wait centuries before India can be evangelized. We must stop waiting and give God no rest until He gives this land to Christ. If we are to calculate simply the capabilities of Christians, why centuries and a century of centuries will be insufficient. If we are to have only the same ratio of divine aid we have hitherto had, these centuries will be needed, and even then India will not be Christ's perhaps. But what reason have we to affirm that

God has gone as far in modern times in the dispensation of His Spirit as He ever will. I cannot tolerate the thought. I believe India may be evangelized in this very generation. But there must first be a mighty increase of vitality in the church.

The fullest expression of Bowen's mind and spirit during this first year in India, except in his journal, was in a letter to his Seminary classmate, Robert Aikman:

Bombay, March 31, 1848.

Dear Brother Aikman:

I thank you for your good long letter begun Sept. 30, and finished ten months later. For the information it contains in regard to the brethren, in regard to your field, and in regard to the work of the Holy Ghost in your own heart—your letter is pleasant to me, because I find yourself in it. I seem to be again sitting with you in that upper chamber, conversing on the most important and precious of all topics, even on the very topics that we shall converse about in Heaven a thousand years hence. Was not our season of preparation for the ministry a delightful season? Is not the retrospect a pleasant one? And can we reasonably look forward to anything closely similar this side of the grave? But it was long enough; for our working time, even the remainder of life, will prove short enough doubtless.

I was thinking this morning that here thirty-two years of my life had rolled away, and I had not yet begun to live. That is, to work—for to work is to live. All my past life, has been a long and strangely circuitous avenue to my present position, a wandering maze whose issue God alone discerned. Only to think of it, thirty-two solid years cast away, and who knows whether my allotted time is not comprehended in them. Surely if any individual should resolve to do with might what his hand findeth to do, that purpose should be mine. But after all it is not time that we want so much. If the choice were now offered me to live twenty-five years with my present measure of grace, or to live six months with that measure of the Spirit's influence which I sometimes crave from God, I would certainly choose the last. Yes, I believe that three days with the baptism of the Holy Ghost, will be of more value to this unhappy world than the longest life of mediocre piety.

If you ask how it fares with me, I answer in the language of John, "Herein is love, not that we loved him, but that he loved us." No, if anyone ask what love is, I cannot assist him to understand it by anything in my life, in me, in my heart; no, I could only take him to the cross of our Savior. Dear Brother, it is an infinite condescension in our Savior, to call anything we render Him by the name of love. Take us in our most spiritual and impassioned moments, and gather about us a company of angelic spirits, and what is it that fills them with amazement? Not our love to Christ, but that astounding and baffling enigma of immeasurable love, displayed in not casting us down even in those very moments, to everlasting darkness. Dear Brother, we ought to have a love that should consume us utterly. There are beings in Heaven called "Seraphim," the busy ones. But there is nothing material about them to be preyed upon, else would it quickly be destroyed; if their love were in our heart, if we in any degree responded to the motives of the cross, these bodies of ours would quickly be devoured, we would burn down to the naked soul. Unless indeed the same beneficent Spirit that kindled that fire, should give to the body power to resist.

Dear Brother, how is it to be with us from this time onward? Is it not very manifest that the glow and fervor of religion does not for the most part increase in the Christian as years pass over him? I mean in those that seem to grow in grace all through their course. Now I am convinced that activity of love in the heart demands this expression. It is an essential part of love. It is a characteristic that is not wanting in the Bible saint. It is that which gave to Paul's life much of its power. It is that which most impresses the minds of the mass of hearers; it is that by which love becomes in an eminent degree contagious.

Now I will tell you what I have remarked in myself. The discoveries, the truths that once so affected me that my whole frame seemed to stagger under them, now affect in a far, far less degree. And the reason you will find in Butler's Analogy, or rather in some principles of our constitution noticed by him. 1st. That passive impressions grow weaker as they are repeated. And 2nd. Active habits grow stronger in the same way. The truth which has affected me today, will produce in me a less degree of emotion tomorrow. But then, the obedience rendered to that truth today will be more easily rendered tomorrow, because of the power of habit. So that in respect to duties, a man may in certain respects be making progress in them while in the respect of emotion and fervency he is rather declining. And this I think is what we often see. I see it too much in myself, and deprecate it. For I have never had anything that deserved to be called love. What fervor I have known was but a starting point from which to go forward.—How shall we grow in fervor as we grow in years?—a most important question; it seems to me that the answer lies hereabouts, according to the principle referred to, the highest emotion of our natures are excited by new discoveries. This then is what we need, namely, to be seeking while in life, new discoveries of Christ. And we are warranted to by the infinite loveliness of Jesus. No matter what we have seen of Him, infinitude of excellence remains behind.

Perhaps Stephen has been for 1800 years receiving new discoveries of Christ, and for 1800 years growing in love. And all that He has said is in our Gospel. And though Paul had been caught up to the 3rd heaven he counted all things but loss, for that—for that knowledge of Christ which is communicated in the Gospel. The angels desire to look into these things. Let us then by the grace of God set ourselves about seeking these excellent discoveries, and prosecute the heavenly business while we live. I am convinced, dear brother, that the other things will take care of themselves. Sermons will write themselves, and preach themselves, and sinners be mysteriously converted. In no way possible can we do so much for our hapless fellow-men.

I thank you and I thank the Savior that you have remembered me. Dear Savior, every blessing you give to me, let him have half. And hast Thou not said: "Inasmuch as ye have done it unto one of these, you have done it unto Me." And what cup of cold water is so precious as the prayers of the Saints? What a wonderful precedence Thou Thyself put upon them (Rev. 5:8; 8:3) Lord, Thou hast not forgotten the prayers we have unitedly offered Thee in other days. Make us holy as Thou art holy. May we know nothing but Thee. May we love Thee to the very extent of our faculty of love. May we love Thee as no sinner on the earth ever yet loved Thee. Lord, all our springs are in Thee. We have one desire; for this we give the universe, namely, that at the last we may have this testimony, that we have pleased God.

Oh, this language, Bro. Aikman! It met me at landing, and made a prisoner of me, and promises to keep me one a long time. I beat against it till the tears come. Yesterday morning, my pundit asked why some men were born blind, and what stronger argument could be needed than this class of facts that the Brahminical doctrine of the transmigration of souls is true. My desires were so strong, my arguments so many, his prejudices so deep-rooted, and my powers of expression so limited that a fit of deep depression came over me. I can't tell you how it affects me at times. When I speak in Marathi, I have feelings of the greatest self-contempt. I feel my littleness. But I ought to be grateful to God. Let me not forget the help He has already given.

My present pundit is one I have recently engaged. To give you an idea of the man and of Brahminism, I will mention that, coming recently by sea from Ratnagiri, he abstained from water, that is from all drink for four days, because the water on board had been defiled by being kept in the vessels of the Mussulman crew. And this is a man who has been a pundit for missionaries for twenty-two years, and who has been necessarily made acquainted with the spirit and doctrine of Christianity. He is a grave and dignified elderly man, wears spectacles, takes a great deal of snuff, is kind and amiable, and passionately fond of Sanscrit and the Shasters. Nothing he enjoys so much as to tell me stories out of these Shasters, giving the Sanscrit at length, and then translating it. He persists on affirming, as I find they commonly do, that we all worship one and the same God. We know Him by one name, they by another; we by one incarnation, they by many; our worship and the peculiarities of our revelation are suited to us, and theirs to them. In vain I tell him that God is something more than a name; that what constitutes God is His character; and that our God and theirs are opposite as light and darkness. Ours has declared that He will cast all idolaters into a lake of fire; and theirs has done everything to encourage idolatry. In vain, thus far. These heathen claim to believe in a Supreme Being; but Him they never worship. Everything else they worship. A little paint makes a God (I sometimes remember the strong language of the Old Testament, "They have committed fornication under every green tree and on every high hill"). You come to a tree and you see red paint daubed on it; that paint is worshipped by every passerby. From the branches bells are suspended. The worshipper first rings one of these to awake his God.

There is a plant called the Talasti plant. One of the wives of Vishnu was transformed into that plant; and worship rendered to it, is considered by Vishnu as rendered to himself. One of these is generally placed before the house. In some quarters of the town, I have seen them growing before every house, upon a sort of altar. Some ten days ago there was a festival called the Holi, lasting for some days. It is a time of universal license, when anything can be said or done. Their principle is that the heart is to be purified by letting all the bad out. And they rack their brains to utter obscenity, and it is not to be conceived what language they use to one another in the streets. All business is suspended. All the people in the streets are covered with paint and powder, with which they besmear one another.

I like my field. I would rather be here than anywhere else. I am interested in the people. It does not appear to me near so difficult as I thought it would to take an interest in this people that would make one glad to spend and be spent for them alone. I shall seek to realize more and more the love of the Savior to them. Oh, how little is done for them! Bombay has more than 300,000 inhabitants, and I think your room in the Five Points would hold all that hear the Gospel here, or nearly all. True, there are nominally eight or nine missionaries. But I cannot bring myself to consider that those who are engaged in teaching schools are really missionaries, or that by such means the heathen are to be converted. The Konkan is a strip of land on the seashore, thirty or fifty miles wide, 300 long, crowded with inhabitants, with not one missionary, not one Christian school teacher. And no country in the world more accessible to the preachers of the Gospel. Nothing can be desired in this respect. From too large a part of Christendom is the Gospel virtually excluded, or its preachers trammeled. But in this land of 140 millions of heathen, there is the most perfect freedom for the missionary. How does this fact speak to the church? See what you can do in behalf of this good cause at home, dear brother. Especially stir up the church to prayer in behalf of missionaries, not that they may have comforts or health or happiness or life, but that they may have souls.

Remember me to any of the brethren you may fall in with.

I have been thinking of late that the 15th chapter of Matthew is a neglected portion of Scripture—that it was designed to have a prominence in the Christian Church it has not, that it is a great treasury of instruction to the Christian minister. Remember me to every member of your father's family. My Christian love to them and to your wife, if now you have one. And may the blessing of the Lord be upon your flock, and may you be united to them as in Isaiah 62:5. (Read Edwards' sermon).

In May, Bowen received the home letters reporting the death of his father, and on May 7 he writes to Harriet:

My emotions have been deep, but I have not experienced a moment's unhappiness. I am led to praise God as often as I come to the throne of grace. Grace has so abounded towards our father, first in sparing him during fifty-seven years of impenitence and ungodliness, next in accomplishing what is perhaps one of the rarest of God's works of mercy, namely, the genuine, unequivocal conversion of a heart frosted by so many of this world's winters; and finally in giving him such a beautiful and happy exit from the world. . . . One prayer I have many times and with much fervor offered when at home to God, namely, that there might be the destruction of all reserve in our family, and a fusion of all our hearts in Christ. Perhaps this prayer was in a measure fulfilled during my father's sickness; and that it was a season of greatly augmented love one to another. So I should judge from your letter. For this I thank God and shall thank Him. One of the first things to come into my mind was this, that if Frank had been home, and if tidings had been received of my arrival, the trial might have been less to him. But it seemed so manifestly ordered that I could not but be reconciled. And there is not a word in your letters that exhibits anxiety as to my safety, so that I feel rebuked for doubting your faith and his. Among his sayings reported by you there is none that has any reference to myself. Of this I am rather glad. His affection for me seemed of old to be inordinate, and I rejoice to see the evidence that Christ had become all in all to him. Of Christ he could speak, you say, but of everything else was apathetic. I praise God for giving him not only grace but opportunity to exhibit in his dying hours to others the spirit that had been put in him. . . . Oh, why should

Beginning Work in India

Frank have gone away on another long voyage without having come to the knowledge of Christ. The Savior seemed so favorable. But I will not doubt.

For a time Bowen contemplated the possibility of having to return to America, in view of his father's death, to care for his mother and sisters, as Frank was continuing his roving life and showing no sense of responsibility. Bowen decided, however, to remain in India, sending home about $20 a month from his salary to aid the family. Harriet took up the work of teaching and there was a small income from rent of a factory belonging to the family. In his diary of May 6, 1848, Bowen wrote:

> I have received a letter representing the present condition of the family as forlorn, their prospects cheerless. They themselves in writing evince an entire trust in God that all will be well, and that they shall be provided for. N. B. evidently considers it my duty to return. But surely this is not the moment to doubt the Savior's faithfulness to us. My course is plain. I belong among the Marathas, and trust to spend and be spent for them. I see not from whence help will come, but I know it will come. My salary here is about $40 a month. During the three and a half months since my arrival, my ordinary personal expenses have amounted to a little less than half that sum. I have been intending to give the surplus to the missionary cause. As long as the family had the means of subsistence, I felt it my duty to give this money to the heathen. But it now seems to me no unjustifiable use of it to relieve the actual wants of the family. I trust that I shall be able to transmit them $20 a month.

The entries in Bowen's journals are conflicting as to the family's circumstances:

> *Diary May 14, 1848.* On the 6th of May at 10 o'clock I received intelligence of the death of my dear father. Nothing was more unexpected hardly. He died blessedly and in the grace that was shown to him during his painful sickness, the overflowing and incomparable love of the Savior, in this I have incurred a new weight of obligation to Christ. Words cannot tell, time cannot tell, Angels cannot tell what God has wrought in our house. I am amazed and confounded, lost in wonder, love and praise. I should be, but I am too stupid and sensual. Frank has sailed on a sixteen months' voyage. My mother and two sisters are left, I think, destitute. Jehovah Jireh. "I will never leave thee nor forsake thee." On these words of my Savior I stretch myself and rest quietly.
>
> *Diary June 24, 1866.* My father died and now these many years they (*i. e.,* the family at home) have been in receipt of £750 a year, a

sum much larger than I could have hoped to provide them with if I had followed the ministry at home.

In August another temptation came to quit his work and go home. An undated clipping from the *New York Evangelist* of 1848 states:

> Letters from India received during the week, bring the sorrowful intelligence of the dangerous illness of the Rev. George Bowen, one of the most zealous and best qualified missionaries ever sent to the heathen world. He was a man of eminent talents and piety. It will be remembered that he embarked for Bombay little more than a year since, and now has been only nine months in that city. Such, however, was his enthusiasm in the service of the people for whose sake he so willingly gave up all that is dear to a young man's heart, and such his wondrous facility in acquiring languages that he was enabled to commence preaching the Marathi language about the latter end of June. His short labor is in all probability at an end ere this time. A letter from his fellow laborer, Mr. Wood, intimates that it was the opinion of two physicians that he could not long survive. His disease is pronounced to be ulceration of the larynx; there is also an enlargement of the liver. It appeared to be his own conviction that he has "finished his course." That he murmurs not, but is entirely reconciled to the will of God need hardly be said. God does not always spare those who seem best prepared for His work. The early sickness or death of Mr. Bowen may be an admonition with reference to this very matter, both to the church with which he was connected and to whose prayers he is commended, and also to the society under whose care he commenced his work of love. God will have all the glory of this world's regeneration.

In full expectation that he was about to die, Bowen wrote in August to his mother and sisters:

> May God enable you, dearest friends, to receive this intelligence in a Christian manner. It is my earnest wish that you may not for a moment murmur, but immediately be reconciled to the will of God. The physicians say that there is no prospect of my recovery and that my end may be at hand.... The prospect of departing and living with Christ is delightful beyond expression. Took six drops morphine last night. Slept well after midnight. One of the happiest nights of my life.

In spite of the judgment of the doctors, Bowen recovered and in spite of their recommendation that he should leave Bombay, because he could not hope to be well and to work there, he remained and without vacations or furloughs lived and toiled for forty years. On Sept. 12 he writes home:

Beginning Work in India

> The fact is the physicians here are very ready to recommend a person's leaving the country. It is the most welcome of all prescriptions to the great mass of English in the Company's service and of Europeans generally here. My own persuasion is that this climate is less unfavorable to my general constitution, than to that of most others who come here. In a word I feel no disposition to leave this country even for a season at this time. When I first heard this opinion of the physicians, I thought that perhaps it might be the will of God I should change my station, and go to Fuchow or to Aleppo. But on further consideration, I am led to the conclusion that this is my field. I am confident that it is not without the guidance of God I have come to this field, nor without His aid that I have been enabled to prosecute the language as I have. Still I wish to lie in the hands of God, and seek His will alone, and disesteem all my own opinions and preconceptions; and pray that I may have years to see and follow His blessed will. However strange, irreconcilable, or even fantastic it may seem to our purblind minds, it indicates the only path of wisdom, of safety, of happiness.

His illness left him weighing 100 pounds, and thirty-four years later he says that this had been his weight ever since. He was so far recovered that he made a long missionary tour with Mr. Hume (R. W.) in the Southern Konkan in October and November, selling Christian books and preaching, of which he wrote a full report to the American Board:

> Returning through the bazaar about sundown, a crowd gathered round us, whom Br. Hume addressed concerning the way of life. One person, as is generally the case, took the lead in defending their doctrines and practices; but after a while the crowd opened and admitted another who had been sent for as better able to manage the discussion. "If you believe in one only and spiritual God," said he among other things, "why do you have temples?" "We assemble in churches not because we think them holier than other places, but for the sake of social worship, and of hearing God's word expounded."
> Br. H. had been urging on them the folly of pilgrimages to distant places to find an omnipresent God. After a while the man came out with a declaration which we considered a leveler, namely that there was no proper distinction between sin and righteousness, seeing that all things and all acts were of God. Br. H. called upon all present to look on this man: "He considers thieving no sin, take care then of your property; he considers adultery no sin, be careful therefore that he does not cross your threshold; falsehood is no sin, put no confidence then in what he says. When he speaks shut your ears, having nothing to do with his doctrines, for he is a man that says there is no sin in teaching false doctrines." The

man was utterly confounded. The people seemed gratified, and we came away. . . .

Wherever the Mohammedans came, Hindu temples disappeared, idols were demolished, and Hindu idolaters became Mussulmans. Wherever the English have come, the idols and temples have been left uninjured, annual allowances in some instances made for the support of them, and Hindus have not become Christians. But a bright day is to dawn, and we ought to be grateful that the restrictions formerly placed on missionary effort have been taken away. In one of these ruined mosques we found a compartment bearing evident signs that the Catholics had at some time appropriated it to their use.

I once saw in Lombardy the ruins of an ancient temple built upon the ruins of some still more antique structure. So here we saw one ruinous religion resting on the ruins of another. . . . So here we see the three religions in juxtapositon. What a vitality in Hinduism. Two religions have swept over it, and Hinduism starts up and simply takes from their ruins stones to make new gods of. When shall He come Whose right it is? . . .

We had been visiting populous villages and towns, without seeing anywhere a single Englishman to represent the government. The people live under an invisible government. Doubtless many in India live and die without seeing one of the conquering race. And the government does wisely and well, no doubt, in employing natives in so many of its official departments. Before coming to this country I supposed it was governed in a great measure by force; but not so; it is another power of some kind or other that controls the people. Nothing can be more pacific and tranquil than the general appearance of this part of the country, as it strikes the traveler's eyes. How many have contended for these regions. For centuries how unceasingly have they been the prey of war. But there is now a pause. This seems to be the auspicious moment for the church to awake, and pour in her forces. . . .

One of a company of Mussulmans called to us, made us sit down, and asked Mr. H. to talk to them. "What shall I talk to you about?" "About God: tell us your views." How singular would be such an invitation at home. But here religion is a legitimate subject of conversation everywhere and at all times. . . . We had cause for great gratitude because of the mercies vouchsafed to us during our tour of three weeks, and the truth we had been permitted and assisted to communicate; and also reason for great humiliation because of our want of zeal and faith. Let the church of Christ pray for the sanctification of missionaries—not so much for their comfort and health and physical well being, and happiness, not much for these—but for their sanctification. Let her make this a matter of leading importance, and consider all her own interests to be some way or other involved in the blessing. When I bring to mind how vast the results that might be expected from a baptism of the Spirit upon all missionaries, how unspeakably desirable, of how world-wide importance, I am convinced that so incomparable a blessing will not be granted to a moderate degree of faith and prayerfulness.

In the late fall Bowen was present at a hook-swinging festival which he described in a letter to the *Dayspring,* a publication of the Board:

Bombay, Dec. 15, 1848.

I lately witnessed the hook-swinging near a temple of Khandoba in a part of Bombay called Kammatty Poor. I remained about an hour and a half, during which time I was surrounded by natives asking my opinion of what was going on, and discussing serious religious topics. There was in an open space a red cart, with a long shaft so arranged that many might take hold and draw. In the center of the cart was an upright post, and upon this was poised a yard or mast some forty feet long, and elevated at one end about that distance from the ground, the other end being depressed. At the upper end a red canopy was extended, under which the performers were to swing. Seated on the cart were drummers who kept up an almost incessant racket. The assembled multitude formed a circle some two or three hundred feet in diameter, in the center of which was a block of houses. A space was left between the houses and the crowd, for the performing parties to circumambulate in.

About five o'clock, appeared an individual, of the Mahar caste, who represented the god Khandoba. "This is our god," they said to me. The face of this man was all smeared with red paint; he had black hair half a yard long, all disheveled and lying about his face, the upper part of his body naked and covered with yellow powder. His garments were cut in slashes of different colors. His legs were covered with bells that tinkled and jingled as he danced wildly along. In each hand was a long brimstone colored whip of twisted cords which he kept snapping about his head. I have seen horrid objects, but it struck me at once that I had never seen a more repulsive and abominable one than this. He made the circuit of the ground five times, preceded by drummers and others clearing the way. The third time he came round, he held in his hand a live black kid, offered with religious worship to this man as to Khandoba, that a blessing might attend the performance about to take place. He tore open the throat of this kid and putting it to his mouth, drank the blood. Having reached the place where I was, he stood still, and while others helped him to hold the animal on high, in which some life was still remaining, he drained the blood out of it greedily, and as it were with fiendish joy. I cannot conceive of an object more resembling a devil of hell, than the man at this moment appeared. And all the people shouted and admired and worshipped. A person said to me, if there were not a divine power in him, how could he drink this blood?

After a while appeared the man who was to swing. I saw the hooks in his naked back, held by another who walked behind him. About his neck were garlands of flowers; a child was upon his shoulders. He or perhaps someone else whose substitute he was, had made a vow to perform this rite, if Khandoba would restore the child from sickness. He also walked several times about the area mentioned. After this, the elevated extremity of the yard was lowered, the hooks were made fast to it, and he grasped a rope that also hung from it. He was then lifted up, and a crowd of people seizing the shaft of the car, began to draw it with shoutings in the aforesaid circle. As the man was in this way drawn around, he showered down turmeric powder on the people, which they received on their persons as though it was the embodied grace of God. Having made the circuit a number of times, the man came down and I saw no more of him. But a woman now came forward to undergo the same operation. She too had an infant, obtained as was supposed in consequence of a vow, which she was now to fulfill. She was young and strong and rather good looking. After going round the course on foot, with the hooks in her back, she also was elevated and carried around several times amid the shouts and acclamations of the people. An Englishman, it is said, once caused a person who was swinging in this way to go round twenty-five times, and afterwards made him a present of a large sum of money as an expression of approbation. I was told concerning the woman there swinging, that many would fall down at her feet and worship her, giving her offerings, believing the act now performed by her to be of such great righteousness as to entitle her to the homage of sinful mortals.

I freely expressed to all around the sentiments inspired by what I saw. Some allowed that this was not the way to please God; others remained silent; others loudly eulogized the act. They asked me my opinion of God, what sort of a being He is, what is His name, and how men are to become acquainted with Him. I told them He was a holy God and without a new heart no one could be saved. He was a Spirit and abominated the worship of idols. They asked about Khandoba. I said he was a fictitious god, and moreover a new god, never heard of till within two or three centuries. He was a god not found in their own Shasters even. One asked about Maruti, whether he was to be worshipped or not, another about Ganpati, and another about another, and they seemed astonished, that I would allow no one of them to be true. I told them about Christ.

Beginning Work in India

"But if He gave His life for people, He is dead," said they, "and can help no one."

"He rose from the dead and ascended into Heaven."

"Oh, like our Tukaram."

"Your Tukaram never ascended into Heaven. The people of Pandhapur said he went to Heaven from thence, and those of other places said he ascended thence; and thus their testimonials balance one another."

"What proof have we that Jesus went to Heaven?"

"Sincerely pray to God, to the one true God, in His Name, and you will receive the Holy Ghost and a new heart."

"Jesus Christ, I do not like that name."

"Jesus means Savior; if you do not like that name, you do not like salvation." In this sort of way we conversed as well as the drums and shouting would allow. I was the only European there, though there were thousands of natives.

The ceremony of marrying their god took place on the preceding evening when some more were added to the number of females espoused to the idol in this temple. There are about fifteen or twenty, I understand, though there are temples in the interior where they are counted by hundreds. Becoming consecrated to this god, they are rendered incapable of contracting any other marriage; and their life becomes henceforth one of outrageous prostitution. Such is heathenism, defying its sins and foaming out its shame.

These things have often been mentioned before; but there is a circumstance that seems to render their occasional repetition necessary. In the civilized world this is an age of progress. The church sees on every side of her unprecedented tokens of movement, life and light. And there is a tendency at home to believe that the heathen are participating in this movement; that there is a virtue in the times we live in, sufficient of itself, without other instrumentality, for the healing of the nations. This is an illusion. They that will benefit the heathen must work as though they were thrown into the very heart of the dark age.

I have lately adopted the habit of going out at six in the morning, and spending two or three hours in the bazaars and other thoroughfares distributing books and talking to the people. I have always a crowd about me, sometimes as many as forty or fifty, who pay readily the small sum demanded for the books, and hear what I have to say. Their conduct is generally respectful. On one or two occasions, some zealous opposers have put themselves forward, reviled the Christian religion, blasphemed the name and character of the Lord Jesus, and purchasing books torn them up and showered the fragments upon me.

One of the persons declared himself holy; I called the attention of the crowd to this sentiment, and asked them what they thought of it.

Afterwards this person used some English words of such obscenity that I could not but put my hand on his mouth and stop him. These things irritated him, and caused him to destroy the books. I find my power of influencing them dependent very much on the control of my temper, and the degree of kindness evinced in my deportment.

I think they are not wholly insensible to an affectionate Christian treatment. They ask the most absurd questions. One man insisted upon knowing who God's father was. . . . He could not understand how God could exist without a father. The heterogeneousness of this population surpasses anything I have ever seen. A person going into the streets with books, needs to have them in the following languages in order to answer all demands: viz., Marathi, Gujariti, Hindustani, Hindi, Persian, Arabic, English, Chinese, Portuguese, Telugu. He will also meet with Abyssinians and Malays.

I send the above notices thinking they may occupy a corner in the *Dayspring*. Since writing, in the accompanying letter of the Mission, my views concerning a new station, I have become more and more convinced of the importance of laying out a great deal of strength in Bombay. It becomes to myself every day a field of increasing interest.

Bowen's report of his tour with Mr. Hume and his account of the hook-swinging festival appear in full in his journal. Probably it was just a transcript of his journal which he sent home. The journal is extraordinarily full both of meditations and experiences and it must have taken hours daily, probably late at night, for Bowen to have produced and maintained such a remarkable record. The main features of the journal for his first year in India are its religious reflections, its penetrating examination of Hinduism, its severe self-questioning as to the mode of missionary living and its dissatisfaction with the idea of the cessation of miracles in the propagation of Christianity. As will appear, Bowen's self-denial was severely and contentedly frugal. Physical hardships were not hardships at all to him and as in the case of Henry Martyn and Lydia Grenfell, his disappointed love left him happy in celibacy. On April 29, 1848, he wrote to his mother:

I enjoy all the opportunities of privacy that I could wish, and you know my appetite is rather large for this. At the same time I expect to become every day less and less of a recluse; the measure of my progress in the language is the measure of my emergence; and probably by the time I have mastered it, I shall be fairly launched out into the sea of human life, finding my communion with the Savior as I make Him known to others. The climate is very agreeable. Bombay is more favored than perhaps any other part of India. They come to it from many parts to recruit. The heat here is less intense than it is in the interior. People talk a great deal of hot weather, but I cannot find it. Indeed, I appear to be less affected by it than some of the natives. I don't know how it will be in the sequel. One thing elicits gratitude as often as I think of it, namely, that I am not as other men are in respect to having a wife. The inconveniences are enormous in India.

In his journal Bowen writes:

Feb. 5. If we would come to the natives simply to know them and be known of them, holding ourselves aloof from Europeans renouncing the dignity and advantages of sahibship, to see what we could do by our minds, our hearts, our bodies, our Christ, independently of all adventitious distinctions, I would like it.

We come to very different opinions concerning missionary life here, according as we view them as members of European society in India, or as belonging to the population of the country. If we say that they are properly to be classed with Europeans here, and their style of living judged of, as it compares with that of Europeans, then there will not be a shadow of fault. Only it may be observed that the churches by which they are sent forth, have sometimes a different conception of the matter. On the other hand, if they are viewed simply as ministers of the natives, as belonging to that population, then they are living in noble style. The natives are generally so poor and frugal, that a little luxury and expenditure are more imposing than they would be at home. In the presence of a missionary Sahib, they have generally the feeling that an English plebeian would have in the presence of an earl or duke, not because he is a missionary, but because he is a Sahib, keeps a carriage and has many servants. The question arises by what standard should the style of life be judged, by that of European society or by that of the natives?

Again, it may be a matter of enquiry whether, in assimilating to Europeans, we may not render more difficult the task of exhibiting our spiritual dissimilarity. From the outset the tendency in the native mind is to confound us with them, coming as we do from the same countries; much more will it be so, when they see us living as they live, I mean in many of the obvious respects wherein they differ from the native. The great task is to convince them that we are a peculiar people, born again of the Holy Spirit, while most of the Europeans are in an unconverted state. And the principal impression we want to produce is not that we are Europeans, but that we are Christians. . . . Let it not be said that a devoted heart is the main thing, and these outward matters insignificant. When Christ sent out the Twelve, and again when He sent out the Seventy, it is surprising how much He dwelt on such matters. Concerning what they should say He was very brief; but concerning their mode of life, the style in which they should appear, He was wonderfully minute. It is very evident that there is a connection between devotedness of heart and disregard of worldly adjuncts and appliances.

Feb. 15. Considering Luke 9:22-23, the question arises, Can I be happy with Christ alone? My heart answers, Take away all the comforts I now enjoy, and I can be happy. I do not value these things and would rather be without them. Let me suffer from hunger and thirst and temporal calamities generally, and I feel that I can still be happy. Let me be treated with contempt and scorn and cruelty, let my pride be warred upon utterly, I believe—I don't know; I should need more of Christ than I have now. Let my labors be in vain, let fruit be wanting, and I feel in this I could not be happy. I would be miserable. But if it be God's will I am willing that it be so.

Sometime this spring Bowen found in the library of the mission station a volume of Edward Irving's orations, including the famous sermon preached at the London Missionary Society anniversary in 1825, in which as Eugene Stock says: "He denounced the Societies for their prudential care about money matters, and called upon Christians to go forth into all the world as the apostles went round the familiar villages of their own little Galilee, without scrip or purse, shoes or staves." *(History of the C. M. S.* Vol. 1, p. 282). Bowen was deeply impressed by Irving's argument that "missionaries should be strictly guided," as Bowen says, "by the rules laid down by Christ in sending forth the Twelve and the Seventy." And he copied in his journal the two following passages from Irving's sermon:

> It was a spiritual work they had to do, therefore Christ spiritualized the men who were to do it. It was faith they had to plant, therefore He made His missionaries men of faith, that they might plant faith and faith alone; they had to deliver the nations from the idolatry of the Gold, the Silver, therefore He took care of His messengers should have none; they had to deliver them from the idolatry of Wisdom, therefore He took care they should be foolish; they had to deliver the world from the idolatry of Power and Might, therefore He took care they should be weak; they had to deliver the world from the idolatry of Fame and Reputation, therefore He took care that they should be despised; they had to deliver the world from the idolatry of Things that Are, therefore He took care they should be as things that are not, making them in all respects Types and Representatives of the Ritual they were to establish, models of the doctrine which they went forth to preach.

Beginning Work in India

Though a missionary should go forth in the first instance stocked like a trader, fitted out like a discoverer, accredited like a royal envoy, and three times armed with prudence like a hostile spy, when he cometh into close communication with the Spirit of God and the spirit of the people, in order to be the mediator between these natural enemies, he will, if his mind be open to light, be taught to utter helplessness of all these helps, the utter uselessness of all these useless things, to that work in which he had embarked; that though they may commend him to the proud and worldly part of the people, give him a place in their regards as a man of some consequence and reputation, they are so far from bringing him into contact with their spiritual feelings, which alone he careth for or ought to care for, that they set him more remote from them and induce a mistake with respect to his unearthly purpose which it will require him much time and labor to correct, and if he be a true man a change will speedily pass over his outward state.

The journal goes on:

March 26. Translating some of Baxter's *Call to the Unconverted* today with the Pundit, where he is speaking of hell and says something about infidels that do not believe in it. Saccaram expressed his astonishment that any man in his senses could doubt the existence of such a place. Infidels are not found among the heathen.

It would seem as though a hearty love for the work of preaching the Gospel to the heathen of this country, were not very prevalent among missionaries. There seems to be such a proclivity to slide into some other occupation. One missionary whom I asked about his preaching, replied that he was sorry to say that he had been for some years very little engaged in preaching, he had been chiefly engaged in building. Others engage in translations; the Bible is translated over and over again; and other books. Some engage in the composition of books and tracts. Some superintend printing establishments. Some spend their time in learning many languages. Great numbers engage in educational labors. It requires but a little interruption of one's health, to induce a visit to the mountains or a voyage at sea for health, and no very severe pressure of motives is needed to take them home. Of course there are exceptions. There are some missionaries who delight in preaching the unsearchable riches of Christ. It remains to be seen whether I will be one of them.

March 30. Was yesterday speaking with Mr. H. of the life of Paul and said, "Would it not be well to publish it in Marathi for the special purpose of showing that the Christian doctrine of salvation through another's righteousness does not lead to license? And also that while we exercise no austerities for their own sake, we gladly endure in the carrying out of God's commands?" Whereupon presently it came into my mind that there was needed such a life of Paul as could not by any means be issued from any printing-press. We wanted Paul himself, embodied, breathing, moving and repeating before our eyes the life described in the New Testament. One of us must become Paul himself. What other way is there? What effect follows from the dissemination of memories of holy men but that our deficiencies stand more prominently out before the heathen mind? We give them a standard by which to try us and condemn us. What a roundabout way we do go to preach the Gospel! The obvious and direct way is to go to the throne of grace, and there be ourselves, converted into living epistles. What was the life of Paul? It was a striking manifestation of Christ Himself. "Not I, but Christ liveth in me."

May 14. Miracles seem to be unspeakably necessary at this time among the heathen. They ask for them. They cannot be profited by our books on the Evidences, which suppose knowledge that they have not. But the Savior has said, Whatsoever ye shall ask in My name, I will do it. The promise is addressed to all believers. Now if we could show the heathen that we actually obtain what we ask, I think a deep impression would be made upon them. I pray with the servants every day. I might do it as I have done, for a year, without any deep impression being made upon their minds. I tremble at the thought of going on to offer prayer in this way—I mean unfulfilled prayer. Each prayer supposes that the preceding has not been answered, and implies that no humiliation or surprise is felt on account thereof. I proceed as though it were a matter of course that prayer should be offered in vain, and that it would be doing remarkably well if one prayer in a hundred were answered. But what is there in this to loosen their attachment to idolatry? They declare that they receive answers from their idols. It is a solemn thing for the Christian to pray in their presence. That is the moment for bringing out the evidence of the truth of his religion; the time for the exhibition of his credentials. Christ has declared that prayer, i.e., the prayer of faith, shall always be heeded and fulfilled. God, almighty and ever-blessed, save me from offering up any other than believing and triumphant prayers. Oh that my prayers may be as miracles to draw this people to Christ!

My Pundit, the other day, defending transmigration, said that our view required that God should continually be engaged in the work of creating. But God was *swasth*, quiet; He had not upon Him the burden of this world. I answered that all such reasonings sprang out of their contracted notions of the greatness of God. Nothing could be a burden to Him. Omnipotence made all things infinitely easy to Him. He could conduct the whole universe as easily as I could move my pen over paper. There was infinite calm and infinite rest in the soul of God at the same time that He was presiding over all the parts of the universe. Finite beings might be tasked, an infinite One could not be. Perhaps the sun might be used as an example. It shines without an effort, yet by its shining gives life to beings and worlds. It is an idea altogether derogatory to God, that He should be burdened by upholding the universe. He upholds it by the simple word of His power. He said, "Let there be light," and there was light. As easily as one can say, Caba, can He create all the souls of a generation. This argument appeared to produce some impression on Saccaram, a very unusual thing.

In regard to this it may be well to show that the work of upholding is essentially the work of creation. Creatures can no more sustain themselves than they can create themselves. Infinite power and infinite wisdom are found in every particular point of space, so that there is the same power to take care of the least point of space, that there is to watch over the universe itself. It is no more to uphold the universe than it is to uphold an ant.

June 29. Today I made my first essay in the distribution of tracts in the streets. Have much reason to be dissatisfied with myself. Indeed have I any reason to be otherwise than utterly disgusted with myself? I ought to have nothing more to do with myself, but live solely by the faith of the Son of God. This is my crime and all my crime, that I am not strong in the grace of the Lord Jesus Christ. I can truly say that I am happy in that grace and I find it hard to believe that any other being in the world receives such amazing communications from his God and Savior. It seems to me that the promise of John 14:23 is fulfilled in me. But I feel that an immense change is to take place in me. I see what I am to aim at.

I want to have Christ walking about the streets of Bombay as He did about those of Jerusalem, and living among this people as He did among the Jews. He was emphatically the friend of the people. They were His family, His home. He had business with every man, and hesitated not to address men. And He had in perfection the talent of talking with all classes of men in a way to interest them. My habits are all sedentary. There is nothing friendly, encouraging, easy about my manner. When in the streets I feel bound home. Home is my goal and I walk till I get to it. The street is something to be got out of, not to stay in. It seems at times infinitely preposterous that I should be engaged in a missionary life. But I have a strong desire that these inveterate habits and tendencies should be battered to pieces. I want to have Jesus the missionary in my mind's eye continually. By the grace of God I may at length learn to love. Love overcometh everything. It will be a blessed day when I feel at home in these streets, and can linger in them without any desire save to continue preaching the Word.

Is there any room for the display of God's power short of miracles? As I look around, I see that there is. There is a great deal of room for His Spirit in my own heart. No telling how much. Then when I shall be filled with all the fullness of God, and strengthened with all might according to His glorious power, there is my fellow-laborer. When his heart is as full of love to Christ as it can be, there are other laborers about us. There is the whole Christian community. There are those native converts between whose piety and that of Paul, there is a vast deal of room for the Spirit and power of God to be manifested. Then there is the preaching of the Gospel which is lifeless and inefficacious, and which may be more and more blest until it becomes the power of God unto the salvation of vast multitudes. Yes, I see that in the channels actually existing there is room for a display of the power of God greater than has ever been made. When these channels are filled up to the brim, then we may ask for miracles.

If miracles were granted would it not diminish the sense of our responsibility to become holy as God is holy, and have the mind that was in Christ? I believe God intends to shut us up to this, and make the entire church sensible that either the world must perish or the church must put on Christ. There is a great unwillingness to learn this. We are expecting displays of the mighty power of God in Providence and otherwise, that shall subdue His enemies and fulfill the prophecies. Let me not be expecting such; but remembering Christ's words, "I am glorified in them," shut myself up to this mode, and seek the outpouring of the Spirit with all desire and prayer.... Looking unto Jesus as unto our one Model and Guide—as a painter who is making a copy of some great painting, looks unto it continually, drawing no stroke without a close reference to the original. His work will be valuable only as he makes it conformable to that original. If he draws upon his own invention at all, no matter how excellent his creative powers, the work is spoiled, for the value consists in its resemblance to the other. Our business is that of a copyist; we must not dare to think of framing our lives in any degree after our own fancies or wisdom; we must simply look unto Jesus; and when we faithfully imitate Him, then we have well done, then only. We must look unto Jesus and not to any other original.

If I tell a man to make me a copy of the Apollo Belvedere, and he takes it into his head that he can make a better statue by copying the Apollo in some respects, and the statue of Antinous in others, his work will be altogether unsatisfactory and will be left on his hands. Now if the first sin is common among Christians, perhaps the second is more so. And the consequences are very mischievous. To this mainly is it owing that our standard of holy living is so low. In very many respects our manner of living differs materially from that which is exemplified in the N. T. without our being conscious of it, or at least without our being sensible of the sin of it. If we had nothing but Jesus to look to, to know how a servant of Jesus should live, we would necessarily conclude that our lives must be characterized by poverty, (what the world regards as) discomfort, self-forgetfulness, love of our fellow-men, association with the poor, long-suffering, indefatigableness, singleness of aim, intense, consuming zeal, great prayerfulness. We should take up our cross daily and follow Him. We would abhor anything in the shape of luxury, as much as we now shrink from discomfort.

The features of the life of Christ are wonderfully distinct and unequivocal. Once conceded that this is the only model, there would be no room for difference of opinion among candid men as to what was duty. Our lives are painted before us in colors more fresh and vivid than those of Raphael's Transfiguration. Why then this wonderful discrepancy in many things between His life and ours? And why this unbroken tranquility of ours, as though the fault were of no consequence? What missionary, what minister, what private Christian thinks of making his course of life resemble that of Christ?

Now if by the grace of God a man becomes conscientiously acquainted with the N. T. standard, and feels the absolute necessity of putting away every superfluity, renouncing all honors, making himself nobody and the good of others his own aim, he will be exposed to the reproof of the church. The world of course will reprove, and will call him madman and fanatic; but more than this, the church to some extent will do so; and, to a large extent, conscientiously. But he must look unto Jesus and leave the result with God. He will have difficulties to contend with in himself. He will be continually liable to suspect that after all, these particulars cannot be of so much consequence; since the church so universally disregards them; that he is troubling himself about the mint and the cumin, to the neglect of weightier matters of the law. His only safety will be in burying himself in the Gospel, till he become thoroughly imbued with its spirit, and knows what is important and what is not. It is painful to be a reprover of holy men, to come out and say, You are all wrong, in some things you are denying Christ, you are living in a way that, taken as a whole, tends to frustrate the grace of God. But as it is love for our impenitent fellow-men that constrains us to come against them like enemies and make war upon all they value, so should love constrain us to oppose, where it is needful, the practice of our fellow-Christians. It is not a small matter whether the visible life of a Christian, urges all that look upon it to count all things but loss for the excellency of the knowledge of Christ, to count one thing alone as needful, to set our affections on things above not on things on the earth, to seek not the honor which cometh from man; or whether it preaches that the religion of Christ is not incompatible with the enjoyments and comforts that men generally desire, that its blessings do not inspire distaste for them and that Christians may to a certain extent take pleasure in the honor that cometh from man. Instructions on this head are perhaps more abundant in the Gospel than on any other. It is not enough to have a real love for Christ in our hearts and to be not injuriously interested in the comforts of life; we have another most important duty, viz., to make known that love to our fellow-men, and in the way which will most impress their minds. Christ knew that among men self-denial is the most unequivocal expression of love, therefore He labored so much to exemplify it and enjoin it. And it is probably because we have forgotten this portion of the Gospel that what love there is in us exerts so little influence.

Our religion is ineffective because it lacks completeness. To have the heart right is the great thing; to perform our duties prayerfully, spiritually and trustingly, and whether our habits be ascetic or not, is of little moment. We leave that to Romish friars and the self-righteous of every religion. But if these things are insignificant, why, in the first place, is there such an immense reluctance to adopt them? And in the second, why did Christ so insist upon them? We have essentially the same world to influence that Christ had; and men are to know us in the same way that He and His apostles were known.

Hardly anything was more common with the Savior than to argue with people from the stand-point of their own opinions, though these opinions were false. For example, "by whom do your sons cast them out?" As though their sons were casting out devils. "I came not to call the righteous but the sinners" as though the Pharisees were righteous. Allowing you to be as righteous as you say, I do rightly in consorting with sinners. Simon the Pharisee, where He takes Simon's opinion of his own religious standing and builds an argument upon it. The rich young man, whose opinion of his own blamelessness regarding the commandments, he takes as a basis of argument. Peter, who said, "We have left all to follow thee." He accepts the statement, though erroneous, that He may introduce a precious promise. In the parable of the talents, "Thou knewest me to be a hard and austere man," &c. This method of meeting men is powerful, and is perhaps too much slighted. If people are self-righteous, perhaps there is no better way to enlighten them than to exhibit God's love to sinners. They imagine that they have the favor of God above others; if they find themselves excluded for their very righteousness and sinners preferred before them, they will be more willing to recognize their sins and their need of repentance.

There is an inveterate self-consciousness in me that is hostile to all effectual preaching of Christ.

Beginning Work in India

After his recovery from his illness in August, when both he and his associates had despaired of his life, he wrote:

> I call upon my soul to praise a benignant and long-suffering God especially for these thoughts and impressions, viz.:
>
> 1. That there is no necessity for dating the conquest of India to Christ centuries hence. I was disturbed by a conversation held with a missionary brother holding such a view and supporting it by strong arguments and facts. The moral degradation and intellectual feebleness of the people were such that there was nothing for the Gospel to take hold upon. And afterwards I thought of the preparation that seemed made in the world for Christ at His advent. He came in the fullness of time. But has there not been a vast work of preparation going on in India for 100 years? What amazing things hath God wrought! Viewed politically and externally it would seem as though God were saying, Now is the accepted time. But the all-comforting reflection was concerning the power of the Holy Spirit. The greater the difficulties the greater the need of the Spirit; I mean, the greater the measure of spiritual influence needed. God the Father is all-powerful for His work; God the Son for His; God the Spirit for His.
>
> 2. But the measure of the Spirit given will be according to the measure of desire and faith exerted in prayer. Hence there must be new prayer in order to have these great successes.
>
> 3. I must have nothing to do with conscience as a Master; Christ must be my only Master. It is a grievous sin against Christ to go about anything merely because conscience dictates it. I must be scrupulous to guard against this in everything. Love and joy must characterize my doings, and my attempts. (Constrained by love, not by a painful sense of obligation).
>
> 4. Christ is with me always, whether I recognize it or not. Hence the greatness of the sin of unbelief. I must cultivate very sedulously all the day long the habit of abiding in Him, drawing from His fullness, having Him to guide me at every step. It is strange how I have declined here, and how hard it is to rise again.
>
> 5. Rigid self-denial must be cultivated till it become as pleasant as nature itself.
>
> 6. Faith must be cultivated with regard to the condition of the Hindus under the wrath of God.
>
> 7. It is necessary to guard against forgetting the value of time, of its moments; and especially as it is employed in reading. There should be no reading without rumination, and reference to future use.
>
> But the great thing is prayer, prayer, prayer. In true prayer all omissions and transgressions become manifest and the true way becomes clear as day.

In November he quotes approvingly from John Wilson:

> "In instituting a discussion of religious creeds, we have not in view the expression of our own feelings, but a kindly influence over our opponents." I am prone to this error. I seek the expression of my own feelings too exclusively. I do not study enough the expression that will be most likely to convince.
>
> "We are not contending for victory, but conviction; we seek not to humble or incense our adversaries, but to conciliate their confidence and direct their judgment. We seek to work a salutary change in their principles, and in this we shall most assuredly fail if we begin by disregarding their prejudices and provoking their resentment." God drew me with cords of a man, with bands of love, so let me draw others. He took into account my nature, my disposition, my characteristics, and then found motives adapted to operate upon me. So let me do with others. Had anyone come to me and angrily denounced my prejudice, and asserted the truth, I would only have been embittered against the truth, and invested it with the unlovely features of its advocate. "Speaking the truth in love." "Let your words be always with grace." Christ spoke gracious words in the presence of a congregation ready to kill Him.

During this first year he records instances of unfriendly treatment, violence, assault with offal, shouting and clamor, but even now there began the reverent respect for Bowen as a holy man which grew with the passing years. On Dec. 15, 1848, he writes to Harriet:

> Sometimes I have to hear the most dreadful blasphemies concerning Christ, and am myself sometimes rudely treated. I have been quite astonished at the composure and forgiveness with which I have been enabled to meet this treatment. This is surely the finger of God. This morning when surrounded by a large crowd, a devotee made his way towards me, the crowd giving way, and prostrated himself at my feet, folding his hands and touching his forehead to the ground. He was not a beggar; said not a word; but having performed this act of worship, arose and took his departure. You may conceive my feelings. While he was yet prostrate on the ground, I broke forth into a vehement deprecation of such wickedness, and told the assembled multitude that there was no more certain way of drawing down the indignation of God, than to perform and receive such acts. The crowd which was before tumultuous and noisy, were hushed at once, and seemed as I spoke to get a new idea of the holiness of God. They seemed astonished that I should be affected in such a way and so greatly by the circumstances.

Beginning Work in India

Dec. 14. I am longing to see the power of Christ more fully manifested to this people through me. He has promised that believers shall do greater works than He Himself did; and it seems to me that in such a population as this, there is absolute need of these greater works, that the Father may be glorified in the Son. May the Lord guide me.

Dec. 15. I have heard it said that if we were enabled to work miracles it would not follow that the Gospel would spread any more than now. I think this is an error. I think the testimony concerning the effect of miracles, in the Word of God, shows it to be. Christ's heart was set upon working miracles; and He was displeased with the Nazarenes, because through their unbelief He could not do many mighty works there. And in the case of the demoniac, He reproached the apostles for their unbelief and unsuccess: "This sickness is for the glory of God, that the Son of God might be glorified thereby." "Jesus of Nazareth, a man approved of God among you by miracles and wonders and signs."

All true faith must be based upon the Word of God. The faith that wrought miracles must have been excited by some promises of the Word of God. How came the miracle-working power to leave the church? It was not by taking away any portion of the Word of God, and so leaving faith without a basis. The Bible of the primitive times is our Bible. Faith in God's Word declined in the church, therefore the miracle working power disappeared. But there is just as much for us to rest our faith upon as there was for them. Supposing that God were especially challenging the exercise of such faith, how could He do it more explicitly than in Mark 16:17-18, and John 14:12?

The journal for this month of December is full of reflections on the subject of miracles and of argument for the availability of the miracle-working power today. It appears also that he attempted to perform a miracle and failed.

Dec. 22. A Hindu this morning declared in the presence of a multitude that I was an imposter because I wrought no miracles. For he had read in the Gospel of Mark that believers should heal the sick, drink poison without suffering any evil effects, &c. Therefore either the religion was false or I was no believer. And he went away triumphing. It appears to me that if the Savior had not intended those promises to apply to all times, there would have been some word signifying it, inserted, that would have saved His people from the reproach so sure to come upon them, by the contradiction of this promise and their own works. For what answer can be made to such a charge? If we say that miracles are only necessary for the establishment of a religion, and that when once established they are unnecessary, it would be answered that Christianity is established in Christendom, but not in India. That it is here a new religion, as much so as it was in Ephesus and Corinth in the days of Paul, and in order to its establishment, requires as powerful evidence as it then enjoyed. But more than this, it might be answered that the words of Christ are unequivocal, point blank to the effect that believers will work miracles. Not perhaps that everyone will work miracles; but in every body of believers, or in every place where there is faith in Christ, there will be the power of working miracles. The promise is given for the sake of the world, as Paul says, "Tongues are for a sign, not to them that believe, but to them that believe not," and all that the world requires is that in connection with the church of Christ there exist the power of working miracles. Therefore it seems to me that if the promise in Mark was intended for the primitive times alone, the Savior has by the peculiar wording of it, given an argument to idolaters and infidels.

Our unbelieving hearts rise up in rebellion against such an enterprise as that of healing the blind and the deaf by a word. Words have power over moral agents, and over nothing else; over the physical world they are powerless. To effect the removal of a stone, or any change in material acts, these are needed not words but an exertion of physical power. For physical things there is physical power; and for moral things there is moral power. Such is our experience, and we shrink back from the proposition to open the eyes of the blind by a word as from a proposition to remove a great mountain by a glance. But in fact words are sovereign. They have done and are doing more than any physical power could do. By the Word of God the heavens were of old and the earth. God spake and it was done. By His Word also, the deluge was brought on earth. By a word did Christ control the wind and sea and storms and all sickness and all infirmities, and the fishes of the sea and the dead. And He upholdeth all things by the Word of His power. Wherever I may be, I am surrounded by objects attesting the supremacy of the words; the ground I stand on, the air I breathe, the sky I see, all tell me that they are there and so, at that time, in obedience to a word, and that they only wait for a word, to become different. And the word of faith is the Word of God. "If ye shall say to this mountain be thou removed and be thou cast into the sea, it shall be done." God hath commanded all things to obey the word of faith.

Dec. 26. The doctrine of the resurrection of Christ is perhaps of greater importance than I have been in the habit of supposing. The Jews saw Christ crucified; and though they returned to the city beating their breasts, yet they repented not. It was when Christ had risen, and on the day of Pentecost gave evidence of His resurrection, that they were pricked in their hearts and cried out for salvation. We tell men now of the crucifixion of Christ, and perhaps they believe it; and they see nothing wonderful in the statement that men did these things unto Him; they hear of His death very much as they would of that of a mere malefactor, or at the most of one unjustly executed; but if they can be shown that He rose from the dead, then the crucifixion assumes a vast importance. Everything turns on this doctrine. This is the first great thing for the preacher to accomplish. He must give them evidence that He Who was crucified, actually left the dead and ascended to Heaven, and they will immediately be full of curiosity to know all about His life and death.

How can we show the heathen that Christ is in Heaven and on the throne? As the disciples did on Pentecost; as Christ showed that God was His Father. "If I do not the works of my Father, believe me not." If we do not the works of Christ, how can they believe? Whether I ever have faith to glorify my Redeemer in this way or not, I have the most perfect conviction that the latter day glory is to be ushered in this way. For this conviction I thank God. The very painfulness of the remaining load of unbelief upon my soul is a proof that my faith has been much increased. I have become acquainted with an obligation that I was an entire stranger to, before.

Dec. 27. We have no evidence that any idolatrous nation was ever converted without miracles. So long as miracles continued in the church, so long she was victorious; since miracles departed, she has not subdued nations. The Sandwich Islanders have cast off idolatry and were without any religion, when the missionaries arrived there; and they were only a hundred thousand in all. The necessity for miracles arises out of the depravity of man; if there were the least proclivity to truth and the knowledge of God in the minds of men, then the moral evidence of the Christian religion would suffice.

The Sermon on the Mount would be sufficient to satisfy angels that the preacher was God's Son. But it is because the carnal heart is enmity against God that the evidence of miracles is required. The amount of evidence required is according to the disposition of the mind; according to the mind's unwillingness to believe anything will be the amount of proof required. It will take much to convince a wife that her beloved has done a dishonorable action; it will require strong evidence to convince an enemy that the hated person is one of the excellent of the earth. Impenitent persons are converted by becoming convinced that the works recorded of Christ were really performed; at least this is a step in the process of their conversion, and a necessary one; the historical chain enables them to accede to this evidence and embrace it. But the Hindus know nothing of history and our histories are to them just as worthy of suspicion as the Gospel itself. It is then only by doing the works of Christ that we can prove to them that Christ wrought the works related in the Gospel.

The cross is not the power of God, till the doctrine of Christ's resurrection and divinity is established. Until this is done, the Cross of Christ has very little more power than the cross of the thief at His right hand. The person crucified is the essential thing.

The greatest achievement of God is not in performing a miracle, but in creating the faith by which it is to be performed. To open the eyes of the blind is really an insignificant work compared with that operation by which God brings a mind into a state of sufficient faith to command in the Name of Christ that the eyes of the blind be opened.

For three weeks God has been carrying on a work of immense power in my heart. Scarce one of my waking hours, in which His Spirit has not been bringing some truth to bear upon my mind in order to the increase of faith. The power of unbelief within me has seemed something altogether colossal, terrible. It is easy to throw down the pyramids or cast mountains into the sea, but not easy to bring me to the exercise of that faith which the Gospel demands and challenges. The works that I am desiring from God, those by which His glory shall be revealed to this people will have been first performed in my own mind. Here are the difficulties, the impediments; here the power of the enemy; here the battlefield; here the victory; and the word which opens the eyes of the blind and cleanses the lepers is simply the external evidence of that victory.

It is at this time my conviction, that God has put the whole universe in a state of preparation, that He has carefully taken out of the universe everything of the nature of an absolute impediment; that He is present with all His omnipotent energy and untold love to glorify Himself in the eyes of the nation, and that there is but one thing delays the blessed hour, namely the imperfection of my faith. What a thought is this? That I should be at this time a stone to check the wheels of the chariot of salvation. And yet an altogether scriptural thought. As true as that Christ has all power in Heaven and earth, and has declared all things to be possible to him that believeth.

It is now midnight. Why should not the next six or seven hours witness the perfecting of my faith, so that I might open a broad door for Jesus in this world? The Word of God is here, the material out of which faith is made, and the Spirit of God is here, the Agent by Whom it is made. I have the infinitude of God's love on my side.

I begin to see how greatly the Spirit of God is glorified by miracles. For they are His work, inasmuch as faith is all His work. I feel that He is waging a mighty battle within me. As the seed, the sprout, the tree, the branches, the leaves, the blossoms constitute a great process of which fruit is the simple and easy result, so the preparatory work of faith when perfected terminates without any difficulty in the working of miracles, that is, in the external revelation of the power of God. So that in fact this is not a material and secondary work as I used to think, but eminently spiritual. There is sanctification at every step of it, for the destruction of unbelief is this; and there is an abundant creation of holiness as the result.

From the rigid uniformity of nature, from the manifest appearance of law in every part, of a plan relating to the whole, men are apt to think that nature is opposed to the working of miracles. She seems to us to frown upon such faith. But in fact we know that the whole creation groaneth and travaileth in pain, waiting for the manifestation of the sons of God. It is the great desire of all the material universe, and the great interest,—that Christ's glory should be revealed, and superstition, sin, be destroyed.

Dec. 28. Spent the entire night in prayer and precious was my communion with God. I went forth expecting to have an indication but had none, and my faith is yet unfruitful. All I have asked for is an indication such as I have already had, such as being challenged for proof, and taunted with the promise in Mark. Christ seems to have waited for an intimation of providence on the occasion of His first miracle. "Mine hour is not yet come," He said; "I see not yet that arrangement of things which indicates that My power is to be now exerted." I am not exactly certain with regard to this instance. . . . Perhaps He meant that the necessity and desire were not yet marked enough; for men must thirst before He will give. Peter and John, Acts 3rd, waited for no intimation of providence. They saw the lame man by the temple gate, and healed him. Perhaps in my present course I am not enough knowing the Word of God. It may be this that vitiated my faith this morning.

Then came on the following day the supreme attempt (apparently to restore sight to a blind man) and the bitter disappointment, the circumstances remaining unrecorded and unknown.

"It was strongly borne in upon his soul," wrote Bishop Robinson, "that it was his duty and privilege to authenticate his divine commission to the ignorant people among whom he toiled with so little success by 'signs following.' The references in his journal are scanty and somewhat vague, but it seems that after days and nights of prayer and study of the Word, he on one occasion essayed the healing of a sick or disabled person by a command of faith and was signally unsuccessful. He was greatly humbled and confounded, but God held him in the hollow of His hand, and he suffered no eclipse of faith. He never, however, abandoned the conviction that the miracle-working power was recoverable by the Church and ought to be an adjunct for missionary labors among idolatrous peoples; but we do not find any further attempts on his part to manifest or exert this power, though he appears to have sought it with prayer and fasting and many tears."

> *Dec. 29.* It has pleased God to confound me before His enemies. The Lord knows I have not rashly rushed upon this business; I was driven to it by the Word of God. . . . My attempt to glorify Him has proved a signal, utter failure. I now desire death more than anything else. For if God's Word is dead, why should I live? The stability of God's Word is all that makes life endurable. Everything in the universe the Christian can endure; but a covenant-breaking God makes him of all men most miserable. The promise stands "he that believeth on me the works that I do shall he do also." It is not said the first disciples shall do it, but the believer. "These signs shall follow them that believe." "All things are possible to him that believeth," and a thousand corroborative texts. I searched long for one text that might limit these promises and could not find it. If ever in anything I was impelled by the Word of God, it was in what I undertook this morning. If the Scripture can be broken, what is the use of living? What is there for a man to depend upon? I feel somewhat as the Savior when on the cross He cried out, "My God, my God, why hast thou forsaken me?" "Our fathers trusted in Thee and were not confounded, but I am a worm and no man."

Years before, Savonarola essayed his miracle in Florence, but was spared the final test to which Bowen carried his faith. Is George Eliot's comment on the Florentine, in *Romola*, relevant in any degree to the modern missionary in Bombay: "Perhaps no man has ever had a mighty influence over his fellows without having the innate need to dominate, and this need usually becomes the more imperious in proportion as the complications of life make self inseparable from a purpose which is not selfish"? How far was it self which was crucifying self? What was this impotence which was venturing to exercise omnipotence?

So Bowen's first year in India ended with this collapse. Or did it end so? As it proved, this was the beginning of as devoted, patient, persistent, holy a life as was ever lived in India.

11. A Decisive Year, 1849

The failure of the miracle led to no abatement of the courageous adventuresomeness of faith. The new year began with fresh and radical purposes:

Jan 1, 1849. The great truth is this that God is able to do exceeding abundantly above all that we can ask or think. I have asked great things the last month. I have perhaps gone beyond the whole church in what I have asked, and asked in faith. Yet God is able to do more. And behind this truth is another precious truth, viz., that there is love as vast as this power. An infinite love within which the whole finite universe with all its capacities for receiving is contained as the smallest possible grain of sand is contained in the hand of a man. He takes up the isles as one would take up a very little thing from the ground, and His exhaustless love takes up the entire sum of His children's wants in like manner. Its length and breadth and depth and height, one must be an infinite God to ascertain. . . . Now about the manner of displaying this, I may not be able to judge; but that is of no consequence. So that it is displayed, and His glorious transcendent power seen in conjunction with Zion, I am satisfied. Why then should I be cast down? Why should I be as one fallen into a pit? The eclipse that has come over God's Word, is merely the mist of my own error and shortsightedness. Let God be true, though every man a liar. I cannot possibly have caught a glimpse of the Savior's love and ability toward Zion, greater than the reality. Satan does not deceive in this way, but in the other. It is not God that is making war upon my faith, but Satan. Though God has struck a heavy blow at me, it was not meant to harm me. If I understand not its meaning, no matter. Behind a frowning Providence, He hides a smiling face. Let me resume the faith that I was tempted to cast off. It is as much our duty to believe all things and hope all things as it is to endure all things.

I want at this time to learn the lesson that God would have me learn. It seems to relate to my position. My position is a false one. I am not living in the style in which Christ lived, or His apostles, or that He points out in His Word. I am not living in such a way as to enunciate by my life the great Gospel principles that can only be effectually enunciated in this way. The glory of the Gospel does not appear by my life. I am living in a way, with a degree of comfort and expenditure, that must make me the object of envy to the great mass of Hindus. Whereas the great power of Christianity is in this that it raises men above the need of these things.

It consists in this that it gives men a treasure in Heaven by the side of which all in this world seems dross to them. . . . How can a man teach that money is the root of all evil, while he has more of it in his hands than any of his hearers?

As far as I am personally concerned, the laying off of these superfluities, will cost me no more than the laying off an old coat. I think this is the state of my mind with regard to them. But the trial of trials is to pursue a course which will be or may seem to be condemnatory of my brethren. I intimated at the Missionary conference this morning something of what is going on within me.

On rising this New Year's day, I read the first chapter of Paul to the Galatians. When converted and commissioned, he did not confer with flesh and blood. And whom does he mean by flesh and blood? Why Christians, the best Christians in the church, even the apostles themselves. "If I yet pleased men I should not be the servant of Christ." And by men he means Peter and John and James. He did not take counsel of them, but the commandment of Christ sufficed for him. He might have said, "Who am I that I should pursue a different course from these beloved disciples of my Master, who were associated with Him in all His ministry, who have been placed by Him over the church, who have had so many years of experience, who have made such great attainments?" But instead of saying this and going to Jerusalem, he went into Arabia. He had been raised up by the Lord to fulfill that great command which they had neglected to fulfill. With all their holiness and devotedness they would have told him, if he had asked their advice, to preach the Gospel to the Jews and not to the Gentiles. He regarded himself therefore as an apostle not of men, but of Jesus Christ.

If the church is always to be deferred to, how can the measure of consecration, the estimate of duty, ever be elevated? The only way in which it can be elevated, is for one individual to hearken to the Word of God which the others neglect, and give it power in the church by fulfilling it in the eyes of men. . . . Strange as it may seem, the greatest benefactors of the church such as Luther, are those who give most offense to the church. To neglect a command of God, from fear of wounding those who neglect it, is to give a wound to Christ and to religion.

May the Lord my Savior, guide me and bless me with the indication of His providence. Although His Word should be abundantly sufficient, yet He has never refused to grant also the leadings of His providence, to poor weak sinners groping for the light of life.

As the Lord is light and in Him is no darkness at all, so His Word is light and in it is no darkness at all. It is my privilege to know His will certainly, and to proceed in fulfilling it, with a mind purged from every doubt. It was said this morning that men are responsible for their errors no matter how strong their conviction that they are right. Their sincerity and thoroughness of conviction did not free them from blame-worthiness for their errors. I said, True; and what is implied in this truth, but that men may know the truth? It is the fact that God is willing to give perfect light to everyone respecting all parts of his duty, that makes him guilty for erring.

Jan. 4. I have not yet sufficiently realized the importance of a Gospel manner of life, I mean as regards externals. I have been content to live with a mind detached from the things of life; this is not enough, I must so live as to give the world the evidence that my mind is detached from them. The world will only know the work of Christ in our soul by the evidences given in our visible conduct. Men are amazingly under the power of their appetites, and nothing startles them so much as to see a man (or set of men) having his appetites all in perfect subjection. A man may preach with the eloquence of an angel, and make no impression upon them; but deadness to the world exemplified in the life cannot fail to impress them. It is something they can understand. It is a proof of divine power and of sincerity, level to their degraded understandings and sensual natures. . . . Christians have laid heavy chains upon me, for which God forgive them. I loathe the style of life they have inveigled me into. How easy would Paul's style of life be to me, once in it. How difficult to break from the associations and habits in which I am bound, and which cannot be broken without much pain to my brethren. But has Christ ever refused to help me? Let me remember how many a similar mountain has been made a plain, by trusting Him. I feel that there is one thing for me to do, namely as soon as possible to get into that position of frugality and self-denial that Paul occupied. Till then God will do no great things by me.

A man that emerges from his study occasionally and traverses a heathen city will not be fully known to them. In order to be fully known as Christ and Paul were, we must live abroad, in the haunts of men. I must be a pattern to my brother missionaries. What an abominable thing is it to neglect doing my Master's will, because my fellow servants neglect it and if I fulfill it they will be hurt and suppose me to be impugning them. And yet this is a most taking snare. It seems unkind and un-Christian to be charging error upon my brethren, to be inflicting pain upon those whom Christ loves. But I am bound to please Christ, and not men. Will a master accept such an excuse? "My fellow servants omitted to do what you commanded and I thought that if I did it, they would consider themselves reproached, therefore I did it not." And why should they not be reproached? Must not everyone who transgresses be reproached? To withhold the reproach is to divide with him the burden of his sin. The command is "reprove, rebuke, exhort."

There can be no progressive holiness without progressive boldness. We cultivate boldness to reprove our fellow Christians and fellow laborers very little. But after all if Satan defeats us here does he not gain his greatest victory? Is there anything so near his heart as the perpetuation of the sins of Christians? If he can only do this, he does all. He may let the heathen alone, if he can only retain a certain degree of power in Christian minds. This is his short route to universal dominion. If he can hinder me from being that pattern of a missionary to my brethren, which Christ would have me to be, it will be as much gain to him as the introduction of one more deity among these idolaters. My business here is to be a pattern missionary not only to those here, but to all missionaries throughout the world.

My prayer years ago was that I might recreate in the eyes of men Paul's standard of ministerial character. That I might be a model missionary and the most useful of men. This text is then for me. . . . "In all things showing thyself a pattern of good works." I have sinned greatly though unwittingly during the past year, by submitting in silence to things that grieved me. Perhaps I ought at the very outset to have exhibited what was in me. I do more earnestly desire from this time to be a true man, and disembosom upon every opportunity the truth that is in me. This fear of offending by our virtue, has great influence in the church I am persuaded. This charity is of Satan. True charity "rejoiceth in the truth."

Jan. 9. "He is a chosen vessel unto Me to bear My name before the Gentiles and kings and the children of Israel." Paul was raised up to bear the Name of Christ, not to declare it, but far more. As a vessel receives some treasure, which is conveyed in it hither and thither; such a vessel was Paul. An earthen vessel, he says, that the excellency of the power might be of God. The Name of Christ is the character of Christ. Paul was raised up for the manifestation of Christ; and this he could only do by becoming as Christ; Paul died out of him and Christ arose in him; not I, but Christ liveth in me. Therefore it was his passionate desire to be in all things conformed to Christ.

Is there an individual living who should feel himself under greater obligations to be what Paul was, and bear Christ's Name before the Gentiles? . . . How much does it become me to be bold, fearless, enterprising? Because others shrink, must I shrink? Because others see not the truth, must I disobey the truth which God has taught me? Why has it been revealed to me, but that I may embody it in action? How can a man conquer unless he enter into the fight? If others are enslaved to customs, and wedded to comforts, must I feign myself to be so too, that I may not displease them? I have been sinning long, while my conscience flattered me. My docility is a crime. I am wedded to Jesus, and must please Him. The thought of Heaven is not near so dear to me as the thought of glorifying Christ on the earth, of manifesting His Name to the Gentiles. Who put this desire within me? Who has fed it? Who has prepared me in so many respects to do it? Who has taught me the all-sufficiency of Christ? Who has raised up so many to pray for me? Who has relieved me of so many incumbrances that press on others? Who has raised me up lately from the brink of the grave? The same Who will doubtless fulfill all these desires. Why should I doubt? Why should I fret because the few remaining difficulties are to be encountered?

I have been led to admire greatly the dealings of God with me. They are those of a master-workman. His wisdom is amazing. How little I understood last month the end He was driving at. He took me up to a high pinnacle and then dashed me into a profound abyss, and yet He had but one end in view in all. These were necessary steps to a still higher consummation. I do not know how the sense of my responsibility could have been otherwise made what it is. . . . There is lying on my table a letter to the missionaries of Bombay, which I have written as I think under strong constraining hand of the Spirit; and which I trust that the Spirit will make productive of good of some kind or other in some quarter or other.

Jan. 10. The promises are given to enable us to obey the commands. . . . God is under obligation to give us what we ask, when His words abide in us, when they become our laws, our guides; when the heart's supreme desire is, at any cost, to have them fulfilled.

The letter which was lying on his table was dated Jan. 8, 1849 and Bowen now sent it forth. It was as follows:

WHAT IS THE TRUE MISSIONARY LIFE?
Discussed in a letter from a Missionary to his brethren.
Dear Brethren in the Lord,

My mind has been much at work of late upon the question: What mode of life should a missionary adopt in order to have the approbation of his Master? Believing that Christ would not willingly have us remain in the dark concerning a question of this kind I have studied the Word of God in the sure expectation of finding the needed light. The conclusions to which I find myself tending are so different from those which I suppose to be entertained by my brethren in this ministry, that it has seemed best before definitely making up my mind as to what is duty, to submit to them my views so far as they are formed, and solicit an expression of their opinion concerning them. I have felt considerable pain while revolving this matter in view of the pain I might possibly give you by adopting a new standard of missionary life; but this is in a measure removed by the reflection, that in adopting your present style of life you have acted on principle and conscientiously, as truly as I now am in addressing you; and that it will be no more difficult for you and less painful, to give the reasons why your style of life is what it is, than for me to state the thoughts which have arisen in my own mind. Light is as much an object to you as to me; by an amicable and earnest discussion light may be evolved, and cannot possibly be extinguished or diminished: and I conclude that you will welcome this discussion, and spare me a portion of your time sufficient to read, digest and perhaps reply to the following considerations.

The question more fully stated is this: Shall the missionary live as a rich man or as a poor man? If as a poor man, shall it be according to the European idea of poverty or the Hindu? Shall his style of living be luxurious, or comfortable, or self-denying? Shall his salary be large, or moderate, or as little as possible? Shall he have any expensive equipage, or a plain one, or none at all? Shall he have many servants, few, or none at all?

Perhaps the opinion of some may be that this question is an unimportant one. The things upon which the Bible lays stress are of another and higher character. The great scope of the Bible is to lead Christians to set their affections upon things above, not on things on the earth; and if they live with their affections detached from these things, it is a matter of comparatively little consequence, whether they detach these things from their lives or not. Two persons may live together in the same style and participate in the same comforts; but God Who sees the heart, may know that the one is bound up in these comforts, while the other disregards them and has his treasure in Heaven. There is a wide interval between their spiritual nature; this interval if not represented in their use of worldly goods, is in many more important things; and this suffices to God. I have at times been disposed to entertain this opinion; but recent study of the Scriptures leads me to reject it.

The Bible does not represent the externals of a Christian life as unimportant. When Christ sent forth the Twelve (see 9th of Luke), He with remarkable conciseness bade them preach the kingdom of God, and with equally remarkable amplitude instructs them as to the mode of life they were to follow, taking up successively the questions of a scrip, a staff, gold, silver, clothes, coats, shoes, food and lodging. The same thing is observable in His directions to the Seventy. Whether these commands related exclusively to the disciples of that day, or otherwise, is a question I do not here agitate. I quote them to show that the question—what sort of life is suited to the missionary—is one considered by the Lord Jesus Christ not unimportant. He has expressly declared it to be important, even in all its particulars and to its minutest details. He has caused these instructions to be recorded no less than four times in the everlasting Gospel. See Matt. 10; Mark 6; Luke 9 and 10. He has taken care to notify us concerning His own mode of life, that He hungered, thirsted, and had not where to lay His head.

The mode of life of the apostles is described with a particularity and a frequency and an emphasis, that utterly forbid the supposition that this is a matter of inferior importance. It seems to have been the earnest endeavor of Paul to exhibit himself to the church as a model minister of Jesus Christ; and it cannot escape the notice of anyone who contemplates his picture as it is portrayed in the Epistles, that the details of his manner of living have a prominent part in that picture. In 1 Cor. 4:11-12, he writes: "Even unto this present hour we both hunger and thirst and are naked and are buffeted, and have no certain dwelling place, and labor working with our own hands." And that this was voluntary appears from the 9th Chapter, where he says: "Have we not power to eat and to drink? have we not power to forbear working? We have not used this power, but suffer all things, lest we should hinder the Gospel of Christ." And to the Thessalonians he writes: "Not because we have not power, but to make ourselves an example unto you to follow us." In 2 Cor. 6 he gives a catalogue of the proofs by which he substantiates himself among men as a true minister of a true God; and among them appear "necessities, distresses, poverty, utter destitution." "As poor yet making many rich; as having nothing and yet possessing all things." See also 2 Cor. 11:27.

It is impossible for me, in view of these and many similar passages, to escape the conviction that the question which I have introduced, is one of consequence. We are, I think, to believe, upon the testimony of God's Word, but there is a style of life peculiarly adapted to the missionary, and which Christ for reasons well known to Himself, whether obvious to us or not, greatly desires to see His servants adopt.

What now is that style of life? It is that style which is best calculated to convince an ungodly, sensual world, that a divine power has been at work within us transforming us, so that we are no longer like them engrossed by the pleasures of this world, but are possessed of a something that satisfies us independently of what this world can give. Men are carnal, and as carnal God addresses them. He would give them sensible proofs of the Christian religion. The eloquence and logic of an angel would fail to arrest them, for the very reason that he is an angel; but let a servant of God give full proof of deadness to the world, that world to which they are so enslaved, and their attention is arrested. They are amazingly under the power of their appetites and lusts; and the sight of a man having all these in perfect subjection must startle them. But this inward victory will never be known to them, till its troubles are exhibited to their senses through the medium of the life.

The high aims of the Christian can only be known to them by a demonstration parallel to their senses. So long as there is the least supposable foundation for skepticism, they will be skeptical about those high aims; and will refuse to believe the minister of Christ indifferent to comforts, and luxuries, and the gratifications of sense, and reputation, and distinction, until they see him throwing these all behind his back, and signifying by his treatment of them the disesteem in which he holds them. Until that moment, though the Spirit be really in his heart, though he be truly seeking the glory of God and the good of men, though his affections be truly alienated from the objects of sense, yet the world will not believe in his transformation, or impute to him any principles superior to those that govern themselves. And if it should so happen that the very things they seek after, which they feed their imaginations on when alone, dream about by night, converse about among themselves, labor year after year by fair means or foul to obtain, if these very things should happen to be found in the missionary's life, will they not be fatal to the production of that evidence which the Gospel is aiming to produce?

Let a man with one hand offer the Gospel to a crowd of heathen, and at the same time be handling a purse of gold in the other, will they give much heed to his message? No, he must put the gold out of sight if he would have them listen to his words. There is a fascination to them about the gold which binds up all their senses, and baffles all attempts to secure their attention to the Gospel. Money is their God; they worship it and the things which it procures. If when they come to see us, they find their gods with us, viz., money, authority, luxury, distinction, they will honor us because their gods are with us, and will envy us. But their respect will not be of a kind favorable to religious influence; nor will they be ready to discover the evidence that we are transformed from our original nature, or that omnipotence dwells in the bosom of the Christian Church.

It is not sufficient that we do not idolize the things they idolize; we must openly and unequivocally disown those things. It is not enough that we can use those things without being contaminated by them; we are to reject them because they contaminate others and because others will not reject them while we retain them. Men are carnal; and the evidences which spiritual persons can detect, are hid from them. Therefore the style of life which Christ enjoins upon us, is that which will tend to flash upon their very vision the evidence that we are born of God, and are looking to things unseen and eternal. This species of proof should come first; in itself insufficient, but indispensable as a preliminary. When they have received this, they will be ready to inquire for others; but till then they will be indifferent to others.

The glory of the Christian religion is not only in the purity of its law, but in the sanctions of that law, not only in the beauty of its morality, but in its power to engrave that morality in the hearts of its believers. There is much excellent morality to be found in some of the sacred books of the Hindus; but then their religion is utterly impotent to enforce the observance of that morality. There is but one religion that can really transform; and Christ would have the transformations it effects exhibited to the eyes of man. "Let your light so shine before men that they may see your good works, and glorify" not you, but "your Father which is in heaven." It is not enough that God is the witness of our renewed nature; that the spiritual in Heaven and earth behold it; but an ungodly carnal world must see it. The apostles could say, "We are made a spectacle unto the world, and to angels, and to men."

The style of life which is adapted to give proof in favor of Christianity, is also adapted to exhibit it, and make beholders acquainted with the great characteristics of the Gospel. In 2 Thess. 3:8-9 Paul says, "We wrought with labor and travail, night and day, not because we have not power, but to make ourselves an example unto you to follow us." Paul was not necessitated to support himself by his own hands there; and seeing that he was a solitary representative of Christ and depository of Christian truth in the midst of that heathen city, seeing that his time as a minister of the Gospel was of unspeakable, incomparable value, it is a thing to be wondered at that he did not avail himself of the means of subsistence furnished him in the providence of God. It would seem that if ever there was a minister of the Gospel called upon by his position to let work alone and give himself exclusively to the Gospel, it was Paul in Thessalonica. If then he could so profusely sacrifice his time, how much importance must he have attached to the end in view, viz.: the exhibition of a model life.

I do not cite this in favor of the notion that ministers should support themselves by their own hands; but as showing in what great account he held the outward exhibition of those principles which Christ had implanted in him. Though filled with the Holy Ghost, he left off preaching and went to work; and what for? Why, he aimed at no other thing in working than in preaching. In fact it was a part of his preaching, and regarded by himself as indispensable. It was, as it were, the interpreter of his oral preaching, without which the latter would not have been understood by the people. And we may preach the Gospel for hundreds of years in India by word of mouth, and by the printed page; but until it be incorporated in our life, and that too in a way adapted to the full apprehensions and sensuous natures of the Hindus, they will not understand it.

The power of the human mind to remain ignorant of divine truth under the most vigorous and long continued efforts to enlighten it, is one of the mysteries of human depravity, and one which will continue to meet us and dishearten us till we adopt the apostolic way of blending the language and the life. Whether we will it or no our manner of life is the great interpreter of our Gospel, to the people we dwell among. They hear us say: "Whosoever he be of you that forsaketh not all that he hath, he cannot be my disciple"; and to know the meaning of these words they look to our life. If its true interpretation is not found in this, then its true interpretation will never reach them. If they see there, instead of a vacuum of the things they covet, an abundance of them, the words have at once lost all their life and power. Five times, speaking by the Holy Ghost, Paul enjoins upon us to follow him, as he followed Christ. To Timothy he says: "Be thou an example of the believers." To Titus: "In all things thyself a pattern of good works." The missionary must be a pattern man; and render his life an irresistible sermon on the words: "Love not the world, neither the things that are in the world."

These considerations lead inevitably to the conclusion that Christ would have us exhibit in our mode of living, to those we preach to, and in a manner comprehensible to them, those principles of the Gospel which are susceptible of being so exhibited. And here one remarkable feature in the position of a missionary to the heathen, presents itself to our notice. He may go so far in self-denial as to exhibit this grace to the circle in which he was brought up. He may go farther, even so far as to exhibit it to the church at home generally. He may go farther, even so far as to exhibit it to his brother missionaries. Yet after all this, he has not even begun to exhibit it to the heathen. This is owing to the great poverty, plainness of living and absence of comforts of the heathen, compared with Christian nations. That style of living which would be decidedly moderate at home, is princely in the eyes of the natives of India. One or two hundred pounds a year, makes a man almost a nobleman in the estimation of the mass of these natives, and they are utterly without a faculty to discern in the life of such a one, the exhibition of self-denial.

There exists between the Sahib-lok and the natives a vast interval; and the former are virtually, in respect to the position they occupy, the nobility of the land. To see them the people must look up. In their hands are the treasures of the land, at their disposal the offices, and in their favor reputation; and those whose aspirations are for these things, look to them. They occupy one level and the people another.

Now if the missionary of the Gospel be identified with them, he will be clothed with a certain external superiority, altogether in the way of his exerting such an influence as flowed from the life of Paul and his fellow-laborers. When the Missionary Sahib goes into the Bazaar to make known the Gospel, he will be as one standing on a pedestal. The people will look upon him as one who is above them in the worldly scale; and while he and they occupy positions so unequal, they will remain ignorant of the true principles of the Gospel. It may be that in order to reach a position which seems to them elevated, the missionary has really descended much; it may be that in leaving his native land and the bosom of his loved Church to take up his abode among heathen, he has made a sacrifice greater than they can conceive of; but it is not a sacrifice palpable to their apprehensions; and they will simply view him as occupying a position which they would love to occupy.

He must destroy that pedestal from under him, if he would embody to their eyes the doctrine which Christ made so prominent, "Deny thyself and take up thy cross and follow Me." As he has renounced his native land, he must renounce his Sahibship. In the providence of God there is given him this opportunity of showing to the heathen the all-sufficiency of Christ, and the indifference felt by Christians for those things which constitute the Elysium of the world. Those steps in his course of self-renunciation, which preceded his arrival among the heathen, are hid from them; but this is one that will meet their eye, and deeply impress their minds.

If it be said that there is something in these adventitious distinctions that gives us an influence over the native mind, and that we have no right to throw away this influence, I would in the first place suggest that no account is made of this sort of influence in the Bible, and in the next place ask whether anything in actual experience shows it to be of value. How long and in what plenitude have we enjoyed it, how ample the experiment made; yet what are the results! Those who have been attracted to us by means of the worldly advantages connected with our position, how insensible have they remained to the religious influences we have sought to exert. How common the remark that those who have served us longest, and derived the largest emoluments, are those who appear least affected by the Gospel. And if from this number, in the course of many years, one, two or three converts be gathered, the mixture of worldly and religious influence to which they have been subjected, manifests itself in a vitiated and obscure piety. Our true weapons are not carnal. If we have worldly ends to accomplish, then this worldly influence is valuable; but if we aim at Gospel ends, it is at the best worthless. It may be favorable to false religions but is doubtless adverse to the true. We conquer by renouncing such advantages. When we are weak we are strong.

If it be said that the church at large, even the most pious and devoted portion of it, demand no such thing at our hands and pass no censure upon our present manner of life, I admit it; and beg in reply to present the following consideration. Missionaries are placed by Christ in the van of the church; and He does not expect that the main body of the church will be keener sighted to discover truth than they; but on the contrary that they as true pioneers, will be first to see what is yet unseen, and afterwards instruct the church to see it. In the body of the church there exists no power to redeem the church from a low state of piety to a higher. How to effect this, is the problem of problems. The tendency in the world is for each man to model his conscience upon that of his neighbor; and this tendency is of overwhelming power and universality. The same tendency exists in the church; and the members of it generally, cannot possibly find in the Word of God any higher standard of Christian duty, than is reflected in the lives of the more pious of their number.

How stupendous the measures adopted by Christ at the beginning of our dispensation to re-create the conscience of the church. Having become a man, He selected twelve from the lower walks of life, separated them from the mass of believers, and, taking them into closest intimacy with Himself, proceeded to delineate before their eyes in His own life, the true standard. Finally, having by His example and instructions and by the Holy Spirit molded them to His liking, He gave them, and in them a new and right Christian conscience to the church. How unspeakable the gift! And vast consequences depended on the careful perpetuation of that standard! For when, after a century or two it was lost, it remained lost.

For more than twelve centuries a darkness brooded on the church, which she was impotent to remove. There appear to have existed some few true Christians in the Roman Church, as Thomas à Kempis and others; but these good men, though lovers and students of the Bible, could study it to the end of their lives without ever surmising that popery with her monstrous errors was not in it, or that it contained doctrines unmitigably hostile to the system of popery. And let us hearken to Luther. "Learn from me," he says, "how difficult a thing it is to throw off errors confirmed by the example of all the world, and which through long habits have become a second nature to us. Though I had been seven years reading and publicly explaining the Holy Scriptures with great zeal, so that I know them almost by heart, I yet clung with obstinacy to popery." And what a striking illustration of this have we in the utter and universal disregard shown for fifteen centuries to the last great command of our Savior. During all that time this ponderous command lay lightly as a feather on the conscience of the church, and good men could live and die without ever once suspecting their obligations to evangelize the heathen.

It was by the work of the Holy Ghost upon the conscience of individuals, that God effected the Reformation; and it was in the same way that Christ brought again to the understanding of the church His last command. And in all probability this piecemeal resurrection of the Word of God has but begun, and magnificent truths are lying there, as in a mausoleum, undreamt of by us; yes, doubtless there are discoveries of Christian duty, as well as of the riches of Christ's grace, yet to be made, no less startling than those we now rejoice over. Therefore it will by no means do for us to adopt the conscience of the church as the measure of our own, but rather resist it in its poverty and narrowness; and with great ardor seek to vivify and embody in our own lives, those principles which are yet uncomprehended in it. All things considered, it were a burning shame for us to be satisfied with that meager view of our responsibility which the church entertains. And if the church makes a disproportionate estimate of the comparative responsibility resting on her and on us, with that mistake we have nothing to do; the great mistake which it concerns us to rectify is in the defective notion entertained of our responsibility compared with that which Christ entertains, and so abundantly displays in His Word. He has written our responsibility in the lives of Paul and Peter and John; has promised us grace as unbounded as they enjoyed; and will expect us to answer for any falsification or reduction of the apostolic standard, brought to pass through our lives. The leaders of the church and the main body of the church are connected by a chain, and by the full length of that chain are separated. She considers it her privilege to be at a certain distance from them; and while so much of her pristine corruption remains, she will use that privilege. They, seeing her inferior standard, make war upon it, but in vain. There is but one way in which they can elevate her; it is by going higher themselves. She will rigidly maintain the existing interval and the existing connection; in order to maintain them, she must reach a higher consecration. Then will be fulfilled the word of the prophet Isaiah: "For brass I will bring gold, and for iron I will bring silver, and for wood brass, and for stones iron."

The Gospel is represented as something swift-moving and powerful. It is compared to fire, to a runner, and the wings of an angel flying in the free heaven are given to it. But what has it been in India? Like an eagle shorn of its wings, a smothered flame, a sword all hacked and rusty. To account for this modern paralysis of our glorious Gospel, we have had recourse to the strength of human depravity on the one hand, and on the other to the sovereignty of Him we serve. But the glory of the Gospel is in this very thing that it is omnipotent in the face of human depravity, and of the allied forces marshaled under Satan; that it is omnipotent with respect to the very maturity and utmost perfection of sin.

As respects the Divine sovereignty, I acknowledge that it becomes us blind mortals, led in a path we know not, greatly to reverence this attribute of God. But until we have made full proof of the measures indicated in the Gospel, until we have done the things commanded us, we cannot conscientiously account for the apparent decrepitude of the Gospel by referring it to a decree of God. There are decrees of God which relate to our present conduct; and there is good reason to believe that by obeying these we shall fulfill the conditions upon which success is depending.

I do not suppose that by conforming to apostolic simplicity and self-renunciation, we shall necessarily convert souls. We might make all the sacrifices mentioned, and without the descent of the Spirit things would go on as they have hitherto done. But the great argument is this, that we would thereby honor the Word, and Him that gave it, and secure a larger measure of the approbation of our Master than we now enjoy; and would consequently be justified in expecting the answer to our prayers for an outpouring of the Spirit. Our Savior, though the Lord of all grace, is an absolute Master.

In all His dispensations from the foundation of the world to the present time, we clearly discern this controlling principle, namely, a withholding of the blessing until the appointed conditions be fulfilled. Though we believe not, He abideth faithful. If we dishonor His Word, He will honor it. With all His boundless compassion to a dying world, He does not hesitate to stretch a heaven of brass over the whole circumference of a disobedient Christendom, until His servants arise and loose the Bible from its convent chains. He leaves the heathen under the unbroken sway of the prince of this world, for fifteen centuries, till individuals present themselves in the church and re-utter the long-lost words: "Go ye into all the world and preach the Gospel to every creature."

If then it appears that the standard of self-denial in the primitive church is in any sense a standard given to us, we may well believe that the decree concerning the salvation of the heathen is a decree postponed to that which requires our conformity to that standard; and that this our conformity will be the signal for the out-pouring of those treasures which have been hitherto detained so unwillingly upon the throne of grace. The exceedingly great and precious promises that stand out upon the front of God's Word, how long have they refused to yield virtue to our touch! They have seemed to say to us: "Jesus we know, and Paul we know, but who are ye?" Our garb and lineaments are strange to them. In vain we protest that Christ is in our hearts: "We know you not," they say, and add: "He that saith he abideth in Him, ought himself also so to walk even as He walked." To show that Christ is in us, we must put on Christ, as one puts on armor; we must be found in Him; we must bear about in our bodies the dying of the Lord Jesus; we must be conformed to Him in His terrestrial and mortal image, that we may hereafter wear His celestial and incorruptible likeness. As there was a twofold transfiguration of Christ, one downward, from glory to deepest abasement, and the other to glory again; so there is to be a twofold transfiguration on our part, first, through the deposition of the world's vain paraphernalia, and afterwards by our glorification in the likeness of the heavenly Christ. If we suffer with Him, we shall also reign with Him.

Therefore did Paul so passionately desire to experience the fellowship of His sufferings, to fill up that which was behind of His afflictions, and be made conformable to His death. "Let this mind be in you which was also in Christ Jesus; Who being in the form of God, thought it not robbery to be equal with God; but made Himself of no reputation, and took upon Him the form of a servant, and was made in the likeness of men, and became obedient unto death, even the death of the cross." Let this mind be in us.

The objection may be made: "We are in a hostile climate, and a due regard to the preservation of health demands the observance of the habits we have adopted." But this objection fails, if there is any force in what has been urged. The adoption of the primitive standard has been urged on the ground that it is authoritatively enjoined, that the command "Go preach the Gospel," cannot possibly be fulfilled without it, that it is essential to the triumphs of the Gospel. We are under obligations to preserve our health as we are to love father and mother and wife and children and brethren and sisters; but in Luke XIV:26 Christ has subordinated these obligations to a higher. Our great end is to be the glory of Christ; when the preservation of life and health may be a means to that end, we are to preserve them; when the sacrifice of them may be a means, we are to sacrifice them. "Christ is to be magnified in our bodies whether it be by life or by death." Christ and His glorious characteristics must be manifested; this is necessary, and nothing else is.

Beloved brethren, as we are to stand before the great God and our Savior in the day of account, let us remember the Word of Christ: "The servant is not greater than his Lord." It is to be feared we have made ourselves greater than our Lord. The servant who labors less than his master, consults ease, comfort, luxury, more than his master does, moves in a social sphere higher than that in which his master generally is found, refuses to be partaker of his master's penury, ignominy and danger, such a servant makes himself greater than his lord, such a disciple makes himself greater than his Master. The relations are thereby reversed, and everyone would be ready to exclaim at a glance that the master is the servant, and the servant the master. Is it not enough that the world disdains Christ, desires His abasement and humiliation, and would be content to have Him for its galley-slave? Is it not enough that the world has a hand to smite Him with? A rod to scourge Him with? A mouth to mock Him with? Has thorns for His head, nails for His hands and feet, and a spear for His side, but must we too lord it over Him? Must we sit when He stands, ride when He walks, live in fine mansions when He has no place to lay His head, and fare sumptuously when He hungers and thirsts?

O shall we not, my brethren, in the midst of this apostate, Christ-despising world, manifest a generous and true-hearted devotion to our Master? Shall we not take up the language of John, "He must increase, but I must decrease"? "If any man serve me," said Christ, "let him follow Me; he that hateth his life in this world, shall keep it unto life eternal; except a corn of wheat fall into the ground and die it abideth alone, but if it die it bringeth forth much fruit." Here is a precious promise of much fruit; but it is at the other side of a certain death to be accomplished, the death of self, of honor, of distinction, of ease. Let us die this death; let us be crucified unto the world and the world unto us. A master commits no injustice when he says to the servant who is come from the field: "Make ready wherewith I may sup and gird thyself and serve me"; and surely Christ makes no unjust requisites when He says: "The disciple shall be as his master."

Other arguments which will present themselves to your mind, I forbear to dwell upon. One, respecting the influence our manner of life will have in determining the tone of piety and consecration in the native church of India, seems to me of incalculable weight.

My dear brethren and fellow-servants, are the views I have stated erroneous? Are they without a proper warrant in Scripture? And am I chargeable with rashness or arrogance in thus making them known to you? I hope I may not incur this censure. I have gone warily and reluctantly about this business, chastised to it as it seems to me, by the Spirit of God. May that Spirit guide us into the truth and make us mighty in the Scriptures, those Scriptures which were given that the man of God might be perfect, thoroughly furnished unto every good work. . . . And whatever opinion you may form of the views I have expressed, believe that my earnest desire and unceasing prayer shall ever be for your most intimate union to Christ, and your much fruitfulness in Him.

Holding these opinions, the obvious question for Bowen was whether he should continue as a missionary of the American Board and draw his missionary salary:

Jan. 20, 1849. It is a question that occupies my thoughts considerably, whether I ought not to renounce my salary, and seek to support myself in some way. It is not an absolute duty. There is no sin in receiving my support from the church. Even the apostle Paul received assistance from the churches. But the question arises, will not good follow from such a course? Would not the influence of such a course be important to the church, to ministers and to the heathen? There is reason to fear that very many ministers are influenced by the love of filthy lucre; and as many more are liable to have such motives ascribed to them by the world, seeing that they receive large salaries, which they spend upon themselves and families. The world is enslaved to money, and the world thinks the church also is enslaved to it, and will think so just so long as by any possibility it can. I am convinced that it is of primary importance that there should be unequivocal examples of self-denial in the church, and especially on the part of ministers. In the 9th of 1st Cor. Paul labors to establish two points, first that he had a right to be sustained by the church, and 2ndly that it was right for him to renounce this right. And he uses the very strongest language to express the importance he attached to this last. "It were better for me to die than that any man should make my glorying void." He attached so much importance to it, that he would rather die than not do it. This is amazing, and shows that he had very different notions from ours concerning the best means of extending the Gospel.

Jan. 21. Dr. Anderson, in a letter to the Mission, says: "I have no expectation that the Christian community will ever appreciate their duty in the use of money, unless they are incited to it by the strongest examples of personal self-denial in respect to that very thing in the great body of their brethren laboring among the heathen." . . .

Ps. 62:5. "My soul, wait thou only upon God; for my expectation is from Him." The word "only" is the emphatic word here. It is when we cut ourselves adrift from everything else, and put ourselves in a position where we must either sink, or be saved through God alone, that the salvation of God is revealed. The tendency of the church is to arm herself with everything she can, and rely on God for what else may be necessary. And it is thought wrong and fanatical not to do so. But if we are truly jealous for the glory of God, we shall desire to see His power manifested in a way least liable to misinterpretation. God in great goodness has condescended in some measure to act according to the prayers of the church and the consequence is that all which He has done is ascribed by the world to natural causes. If our faith would let Him, God would delight to put forth His power in Zion in such modes that all should recognize the presence of something more than nature. My soul, wait thou only upon God. I want to get rid of everything but Christ. I want to be rid of everything that carnal men respect. The more they cast off respect, and speak out their contempt of me and my words, the more unreservedly they manifest their hatred to my work, so much the more let me rejoice, for it is a sign I am losing adventitious distinctions, and approaching a state of entire dependence on God. So Gideon drew nigh to victory, just according as he diminished his army. When he had nothing but a few pitchers, lamps and trumpets left and men to carry them, then he triumphed, and God was glorified. The Israelites could not vanquish Goliath, because they were strong and valorous and armed from head to foot. When a stripling appeared with his sling, that is to say, with nothing but his God, then the giant was vanquished.

1 Sam. 17:38. "And Saul armed David with his armor, and he put a helmet of brass upon his head, also he armed him with a coat of mail." This is much the way the church treats the converts, and the missionaries treat the young missionary that comes among them. They are sincere and mean well; but the helps and appliances they direct him to, are in fact his great cumbrances. They forget that the shield of faith, the sling and pebbles of faith are the true armor of God. David said to Goliath, "All this assembly shall know that the Lord saveth not with sword and spear." For in this way there could be no manifestation of God. Afterwards when by the defenselessness of David, God had manifested Himself, the entire host of the Israelites became at once filled with courage, and rose up and used their weapons to advantage. They were all as dead men in influence till the Lord's stripling had glorified God. And it may be when once the true missionary, formed of God after the Gospel model, has made his appearance, then the entire body of Christ's servants will be filled with new faith and energy, and will turn to good account the position in which the Lord has placed them.

Matt. 6:19, 21. The substance is simply this, cut yourself loose from all resources but Christ. The reason is given in the 21st verse, namely that we may be thus bound more closely and intimately to Christ. As an infant at the breast is attached to the mother by the tie of absolute necessity, so Christ would have us bound to Him. He hates everything that tends to weaken our sense of dependence on Him. Therefore He would have His disciples live like the ravens, not knowing whence tomorrow's bread shall come, save that Christ shall give it. He would have them live by the faith of the Son of God. It is love that urges Him to make war upon our temporal possessions. For the same cause He hated the horses which the Jews brought up from Egypt.

Jan. 29. As usual this morning reviled, pushed, threatened, &c., and my books torn up. This thought afterwards came into my mind: in suffering these things, I do for Christ what He has done for me. The rage and enmity of the people are not against me, but against my Master. If I would only let the Name of Christ alone, they would bow down to me. I stand in His place, and receive the reproaches meant for Him. Now this is what He did for me, only a million times more. He was my substitute and suffered the wrath that would otherwise have fallen on me. He manifested His amazing love by standing between me and wrath; and

I manifest what love I have by standing between Him and wrath. Should I not rejoice unspeakably in this blessed prerogative? In this way let me fill up that which is behind of the afflictions of Christ. These afflictions are Christ's because they are intended for Him, and are inflicted by His enemies. And if we suffer with Him we shall also reign with Him.

A man told me this morning that he had never seen a Christian who showed by his conduct that he was different from other men.

Jan. 30. It is five years today since E. M. died. How slowly has the seed then sown by Christ expanded. How immature and far from proper fruitfulness. A most ungenial soil received that seed. The tree has still to contend with choking thorns and briars.

Where am I now? In this resolution, viz., that come what will, by the grace of God I will put myself in a position where all men shall see that I am the disinterested servant of Christ. By the help of God, I will honor the Gospel and conform myself to it with all strictness. I will forsake all that I have, and follow Christ. In the *Daily Food* is this text for the day: "He that hath begun a good work in you will perform it until the day of Jesus Christ."

The mob this day tore the books out of my hands and carried off between thirty and forty. I think they must have been surprised by my equanimity. I was as unmoved as I was in my own room. The people gnash with their teeth upon me; and in many ways testify, as I pass along, their hatred. I am a good way from Calvary yet.

Told Bro. W. this day the resolution lately formed. He, of course, disapproved of it and said there was not a missionary here, nor anyone at home, who would approve. . . . I know how it will be. I shall be considered presumptuous in disregarding the examples and opinions of all my predecessors in this work. "Heady, high minded, wise in his own conceit," some will say. Others, "enthusiast, fanatic."

A brother sitting in his carriage, was drawn up the ghat by sixteen men.

Feb. 2. "When a man is so far advanced in the Christian life, as not to seek consolation from any created thing, then does he first begin perfectly to enjoy God." It is long I think since I have realized and leaned upon the all-sufficiency of Christ; but I have not glorified Him, nor benefited His cause by giving proof of it to the world. It was my duty so to live that men might see with their eyes, that Christ is all-sufficient to me, and having Him, I need nothing else. A man does not light a candle to put it under a bushel. There are greater obligations resting on me, to forsake all things, than on others; for others are not acquainted with the all-sufficiency of Christ as I am; and they have yet to experience a struggle already experienced by me.

His right course of action was perfectly clear to Bowen's mind and he wrote, accordingly, "To the Members of the Bombay Mission" as follows:

Bombay, Feb. 1, 1849.

After much reading of the Word of God, reflection and prayer, I have come to the conclusion that God would have me adopt a different mode of life from that I have hitherto led.

Ever since I joined this Mission my mind has been more or less dissatisfied, and more or less the subject of doubt as to the propriety of my conforming to the example of my brethren of this and other missions. But through fear of being charged with presumption, through deference to those whose experience and years give weight to their example, through a sense of the importance of caution in a question of this kind, I have refrained from any decided action hitherto. I have suffered an entire year to go by, during which I have had ample opportunities, I think, of becoming acquainted with the arguments in favor of the mode of life hitherto observed by missionaries in India; and the result is a conviction that as far as I am myself concerned, a change of life is imperatively required.

It has been impressed upon me that in order to have the blessing of God resting on me and on my labors, I must conform my life so far as circumstances will permit, to that which was delineated by Christ in His instructions to His disciples, and which they afterwards exhibited, as we find it recorded in the Acts and Epistles. And I have come to the resolution, that by the grace of God, I will strenuously endeavor to lead a life like that of the first preachers of the Gospel, who received more signal tokens of the favor of God than have been enjoyed by any since, and who have been repeatedly and expressly recommended to the church as models, by the Holy Ghost.

So far as this I think every true Christian must go with me and wish me well. But when I state my views of what it is to imitate the first disciples, some true Christians may possibly withhold their approbation and sympathy. Sensible—as before said—of the great need of caution in adopting views different from those entertained by the church, I have borne my burden of doubt, indecision, self-condemnation, long; and it is only after many a struggle and the most assiduous study of the Word of God, that I have adopted views of duty in this matter different from those entertained by my brethren. The views substantially are these:

It is of sovereign importance that those great features of Christianity upon which our Savior so urgently insisted, such as self-denial, humility, disregard for wealth, ease, comforts, honors, etc., should be embodied in the lives of those that preach the Gospel. It is not enough to be conscious of possessing those characteristics; the manifestation of them to those we preach to, is a great exigency of the Gospel, set forth by our Lord in language most unequivocal. The plea that some superiority of position is needed for the sake of influence, however specious, must be illusive, because no value is set upon it in the Gospel.

It is of great importance that there should be an exhibition of faith in Christ. Not simply that there should be faith; but that there should be given the most decided and undeniable proof of it by the preacher of the Gospel; and there proof should be of a character suited to the peculiar condition of those he addresses. This principle of faith should be embodied in his life. It was wonderfully exhibited by the apostles. There was that in their lives which forced upon all beholders the conviction that they were living by the faith of the Son of God.

I am at a loss to see how by any possibility, living as I now do, I can fairly exhibit these things to the mass of those I preach to. The house I live in, the servants that wait upon me, the food prepared for me, and numberless other particulars hinder them from discovering in my life the characteristics mentioned. I may manifest them to others, but not to the heathen. They will not discover self-denial in my conduct, perhaps not even disinterestedness, so long as I occupy a position which they regard as superior to theirs in worldly advantages.

It will perhaps be said that these remarks are grounded upon ignorance of the native character. Their respect for us is based solely upon our superior social position; and if we bring ourselves down to their level, the only result will be that they will cast off restraint, and express in their conduct the feelings of aversion and hatred they entertain for the Gospel. I would say in reply that the question of native character has nothing to do with the question of my duty. Christ knew the character of all men. He knew that the manifestation of self-denial, faith in Him, disregard of worldly possessions, repentance, humility, would be the poorest of recommendations to His disciples in the sight of the world; nevertheless, He commanded these things. My view is this, that by a life favorable to the exhibition of these things, I shall enjoy a larger measure of His favor, and may expect a more decided display of His power in conjunction with my preaching. This is my one ground of confidence. My faith is altogether in Christ and not at all in the life which I propose leading.

The question has been with me, What is *my* duty, rather than, What is the duty of missionaries. It has seemed to me that my position was in some respects a peculiar one, and that a line of conduct might be proper for me which would not be for others, and vice versa. And I am not at this time discussing the duty of others, but simply what I conceive to be my own.

From what I have written, dear brethren, you may gather that I propose with your consent adopting a style of life calculated to exhibit to the heathen self-denial and indifference to the world, in other words, a life of poverty.

Furthermore I have concluded to renounce from this day the salary which I have hitherto received, and to support myself in some way, other than by the Gospel. I do this upon the ground of expediency; it seems to me the end I have in view may be more perfectly attained in this way. Expedient for myself I say; I have no thought of deciding for others. I plead in this the example of Paul. Peter with a sound conscience could live by the Gospel; but Paul attached so much importance to a contrary course, that he declared he would sooner die than abandon it. I suppose that in order to obtain the means of subsistence, it will only be necessary for me to devote a few hours daily to secular business.

It is with pain I submit these views to you, because I know they do not correspond with your view. Indeed the greatness of this trial is more than I can express. The trial I refer to is in adopting a course that may meet with the disapprobation of those I love and respect. All the rest is light and bearable.

That the Lord Jesus Christ, our common Savior and Master, may guide both you and me, and cause all that we do to work together for the advancement of His kingdom is the prayer of your affectionate brother and co-laborer,

George Bowen

How did this action of Bowen's affect his four relationships: to his family at home, to the American Board which had sent him to India, to his fellow missionaries and to the people for whom he had come to labor?

First, from his home letters:

Jan. 16, 1849. About the new year I went on a little tour through the Island Salsette, in company with a dear native brother. We went on foot and without a servant, and nothing could be more agreeable and less troublesome than our mode of journeying. At night, for instance, we would stop in the porch of some native house, or wherever we discovered a vacant piece of ground with a roof over it. We would always find somebody to cook for us, (bread was all we wanted generally, sometimes vegetables); and I learned a good many years ago you know that knives and forks and the like were by no means indispensable. We would arise before daybreak and travel by moonlight. I judge we walked about eighty miles. Opportunities of preaching, arguing and distributing books were frequent. On reaching my house in Bombay again, I found that quite a metamorphosis had been effected through the kindness of Mrs. Hume, who had asked me for the key when I left. She had sent her servants and whitewashed the walls, covered the floor with matting, filled the handy with ice, the canisters with tea and sugar, the kitchen with wood, the bottles with oil, etc., etc. She did it, I understand, with trepidation, but how could I be otherwise than grateful for the kindness? I know this will please Ma; for it is much in her way. At present I overflow; I don't know what to do with my temporal superabundance. It seems as though the poorer I tried to make myself the richer I become.

I continue teaching and enjoy very much the time I spend in that family. Mr. Miles (the head of it) is collector. Mrs. M. is a converted Jewess, a zealous Christian. There are eight or nine children. I teach about half of these. I go at 8.30 a.m. and conduct family worship. I eat breakfast with them, and then spend an hour in teaching, that is all. Nothing could exceed their kindness, and they seem to regard it as a great favor on my part.

Those discussions at the seaside, continue. I was surprised to find the report of them spread abroad through the country. . . . I will tell you of a little incident. Narayan sent to me to know if I would go with them on that excursion. I didn't know whether the Lord wanted me in Bombay or in Salsette; so I could give no answer, but promised to let him know in the afternoon. About noon I examined into my finances, and found I should only have money enough to fulfill certain impending obligations; and came to the conclusion that it was not the Lord's will I should go. But if it should be, He could still manifest it in some way. Not a quarter of an hour after these conclusions the postman came with a letter which was merely an envelope covering ten rupees, abundantly enough for my expenses. So I knew that I was to go.

Feb. 12, 1849. I believe when I wrote last, I had begun the practice of visiting the thoroughfares of this city every morning with books. I have kept it up regularly till the present time. Since the beginning of the year, I have disposed of 1,200 books, and we are obliged to sell them to keep them from being destroyed. I am out about three hours, and have abundant opportunity of making known the Gospel. I am pretty well known all over the city, and, must I say it, exceedingly hated. But it is not me they hate, it is my Master, and because they cannot reach Him, they lay hands on me. I have been pretty roughly treated. I am often struck and pushed; they have many times knocked off my hat and tried to throw me down; sometimes they have wrenched all my books out of my hand, and either destroyed them or carried them off; and on one occasion I walked for more than a quarter of a mile, pelted with stones, and followed by perhaps a hundred Mussulmans. A Parsi was much moved at the sight, took me by the hand and led me into his store, where I sat for a few minutes, and then went on my way, still followed, and molested.

I have been warned at certain times not to go into certain quarters, for the people were preparing to beat me. I may say that in the exceeding goodness of God, my soul is kept at such times in perfect peace. There is not the least rising of fear or anger. The policemen do not interfere; I feel that I am alone with my God; but what more do I want? He is able to make me triumph single-handed over this great population. Their hostility is more marked from day to day as they see my evident purpose of forcing the Gospel before their notice. I am looking for speedy displays of the power and grace of God. I have written, printed and sent a letter to my missionary brethren of all denominations, upon the proper mode of life for a missionary. My mind has been much drawn to the subject, and I have become thoroughly convinced that we have hitherto been in error on the subject, and that the ministerial standard of the New Testament is the only safe standard for us. And I have determined that by the grace of God, I will put myself in that position which I think Christ has marked out for me, and in which alone I think I can enjoy the ample blessing of God upon my labors.

My dear, dear friends, I had anticipated the happiness of contributing somewhat to your support; but the time has come when I must commit you again to my Savior, trusting to Him to make up many-fold my deficiencies. I have felt it incumbent on me, for reasons perhaps, that no one not occupying my position can appreciate, to renounce my salary; and I have done so. I expect henceforth to support myself. In this there will be no difficulty. The style in which I expect to live will not require me to spend more than two or three hours a day, as a writer probably in some public office. Why do I do this? Because I feel the absolute importance of exhibiting Christianity in its strong distinctive features in my life. It must be acted out, or this people will never know it, though hundreds of missionaries live and die preaching the Gospel among them. There is no precept requiring me to renounce my salary but I have the example of Paul, and I think the spirit of the Gospel carried to its full length would lead a person situated as I am to adopt this course. My situation is in many respects different from other missionaries.

Tomorrow I expect to leave the mission premises, and take up my abode in another and very different place, in the house of a poor man, a Christian. Of course I give pain to my brethren. But the fear of giving pain has kept me silent, a whole year, and I concluded it is better to give them pain than to give it to Christ. For I found a wall in my path, and a vault of brass over me; and God told me that I would in vain beat against that wall and my prayers in vain assail that vault, till I obeyed the word of His Gospels and destroyed the discrepancy which the natives saw between my life and my preaching.

Since writing the foregoing I have taken the step referred to and am now occupying a humble room in a humble house, probably such a one as Simon the Fisherman lived in in Capernaum and who had Christ for his guest. My soul is filled with peculiar joy and gratitude. A load is removed that I have borne a long time. Things are told in a few words which have cost me long, long struggles. I am living with a Christian in the style that native converts would be expected to live in. I have often heard the question agitated, how shall converts live? If they live like missionaries, and are admitted to their table, they will be lifted up with pride; and if they do not, invidious comparisons will be made, and discontent be engendered. I think this difficulty is only to be solved by a course like that I am now pursuing.

Bowen wrote, of course, to Dr. Anderson, the Secretary of the American Board in Boston, explaining the course which he felt obliged to take. His letter was dated February 14, 1849:

Bombay

Dear Brother in Christ,

I beg to call your attention to the enclosed pamphlet, as your perusal of it will spare me the necessity of writing you at great length, concerning certain views that have been lately matured in my mind, and certain steps that I have deemed it advisable to take. Ever since my arrival in this country my mind has been more or less occupied with the question, Is the mode of life followed by my missionary-brethren, exactly that which is most favorable to their success as missionaries? Is it not possible that some other life might be more favorable? And as these brethren, even, would not assert that this mode of life is positively insusceptible of improvement, I judged that I was not at all sinning against the law of love, in taking up this question seriously and with reference to personal duty. To personal duty I say; for I have not so much occupied myself with the question what ought missionaries in general to do, as with this. What does it become me in my circumstances to do? For it seemed to me that there was something peculiar in my circumstances, and that a course might possibly be expedient for me, which would not do for others. The two questions are connected, and the one could not well be agitated without the other; but as I have said, my attention has been chiefly directed to this last.

There has been for years in my mind a growing sense of the importance of being conformed, in kind as well as degree, to the Gospel standard. That standard was given by a Being of infinite wisdom; One Who had perfect knowledge of man, and of the means best adapted to influence him; One Whose words were uttered with a prescience of all coming things. The apostles were conformed to that standard, and in the success of their labors, God gave full proof of the suitableness of that standard. The apostles were missionaries. Were missionary operations a new thing in the world, the missionary character a new character, and not even noticed in prophecy, we would be left to the guidance of our own wisdom to the gradual teaching of experience in determining what constitutes the true missionary life. But it is not so. There are few subjects on which more copious information is given, directly or incidentally, in the New Testament than this; and perhaps none whose details are more nicely marked out. And the world at the present day to be operated on by missionaries, is substantially the same with that which the apostles were sent to operate upon. In view of these things, it seemed to me that a prayerful study of the New Testament with reference to a decision of this question, was a course not to be reprehended.

I have pursued this course; and the results have been a conviction that God would have me adopt a style of life different from that in which I have hitherto lived. I made known this conviction to the brethren of this Mission about a fortnight ago. While they could not adopt it themselves or admit the expediency of the course I had determined upon, they would not throw any obstacle in my way. I have since then left the mission premises, and am now living in a very humble style. I could not live in this way, and continue in receipt of my salary; for the impression on many would then be that I had adopted this life in order to save money. Other reasons conspired, in a word I felt it necessary in order fully to carry out the principles which I had adopted for my own guidance, that I should renounce my salary altogether. This involves the necessity of resorting to some means of livelihood out of the Gospel; but there seems no doubt that by spending two or three hours a day as a writer in some office, I may earn all that I shall require for my support, viz., fifteen or twenty Rupees a month. The great trial in this is of a moral nature. I regard the physical privations as not worthy to be named. It will be a considerable trial to abstract any time for secular pursuits, for which I have no manner of taste. But the chief trial is in taking a step that will not be approved by my brethren here, perhaps not by the Secretaries and Committee of the A. B., perhaps not by any portion of the church at home. It is not without much suffering that I have brought myself to this step. I have not counted upon the sympathy of a single individual in adopting this course. I have been led to it, by a deep persuasion that God would withhold His blessing from my labors, if I did not adopt it. Nor has it been with any expectation that my new life would tend to propitiate the natives with the Gospel. I have been prepared even to meet with increased opposition from them. But I am convinced that all true progress of the Gospel, must be through the displayed power of God alone. He works by means, but what means? Not such as men use to effect their purposes; but those which will favor the manifestation of His own glory. My confidence is not in the life I am adopting, but in that favor of God which I think will rest upon me, if I conform to the regulations of the Gospel.

On the 1st of this month, I made known to the Mission my intention of renouncing my salary from that date. It may be said in connection with this, that such a course tends to ease the church of her obligations and in just that measure to inflict an injury upon her. But not so. Missionary operations are everywhere greatly contracted and curtailed, by the deficiency of funds. Those operations might well be enlarged ten times. This is the great plea urged upon the church, namely, that our operations need to be greatly enlarged. So that when a missionary gives up his salary, the church is not relieved of her burden, but an opportunity given for expansion in other directions.

I feel very thankful to God, that my brethren of this Mission have shown a disposition to bear with me in what they regard as an unscriptural and erroneous course; and that it does not at all appear, that our feelings of sympathy and affection will be marred. My desire was never greater than it is now, to labor in the mission and for the Mission.

I very earnestly desire that the Board will not see it necessary to dissolve my connection with them.

If there is anything in my course which still calls for explanation, I can only refer to the Sermon on the Mount; and also, to the enclosed pamphlet, in which the process by which I have reached this decision is sufficiently indicated, to come to light, when a steady attention is directed to it.

May the Lord Jesus Christ give you of those treasures of wisdom that dwell in Him, to guide you in your most responsible situation. Believe me ever affectionately,

Yours,
George Bowen.

Dr. Anderson replied in a way that indicated that Bowen's surrender of salary need not involve his separation from the Board, and Bowen answered on Dec. 15, 1849:

Bombay.

My dear Brother,

I have to acknowledge yours of July 21, 1849, which was a letter grateful to my feelings, assuring me as it did that my present course is not regarded as necessitating a rupture of the relations between us. And I am thankful for the measure of approbation you are kind enough to pronounce, which, though limited, is greater than I have received from other quarters. (I allude to missionary stations). In conformity with your advice I have given up my intention of writing in a public office, and am now supporting myself by giving instruction in a private (Christian) family. I teach during an hour and a half daily, and receive ten Rupees monthly, which suffices for my expenses. And let me add that I was never living more comfortably or pleasantly, or with less of household embarrassment; and further I have never enjoyed better health than during the past year. You err in regarding my course as an experiment. I do not think I would have had the moral courage to deviate thus from the course of all my brethren, unless urged by deep convictions of duty. I expect by the grace of God to pursue my present course while I live. Should I fall sick I would thankfully avail myself of the privileges of every poor European, and go to the hospital. I am willing to be regarded as having no more claim on the American Board of support, than before I became connected with it.

I am on the same terms of friendly intercourse with the brethren of this Mission that I was before. There does not appear to be the slightest interruption to the kindly feelings that existed from the beginning and there was no occasion for your soliciting their favorable regard for me.

I thank you for the encouragement "to write on all subjects with the utmost freedom," and for the promise of "such strictures and suggestions as you may be able to make."

I do not altogether assent to what you say about the avoidance of violent extremes, and the example of Paul in that respect. It seems to me that Paul was in things he deemed important, a man of extreme measures. He made himself all things to all men, where the great principles of Christianity were not involved, but then great principles could not receive a fit embodiment in his life without such measures as would shock public sentiment.

The Sermon on the Mount manifestly and copiously enjoins violent extremes. Almost every word of it did violence to the public sentiment of those days, and a great deal of it to the public sentiment of these. For instance 5:39 to the end and 6:19 to the end. To eat with publicans, sinners, was an extreme measure; to cast out the traders from the temple was another; to wash the disciples' feet another. His friends and others thought Him mad, and sought to restrain Him. Paul was also judged to be beside himself. The first measures adopted by the church after Pentecost, and they are recorded with evident commendation, were violent measures, such as must have given a shock to society in

Jerusalem. See Acts 2 the end and 4 the end. We are to be a peculiar people. Luther went to an extreme on the Nov. 1, 1579; and the Puritans won their name by the violence of their measures.

I dwell on this because I think it is just here the church is lacking. There is a great shrinking from abrupt measures. Christ commands the church to go five miles an hour. She is actually going two, and if an individual would give an example of obedience, let him go two and a half. No, I say, let him go five and shock the church into a sense of her supineness and a recollection of the true commands. In most things processes are desirable; in some things abruptness is necessary. Ask the heads of families, one rich and now bankrupt, and who are seeking by a slow and long drawn out process of retrenchment to descend into a lower position in society, if they do not find the attempt prodigiously difficult. A change of conduct, to be in the nature of example and influence others, must be apparent; the more apparent the better; but if gradual it is unobserved. See Luke 19:8, and 18:22. Earthquakes are predicted in the latter times; moral earthquakes doubtless, churchquakes, I think.

It seems to me that everyone who has fed much upon the promises of the Bible must be surprised at the quantity of results witnessed hitherto at missionary stations, or rather at the little that is actually accomplished by the church generally. Up to the present moment the world's population has been gaining on that of the church. There probably were never more idolaters in the world than there are this moment.

Brother Ford says in a recent letter there must be some worm at the root of the tree of modern missions which withers its leaves and blights its fruit. This is my conviction. Man pines to think, when success does not appear, that our methods or instrumentalities must be wrong. We give too much attention to educational measures. Or we do not give enough. Or we do not tour enough. Or we must train up native teachers. Or we must print more. But I do not think the fault is in our mode of presenting the Gospel. If in other respects we were right, none of these instrumentalities would be so feeble as they are. The difficulty is that our communication with God, the source of all right influence, is not what it should be. We want power with God. And what is worse, there is no adequate sense of the deficiency. The many discoveries of modern times, the numerous means of facilities for carrying on the work of missions, the elaborate organizations at home and abroad, the spirit of the age itself, all these have proved a snare to the church. It has led Christians, ministers and missions to trust in these things.

God, I think, has become less prominent in the scheme of modern missions, just in proportion to the increase and perfection of machinery, literal and moral, in that scheme. Obedience and faith are the great disiderata. Probably the church will not make a great progress in these things until she has been brought to an almost despairing sense of helplessness. For myself I feel that just according as I make progress in these things, I advance towards the goal of my hopes, namely an abundant harvest of Maratha souls.

I have been considerably interested in a discussion lately carried on with some Parsis. It is now eight or ten weeks since they began, between myself and a converted Brahmin of the Free Sc. Church on the one side, and a Parsi on the other. The discussions have been carried on, by the seaside, at a place where the Parsis come to worship the sea and the setting sun, and we have often had as many as 200 auditors. We are accustomed to sit down on the sand, the multitude standing about, and sometimes have continued disputing till two hours after dark. It shows how much this people are interested in religious discussions, that they would be willing to stand for three hours or more, hearkening to us. Occasionally the Parsi speaker has given way to Hindu, Mussulman and Jewish interlocutors. On one occasion, even a Roman Catholic priest took part. Tom Paine has also acted a considerable part, with Voltaire and other infidel writers, with whose works or arguments, the educated Parsis and Hindus are surprisingly familiar. I cannot see that any change has been effected in the mind of the principal speaker, who up to the present time maintains the doctrine with which he set out, that God is the author of all sins, and that we have no responsibility connected with them.

I close with the remark that I am altogether satisfied with my present field of labor, and am grateful to God for the privilege of laboring in this important place.

Yours affectionately in the Gospel,
George Bowen

Jan 10, 1850. This letter has been unintentionally delayed a month. A part of this month I have spent in a tour among the towns and villages of Salsette, made in company with the convert mentioned above. We went on foot and took no servant. We walked about eighty miles, generally taking the earliest and the closing hours of the day. I never performed any journey with less trouble. We never failed of finding a spot of ground to lay our quilt on with a roof overhead, or somebody (Mussulman, Parsi or Portuguese) to bake bread for us. I was surprised to find even in these villages, many who have reached what I regard as the *ne plus ultra* of depravity, namely boldness to deny their own sinfulness and responsibility, and to blame God for all that is called sin. I conclude my letter with a couple of items of rather painful interest, one is that at this present moment, A. D. 1850, they are erecting in Bombay, massive substantial Hindu temples that look as though designed to stand the shocks of ten centuries; the other, that the principal of the Government College in Bombay where 1000 pupils receive an education from English professors, is an infidel and freely ridicules the Christian religion before the pupils.

Yours,
G. B.

Bowen's fellow missionaries behaved toward him as the true Christians they were. His course, as his statements clearly indicated, was an indictment of the mode of life of the missionary body and of the consecration of his associates, but the relations between him and them were undisturbed for five years. Mr. Hume evidently replied to the communication of Feb. 1, addressed to the Mission, and Bowen answered under date of Feb. 13, 1849:

Dear Brother Hume,

I thank you for your note, which seems to have been dictated by a spirit of true kindness, and in which you do me all the justice I could expect. To conclude this subject, I beg leave to suggest:

1. That while missionaries may be firmly convinced that their mode of life is most suitable, they ought not to demand of every new missionary that he should judge it to be so, or find fault if he thinks some other mode more suitable. The missionary receives no instructions at home binding him to adopt on matters of this kind the example of his brethren already in the field; his liberty on arriving must be unimpaired in this respect. And if he through deference to his brethren or desire for information postpone the decision for a year, much less should fault be found with him.

2. The mode of life generally observed by missionaries has not received that signal and unequivocal attestation from Heaven, has not been attended with that triumphant success, which would forbid our trying a different mode of life. No great fault is found if a missionary comes out and spends thrice three times or four times the salary of an American missionary; but when a step is taken in the other direction the greatest apprehensions are entertained. Everyone that loves the Lord Jesus Christ must be intensely interested in the question, What is the best way of obeying the last command? If it shall soon appear that I move in this matter without the blessing of God, then will the confidence of other missionaries in their own course be strengthened, and new missionaries will be less embarrassed in settling the question of their duty.

3. "Who is he that will harm you, if ye be followers of that which is good?" However much pain this step may cause, I believe that God will not let any permanent injury to the cause come out of it. The more the step I am now taking may be a deviation from the Gospel standard, so much the more honor will eventually redound to those who have not taken this step. And when one remembers that there are some at home who entertain suspicions as to the expediency of the life now observed by missionaries, it will surely be a good thing to be able, by my example, to remove those doubts; I mean in case God should disown my present course.

Dear Brother, I heartily reciprocate your expression of amity, and shall earnestly pray that this matter may be overruled for our more intimate union eventually.

Yours in Christ,
George Bowen

This course of action adopted by Bowen was warmly commended by the non-missionary foreign community, which had no thought of imitating it, but which regarded this as the way missionaries should live. His fellow missionaries disapproved but sought to help him as fully as he would allow. Mr. Hume thoughtfully wrote to Mrs. Bowen and the sisters on June 21, 1849:

Since our dear brother Bowen joined us, now nearly eighteen months since, I have often, very often, thought of you, and of the anxieties you would feel on his account. This was the case particularly during the time of his illness when we thought it more than probable you would soon hear that his work on earth was ended, and that he had been removed to a higher service and a better world. Had such been the will of God we should have sorrowed not for him, but for the poor benighted heathen to whom he had come, to publish the glad tidings of salvation. And I need hardly add, that our hearts would have bled for you. But the Lord had mercy on us and on the poor heathen, and still spares him to labor for the salvation of souls.

Since our Brother relinquished his salary and moved from the mission premises, we have thought of you, and feared that you might, in consequence of this step on his part, have much painful anxiety on his account. You will naturally think of him as destitute of comforts and exposed to hardships which may affect his health and his usefulness. My object in writing this note is, if possible, to relieve in a measure these anxieties. Let it then be a comfort to you to know that one so dear to you is among those who love him as a Brother, and who are disposed to do all in their power to render him comfortable and happy. In case of sickness we should endeavor to have him removed to our house where we might watch over him as much as in us lies, supply the want of his own dear Mother and Sisters. And although Bombay is a heathen city, there are a number of the Lord's chosen people among the English residents, who would count it a privilege to do for him all that his circumstances might require. He has relinquished his support from the Board, but his salary is still at his service as before in case he should wish or require it.

We are all very sorry that our dear Brother saw it his duty to adopt his present course, which we cannot see to be required by Scripture nor to be fitted in any way to promote his usefulness. But we ceased to dissuade him as soon as we saw that he felt constrained by a sense of duty. We would have him act not according to our opinions and wishes, but according to his own conscientious convictions of duty. In this way and only in this way, could he be happy. And with an approving conscience he will not be unhappy. Would that many who expend their hundreds and thousands on bodily comforts were as comfortable and happy as he. I do not think that any serious evil can arise from the course which Bro. Bowen sees it his duty to pursue. The only fear is that his health may suffer, but such does not thus far appear to be the case. He is always with us on Wednesday eve. at our Mission prayer meeting, and we see him once or twice a week besides in addition to the Sabbath. He always appears cheerful and well, as well now for aught I can see, as at any time since he came to the country. We have again and again warned him against exposing himself too much to the sun from which I think there is more to fear than any other cause. He, I doubt not, suffered from the effect of this formerly and I fear he is still not so careful as he should be. You may caution him strongly on this point, but I do not think you need to press him to change the plan of life he has adopted in other respects. We would often try to do something for his comfort which we do not attempt, lest it should be a trouble instead of a comfort.

The course which Bowen had now adopted he pursued consistently for his whole remaining life of nearly forty years. He received no salary from any missionary board, but supported himself by his teaching and writing. How he fared for the first year of his experiment is set forth in his journal and "Reminiscences":

"Reminiscences, 203." The stipend of an unmarried missionary of the A. B. C. F. M. was Rs. 90 a month, and after his father's death, Homunculus had been sending about half of this to his mother and sisters. This he could no longer do. But there proved to be no need. In other ways the Lord supplied their need.

Mention has been made (Feb. 3) of a miserable man encountered in the streets, who had once been a soldier and tried for murder, and who seemed to be desirous of turning to the Lord. His name was Whitefield. He was living with an old couple, a pensioner and his wife, near Waree Bunder, under Nowrojee Hill. The house had a mud floor and mud walls. A tree was growing out of one of the walls; it was in the midst of a cluster of similar houses occupied by Portuguese and Natives; there was a spare room; and H. was quite delighted when the old people agreed to give him this room and mess him. (The house has long since been swept away and the whole neighborhood altered). So on the 13th of February he left the Mission House and repaired to this place. Before he left, Mrs. H. for whom he had the highest regard and to please whom he would have made any sacrifice except of what he believed to be duty, and who thought his course a most unhappy one for himself and the Mission, besought him with tears not to take this step. It was most painful to go contrary to the wishes and convictions of his best friends in this country; but the same Lord that enabled him to obey his convictions, enabled him to retain the friendship and regard of those whom he thus grieved, from whom he never ceased to receive tokens of kindness.

Journal Feb. 13. At length, thanks be to God, I am in that situation which I have so long desired to be in. . . . The Lord did not more truly guide me to India, than He has guided me to this humble spot. Were the apostle Paul in Bombay, I should be far more content in receiving him where I now am, than where I have hitherto been. The brethren think my course unwise and unscriptural and my views contracted. God will show in due time. . . . Lord God, I give Thee thanks. . . . On opening my Bible the first text that met my eye was "Now there was found in it a poor wise man, and he by his wisdom delivered the city."

April 16. Have this day removed to other quarters. Satan, from the beginning, was endeavoring to drive me out of that house. There was a wonderful manifestation of his power there. I do not remember to have ever been in the midst of greater wickedness. I suppose this formed a part of the trial to which it pleased God at this time to subject my faith. But with great thankfulness to God I can testify that the tempter was quite unable to make me swerve a moment from my path, or cease to confide in Him that leadeth me in a way unknown. I am now very agreeably situated in a little house formerly occupied by some Native members of our church, where I am all the day alone, and at night my companion is a man whom God has made me I trust the means of delivering.

"Reminiscences, 213." The house referred to was engaged at a monthly rental of Rs. 8. It was situated in the heart of Oomerkhady. Some five years were spent in it. Perhaps it should be stated that the writer continued, as before, to work with the missionaries, taking part in the services, preaching in his turn, visiting some half a dozen vernacular schools regularly, and was generally ready to do whatever he was asked to. He visited the missionaries frequently and was always kindly welcomed by them.

July 16. Missionary friends would dissuade me from taking a situation of writer and supporting myself by my own hands. . . . One says: "We are not to degrade the Gospel, or do evil that good may come. . . . When they see you, a regularly ordained missionary go to seek employment as a common clerk, I am afraid it will at least have the appearance of evil in two ways—it will lower the work in which you are engaged, and it will injure the credit of our country as not being willing to support you." If the work is lowered, the Gospel degraded by a missionary's supporting himself, would Paul have done it and gloried in it? Would God have allowed him to do it?

My reasons are these. When I believed in Christ and surrendered myself to Him, it was with a very deep sense of obligation. I felt that while I could never dream of liquidating the debt I owed, yet it was my privilege to give the most explicit proofs of love to the Savior, by devoting myself and all my resources to Him. I could not tolerate the thought of the Gospel being my servant, to work for me; I wanted only to work for it. And when I went out as a Colporteur for two successive years, I refused to take any pecuniary compensation. I shrank back from receiving anything for service rendered Christ. I wonder that the influence of other Christians did not sweep away these romantic notions, as they generally seem. I believe, too, that if I had not associated with theological students and other Christians for three years, I would have come out before the mast, rather than suffer $300 to be paid for my passage. But the influence of the church had so far got the victory over the influence of the Gospel in my heart, that I suffered this expense and others connected with my coming out, to be paid out of the church's funds; and for a year I drew my salary. But God has restored me to my first and better self, and henceforth I desire to give proof to all that I preach the Gospel of Christ purely from love to Christ.

1. I aim to be perfectly conformed to the Gospel standard. Everybody is asking to see this standard embodied; the better the heathen become acquainted with the Gospel, the more they censure Christians.

2. The society I am connected with is in debt. The church does not contribute money enough to carry on the present system of missionary operations. There is a universal cry of money wanted for the work. If missionaries part with their salaries there will be more money for schools, books, &c.

3. Some missionaries receive very large salaries; and in the missionary body generally, there is altogether too much that looks to ordinary men like love of money; and a very strong and startling example is necessary.

4. The work of the Gospel needs to be lowered. It is altogether too elevated. It is away up in the skies above poor publicans and sinners.

5. It is more blessed to give than to receive. Paul quotes these words of Christ in justification of the course pursued by him at Ephesus, and by him recommended to the ministers of Ephesus. If it be said, Give out of your salary, I answer, that would not be my gift, but the church's. It is her liberality and not mine that would appear. I cannot be liberal with that which is another's. I must do as Paul, work that I may have to give.

There were times of great want, however, when not only he had nothing to give but also could not even pay his washerman:

"Reminiscences 230." When the dhobi brought his clothes he had no money to pay him with. He had solemnly promised the Lord that he would never seek any personal aid from any man, either directly or indirectly, as by letting his need be known, and from this engagement has never departed. On the occasion above referred to he carried the matter to the Lord, and help came in due time, though not till patience had been tried.

October 31. Next Monday it falls to my turn to receive the Missionary Conference and breakfast them. But I have no means; scarcely room to receive them, no table-room, no cups, saucers, plates, knives, &c; no money to buy provisions. What is to be done? I leave the matter with my Master.

Nov. 5. The Conference assembled this morning. I was determined to be led by God, whithersoever He might lead me. I imagined that succor might come from some quarter, even at the last moment. I could not bear to think that after partaking of their sumptuous entertainments, I should give them a crust of dry bread. But no succor came, and it became manifest that I must go forward and expose the nakedness of my cupboard to the brethren. I had four pice; the boy who lives with me (Geo. Williams, an orphan boy, whom Mrs. H. had asked me to take charge of, sending him to school) had two; and I was enabled to spread my table with a plate of dry bread, some cold tea and a few plantains. I said, It gives me pain to be so shortcoming in hospitality, but in the providence of God I find myself obliged to treat my brethren to such as I am accustomed to myself.

Nov. 20. Until yesterday for eight days I had not possessed a single pice.

Until now he had been living with a Parsi contractor named Nowroji, as Bowen writes, "a person of some bluster and infinite assurance, and who was never happier than when railing against Christians and Christianity in the midst of a crowd of Parsis and Hindus. He was good-tempered on the whole, but, if one could believe his own statements, something of a libertine; he was ready to uphold Hinduism and Mohammedanism against Christianity, and was very unwilling to have Parseeism brought into the discussion. The Rev. Narayan Sheshadri and the writer were in the habit of going to the Back Bay to preach, and Mr. Nowroji always took care to be there, and bring on a discussion, and large crowds came together, specially to listen to the debates."

Under date of Dec. 15, 1849 Bowen wrote to the Board a letter of which a paragraph about the meetings for Parsis was published in the *Missionary Herald,* May, 1850, p. 175 f:

> I have been considerably interested in a discussion lately carried on with some Parsis. It is now eight or ten weeks since it began between myself and a converted Brahmin of the Scotch Free Church, on the one side, and a Parsi on the other. The scene of debate has been the seaside, at a place where the Parsis assemble to worship the sea and the setting sun; and we have often had as many as 200 auditors. We are accustomed to sit down on the sand, the multitude standing about us; and we have sometimes continued disputing till two hours after dark. It shows how much these people are interested in religious discussions, that they should be willing to stand for three hours or more, listening to us. Occasionally the Parsi spokesman has given way to the Hindu, Mussulman or Jewish interlocutors. On one occasion a Roman Catholic priest participated. These Parsis have also acted a considerable part, with Voltaire and other infidel writers, with whose works or arguments the educated Parsis and Hindus are surprisingly familiar.
>
> *Dec. 3.* It is a year now since I entered on my present phase and since God's truth is in abeyance. How long will the heavenly visitant remain in mid heaven suspended? It seems incredible that I should be thus far and not arrived. I enjoy a sweet serenity today. How many unpossessed of a penny can say the same? I have today entered upon the work of giving instruction in a private family. They offer me Rs. 25. I take Rs. 10 a month. The Lord's goodness appears distinctly in this. Also in delivering me from the evil man who was living with me. I enjoy the luxury of a home again.... The discussions go on, but are very painful, because of the constant demands for miracles.

"Reminiscences 234." The family in which the diarist now became a daily tutor, was that of Mr. H. M., a gentleman occupying a good position in the Customs, a very worthy man, much respected by all who knew him, observant of Christian usages though perhaps not at the time a converted man, very much attached to his family. His wife was a converted Jewess of Cochin, as fair as any European, with a deep sense of religious obligation and a great respect for religious people The family attended the Free Church, of which Dr. Fraser was then pastor. There were eight daughters ranging from infancy to young ladyhood, and one son, George, about sixteen. The tutor continued to teach the elder girls and their successors for about twelve years. His duties were light enough. Going to the house at 8:30 a.m. there would be family worship, then breakfast, and then about an hour of instruction, the aim being to guide their studies for the day and take account of those of the previous day. Once for all, the writer may here express his thankfulness for unmeasured kindness received in this family, during all subsequent years. Great spiritual blessings came to them when the Rev. Wm. Taylor began his work in Bombay, and no scant mention is made of them in his book, *Four Years' Campaign in India.*

Shortly after this he earned a little from his editorship of the *Bombay Guardian* but he lived always in the utmost frugality and self-denial. A few bananas and bread sufficed for his meals. He wore old but clean clothes, giving away any new clothing presented to him. His missionary associates, as already reported, furnished his room for him but he sold or gave away the furniture. A charpoy or a table sufficed for a bed. He took no thought for himself for food or raiment but friends constantly took thought for him. In sending Bowen's letters of Feb. 1 and 13, 1849, found among the papers of Mrs. R. W. Hume, her son, the Rev. E. S. Hume, who followed his parents as a missionary in India for thirty-two years, wrote on March 21, 1906:

> In these letters Mr. Bowen has certainly shown a Christian spirit. Could he have foreseen that, forty years later he would feel moved to say that he did not know of a single person, who had been led to Christ by him, he might have written differently, but perhaps not. He based his action on other grounds than results. He certainly lacked the power to effectually "Draw the net." Also it should be borne in mind that although he refused to draw a salary from any Mission Board, he took most of his meals with missionaries and other Christians, thus saving expense. He knew that he could go at any time to the houses of friends and that he need lack for nothing. Thus he did not live in as inexpensive a way as one might suppose, who hears that he lived on a very small pecuniary income. His income was not money, but free board.

Bowen's mode of life demonstrated to everyone the utter disinterestedness and conscientiousness of the man, but it did not yield the fruitage in persuasive influence which Bowen anticipated. No one, not even St. Francis, has ever been more sincere or thoroughgoing in the subordination of all the comforts and appurtenances of life to life itself and to the great ends of life in the service of God and man, but it would seem to be the lesson of Bowen's life that the main source of fruitfulness and power lies elsewhere then here, that just as the accoutrements of life are to be only means to life's true ends, so the depreciation and repudiation of these means is also to be only means to something deeper and more significant. How far was it so with Bowen? What was the course of his inner life during this year which determined the whole future of his career and work in India? And what developed as to the apparent success or failure of his preaching and teaching? Was there still an element of spiritual ambition and pride in his self-denial?

> *Feb. 3.* Was this morning beaten and pelted with stones. I walked for more than a quarter of a mile with stones falling upon and around me. A Parsi watchmaker felt very much concerned for me, and made me come into his shop. I sat there a few minutes, and then went on my way, still followed, and maltreated by the mob. A man told me that the people were preparing to give me a beating, in a certain place and advised me to turn aside, which I did. . . . The Lord kept me in perfect peace. But I feel that the time of trial is begun. I expect to see the people waxing more and more violent.
>
> *Feb. 7.* Was this day much abused by a Mussulman mob. They ordered me away from the place where I was standing, with threats, took books and tore them up before my face, endeavored to throw me down, and finally tore all the books out of my hand, destroying and carrying off about fifty. They wax more and more violent, and I have much worse to expect. I thank God for the grace given me at such times. But I feel lonely today. My brethren are cool towards me, I think; the people hate me; whom have I but Thee, my Savior? I wait for Thy appearing.
>
> Dreamed last night that I was fishing in a certain place. Suddenly I discovered that there were other nets in the water, cast there by some persons on the other side of a wall, and whom I could not see. I learn by this that if I want to be the first to glorify Christ I have no time to lose. Others in some other part of the world will be before me. How good the Lord to speak unto me thus in the night seasons. I reproach God for His tardiness, and He reproaches me for mine.
>
> *Feb. 15.* I have to drink every morning a cup of contempt and injuries. The people are very bitter. They buy very few books, destroying more than they keep. How long, oh Lord! How long? I spend half the night in prayer, and go forth seeking Him, but find Him not. This book instrumentality is worthless in itself. I have not a single evidence that the 2,000 books lately distributed have done good. . . . Everything is vain. . . . One thing is needful. How long, oh Lord! how long? I desire

death rather than this unprofitableness. My prayer is: Reveal Thy glory, or let me die. . . . My absorbing desire is that these heathen should know God.

16th. The open door seems to be closing. I sell scarcely any books now. As many are destroyed as carried away. The people rage more and more in some quarters.

17th. When Christianity assumes an aggressive attitude, the first result is a great exhibition of Satanic power. Satan's power to be manifested, must be assaulted. The world is now lying in wickedness, as a woman in the arms of her paramour. Nobody knows the power of the god of this world till Christ's soldiers begin their irruptions. There must necessarily be a complete exhibition of Satan's power, before there can be a complete revelation of the power of Christ. This last is the second result of Christian aggression. It is by what He conquers, that Christ's power is to be discovered. . . . The battle-day is dawning. . . . Christianity in India is now pursuing an insidious policy. She deals in ambushes. She employs baits. She has schools where human science and literature are taught, with a slight admixture of religion. She has books that please the eye and hold out promise of entertainment, and which have a few grains of religion hid under the crust. She hires Hindus to do secular work for her, that she may insinuate her doctrines into their ears. I am ashamed of the stand she takes. It does not become a system with which infinite power and infinite grace stand indissolubly connected, to be pursuing this policy. It does not become one possessed of the whole armor of God, to be shooting arrows from a place of ambush. There is nothing in her tactics that sets her forth as the credentialed ambassador of the living God, the bride of God's Son, the possessor of the promises.

Feb. 26. "Thou hast enlarged me when I was in distress." The recollection of what God has done for me in other days, is wonderfully strengthening to my faith and hope. I feel confident that in His own good time God will bring me out into a broad place. Since yesterday I am rejoicing in the love of Christ more than usual. I do not generally feel as I should a lively sense of Christ's love; I get absorbed in an aim, and neglect to meditate upon the secret of the Lord, to look at the name on the white stone which only he that hath the stone can read, in a word, upon that love which passeth knowledge and which is so wonderfully portrayed in the Canticles. I want to feel henceforth the obligation to commune with this most loving Bridegroom when in the streets and surrounded by men. If I may retain at such times a sense of the Savior's presence, and a suitable recollection of who the Savior is, I shall be mightier than all who come against me.

One thought is precious to me this morning, viz., that when Christ's truth is in my heart, Christ is in my heart. "Abide in me and I in you"; and, "If my words abide in you." This is the only way Christ manifests Himself to me, by the Word. He is the Truth, the Word. There is infinite power and infinite love in the Word. The Word is the throne of Christ. Just as a man has true faith, Christ's Word will be to him a manifestation of Christ. I conceive that this thought, with the aid of the Holy Spirit, may be prolific of great results. All things are possible to him that believeth that Christ is in the Word. All my blessings have been out of the Word. What an effect should this thought have on me, leading me to seek the treasures of that Word. God in fact gave me all blessings when He gave me the Word, and I am responsible to take them out. In the Word is that manifold grace of which I have been a steward.

March 4. I am to do a work as great as the apostles did; why should I expect to do it by means inferior to those employed by them? Is there anything in me to compensate for such a deficiency? On the contrary.... Why should I expect to do it with a less measure of the Spirit than they enjoyed? The same end naturally calls for the same means.

I am under no more obligation to obey the commandments of God, than He is to obey His promises. It is no greater transgression in me to break His commandment, than in Him to break His promise. It is not optional with Him to fulfill His promise or not.

March 6. Mark 9:41. "Ye belong to Christ." This is our greatness. Our greatness like our righteousness is imputed. We are great only because all greatness is Christ's, and we belong to Him. If we be the merest infant and belong to Him, we have it. We cannot then esteem ourselves above others. To do so is to put ourselves above Christ.

March 10. He is the head of the body, the Church. What an intimacy! What an interdependence! What can a body do without the head, or a head without the body? So far as regards the manifestation of Himself in this world, Christ can do nothing so long as the church remains divorced from Him. When the body goes, the head goes, and only then.... What is done to the body is done to the head; so we pray for Christ when we pray for ourselves. He is glorified in us. As two lovers violently separated, are only intent on a reunion, so Christ and myself. His desire is towards me and mine towards Him.

March 14. I have been impressed with the thought lately that Christ is a wonderfully jealous Savior. He cannot bear to have us turn our eyes for a moment to anything but Him. And He has a fearful hatred of certain things that entice away the souls of His people, such as money, clothes, &c. ... I was so profoundly impressed with this the other morning on awakening that I felt it absolutely necessary to get rid of what money I had and forthwith proceeded to do it. So that I have not now a penny that I can call my own in the world. I have other things, a great superabundance of clothes, &c., and they weigh heavily on my conscience. I would be exceedingly thankful for an opportunity of getting rid of them. I abhor myself for having suffered these dreadful enemies to come near me. I ought to be at work, earning something for my support; but have no heart to do anything whatever till I get the blessing I seek. I can do nothing but pray night and day. Have fasted for a fortnight.

17th. It bespeaks admirable wisdom in God to take the worst of sinners for the most exalted positions in the church. In this way they are saved from pride. They know that their only merit, the only thing that led God to choose them for these exalted places, has been their preeminence in sin. I pray earnestly that I may be always deeply convinced of this, and remember that I was worse than my fellow-creatures, and chosen on this account. If I remember this, then the more grace I experience, the more my fruitfulness, the greater discovery will there be of my sin. Let me say to myself then, in the day I wait for, my sin must have been immense, to justify God in bestowing such grace upon me.

All nature is full of Christ to me. There are hundreds of birds singing delightfully all the day long about me; and their songs are full of the promises of Christ. Do they not every one of them bear testimony to the cross of Christ, to the truth that God is love? Do they not repeat in my ears, "Ask and it shall be given you." "Whatsoever ye shall ask in My name I will do it." "He that feedeth the ravens will He not much more, &c." Christ created these things to bear His messages to me. This was the great object He had in their creation. They tell me that He is the same yesterday, today and forever. So with the trees, even their tiniest leaf says ever to me, He that hath begun a good work, will He not carry it on to the end? It says, "Though I be nothing but a little leaf, yet God is mine, Christ is mine, all things are mine. The sun, the wind, the air, the rain, all things are made to work together for my good. Therefore have faith in God." . . . The stars that twinkle through the leaves, tell me the same thing, revealing at the same time His mighty power which He is offering to me.

18th. I desire while I live to remember the dealings of God with me since this year set in, in respect to the gracious facility with which He has removed what seemed unspeakable difficulties. I saw myself opposed by obstacles which it seemed to me could not be overcome without very considerable suffering; yet they have been actually removed without any suffering at all. I went forward, trusting in Him, and found the mountain a plain. Christ cannot bear the least suffering on the part of His disciples;

He can better bear all Calvary, and He will only let us suffer when our disobedience and unbelief make it absolutely necessary.

In his diary of May 3, 1849, there is a long covenant into which Bowen entered. He did not refer to this in his "Reminiscences," but it should be quoted as indicating the state of mind and soul in which he was at this time:

I covenant then, from this hour forward, world without end, whithersoever He goeth, to walk as He also walked. To be the light of the world as He was the light of the world. To do as He did always those things that please God. To be the reproduction of Jesus Christ. To live as though mankind were only to have the knowledge of Jesus Christ through me. To be the beginning of the New Jerusalem come down of God out of Heaven. To be the salt of the earth, and live as though I were a mold into which God were to be cast, into which to receive the everlasting stamp of holiness. To be the Truth, as Christ was. To feel that a departure from God's will would be as treasonable and dreadful on my part as it would have been on that of Christ. To be the manifestation of God as Christ was. To be the first-born among my brethren of these latter days, as Christ is the first-born among all. To give the most advanced Christians, higher conceptions of Christ than they have ever had. To fulfill in my own person all the prophecies relating to the coming of the Son of man, the Messiah, the Son of God, God, the Lamb of God, the Judge of all things; the Ancient of days, knowing His words, "I am glorified in them."

I covenant, moreover, to honor the Word of God to the highest possible degree. To give each jot and tittle of it regal authority and dignity. To abase myself in the dust before its least data. To make as much of its least commandments as ever has been made of its greatest. To urge it upon men as something given to be thoroughly fulfilled, which must be fulfilled.

I covenant to honor and reveal the Holy Spirit in all His glorious fullness. To be the reproduction of the Holy Spirit; to give the Holy Ghost more room in the world for the manifestation of Himself, than He has ever had. To give Him that surpassing glory which the Scripture allots to Him in these latter days, when it speaks of the manifestation of the Sons of God.

I covenant to honor and make war upon the pride of man, and lay all his glory in the dust, that God alone may be exalted in that day. To tear away all filthy rags of his righteousness, and show him all his nakedness. I will put the worm and the moth above him. I will make him to loathe his own pride more than the flames of hell. I will take his works of pride all out of his own hand, and lay them at the feet of God. I will stain the pride of all greatness, and the name of every hero shall be as fire in the mouths of those who have paid homage to heroes. I will efface the name of man from the title page of all books, from all monuments, from all works reputed to be of man, and show that all things are of Him, through Him and to Him.

I covenant to be poor in spirit as Christ was, carefully treasuring up the great truth of my own nothingness, and that I only live as God liveth in me, that I can of my own self do nothing, that there is none good save one, that is God. That as regards spiritual life, as regards doing the will of God, there is in me an absolute destitution of resources. There is no more wisdom, strength, holiness or love in me than in a stone; and to commend me for any of these things were as foolish as to commend a stone for them.

I will hate and detest the honor which comes from men, feeling that no man can honor me without robbing God, and I cannot receive it without treason and embezzlement. To fight against this temptation, as against death and hell. I cannot receive the honor of men without receiving their sin. To receive it, to be pleased with it, to desire it, is to make a recantation of all I have yet attained to, and authorize God to break in sunder every golden promise He has given me.

I covenant to receive and welcome the persecution and contempt of man, and all sufferings whatsoever that it may please God to lay upon me. To bear about in my body the dying of the Lord Jesus, that is, to take up my cross daily and follow Him. I covenant to rejoice in soul, however He, for the good of Zion, may see good to afflict me. I covenant to be happy in God, and give the world evidence that He is my satisfying portion, and that a storm of brimstone has no power to take away the bliss He gives me. I covenant to be though sorrowful, yet always rejoicing, that men may know the blessed spiritual nature of that heaven into which we are introduced by faith.

I covenant to show the world and maintain with unbending rigidness the very terms of discipleship laid down by Christ. To say to the rich man, one thing thou lackest, and to all, provide not for yourselves treasures on earth. Except a man forsake all that he hath. Let the dead bury the dead. Consider the ravens.

Above all things, I covenant to labor with my heart, soul, mind and strength, to redeem the church from all iniquity, and purify her unto my Master a peculiar body without spot or blemish or any such thing. To combat with every sin in every member, as I have ever combated with my own sins. To consider the redemption of the world as involved in the sanctification of even the obscurest. To tolerate no sin for any earthly consideration whatever. To look upon the church as Heaven, and her sin as odious as sin would be in Heaven. To regard this as the keystone of this my covenant with God. To look upon every church member, high or low, rich or poor, as Peter, Paul and John; and labor with them, love them, sweat and agonize for them, suffer and die for them, as Christ did for those. This is the special mission on which Christ has sent me into the world. Oh, my God, I beseech Thee write this responsibility in me, in letters of living fire. In order that this commission may be perfectly discharged, dwell Thou perpetually within me with all Thy love and wisdom. By this I shall know that Thou art in me of a truth.

To have no personal privilege, no privacy, no time of my own. To establish Christ's kingdom and the authority of God throughout the world, and cause the whole world to be filled with the knowledge of the glory of God as the waters cover the sea, and perfectly upbuild the new heaven and the new earth wherein dwelleth righteousness, and present every man perfect in Christ Jesus.

All this, which is simply one thing, namely, to serve the Son of God, I covenant to do, by virtue of the covenant which God makes with me, that He will be unto me a God, and will never leave me nor forsake me.

I have made this covenant with Thee by sacrifice, that is by the sacrifice of Thy Son, Whose blood is the blood of the covenant.

Oh, my God, if Thou hast taught me to desire the whole earth be filled with the knowledge of Thy glory, haste, haste, haste Thee to help me.

May 7. Probably the holiest man in the world is he who retains most keenly and unceasingly the sense of his liability to sin. I desire to be that man.

May 20. Preached this afternoon the seventh of a series of discourses on the sufferings of Christ, which have been advantageous to me if not to others. I wonder if there is any other minister, who on the average has preached for the last three-and-a-half years to smaller audiences? This average would be under twenty, I think. And often when I am preaching it seems to me that I have no other auditor than God. The rest are asleep or laughing or musing. . . . I don't know of any good ever being done by my preaching. This has been the particular point of my trial.

To the eye of the Christian, a new creation is going on from day to day around him; he sees the common and despised trees around him becoming trees of paradise. He finds sanctifying influence in everything. The Holy Ghost is exhaled from the leaves of plants. On reaching those high experiences lately, I thought that a great deal I had been learning was now useless; that the laws of God's operations, even of His spiritual operations, were now obsolete, and I was introduced into a world where everything was differently ordered. But I was soon corrected. I found, it is true, that instead of the thorn tree was the fir-tree, and instead of the brier the myrtle; nevertheless the laws of their growth were the same. I find that directions to the impenitent are profitable to me. All the results of my experience were precious to me. Whatever a man soweth that shall he also reap. We shall be astonished to find how much of earth there is in heaven, or rather how much of heaven there was in earth all along. All natural history should be natural theology; for in this shape it is an everlasting science. But natural theology must have a cross on its title page, and over every page.

"Servant of the Lord." "The servant is not greater than his Lord." John 13:15 and 16. 2 Tim. 2:25. "In meekness instructing those that oppose themselves." One great temptation to which I am and shall be exposed, in my zeal for the truth, and against the dishonoring views of God's truth so widely entertained, is to have the command of myself in discussion. The tendency of my nature is to try and bear down all opposition at once, to be violent and headstrong in argument, to be intemperate. I am wanting in meekness at such times, and forget that there is any place then for meekness.

These verses teach that when men oppose, we must:

1. Instruct them, as distinctly and impressively as possible set the truth before them.

2. Do it in meekness, not as though we were any better than they, for what have I that I have not received? and if I have received it, why do I glory, as though I had not received it? I am to remember that God has called me out of still deeper darkness than my opponent is in. And how did He do it? Not by violent and headstrong denunciation, not by sending bitter censors, but by the meekness and long-suffering of a dying Savior. It is love that alone does any good in this world; and it were a poor way to honor the Word of God, to cast away love, in the heat of vindication. Those that have the truth can afford to use meekness, for God is on their side, and all the promises; the meek shall inherit the earth. There is nothing hinders an opponent from seeing the truth, so effectually as violence and bitterness.

3. Do it with a sense of entire dependence on God, for fruit. If God peradventure will give them repentance. . . . The difficulty is in the heart, rather than in the judgment. They are averse to the truth, so that the mere exhibition will, so far from leading them to acknowledge it, only make then the more opposed. What we are trying to bring before their minds is the very thing they hate; and unless God remove their aversion how can our arguments affect them?

4. Consequently do it with prayer—incessant prayer. And by this may be measured the spirit of meekness. We will only be able to offer up true, affectionate prayer, as we have meekness. If we find a repugnance

A Decisive Year, 1849

to prayer, we must take the alarm, let our opponent alone and turn against ourselves.

5. Do it with a recollection of what is really at stake. If they are in error, they are in the snare of the devil. This wily fowler has succeeded in snaring them, and if they are not presently recovered, they will be lost forever. Their immortal souls are at stake.

Remember Dr. White's precept: Grow cool as he grows warm; aggregate amount of temperature in both the same. Distinguish between great things and small.

Matt. 4:4. Man shall not live by bread alone. Satan says, "If thou be the Son of God." Christ answers, "Though I be the Son of God, yet am I man, and am subject to all the appointments of God concerning man." It pleased Christ to bury Himself in His humanity, and to refuse any privileges in which men might not participate.

June 4. It is today three-and-a-half years from the day when He showed His covenant unto me. What a blessed day of confidence was that. How would my joy have been embittered could I have foreseen this heavy day. The 102nd Psalm seems to have been written for me. My bones are burned as an hearth, and my days are consumed like smoke. Smoke is the result of my days. I am accomplishing nothing. God is a scorching sun to me, my heart is smitten and withered like grass. Truly and literally, my bones cleave to my skin, and that probably by reason of the voice of my groaning.

Sept. 12. The same reasons that required me to enter on my present course, probably require that I should remain in it a considerable time. It is to be seen whether I have acted upon impulse or not, and can endure the trials incident to a life of faith. I have had such. Often without a farthing and much distressed because of small debts, (not able to pay the dhobi on his usual day, &c.) I have found myself in the company of drunkards, fornicators and adulterers when I thought myself among Christians. Yet my faith has not failed. I have not dreamed of retracing my steps. It has cost me too much to get here to think of going back again.

Oct. 29. It strikes me at this time that it was a most kindly and blessed providence that selected Paley's *Evidences* as the instrument of my conversion. For the grand argument of Paley is built upon the life which was led by the apostles, their self-denial, perfect disinterestedness, superhuman zeal for the good of man, willingness to suffer, joy in unheard of sufferings, voluntary poverty, meanness of condition and the like. So that the nature of evidences by which I became convinced of the truth of Christianity, was also the means of presenting Christianity to me under one of its most interesting features. My first conceptions of Christianity, when brought to view it as a true system, were of Christianity as revealed in the lives of the apostles. In their lives I found not only the proof, but the thing proved. The religion which I embraced was not the religion of the modern church; no evidence in favor of this could have overcome, I think, my skepticism; but it was the religion of Paul and John. Up to the present moment the church has been trying to alter my standard, and make me a convert to modern Christianity, but without success. And so help me, God, I will never forsake that religion which I have embraced, namely, that which Christ implanted in the hearts of the Twelve. I believe before God that the modern church has been a greater hindrance to me than a help. Why should I profess and follow a religion to which I have never been converted? I was converted by him that converted Timothy; and him will I follow so far as he followed Christ.

Oct. 31. I have been in the habit of looking back on the time spent in the seminary as one in which I was exerting an important influence for Christ. While plainly seeing that all my other Christian work was barren, I fondly thought that I was useful there. But from present indications I must give up even that. Those from whom I hoped the most, do not seem to be any better for my influence. I have now fulfilled five-and-a-half years of Christian sterility, the most useless being in the church. The most pathetic language I ever saw occurred in one of my sister's letters lately. She said that before coming to the knowledge of Christ, a constant source of unhappiness to her was her uselessness. On becoming a Christian she rejoiced in the assurance that now at last she would find a means of benefiting her fellow-creatures. But in this she had been disappointed. And it has been my own experience. Only I know that some day or other we will emerge into usefulness. Our barrenness is God's barrenness. It is He that worketh in us hitherto, and if our working be in vain, His is in vain. But every tree is sterile till the time of fruit comes.

These quotations will be sufficiently illustrative. It must not be inferred from them that Bowen was living unhappily. The Gospel was a joy to him:

May 13. Beloved, if God so love us, we ought also to love one another. Nothing is clearer in my experience than this, that it is only as we have a sense of God's love to us, that we are able to love one another. In order to love our fellow-men it is necessary to know and retain in mind Christ's soul-subduing love to us. In this way God has the glory of all the love we exercise. It is the inevitable effect of the happiness bestowed upon us. Hence the obligation to be happy in Christ.

His diary is a Bible commentary of the richest kind ranging over the Old and New Testaments alike and very full, in this year of Bowen's life, of his interest in prophecy and the prophetic interpretation of human history. In reviewing his journal for 1849 Bowen wrote in 1882:

> The writer of these notes was in 1849 continually looking for the manifestation of Christ's glory, and the eagerness of his expectation enhanced greatly the severity of the trial caused by each day's delay. God had given him his heart's desire with regard to personal experiences revealing His glory in the depths of his soul, and he could not but look upon these inward revelations as the day star betokening the immediate rising of the Sun of Righteousness. But we find that it has not been an unusual thing for God to give great discoveries of Himself to prepare the subject for protracted seasons of comparative desolation. There were exceedingly glorious revelations made to Ezekiel (chs. 1-11) at the beginning of the captivity, introductory to the seventy years of exile and humiliation. Homunculus eagerly scanned the features of each coming day in succession, to see if he could distinguish any tokens of an angelic messenger. The record of his many disappointments would be wearisome, but it may be well to note how far the temptation was often permitted to go.

And he proceeds to quote the journal for May 26-29:

> May 26. I cannot help but pray as Elijah did under the juniper tree. I want to die, I claim the common privilege of dying, rather than living on under these conditions. The blessing of 20th Rev. is no blessing, if I am to be thwarted here. I seem to reach now a point where my solitary life must end, and I am, whether or no, to begin to work again among the people. But to come back among them without any blessing, as poor and denuded as I was before, in fact every way more unfit for laboring among them, would be horrible.
>
> May 27. The most wretched day of my life. God is dealing with me as they sometimes deal with soldiers to whom 500 or 1000 lashes are to be given. They whip them until there is danger of their dying outright and then send them to the hospital. As soon as they are sufficiently recovered, they give them a couple of hundred more, reducing them to death's door again, and then send them back to the hospital and so on. God bruises and crushes me with disappointments, till I am ready to die outright, faith, hope and all; and then He goes to work building me up again in these things; as soon as they have got some maturity again, down comes God again upon me, beating me almost to nothing. And so on. I am weary of hope. God sent me a dozen angels successively to tell me I should find Him today, and now, where is He? I would give much for death. I envy every little bird that sings and flies. I envy the poor blind

heathen beggar, whom no one knows or speaks to, who sits in the sun all the day long, and lies in the damp all night long. It seems as though the curse of God were on me. What greater curse can there be than this, to be consumed by one desire, and to have God utterly hostile to that desire. God seems to me a very dreadful and implacable God, glorying in His power to laugh at suppliants. He is God and I am a worm; and if He has created me to suffer, why, I must suffer. Why has God taken such a mask as this? His own character is not so. But of what avail is His love if He keeps it shut up, and puts on its opposite? I should like to sit with Job on his dunghill, and curse the day of my birth. I can sympathize with Elijah, for I have been very zealous for the Lord God of hosts.

The painful element in it is, that the character of God suffers. His glory is that He is a prayer hearing God, answering speedily, and delighting in mercy, ready to do anything for Christ's sake. How shall I ever pray in faith again? May not every unbelieving Christian mock me for my vain confidence? "Wilt thou break a leaf driven to and fro?" O God, what sort of a victory is this? What glory will there be in breaking a poor withered leaf driven by every puff of wind? Lord, kill me outright at once, and not piecemeal. Let there be no more vain hopes enkindled in me. "Oh that Thou wouldst hide me in the grave, that Thou wouldst keep me secret, until Thy wrath be past, that thou wouldst appoint me a set time and remember me." "He hath taken me by my neck and set me up for His mark." But is He not the potter and I the clay? And what business have I to find fault with His processes? Did I not years ago offer up the prayer that He would make me perfect through sufferings, seeing the inefficacy of other ways? And if this is what He is now engaged about, let me say with Peter, "not my feet only, but my hands and my head." I can but trust in Him, though He slay me.

May 28. God is like a king who should build a tower, and afterwards bring out all His heavy ordinance and endeavor for three days together, by opening the most terrible batteries upon it, to knock it down. But when He saw it could not be destroyed, nor even injured, by this terrible ordeal, then He said to it, "Well done, thou good tower, I confide in thee." God by all manner of winning processes, gently builds up my faith; then after some months He turns right round, even like a lion, and lays a lion's grasp upon me. He brings with His soft sunshine and showers of spring the little twig to maturity and robustness; then comes as a hurricane, seizes it by the scalp and pulls as though He were determined to have it up roots and all. What a horrible pit the disciples found themselves in, the day of the crucifixion! Their God was dead. But they reaped all their life long the fruits of that experience.

There is this that is admirable about God's ways; that it is only those who have faith who are treated by Him in this way. The disciple whose faith is weak and incipient, is heard at once. God exhibits a wonderful alacrity in answering him. And it is only the disciple whose faith is considerably matured, and who has in memory a thousand instances of God's faithfulness, who is thus hammered and battered and bruised.

It is certain that God's truth suffers with me. Many have said and written to me: "If your course be indeed the true one, God will make it manifest, He will give you decided success; and we shall then feel ourselves bound to give more attention to your advice." Others who are really interested in my course, are waiting in hope that God will bear testimony to it, so that the truth of the Gospel is in some degree implicated with me. Now there is nothing God loves better than His truth. If then He is willing for some great end to let that suffer for a season I should be resigned to bear my part; knowing this, that there is no suspension of God's love, in these trying dispensations. I cannot possibly desire anything better than to be treated on the whole as He treats His truth. When He shall speak to it from Heaven saying, "Come up hither," may I be there to ascend with it.

29th. I think that God bestowed upon me last evening a great blessing (time will show) in leading me to look at all that is said of Heaven in the Bible, as describing the present privileges of Christians. I was reading a sermon of Edwards on Heaven and its employments and it came into my mind that the functions, duties, enjoyments, characteristics of its inhabitants should all be mine. There was a measure of responsibility suited to earth, and another to Heaven, and this last should be mine. He remarked that "they saw God." God has showed me two months since, how I might see Him, how I might at all times behold Him Whom the Seraphim praised, crying, "Holy, Holy, Holy, Lord God of Hosts, the whole earth is full of His glory." The earth is to be transfigured, just as the Bible was in Dec.—Jan. '45-'46. That is, I am to concentrate my mind upon the details, and by patient, laborious, microscopic searching, finishing one thing and passing to another, in patient contentedness, discover the All Glorious God. I should have gone on doing this, if it had not been for that absorbing desire, which leaves me without peace or life or strength, until it be fulfilled.

As he brings his "Reminiscences" to a close he says:

Homunculus was seeking not a private blessing, but one pertaining to the church of Christ, and he was led to see that there would necessarily be a congruity with the condition of matters in the church and in the world, in the time chosen for its bestowal. He was led accordingly to scrutinize the coming days and seasons to discover if possible when the congruity would present itself; that is, he was led carefully to study the subject of prophecy, fulfilled and unfulfilled and to notice with equal care the signs of the times, both within the church and beyond its borders. But who is sufficient for these things? In common with many others who have sought to find out the application of unfulfilled prophecy to our own time and the immediate future, he often fancied that he could distinguish the day of the manifestation, and under the influence of this bias found a multitude of things in Heaven and earth and Scripture and his own experience to make him positively sure that he was right in his calculations, till the expected day came and carried them all away as by a desolating flood, leaving something like chaos behind, until reviving hope caught a glimpse of some new golden summit in the distance, the Pisgah of many succeeding days.

Like many others too he found the blunders in this field of investigation not unaccompanied by blessings. The ordeal is a terrible one, and many have lost what faith they had in finding that their cherished calculations have failed. They allowed themselves to be persuaded that the Spirit of God had inspired these calculations, and when they failed, they were tempted to believe that there was no such thing as spiritual guidance. We learn from the Scriptures that holy men of old, men who were undoubtedly taught of God, often sought to understand the seasons and signs of future manifestations and were baffled. Says John, at the beginning of the Apocalypse: "Blessed is he that readeth (aloud, in the assembly) and they that hear the words of this prophecy, and keep those things which are written therein." It is not the mere study of prophecy that is blessed; but the study that is accompanied by practice of the things indicated. Prophecy must be converted into experience. The mere study of prophecy disposes a person to neglect or make light of the duties and privileges of the passing hour, and to lose himself in an ideal region. But every man belongs primarily to the passing moment, and must be on his guard against any influence that would snatch him away from it, or hinder him from giving his heart to it.

The last quotations from his diaries which are preserved in the "Reminiscences" are of a gentle and peaceful and reassuring tone:

Feb. 4, 1850. My soul is greatly rejoicing. Since the beginning of December the Lord seems to be leading me more gently. He has given me a sweet resignation, a disposition to wait as long as it may please Him. The idea was sometimes in my mind that there were to be eighteen years yet. I know the time and it does not seem to be long.

Memo. Not to expect, because I have passed, by the grace of God, triumphantly through certain stern trials, that therefore I do not need to arm myself against the recurrence of the same. In other words, not to think because I have given unusual proof of any grace that I will naturally and necessarily continue to exhibit that grace. Not to be disheartened when the necessity of striving for the retention of the best graces, discloses itself. It springs out of the very constitution that God has given.

Because my mind requires the same applications of truth now that it did years ago, it does not follow that I am just where I then was. A man half way up the mountain needs to use his feet just as he did when at the bottom. But our mount is without a summit. It grows as we ascend and will forever. Blessed be God Who teaches me at this time that I am to use all diligence now and henceforth, just as though I were setting out in my Christian course. May I not forget this oft-reiterated lesson. Nothing can be more deplorable than to entertain a settled and unquestioned notion concerning any part of our conduct, that it is faultless. Better the opposite notion, that is, suppose it faulty, unless there be positive proof to the contrary.

Cherish a more peaceful, unruffled frame. Not to be impatient for the termination of anything. If I can do nothing to terminate it, then of course impatience is vain. My strength at such times is to sit still. Impatience is good when it can accomplish some good; at all other times, bad.

It is very certain that I have been paying too little respect to present time. The glory of the future has rapt me away. I want to feel that today and tomorrow are just as important as any day in the future. And I fondly anticipate that the Lord will enable me to have as high an appreciation of time in the interim, as I ever had; which will be greatly to His glory.

My mind is never in a more delightful frame than when realizing that all bestowed upon me has been given as one gives to a messenger, that I may convey it to others. All the love shown to me, was love to others rather than to me, and in all this I have been simply a means. God has seen in me and addressed in me the entire company of my fellow-sinners. I ought to have just as much confidence in praying for others, as in praying for myself. My business in life is to be an intercessor. I desire no blessing more than to be able all the time to realize that God loves every other sinner at least as much as He does me. Any other supposition is stupidity and pride. Why should God take any more pleasure in blessing me, than in blessing another? Is there anything less odious and repulsive in my natural character? May God scourge me when I think so. I have long ago covenanted to desire no happiness save as is to be found in the communication of happiness. Selfishness is hell. Selfishness is Satan.

With these words the "Reminiscences" and their quotations from the diaries of the years 1834-1850 come to a close.

Some journals, worm-eaten and mutilated, are in the archives of the Methodist Church Executive Board in Western India. They were kindly lent me for use in preparing this memoir. There are four volumes. One of them goes back to notes of his Union Seminary courses and one is largely of Bible studies. All but the Seminary diary are in a different hand-writing and are evidently copies, with great gaps of omission. They extend from 1846 to 1870.

One other matter should be referred to in connection with the diary of 1849. Bowen still cherished the conviction that he ought to expect the attestation of his preaching by miracle. In this as in much else, despite their differences, there was a striking resemblance between Bowen and Edward Irving. Bowen was no such preacher as Irving, but in the breadth of his reading and scholarship and in his survey of history and of contemporary life he surpassed Irving. They were alike in their conception or misconception of prophecy, their deep and introspective piety and their estimation of their own unique mission in the plan and providence of God. In his diary Bowen writes:

Feb. 19, 1849. Yesterday was a precious Sabbath. My faith was strengthened by reviewing all that truth which occupied me in December. There seemed to be a very strong light shed from on high upon my path. I spent most of the night in prayer. I went forth this morning expecting very confidently a display of God's powers. But my heart sank within me, unbelief was too strong for me, and I have returned after a long, vain walk through the city. As in the autumn of 1845 when absorbed by desires after an increase of faith, my energy seemed to be paralyzed, so that I could not perform my duties as well as I had done before, so it is now. I have become indifferent to the work of book distribution and street-preaching. It all seems perfectly idle, till by faith I can give the appropriate evidence of a risen Christ.

Feb. 22. As far as my observation goes, God observes processes and will not work without them. There must be the sowing of a seed and the growing up of a plant and the ripening of fruit. These processes are wonderfully rapid sometimes. Some plants shoot up in a day or two, others take years. Even in creating the world, and also in destroying it by the deluge, God wrought thus. In many of His miracles even Christ used processes; and with regard to all of them there was the process of Christ's own preparation. In my own experience it is altogether so.

"If I do not the works of my Father, believe me not," said Christ. And may not the believer say, "If I do not the works of my Savior, believe me not?" For Christ has promised that the believer shall do His works. Are not the heathen authorized to disbelieve us, till we do the works of Christ?

23rd. I think I am declining in courage and in boldness to confess Christ. This people are beginning to convert me instead of I them. Yet I have never prayed more assiduously than in the last few days. The moment the influences of the Spirit cease, my pristine nature rises in all its power. As a watch goes till the chain is run out, so I can only do the work of God while under the immediate influence of the Spirit. Talk about holy habits, the earth might as well imagine it could shed light upon itself, if the sun failed to arise, as I might imagine that I could hold off my own depravity for one minute by any effort of my own. I am no more holy than when I began to be a Christian. Only the aperture to my soul is perhaps larger, and more of God comes in when I have faith. I frequently rise at two o'clock and spend a couple of hours on my knees. It is a precious season.

Miracles were given originally to prove the doctrine. The doctrines of Scripture were not regarded as carrying their own evidence with them; but as standing in need of evidence; for man is apostate, and the truths of Scripture find no response in him. The writing of God in his heart is effaced, not a trace remains, by which to verify the writing of God in Scripture. But instead of our working miracles to prove the doctrine, we are obliged to prove the miracles of Christianity by the doctrine. When called upon by the people to give proofs of the Christian religion, I refer to the doctrines. I try to show that the doctrines are good, are worthy of God, are favorable to society, involve the happiness of man, &c. But thus did not Jesus. Even when John the Baptist, that man of God, sent for evidence, Jesus answered only by miracles, with the exception of one word, "The Gospel is preached to the poor." The miracles of the Gospel are that part of it which offer most difficulties to the people. When reading about them in the school or chapel, I am straitened and oppressed; the people's incredulity is a load upon me, which I cannot shake off, and I breathe freer when I get on the terra firma of the precepts. But there is something wrong about this. The people hate God's holiness as well as His power. We need miracles to substantiate both the miracles and the precepts of the Gospel.

The great success of the Gospel at the outset, was intended by God to be a standing condemnation of the church in all her subsequent lethargy and impotency. But the force of this reproof is nullified by the remark so constantly made, that the primitive church had miracles, and we have none. The church in her unbelief hinders the Holy Ghost from working miracles, and then declares herself absolved from primitive obligations. Nothing I think will bring the church to a sense of her obligation to equal the first disciples in consecration, but the reproduction of the miracle-working power.

On the *29th of December,* the Lord frustrated my attempt it is true; but it is also true and wonderful that He did not suffer me to be ashamed and confounded before my enemies. After that vain attempt I thought that I should be the object of great ridicule; but it is remarkable that not a soul has ever alluded to it since, or intimated that he knew of it. The Lord found it necessary to let me fail in that instance, and I can see now how indispensable it was that He should; but He took care that His enemies should not triumph. It is a great comfort to me to remember this, for I have in it an additional encouragement to go forward. He will not suffer me to be confounded before His enemies; He would sooner cause the earth to open and swallow them all up and me too, than let His Name be reproached through my unanswered prayer. My faith is strengthened by considering the many ways in which God, if any dire necessity hindered the working of a miracle, could in the very last moment, break up the assembly without letting me be put to shame. There is no instance in the Bible of anyone's trusting in the Lord and being confounded.

And the journal is full also of amazing dreams and visions such as these:

July 28. Last night, I was spoken to again. I was abroad in the night, and saw in mid heaven, that is, in the very zenith, a blazing comet, above the brightness of all stars and traveling rapidly. But presently it descended and came to me, and I found it in my hand, in the form of a book. A little volume, several centuries old, in antique language, which I could read very well. I went into a house and when it was day two men arose and came out of their rooms, to whom I read a portion of it. One of the men was immensely old.

Sept. 1. Night before last, had in my hands a sword, grasping it by the hilt firmly with both hands. A dog flew at me, and seized my hands in his mouth, to make me let go the sword. The temptation was strong but I resisted it. Finally the dog had to let go my hand, and lo! not a drop of blood had been drawn:

Oct. 7. I dreamed last night that lightning fell from heaven and set fire to everything, and around my dwelling. I saw all the trees blazing in the darkness, and it was a time of universal confusion and destruction. I was lying on the hearth, and looking up the chimney I saw the fire raging and the stones of the chimney came tumbling down besides me, but nothing touched me, nor had I the slightest apprehension.

Bowen's letters to his mother and sisters embody much that he wrote in his journal but there are also many home touches regarding his new manner of life and his inner thoughts and hopes.

To Harriet, *April 14, 1849:* I don't like to see you anxious about my comforts. I am more solicitous about my own comfort than anyone can possibly be. I am seeking my comfort as diligently as any luxurious Englishman or New Englander is, and probably a great deal more successfully. But you know what is comfort to one man is not to another. Tastes and appetites and constitutions differ; and it is the privilege of every man in the restaurant to call for what he pleases. We could easily dispense with the hospitality of the Laplander who should set before us dishes of whale oil. Now this I say, that I suffer no discomfort from the absence of what people generally regard as the comforts and conveniences of life. If I were to sit down to a most sumptuous banquet every day, I would choose from all, bread and water, as that which suited my taste best. The impenitent don't understand this; and they suppose, that it is merely under the pressure of some strange dream of duty, that a man does this; they entirely refuse to believe that he is in heart indifferent. Now it is our wonder if they think so, but it seems to me that it is a wonder when Christians adopt this way of thinking.

If there is one distinctive thing in the Gospel it is this, that the believer in Christ is made independent of earthly comforts. And one great end of his calling is to give the evidence of this to the world, and cause them to know by his daily life that the knowledge of Christ is satisfying, and tends to appease not one want of our nature, but all wants. There is something in my opinion very dishonoring and criminal in the regard shown by Christians to the matter of their personal comfort. . . .

Is not self-denial as conspicuous a feature in the Gospel as any other grace? Is it not the great thing exhibited in a dying Savior? Is not the Cross a tremendous effort to wean us from self? From first to last, it is the aim of Christ, as it is His glory to be our All-sufficiency. He hates our earthly comforts, why? Because He grudges us the pleasure we derive from them? Not so; but because He grudges them the privilege of blessing us. I tell you, and whatever Christian will faithfully consider it, will acknowledge it, that the more we cut ourselves off from earthly comforts, and forbid them to give us satisfaction, the intenser will be our desire for Christ; and I do not need to tell you that such desires are the prelude to joys unspeakable. I hear people speak about these things as the small dust of the balance. If it be so, then the Savior spent much of His time in weighing small dust, and the apostles very much misunderstood the Christian calling. Christ says, "he that breaketh one of these least commandments, and teacheth men so, shall be esteemed least in the kingdom of heaven." That is, he who regards any of the things enjoined in the Sermon on the Mount, as insignificant, will himself appear insignificant and good for nothing in the day when the church exhibits the true standard. And I incline to think that these things which many Christians speak so contemptuously of, are really the most formidable mountains in their way. Why is there such an intense reluctance to make this trial? When individuals or the churches are in a state of depression, why is it that we see this and that measure adopted, but never an individual rising up to obey the command, "Sell that thou hast, and give to the poor, and come, follow me"? "Provide not for yourselves treasures on the earth." "Forsake all things and follow me." "Take no thought what ye shall eat," etc.

Self-denial is frightful to those who are without faith; but surely it is an unspeakable shame that those who have faith in Christ, should shrink from it. And I am convinced that there is no growth of faith where there is not a corresponding readiness to evince our faith in self-denial. You may be sure that there is to be a tremendous earthquake in the church, and that Christians are to be emptied out of their fine houses and worldly comforts, and shrink from the things they now delight in, as from venomous serpents, and the stern uncompromising standard of Pentecostal times be again recovered....

Why is it that so many missionaries return, that there is such a readiness on their part to go home? It is because in consequence of their want of faith, they have trials that are unendurable, and which the Savior never meant to lay upon them. I may be wrong, but this is my view. The apostles had no such trials. Everything can be done and everything borne where there is an adequate hope. The apostles felt it their privilege to triumph always in Christ Jesus, and they did triumph. They knew that their triumph was Christ's triumph, and their very love to Christ would have made the prospect of laboring a life long without bringing forth fruit, in other words laboring simply to make Christ more and more contemned, (which is the inevitable result of unfruitfulness)— their love to Him, I say, would have made such a prospect unbearable. When Christ said, "Go preach the Gospel to every creature," He also said, "Tarry ye until ye be endued with power from on high." Without the baptism of the Spirit that last commandment is most grievous. My own dependence is altogether withdrawn now from other things, and placed exclusively on the expected Spirit.

To Kate, *April 16.* I have changed my quarters today, and am living in a little house situated in the midst of a block of houses occupied by natives. No one lives in the house but a Mr. Whitefield, who I hope is destined to be a useful Christian. I could not be more comfortable than I am. I sincerely hope Frank will not go to California. I believe that Satan has desired to have the world to sift as wheat; and these gold mines of California are one evidence that God is giving it to him. This California is the world's New Jerusalem and they are all rushing to it as the crusaders of old. Mammon was never more the god of this world, than at this moment; when the true God is revealing Himself so remarkably in Providence, when the sign of the Son of Man has appeared in Heaven and He Himself is about to follow. "Watch, therefore, and pray always." Unwatchfulness was not a more flagrant crime in Gethsemane, than at this moment. I warn you and all, be afraid of any standard you see in the church. The bed is shorter than that a man can stretch himself on it. "Behold I come as a thief," and "Blessed is he that keepeth his garments lest they see his shame." That is, a day is coming when the flimsy and scanty garments of our present piety will be seen as they are. The true standard is to be revealed, and they who now walk in honor, apparently clothed, will be terrified at their nakedness. That which is considered clothes among the Hindus is regarded as nakedness among Europeans; and in like manner what is now creditable piety, will soon be utterly contemned for its inadequacy.

To Kate, *June 13.* I am convinced that the Gospel has surprisingly little power here, even upon the religious portion of the European community. I cannot find anywhere such a thing as a deep Christian sense of responsibility. There is nobody who trembles at the Word of God. It seems to be so all over the world. In other words, the Spirit of God is almost clean gone from the world. A great deal of what is called piety in England and America may be accounted for otherwise than by supposing a divine agent. This does not look like the dispensation of the Spirit at all. I doubt if our piety is superior to that of the church, before this dispensation began. We have a great deal of truth the pious Jew has not, but piety does not consist in truth, but in the degree of influence truth has upon us.

To Harriet, *Sep. 14.* I very deeply sympathize with you in your spiritual exercises. I confidently believe that there is a broad bright place to which you will be brought ere long. Christ saw I think that your Christian character was not going up exactly right; so He has pulled down some of the walls, and made bare the foundations. At present the basement is filled with rubbish; but the building—let us hope it is going up right, and will never need any overturnings more. Christian experience is like a revolving wheel. We go up and then we go down; but even when going down we are going forward. We make the circuit, and come around as it seems to us to just the place where we were before; but on examination we find that while our present experience has many points of resemblance with some past experience, yet it also differs on some important points. Thus Christ found Peter fishing on the sea of Tiberias; ordained the miraculous draught of fishes; and said unto him: "Follow me." There years after he found him in the same place, in the same employments with the same companions, in many respects the same man, namely, Simon Barjonas, the fisherman. Again He ordained a miraculous draught of fishes, and again said unto him: "Follow me." But still it was not altogether the same man; his character was different in its substructure and he followed the Savior right on to Pentecost. May it be so with you! . . . We must have a right notion of patience. The word is used in Scripture in a somewhat different sense from the common. There is action and not inaction in the idea. We are to *run* with patience, and not sit down.

His last home letter of the year was a long one to the family, Nov. 15, 1849:

> I have heard repeated instances of stations being abandoned because no house could be procured fit for the missionaries. . . . You can have little notion how greatly a missionary is affected, not to say impeded, by the wife. . . .
>
> If you ask what I have been about in the last two months, what missionary work I have been doing, why, you must know that my doings do not amount to much. I am a very paltry missionary at the best, and you might as well make up your minds to it. If you ever had the idea that I am somebody, and that in consequence of my coming into the field, something is to be expected, I beg of you to renounce the idea. I assure you I am a missionary of very small stature, coming short in everything. To this day, my knowledge of the Marathi is meager and unsatisfactory, and humanly speaking I never can expect to attain even the limited measure of success enjoyed by many of my brethren. I do not believe there is a minister in the world whose words fall more powerless than mine do now and have done for years. And if in some matters my life is more conformed to the truth than that of others, that in itself is not a guarantee of success. And besides what success has been witnessed in modern missionary operations, has been reaped only after many years of labor. Therefore while you pray earnestly and constantly for me, be prepared for a long trial of your faith.
>
> I really think that I am not sent in vain into this land, and God in His time will accomplish a work by me. But the times and the seasons He has put in His own power. My expectation of success is based not upon any fitness for the work in myself, but springs out of that faith which God has given me, in His own Word, and which is perhaps peculiar in its strength and tenacity.
>
> I am glad to see by Harriet's letters that she and others have realized that it is quite possible for me to fall, and become guilty even of gross

sin. It is impossible to offer up genuine prayer for anyone unless we have that realization. The greatest of all falls is to lose the sense of our liability to fall. If by the grace of God I have any peculiar stability, I have it in virtue only of a constant attention to the fact that a deep precipice of sin is close to my feet. At the same time I would say to you that I have not for years perceived in myself the rising of any unlawful lust or affection. My experience of the Christian warfare is conflict with victory and not conflict with defeat, and this I think is the N. T. idea. Vain conflict is the doom of the unregenerate. I can do all things through Christ, and nothing save through Him, sums up my experience. Mark you, I speak only of conflict with the world within. The war I have waged upon the sins of others has been deplorably successless. The internal harvest is more rapid than the external, but I regard it also as a pledge of the external. If this language seems vanity, why, *it must seem so.* I speak what I think, and God is the judge.

For the last five weeks I have been accustomed to go in the afternoon to a spot on the beach where a good many Parsis assemble to worship the elements. I go with a native convert belonging to the Scotch Mission, and we have long discussions with Parsis and other natives. There is generally one person who acts as their spokesman or advocate; we sit on the sand; sometimes the discussion is prolonged till 8 o'clock. They seem to take a great deal of interest in it, and at the appointed time there are generally as many as 200 persons congregated. I cannot see that a desire for the truth attracts them, but rather hostility to the truth, and a desire to show off their attainments in infidel literature. They have been stirred up to look into the Bible considerably; but also to hunt up the works of Paine, Collins, Voltaire and other infidels. The chief speaker is one who has but little religion of any kind. He regards God as the only agent; a necessary inference from which is (though he will not explicitly avow it) that God is the only sinner. The Trinity, the twofold nature of Christ, His divinity, salvation by faith in Him, these doctrines they really hate and constantly assail.

Yesterday they alleged that Christ was no better than Krishna and their Hindu avatars; that He was guilty of stealing, and in proof of this strange accusation they referred to the disciples plucking even as they were passing through the field, and to His sending two of them for an ass. Also to His overthrowing the tables of the money changers. They are constantly calling upon us to work miracles, and indeed this is one of the first results of reading the Gospels and the Acts, upon the people of this country, they ask to see miracles like those recorded. And it is sad to think that the entire mass of historical evidence is lost upon this people, who are unacquainted with European history; and as for the moral evidence embosomed in the truth itself, they must receive the love of the truth, before they will have any aptitude to receive that evidence. If ever special displays of divine power were needed, they are needed now and here. And all my reliance is upon the holy arm of God, yet to be made bare.

I have spoken to you several times of dear brother here, Mr. Fraser, minister of the Free Church of Scotland. His wife and child have gone home to Scotland lately on account of ill health. Immediately on their departure he hastened to inform me that from the very outset he had been convinced that my course was the true one for preachers of the Gospel in India, and that he was now determined to adopt it. And he is desirous not only of living like me but with me. If God favors this proposition, and permits us to live and labor unitedly, I shall regard it as a very peculiar kindness, for there is no one in this part of the world with whom I seem to sympathize so fully as with this brother. But I cannot take the least step upward from my adopted habits. I have such a keen recollection of the difficulties encountered in making my way down, that I have almost a morbid sensitiveness on the subject. When I was in my former position it used to be my daily and hourly resolution that if I ever escaped from that net, nothing should suffer me to return to it.

The secretaries have written me in an encouraging and gratifying manner, approving of my experiment, (as they consider it) and adding some friendly admonitions about avoiding extremes. But letters which I have received from missionaries in answer to my printed letter, have one and all been condemnatory. For this I was fully prepared. Why do I write so much about this thing? Because I think you are interested in it. And I feel disposed to tell you about a breakfast I gave lately to the missionary circle. I will do so if you will promise to view it as I do, and be very much amused by it.

You must know that the custom is to meet on the 1st Monday at the house of some missionary, spend some time in prayer and reading the Bible, and afterwards partake of breakfast. This breakfast is generally a stylish affair, six or eight servants, a display of silver, a loaded table, and perhaps moving of punkahs overhead. It fell to my turn to receive and entertain the conference this month. But what was I to do, in my little house, one little table, a few chairs, two spoons, two teacups, one knife and two plates? I was determined to be led by providence, and sent out the invitations. Mr. Hume told me to get whatever I wanted from his house and promised his servants. But as I had no money to procure a costly breakfast, I felt that it would be very foolish to have a quantity of plates, etc., sent, and so I borrowed nothing.

Monday morning came and I had but four pice (three cents) and nothing in the house but bread and a little milk. I concluded therefore that God did not mean that they should be feasted by me, and that they would either not come or else not remain to breakfast. But some came, and to my surprise three remained for breakfast. Now what is to be done, thought I? And for a moment I was undecided what course to pursue. I was half disposed to confess my inability and dismiss them; but finally concluded to do what I could. So I spread a napkin on the table, brought out some cold tea, left from the night before, and some bread. I found then that there was no sugar in the house, and my four pice had to go for that; but George had two pice of his own and with these obtained some plantains. I borrowed two cups and saucers and spoons from a neighbor, and as there was nothing but bread we did not need any plates. I then said to my guests, "I am sorry to be so short-coming in the rites of hospitality, but in the providence of God I find myself compelled to treat you just as I am accustomed to treat myself." And they ate it with a good grace, apparently; though probably no missionary conference in India ever sat down to such a breakfast. I have hardly been able to think of this since without laughing; and I hope you may be greatly diverted by the account of it.

So there was a saving sense of humor which later gave a distinct flavor to the *Bombay Guardian.*

In this same letter he wrote to Harriet:

One thing is necessary, namely, to acquire a thorough knowledge of the fact that God is sufficient to us, and that His presence and favor can cheer up the most desolate scene imaginable. The desert was no desert to those Israelites that trusted in God; the very heavens became their fruitful fields. I observe two things, that if I dread anything very much, that thing is sure to come to pass; but when it is come to pass I find it a very different thing from what I anticipated, so that I wonder how I could have dreaded it. So that now impending evils alarm me not. The cup did not pass away from Christ; but when He came to drink it, He found He could drink it. If God does not change the dispensation, He changes us into a fitness for the dispensation which comes to just the same thing.

When I was young I used to dream of falling from a great height. And at first these dreams were attended with great terror, but as I found I always landed safely and softly in my bed, I soon ceased to be afraid, and afterwards when I found myself falling in my dreams, I said, "Well, no matter, I shall come down all right and no bones broke." In this same way does God deal with me, so that I have learned to look at every stern-visaged Providence without alarm. But with regard to you, if any privations are to be endured I would rather have them fall to me than to you. It seems to me, however, from the sums which you have mentioned to me as received, there must be money for a year or two. If so, go on and spend it; and don't abstain from giving away. I have never given away more to the poor than during this year. I am not at all in favor of laying up against the future. I don't think it Scriptural. I have read lately with much satisfaction a little book called, "God's dealings with George Müller," a German by birth, who became a minister in Bristol, England. If you can get hold of if, read it and be strengthened in faith. Our family for years have been living above their circumstances. We ought long, long ago to have given up all pretensions to appearance, and come down to a poor man's way of living. We ought to have confessed our poverty before the world. . . .

I see in the native papers that our seashore discussions are exciting considerable attention in the Parsi and Hindu community I have just read in the Gujarathi paper an article three columns long on the subject. It represents the discussion as starting with the following conditions, viz.: if our Parsi antagonist be defeated, he, as well as his wife, children and relatives is to become a Christian; if we (Narayan and myself) be defeated, we are to turn Mussulmans. This is of course mere fancy. The Mussulman religion is substituted because the Parsis, like the Hindus, would not receive converts. We have been treated very well during these discussions; what I mean is, no violence or very little has been offered to us, though abusive language has not been wanting, and our ears are often pained with blasphemies against Christ. So long as they find themselves able to answer at all, and to keep up the semblance of successful resistance, so long they will probably refrain from violence; but if they should find themselves confounded in argument, they would quickly take to stones.

12. From 1850 to 1855

For the ensuing five years Bowen continued as a member of the Mission of the American Board, receiving no salary but supporting himself by teaching an hour or more daily in a private family. He had thought of seeking employment as a writer in one of the public offices but, as already noted, the secretaries of the Board who looked with favor upon the experiment which they considered he was making, disapproved of this course. For this period from 1850 to 1855 we have no diary records, but there are five letters written to the Board in Boston, and there are some thirty letters to his mother and sisters, both the originals in Bowen's fine steel-plate handwriting and careful copies in the letter book preserved by Harriet in her larger hand.

To the family, Jan. 16, 1850:

> Although I have not yet the happiness of seeing the Lord's work prospering in my hands, yet is my soul kept in perfect peace; and frequently favored with seasons of the highest spiritual joys. My experiences at the commencement of this year are very much akin to those I had at the beginning of 1846; and you know how much I say in saying this. I marvel how the Lord enables me to endure the iron pressure of these times, when "vanity, vanity, vanity" seems to be the only product of my labor. But the thing is this: He has given me an eye capable of piercing the brazen vault He has stretched over us, and I can see smiles and glory and undreamed of grace beyond and ready to be revealed. The instant before God said "let there be light" the world was without form and void.
>
> Since my last I have received a little letter, the joint production of Harriet, Kate and Frank, which was most welcome. I bless God for His signal care of you all; and far be it from me to cherish doubts of His future faithfulness. What could the Lord have done for us that He hath not done? Never it seems to me was a family so distinguished by His loving kindness. My heart is almost broken with emotion sometimes as I think of it. Also that there should be any defect of consecration on the part of any of us.

To the family, March 14, 1850:

> The paralysis of the Gospel still continues in this part of the world. Those discussions by the seaside yet go on, though without any notable

results. The Parsis, Hindus and others that attend them manifest an unmitigated bitterness toward the Christian religion, and an interest in the discussion that is surprising. They spare no pains to familiarize themselves with all the arguments brought against Christianity by its enemies of all ages and countries. I have seen in the hands of one of them a work against Christianity in the Parsi dialect, in four large octavo volumes.

The thought used to come into my mind sometimes before leaving America, that in some respects my former character, sentiments and manner of life, rather fitted me to labor among an infidel Christian population, and I was sometimes inclined to wonder that the Lord should send me to the heathen. But I am confident that in the last six months I have had to encounter a greater amount of infidel argumentation, than I would have found in the same time anywhere in Europe or America. And in this as in everything, I find proofs of the perfect wisdom and condescension of Him Who is my Leader and Commander.

I suppose it is pretty generally known throughout Bombay, that if anybody has any arguments to bring against Christianity, he will find at the seashore, near where they burn the dead, at five o'clock in the afternoon, a Padre (as they unhappily designate the missionary) and a converted Brahmin, ready to hear their objections and to answer them. Many of the persons who constitute this audience are, to my mind, a striking proof of the insufficiency of mere science to open a door for the Gospel. Science so far as they have cultivated it, has only armed them with new weapons against the Gospel. Enlightened Christians are fully aware that science has nothing among her genuine treasures that is inimical to the religion of the Bible, but Christians have not yet learned that science is no auxiliary to the Gospel. . . . The Church imagines that the progress she sees going on around her is her progress, that all the marvelous inventions of the day are contributing to the spread of the Gospel. But what proportion of the scientific professors of Europe and America is Christian? A very small one. Do we find that in proportion to the number of steamboats, railroads, telegraphs, etc., in a region, is the prevalence of piety in that region? God may make use of these things at some future day; but they are not doing any more for the propagation of Christianity, than they are for that of infidelity, pantheism, etc. . . .

You are interested in the matter of my personal experiences. It may surprise you to hear that notwithstanding the desolate aspect of things without, I am rejoicing continually with joy unspeakable in God and in His Son. I never in my life, have enjoyed such a serene, unbroken flow of spirits as since the commencement of this year, and this you (who saw me in 1846 and '47) know to be saying much. And you must not infer that I am any the less interested in those around me; for a large element in my happiness is the assurance that He, Who delighteth in mercy, loves these poor souls, and will without any great delay begin to do exceeding abundantly above all that we can ask or think. Probably not immediately; by next autumn; but at all events in the very best day and hour. You that love the Lord give Him no rest, until He arise and make Jerusalem a praise in the earth. You that love me, praise Him for all His surprising goodness to my soul. Before the end of this year I hope to tell you some admirable and glorious things, which He has told me. But have you not His Word? and His Spirit? and His intercessions? Remember that the secret of the Lord is with them that fear Him, and that "they who will do His will" shall know. . . .

Afterwards a present of some large and delightful grapes was sent by a friend. Then I went to the examination of the Free Church missionary institution. Dr. Duff, just arrived in Bombay on his way to Scotland, presided and afterwards delivered an address. He is an admirable speaker, and I have not had such a treat for a long time. His speech was principally against the notion that mere secular education could regenerate India. His plan is to teach them everything, religion included, perhaps I might say religion prominent. Not so prominent, however, as you would suppose. I heartily sympathize with all that was aggressive in his discourse: the infidel principal of the government institution was present and must have suffered, I think, under the volleys of eloquent crimination. But I think that Dr. D., like almost everybody else, errs with respect to the way in which the conversion of India will be effected.

Afterwards I accompanied my friend Narayan to his house close by, and made use of a leisure hour in writing a note to Mrs. Lee which I enclose. Please transmit. Took a brief dinner with Narayan, and then we went to the sea shore, and had our discussion. At least 200 were there. Towards seven we left. A half dozen educated youths from the Government Institution followed us. They expressed themselves to be skeptics; they rejected the Hindu Shastras, but saw no reason to believe that God had given any revelation whatever, nor that any was needed. They wanted to discuss with us this point. So after a little debate, we agreed to meet them tomorrow afternoon at the house of Narayan. I then came home, lighted a fire to cook some rice with, taught a little English to the two converts living with me, afterwards took supper, had evening worship, and am now, ten o'clock, in my little room (ten feet square) writing these lines to some whom I love much.

To the family, May 9, 1850:

> We should look upon every human being as the raw material of something precious. The Manchester merchant, when he brings a bale of cotton, sees in it future prints of choicest patterns....
>
> My own health is perfect. I have never been better than during the last year and a half. I may tell you freely that the number of those in Bombay who admire and approve my course is increasing, and that some European Christians are awakening to the importance of shaping their lives in more strict conformity with the Gospel. I know a little circle of praying ones, men of wealth and station, who are anxiously waiting upon the Lord, to know what He would have them to do. Since this year set in I have not known a heavy or desponding hour, having the most unwavering assurance that the Lord is bringing me into the promised land.
>
> The discussions at the sea side continue and are numerously attended. There are no heathen pressing into the kingdom, but on the contrary, some converts are falling away. You remember that once there was chaos, and in the very next moment, light, and the sons of God shouting for joy. So it will be again, presently. A nation shall be born in a day. All that has yet been in the world, was but the auroral light preceding the rising of the Son of Righteousness.
>
> I have one very dear friend here by the name of Larkins, a lawyer, one of the most devoted Christians. He loves me much and I him. Remember his name; you will probably hear it again. I continue teaching, as before....
>
> There has been lately a great discussion in the Bombay English papers touching the true mode of missionary operations, infidels as well as others taking part in it. The discussion has had special reference to mission schools. The directors of Government schools aver that it is not their schools that make the rising generations of heathen infidel, but the mission schools. Their opponents point to refuting facts and are in return withered by the question, Where are your converts? The Hindus read and wonder. When salt without saline qualities can do all that genuine salt can, it will be proper to expect the conversion of the heathen, while the church remains as she is. But as that day will never come, my absolute conviction is that the first thing needed and to be expected is the revelation of God in the church. Zion must arise and shine, then will the gross darkness of the earth be removed.
>
> On Sabbath next, the 12th, I am to distribute the elements to the members of the Free Church here, and I purpose to urge upon them, "Conformity to the spirit and letter of the Gospel. 1. If any man have not the Spirit of Christ and 2. *Put ye on* the Lord Jesus Christ." It is a

thing to be noticed that people will listen with all benignity when told to conform to the spirit of the Gospel, but are instantly thrown into convulsions if the letter of it is pressed upon them. The reason is that we divorce spiritual religion from its external manifestation, and settle it that there is no one style of life that properly and exclusively expresses it; why then one man's profession is a valid as another's. It becomes impossible to impeach the piety of professors. But Christ has legislated not only concerning the heart but the life; and He has done it concerning the latter, in order to have His laws concerning the heart obeyed. The two go together. He who breaks the letter of the law, breaks both the spirit and the letter. Let me relate a little incident.

I was lately in company with Dr. Wilson and others. Dr. W. was complaining of the want of missionary interest among the Christians of Bombay, that they were reluctant to contribute, etc. A Christian brother present in the Civil Service (Capt. Trewen) spoke in reply thus: "Dr. Wilson, do you want me to tell you the reason why Christians here are so indisposed to give to the cause of missions? It is simply this, that they are dissatisfied with the way in which missionaries are living. When they see you living less expensively, they will begin to answer your appeals."

To Harriet, May 10, 1850:

How I would love a few hours conversation with you. For a long time the secret of the Lord has been with me, but my mouth has been necessarily closed. And it has been a part of my peculiar probation to carry about in my bosom so much of great value and importance, without being privileged to communicate it to a soul But the day is at hand, May 24, when the voice shall say "cry," and "I shall speak and be no more dumb," Ezek. 24:27. And again a little while, and "the glory of the Lord shall be revealed and all flesh shall see it together." Read the 24th of Isaiah. The first half of it has been in process of fulfillment during the last two years and more. In the 15th v. for "fires," read "auroral lights," *i.e.,* the Orient, indicating as Gesenius observes, direction, namely that of the rising sun. In a time of desolation and confusion, there shall be a few to lift up the voice, in praise of the majesty of God, in an isle of the Sea, in the distant Orient. The word "Righteous" is singular, the Righteous One. The treacherous dealers whom the church upbraids are her spiritual teachers, who have been teaching her another gospel. And in a day very proximate, the rest of the chapter will be strictly and literally fulfilled, even the 20th verse. That will be the great and terrible day of the Lord, when Isaiah 28:20 will be fulfilled, and a thousand other awful texts of Scripture. Be ye also ready.

No one knows me better than you do, and perhaps no one knows the Lord in me better than you do; therefore things that would make anyone else smile will have their due weight with you. The Lord knoweth how little I care to be a prophet. I am and long have been purely dead to this world's judgments, good and bad. I write this for the safety of your soul, and that you may with all prudence and all earnestness seek the salvation of Christian souls around you, devoting yourself especially to the most devoted. I wish you to act as you would if fully persuaded that in about two months from the reception of this letter, the day which is to witness the consummation of all things, were to break upon the world. And may God fill you with His Spirit, Who is the Spirit of wisdom and understanding, of counsel and might. And my trust is that from this day until that in which this letter reaches you, the Lord may be powerfully preparing you to witness for Him.

I would like, if I were with you, to explain the 18th of Isaiah, the 3rd of Habakkuk, the whole of the Revelation, the 36th and 37th of Ezekiel, the 41st of Job, and many other parts of the Bible containing things undreamt of. But He that taught me will teach you, if you are strictly careful to use the light received. If we want to make progress in knowledge, we must make progress in obedience. Remember, dear Harriet, that He Who dwelleth in you is an Omnipotent and All Holy Being. Make much use of these two facts. What to you were all other miracles, if you have not first this miracle of sanctification wrought in your heart?

To the family, Oct. 15, 1850:

All things continue with me as from the beginning. I have been now three and a half years a licensed minister, yet do not know that my ministry has been blessed to the salvation of a soul, nor is there any visible evidence that I have been of any use in the world. Yet I was never more serene, hopeful, patient or confident than now. Paul could not more cordially bless God for having put him in the ministry than I can. Looking at results, my hope seems a disease of the mind. It is true, charity hopeth all things, believeth all things. But the simple explanation in my case is that God reveals Himself so graciously to my soul that I cannot but commit my way unto Him with tranquility and trust. My former views of the love of God to sinners and of His desire for their salvation have lost nothing of their intensity. He shows me that the best thing for me, and the best thing for the world, and the best thing for the universe, is that He should do as He doeth. If we know that we have faith, we know that God is propitious, and will declare it, though 10,000 providences browbeat us. We, standing at a distance, see Job beneath the cloud, pining and almost despairing; and God above the cloud, listening and loving; and the cloud gradually evaporating.

I am kept in perfect health. For nearly two years I have not been hindered by sickness from the performance of single duty. I live in the same little house, with the same house mates. Unfortunately Mr. Brown, my fellow lodger, is about to commit the folly of marriage, and thus I shall lose him. I shall be content if Christ lose him not. I cannot credit the report you mention that the Am. Board intend sending no more unmarried missionaries. It seems impossible they should be so blinded.

Last week the missionary conference met at my house. We were seven. In the good providence of God I was enabled to treat them somewhat better than last year. For instance we had hot tea instead of cold, of which they so complained. The entire breakfast cost me fifteen cents. My spirit was refreshed lately by a visit from Mr. Cassidy of Poona, a young missionary not yet ordained, who for almost a year has been pursuing my course. He is a devoted servant of the Lord, and through many trials and some obloquy, pursues his way humbly, patiently and laboriously, taking nothing from any society. He expects to spend next month with me in Bombay, and I will perhaps spend December with him, touring in the Deccan.

I pass some hours daily in street labors, meeting with less violence than formerly, though aversion for the truth seems unmitigated. Christians at home wonder that the heathen are not converted. The wonder is that any should be converted. For you must understand that they are conscientious in their religion. The conscience of a man is his own child. God gives the child, but the parent educates it for good or evil. Each man is the potter and his conscience the clay. Paul's superior conscientiousness made him a persecutor. The Mussulman who this morning bought a book of me and then returned it, because Christ was said therein to be the Son of God, acted from conscientious motives. And it is to be feared that some of those who come to us for baptism, do so from inferior conscientiousness. A man is responsible to obey his conscience; but he is also responsible to have a right conscience. To transform a conscience matured in error, oh, how divine a work is this!

That circle of praying Europeans of whom I spoke sometimes—we have weekly a precious evening. Some of the brethren are Plymouth brethren, or pre-millenarians, but the love of Christ unites us. I think God is answering our prayers by awakening other Christians in Bombay. We are having special meetings for prayer, for the out-pouring of the Spirit, and these are crowded. The doctrine of the Spirit is beginning to be better understood in Bombay. The Evangelical Alliance is making progress here; you know how much attached I am to its principles. A Swiss brother has well said that it is the church of the future.

Mr. John Sands, one of the first merchants of London, spent a couple of months here, some time ago. Since I left home I have met none whose spirit so fully met mine.

To Harriet, Oct. 15, 1850:

My letter to you of May last has caused you much perturbation of spirit and perhaps grief. I could not bear at first to think that I had drawn you into the net of my own disappointments. But I believe that I was moved of God to communicate what I did and therefore I assure myself that in some way God will bring good out of it. You are the only soul I breathed those persuasions to; and it was altogether a strange thing that I should have made an exception in your favor. Yes, it will turn out to be in your favor. I feel myself bound to be a little explicit in speaking to you now of my views so far as they are peculiar.

If you read the New Testament with a sedulous abnegation of opinions derived from extraneous sources, you will see that the primitive church were expecting the return of the Lord Jesus. How lucid the testimony in 1st Thessalonians! The 2nd. Th. does not contradict the 1st. It mentions things that must intervene, but did not require the Thessalonian church to place that event beyond their own life time. I gather from the Gospels and Epistles that God's intention was that the church of every generation should be expecting and hastening unto the Day of the Lord. Again the Bible declares abundantly that the world is to be converted under this present dispensation, by the Word of God and the Spirit of God; and the whole earth be filled with the knowledge of His glory. But if I believe that the Holy Ghost will convert the world by the agency of the church, how can I look for the immediate coming of our Lord? The first must necessarily precede. For Christ cometh to judge the world; probation ends with His advent. Consider the 60th of Isaiah. Suddenness and haste seem implied. Notice especially the last word, "The Lord will hasten it in its time." A short work will He make in the earth. I believe then that there is to be a glorious manifestation of God in the church, sufficiently preternatural to fill the earth with evidence, and to make all men understand, in the church and out of it, that the Great Day of the Lord God Almighty is at hand, and that all who desire salvation must flee to Christ as a cloud of doves to their windows. This manifestation will be the work of the Spirit. We must not get our ideas of this present dispensation from what we now see; but consider the apostolic works; consider what Christ wrought; remember that the believer is to do great works. Miracles (remember) continued in the church so long as faith and consecration continued. But I expect that the Spirit of God will choose for this latter day revelation of Himself, something far transcending the miracles of the primitive church, the work to be now performed (the conversion of the entire world) being a far greater one than theirs.

The Spirit reveals Christ; so that in the manifestation above spoken of, there will be a fulfillment of many prophecies found in the Gospel, teaching that the Son of Man will come in an hour when we think not, and His coming will be like a snare upon the face of the whole earth. Remember that the bridegroom has not quite come when the cry is raised, "Behold, the bridegroom cometh"; and the "sign of the Son of Man" is seen in the heavens before the Son of Man Himself.

In connection with this notice the providential preparation of the earth. The invention of steamboats is a drying up of the Euphrates, by which the most perfect intercommunications are established throughout the whole earth. The seas that once separated nations, now unite them. The electric telegraph is a pouring out of the vial upon the air, effecting in the air, what steam effects on the sea and land, annihilating distances. Even now there is no part of the world that cannot (with a right use of existing means) be reached in fifty days from Bombay. Now why is the Lord diminishing this entire planet to the dimensions of a city, with streets from London to Constantinople, and from New Orleans to London? In Ps. 19:4 the word *line* has troubled many, and Gesenius is bold enough to propose changing it, because of its unintelligibleness; but it is right and refers to the line of telegraphic wire. All these things are over and over mentioned in the Bible, and the reason of it will soon appear, when a supine church shall suddenly find that the work she has been these eighteen centuries neglecting, must be speedily done or not at all. And I think I could prove to you in a hour from the Bible, that the year 6000 will end in the course of A. D. 1857. But I do not ask you to adopt any opinion because it is mine. Rather be wary of my opinion and ask the Spirit of God to teach you.

I truly coincide with what you say that this world is of all others the place best fitted for the attainment of holiness. I think I can add that all my discoveries in the region of prophecy were made while searching the Bible for sanctifying truth. What you and I supremely need is that we should be holy as Christ is. If we may only have His spiritual image, we may patiently wait till He transfigure our bodies (2 Cor 3:18, orig.) and conform us to the image of the Son of God. After we have done His will we have need of patience that we should receive the promise.

I receive with much pleasure the salutations of Mr. Denny and Mr. William Hall. I remember them cordially. Give my Christian love to them, to Dr. Skinner and Mr. Styles, to the Masons, Lockwoods, Gibsons,

Atterburys, Chesters and church members and friends generally. Send my love to Fred King. I am getting somewhat heretical on the subject of infant baptism; mean to write to the Presbytery before long. Ask all good Christian people to pray for me. Love to Aunt Weston and her daughters. Say unto Kate that from him that hath not (doth not avail himself of) shall be taken away that which he seemeth to have. I fear it is only a *seeming to have* with her. I may do her wrong. Her letters are dear to me. In some respects she is evidently improving. The Lord bless her and my dear Mama, and preserve them unto His heavenly kingdom. It is delightful to hear of Mama's continued health and activity.

To his mother, Dec. 16, 1850:

I don't know that there ever was a year of greater stagnation in the missionary work than this. I speak of results, not of attempts. Many here in India have a sort of compassionate feeling towards missionaries and the church of Christ, such as we feel when we see a little child undertaking to roll an immense rock up hill.

To the family, March 15, 1851:

It is a bitter thing to love those who treat our persons, deeds and professions with contempt. What perpetual bitterness for Him Whose Name is love, Whose goodness is on all His works, and whose heart once sent forth its streams in the sweat of Gethsemane and the blood of Calvary, to meet the returns He does. I continue to enjoy much precious communion with a few souls. There was a sea captain (Capt. Hamlin) here from Glasgow, who was a very dear brother in Christ, the rigidness of his Baptist views being his principal fault. By the by, he gave me a new suit of clothes. I mention this for the sake of Ma.

There has been much cholera here, in January and February, 2,800 deaths by it alone. Just at this time occurs the abominable Holi festival, when there is a universal license to sin. The Jews here think that this is simply their *purim*, adopted and embellished. The purim occurs at the same time, and is observed by the Jews as a time of license. Its origin you know was a day of license to kill; and as men don't want to kill at the time, they celebrate it by the suspension of some of the other commandments of God.

From my heart I bless the Lord for His goodness in raising up Ma again and giving her strength to resume her avocations. May she make haste to love the Lord, and be all that He would have her. I trust she is kept in life that she may be presented unblemished before the throne of His glory. I do beseech you, one and all, make much of your time. Make much or every day, every hour. Time is narrowing down with fearful rapidity. The Lord is at hand. His shadow is even now on the earth. But men are drunk with their own greatness, and are hastening to the apotheosis of humanity in London. Men are making a New Jerusalem of their own there, but the Lamb is not the light thereof. Their New Jerusalem will turn but simply Babylonia Rediviva. Christians err in supposing that Satan changes not. There is a Satan of the 19th century as much in advance of all previous Satans as the 19th century is of all previous centuries. They are looking for the Satan whom they heard about in their infant days, and thus fail to see the polished, philanthropic, scientific utilitarian, perfectionist Satan of the year 1000. There is but one vehicle in which man can safely sail through all centuries, and that is the Gospel. But Christians make the spirit of the age interpret the Gospel, instead of making the Gospel interpret all things.

To the family, July 4, 1851:

You enquire about my finances. They have not given me a moment's solicitude for a year. I have not seen a moment, that I remember, when I wanted money. Yet I have received nothing but my $5 per month, with the exception of sundry articles of clothing from the kind friends of Christ. . . . ——— has strong views on the sovereignty of God, and defective views of man's responsibility. This is the common blemish of piety as it is found here. Nowhere, I think, is the nice balance of these things so apprehended as in America. The way I regard it, is that God does everything and the believer does everything. For every act of the believer there are two wills, the will of himself and the will of God. Whatever is to be done, the believer must do it because it is God that worketh in him to will and to do.

To the family, Dec. 16, 1851:

I forgot to tell you I had been sick since I last wrote, a thing so extraordinary that it should not be overlooked. A kind concern was manifested, but really it was nothing serious. Mr. and Mrs. Hume insisted upon my spending a few days with them, and I did so. I don't know what the matter was. This was the latter part of September. Afterwards, I went out with Bros. Fairbank and Fraser, for a little tour visiting some five or six posts, which was pleasant and restorative. . . . You ask about my ability to write Marathi. I can write it without difficulty though not rapidly. Indeed it cannot well be written rapidly.

To the family from Seroor, Feb. 5, 1852:

We were invited to witness a miracle that was about to be performed by a votary of Khundoba. We repaired to the spot, where a great crowd assembled in front of the idol, and sixteen carts from neighboring villages were brought and fastened one to another. Said devotee was to have hooks inserted into the flesh of his back to which the sixteen carts were to be fastened and so he was to draw them, and give unimpeachable evidence that Khundoba was in him. It was not till after nightfall that the man appeared, and it was quite impossible to see how much was imposture and how much was not. I suppose the hooks were actually inserted in his back. The carts were placed where the road just begins to slope downward toward the river. All that was necessary was to get a start and the train would move on of itself. Darkness and the crowds of friends about the foremost cart hindered from seeing much, but I saw some tugging away at the reluctant wheels till the train was started. After this there was no difficulty. The devotee left the people to bring the carts up again, and came back to receive the worship and the gifts of the deluded people. They then triumphantly asked what I thought, and I frankly told them. When asked why their god did not drag the carts up some steep hill, they said their god was there and not at the hills....

I am urged to visit Ahmednagar and will probably do so sometime this month. Mr. and Mrs. Bissell you know are stationed here. They are studying the language. I find them very agreeable companions. They together had charge of a school in Ohio, for a year before marrying. I find myself obliged to modify in some degree my way of living. Under the circumstances I seem to be obliged to conform more to the habits of those I am with, for a brief season.

His letter home of June 4, 1852 seems to indicate some change of attitude on the subject of miracles:

I little thought when I left America that I should have to combat Mormonism in Bombay. But there has actually arrived a Mormon missionary here from England, and he has been most industriously engaged since his arrival, in seeking to make converts. He found his way to the meetings held at my house. He afterwards came at an appointed time to hold a discussion with Mr. Cassidy and myself. After some random talk, I reminded him of what he professed, namely to have all the apostolic gifts, and requested him to give such evidence as the apostles were accustomed to give. He said it was an evil and adulterous generation that asked for a sign. I replied that Christ was performing the most surprising miracles when He said this, and that He said, "If I do not the works of Him that sent Me, believe Me not." He replied that if anyone would embrace the Mormon faith he should behold the miracles. I told him that tongues were for a sign not to them that believe but to them that believe not.

To the family, Oct. 14, 1852:

Today then you see me in Oomerkhardy in the same little house (pretty ample now that I am all alone excepting the half dozen mice who come out regularly at two o'clock to help me eat my bread and who seem to suppose their company indispensable and to look upon themselves as constituting the life and light of the mansion; and the rats who live overhead and who occasionally get up a kind of imitation thunderstorm; and the lizards who live in my pantry, the self constituted commissioners to taste of the bread which my baker furnishes; and the ants between whose wisdom and my wisdom there was a long and almost desperate conflict, but they appear now to have given in) in which I have been living three and one half years, singularly cheerful as you see, and unusually loving as you cannot see. There is no use in living except to love.

I wish some people would not make it so hard to love them. I have in my mind a group that followed me the other night saying every little thing that malice could invent. One feels the inclination at the time to show his love by a good shaking first, and afterwards by looks and words of kindness. But what a wonderful world will that be where everyone is easy to love, where love finds the most interesting facilitations of itself. That is the world for me. I shall come there with an appetite. But on the other hand, love triumphs most when circumstances are most adverse. Harriet once proposed certain queries on this subject. Does she want me to give her a *carte blanche* to dislike some people? Or to love some fanatically, ignoring the rest? I'll not do it. Let us love God very much; and let all our love to man be the expression of our love to God. Any mistakes in our love to men are best corrected by increased love to God. I am lost in amazement as I contemplate God the lover. The Bible is such a love letter. And the universe is so pressed down and running over with love.

To Harriet, Jan. 27, 1853:

God cannot lie; He can wait, and that's all. And if we wait too, we win. An old prayer must have as much power with God as a new one. More indeed, for it accumulates power, as deposited money gathers interest. The past is present with God, until a balance is struck and the account squared. If a former prayer is unanswered, forgotten before God, we have no reason to rely upon a present prayer. We need a most thorough persuasion that He is the rewarder of all who diligently seek Him, and that we have the petitions which we ask of Him, and that there is no seeking His face in vain; without this persuasion there can be but little life in us; but if we relinquish past prayers, we show that such persuasion is weak in us. We hold God fast, by the sum of all the prayers we have offered up in Christ's Name, yet unanswered; fast, if we have faith now; they are adamantine and continue so, if our faith continues; they are mere threads if we be unbelieving. I, for my part, have all along said and do still say, I will not let Thee go. Think not that I have relinquished the things anticipated in 1851; I erred as to their distance, not, I am persuaded, as to their reality; and my eye is at this moment as intently fixed upon them as ever.

To the family, June 18, 1853:

We are yet at a loss to say how India is to be governed, whether the E. I. Co. will get a renewal of their charter or some new system be devised. The present is a most preposterous form of government. A perfect Hydra. The Bombay Government is not governed by the Governor of Bombay, nor by his council, nor by the Governor General of India, nor by the supreme council of India, nor by the twenty-four directors constituting the E. I. Co. in London, nor by the Board of Control, nor by Parliament, nor by the Queen, but a little by each of these. The principal power residing in the different parties mentioned, is to frustrate one another, and to retard the improvement of the country. A Native finds it quite impossible to understand what government he is living under. An immense deal of odium has fallen upon America through the publication of Mrs. Stowe's book *(Uncle Tom's Cabin)*.

To Harriet, Sept. 27, 1853:

Narayan and I go out as of old to preach, though not to the seaside generally but to different parts of the city. Only the other day we were regularly mobbed, and both of us covered with mud and filth. . . . Are the Apostolic Christians you speak of, Irvingites? If they claim to have the gift of tongues, prove them. They themselves furnish you with a text. Irvingism is a delusion, even tho' it should be found to have some right things which other Christians have not.

One can easily note in the letters and in the man a maturing, satisfying growth and a better balance and stability.

To the family, Oct. 27, 1853:

When we do our duty something more than our duty is done, namely, other people are made to open their eyes upon their duties. We can't do anything alone. If we shut our eyes, somebody else will shut his eyes; if we speak a word, somebody else or a hundred somebody elses insist upon speaking that same word; whatever we do a lot of people stand consecrated to do the same thing. "Then went in that other disciple."

Long ago this was deeply impressed upon my mind, and the question is never with me, "What can I safely do?" but, "What can I, in conjunction with my unseen army of imitators, safely do?" Had I no other observer than God, I would in many things act differently from what I do. We should act as mothers of spoilt children sometimes act: keep certain delicacies away from the table, away from themselves lest their sick children should want them; to the weak becoming as weak. Let love lead and rule us. I always feel ashamed to eat anything at the bedside of a sick person. . . .

Every sinner ought to believe in God's willingness to justify him, and every Christian ought to believe in sanctification. But it is of vast importance to have a right conception of sanctification. Very many of the Methodists mistake here. It is of exceeding importance that we should be willing to have God enlarge our conceptions of true holiness. The standard of God grows with our growth. It will always do so. The piety of today carried over to tomorrow is not sufficient for tomorrow. To that, in one sense, we shall never have attained. In this, namely, that we may stay contented at the point we have reached. It is the perfect that are most bent on pressing forward, even when they have a heavenly consciousness of holiness and a peace inviolable. Even God Himself is always exceeding Himself. I have not the disposition I once had to speak of myself to people. When people speak as though it were forbidden us to hope for entire holiness in this life, I cannot but endeavor to vindicate the Word of God and the Spirit of God. But remembering the self-deceivableness of the heart, I make no report of myself, other than that of utter vileness and unworthiness, and throw on God the obligation to make a report of me, if He sees it important that there should be one. It is His matter more than mine. Yet would I not say that Christians should never verbally declare what they believe the grace of God hath wrought in them. I myself have profited by such declarations.

To the family, Nov. 26, 1853:

This is truly the year of reform and progress, and I must not be caught lagging behind the age. Perhaps as India and America are brought nearer to one another by the sixth vial, drying up the intermediate waters, and by the seventh vial drying up the intermediate air, in one word by steamboats and electric telegraph, we may catch the spirit of the times, and our correspondence become more and more frequent. The time is not far distant when America will be brought within thirty days of India. Soon, in fact, one half the distance that separated us on my arrival here, will be as good as annihilated. When we have reached that height, we shall be able to see looming not far off New York and Bombay fifteen days apart. Then shall we see another height and upon its pleasant summit Bombay, and New York, and all other localities of the New Jerusalem side by side. But in the meantime what things shall come to pass? In 2 Pet. 3, observe "the world that then was," "the world that is," "the world that it is to be." The latter is the new heaven and earth. The first, an old heaven and earth. The second, an intermediate one. The flood of water came between the first and second. The flood of fire or of something like fire comes between the second and third. We see that absolute destruction is not necessarily the fulfillment of the words. There shall be everlasting destruction of the wicked from the presence of the Lord and there shall be sanctification and glory for believers, the New Jerusalem coming down from God out of Heaven, with gates open for the reception of the converted nations. We are to haste unto this day, and it is doubtless at hand. . . .

Perfection consists in desire. The angels in Heaven excel us in this. Desire with faith is the essential condition of happiness. Our souls expand as they receive, so that in the very moment we are sanctified and ready to exclaim, now we are perfect, we find our capacities have grown, and we are in want of more. With all this, perfect contentment and exulting joy are consistent. . . . I still go about preaching now in one street and now in another, and distributing tracts, of which we have a gratuitous series.

To the family, Dec. 25, 1853:

With regard to entire sanctification, I commend to you the following thought, which has long been present to me, and which perhaps I may have spoken of before; if made entirely holy today an increase of holiness will be needed tomorrow, because our moral capacity expands just as we press upon its limits; so that in the unending life of all holy beings there must be pursuit, aspiration. No angel has time to say, I am perfectly holy, for scarcely can the words leave his mouth before he is made sensible of the need of reaching forward. His ideal has risen—what was just now full sanctification has ceased to be so.

To the family, March 10, 1854:

It is a great thing to get the eyes of our understanding open to the fact that God is willing to do great things for us; but it is not good when we have experienced them to say, "These are the greatest, we must stop here." There is one thing that tests all heterodoxy, and that is, progress; it makes but little difference comparatively how defective a man's views may be, if he has a mighty impulse onward. Errors will vanish one by one from the path of such a one. Honor the Spirit of God, and you shall never fall. . . . Many Christians that one meets with here, believe in the restoration of the Jews to their land in an unconverted state, and a great assault made upon them by Gentiles, and a manifestation of Christ resulting in the overthrow of their enemies and their own conversion. One would think the Epistle to the Galatians had no existence. One of these told me the other night that our dispensation was but parenthetical; he was quite unable to see that the Jewish dispensation was truly so; the law being a schoolmaster to bring us to Christ. You will not wonder that these people go further, and believe in the rebuilding of the Temple, the reconstitution of sacrifices and cognate rites. And to deny the validity of their tenets seems to them to savor of infidelity.

To the family, May 12, 1854:

We are about commencing here an Educational Institution like those that are connected with the other Missions in Bombay, where natives may receive a pretty thorough education, largely religious. We have been in correspondence with the Prudential Committee about this for a year. I was not formerly in favor of such institutions conducted by missionaries; at least I thought it more desirable that they should give themselves to direct evangelistic efforts. I do not retract my former opinion; but it is evident to me that missionaries will not spend their time in such efforts, and that if disposed to preach, they will do so none the less because they have an educational institution. The principal reason for establishing this, is that converts of our Mission at Ahmednagar come down to Bombay in considerable numbers to get a better education than is given in the Deccan, enter institutions connected with the Missions, and our best men are thus withdrawn from us, as they often end by joining these other Missions. And if there be a school at all it may as well be as large as we can make it. So our Mission here has hired a large building, and engaged a Mr. Firth as a teacher. It is expected that I will take a considerable part in this, and I am willing to do so. We begin next month.

There is quite a passion for education on the part of the native youth, chiefly, however, as it is considered to be the chief avenue to employment and promotion. Since March 31 inclusive, in consequence of the departure of Dr. Stevenson for home, and removal of Mr. Mitchell to Poona, the *Bombay Guardian* has fallen entirely under my management. I find it easy to supply all the editorial matter. I will send some numbers by this mail or the next. Tell me please what they cost you, if anything. I want to know, as a matter of curiosity.

Dr. Stevenson has many friends in this community. He came out from Scotland as a missionary thirty years ago, and twenty years ago accepted a chaplaincy in the Scotch Established Church. The fact that a salary of £1,400 a year is connected with it, leads many to impute a worldly motive. He has conducted himself well, however, being generally ready for good works, and not renouncing his interest in the natives. He is a very decided premillenarian, and has all sorts of wild views (as they appear to me) about the Jews, but is a humble, pious man as well as a learned one. He is President of the Bombay Branch of the Royal Asiatic Society, and has troubled himself much about inscriptions on the ancient caves of India. A large quantity of sculptures have been brought to Bombay on their way to England from the Persian Gulf, exhumed by Col. Rawlinson in Assyria. He has had much success in deciphering the inscriptions on them, though it is quite another thing to translate them. He has discovered the name of Belshazzar, the only Scripture name that was wanting. Up to this moment we see that the English and French fleets have not been able to help Turkey. "None shall help him." They only precipitate his fall. At the same time God will take care of His infant churches in Asia Minor, and give them enlargement. I am quite willing to see in these Protestant churches, the "people brought back," of Ezekiel 38 and 39. This Armenian Church is the church founded in Apostolic times which got shifted from its foundation, and is now being restored. This is the true restoration of the Jews, Rev. 3:9.

Mrs. Hume and most of her children are at the hills (Mahableshwar). This is a great year for return of missionaries. Mr. Clarkson, a very useful missionary in Gujerat, goes home by the next steamer. At the present moment there are only half a dozen missionaries in Bombay. I suppose you will have heard Dr. Duff and rejoiced in his eloquence and ardor. With all his zeal he manages to spend very little time in India, and thinks nothing of being away four or five years at a time. He has never acquired a native language. But he may be made the instrument of good. I got a letter the other day from Mrs. Graves, Mahableshwar, who has been here now some thirty-six years and is much loved by all. She still talks of returning to America. The return of the Humes would be a good opportunity for her.

We get sad news of the Jews at Jerusalem; they are perishing from want in consequence of the war. This must create, if prolonged, distress all over Europe. Americans abroad deeply deplore the action of Congress in the Nebraska matter. American slavery is everywhere regarded as the anomaly of the age. We are pretty much cured of a desire to boast of our country; for though we should bring forward a thousand admirable things, this one would outweigh them all. I often feel as though I would prefer a severance of the Union.

To Harriet, June 19, 1854:

I find myself now to my own astonishment Principal of an Educational Institution, as they phrase it, in other words, where natives learn English, English Literature, Science and Religion. Nothing was further from my thoughts than putting myself in such a position; I have been very quietly put into it. There has never been such an Institution in connection with our Mission, though the other Missions in Bombay (Ch. of England, Ch. of Scotland, Free Church of Scot.) all have them. If I do not mistake I have sometimes spoken unfavorably of them, as withdrawing a missionary from other work. They need not do so. An hour or so of daily street preaching is as much as any ordinary man is fit for, in that way, while there is no outpouring of the Spirit of God upon the hearers. This last would make everything easy. I approve of schools for the present distress, viz., suspension of spiritual influence. There is an earnest desire for English education on the part of the natives, and to obtain it they consent to receive the religious instruction that is mingled with it. I do not at all suppose that India will be converted in this way. Alas! But few of those who pass through missionary institutions ever embrace the truth. But God's hand is in His bosom, and till it is plucked out we have but a choice of stagnations. The great thing is to stand ready, so that the moment His glory begins to appear we may press forward in the opening path. I have greater scope in this Institution for utilizing the various knowledge I possess.

The *Guardian* goes on under my sole editorship. It is valued by a few. It is too exclusive, i. e., too religious, say the most. As a man on board an American ship in the harbor last year, said, we in Bombay may say, "religion is at a discount here." Dr. Wilson, the Free Church missionary, has been joined lately by his son from England, one of the two mentioned in the Memoir of Mrs. Wilson, as sent home when children. He returns to India an infidel. Thinks Carlyle a greater prophet than Isaiah. He spent two years in Germany and became thoroughly infected with the infidel philosophy of Germany. Unhappily he has become editor of a daily paper here, the *Bombay Times*. I think he is wanting, however, in the ability and prudence to maintain himself in that position. This is a great trial to his father, you may be sure.

There are now about 150 boys in the school, and the number will probably double by the end of the rains. Four or five native teachers are employed. Ramizi, a convert, is useful. I live where I did; Ludru, a convert, with me. Upstairs an Armenian, imprisoned last year in Russia for Protestantism, and a Mussulman from the North of India, who came to this port on his way to Mecca, but was here led to seek Christian instruction. He appears very well. I must mention that I support myself as of old, by teaching in Mr. Miles' excellent family.

We got lately some copies of the "Sharon" from America, containing Daniel's Cantata composed by Mr. Root and Mr. Bradbury. Scarcely had I begun to read this music when it affected me inexpressibly and afterwards when I sat down to a piano and worked it out I was delighted beyond measure. A solo of Daniel with chorus, near the beginning, prayer of Daniel, duet of King and Queen, solo near the end, are quite to my taste. If not utterly originals they are the better for it. They are of the school that I like.

To the family, Jan. 30, 1855:

Some people think I have a great deal on my hands. There is the *Guardian,* for instance, edited by me. There is our Institution, of which I have the charge. I preach in the hospitals, visit ships in the harbor sometimes. I have with Bro. Fairbank the chapel services. Have meetings every night somewhere. Preach to the heathen as much as any other missionary, I suppose. Am Secretary to the Bombay Tract and Book Society, having been chosen about a fortnight ago. Am president of the Temperance Society, though that does not involve much labor. And with all this am not without leisure for social recreation. I wish to be led by the Lord in all things, and cannot refuse anything to which He seems to call me. I would like to be a model missionary, but find that I come short in many things, and perhaps am not worthy to be called a missionary. Doubtless I am outstripped by many in usefulness.

To the family, Apr. 30, 1855:

The P. & O. Co. have the monopoly of steam communication between this and the Mediterranean and they charge enormously. Bombay is one of the most difficult ports for an American to get away from. There is almost no trade from thence to the United States, and the ships that come from America are generally obliged to take freight for some other port and there obtain a cargo for America. Yet though there are such difficulties, our missionaries manage to surmount them bravely. Since I arrived in the country, I may say, indeed, since Jan. 1849, there have left this for America no less than eight missionaries.... Our English institution, started with so much trouble and no little expense, has been broken up. Saturday was the last day. It gave promise of answering the expectations that have been formed of it. Some of the pupils were evidently much interested in the religious instruction, and showed much seriousness towards the last. They are scattered It would have been a most painful thing for Mr. Hume to hear of the dissolution of this school, which was principally got up through his endeavors, and for the success of which his interest was greatly awakened. However, this is not a very pleasant subject. . . .

I am not sure but my connection with the Board may before long be dissolved. One of the converts has adopted views, such as I hold in regard to infant baptism. I wrote you, I think, in 1850 with regard to my change of views. I wrote also to the Presbytery; but as no answer was sent to my letter, I took no step with regard to the American Board. I had some conversation with Dr. Anderson on the subject, and he seemed to agree with me that I might labor with propriety in connection with the Board. He viewed the matter in a liberal spirit. But some are much grieved by the defection of Sador. They know well that I have exerted no influence directly to overturn his conviction in favor of infant baptism; but it strikes me as not unlikely, as most natural indeed, that they should ascribe the change somewhat to the indirect influence exerted by the fact that I was known to be opposed to infant baptism. So I have thought it best to write to them as a body and ask their opinion with regard to the course I should pursue; whether they would consider that the interests of the Mission might be promoted by my dissolving the official connection between me and it, and labor with them as heretofore, though not officially, or otherwise. I told them I would not consider an answer in the affirmative as having the least shadow of unkindness attending it. It seems to me better that there should be a disruption. I have no very proselytizing tendencies with respect to the subject of baptism; at the same time I must be free to express and maintain my convictions on this head, which are deep and settled. I have received no answer from them yet; but will receive one no doubt in the course of a week or so.. Thus I shall probably become disconnected from Missionary Societies except in sympathy and hearty cooperation. I have not the slightest idea of connecting myself with the Baptists. The Baptists (of America certainly) attach an importance to the mode which I cannot find to be warranted by Scripture.

To Harriet, July 9, 1855:

It is nearly five years since I have taken a dose of medicine of any kind. I think I have seldom been more free from headaches than this year. People here, especially when they first know me, find much fault with what they call my exposure of myself. It is regarded as a frightful thing for anyone to get wet and keep wet. However, when they see that I flourish under it, and that I am more free from colds, etc., than others, they reconcile themselves to it. I am now in my eighth monsoon. The rain has been falling for nearly a month. 38½ inches have fallen. I will continue to work on the Bible revision Committee. (On which he began to serve this year—revising the Marathi New Testament).¹

The files of the American Board in Boston have five letters of Bowen to Dr. Anderson written during these five years, 1850-1855:

Seroor, Feb. 14, 1852.

I see nothing in India but a providential and preparatory work, important indeed with reference to that which it introduces, but viewed apart, not satisfactory. The difficulty is that the church is disposed to aggrandize these outside things and put its trust in them. The times are pregnant; but there must be throes and agonizings before the nations are born. There is no chloroform in the inventions and facilities of the age we live in, that will obviate the necessity of travailing in birth for the world's regeneration. . . . Dr. Bissell and I returned this day from a tour of the villages. The work is interesting, and the field quite as promising as any I know of. The Mahars (outcastes) are well disposed to listen; and if there were a more unequivocal display of the co-operating Spirit, things would bid fair for a harvest consisting of many little heaps gathered here and there from a hundred villages. Some persons in this country think it desirable that converts should be gathered into a Christian village, to support themselves by agriculture and manufactures and be as a city set upon a hill to all around. . . . Night and day I praise the Lord for all the ways by which He has led me. My views of my own duty are precisely what I made known in 1849 and '50. I greatly prize the unceasing friendship and kindness of my brethren here. I do not feel prepared to urge any more forcibly than I have already done, those views.

Bombay, Jan. 28, 1853.

I would not have it supposed that I disvalue my connection with the Board. I value it, and should be sorry to see it dissolved. As you have

---

1. Note from American Board: "In 1855 the Marathi translation of the Bible had occupied much time. Messrs. Hazen and Fairbank were appointed members of a sub-committee of the Bombay Auxiliary Bible Society, for revising and carrying through the press two editions of the New Testament. After the departure of Mr. Fairbank, Mr. Bowen was appointed in his place. The work was pursued by this committee very diligently. In addition to the revision the preparation of the clean copy for the printer devolved on Mr. Hazzen; and the reading of the proofs came mainly upon him. The first edition to complete the whole Bible in one volume, was finished in September, the other edition of five thousand copies was brought to a satisfactory termination in December. The result of this year of toil is a New Testament, which is generally satisfactory."

before remarked, the mere fact that I am not supported by the Board, does not in itself destroy and should not relax the ties by which I am bound to it. . . . To be candid, while I see many encouraging, I see also many discouraging things. There is progress of a relinquishment of many falsehoods and an adoption of many truths. But the measure of spiritual illumination is faint indeed. The numbers of sincere enquirers is few; of persons convinced of sin in any emphatic sense, too small to be estimated. In fact I have not seen a single native of India that appeared deeply distressed on account of sin. It is only in the last year that I have seen Europeans in this state. The native church connected with our Mission here has not increased since I came to this country. Whether it has increased in twenty years or not, you know better than I do. I have never known it to exceed a dozen members, unless by the addition of Ahmednagar converts. These apart, there is no Hindu male convert connected with it. And we are all disposed to shrink from severely scrutinizing the measure of grace in the hearts of its members. If a sincere enquirer presents himself, he comes as far as the wicket gate, there lingers a while, and then goes back with a killed conscience. Others present themselves who afflict us by their ill-disguised interested motives, and who withdraw when they find that we have not gain but godliness to offer. You will say there is nevertheless manifest progress in many things. Yes, in too many things.

The harvest is perhaps near; and the tares and the wheat are ripening together. There is progress in the matter of a native Christian literature, and of its dissemination but there is equal progress in the matter of a native heathen literature; of a native Mohammedan literature; of a native infidel literature. If one mission has had a more notable triumph than another in this land, it is the mission of infidelity. The spirit of the age invades everything; and we are liable delusively to ascribe to the Truth, and to connect with the interests of the Truth, results that spring out of that spirit, and that connect themselves simply with the pride and self-confidence of man. Catching the spirit of the age, one native comes forward to lecture against Christianity and in his support of Hinduism; another establishes an infidel periodical; another rears a Hindu Temple, substantial and costly, just where the railroad leaves Bombay; another charters a steamboat to convey Mussulman pilgrims to Mecca, etc, etc. The thing is very delusive, and we need to be on our guard. I have long felt that the Christian public at home are addressed in too flattering a strain with respect to the progress of Christian Missions. These are not making a progress corresponding to the progress of the age. If the church be growing at all, the world is growing much faster. Some two millions are added to its population yearly.

The faith of the church at home in missions is not of the right sort; it is based too much upon what they think is; and if this should be taken away, there would be a great crash of their faith, and a wide gulf of skepticism would be revealed. And it is the fear of this that makes many careful, when addressing the church, whether by communications or personally, to give prominence to the signs that encourage, and keep in the dark background facts unsuspected but stubborn. I have myself felt the influence of this fear, and have preferred not to write rather than to exclude from my communications things which would offend, and which some might even call in question, or ascribe to my own perceptions. Perhaps, however, greater boldness, as it would honor God, would lead eventually to a better state of things, namely to a quest after the true ground and the true aliment of faith in this matter. I do not find that my own faith in the future successes and glories of the missionary work, is any the weaker because it rests exclusively on the Word of God. . . . I continue to receive for teaching ten Rupees a month, a fraction of what the parties would willingly give me, and on this I easily and very much to my own content support myself. Over this whatever comes to me I bestow. I have been permitted to give 500 Rupees the last year to the cause of missions, to say nothing of renounced salary.

Bombay, May 30, 1853.

A conversation with Brother Hume the other day, brought to light the fact that we were both in favor of having an Educational Institution in Bombay. It has since appeared that Brother Fairbank coincides with us; and so we are led to forward by this opportunity an exhibition of our views and of the arguments that support them. As Brothers F. & H. will write you rather copiously, it will be enough if I submit to your consideration, the reasons that have led me to look favorably upon the plan:

1. Among the young men of this country the desire for education is very strong and is daily becoming stronger. What they principally seek is an English education. They regard it as the avenue to success and influence. We may find fault with that desire; we may prefer to see them cling to their vernaculars; we may exert ourselves to make them do so; the fact remains. We cannot overcome it. We should incur odium by attempting to do so. And having the appearance of being something providential, it commands our respect.

2. Young men connected with our Missions in W. India, have their full share of this desire for what is termed a liberal education. And they are drawn to Institutions, superintended by other Missionaries, and the consequence is that they join other Missions. This though not a great evil, is still I think, not the most desirable state of things. It is a reproach

to our Missions in the public estimation that they should be parting with their converts in this way. It was this circumstance that first led us to doubt the expedience of our existing arrangements. The first impulse then was to seek to change the minds of those young men. In one or two instances, this endeavor was successful. Mr. Ballantine induced Sudoo, who had come to Bombay with the view mentioned to go back to Satara. But in almost all instances such persuasion is quite ineffectual. And there is no guarantee that Sudoo will not resume his abandoned design. The fact remains; it will not accommodate itself to us; must we not accommodate ourselves to it?

3. If missionaries have not a mind to preach, (i. e., to make this their principal business) you cannot make them preach by shutting up their schools, or withholding the liberty to found an Educational Institution. If missionaries have a mind to preach, the fact of their being engaged in teaching some hours in the middle of every day, will not hinder them from preaching. Taking the year round, I doubt if there be in India a missionary who preaches (in the technical sense) on an average, two hours a day. No missionary connected with the Educational Institutions of Bombay is actually employed in them more than twenty-four hours in the week.

4. I believe, as I have always believed, that the greatest results of missionary efforts, shall eventually be seen in connection with the preaching of the Gospel. I look for no great and splendid spiritual results from educational efforts. As things now are they seem to be expedient, they seem to be necessary. A day is coming doubtless when the preaching of the Gospel will be attended by such displays of the power of God, as have never yet been witnessed. That day may be at hand. But at present, street preaching is little else than street quarreling. Wherever you go in Bombay, men present themselves armed with infidel objections against Christianity, or with obscene descriptions of its origin, or with a treasury of personal insults, or with an overwhelming volume of voice, or in default of all, with handfuls of sand. And the most complete refutation of their objections, though repeated a hundred times, never induces them to relinquish a single one of those objections. Truth-seekers, as a class, have no existence. Distress on account of sin is never met with among these people.

5. If young men are not afforded the means of getting an education such as I have just indicated, they will go to the Government Schools, and get an education from which the more beneficent features of the above list are excluded. They will thus become infidels.

6. I believe that this Mission is possessed of the pecuniary means of commencing such an Establishment. The fund in my opinion, should be used; and I see no better way than this.

7. I am willing to aid in such an Institution, to any extent that may be thought desirable. I am also willing to remain disconnected with it. With these remarks, I let the matter rest, so far as I am concerned.[2]

Bombay, Jan. 13, 1854.

With reference to yours of Sept. 9, I am glad to see that you appreciate in some measure the difficulty and disadvantages under which we as a Mission labor. You say, "it is clear that you ought not to remain in your present helpless state," in other words that some means should be found of placing our Mission on a footing equal to others, with respect to the ability of presenting attractions to Christian young men who are desirous of obtaining an education. You are, however, unwilling that we should enter into competition with other educational institutions, or become too prominently educational. You suggest that a Seminary at Ahmednagar would answer the purpose.

I do not think this would obviate the difficulty. The town of Bombay is swallowing up the Presidency. It is the metropolis of W. India in a different sense from that in which our great cities are metropolises. The current sets more and more strongly heathenward. I could not do more than repeat, so I will only refer to our letters written in May and June past upon this subject and upon the strong desire which possesses the younger portion of the community for an education. India is awakening

---

2. In his lectures in Scotland entitled *The Missionary Ideal in the Scottish Churches* (p. 171 f), Dr. Mackichan, for many years principal of Wilson College in Bombay, speaking of the people in the home church who judge foreign mission work by the number of conversions, says:

"They need to be reminded that the crude test which they are applying is not the only measure by which such work is to be tested, and that their obedience to their Lord's command to go into all the world is not to be guided by the visible result as they are wont to measure it.

"In this connection the writer recalls a conversation he had with the sainted George Bowen, one of the most devoted missionaries that India has known. When the question of educational work in the mission field was exercising the minds of some within the church at home, the writer on one occasion took counsel with George Bowen in regard to this matter. George Bowen in this conversation vindicated educational work of every grade, claiming that the converts to Christianity among all classes of the people had been gathered into the Church of Christ mainly through mission schools. He held at the same time, that our duty as missionaries was not to be measured by results in any department of our work. Referring to his own special work, evangelistic work carried on mainly by preaching in the streets and open spaces of the city of Bombay, he added that, although he could not trace a single conversion to the street preaching in which for years he had been engaged, he would continue to preach in the streets of the city to the end of his life. And he did."

and like a Caspar Hauser, needs to be taught everything. The young men who are likely to be withdrawn from us, wish to know not only Western Theology, but everything Western. To run the gauntlet of merely secular instruction in Government Schools, is a more dangerous thing here, than it is in our country.

I do not wonder that you shrink from encouraging us to launch ourselves into an educational sea. You feel that while education is a great want of India, we are here to supply a greater want. But would the Gospel be less preached under the proposed circumstances than it is now? I do not think so. I believe the contrary would be the case. The Free Church Mission are building an edifice now for the first time, after carrying on their Institution for twenty years. I do not see any necessity of building now, should we begin an Institution. A good enough house could easily be obtained for Rs. 150 a month, and I think the whole monthly expense need not exceed Rs. 400—under $250. We might expect considerable help from parties here.

I continue to preach in the streets and wherever the people so congregate that I can quietly talk to them. They have many inquiries to make and difficulties to start. Occasionally I am maltreated or mobbed. But I do not suffer my mind to dwell on these occasional unpleasantnesses. May this upon which we have entered prove a year of the right hand of the most high.

I have never forgotten what you said to me upon my embarkation, viz., that I should consider myself rather the servant of the Lord Jesus Christ, then of the Board. Upon this I have acted, feeling that the highest interests, indeed the only interest of the American Board is that I should fulfill my course, and then hear from my heavenly Master, hail, well done. To this end pray for me. Pray for us. I am in heart as friendly to the American Board as any, and value my connection with it.

The Providence of God is causing a great deal of attention to be directed to the Mission of the Board among the Armenians, and it is felt that Americans have been highly favored in being sent into that harvest. I love my own field best, however, with all its barenesses. We are alike barren till the Lord alters the quality of the soil.

In the winter of 1854-'55 the famous deputation of the American Board, consisting of Dr. Rufus Anderson, Secretary, and the Rev. A. C. Thompson of the Prudential Committee, visited India and introduced some radical changes in the work of the Board's Missions, especially in the matter of closing schools and restricting the use of education as a missionary agency. The deputation re-emphasized the duty of direct preaching. In his home letters Bowen refers to the visit.

To the family, Nov. 27, 1854:

> The deputation, with Mr. and Mrs. Munger, reached here Nov. 3, twenty-four hours after our dreadful hurricane. I have seen something like this at sea, but never on land. The pressure of the wind was thirty-five pounds the square foot. The number of lives lost probably exceeded 800. It seems to have been aimed point blank at our harbor, our admirable harbor where the vessels thought they could ride in safety. We hear very little of it anywhere else. At least 1000 trees were torn down. A tract was written (by me) on the evening following, and published the next day. The deputation spent ten days in Bombay. They have very much the same views that all missionaries have on arriving. Admirable in theory, but needing to be modified in practice. We have to consult the circumstances and exigencies of our case, and recognize the necessity of adaptation. They are disposed to make many changes. Some of them good no doubt. But there is to be a Convention, or General Conference at Ahmednagar next week. . . . The Deputation look askance at our Seminary, and it remains to be seen whether they will retain it or not. They want to have the missionaries preaching almost exclusively. I enjoyed the intercourse with Dr. Anderson and Mr. Thompson very much. Dr. A. appeared to enjoy hearing me preach in front of a Hindu temple one night, about as much as anything. But our one need is the outpouring of God's Spirit. In whatever manner truth is presented it will come with power *then*. The kind of instrumentality is not the great thing. We all look forward with interest, and some perhaps with apprehension, to the Conference at "Nuggur." Some change may be made that some will deprecate. The gathering of Missionaries will be interesting.

To the family, Jan. 30, 1855:

> I was absent at "Nuggar" from Dec. 1 to 27. Our Conference lasted twenty-one days. The minutes and reports are to be printed. It was delightful to be thrown so much into the Society of American brothers and sisters. I was much drawn to them and received ever so much kindness. . . . Our Deputation has gone to Madura by way of Cochin. We could not but form a high opinion of these brethren. Their views in many respects were just, in others crude, like those of young missionaries. I hope good will come from their visit. Two native brethren were ordained. . . . The Deputation tried to do some things that they did not succeed in accomplishing. They tried to get the brethren to consent to a diminution of their salaries. They made some strong appeals which were not responded to, and they were obliged to give it up. Our printing press, so far as it is secular, is to be given up. This is right.

As indicated in his letter of Apr 30, 1855, to the family, Bowen had come to adopt views on the subject of baptism which led him to feel that his continued relationship to the Mission might be open to question by his associates. On May 9, 1855, accordingly, he addressed the Deputation:

On the 19th ult. I addressed to my brethren the missionaries of the American Board in Western India, a letter, of which I beg leave here to introduce a copy:

"Rev. S. B. Fairbank
Rev. A. Hazen
Rev. S. B. Munger
Rev. H. Ballantine
Rev. R. G. Wilder
Rev. L. Bissell
Rev W. P. Barker

"I have lately come to the knowledge that Sudoo has adopted the views of those who oppose paedo-baptism. This change has not been brought about through any effort on my part. It is quite possible that we may have exchanged some words on the subject a year or two ago. But I had not the least idea that his mind was awakened on the subject, till he informed me lately of his change of sentiments, and in doing so, he ascribed the change to something that he had read while studying in the Free Church Institution.

"On reflection it has seemed to me not impossible that he may have been more or less influenced in his enquiries by the fact of my holding views in opposition to paedo-baptism. At all events the idea will naturally arise in the minds of some that there is a kind of connection between the fact of my holding such views and his embracing them.

"Further, I have been led to consider that possibly the brethren with whom I am now associated in the Missions of the American Board in Western India may look with some apprehension on my relations to them as being likely to beget a difference of views among the converts and inquirers connected with those Missions. They are aware that I hold the views in question without any disposition to proselytize. But they are also aware that I cannot disguise those views nor hold them in abeyance when I seem called upon to speak of them, and that this without any special design, I may be exerting an influence with respect to this thing, in opposition to the influence of my brethren.

"I have thought it proper therefore to write to you with regard to this matter and ask you what course you think I ought to pursue. And I write you to speak with all frankness. Should you judge that on the whole it would be better that I should not stand in my present relation to you as a missionary of the same Board, I will at once act upon your advice, and take measures for dissolving my connection with the American Board. I do not suppose that my relation to you as a Christian brother and minister of the Lord Jesus Christ will be in the least degree affected by the change spoken of. In fact I should expect to stand upon the same footing with respect to you all as I have hitherto; with the advantage (as you may perhaps regard it) that there will be a distincter line of demarcation between the views held by you and those held by me, with regard to infant baptism

"Again I say and more emphatically that I will not look upon your recommendation of the course spoken of, as in the least degree implying any diminution of that Christian love, which I have so good reason to believe you entertain for me, and which you know is—and by the grace of God—ever will be cordially reciprocated by me."

Bro. Fairbank in the very kind remarks made by him deprecated my adoption of the course proposed in the above letter. "I earnestly hope (he says) that existing relations may abide unchanged." He dwells particularly upon the fact that I had never objected to the baptism of infants by the other members of the Mission, nor endeavored to propagate my views on this subject. Had the expressed opinion of the other brethren coincided with that of Mr. F., I would not now be writing to you on the subject of my relation to the Board. Br. Hazen agreed in general with Br. F. Br. Bissell thought that nothing would be gained by my dissolving the connections. The other four brethren, however, decline expressing any opinion or offering any advice; saying at the same time, "Br. Bowen is a brother whom we greatly love." As a majority of my beloved associates in these Missions say nothing to dissuade me from pursuing the course proposed, I conclude after prayer and deliberation, that this course is the most eligible.

I therefore beg of you to accept and to transmit to the Prudential Committee of the American Board of Commissioners for Foreign Missions, the resignation of my status as missionary of that Board.

My relations with that Board have been throughout of an amicable character, and will ever be remembered by me with feelings of gratitude for the kindness and consideration shown to me by the Secretaries and Prudential Committee. I trust that I shall still be united to the Board and to its missionaries by the ties of fraternal affection, and may be enabled to approve myself, hereafter as heretofore, a staunch friend and willing fellow-workman.

Believe me, honored sirs and dear brethren,
Yours in Christian affection,
George Bowen

To Harriet, July 9, 1855:

> I have sent in my resignation and it has been accepted, or rather forwarded to the rooms by the Deputation, recommending its acceptance which amounts to the same thing. Ever since it was hinted by Dr. Anderson to me last December that it would hardly be right to commit to my instruction a theological class, I have had the idea that a dissolution of this connection must take place. I must be free to serve the Lord as I think best. However, nothing that occurred in my intercourse with these revered brethren would have led me to resign. You will see by the last *Guardian* my reason. Perhaps it would be well to send this to be extracted into the *Evangelist.* Practically, my position remains unchanged. I labor in connection with the American Mission, as I always have, dividing the services with Bro. Hazen. I have received very kind letters from the brethren, expressive of warm affection and sincere attachment. I am perfectly persuaded that I have been led of God in this matter. He has determined all my ways from the beginning, and He must determine them to the end. The path I am in may lead whither it will, it is the path that God has chosen for one. This is enough for me.[3]

For the next ten years Bowen worked in Bombay with no specific missionary connection. Then for a period of six years his relation to the American Board Mission, as we shall see, was resumed.

Bowen's home letters for the five-year period just reviewed are full of observations on world affairs: the Taiping Rebellion in China, France and Napoleon the Third, the Papacy and the anti-Slavery struggle in America. He continued his simple life with steadily enlarging influence in Bombay. Derelicts from England and America floated to his care and his circle of friends embraced all classes high and low. Even now he was beginning to command that respect for his character and talents which made him in time the most conspicuous and most highly regarded citizen of the city.

---

3. In Dr. Rufus Anderson's *Missions to India,* published in 1874, in the chapter on "Missions to the Mahrattas, 1854-1862," Dr. Anderson says (p. 268): "Mr. Bowen having adopted sentiments adverse to the baptism of infant children, resigned his connection with the Board but continued his acceptable aid as a preacher which he has done to the present time." In a footnote Dr. Anderson adds: "Since the above was written my attention has been called to the *Bombay Guardian,* edited by Mr. Bowen, of Nov. 1, 1873, in which he announces his return to his former views on this subject. This he does in the following language: 'Lately we have come to look at this matter under another light, and believe now that we have been in error in denying the Scriptural warrant for the baptism of the infant children of believers.'"

The picture of the little Indian church in its infancy presented by Bowen in these years is a pitiful picture. In his diary of Dec. 19, 1848, he writes of the poverty of the results and the need of miracle or at least of more miraculous power:

> Can it be the Father's good pleasure that a mission should be established forty years in a heathen land, without bringing forth fruit? It will soon be forty years since this mission was established, and there are six members of the church, not one of them a Hindu. How long shall I be with you, how long shall I suffer you, is the language of Christ. Our want of faith hinders people from believing on Him. Christians are like reservoirs with an outlet at the top, which require to be filled before they can send out the streams of life. In this way travels the grace of God. It comes to a soul, and flows, flows, flows into it, until it has filled it, then it overflows and goes to another soul, and little by little fills that, overflows and goes on to another. Sometimes indeed when it overflows it reaches a great many souls at once as in the day of Pentecost, but there must always be one full and overflowing reservoir. For forty years the utterance of God from Heaven has been thus to us, "It is your Father's good pleasure to give you the kingdom." Let me henceforth believe this word and show my faith by my works. . . .
>
> Whether we are to have miracles or not, it is certain that we have the promise of boundless power, sufficient to give us the kingdom. But is not the reason why we shrink back from miracles this, that they involve such an immense exercise of power? This unbelieving generation of Christians has not real faith in the power of God to be thus grandly exerted for them. Their notions are cramped and contracted. They are expecting the world to be somehow or other saved without the grander and simpler displays of divine power.

A year later he describes the church in a letter to Harriet, Nov. 19, 1849:

> We had lately the communion in our native church. Shall I tell you of our members? You will be much pained; but the truth might as well be known. If the truth concerning the churches of India were known in America, I think there would be a greater realization of the difficulties of the work and of the need of consecration and prayer in the church. Fifteen persons in all sat down. Deduct three missionaries and one missionary's wife, two European members of other churches, Mr. Graham, the printer and his wife, who are Indo-Britons, and by birth, nominal Christians, there remain seven persons as the number of

converts from false religions. Of these two males, originally Catholics, one married female and three girls originally Catholics, and one girl of Hindu origin. Not one converted heathen man. . . . There remain seven missionaries (of all denominations) to the vast heathen population of Bombay.

In July, 1851 he writes home:

Tomorrow we have the communion in our little native church, which grows not any. The secular papers here say that every convert has cost a missionary. It is a day of deep unmitigated rebuke with us. But as a body we live unconcerned. A proposition to reduce salaries would excite the greatest emotion; but the stagnancy of the gospel Bethesda awakes little concern.

In 1854 he writes:

Baptisms in Western India continue to be few and far between. We talk about progress but the increase of population makes increasing idolaters in a proportion vastly greater than that of the church's increase.

Not now. The decennial census in India has shown for half a century a ratio of growth in the numbers of Indian Christians far exceeding the ratio of increase in the population and in the non-Christian communities. This is the table:

Proportion for 10,000 of population:

1881	73	1911	124
1891	79	1921	150
1901	99	1931	179

In 1881 there were 2,284,380 Christians in a total population of 253,896,330, and in 1931, 6,297,000 out of a total population of 352,837,778.

Bowen ought to have seen in the patience and courage of the little band of seven some larger assurance of faith. It is good to think that he sees now in Bombay and throughout India the vast growth of the seed which he and others planted and watered with their life blood.

13. Ten Years of Independent Work
1855—1865

At the time of his disconnection from the American Board Mission, Bowen was urged by English friends to undertake a mission to some of the Hill Tribes: To Harriet, Jan. 30, 1855:

> I received the other day a letter from a gentleman at Mt. Aboo, an acquaintance of mine, saying that he and a Christian friend (Sir Richmond Shakespeare) were desirous of having a mission commenced among the Bhils, an aboriginal tribe inhabiting the hill country north of the Nerbudda, and in a complementary manner, inviting me to undertake it. I have no objection to the work itself, and am as able to go as any missionary in Bombay, I suppose. But I have no knowledge of the language spoken by these people, and among them would nave no occasion for the Marathi which I have acquired with so much pains. They need missionaries. But there are maybe 100,000 people in Bombay as ignorant of the Gospel as they are. I cannot see my way to go, not now, at least.

To the family, Sept. 11, 1855:

> You will have heard of the death of Mr. Nesbit, the Free Church missionary here, one of he best men I ever knew, one to whom I was strongly attached. The whole Christian community here regarded him with great veneration. He had a remarkable love of the Word of God and a most happy manner of expounding it. Great humility. Readiness to prefer others to himself. Scarcely read any book but the Bible. Shunned (in English society) by all but Christians. A single eye. Great power of interesting and attaching to himself the natives. He died most suddenly. . . . One Hindu has embraced or is about to embrace Christianity in connection with the established Church of Scotland. This, I believe, is their first convert from Hinduism. There have been some painful developments in the church at Ahmednagar. Some members of long standing and good repute have turned out to be great transgressors; to have been so all along. . . . I almost forgot to mention that I had a bad cold all last month. You can't imagine how solicitous all are here when anything is the matter with me. They seem to have the erroneous notion

that I don't care for myself and they must care for me. I am now, thank God, as well as ever.

I labor in connection with the American Mission as of old. Preach besides in the thoroughfares. Have the charge of the Tract Society. We are rejoicing this week over the completely printed New Testament in Marathi.

To the family, Nov. 15, 1855:

I have removed since I wrote you. After having spent 6½ years in Oomerkhadi (in two houses) I have come to another part of Bombay called Hamatipur. I took the place first for a preaching station, and after using it for that about a week, I concluded to come and live here. I have a pretty good-sized room, some twenty feet square, opening on the street. The front consists altogether of folding doors which can be thrown entirely open.

I preach two afternoons in the week, as we have discussions in the Chapel on two other afternoons. The people come in pretty well, sometimes filling the room and the sidewalks in front. In one corner of this room is my desk, books, and settee. On this latter I sleep, having had no other bed since last year when I gave my bed and bedding to a sick man in Oomerkhadi whose furniture had been seized. (Here, by the way, is something that does not look much like keeping your right hand in ignorance of what your left hand doeth). I had not used either bed or bedding for a long time before, so of course there was not the shadow of privation about it. (I think I have snubbed myself pretty well for the miserable attempt at self-glorification. A man must be reduced to great straits when he resorts to such means as this to get himself praise).

I continue to preach as of old in the Chapel on the Sabbath and also in the Hospital. Have also done considerable in the way of street preaching since I last wrote. Sudoo, a young man that formerly lived with me, a member of the Ahmednagar church and studying for the ministry, embraced my views about baptism, not, however, through any influence of mine, and the American Mission dismissed him from their employ. I felt bound to give him employment. He preaches with me and pursues his studies in the Free Church Institute. I had no particular desire to adopt him, not caring to build on others' foundations; and I know not how long he may remain connected with me. The American missionaries are quite content that I should support him. If you ask how I am able to do so, I answer, I have funds supplied by friends in this country, for mission purposes. . . .

> About twenty works have passed through my hands as Secretary of the Tract Society this year. I have to read all these in manuscript and in type. They are in Marathi, Gujarati, Hindustani, and English. . . . Yesterday we were discussing the attributes of God in the Chapel. Brother Hazen set them forth and proved them at some length. Afterwards objections were raised. Nourojse, the Parsi, who opposed me for two years at the seaside was there and talked as of old. His favorite position is that God is the author of all and that it is impiety to doubt it. He puts it into one man's heart to steal and into another's to arrest him and punish him; and He has created hell for the wicked (whose wickedness is from Himself) and Heaven for the good (whose goodness is from Himself). All is from Himself, yet He makes these distinctions in dealing with men. There are thousands in the community who regard this as a highly religious tenet.
>
> I write little to you about my inner life. The *Guardian* will help you somewhat. But, after all, I leave much more unsaid than said. It will be time enough when we are among the pastures of everlasting green, together, to talk of much that seems to be incommunicable in this world. I had the thought, one sleepless night lately, with regard to the expression, "He putteth all their tears in His bottle"—that there are to be future expressions of the sympathy of God with our present sorrows. Our wounds are not merely to be cicatrized—by time. If God now sees it necessary to withhold the expressions that our hearts demand, He will nevertheless find it due to Himself, hereafter, to give special tokens that in all our afflictions He condoled and felt all we felt. Therefore the tears are bottled. We may forget them but God will reproduce them for the vindication of His own infinite loving kindness.

As the letters show, Bowen's relations with his fellow missionaries continued close and affectionate. One of the new-comers, Mrs. Munger, wrote to Bowen's mother and sisters on January 15, 1856, surviving her letter only six months:

> The esteem and I have for your dear son and brother and the frequent opportunities I have had since I came to this land of seeing him and speaking with him of you has drawn you so near my heart that you seem to me more like the friends I have known for years than those of so brief an acquaintance. It is some months since this good brother gave me your address and I fully intended writing but the early loss of my American vigor and an unceasing round of missionary duties kept me from telling you many things about the beloved absent one, which I thought it would give you pleasure to know. When I first saw brother

Bowen I was troubled to see him so thin. It seemed as if instead of going about prosecuting his daily labors, he ought to be on his couch under the care of a kind nurse. But he always affirmed he was well, and I recalled what one of you told me, that he has a wiry constitution. Your message, dear Mrs. Bowen, I delivered to him, to which he pleasantly replied that his mother gave herself too much trouble about him.

He has here a circle of dear devoted friends among different denominations of Christians, all of whom would esteem it a privilege to do something for his comfort and happiness. His agreeable conversation, enriched as it is from the storehouse of his intellectual treasures and his deep earnest piety, cause his society to be sought for by the pious and intelligent portion of the community. He is a very dear brother in our Mission. We all feel that he is prone to pay too little attention to his personal comfort, therefore we would fain in some way add to it. Today he is going on a little tour. Mrs. Hazen tried to force some delicacies upon him for his journey but he said he had "everything." He had been looking around for some poor person on whom to bestow some sugar and tea. His European friends, knowing his unwillingness to receive anything from their hands, sometimes send supplies to his house during his absence so that he knows not where to return them.

Such is your son and brother, a happy man with everything that he wants, an example of humility and self-denial to the world around him. I often wish you could see him, it would so comfort your heart. I feel that in giving him up for the sake of Christ to labor in this land of night shade and death you have indeed made a great sacrifice. If maternal tenderness and sisterly affection sometimes plead that his presence is necessary as one earthly friend after another is taken away, all these feelings would be hushed could you witness the great work in which this beloved one of your heart is engaged. Could you see the hundreds of thousands in this great city who are mad upon their idols, and then see the cities, towns and villages teeming with idolaters all over this vast country, you would renewedly dedicate him to this glorious work.

Bowen to the family, Feb. 16, 1856:

The new Governor General, Lord Canning, visited Bombay last month on his way to Calcutta. I attended his levee in the Town Hall. Lord Dalhousie haw been eight years our Gov.-General, and has greatly distinguished himself by his administration of the Government. These eight years have seen the most mighty changes and improvements in India. The Punjab, Pegu, a part of the Nizam's territories, and just now, Oudh, have been annexed. We have a new opening for missionaries in

Oudh. It is unspeakably desirable that the whole of the Nizam's territory should be brought under the Company's sway.

I was absent a fortnight on my late tour. I have such a multiplicity of engagements in Bombay that I find it difficult to remain long away. I have abundant opportunities of preaching. These I have everywhere indeed. The preaching at my own house goes on as usual. Large numbers attend, but there is no permanent audience. People come and go. On returning from my tour, I found that some persons had possessed themselves of a key and entered my house, unabashed. I suspect two ladies, Mrs. Munger and Mrs. Hazen. A cot, etc., had been placed there, my couch mended. One can get no redress for these things. The same happened before in the days of Mrs. Hume. I only wish everybody could sleep as comfortably as I do whenever I lie down and fare as well as I do whatever I eat. I have no ungratified desires with respect to worldly things. I seem to have had more of the life of God in my soul since the first Sabbath of the year.

The great thing impressed upon me is the importance of manifesting God in everything I do, and without reference to anything ulterior. And I seek ever to bear in mind that I have no manner of right to exist for any other purpose. It is arch treason in me to be exhibiting myself. My faculties, my members, my organs are given me that I may do, not my own will, but His. Self-consecration is not good for a day. It must be renewed hourly and still more often. A perpetual consciousness of a present God, to Whom belong all my powers and opportunities for the showing forth of His glory is what I seek to have. I find that in company there is a perpetual remembrance of the company, and a necessary adaptation of oneself to the company. Not a word is spoken without some kind of preliminary reference in the mind to the parties hearing and consideration of the way in which they are likely to be affected. Why should not God be equally remembered? Nothing is more important than praying without ceasing, and giving way to God.

Had some pleasant thoughts last night as I lay awake in bed. First the idea came into mind, suppose this great building should tumble down upon me as I lie here. Then I said, it cannot. God upholds it. All the night long He holds up this ceiling over my head so that I can sleep in peace. The building in itself can just as easily fall up as fall down. You see that my notions of Natural Philosophy are very unphilosophical, judged by ordinary standards. But I thoroughly hold, and have for many years, that it is absolutely impossible to account for the fall of anything, or for any movement or change in the material universe, except upon the hypothesis of a present, willing and efficient God. I thought also that there was no motive so powerful as an intense desire to please another, and resolved to lay myself out in everything just to please God. Of course such resolutions have been made a thousand times; words cannot picture forth the particular phases of experience. It seems to me generally sheer nonsense to speak about myself, for I cannot convey any proper impression of the kind of converse my soul has with God. Everybody can say the same. . . .

Eight years in Bombay and not the beginning of fruit! I hope you have learned to bother yourselves with no more hopes concerning me than that I should humbly accomplish the good pleasure of His will, and be found with you at His right hand in that day. And that you have quite got over any delusive expectation, that your brother, your son, would be a distinguished missionary, a distinguishingly useful missionary.

To Harriet, April 16, 1856:

Mr. Fairbank's calumniatory remarks about my white pantaloons I strongly deprecate. You ought not to listen for a moment to such representations. You may be sure that he looked upon my pants with a jaundiced eye, else he would have seen them to be immaculately white—considering. I don't know why he should stab me thus behind the back and destroy among you my hitherto unimpeached reputation for cleanliness. As for my shirt collars, there is not the shadow of a foundation for the remark he makes upon them. They will look defiantly upon him when he returns and notwithstanding all the serenity and amiability of my countenance will, I dare say, make him turn pale with a sense of the wrong he has done. And if I could bring myself to it I could tell you tales of him that would convince you that he is not at all the one who should come forth as the champion of missionary neatness. But in all generosity I forbear. Yet if I hear any more insinuations to the effect that my dhobi (washerman) is a myth, I think I shall just transfer his monthly bills to the authors of these insinuations. I think that will effectually cure them. I had it on my mind to get myself photographed and the likeness of myself, pants and all, sent to you that you might judge for yourself and that Mr. F. might stare confounded and abashed.

To Kate, August 29, 1856:

You will read in the *Guardian* about our attempt on Cocoanut Fair Day. This is the great festival of Western India. On that day there are at least 100,000 people in the Esplanade and beach. A friend of mine, Mr. Peyton, conceived the idea of getting a pulpit made and conveyed there. I promised to preach. The pulpit or scaffold was covered with red cloth and, borne on the shoulders of four coolies (porters), was a conspicuous object. No sooner was it planted and I had got into it, than a sea of heads of all castes assembled around it. I raised my voice to its utmost pitch and for a little while, I hope, was heard by many. Afterwards "some lewd fellows of the baser sort" resolved to extinguish my voice by their clamor and succeeded. Mr. Narayan Sheshadri attempted to carry on the preaching, but with no better success. Thus we alternated for some time. The people became more unruly, tore up tracts and threw them at us, and finally got up in the pulpit. Seeing that there was likely to be a riot, we desisted, and sent away the pulpit. The attempt was not successful but it was as well to make it. The whole difficulty was caused by one or two individuals. Afterwards we found opportunities of preaching and discussing.

To the family, Oct. 3, 1856, recalling the vanished manuscript on which he was working at the time of his conversion and of which his journals have spoken:

> I thought I had effectually damaged, in fact given a death blow to that manuscript work, by burning up the chief part of it before I left. I am sure I must have done so, and that what you have is an inconsequential fragment. The only good (I can perceive) that this work could have wrought would have been by showing to a class not very numerous in the community but still having a definite existence that a person viewing the world as they viewed it, having their aspirations, their sorrows, their doubts, their religion, as they choose to call it, their sins and their natures, did yet become a most sincere believer in orthodox Christianity and profess to have found by faith in Christ, what he had so vainly rummaged literature, philosophy, and the dream world in quest of for many long years.
>
> I really remember scarcely anything about it. I was engaged upon it up to the very moment when I was shown the truth of Christianity; its completion and my own new life were, as near as might be, simultaneous. The engrossing nature of my new perceptions and the disgust for my old errors which they naturally brought with them, hindered me from looking to that former condition and it is surprising how entirely a multitude of things have faded from my mind that were formerly its constant tenants. Is that *Agathon* in existence? Probably not. I believe I have never told any human being what I designed in that. My idea was to take Christ, in the period of His life before His ministry, and represent Him subject to various temptations, availing myself of the silence of Scripture with

regard to His early manhood. This idea was cherished by me as long ago as when I was in Europe. I find references to it in my diary. I got a New Testament (French) when I was in Paris, just to see what scope it would give me in this respect. In all this I was a perfect unbeliever, and took Christ just as I would have taken Prometheus, regarding Him (that is, the incarnation) as a mythological character. Under these views, I wrote some strange things. I have most of the original matter of this in a MS book.

Bowen must have been a slight figure, considering his weight of only one hundred pounds and his conception of tallness:

Mr. Robert Brown, one of my best Christian friends, goes home by this mail. He is a wealthy merchant, very tall, 5 (6?) feet 7½. He goes home for his health. The rain is over and gone. I have frequent opportunities of preaching in the streets and on the Esplanade. Was at a lecture in defense of Hinduism last Saturday evening, and replied to the Brahmin's arguments.

To the family, Dec. 17, 1856:

I enjoyed your last letter very much. It is very grateful to think that I write anything that is helpful to you and others, be it but one or two others. I feel that I am called to give out what is in me, so far as providence intimates, and to leave what I have uttered to be used by providence. If it should be neglected 100 years, what of that? I suppose that by a very little concession to the spirit of the world, I could write something that would be far more attractive generally. But I ever feel that I must look to the standard which God has given me, weigh every line in the balances set before me. I often feel as I add a line or two to an article, This is spoiling this for the world, destroying its influence. There is a very great temptation to a writer or speaker to make a little more of the human auditors than of the One divine Auditor. I suppose there is a very little written that the writer would like to read aloud *every word of it* in the presence of Christ. Many a long year ago I asked from God grace to live a life of faith and it will not do for me to shrink from a life of sterility if this is to be the answer. I suppose it is. I never dreamed that God would take me so literally at my word, in the promises I made Him. It is very easy to make promises to one who you think will not require you to fulfill them. But if I hold the Lord to the letter of His Word He may and will hold me to the letter of mine.

To Harriet, March, 1857:

I have only been induced to write today by the necessity, real or supposed, of administering—a reproof shall I say—a criticism. I may perhaps be all in the wrong, and it may be that there is not the slightest necessity for me to give myself any uneasiness; but some remarks of yours about a book that you have read and which I have never seen, entitled *Seed-grain for Thought and Discussion,* by a Mrs. Lowell, rather jar upon my feelings. This book you say contains extracts from Emerson, Martineau and Carlyle; and you write in a rather commendatory way of these writers saying that "they give virtue a high place, the highest, in fact do everything but humble themselves at the feet of Jesus." I look upon these persons as the enemies of all righteousness and the deadliest foes of virtue. Miss Martineau is that most hideous of beings, an atheistic woman, the translator and panegyrist of Comte who would have the works of man substituted for that of God. Carlyle too is a pantheist, and avows sentiments that tend directly to the annihilation of the very idea of virtue. Like the heathen around me he looks upon sin as a necessary infelicity of our condition. Sin is not sin, in his theory; man not really guilty. Emerson uses the same language. Now if these persons just uttered their atheism and ungodliness and left it there, there would not be much to apprehend from them. But they wish to be thought humble and loving Christians, at the same time that they hate the true Christ with a most uncompromising hatred. This it is that gives them an influence. But the Christian is one whom God hath gifted with power to detect the true character of these teachers, and whom God has commissioned to testify against them with unflinching faithfulness.

Be not deceived. These writers are infinitely more mischievous than Tom Paine and his crew. They wear sheep's clothing which he did not. It is impossible for blasphemy to go further than it does in their writings; and that too in the very virtues which are intermingled with the phraseology of the Gospel. I write not from prejudice but from conviction. I bear about with me the scar of the deep and venomous wound which they inflicted upon me in the days of my infidelity. I can well forgive them the injury they did me, though that injury if it had worked itself out would have destroyed my soul forever and involved the perdition of others. But can I ever fall in with the world's way of viewing these men and their doctrines! Can I be led captive by their guile, so far as to look upon them as sincere, truth-seeking men? Can you? I trust not.

On reflection I conclude that you did wrong in reading those old manuscripts of mine on which you lately stumbled. I fear they have done you harm. You have interested yourself in the sentiments there brought forward, because they were those of your brother. But no, they are those that I hate. So burn up those manuscripts, I conjure you, and let not my old self come up again from its proper hell to do mischief when I am seeking to do good. I would not have you read such books as you speak of. I believe you can do it with less harm than others. But you cannot read them without mentioning the reading of them, and thus some weak brother may perish. My dear Harriet, there is something in you that you need much to beware of: your love for the intellectual, the uncommon, the out of the way, your power of appreciating and sympathizing with elevated views, poetic ideas. *Mind not high things.* Even in religion there is danger of your suffering from this tendency. You may be much taken up with a Madame Guyon, a Fénelon or a Pascal, when some much better Christian, whose society is far more to be prized, who is unspeakably dearer to Christ, living next door to you, is perhaps overlooked, unthought of, because commonplace.

His letters of the summer of 1857 give a contemporary picture of the shock of the Indian Mutiny. To the family, June 10, 1857:

Since I wrote last, India has become the scene of a vast and dangerous revolution. It has been hitherto confined to the Bengal army, but you must bear in mind that this army is scattered over the whole of non-peninsular India, that is from Burmah to Afghanistan. It consists of about 120 regiments which if they could effectually combine would of course be irresistible. The English (troops and all others) are a mere handful comparatively. The first mutiny took place at Barrackpore (Calcutta) in April. The disaffection was caused by an idea, that government had planned to destroy their caste by giving them cartridges prepared with animal matter, beef fat for the Hindus and lard for the Mussulmans. The mutiny was speedily suppressed; but the disaffected were just disbanded and allowed to go their way. Nothing was thought of this mutiny. But on the 10th day of May, at Meerut (thirty miles from Delhi) some sixty-five soldiers having been put in prison on account of this cartridge fantasy (for there was really no objectionable matter in the cartridges), the rest of the soldiers mutinied, released their companions, and the whole fell upon the European population and massacred all they could find, men, women, and children, with every circumstance of brutality and aggravation. They then made off to Delhi, where they induced the native troops to join them and so get possession of the town and fort.

The Emperor of Delhi you must know has been allowed by the Honorable Company to retain his title, though he is a mere stipendiary of the British with a shadow of authority. But the mutineers have rendered allegiance to him or his son, and are seeking to set up an independent sovereignty. At Delhi there were frightful massacres of the English.

Since then, almost every day has brought us the account of some new outbreak, until it seems as though the panic were to spread through the entire Bengal army. Happily this army is distributed among thirty or forty different military stations, far separated. At these stations there is generally a regiment or more of European troops. In most cases the mutineers have been subdued and disbanded, after a conflict, after murders and arsons, and have gone off in the direction of Delhi without arms.

There has been very great delay on the part of the British army in marching upon Delhi. One reason I suppose, has been the danger of leaving the country unprotected behind them. Just as he was setting forward from Hurwaul the Commander-in-chief died, of cholera, it is said. We have no details; and suicides have been so common of late that one naturally surmises this. We are momentarily expecting to hear that Delhi has been taken and the revolt suppressed at that place, now its great center. But we may be disappointed. The insurgents may be able to defend themselves and even to get some victories over the British; there may be massacres more fearful than we have yet had; the flames of revolution may rage throughout the North West Provinces, Punjab and Bengal. I cannot doubt, however, that God will enable the British to maintain themselves in the country and ultimately to recover their authority. Matters will then be placed I trust on a better footing.

There has been too much caste in the army. The Brahmins have had everything their own way. There has been some fear entertained in Bombay, though I know of no ground for it. One missionary I understand has just come down to Bombay, for the purpose of sending his family to England, under the idea that they are not safe here. But the Bombay army has not shown the slightest disposition to sympathize with the Bengalis. What an age it is! What revolutions, what conflicts, what a spirit of madness! China, that third of the world, destroying itself as fast as it can. China and India together are one-half the world. Add the Persian wars and the massacres in Borneo, and what a year this 1857 is!

June 11. The mail leaves today. It is not likely that we shall get tidings of the fall of Delhi before the steamer leaves. The army probably reached that place the day before yesterday and may even now be assaulting it. The telegraph is broken between Delhi and Agra and there will be some delay in communicating the result.

To Harriet, July 13, 1857:

As yet the mutinies have been confined to the Bengal Presidency, though they have advanced to our very borders. At Indore and Mhow, there have been risings and massacres quite lately. These places are just over our frontier. There was also a rising of Nizam's troops at Aurungabad, within this Presidency, but it was quickly suppressed. Thus we have been wonderfully preserved up to the present time. The possibility of a rising in Bombay has been contemplated since the beginning as the Mussulman population is large (120,000) and dangerous just now. The proclamations of the emperor of Delhi have been in circulation, I understand, among them for some time, inviting them for the sake of their religion to rise and drive the Europeans from the country or destroy them. But there is not much fear entertained, I think, of an outbreak, as it would be necessary for the Mussulmans to have an understanding with the Native army and our Bombay army is mostly composed of low caste Hindus.

We are sending a force northward towards Indore and Mhow. Whether the Bombay native troops will be staunch when called upon to fight their brethren of Bengal is doubted by some. There is of course a great demand for European troops. But a few thousands can be brought to bear at the present emergency, (I mean, in all the disturbed provinces) and this in a country peopled by half a hundred million of souls. It has been hoped that the troops departed from England to China would be diverted to this country, but there is some doubt now of this, as we hear that war is broken out in China, worse than before, and all help will be needed there. Still, on the whole, I have the impression that things are improving. Delhi is not yet taken, but the condition of its inhabitants and defenders is said to be bad in the extreme, and I cannot but hope that we may soon be permitted to hear of its downfall.

But it seems to me that even the rulers must see that we need something more than earthly resources to bring this country again in their power. Alas, that there should be so little willingness to seek the Lord and give honor to Him. There is no telling the amount of ruin and desolation wrought in the North of India by these mutinies. The amount of Government money stolen from the local treasuries is something enormous, and the ruin in the destruction of property is beyond computation. But of course the saddest thing is the destruction of life that has taken place, and the unspeakable barbarities perpetrated upon helpless women and children. Delicate ladies that would never set their foot upon the ground have been subjected to indignities that cannot be described. I have only heard of the death of one missionary but it will be wonderful indeed if many have not perished. And yet I think we should have heard of it, if many had been killed. It will be a most important fact, on many accounts, if missionaries and converts have generally escaped.

It is not missionary efforts that have provoked this rebellion. The wrath is against Government, and has been excited by the diminution of regard shown to caste and native prejudices. Such a result would never have been witnessed if Government had not so long and so extravagantly pampered these prejudices. It is really and strictly the fruit of the long and wicked alliance of the Government with idolatry, caste, etc. If the abominable things had never been hugged to the bosom of the Government, their repudiation would not have excited this ire and this alarm. This is the earthly rationale of the matter. But there is a heavenly, and from this we learn that God is not mocked, any more in modern times than in ancient. I continue preaching, writing, praying, conversing, hoping, sorrowing, rejoicing, believing. . . .

The Lord was never more manifest to me than of late. I am sometimes overpowered, and physically weakened by these manifestations. The rains have been holding off very much of late. Only about twenty inches so far. I have this evening read a letter from an officer at Indore who was in the midst of the mutiny, in the hands of the mutineers even, and in great danger. It described the entire outbreak. The mutineers did their utmost to make the Holkar (their active sovereign) lead them against the British. There was great slaughter. Sixteen bodies of men, women and children, Europeans, were to be seen in one place. At another time thirty-two were counted in various parts of the city. They completely destroyed the residences and European houses.

To his mother, July 29, 1857:

Perhaps I ought to address my letters occasionally especially to yourself, instead of addressing them to the family. Who knows but it may have the effect of eliciting some special letter from you. Year after year goes by without my getting anything direct from you. . . . I write at the present time from a feeling that you will all be, if not anxious, exceedingly desirous to know how matters are going on in India. Up to the present time I cannot say that they are improving. The late horrors indeed far exceed those previously announced. The idea has distinctly dawned upon my mind as a possibility that the rebels may succeed in entirely exterminating the Europeans in the upper province, and in banishing the Europeans, Governor-General and all from the northern half of India. And all in Bombay have felt it to be quite possible that they may be driven hence. But without speculation on the future let us consider what is actually brought before us in the Providence of God.

Delhi is not yet taken. The besieging force is still there, and there are frequent encounters between the rebels and them. But there has been no assault. General Barward, the commander-in-chief, has died. It is the non capture of Delhi that had led to all the mutinies and massacres of the last six weeks. General Sir Hugh Wheeler who was holding the fort of Cawnpore died with a wound and afterwards the entire company of Europeans (including about 240 women and children, many of them the families of officers) were treacherously and horribly assassinated. Sir Henry Lawrence, regarded as the best man in India for the present emergency, has been killed at Lucknow. The three foremost men cut down almost at a stroke. Nana Sahib, Raja of Bethoor, (near Cawnpore) at the head of 10,000 or 15,000 men, advanced as far as Fatehpur, and it seemed at one time, as though he might march on Calcutta. For you must understand that the European troops in the country are very few, and very scattered. General Havelock met Nana Sahib at Fatehpur, and gained several victories over him, having only about 1,700 men with him. He has reoccupied Cawnpore. This is the first news of a cheering character we have had. But between Havelock and Delhi there are two large bodies of insurgents in undisturbed possession of the country. Agra has been burnt and pillaged by the mutineers, the Europeans escaping in the Fort.

Wonderful to relate the rebellion has not yet crossed the frontiers of the Bombay presidency. Some of the Bombay native troops have been sent to the disturbed frontier and it remains to be seen how they will behave in presence of the Bengal mutineers. I have no confidence in them. I know that some of the corps most trusted in, sympathize with the mutineers. But what all are now apprehending in Bombay is the Moharrem, the Mahomedan 1st month, commencing Aug. 20, when they have their great festival. This is always a time of great license with them, and many feel that they are likely as not to raise the standard of the king of Delhi then. We have now no European troops, they having been sent up country; whether any other will arrive before that is a question. I need not say to you that I am unacquainted with such a thing as fear or apprehension for myself.

During all these months my mind has been as serene, my sleep as sweet as ever it was. I feel that it is God Who has come forth to work His strange work, and I wait to see the accomplishment of the same. My soul is of course wrung at times by the tidings that burst upon us. And I have many dear friends here for whose safety I am tenderly solicitous. Up to the present time I continue to have good opportunities of preaching the Gospel. One day lately I made a pleasant excursion with Mr. White and Narayan Sheshadri to Salsette where there are 1,500 workmen employed on the water works, and we preached to them and to bodies of workmen on the road.

A vast missionary field occupied by missionaries of a number of societies, English and American, (not by the Am. Board) has been entirely swept by the rebellion and it will be a long time, to human appearance, supposing the English succeed in recovering their ground, before the stations can be occupied. Missionaries have been killed, native Christians too and mission property has been destroyed. The names of a few missionaries have been given in the *Guardian*. We are very much cut off from obtaining information. We were all greatly distressed last Sabbath to hear of the massacre of a Mr. Hunter, his wife and infant at Sialcot. He was a Scotch missionary and was some time in Bombay. They were excellent people; I saw them go from here with great regret. They went only last November to the Punjab to commence a new mission there. He had some native Christians with him; they too were probably killed. General Havelock, whose name I mentioned, is a good Christian man. I knew him intimately. With Sir Henry Lawrence, too, I have had correspondence. He was regarded as a Christian. So, too, I believe was Sir Hugh Wheeler. It is altogether singular that there should have been three such men in supreme command in one district. As a rule, irreligion and immorality prevailed among the European officers of the Bengal army to a fearful extent. As they have done things that could not be told, so there have now been done to them and their families things that cannot be told.

To Harriet, Aug. 28, 1857:

The aspect of things has not improved; it has even assumed some darker shades. The mutiny has extended to the Bombay army. July 31 at midnight a mutiny broke out at Kolhapur. For some weeks the papers here were not allowed to speak of it. Three officers were killed. It was put down after some fighting. Many of the rebels were killed. Some 120 or 130 were made prisoners, and they are being blown away from guns. Within a few days we have heard of mutinous conduct in the twelve Bombay regiments stationed at Nassurabad. There was a great panic in Bombay on the 1st of the month. A Mussulman conspiracy with a view to a general rising through the country on the Bucru Eed (Baqarah Id) feast of the sacrifice of a cow, Aug. 1, had been by the goodness of God, detected; and it was believed that it extended to Bombay. A great many of the European inhabitants fled to the Fort; many went on board of ship; others made preparations in their houses for receiving the enemy. All passed off quietly. There was a tremendous downpour of rain that day (6 inches), and it would have been an uncomfortable time for insurgents.

Though living more exposed than anybody else, I yet saw no occasion for departing from my usual routine. I sleep where anybody may shoot me from the streets, that chooses; but the thought of danger has not yet come to me. The Hazens went on board of ship, which was well on Mrs. Hazen's account. We had a day of humiliation, not, however, appointed by Government. We have been greatly favored by Providence. A regiment of European soldiers has arrived from the Mauritius. When people have had one good panic and nothing has happened, it is very difficult to alarm them again.

We are now in the midst of the Moharrem, the great feast of the Mohammedans, and there would naturally be a good deal of alarm, were it not for the reaction from the previous fear. The Mohammedans get very wild in this feast. At this moment, twelve at night, they are making a most deafening noise just before my door, and the light of their torches flares into the room where I am sitting, and I see men made to appear like tigers, rushing by with a rabble at their heels. They paint themselves a brimstone yellow from head to foot, with black stripes and spots all over their body, with a long tail borne by attendants, and go dancing and prancing along. Matters have got a good deal worse in the Bengal Presidency. From Benares to Patna the country near the Ganges is in the hands of the mutineers. General Havelock has been unsuccessful in his attempt to relieve Lucknow, and it is awful to think of the fate that, humanly speaking, awaits that garrison. There are the families of some friends of mine there. I know a lady in Bombay, seven of whose relations perished in that bloody massacre at Cawnpore. It will strike you, I think, as the most awful thing you ever read of. Not far from a thousand in all, men, women, and children, perished thus and that, too, under the most frightful circumstances. It is even a question, I think, whether Havelock and Neil may not be invested by the enemy at Cawnpore and be destroyed before reinforcements can reach them. The English force is still before Delhi; acting on the defensive. We shall have great cause for thankfulness if they are not greatly reduced before large reinforcements reach them, if not overwhelmed.

The next two months will decide, I think, whether the British Empire in India will endure or not. The entire country from Calcutta to the Punjab has been forsaken by missionaries, those of them that have survived. I have seen the names of eleven missionaries, who with their families and the family of another missionary, have been killed. If God has sent these judgments in consequence of the iniquity of the Government in honoring the things that He hates, it would seem to follow that He will not turn away His wrath while the Government refuses to change its policy. *This the Government will not do.* What then?

To Harriet, Aug. 29, 1857:

I think I have never seen the Mussulmans enter into this festival with so much earnestness. Every five minutes some company is going by with music. One large company just went by with green flags and with certain religious symbols borne on horseback, and fanned by men walking at the side. We have a man of great energy at the head of the police, Mr. Forsett. The departure of the mail has been postponed to the 31st evening, in order doubtless that it may take the news of how we got through the Moharrem. *30.* Sabbath evening. This afternoon as I was going down to the Chapel to preach I met a company of artillery with four heavy guns drawn by six horses each. They were on their way to take up positions at certain points in the town, in case there should be any disturbance tonight, or simply as a precaution against it. Tonight is the night of the great midnight procession; the taboots which are to be thrown into the sea tomorrow are tonight conducted through the city. These taboots you know are gaily ornamented structures representing the mausoleums of Hossein and Hassan. Intelligence has been received, I hear, of a mutiny at Kolhapur. No details. There are cavalry and infantry there. The ladies of that station came to Bombay a week or so ago. *31.* Some doubt about the Kolhapur news. The night has passed off quietly, and there is no more apprehension felt with regard to this festival. It appears there was a fight on Saturday evening, between the native soldiers of a regiment here and the police. The regiment should be disarmed at once.

To Harriet, Oct. 16, 1857:

I last wrote you about the 1st of September, at the close of the Moharrem. Since then the numbers of the *Guardian* will have enabled you to trace the course of events in India. There have been a number of outbreaks in the Bombay army, at points remote from each other, but they were one and all wonderfully unsuccessful. It is matter of admiration that notwithstanding the revelation of such elements of mischief in the midst of us, we have been kept in perfect safety. Those that entertain mutinous design, at this hour, after the exhibition of enormous wickedness made by the mutineers of northern India, declare by that fact that they approve of that wickedness and are prepared to imitate it. Their guilt is equal to their infatuations.

In Bombay we have just been passing through a crisis without knowing it. There are here three native regiments that ought to have been disarmed long ago. Men and native officers belonging to these regiments met in a hired house in the native town, for the purpose of organizing a simultaneous outbreak with massacre of the European inhabitants, and plunder of the shops of Marwadis and Wanis (money lenders and grain dealers). The time was well chosen.... But Mr. Forsett, our superintendent of police, a Fouche in cunning, though a better man, ascertained about the meeting, and attended it as one of the conspirators, made it known to an officer of one of the regiments, and a number of the mutineers have been seized. Two were yesterday blown away from guns on the Esplanade, and there are more to be tried. A friend of mine present at the execution stood behind the guns at some distance, yet the *disjecta membra* of these unhappy wretches fell around him.

The Lord has favored us in this Presidency in a most surprising manner, and I am quite at a loss to account for it. Delhi was taken on the 21st after seven days of desperate fighting within the walls. The mutineers that survived are dispersing in bands through the country and may do a great deal of mischief before they are destroyed. Lucknow, I am glad to say, has been relieved and we have been spared a repetition of the Cawnpore tragedy. It remains to be seen if the force and the relieved succeeded in making their way safely to Cawnpore.

Weekly prayer meetings in connection with these disturbances have been kept up on Bombay, and have been pretty well attended. Can I say so? Perhaps not one in ten of those who make a profession of Christianity, have been present. I have never had better opportunities of preaching than during these months past. It is still apparently water spilt upon the ground, but I thank God that I am enabled heartily and energetically to work in this appointed and therefore excellent work of spilling water on the ground. I have been very much troubled of late with prickly heat, so that for five weeks I have not slept on an average three hours a night. It is perfectly astonishing to me how I can lose so much sleep with impunity. I wonder how much sleep we really need. I am as well as ever I was in all other respects, but I have been such a spoilt child with respect to physical suffering that this appears to me like a real affliction. It only troubles me at night, and then it comes on like a paroxysm sometimes.

To the family, Dec. 24, 1857:

The mutiny is now fast dying out. We are much interested to see the state of the public mind in England with regard to India, the decided conviction of the necessity of an entire reformation of Governmental abuses. Some things that I have seen in the American papers indicate a wrong apprehension of the Company's rule. It has on the whole been beneficent rather than oppressive, especially of late. Yet there has been a good deal that would appear to the Americans very like extortion. For instance, taking 1/3, sometimes 2/5 of the produce from the poor cultivators. Yet they have never been used to anything better. It is a pernicious policy, however, detrimental to the interests of the country and Government.

You must not believe all that is said about torture. What torture there has been has generally been inflicted by native officials without the knowledge of Europeans. The tendency to tyrannize is far stronger in the Natives than in the Europeans. No missionary in India but desires to see the entire annexation of the Native States by the Company. It is beyond a question that such annexation would be greatly for the benefit of the masses in these states. But the connection of the Government with idolatry, caste, opium traffic, etc., is abominable without the shadow of extenuation.

I have been out of health since I wrote you last. I thought for a long time it was prickly heat, but when I came under the doctor's hands it turned out to be a cutaneous disease. Whether I caught it in the hospital or not I don't know. I never had anything that gave me so much physical discomfort. For two months and a half the only sleep I had ordinarily was between 4 and 6 a.m. and often I passed the entire night without a wink of sleep. I do not reject this trial of faith, and hope that patience was thus assisted to have her perfect work. The wonder was that I could go about all my duties just as usual. At length, Dr. Leith, hearing about me, called on me, and required me to remain at home, which I did for a fortnight. It is now a wonder to me to find myself well, the malady seemed so ineradicable. I hope that I may not lose the benefit of this trial.

His work during these years continued to be preaching and writing and service to all sorts of folks, Indians and Americans, British and European castaways, with access to all grades of society from the Governor-General to the lowest.

To Harriet, Jan. 23, 1858:

I preach daily, as a general rule, sometimes necessarily broken in upon, either at my own house or in some of the thoroughfares of Bombay, to Hindus of all castes, Mussulmans, Parsis and Jews. This letter would be very long if I gave you a report of but a few days' experience on these occasions. The spirit of opposition seems as intensified as ever. I have much cause for thankfulness in that God enables me to keep at this work without disinclination, with more zest than formerly even, though the results are *nil*.

The process of converting rags into a piece of fair paper for the King to write His Name upon is you know one of prodigious severities and crushings. I speak of myself. But I have only to make mention of loving kindness and gentleness on the part of our (speaking reverently) Secretary of Missions.

My health is not yet quite re-established. I am rid, thanks to the Lord, of that which hung upon me last Oct. and Nov. But my digestive organs have never got altogether right. A greatly esteemed Christian brother, Mr. Molesworth, has come down from the Deccan, to live in Bombay, and I have been permitted to see him face to face. He is somewhat of a Plymouth Brother in sentiment. Christians generally delight to hear him expound the Scriptures. He was in the army, but left it through conscientious scruples and through the same has refused ever since to receive his pension. He lives a life of faith beyond most men; giving away almost everything and spending little upon himself.

The book into which Harriet had copied Bowen's letters ends with his letter of Apr. 5, 1858 and only four letters of the years 1860-65 are preserved. One of these dated Sept. 11, 1860, referred to his brother Frank of whom he had written also on Jan. 23, 1858.

To Harriet, Jan. 23, 1858:

> I told you in my last, written a month ago, that I was going on board of a ship in the harbor to see a person who had sent word to me that he could give me information concerning Frank. I went that same day, and saw Mr. Smith, an American, an officer on board of a ship that was loading opium for China. He told me that he saw a good deal of Frank at Hongkong last August. He had known him before. Frank was first mate in the *Kate Roper,* a Baltimore vessel. But he was expecting to be made captain of a ship coming down there from Shanghai. This vessel was to take coolies, I believe he said, to South America. I cannot say that I received a very satisfactory impression concerning Frank. He said he was *not* married. Had really been in New York as mentioned by you. Did not go to see you because he did not wish to see his friends until he had plenty of money. *Had been in Bombay* within a few years. Looked like a Frenchman, with beard, moustache, imperial. Asked Mr. Smith to find me out in Bombay and tell me he had seen him, though not to let me know anything of his whereabouts. Was quite thin. Only think of his having been in Bombay while I was there, and not making it known to me! Very likely he saw me on some occasion or other. I would probably not have recognized him. Well! It is a ground for thanksgiving that he is alive, and still wanders about the world, which though a world lying in wickedness, is still a world where grace is proffered. It is fourteen years since I have seen him.

To Harriet, Sept. 11, 1860:

> I saw last evening at the house of Mr. Stearns[4] an American paper, and in it a paragraph to the effect that on the barque *Adela,* or more properly *Sultana,* Capt. Bowen, had left New York Jan. 26th, proceeded to Africa,

---

4. Mr. Stearns was a greatly respected American merchant, the father of Alfred E. Stearns, for many years principal of Phillips Academy, Andover, Mass.

taken thence over 2000 negroes to Cuba, and there been burned. It is not an uncommon thing for the captain of a slaver to set fire to her and leave her, when he has landed his cargo, and there is some man-of-war in the neighborhood. I have no doubt that this was Frank, for it tallies very much with the information you gave me of his being in New York at the beginning of the year. The grace of God has been exhibited, during the last three years, in the conversion of just such characters. In many instances these appear to have been singled out whose conversion would most strikingly attest God's readiness to receive the worst sinners. Some of the men of said barque landed at Key West, and made this report. Brought there, I suppose.

To the family, Aug. 12, 1862:

I am laid up with inflammatory rheumatism or gout! You may learn from this what a high liver I am. You would not have thought of my getting the gout, the rich man's disease. Whatever it is it is excruciating enough and I am fastened to my chair. But it is a peculiarity of my ailments that they soon go. I have scarcely time to indent on the sympathy of others.

Apart from the letters to the family which have been cited, our information regarding these ten years of Bowen's life and work comes from letters written by those who knew Bowen during these years, which were fortunately collected for this memoir long ago before these friends of Bowen were gone beyond our reach. Some of these were the missionaries of the American Board with whom during these years he continued to work in close and affectionate relations and for whom in his home letters he expresses the fullest confidence and regard. The reminiscences of some of these friends covered also the later period of Bowen's life but they begin with these years, 1855-65.

From the Rev. Charles Harding, missionary of the American Board from 1857 to 1876:

It was our privilege, while stationed in Bombay, to be intimately associated with Mr. Bowen from Jan. 1857 to 1862, and again from Nov. 1869 to 1876. During the earlier years we met him nearly every day in the week, either at our house or at some religious service in Marathi or English. He used to attend our Sunday afternoon services, himself often preaching, and after the service an hour was spent in preaching to non-Christians from the steps of the church, and then he would come home with us. The evening was spent in singing and in reading letters from friends, and in conversation, finally closing with family prayers, led always by Mr. Bowen. The memory of these Sunday evenings has always been cherished with peculiar gratitude.

Ten Years of Independent Work 1855-1865

In his public speaking Mr. Bowen did not have the elements of an orator. His style in preaching was often conversational. His voice was weak, and he generally had the appearance of one in feeble health. In preaching to a native audience, I have more than once seen him rest his elbow upon the desk, and his head upon his left hand. There was uniformly an absence of those expressions of face and inflections of voice, and gestures, and apt illustrations, which accompany real eloquence. These characteristics rendered his preaching to non-Christians less effective.

He was sedate in manner and in preaching, seldom manifesting any special emotion. Once, however, in 1858, on the day the news came of the great Revival in the North of Ireland, he was greatly moved and seemed almost beside himself. The possibility of such a work in India seemed for the time to fill all his thoughts.

In his own unworldliness of spirit and perfect trust in Christ, he seemed sometimes unable to comprehend the imperfections of others. I once heard him say in a sermon, that a man who borrowed money at a high rate of interest from a native banker could not be a Christian.

Those who knew him during his Theological Course said that a missionary spirit was awakened and the whole Seminary quickened by his earnest consecration.

A prominent trait in Mr. Bowen's character was that he never seemed discouraged, though seeing very little fruit of his labors. Up to 1876, when I left Bombay, I repeatedly heard him say that after twenty-five or thirty years of faithful labor in Bombay, he did not know of a single person who had been brought to Christ through his influence, yet he labored as he believed Christ would have him, and he apparently believed that his services were accepted of Christ.

It is, however, undeniably true that during all those years he had had a decided influence both among Christians and non-Christians.

As to his habits of prayer, several incidents will illustrate what he was accustomed to do. About the year 1870 or 1871 he was seriously ill, and two Christian physicians living together on Malabar Hill took him to their house and tenderly cared for him. On his recovery, a number of his special friends were invited to meet and render thanks to Christ for sparing his life. In Mr. Bowen's remarks near the close of the meeting, he said: "I have been praying daily for everyone of you." He once told us that for twenty-five years he had been praying every day for a relation in the homeland, who had been, and was still living a very ungodly life. About that time, this friend, who was an officer of a ship, came to Bombay and was present incognito among a company of natives to whom Mr. Bowen was preaching near the Tract House. This fact came to Mr. Bowen in a letter from another friend, months afterwards.

At one of our annual meetings at Ahmednagar, there was among the missionaries a very deep longing for a spiritual revival for ourselves and the native churches, and day after day much prayer was offered. Bowen was staying with Mr. Bissell, and it was understood that he spent most of one night in prayer for this object.

Although he dressed like a European, he lived very simply, having no servants and getting many of his meals with his friends, who loved to have him with them. I doubt if this manner of life added much to his influence among the non-Christians. According to their ideas, this was only a way to gain personal righteousness.

A Hindu ascetic, who lives without clothing, with his body covered with ashes, is often the proudest and most conceited of mortals. A certain missionary touring in the Deccan, usually took a tanga or a pony in going from village to village. One year, to save this expense, and hoping it might give him more influence, he decided to walk. This was noticed at once, and the conclusion was: "Oh, well! You will get more righteousness by it."

Mr. Bowen's practical way of handling Scripture, Bible instruction, was with him the chief means of developing Christian character and building our lives. This careful study of the Scriptures with pen in hand fitted him admirably for Bible Readings, which were held weekly for many years at one of the mission houses in Bombay.

A similar meeting for native Christians in the vernacular was also held each week. Mr. Bowen was extremely happy in leading these meetings.

From Mrs. William G. Greenwood, daughter of the Rev. Henry Ballentine, herself a missionary of the American Board from 1835 to 1865:

My childhood's home was in Ahmednagar, 160 miles from Bombay, and in those days of no railroads, no stage coaches, no bridges, the missionaries of the two cities met quite infrequently, so that though I must have seen Mr. Bowen when we came to the seaport to take passage for America on account of my father's health, I do not recall it, as I was but eight years old.

On my return to India in 1864, I tarried in Bombay a fortnight with my parents who had come to meet me, and it was then that I saw Mr. Bowen to remember him. I presume the curiosity I felt about a man of whom I had heard so much all my life heightened the impression he made upon me, for I have a vivid recollection of his looks. . . .

I was not surprised at his appearance, so much in keeping with the stories I had heard of his asceticism. He was tall—at least he looked so on account of his thinness, for "thin as a rail" could have been applied to him more truthfully than to almost any other person I have ever seen. He had on white duck trousers so common in that hot climate, with a long black bombazine coat buttoned above, and he had so little shape that he resembled in figure one of the male members of Noah's family in a child's toy ark. He was quite homely, as I recall him, with his long, thin sallow face, and scanty locks hanging down over his ears, his homeliness being accentuated by his carelessness in dress.

He had severed his connection with the American Board before this time on account of a change in his views on baptism, and, though the Board had urged him to continue in their service, he was too honest to take salary from those whose doctrines he could not preach. He had then taken employment with the Tract Society, receiving a small salary which barely kept him alive, and was, when we were in Bombay, for economy's sake sleeping on the counters of their bookstore.

We looked in upon him once in our journeyings about the city, and were interested in his housekeeping arrangements, for he not only slept in the store, but cooked some if not all his meals there. My mother's tender heart, however, could not bear the thought of his living in so rude a way, her only comfort being that his many devoted friends in the city did not allow him often to eat at home. He might be shabby, his trousers might be fringed round the bottom, as they often were, but he was always welcome in the homes that knew him. All deficiencies, all eccentricities were forgotten in his presence, and especially when he sat down to the piano, and his hands began to run over the keys, even strangers thought no more of his personal appearance, but only of the wonderful gift bestowed upon him. . . .

My nephew, Rev. Henry Fairbank of the Maratha Mission, who has just been visiting me, adds this: that his father, Rev. Dr. S. B. Fairbank, stationed many years in Bombay, used to tell of a preaching tour he made in company with his friend, Mr. Bowen, when Mr. Bowen carried all his belongings for the trip stuffed in a pillow case. One morning, for some unknown reason, they could not make their coffee and Mr. Bowen had a severe headache in consequence, showing that even ascetics allow themselves some luxuries. My nephew also tells me that Mr. Bowen at first believed that a missionary should confine himself entirely to preaching and not waste his time and strength in teaching and on schools. Hence he gave himself to street preaching during the week, but sorrowfully confessed afterwards that he did not know of a single convert he had made in this way.

From the Rev. H. W. Ballantine, missionary of the American Board from 1863 to 1865, nephew of Henry Ballantine:

> Please bear in mind that my acquaintance with Mr. Bowen was confined to the two years between March 1863 and March 1865—more than forty years ago.
>
> While therefore I retain distinct impressions of his look and manner, words and incidents have faded, so that it is unsafe to attempt conveying them to another.
>
> Two afternoons each week he preached on the street at a place not far from the Tract House. Other afternoons he frequently joined me in my preaching from the steps of our Mission Chapel.
>
> In our Chapel he regularly attended on Thursday evenings a Prayer Meeting for English people, taking his turn in leading it.
>
> In manner he was extremely modest; but in convictions clear and strong. As a man he was universally respected and beloved.
>
> The then Governor of Bombay, Sir Bartle Frere, repeatedly consulted him regarding matters affecting education and religion. On the other side I recall an expression of a certain Hindu of high caste whom I encountered one day making disparaging remarks about the Christian Religion. In defense of Christianity I cited Mr. Bowen as an example. At once he made acknowledgment. "Oh! Mr. Bowen of course! But he is different. We all *worship* Mr. Bowen."
>
> The whole city held him in this regard.
>
> He was most charitable towards others; never speaking ill of any; never assuming to judge others' conduct; but extremely exacting with himself. In both dress and food he was frugal—too frugal his friends all thought.
>
> For room, he occupied a corner of the Sales Room of the Tract Society, concealed behind some stacks of books. There he had a desk, a wash-stand and a narrow couch. In the hot season he used to sleep on the counter, with a pile of papers for a pillow.
>
> His clothing, while kept carefully clean, was thin and usually threadbare. Once some unknown friend distressed at sight of his frayed shirt-bosoms sent him Rs. 25 with a request that he use it for a new supply. The next day he turned over the whole sum to our Mission treasury, and continued wearing the old shirts.
>
> He suffered much and often with severe headaches. For myself I have little doubt they came from insufficiency of food. His breakfast was a roll, bought from a near-by bakery, with some simple fruit, usually one or two bananas. His one hearty meal was a noon dinner in a private family, for which he paid by teaching the two or three daughters, then in their teens. The family were in moderate circumstances, and it is

likely their food was lacking at least in variety. His suppers were almost always at the table of some friend, but were little more than bread and tea. Of tea he was very fond, and could drink several cups.

For his evenings he had regular places where he was expected; usually in connection with some religious gathering. Every Tuesday evening there was a Bible Class at Col. Murray's, in which Mr. Bowen was the leader. The study followed light refreshments. Every Wednesday evening there was a Prayer Meeting at Dr. Fraser's (Editor of *Bombay Times*—a member of the Plymouth Brethren).

Thursday evening came the Prayer Meeting in our Mission Chapel, above mentioned, when, as also on Sunday evenings, he usually took supper with us, etc.

Mr. Bowen was very fond of music, had once been himself a skillful player on piano but had given it up. A piano at our Mission House and the playing of Scared Music there by Mrs. Ballentine formed no small part of the attraction that brought him often with us. And we always enjoyed his coming, benefiting by his lovely spirit and his wide and accurate and fresh information.

From Mrs. A. M. Park, a sister of Mrs. Greenwood:

These recollections date back to the days of my childhood, and very pleasant ones they are too.

Mr. Bowen was a peculiarly unique and picturesque figure on the streets of Bombay, the city where he chose to remain, during all his long residence in India. He was a man of medium height but as thin as a rail, and he went about in white duck trousers that were loose enough to hold three of him at once. On his back he wore a threadbare alpaca coat, on his feet shambling slippers and often heel-less stockings, while an old straw hat covered his long hair that curled slightly at the ends. He had somewhat the appearance of an emaciated cowboy, but a cowboy that had a remarkably refined and gentle face. The children of the missionaries, of whom I was one, gave him the nick-name of Bombil Sahib, Bombil being the name of a small dried fish, much used by the lower classes. We called him this because of his dried-up look, but it was only in fun, for we all loved him, he had so much humor himself and was so kindly. He seemed to understand us and took an interest in our pleasures.

I remember that at one time, in making some article of crochet work, I was following the instructions given in a pattern book, when Mr. Bowen came in, and taking up the book, translated the abbreviations denoting the different stitches, in such an amusing way, that we children were convulsed with laughter, and begged for a repetition on future occasions.

Mr. Bowen never allied himself to any missionary society, but preferred to remain independent and to carry on his work in the apostolic way. We often wondered what he lived on and where he got any money at all for his scant expenses. As editor of the *Bombay Guardian,* however, he probably made enough to live on and to spend on his charities. He did not choose to live as the missionaries did, according to the style of Englishmen, but held socialistic ideas, that seemed strange sixty years ago, though they have become common enough now, which led him to bring himself down to the level of the poorer classes, and to live among them.

India, however, with its complicated caste system, was a hard field in which to practice such ideas, and his influence was felt more among the Eurasians, I think, than among the natives themselves. By the English people in general, he was looked upon as a curious freak, scarcely worth notice, though the godly minded among them discerned his rare nature and esteemed him highly. He became widely known through his paper, the *Bombay Guardian,* and was universally respected by all classes. The simple-minded natives even looked upon him as a very pious Yogi, or fakir, of the Sahib-lok.

But in spite of his living with the natives, he could not assimilate himself with them. The color of his skin and his European clothes were barriers that kept him apart, to say nothing of his refined tastes. An educated Brahman in speaking of him once, said, "Mr. Bowen would do more good if he lived on a higher plane. The people now do not look up to him as much as they would if he lived better."

He was a man of keen sensibilities and genuine native refinement, and it must have been a great sacrifice for him to give up the comforts and luxuries of life, for the hardships he endured. Just how he lived no one seemed to know. At times he rented a room in some native or Eurasian house, but when he was connected with the Bible Society, the Society's building was all the home he had. He slept on one of the sales tables, and bought bread, milk and bananas for food, never doing any cooking for himself. His numerous friends among the missionaries, the English people and the Eurasians, however, often invited him to their homes for a meal and tried to keep him supplied with little necessary comforts. The missionary ladies often resorted to some scheming method of getting hold of his clothing that needed repairs; but all these things seemed to distress him, either because he disliked to cause others any trouble, or because he actually held some ascetic idea that he was too great a sinner to have any comforts.

He had a keen love for music and could play on the piano almost any piece he heard from memory. He enjoyed improvising by the hour.

His strong will-power showed itself very often, but once in a special way: He was occupying a small room in some native house, when he became very dangerously ill. The doctor ordered him out of the country, but Mr. Bowen would not hear a word of leaving India, he had gone there to live and to die for the heathen. It was found that a ship was all ready to sail for America, and the doctor declared that Mr. Bowen should be put aboard the next day, as the only remaining remedy for saving his life When the morning dawned and the doctor, with others, came to remove Mr. Bowen, he was nowhere to be found. So determined was he not to be taken to the ship that he had escaped from his bed and gone, no one knew where; but the ship sailed without him and he recovered.

It was a common sight to see Mr. Bowen preaching on the streets of Bombay, to a company of natives, sometimes alone and sometimes accompanied by others. But he never mastered the Marathi language well enough to be quite at home in it. His preaching was too labored to be easily comprehended. It was his life, which was full of kindly deeds, that was more effective than his words.

From Mrs. S. C. Dean, a daughter of the Rev. Amos Abbot, herself an American Board Missionary from 1856-1867 and later from 1901-1905:

I regret that my letters and diaries were lost at sea in a hurricane off Cape L'Agullas (south of Africa) on our way home from India in 1867.

My husband, Rev. S. C. Dean and myself with three other missionary couples left Boston in August 1856 for Bombay. It was not 'till the middle of January 1857 that we arrived in that harbor, and a boat with several missionaries, among them Mr. Bowen, came out to the ship to welcome and take us to shore. During the month we spent in Bombay, before going to the Ahmednagar District to our work, we saw Mr. Bowen several times.

The first distinct recollection I have of him was soon after our arrival, at a gathering of missionaries to welcome us new arrivals. After tea, he sat at the piano and delighted us with several numbers. To us who had just landed, after a voyage of five months, the treat was one never to be forgotten. He was tall and thin, a cultured, well educated gentleman and a devoted missionary.

It was a great source of anxiety and I might say vexation to some of the ladies of the Mission, that his manner of living was so odd and strange, and naturally, he was often a topic of conversation. We new missionaries were told that he slept on the counter of the Bible and Tract Society rooms, that he went early in the mornings to the home of some music pupil of his, and after giving a lesson, stayed in that home for the nine o'clock breakfast, also that his daily luncheon consisted only of bread, butter and plantains (bananas) and that he was so popular among the American and English families that he was engaged to supper somewhere every night in the week and always on Sunday evenings with our own Mission. At one time, several of the ladies surprised him by fitting up a comfortable room with necessary furniture, begging him to accept of the hospitality, but he would have none of it, saying he preferred to live in his own simple way—his idea being that he would by this method make himself one of the people and do more for them.

One Sunday on our way to the church we overtook him walking in the heat through the street with an umbrella over his head. He was dressed like a common Goanese cook, or an Indo-Briton of the lower class. Unfortunately the Hindu is not drawn to such an example. Caste, especially in those years, was too iron bound and massive to receive any impression he intended to make. The natives of India probably looked upon him as low caste European.

Those, however, who knew his worth from long acquaintance must have, at least in their hearts, respected him, while all the Christian community of Bombay loved and honored him.

Later, he left our Mission and joined himself to the American Methodist Mission. We met him now and again during our stay in India and always enjoyed the *Bombay Guardian* edited by him, and used with pleasure a book of *Daily Meditations* which he published. He looked very worn, tanned and exceedingly thin the last time I saw him. At his request I called on his sisters at the old home soon after arriving in New York.

In my recent four years' stay in Bombay, I was greatly interested and pleased to see a fine church edifice erected in his memory in the part of the city called "The Fort," (occupied mostly by Europeans and Parsis) called "The Bowen Memorial" church. It is on a prominent street, has a large audience room, and apartments in the upper story for the residence of the American M. E. pastor and family. The church is well filled by English-speaking people. A good Sunday School is connected with the church, and also a devoted lady from America who acts as deaconess and general helper.

I was told that he regretted some things in his method of work and living, and before his death said he did not know of any whom he had brought to Christ!

It is hard to believe this, and I cannot but feel that the last day will reveal the good, faithful service done by that true servant of God.

The Rev. Edward Fairbank, another of the missionary children who knew Bowen, testified to the love the children had for him and their delight in his company. The Rev. E. S Hume, D. D., who was born in India and served in the American Board Mission from 1875 to 1903, and who knew Bowen well, in an interview many years ago, spoke of Bowen's "proclivity for criticism, his changeableness of conviction, his indiscriminate choice of friends, his warmth of heart, his aversion to all stagnation and routine, his freedom in forgiving and asking forgiveness, his lack of pride, his Christlike expansiveness, his utter lack of bitterness, his carelessness of living, his popularity, his cleanliness and neatness in spite of his shabby clothes, the amazing fineness of his mind and soul in such surroundings, his ceaseless intelligent scrutiny, his tireless fidelity in spite of the want of any apparent success."

"Everybody loved him," said Dr. Hume, and "no one but Dr. Mackichan ever criticized him." "He was an indifferent preacher, and took no pains to make such an impression on his audiences as he might easily have made. When listening to him, I received the impression that he spoke with little or no special preparation—partly because he believed that he would thus be a better channel for the Holy Spirit, and partly because he was always fighting against all tendencies to pride. Most men with his powers and gifts would certainly have harbored and exhibited pride."

In his Chalmers Lectures in Scotland in 1926, however, Dr. Mackichan spoke with unfeigned admiration of "the sainted George Bowen, one of the most devoted missionaries that India has known." (Mackichan, *The Missionary Ideal in the Scottish Churches*, p. 171).

The late George A. Kittredge, brother of the Rev. Abbott Kittredge and one of the leading American business men in India, knew Bowen in Bombay from 1862 till Bowen's death "as a devoted servant of his Master commanding the respect and regard of everyone in Bombay."

Two of Bowen's greatest admirers were the late Samuel J. Barrows, Secretary of the Prison Association of New York, and Mrs. Barrows, both of them very extraordinary personalities. Mrs. Barrows had been Mrs. W. W. Chapin, who went to India in 1864 at the age of eighteen as the wife of a Congregational missionary. Mr. Chapin, who was a brother of Miss Chapin, president of Mt. Holyoke College, died and she came home in the fall of 1865 and later married Mr. Barrows. In an interview in 1906 Mrs. Barrows said that Bowen was nearly fifty and that her feeling toward him was often one of worship. Mrs. Barrows told me:

> Bowen was then living in the book room, sleeping on the table without pillow or mattress. Mrs. Hazen and others had fitted up a bed room for him but he sold all the things. He went out into the bazaar for breakfast, consisting of a little fruit. He ate no lunch. There were seven families where he always went for dinner. "Poorest man in Bombay," said one. "Not poor," said the people, "the richest man in Bombay." The rich had

such confidence in him that he could get any money at once. Charitable toward the poor and the idolatrous. Appreciated the religious side of Hindu life and yet made more sacrifice than anyone else. . . . Bowen brought her an offer of marriage from a man whom he had introduced to her a few nights before. Bowen had made it a matter of prayer that she should be kept in India. She had worn a gymnastic dress with short skirts given by Miss Chapin and so won may people among whom she went lovingly and freely as missionary ladies could not with the big skirts then worn. The offer was from the Presbyterian minister of the big cathedral (!). Bowen had made all the arrangements. She wavered at his insistence that she should stay. Bowen had the man waiting in the next garden and rushed off and got him and the three talked it over as a commercial arrangement. Bowen wooed her for the other man. Mrs. Barrows suggested that Bowen should have asked her for himself.

Mrs. Barrows later (in May, 1906) wrote out her recollections, saying, however, "The trouble was he was all soul and you cannot photograph the soul nor describe it as you know it to exist":

It is like looking through a pane of ground glass at moving figures to recall the image of George Bowen as I first knew him more than forty years ago. His was the first hand to clasp mine as I landed a happy bride, enthusiastic with the bright hopes of work in that far away land of India. His was the last hand I clasped when a little widow of nineteen I said good-by forever to Hindustan.

The impression made on my mind of Mr. Bowen was that of a saint. I can recall no other man ever who so strongly impressed me as a true follower of Jesus. He would have been the first to disclaim such likeness, but we who knew the man all felt it. Like the Master he served he had not where to lay his head. Several times the ladies of the mission had fitted up a room where he might, as they said, be comfortable. Every time he would sell the furniture to meet the wants of some sufferer, and when I knew him he was sleeping on the counter, without mattress or bed, in the book-room of Bombay. Perhaps more from him than from any other person I learned the precious lesson of the needlessness of *things*. Yet no one ever was nicer in person and appearance. He was as tidy as could be asked, and though his clothes were simple and few they were adapted to the climate and always presentable.

But one did not think of the clothes when one saw the man. His abstemious habits and the torrid weather of Bombay gave to him the looks of an ascetic. He was as thin as a rail, and brown as a Hindu, but his eyes had a depth and serenity that showed a soul superior to the flesh.

It seemed as if he needed and had only just enough body to keep his soul from drifting skyward in our very sight.

Mr. Bowen had many friends. First the people who knew and loved him for his inner worth. Then the people to whom he went as teacher, helper, guide—the weak, the sinning, the suffering. His whole life was a gospel. He went about not only doing good, but living the Gospel of good news. Hindu or Parsi, Protestant or Portuguese Catholic, all respected and honored him and those who knew him best loved him best.

To the world he seemed a very poor man, but I used to hear it said in Bombay that there was no man in the city who could command so much money. If famine came, or disaster befell the many or the few, his appeal was always heeded, because people trusted him.

As a companion Mr. Bowen was delightful. Of this I know more from watching him with others than from conversation with him myself. His great store of learning and his rare experiences in life, made him a noble companion for the most gifted. I did not aspire to much of it from my humble standing place of nineteen summers. But he was as genial with the young and even the little children as with the wise and learned who found him their master. I was told also that his thorough musical education in Italy added a great charm to him in society, but in our humble missionary homes we had no chance to hear him play and I do not know how much he used his talent in that direction.

Across the years I look back to him with peculiar reverence and love. He is one of the many who have passed on for whom at times I yearn. It seems as though he were one of the saints on whom, did we canonize our saints, we should gladly call to help us in the day of temptation. His happiness in poverty; his serenity in trouble; his courage in danger; his gentleness to the weak; his charity for all, would seem to have fitted him to be the friend and helper in other worlds as well as in this. It is something always to be grateful for to have had the privilege of calling George Bowen friend.

In the *Christian Register* of Boston, in the issue of March 29, 1888, appeared the following editorial written by Mrs. Barrows, who with her husband was busy in the work of prison reform:

A Devoted Missionary

Many years ago a young missionary about to sail for an Oriental country was greeted by a very solemn woman with the question, "Are you sure you are not going for the romance of the thing?" Whatever may have induced any other man to become a missionary, certainly George

Bowen was never persuaded to go to India from romantic motives. Pure devotion led him to give up home and land, and his life was one of utter consecration.

Less than half a century ago, when the life of the missionary involved far more self-sacrifice than now, he returned from Europe where in Italy he had been studying languages and music, in both of which he was proficient. Life was full of promise, and his friends looked forward to a brilliant career for him. Nothing could have been father from their dreams than the reality which was before him. He was betrothed to a beautiful girl, whose graces equaled his own accomplishments. Through her sweet influence, he was won from a restless, faithless life of idle speculation, to unwavering trust in God. On the eve of marriage, death robbed him of his bride; but, so far from yielding hopelessly to despair, he at once girt up his loins for the conflict, and, strengthened by tender memories, set sail for India as a missionary of the American Board.

From his arrival in Bombay in 1848 till his recent death, that city was his home. Not once did he return for rest or recreation to his native land. Never again did the eyes of his fond mother rest upon her boy, who went from her in the pride and glory of his young manhood. A score of years after he had parted from her, it was the writer's privilege to greet that mother with messages from her son, to sit at her cheerful open fire in a beautiful old-fashioned house in New York, and answer a thousand questions about his life and work. Her longing to see him was intense; but she knew that it could never be gratified, for his entire consecration forbade any thought of return to America. Yet, though she sorrowed that she should see his face no more, mingled with her grief was a mother's pride in a son who was so loyal to duty. Her sweet submission was as beautiful as his own abnegation.

To have known George Bowen and called him friend was a life blessing. He embodied more nearly than any other man whose life has ever crossed our own the ideal of the Christian missionary. After a year or two of connection with the American Board, he severed his relation with it by refusing to take any salary from its treasury. Henceforth, like Paul, he supported himself while doing the Lord's work. In this way, he thought that he could come into closer sympathy with the natives, and thus reach their hearts and do them good. No service that he could render them was too humble, no life which he must live too hard. A part of his work was connected with the Tract Depository; and here, in those days, he made his home. He couch was the hard counter, which he said was better than his Master's, Who had not where to lay His head. Some friends fitted up a small room with a comfortable bed and furniture. He gracefully thanked them, then sold it all, and turned the money into the Lord's treasury.

In food and dress, he was so simple that he himself told a friend that five dollars supplied him with food for a month. Yet, had he chosen, he could have fared like a king; for the best homes were open to him, and he was everywhere a welcome guest. For, though almost an anchorite in his habits, he was far from being morbid or gloomy in his manner. A spirit of sunny trust and cheerfulness accompanied him, and his friends were not made conscious of the presence of an ascetic. He won the confidence and trust of those with whom he came in contact, so that it was said no man in Bombay had the command of so much money for charitable purposes. Year in and year out, he lived this quiet, unobtrusive life of self-denial, known and respected by European and native alike, till his name was a synonym of manly virtue.

Besides preaching and teaching and giving the example of godly living by his daily walk and conversation, Mr. Bowen exercised a wide influence by several religious books which he wrote, and through the *Bombay Guardian,* a weekly religious paper of which he was editor. As proof that his devoted life of self-denial was not the result of fanaticism, nothing could be stronger than this well-edited paper. The *Missionary Review* says of it: It was "one of the most vigorous and best balanced Christian weeklies of the foreign mission field." The same magazine, in referring to Mr. Bowen, says of him with perfect truth: "He was a cheerful, self-sacrificing, devoted missionary and a loving and lovable friend." "There was a man sent from God, and his name was—George Bowen."

Looking back over a vista of three-and-twenty years to that mission field, the images of men and women appear: some lovable for one quality or reverenced for others, some vivid and never to be forgotten, others fading into obscurity; but it is no disparagement to the wisest and best, as they would be the first to acknowledge, to say that clearer, stronger, more inspiring than any is the image of the thin, pale man whose gaunt fingers swept over the organ keys and filled the air with sweetly solemn music, whose deeply earnest tones swept through the soul and stirred vibrations that inspired to holier living. It is a grateful task at this Easter time to pay this tribute to the memory of one whose influence is in itself immortal.

14. The Bombay Guardian

Many times references have been made in this memorial to the *Bombay Guardian* with which Bowen was associated from its establishment until his death in 1888, in which he poured out the rich fruitage of his intellectual and spiritual life and which in the judgment of many was, under his editorship, the most remarkable religious paper in the world.

Of the origin of the paper Bowen gives a brief account in his "Reminiscences, 236":

> In the latter part of 1850 some members of the Bombay Missionary Conference began to arrange for the publication of a weekly religious paper, and on the 7th of March, 1851, the first number of the *Bombay Guardian* appeared. The writer of these "Reminiscences" was from the outset one of the associated editors, and besides writing occasional editorials, prepared the Epitome of News from the beginning, and three years later the entire charge of the paper devolved upon him. Revs. Dr. Stevenson, Dr. J. M. Mitchell, Dr. Fraser, Geo. Candy, and one or two others were the first editors, but one by one all left Bombay except the present editor.[5] There was now less necessity and less scope for diaries, note-books and the like. 1851 was the year of the World's Great Exhibition in London, the first, and a good many extravagant things were written with regard to its phenomenal significance, many hailing it as the inauguration of a new era, when every man should sit under his own fig-tree, and none should make him afraid, and men should learn war no more. The first article of the writer in the *Bombay Guardian* was against this glowing conception of the matter, and elicited from the *Friend of India* a somewhat scathing criticism.

Bowen refers to the launching of the paper also in his home letter of July 4, 1851:

---

[5]. "I have seen it stated that the paper was originally started by Mr. Bowen. It is more correct to say that it was begun by a small company of friends in the city of Bombay, of whom Mr. Bowen was one. They were five in number. Ere long all had left Bombay except Mr. Bowen and myself; and we two carried on the paper for a short time. Then, by and by, I had to live in Poona, and thereafter Mr. Bowen became sole editor." (Letter from the Rev. J. Murray Mitchell, D. D., Edinburgh, June 12, 1903).

> I do not know if I told you that I assist in editing a religious weekly paper called the *Bombay Guardian,* which a number of us (ministers of various denominations) started in March last. There are three Roman Catholic papers in English, and one in Portuguese, one Puseyite Quarterly, three non-religious dailies in English, and a number of anti-religious papers, beside the *Dnyanodaya.* A paper has lately been started in Marathi for the express and sole purpose of combating Christianity. It is distributed like our tracts, at a price merely nominal. I suppose the *Guardian* is doing some good from the opposition it excites. But my articles are the ones generally singled out for animadversion. I write on "The 19th Century," "The Christian in India," "Difficulties of the Bible." Mr. Larkins has gone home since I wrote last, and so indeed has the greater part of the little host of God's elect Europeans here. My eternal relations to the people continue as before. I give them the Gospel, and they give me mud.

From the founding of the paper until 1854 Bowen was one of a group of associated editors. From 1854 to 1865 he was solely responsible. Then the paper was suspended for a time, to be resumed with the issue of March 3, 1866, Vol. 12, New Series No. 1. In an undated fragment of a letter of this period to Kate, Bowen writes: "Some people are talking of reviving the *Guardian.* A gentleman was offering the other day to be responsible for the expense. I have no faith in these tardy attempts. An ample opportunity was given the public. There is now no evangelical organ. One High Church and the rest secular, admitting anti-evangelical articles." He is omitting the *Dnyanodaya,* the little mission paper in the vernacular which has been published without interruption since its establishment in 1842. There are no files of the *Guardian* prior to 1866 in existence so far as can be learned after diligent inquiry. In 1881 Bowen wrote that he himself had no file:

> We have no complete file of the *Bombay Guardian* anterior to March, 1866. We often wish that we had, perhaps an idle wish. We have partial files for some years and for some scarcely any. The white ants have taken considerable liberties with what we have.

From the resumption of the paper, however, there is at least one complete file, and there appears to be only one, now entrusted to the Missions Research Library, for the whole period of Bowen's editorship which ended only with his death, a period of twenty-two years. The opening paragraph of the issue of March 3, 1866 is as follows:

> No one probably is more surprised than ourselves to find the *Bombay Guardian* once more a living entity. This shows that it is wanted by

somebody, whatever view you may take of that somebody. In this world bad things are tenacious of life, as well as good; there is the Beast of Revelation for instance, whose deadly wound was healed; so the mere fact that the *Guardian* has an inextinguishable life is not much in its favor. To have friends one must show himself friendly; but there is a difference between showing oneself friendly and being friendly; the friendliness which keeps back no needed truth is not always appreciated. We intend, however, to be as amicable as possible. The editor is no longer exclusively responsible (as he was from 1854 to 1865) for all that appears in the editorial columns; and it is hoped that the multitude of counselors will clothe our columns henceforth with a wisdom and ability beyond the former.

It does not appear who shared the editorial responsibility, and there is no internal evidence in the character of the articles that any mind but Bowen's was producing and controlling the paper. It is published by the "Oriental Press" and the editor's address is the "Tract and Book Depository." The issue of March 3, 1866 is composed of l. Weekly Review of Occurrences and Opinions, 2. Bible-notes and Editorials, 3. Articles, 4, Epitome of News, 5. Articles quoted from other publications, 6. Domestic Occurrences, i. e., births and deaths, and Advertisements. It was eight pages of three columns each, size 13 by 9 3/4 inches, and it retained its format and style of type throughout its history. It added, however, in due time other departments: a fearless and discerning section of book reviews, comments on the International Bible Lessons, correspondence, telegraphic news and especially series after series of Bowen's expositions and devotional meditations, while the advertisements grew from one inch to five or six pages, including, it must be admitted, some advertisements of proprietary medicines which might have been omitted. Conscience regarding such matters, however, had not been awakened and the *Guardian* was not a great offender. Bowen, moreover, disclaimed any responsibility for the advertisements or business management.

In an undated letter to Harriet, written after his connection with the Methodist Church, he speaks of his financial relation to the *Guardian* and also of his conscience in his editorial work:

> I have made over my pecuniary interest in the *Bombay Guardian* to the printer. He pays me a monthly sum, sufficient to pay my expenses and leave me something to give away.
>
> The great moment in the Methodist Annual Conference is the last, when, just before the dismissal, the Bishop reads out the appointments for the coming year. Bro. and sister Goodwin, for instance, who had

been two years at Karachi, found themselves appointed to Calcutta, 2,000 miles away; Rev. Fox, four years at Poona, to Karachi, etc. These appointments had been previously arranged in what is called the cabinet, consisting of the Bishop and presiding elders. This itinerant feature of Methodism is one of the things that has made it what it is. At request of the conference, I preached a sermon to them on Luke 14:31. The god of this world as enthroned in India was the one with 20,000. The missionary who trusted in his western civilization or his own power, the man with 10,000. But all power in Heaven and earth is offered to us.

Bro. Thoburn brought me out two books, *Love Enthroned* by Dr. Steele, who sent it to me; *Elijah the Prophet* by Dr. Wm. M. Taylor. This last is from Mr. Thos. C. Doremus, who has pasted his own card in it, adding, "Your father's and mother's friend." Dr. Thoburn told me something about the Doremuses. Did you ever see them?

Since writing the above I have seen in Dr. Steele's book a long extract from *Daily Meditations* and a very eulogistic reference to the book. I do not publish anything without a conviction that it is from God and belongs to Him; then when it is praised I do not rob God, I let Him have the praise, and am kept from self-complacency.

Henceforth it will be possible to gather something about Bowen's work from the pages of the *Guardian* and one chapter will have to be devoted to a review of his thought, as set forth in the paper. For the present it will suffice to recall the judgment of the opening note in the issue of Feb. 11, 1888 which reported his death:

> The loss which religious journalism has sustained in his death cannot be estimated; neither can it ever be fully repaired. Few, if indeed any, editors known to India have approached George Bowen in facility of incisive comment on current topics; in masterly analysis of measures, methods and men's characters; in thorough grasp of all religious, social and political subjects; in intelligent acquaintance with, and insight into, the great modern movements; in power to penetrate the core of a proposition, expose the fallacy of an argument, and pierce the vulnerable point in an antagonist's armor; or in general breadth of literary culture and philosophical attainment.

For nearly thirty-five years Bowen conducted the journal week by week, with only the one intermission, with an encyclopedic knowledge, a true sense of humor and proportion, and a knowledge of history, literature, philosophy and religion unsurpassed by any other editor in the world. He poured out in it his inmost heart and his deepest convictions. He wrote to his mother and sisters, Nov. 27, 1865:

> You say the *Guardian* contained my thoughts, and these are not what you want. The *Guardian* contained my inner life as no letters that I ever wrote did. I put things in it that I would have been slow to put in a letter: e.g., the diary of my innermost experience from 1845 to 1848, the sketch of my former life and conversion given in verse. In a true life thoughts are not separable from feelings and character. The thoughts of Christ fill up the Gospels, uttered in words and deeds. The great conflict waged in the arena of this world is of thought with thought, Christ's thoughts with the world's thoughts, and the victory of Christ's thoughts over the world's thoughts. Happy he to whom Christ shall say, "Thou hast uttered all My thoughts, and he that has heard thee has heard Me, he that has rejected thy words has rejected Mine."

On Bowen's death in 1888 the editorial work of the *Guardian* was taken over by the Rev. H. C. Stuntz of the Methodist Mission. He was succeeded in 1889 by Mr. Alfred S. Dyer who conducted the paper for ten years, until his health failed. And in the issue of June 19, 1899, the trustees offered the paper for sale with the statement, "The paper must be carried on as a missionary effort and requires to be subsidized."

The *Bombay Guardian* has filled so large a place in the work of the Christian Church in India that it is desirable to record its history from Bowen's time until now. In a paper contributed to *Our Missions* in 1912 by J. Douglas Maynard of Selly Oak, Birmingham, Mr. Maynard related the history of the paper from Bowen's death in 1888 until 1912, as follows:

> After Bowen's death in 1888 the *Guardian* was edited for a few months by J. E. Robinson, who is now a bishop of the Methodist Episcopal Church in India. At the same time Alfred S. Dyer and his wife, Helen S. Dyer, were traveling in India in connection with the Friends' Repeal Association. The state of matters which they found impressed Alfred Dyer with the desirability of his remaining in India, in order if possible to create a public conscience on moral questions, and especially to try to impress on the mind of Christians in India their responsibility in such matters. The Karmarkar family, their father having died, were anxious to sell the press in order to raise money for their further education in America. Following these leadings, and with the support of Friends in England, Alfred Dyer bought the press and the paper. The Karmarkars carried out their intention of going to America; the eldest of them graduated in theology while his wife studied medicine, and he has been ever since pastor of an Indian Church in Bombay.
>
> Supported from England by the Friends' Association for the Abolition of the State Regulation of Vice, and more especially by the persistent

energy of the late George Gillett, Alfred and Helen S. Dyer made the *Bombay Guardian* the center of a vigorous campaign. A trust was formed in England to hold the *Bombay Guardian* property for the stated purposes of the spreading of the Gospel in Asia, and the extinguishing of the traffic in vice, opium, and intoxicating liquors. Suitable premises were bought for the press and the residence of the workers, and these have been occupied from 1892 to the present time (1912). The place soon became the center of active moral reform propaganda and evangelistic work. Among the helpers were Maurice Gregory and his wife, who were there three years. F. Percy Horne came from England to manage the press and began work in 1891, and Alice Drewett, now Mrs. Horne, was also a helper.

Doing so active a work in causes which were then unpopular in many quarters, it is not surprising that the *Guardian* and its methods were subjected to a good deal of criticism, but its crusade proved in many respects effective. Alfred Dyer's work continued till the end of 1898, when ill-health led to his retirement, and the editorship was taken up by F. Percy Horne.

A crisis in the affairs of the *Guardian* came in a few months, when the death of George Gillett removed the chief supporter of the work in England. There appeared to be no way of continuing the work on the former lines, and a notice was put in the *Guardian* announcing that the press and the paper were for sale to any Christian agency that would keep them on. This announcement brought forth a considerable expression, from many quarters, of regret that the career of the *Guardian* should seem to be so near its close. In the minds of a few Friends it suggested itself as a special opportunity for aiding the Christian cause in India by means of a journal which, while maintaining a broad, inter-denominational character, should be conducted from the best Quaker standpoint. Friends in England seemed slow to realize the opening; to a Friend in India they appeared "unable to see beyond the back bench of an Adult School." It did seem for a time that they would (to quote the same Friend), "with hardly any thought, put away the chance of influencing a continent."

In India at this anxious time the post one day brought a donation of Rs. 400 (£26.13s.4d) from Indian Christians, which enabled the paper to be continued for one month, and Percy Horne was thereby encouraged to enter upon another month at his own risk.

At this juncture Henry Stanley Newman, who had visited India many years before, and had kept up a keen interest in the economic, political and religious progress of the country, came to the rescue, and offered to act as secretary in England for the *Bombay Guardian*. The trustees sold him the machinery, type and furniture as a going concern, and gave him the use of the premises at a peppercorn rent. Many friends generously assisted by subscribing the necessary funds to maintain the work, while Percy Horne worked energetically in Bombay to reduce expenses and enlarge circulation. It was determined to extend the general printing work so as to increase the receipts of the press, and this policy has been continued ever since.

Some change was made in the emphasis given to the subjects treated in the paper, so as to make it of a more general character than during the previous years. The important interests that marked Alfred Dyer's editorship continued, however, to receive special attention. On 30th December, 1899, the editor said: "We earnestly hope that coming years may witness a still greater development, especially in the direction of making the paper more completely interdenominational in its scope and character, embracing if possible additional missionary and church interests, while not losing touch with those already familiar." New trustees were appointed for the property in Bombay, all of them Friends. The crisis was thus met, and the *Guardian* re-established on a principle which gave great promise for its future, and the work has been continued under Percy Horne's editorship with a good measure of success to the present time. Edward Backhouse, of Stockton-on-Tees, succeeded Henry Stanley Newman as secretary in England in 1903, when a committee of management was formed, consisting of a few English Friends. One of the principal members of this committee was the late Elizabeth B. Backhouse.

The later years, however, have not been uneventful. Work in India is always done against certain adverse conditions, mostly attributable to the climate. The development of the general printing work necessitated an addition to the staff. In February, 1902, Charles O'Brien, of Liverpool, and his wife landed in Bombay and entered on work at the Press. But six weeks later he died from Bubonic plague. Later in the same year Percy Horne's health broke down, and he was obliged to leave for a time. His place was filled for a few months by Henry G. E. de St. Dalmas, who was kindly spared by the Friends' Foreign Mission Association from their work in the Central Provinces. About the same time Arthur J. Sharp, then an officer in the mercantile marine, who had been impressed during visits to Bombay with the value of the *Guardian's* work and the courage with which it was being carried on, offered his services for help with the business management. After working for some months at the press, he was adopted as a permanent member of the staff. With his wife,

Josephine B. Sharp, he now assists Percy and Alice D. Horne in carrying on the work.

A word may be said of the employees of the press. When he first went out, Percy Horne made a point of engaging Indian Christians for this work. There were difficulties about it, as many of those engaged began without any previous experience or much industrial character. But the policy has proved successful, and this little piece of industrial mission work has shown that the difficulties are not greater than those that arise in the general employment of Indian workmen.

George Bowen used to speak of the *Bombay Guardian* as "a child of providence." The way of providence has brought it into the hands of Friends. It is a far more effective means of carrying our message than we easily imagine. An Indian student has said, "Hindus and Mohammedans who have never come across a Christian, nor perhaps heard of Christian missionary work, read Christian papers. Christian journalism in India has from its inception stood for righteousness, and the non-Christian knows that he can rely on what the editor of a Christian newspaper says." Quite recently Percy Horne has received letters from the editors of two vernacular papers, both speaking of the usefulness of the *Bombay Guardian* to them, as they frequently translate part of its contents for their own papers. In another direction Friends have a special opportunity. Like George Bowen they are regarded as holding a non-partisan position among the denominations, and they are therefore specially well fitted to conduct a paper which shall be a bond of union among Christian workers, as the *Guardian* is in Western India. The possibilities open to such an agency are large and the responsibility attending it is great.

In 1917 an appeal was issued by Maurice Gregory for £1,000 for the support of the *Bombay Guardian,* and this appeal set forth the history of the paper from the beginning. Supplementing Mr. Maynard's statement is the following account of the years 1914-1917:

> The Hornes returned to England in December 1913, and their place was taken by one of the ablest journalists in India, the late Benjamin Aitken, who was not only persona grata with the missionary community, but also very well known and respected in all the great journalistic offices in India, in most of which, at one time or another of his eventful life, he had been a helper.
>
> It was to assist him in carrying on the paper that the present Committee took it over in 1915. The transfer had not long taken place when his decease occurred. At the request of W. C. Madge, a member

of the legislative Council of the Viceroy, who was also a member of the new Committee of the *Bombay Guardian,* the editorship was temporarily taken up by Miss Dobson, of the Bombay University Settlement for Women.

This appeal asked for help in behalf of the paper because of four purposes for which the paper was maintained and which underlay the trust which for many years had supported it, namely:

- (a) Propagation of the Gospel in the Indian Empire.
- (b) Abolition of Regulation of Vice by the British Government in India, and the general promotion of Social Purity.
- (c) The Suppression of the Opium Traffic in India, and with China.
- (d) The Abolition of the Government Traffics in India in Drink and Intoxicating Drugs.

In a personal letter dated January 1, 1937, Mr. Maynard writes that Mr. Gregory's appeal was not successful and that the publication of the *Guardian* was stopped in 1918. Mr. Maynard adds:

> The Committee of Management of the *Bombay Guardian* Mission Trust then sold the printing press and the property in Bombay, and invested the proceeds in English securities.
>
> In 1923, Joseph Taylor, a Friend missionary who had always taken a great interest in the old *Guardian* and who was then living in Calcutta, restarted the paper in Calcutta, under the name of the *Guardian,* with A. N. Sudarisanam as co-editor, and financed by the interest of the invested funds. They formed an independent committee in Calcutta, which was responsible for the carrying on of the paper, and this included missionaries, Y. M.C. A. and Indian Christians. It was described as "a Christian weekly Journal of Public Affairs," and its aim was to treat all subjects from a Christian standpoint independent of the interests of any sectional body, such as Y. M. C. A. or a missionary society.
>
> After some years, and after Joseph Taylor had left Calcutta, it appeared advisable to transfer to Madras, where A. N. Sudarisanam had gone to live, and a new Committee was formed there, on the same lines as in Calcutta. A. N. Sudarisanam again became editor, and the paper continues on this basis, relying on regular grants from the *Guardian* Mission Trust in London, without which it is very doubtful whether the paper could continue.

15. Re-establishment of Relations with American Board, 1865-1871

In his letter of Nov. 27, 1865, Bowen writes to his family of the happy personal relations with the Congregational missionaries which had not been interrupted by his disconnection from the American Board in 1855. During all the ten years he had continued to work with them in as hearty cooperation as before and his letters home are full of personal notes about them all.

To the family, Nov. 27, 1865:

> I went to Ahmednagar last month leaving on the 13th and returning on the 2nd Nov. I spent two or three days in Poona on my way up. The railway took me to Dhond about forty-five miles from Ahmednagar. Dr. Fraser, Lieut. Brown and Mr. Macdonald, Christian friends (of Harriet's views) entered the carriage at Poona. They were going to Ahmednagar too, but when they found out from me that they were in error as to the time of the general meeting, they hesitated. However, they went on to Dhond and I spent a pleasant day with them in the travelers' bungalow. Dr. F. has now no employment. He is waiting upon Govt. but without success so far. Mr. Harding came on in the evening from Kolhapur and the next morning he and I left for Nuggur in a tanga, the others returning to Poona. A tanga is a little two-wheeled vehicle on which the parties sit back to back, looking forward and hindward, drawn by two ponies.
>
> We reached Ahmednagar in the evening. Mr. Harding stopped with the Hazens, I with the Woods. The Fairbanks and Mr. Abbott were living also with the Woods. The Mungers and Bruces made up the mission party. I spent a very happy fortnight there. We had a daily prayer-meeting in English for the mission families at 9 a.m. The brethren appointed me a corresponding member of their body and I took part with them in their business meetings which occupied some four or five hours daily. It was almost like being in America; all Americans, American books, newspapers, etc., etc., and American food (pancakes, pumpkin pies, etc.). The only children there were the Fairbanks' four, the Hazens' two daughters, and the Bruces' baby.
>
> In the second week, there was the examination of the schools, diversified by certain little pieces of representation. For instance the story of the Merchant of Venice was worked up with two or three colloquies

sustained by the schoolboys. I was interested to observe the absorbing interest of the national Christian spectators. Sir Alex Grant and others of the gentry were present. In these schools the Christian children are educated to be teachers, catechists, pastors, or to fill secular posts, and the wives of such. Several hundred native Christians came in from the districts, and filled the Chapel during the special three days' exercises. There were about forty speakers, on a great variety of subjects. This was followed by the Communion. I should not forget that there was a scene of offerings to the Lord, such as I once before described. One evening we went to what must have been a charming spot in its day, and is pretty and picturesque even now. Fairy-bag it is called, bag being garden, and Fairy for Peri. It is a Mohammedan pleasure-palace, stone, with arches and a dome, three stories of galleries encompassing the domed interior, a flat roof commanding a north view. The building is islanded in the midst of a piece of artificial water, which is surrounded by noble tamarind trees.

After the meetings were over we spent a day in visiting a somewhat similar structure on a hill-top six miles east of Nuggur. It was a strange idea to combine a palace with a tomb. The building was erected by Talabat Khan in honor of a favorite wife, buried in the basement. We dined there alfresco in one of the open galleries near the top. Had a delightful day altogether. I was there before in 1854 when the Deputation was here. We were constantly reminded of the absent: the Ballantines: Bissells, Barkers, Chapins. Nothing could exceed the kindness shown me by all. This, however, is so constant a thing that I might easily have forgotten to make mention of it.

After Br. Harding and I left, there was another Mission meeting, at which they passed the following resolution: "Having enjoyed the presence and counsel of Br. Bowen during this meeting, and reviewing with great satisfaction the course he has pursued in regard to the Am. Board and ourselves since he was outwardly disconnected with us in 1855, the Mission would express the hope that the Prudential committee may again appoint him a missionary of the A. B. C. F. M., and that Br. B. himself may again assume the duties and enjoy all the privileges that such a connection involves." This was communicated to me by Br. F. in a kind letter. I am willing to be connected with the Board as I was before 1855, and shall probably send by this opportunity a letter to this effect. The Lord will hinder it or promote it as He sees fit. I am equally the Lord's servant whether so connected or not.

His letter to the American Board was dated Bombay, Dec. 13, 1865:

My dear Dr. Anderson:

At the meeting of the missionaries of the Marathi Mission in Oct. last in Ahmednagar, a resolution was adopted expressive of their desire that I should again become a member of that Mission.

I was led to resign in 1855 chiefly through a feeling that my views on the subject of paedo-baptism might lead my colleagues to question the advisableness of my continuance in the Mission. A convert in the Ahmednagar Mission had adopted similar views on the subject of infant baptism. He was living in the house with me; I had had no conversation with him on that subject; his change in views had been brought about by another agency altogether; but I feared that a feeling of uneasiness would spring up in the minds of my brethren; so I resigned, and you accepted my resignation.

During the ten years that have since elapsed, I have been in constant intercourse with the missionaries, and have frequently been a fellow laborer with them, without the slightest jar, and it is both their conviction and mine that the views referred to, constitute in this case, no bar to cooperation. I cannot myself baptize any but those whom I regard as believers. I cannot make a secret of this inability. If my connection with the Board placed me in the position of a pastor, some difficulty might arise, but I do not think I hold this view in any way to hinder my acting as a missionary of the American Board.

During the last six years that I was connected with the American Board I declined receiving any salary. I have received none since 1849. During the greater part of this interval I earned the trifling amount necessary by giving an hour's tuition daily. For the last three or four years guided by the providence of God I have not supported myself in this way: that providence has kept me supplied with the necessaries of life. My expenses do not amount to $100 a year. I am quite sure that Providence will never fail me, and I do not seek any other provision.

I think it a matter of congratulation that Bro. Munger is to come to Bombay. The population in this place has immensely increased since you were here. There are three lines of railway connecting it with the interior (N., N-E. and S-E) and its influence is more and more felt in every part of the Presidency. Notwithstanding the very unsatisfactory results of missionary labor here, I am persuaded that its importance as a missionary center cannot be overestimated.

I am grateful to the brethren of the Mission for the honor done me in their resolution. I have written this to show you that I cordially acquiesce in their proposition. I am, my dear Dr. Anderson,

Yours faithfully,
George Bowen.

The American Board approved the resolution of the Mission, and Bowen's official relations became again what they had been prior to 1855. Our knowledge of his life and thought during the six years of this resumed relationship is confined to a dozen or more home letters and to his self-revelation in the *Guardian*. First, some excerpts from the home letters:

To the family, Nov. 12, 1866, referring to the annual meeting of the Mission at Ahmednagar:

> You may see in the *Guardian* account of the meeting, mention of the Chaplain of the station, Mr. Watson. There is a large camp of European (and native) soldiers, and he is the only one to preach to them. He is liberal, but it is broad church liberality. Let me tell you of a conversation I had with him. He asked me if I wrote the Notes from an Interleaved Bible. Yes. "I like them but I think your views are sometimes narrow." They are just what I find in the Bible. My views were once broad enough. I did not believe in a revelation at all. When I knew the Bible to be true, I resolved to take it as my guide, both in doctrine and in practice. "What about inspiration? Do you hold the literal view?" I believe it to be wholly the Word of God. How the writers were influenced is with me of no consequence. God took care that the Bible should be what it is and every page has His imprimatur. Copyists may have made mistakes; but none were allowed that in any way impaired the value of the Bible as God's book. "I was conversing," says he, "today, with a Roman Catholic priest. He maintained the infallibility of the Church. It seems to me your error is a similar one in relying on the Bible as infallible. It was written by fallible men, and of course must partake of their imperfections." In the Bible I hear the voice of God; the infallibility on which I rest is that of God. If I wished to send a message to a man I would take care that the messenger was fitted to convey it. It would be a strange thing if God should commit the most important of all messages to those who might pervert it. He surely has power to get His messages rightly delivered.
>
> I afterwards asked him if he had any difficulties about the supernatural. He said, "Yes," and asked me what I thought of such miracles as that of Joshua stopping the sun. I told him I fully believed it. It was fitting that the material world should be shown to be subordinate to the spiritual, and I believed there were from time to time sent interferences with the ordinary course of nature with a view to the greater manifestation of the divine power. He could not go with this at all. The wonderful works of Christ he believed to be in the exercise of power beyond those of ordinary men, but still not beyond nature. Christ said, I can of my own self do nothing. The Father that dwelleth in Me, He doeth the works. So the power was that of God, and was just the power that was manifest in

creation. And nothing less would have answered. Power that all should recognize as divine, was what was needed. "Yet how small was the result," said he. "Men did not believe. And it is not miracles that men need in order to believe." Why should miracles be wrought if men were not convinced by them? The N. T. does not make light of the evidence of miracles. If I do not the works of Him that sent Me, believe Me not. Look at the first dozen chapters of the Acts, where the greatest effects are connected with them. God gives sufficient evidence, and it is no disparagement of this that sin blinds men to it.

To Kate, Aug. 23, 1867:

I am so glad to hear you speak of Mrs. Chapin. But I have later news of her. She is going to be married. If you get well acquainted with her you will find her an uncommon person. She makes a mark. I fear that you women are getting too much liberty in America. It is observable that the more you get the more you wish. All you wish, you get. Impartial suffrage comes next and then the men will be nowhere. Serve them right, I suppose. What we all want is not so much a wider scope, more elbowroom, but more heart to do the work before us. From all I hear, Mrs. Chapin has this, and I trust wherever she may be she may do much good and glorify the Savior. Capt. Hanscom, my friend, remembers her with great gratitude, for she was the means of leading him to Christ when he was officer in the *Gunga.*

Mrs. Bowen died this winter and Bowen's further letters are to the sisters. To his sisters, March 14, 1868:

I have just been writing to Frank. A gentleman who passed through Bombay on his return to America, a Mr. Chase, told me that he had spent some time with him at Yokohama last August, Captain Frank Bowen he called him. Frank had told him that he had a brother, a missionary, in Bombay. He was there for his health. Is a merchant in Macao (Portuguese port, sixty miles from Canton); is in the coolie business, that is, he sends Chinese emigrants to South America. Mr. Chase said Frank was a most gentlemanly person, moving in very good society. He is thin, it appears. I fancied he was stout. Some friends were leaving in the steamer for America and Frank suddenly decided to go with them. He told Mr. Chase he would return by the January steamer. I suppose he did not go to see you. His business relations are with New York, I believe. Mr. Chase did not hear him speak against religion, but got the idea that he was simply indifferent, careless on the subject. He spoke as though he thought it a strange thing I should be spending my life out here as a missionary.

I have told him about Ma's death, and have urged him if he has occasion to take a run anywhere for his health anytime, to come to Bombay, and have promised to see that he is well cared for.

It is a matter of great thankfulness that we have got such an account of him. I feared worse things. I hope he may be touched by what I told him of Ma's death. It is a good thing that we know where to address him. I cannot but hope that this is the beginning of his restoration. I hope you will be instant in prayer. . . . I spent last evening at the Stearns'. They have a Col. and Mrs. Kirby and a Mr. Charmtrell living with them, Christian people, and they are accustomed to study the Word of God together, and when I come they have a lot of questions to ask me. There is no more delightful subject of conversation than the Word of God. It is that which God has given to form the staple of our intercourse, and we set it aside substituting the weather and other most dreary subjects.

To his sisters, May 18, 1868:

I am sorry not to be able to tell you that I have heard from Frank; but I hope the next China mail may bring a reply from him. Am I too sanguine? It is certainly singular that Kate should have had the dream about him just a few days before I got news of him. My friend Capt. Hanscom left lately for America. I think I must have often mentioned this excellent person to you. He has been in command of one of Stearns, Hubart Co's steamers between this and Suez, and goes home to see his wife and child in Saco, Maine. I hope he will come out again. I gave him a letter to you. My friends, Mr. and Mrs. Stearns, went in this same steamer. To her also I gave letters to you, and I hope you may make her acquaintance. I have spent many pleasant evenings at her house, speaking of the teachings of the Bible. . . . You will have seen in the *Guardian* what a furious controversy has been raging around the Bible here, in reference to the alleged mythical character of its contents. Dr. Budwood, the leader in this onset on the Bible, is secretary of the Asiatic Society here. He is known as the irrepressible. His father is my friend, General Budwood, and all his relatives are Christian people, viewing his aberrations as I do. The educated native drink in with delight these assaults upon the Bible and arm themselves with arguments against it, thus furnished. The missionary here finds all European infidelity between him and the heart of the people.

Re-establishment of Relations with American Board 1865-1871   355

> I had a letter today from General Field. He commanded one of the brigades in the march on Magdala. He speaks very admiringly of the providence of God shown in the ordering of affairs. He is a man of great prayerfulness and great faithfulness. When you do get piety in military men, it is generally unequivocal. This is a dear brother whom I have known since I came to the country.
>
> I agree with you, dear Harriet, in the longing for Christ's coming. I have been expecting the event spoken of as the coming of the Son of Man for a great many years, and shall expect it till it comes. My conceptions of it may differ from yours in various aspects. But I know of nothing that needs to come in between us and that day. Whatever I do, speak and write is with reference to the revelations of that day, which is the explanation of the narrowness that some attribute to me.

Harriet wrote to him of the possibility of her coming out to Bombay to teach and Bowen wrote, June 16, 1858, discouragingly.

To his sister, Oct. 8, 1868:

> About the middle of August I received from a friend in London, marked "Private" a letter, in which he said: "My dear wife and I have more than once, in our conversations regarding yourself, asked the question, how you might be placed in years to come, should sickness or other troubles assail you, refusing as you now do all pecuniary assistance from any Board or Mission. And while we are ready to admit God's ever-present care for the wants of each one of His people, we have pleasure in the belief that it is our duty as well as privilege, as God has given us the means abundantly, to beg your acceptance of the enclosed document." This document was a receipt for Rs. 10,000 deposited by this friend in my name in a Bank in Bombay last May. He adds: "I have placed the amount at interest for a period of years, which may possibly save you some present trouble. The reinvestment, however, and the disposal of principal and interest remain with yourself absolutely It is not our wish in any way to dictate to you as to the particular manner in which it is to be used, but we are inclined to hope that while it may be of service in providing for your personal wants, a portion of the capital may be expended in enabling you to recruit your health by a visit to your own country." Is not this generosity? True Christian love? You will surely pray for these dear Christian friends. I give you their names, but you need not repeat them to others: Mr. and Mrs. C. B. Ker. The money you understand is locked up for five years; only the interest is available.

If the money had not been given in this particular way, I should have felt it my duty to get rid of it in some way.

About a fortnight after receiving this letter, I received another from my friend, Mr. Sands, here in Bombay, referring in the same way to the possibility of my wishing to visit America, and asking me to let him place Rs. 2,500 at my disposal for this purpose. I told him in reply that I had no thought of going, and could not avail myself of his offer. You must hold him in affectionate remembrance.

Connect with all this that I have never during these twenty unsalaried years, asked any human being for a pice for myself. It has been a fixed principle with me never to do it whatever my circumstances. It did not seem consistent with such a life of faith as I wished to lead, to intimate to any mortal, in any way, any pecuniary need. I have never lacked, though sometimes I fancied I did. I have never thought it proper to refer even to any break of faith there may have been.

To Kate, Jan. 1, 1869:

Another year finds us separated by half the circumference of the globe, but still on the globe and with ten thousand causes of thankfulness. Though the Lord has not fulfilled the wish entertained for reunion, He has found, and will find, other ways of expressing His great and tender love. He is willing to show us in Christ a length, breadth, height, depth of love far surpassing our past experiences. Why should we not be strong in faith to appropriate it? But it must be allowed to live and move in the heart according to its own laws. Sometimes on reaching the heart it begins to act very strangely, casting this and that precious thing out of the window, tearing down what we esteemed ornaments, and instead of letting us sit down to a banquet, sending us forth with provisions for some wretched ones. But the angel-guest must be allowed to have His own way, and we shall soon see that His advent is blessedness. Is it not the consciousness that Love divine will act thus, that makes the heart of even the believer content itself with what it knows of that love. Let us forget the things that are behind and press towards the mark for the incomparable prize.

To Harriet, Nov. 25, 1869:

While Frank is with you and unsettled, every letter I get from you stimulates my desire to hear from you. I hope I may soon hear what I wish to. A few weeks ago I was in prayer for Frank and I seemed to have an assurance that the prayer was heard and was being answered. I cannot but hope that before very long I may hear that God has revealed to him

His grace in Christ. . . . What more can I say? What better news can I give you than that I have a delightful sense of the Savior's presence and an unwavering conviction of His faithfulness. Pray always that I may be enabled to endure unto the end, and that the world may get the fruit of all the seed that Christ has sown in my heart. And may God give you and Kate and Frank grace to do all that is pleasing in His sight and give His love expression in your lives.

To his sisters, Apr. 8, 1870:

There is a surplus *Guardian* fund entirely at my disposal. I do not know of any more urgent need for it—at all events, it is impressed upon me that I should send it to you, and I do. Enclosed is an order for $150.

To his sisters, May 30, 1870:

You will have seen in the *Guardian* a brief notice of a united meeting of native Christians. Col. Tripe, a friend of mine in Burmah, some time ago sent me some money for the expenses of such a meeting which he wished me to get up for the promotion of union among native Christians. It was a very nice meeting. The General Assembly's Institution, a large building, was lent me for the evening; about 175 came together, of whom twenty were European ladies and gentlemen.. All the Native churches were represented, though the High Church party were offended because it was Easter evening and did their best to hinder some from coming. In the course of the evening I addressed them from the 17th of John. At the close gave picture cards, etc. All seemed to enjoy the meeting, and I trust it was profitable.

To Harriet, July 19, 1870:

I send the semi-annual Rs. 200. I shall perhaps not send anything more for six months. That money I send I send to you and Kate. Of course I leave it with you to employ as may seem to you best. I regard all money that comes to me, as belonging to the Lord. I am not master of it to do what I like with it, but can only dispose of it in a way that seems accordant with the will of the Lord. Those who put money in my hand have generally first given it to the Lord, and it would be a misappropriation of it to divert it to any other than purposes of Christian benevolence. It seems to me that you and Kate are to some extent providentially connected with me, so that I may very properly assist you to the extent of your need.

With regard to "adokimos," I think it not inaptly rendered "castaway" (tried and found wanting). Paul knew perfectly well that he would not be a castaway; was sure of it as he was of his existence; yet he knew equally well that if he did not keep his body under, if he was not led by the Holy Spirit, he would be a castaway. He knew that not one of the 276 souls in the ship in which he sailed to Melita would be lost; but he knew that except the shipmen abode in the ship, many would be lost. Acts. 27:30. But I have written on this subject in the *Guardian,* May 28th. We should never be afraid to use the language of the Bible. The Arminians find Arminianism in the Bible, and the Calvinists, Calvinism; the better instructed take both, take all Scripture.

To his sisters, Dec. 2, 1870:

I wrote you on October before going to Ahmednagar. I went on the 15th and returned Nov. 3 and had a very happy time. It was delightful being with the brothers and sisters and dear children in Nuggur, and over and above that I had heavenly communion with the Savior in the little chamber which Mrs. Bissell gave me in the top of their house, a little room that looked out on the flat roof. There was a larger gathering of missionaries than had been for some years. The anniversary exercises were very interesting. I stopped at Poona on my way up at Col. Kirby's. The Kirbys are excellent Christian people. He is Adjt. Genl. of the Bombay Army, and they have a great deal to do with the world, but they are consistent and decided in their religious profession. He is about six feet two inches, a noble looking man. For many years they had no children; now they have two. They were intimate with the Stearns. . . . How far it was from the anticipations of anybody that the return of Frank, so long desired and waited for, would involve you in greater suffering than you had ever known. The idea that Frank has been trifling with you this year and a half, I am unwilling to entertain. Not because you have such an unwavering confidence in him, but because it really seems, as you say, that God has been specially and designedly baffling all his schemes until he shall have learned to recognize the hand of the Father, even the pierced hand of Calvary.

To his sisters, Jan. 6, 1871:

God is doing great things for us here. The work of conviction and conversion goes promptly on. The Lord has blessed me in connection with Mr. Taylor's visit, enabling me to see as I have never before done, the way in which He uses us in the recovery of lost men. I have the great happiness daily of instructing burdened souls and leading them to Christ. The great thing is that we expect to see souls saved, expect that God will use us in bestowing salvation. We are witnessing some remarkable conversions, i.e., the conversion of men who seemed to be lost beyond recovery. And there is a gradualness about the development of the work as a whole, that leads us to think that we are going to see a very extensive work before this is done. Bombay is such a widely diffused place, in fact a cluster of large towns, that Mr. Taylor has to shift from one quarter to another. He is now laboring for a fortnight in Mazagon. Most of the people of the upper class dislike his preaching. He troubles himself very little about conventionalities and talks like a man who has to do with the dead and dying and cannot stand on ceremony. He lives for the one object of saving souls, and saving them now, and some of us are catching his spirit.

This is the first letter reference to William Taylor, afterwards Bishop Taylor, of the Methodist Episcopal Church, with whom Bowen was soon to throw in his lot.

In Feb., 1871, he was so seriously ill that his life was despaired of, but influential friends took him into their home, secured the best medical aid and he recovered. In his own judgment his recovery was due to his rejection of the physics prescribed and to prayer and to—buffalo milk (Letters to his sisters, Feb. 23, 1871).

To his sisters: May 20, 1871:

> I send you Rs. 300 for which I have no need, which may help you through the summer. The Lord counsel you in all things.
>
> My dear sisters, we get the most out of every day when we get most love out of it. The love is in Christ, and it should come into our hearts and unite us heart to heart. Our old bronze natures are to be melted down again and run into the mold of Christ that we may be as He was in the world. Love alone gives value to life, and all in us that is unfavorable to love, must be done away at the cross of Christ. Shall we not come to the cross expecting greater things than we have seen? Greater subjugations of our natures? Mightier assimilations? Why not? The past time may suffice us to have lived our own life, to have obeyed what Kate calls the Bowen nature. It is a bad nature. The sooner we get rid of it the better.

Frank had disappeared again. Bowen says he had had no letter from him since 1848.

To his sisters, Aug. 11, 1871:

> One Saturday evening 9 o'clock, I came in and groped my way to the place of matches to light my candle, but found a ladder in a place where it was not when I went out, and wondered whether thieves had entered.

> I had locked the door when I went out. However, the light explained everything. Somebody had entered surreptitiously (getting a key from the clerk) and had left a cabinet organ behind. Opening it I found a letter from Harding saying that some friends begged my acceptance. I was half vexed at first, having a little harmonium given me eight years ago, very inferior of course to this, but equal to my needs. I do not give more than ten minutes a day to it generally. My first instrument I have sent over to Mrs. Cross, wife of the C. M. S. missionary in the Missionary School opposite. But I am not reconciled to having this larger one. I shall try to get the Fairbanks to take it.

Among Bowen's friends in Bombay, during these years 1865-1871, were the leading British officials, all grades of Indians, the riff-raff of Europe and America which drifted through Bombay and practically all the worthy representatives of our own land who came and went through this gateway of the Far East. His letters make frequent mention of the Stearns family and of Captain Hanscom whose ship plied to and fro between India and America. Mrs. Hanscom lived into the present century with her daughter who was on the faculty of Smith College. On Nov. 7, 1906, she wrote:

> A few years ago I went through my husband's papers and among them found some characteristic letters from Mr. Bowen. I remember considering whether I would keep or destroy them, and I thought I decided to preserve them. Now I have looked very carefully and cannot find even one. I remember that one was written at the time he decided to go into the Methodist Church, and he wrote freely about his reasons. My husband knew Mr. Bowen intimately between the years 1865 and '72 and their correspondence continued. They had many talks at night around the office table. Perhaps one conversation you may find of use, although you may have the matter from another source. I remember that Mr. Hanscom told me that in one of their last talks, when they did not expect to meet here again, Mr. Bowen said he did not regret his manner of living in Bombay; he did it because it was right for him, and he should do it again, but he would never advise anybody else to live in the same way. He thought if the people around him saw that he had no worldly motive, if they learned that he was there from love of them and a desire to become "all things to all men" for the sake of serving them, that then they would listen to him, but, he added: "I do not know that I have been the means of gaining one soul by this manner of living."

16. Association with the Methodist Church in India

William Taylor was one of the most distinctive and picturesque personalities of the nineteenth century. He roamed all over the world as a Christian evangelist, looking to no human agency for direction or support. He believed in self-supporting missionaries like Paul, who maintained himself by his trade as a tent-maker. In his book, *Self-Supporting Missions,* published in 1882, he advocated missions established and supported by men "at their own cost without any guarantee of compensation." He did not disapprove of missionary work supported by money, but it should be money earned or contributed on the field and not sent out by the home church. He allowed charity, as such, but not as a form of missionary work subsidized by foreign funds. In Asia, Africa, South America, indeed all over the earth, this heroic, adventurous, undaunted spirit moved, establishing churches and schools, conducting revivals and evangelistic campaigns, laying here and there enduring foundations and, it must be admitted, leaving far and wide also the wreckage of courageous but unenduring sacrifice.

In the early 60's Taylor was working in Australia. Then he went to Africa where, as he wrote in *Four Years' Campaign in India,* his work resulted "in the professed conversion to God of 1,200 colonists and 7,000 Kaffirs as reported in detail in *Christian Adventures in South Africa.*" Then he was at work in Great Britain and then in the West Indies where "an annual loss of 6,000 in Wesleyan membership was turned to a gain of 5,000." From the West Indies he went again to Australia with a resulting gain in church membership of 21,000 in the years following his visit. Next he came to Ceylon and thence at the appeal of the Rev. J. M. Thoburn, afterwards Bishop Thoburn, a most efficient missionary leader of the Methodist Church, to India, arriving in Bombay on Nov. 20, 1870. Taylor at once called on Bowen. "We called for one minute," he says in *Four Years' Campaign in India,* "at the Tract Society's building to see Rev. George Bowen. He is a long, lean brother. I have heard that he is the most devoted man of God in India, and lives very abstemiously that he may have the more to give to those who are in need. If the Roman Catholics had him they would canonize him as a saint. He shook my hand and said, 'Can I do anything for you? Will you have any money?' I thanked him and replied, 'I am in need of nothing, my brother.' He expressed regret that I would not tarry a season in Bombay. I said, 'Perhaps the Lord will bring me back,' and bade him a hurried good-bye." When William Taylor met George Bowen, in the matter of austere frugality and self-denial, it was Greek meeting Greek.

The first mention of Taylor by Bowen in the *Guardian* is in an editorial note in the *Guardian* of Nov. 19, 1870: "The Rev. William Taylor, whose work as an evangelist has been so remarkably blest of God in America, Africa, England, Australia, etc., is expected in Bombay by the incoming Chinese steamer. He comes to India upon the invitation of the Methodist Episcopal missionaries in Northern India. We earnestly hope that his visit may be attended with much fruit." This note is immediately followed by a promise of review of the following books: *Autobiography of an Indian Officer* by Major H. M. Conran: *Thoughts on Brahmanism* by a Native; *On the Physiological Basis of Psychology* by M. L. Sircar, M. D.: *Short Papers for Educated Natives: Babu Keshub Chundra Sen and His Mission.* The next issue of the *Guardian* makes no mention of Taylor but quotes with satisfaction an extract from "A Sermon in Verse, on Christian Self-Denial, by W. S. S." The author had been domestic chaplain of the Bishop of Madras:

> To do the work that God has given us,
> Whate'er, where'er it be; to do the work
> Unto the end, at cost of life and limb.
> In spite of malice and of cruel fraud,
> In spite of violence and treachery,
> In spite of all the varied forms of sin
> And unbelief that mar and vex our world,
> To find the very nourishment of life
> In close obedience to our Father's word,
> And rather starve for want of daily food
> Than leave undone a single duty—this
> Is to deny ourselves and follow Christ.
>
> Yet more. To bear as well as do God's will,
> To find in suff'ring service, and to feel
> That all that He may put on us of pain
> Or sorrow is a needed discipline;
> To see in darkest hours of agony
> The path that leads to light, and to behold
> Beyond the cross—yes, on it even now—
> The glory shining from the golden gates
> Of God's eternal city, and to cry,
> When worst the burden weigheth down the soul,
> "My God," as Christ did—this, my brethren,—is
> A true denial of our sinful self,
> A taking of the cross to follow Christ.

> Patience and zeal; with fervor, self restraint;
> A bridle put upon the undue haste
> And willfulness of proud imaginings;
> Amid all joys a soberness of soul
> That learns the limits of our earthly bliss
> Using the world and not abusing it,
> And keeps God ever in the foremost place,
> As ground and aim of highest happiness,
> Amid calamities, a will resigned,
> Not apathetic but submissive still
> To all the will of God—such character
> Pertains to those who would deny themselves,
> Daily take up their cross and follow Christ.
>
> And Christian love is but the highest form
> Of Christian self-denial, when the heart
> "At leisure from itself" can burst with joy
> Or beat with woe, at others' joy or woe;
> And when the mind kept free from selfish aims,
> Can bend its powers to benefit the world,
> While yet the world regards it not, or looks
> With scorn on the divine philanthropy.

In the *Guardian* of Dec. 3, 1870, Bowen notes that Taylor had spent only two days in Bombay and had then gone on to Lucknow and that "he expects to spend, God willing, a year and a half in India, and we hope that he may find opportunity to visit Bombay and preach here." The editorial note refers to a book by Taylor entitled *The Model Preacher,* presenting Christ as the true model for preachers and suggesting the following characteristics of His preaching: clearness, earnestness, naturalness, literalness and appropriateness. By literalness is meant "literal facts demonstrating the truth and power of the Gospel and literal figures from real life, illustrating the great principles of the Gospel."

Bowen calls attention in the *Guardian* of Apr. 15, 1871, to weaknesses recognized and described in the Report of the American Methodist Mission in North India as revealed by Mr. Taylor's revival: "Nothing can be more evident than that our work has sometimes suffered in the past from the character of many of the workers we have employed. Experience has convinced us that a man who is not a positive help, is usually sure to be a positive hindrance to our work. It is not enough that a man has a good character, ability to preach, a fair education, and willingness to work; he must have in addition to all these, emanating from above, the call of the Holy Ghost. During recent revivals in Lucknow and elsewhere, preachers of established reputation have been found utterly useless in the work of leading souls to Christ. They can *preach* very, very well, can gather up enquirers and bring them to the missionary for baptism, but when a man becomes distressed about his sins, and asks with tears what he must do to find relief for his burdened soul, they look on with bewilderment, or perhaps, with an awkward embarrassment turn and leave him. Such men cannot help us. . . . For the future we shall give no man a place among our helpers, until he has himself not only learned the way of salvation, but demonstrated his ability to show others the way."

Various notes in the paper referring to Taylor before he began his work in Bombay reveal Bowen's growing interest and approval. On Apr. 29, he comments on Taylor's principle of self-support: "He declines all pecuniary aid and supports himself and his family by the income which he derives from the sale of his books. 1 Cor. 9:18." On June 10, 1871, he quotes from Taylor's *Christian Adventures in Africa,* commending the evangelist's "faith and single devotion to God's Word." On Oct. 28, he reports Taylor's visit to Ahmednagar and his method of working through the church and not apart from it, seeking first to awaken church members to their obligations. Bowen evidently heard him at Ahmednagar. On Nov. 4, he says: "It is evident that Mr. Taylor has made a life-long study of the art of bringing the truth of God home to the hearts of men. He does not think to honor the Spirit, by just delivering the message and leaving the Spirit to do what He likes with it; but he thinks to honor the Spirit by consecrating all his powers in all their detail to the work of presenting the truth in its integrity to the minds of men, so presenting it as that they shall feel the power of it. And, beyond all men that it has been the privilege of the writer to hear, he succeeds." A week later he speaks of Taylor's sermon on John 1:12, as the most "powerful" sermon he had ever heard and hopes that he will soon come to Bombay. The next week Taylor came and thereafter Bowen is referring constantly to his work. He wrote to his sisters on Dec. 23, 1871:

> The Lord is working gloriously in the midst of us, blessing the preaching of Mr. Taylor, and we have seen things the like of which men never saw before. Among my own friends, some have been promptly converted, and others who may or may not have been Christians have sought a new life. Mr. Taylor preaches the very Gospel I delight in, fullness of peace and fullness of consecration, making war upon all sin with the banner of good. What we have seen is probably but the very beginning. His aim is to raise up by the end of the year a witnessing, working church. Mr. Taylor has had two or more meetings daily, the evening meeting lasting sometimes four hours.

And the *Guardian* reports the meetings when Taylor spoke both in the vernacular through an interpreter and in English.

Association with the Methodist Church in India

The revival was criticized by some, including the *Bombay Gazette,* and in the *Guardian* of Jan. 20, 1872 Bowen prints a nearly full-page leading editorial in defense, and follows this up in the next issue. On March 2, Bowen reports and defends the proposal for the establishment of a Methodist Church in Bombay. Heretofore there had been none, but now partly because of the attitude of some of the other churches and partly in response to the desire of a number of the converts of the revival that Mr. Taylor should officiate as their pastor, Taylor gathered the various Fellowship Bands that had been formed into a church organization. The work went on more quietly during the succeeding months, with meetings in private houses rather than large halls, and among Christians predominantly. The movement met with increasing opposition and hostility against which Bowen protests in an editorial entitled "Our Revival" (*Guardian,* July 20, 1872) and which evidently only deepened his sympathy and interest, and in November he definitely related himself to the Methodist Church and continued in this relationship until his death sixteen years later. He writes of his new connection to his sisters on Nov. 27, 1872:

> My last letter will have told you something of the blessed work that has been going on here in connection with Mr. Taylor's preaching. The work is going on steadily, not with great demonstration but steadily and surely. Souls are saved every day, and the converts are being built up in love and faith, and learning to work for Christ. The course pursued by the churches here, has had the effect of putting Mr. Taylor upon a new track, the formation of a Methodist Church which will keep him in Bombay some time. Meanwhile he labors as an evangelist four days in the week. Some eight or ten fellowship bands have been formed, of one of which I have charge. There are nearly thirty in my band. . . . ——— was converted through Mr. Taylor's preaching, and has now no desire for drink whatever. He belongs to my band. There are other cases of conversion as striking. God's providence seems to be leading Mr. Taylor in the English-speaking stratum of the population, but Mr. Taylor regards this as preparatory work, believing that when a witnessing, working, aggressive church has been raised up, the heathen will be impressed and drawn. And I think he is right. They need to be made to see that Christ is really risen and at the right hand of Majesty, and is giving gifts to men. . . .
>
> The great thing that I have been taught in these months is the power and importance of the word "now" in addressing sinners. Men naturally have the idea that to get right with God is a gigantic work requiring long-continued, assiduous conflict; and it comes to them with the force of a new revelation when they see that they may now, at once, get into amity with God and get from Him all the help they need to overcome sin. The grand points, in addressing people, are these: Will you *now*

make a full surrender to God, give up all self-justification, acknowledge the truth of what God says about you, consent to be loyal, to let His will be done instead of your own? Will you *now* receive Christ as He is offered, in all His fullness, upon the testimony of God's Word, as your own Savior, Physician, Leader, Friend and Lord, receive Him for all the needs of your soul? The Gospel preached to every creature is a declaration of God's readiness to save, and an invitation from God to every sinner to come and take the water of life; this forbids the idea that God will keep the sinner waiting a moment when this entire surrender of himself and this reception of Christ by faith take place. *His now* follows instantly upon *yours* and He sends forth the Spirit of adoption into your heart, witnessing with your spirit that you are a child of God. The surrender, of course, involves faith, and the faith involves the surrender. In submission we recognize our own utter inability for any good, and take Christ as our goodness, relying upon Him for all the strength needed to carry out His will. It has a wonderful effect upon men, to learn that they may, thus submitting and believing, receive a divine attestation, an earnest from God assuring them of their acceptance; that the acquittal shall actually be communicated to the prisoner setting him free.

Of this new step of Bowen's in joining the Methodists because he approved their evangelistic zeal and the immediacy of their appeal, William Taylor gave a brief account in *Four Years' Campaign in India,* published in 1876 (p. 237 f.):

About the same time (Nov. 1872) Rev. George Bowen joined us. He came to India over twenty-five years before, as a missionary of the American Board of Foreign Missions. After a couple of years' service he became convinced that to succeed in establishing a Native Church in India, on a sound, healthy basis, would require greater self-sacrifice, and a closer assimilation to native life on the part of missionaries than had been generally supposed to be necessary. He embodied his views in a small pamphlet, which he respectfully submitted to most of the missionaries in India at that time; but failing to get any of them to concur in his views, he felt it his duty to give his principles a tangible form in his own example. He resigned his connection with the American Board of Foreign Missions and proceeded in his missionary work on the self-denying, self-supporting principle. He did not propose to set up a mission but became the helper of all. He gave a few hours daily to a few pupils in a private family, and thus earned a living. For more than twenty years he has been the editor of the *Bombay Guardian*—an able, outspoken, religious weekly: for many years also Editor of the Marathi publications of the Bombay Book and Tract Society, and agent of their Tract Department. All the people of this region, high and low, European and native, know George Bowen and set him down without debate as a

Association with the Methodist Church in India

saint. He is a learned man, an author, a clear thinker, a transparent preacher of great humility and usefulness, a good musician—a John the Baptist to prepare the way for the Lord's coming to establish the self-supporting India Mission of which he has now become a member and a minister.

Of the same action of Bowen, Bishop Thoburn wrote long after in his book, *India and Malaysia*, (p. 429):

> It was here (in Bombay) that Bishop Taylor made his first independent stand in the empire. It was here that he was joined by the saintly and venerable George Bowen, a man whose praises were in all the churches of the East, and who brought with him a commanding influence in the city of Bombay itself.... When Mr. Bowen united with the Methodist Episcopal Church he was an independent Protestant missionary, but had been sent to India in the first place by the American Board. He of course continued the work which he was doing, and in this way it may be said that we have always had a vernacular work in Bombay.

In an editorial in the *Guardian* of Nov. 20, 1875, Bowen defends Taylor against the criticism of an article in the *Indian Evangelical Review,* and his defense indicates the wide base of his sympathy with Taylor and his methods and ideas:

> We know not for how much our opinion may count with the writer of the above article, but we are free to confess that often when hearing Mr. Taylor preach, the thought has come up that we had never heard the Gospel preached by any other man so fully, so faithfully, so effectively. And we have had abundant opportunities of seeing educated men as powerfully influenced by him as uneducated.
>
> The writer of the above-mentioned article finds the explanation of Mr. Taylor's success, in these things:
>
> 1. His departure from the rigid and conventional style of preaching now in vogue.
>
> 2. His departure from conventional systems of theology.
>
> 3. His departure from the conventional caste rules of society.
>
> To these are added, Mr. Taylor's triumphant faith in his mission, his boundless energy, his wonderful perseverance, and his marvelous elasticity of principle and disposition.
>
> After a prolonged and intimate acquaintance with Mr. Taylor, we feel constrained to say that we do not find the secret of his success in the things enumerated. Mr. Taylor has made the operations of the Spirit of God the study of his life. He has had a very deep experience of the work of the Spirit in his own heart, and realizing his absolute dependence on the Spirit for success in his work, he has diligently sought to understand

the laws of the Spirit's operations. He is thoroughly consecrated to God; his time, abilities, money, family ties, all are on the altar, and always on the altar. He lives a life of faith. He is constrained by love. His energy, perseverance, zeal, and the other things accredited to him, are just the outcome of this self-sacrificing love, and of his realization of God's love for the souls of men. Where the *Reviewer* finds bad taste and bad reasoning, many others have found a spiritual influence carrying home to their hearts the great truths of the Gospel, as under no other preaching they had ever been brought home to them.

With regard to Mr. Taylor's Mission Policy, the *Reviewer* evidently thinks it somewhat quixotic. "Churches thoroughly bold, burning with missionary zeal and missionary earnestness, and presenting no obstacles to the spread of truth in the lives of their individual members, are beautiful visions not to be realized for many a long day to come." Mr. Taylor's faith is happily stronger, and "all things are possible to him that believeth."

Bowen attached himself to the Methodist Church in India but he did not become a missionary of the Methodist Episcopal Board in America. He continued to be a self-supporting worker and his relation was wholly to the Church in India, although that Church was recognized as a part of the American Methodist Church, which at that time pursued the policy of holding all national sections of the Church as integral parts of the American General Conference. Bowen made no reports to the Methodist Board and the reference to him in the minutes of the Bombay Conference relate little more than his repeated election as Presiding Elder, or District Superintendent as he would now be called, of the Bombay District. *The Gospel in All Lands* of March, 1888, the Methodist missionary magazine, in its article reporting his death said:

> The *Indian Witness* in an account of the South India Conference recently said of him: "The veteran George Bowen still retains his place as the Nestor of the Conference, unchanged and unchanging, unless perhaps a little more ripe for the rest which for twenty years he has seemed about to enter. With an appearance of feebleness he had an amazing reserve of strength and endurance, although carrying on his shoulders the triple burden of an Editor, a Presiding Elder and a Missionary, preaching in two languages to the natives."

The sources of information for this last period of Bowen's life are (1) two score letters to his sisters, none preserved after 1883, (2) some correspondence with Mr. Henry W. Rankin, (3) reminiscences of some of those who knew him in these years, (4) occasional though scanty personal references in the *Guardian*.

Association with the Methodist Church in India

To Harriet, Sept. 23, 1875:

> Your letter (from Lake George) quite carried me back to old times. Do you remember I spent a fortnight or so in 1835 at Plattsburgh. . . . I had a box of rattlesnakes with me at the hotel at Lake George.

To Kate, Nov. 1875:

> I have at last found a medicine that helps my headache. Miss Norris, M. D. of the American Mission has told me about it. It is *Guarana,* a powder. I have been wonderfully well of late.

He seems generally to have been willing to use means in the matter of sickness, just as in his thought of nature and grace he allowed for processes.

In the winter of 1875-76 Edward the 7th, then Prince of Wales, visited India. The *Guardian* chronicles quite fully his movements, his sympathy with the Indian Christians, his hunting expeditions, but neither in the paper nor in Bowen's letters home is there any reference to the Prince's visit to Bowen reported in Alfred S. Deyer's *Occupy Till I Come,* as follows:

> A missionary friend in Western India relates a notable episode in the life of an intimate fellow-missionary, the late George Bowen, the first editor of the *Bombay Guardian,* a Christian weekly newspaper with an Evangelical record of more than sixty years.
>
> During the visit to India, in 1875-6, of the Prince of Wales (afterwards King Edward the 7th), he enquired when in Bombay concerning George Bowen. He was told he was only a poor missionary, living in a poor part of Bombay, and would not expect to be noticed. The Prince informed one of his suite that the next time they were riding in the city, he wished to call on Mr. Bowen. Before leaving England, his royal mother had charged him to deliver a message from her, and he must obey.
>
> The home of the missionary was a very small house in a row named Moos Buildings. It consisted of two rooms and a bathroom, at a monthly rental equal in English money to less than four shillings a week.
>
> The royal visit was accordingly paid. One morning a Government House carriage stopped at the humble dwelling and an A. D. C. announced to George Bowen that the Prince of Wales wished to speak to him. He went out to the carriage. The Prince said he bore a message from his mother, Queen Victoria. She had commanded him to call and tell him that his books had been a great comfort and blessing to her, and to thank him for them. He then shook hands and drove away.
>
> The works referred to were entitled, *Daily Meditations, Love Revealed,* and *The Amens of Christ.*

Bowen's editorial reference is:

> H. R. H. the Prince of Wales arrived in Bombay harbor early on Monday morning, landed in the afternoon and since then has been about as hard worked as a Royal Prince ever was. Just to think of having to stand and bow and look pleased to a thousand gentlemen, European and Natives, in immediate succession, not one in fifty of whom he expects ever to see again. But this was only one item. We really think that the Prince should be excused from these monster levees. He does show himself very gracious and complaisant and has made, we believe, a very pleasant impression upon all (*Guardian,* Nov. 13, 1875).

To his sisters, Feb. 14, 1876:

> In January I made a long journey, to Cawnpore, to attend the Annual Conference of the M. E. Church in India. I never before had been beyond this Presidency to the North. It was altogether a journey going and coming of near 2,000 miles. I made halts at Jubbulpur, Allahabad, and two other points. At Cawnpore I was entertained by a kind Swiss gentleman who has been some years in India. He was converted a year ago, and is now a warm-hearted Methodist. He had eight of us in the house and was hardly satisfied then: placed several carriages at our disposal for daily use. He was a cheery, joyous, generous host with a genuine experience in religion. I enjoyed my intercourse with the brethren and sisters of the North India Conference very much. I was there about a week. You may see how much they made of your foolish brother by the enclosed resolutions, which you must not show to anybody. We had devotional meetings every morning that were full of blessing.
>
> You know the distinction between this older mission work and ours. The mission in Oudh and Rohilkhand was established after the meeting; it labors directly among the natives; it is supported by funds received from the missionary board in America. Our work organized by Brother Taylor on a district basis, as the Bombay Bengal and Madras Mission, is independent of home funds, though we are at present connected with the N. I. Conference. The Board in New York was to pay the passages of missionaries coming to us from America, but they have failed even in this. Brother Taylor would not go to see his family in California until he had obtained seven men for our work, and finding then that the Board was not prepared to pay their passage money, paid it himself, trusting that the Lord would enable him to sell books enough to meet the wants of his own family. I hope before this he has got home to them. He will be at the General Conference in May next. This Conference is quadrennial.
>
> Dear Harriet, you saw that I took the liberty of extracting part of your letter in the *Guardian* in an article entitled Self-Torment. I shall be very glad to hear that my remarks have been of some use. . . .

Association with the Methodist Church in India 371

Dr. Field of the *Evangelist* and his niece were in Bombay lately and called upon me and were most kind. I was much drawn to him. I hope you will see him when he gets home.

We have been enjoying the visit of Philip Phillips and his wife. They are excellent people, full of love and Christian feeling. He gave a service of sacred song last evening at the Falkland Road Hall; there was an after-meeting and the men sought the Lord and found peace in believing.

You will have heard Mr. Moody before this. I trust his visit to New York will be greatly blessed. So many members of your churches dwell in a cloudland of undefined experience, the objects of faith shadowy and ungrasped. He has the gift of making them appear real. Christ must be apprehended. He that hath the Son hath life. And he shows Christians how to seek and labor for the conversion of others. His great work is to get new life, the true life, into the churches. Have you read his life by Daniels? It is a delightful book.

In this letter he enclosed a printed copy of the resolutions of the Conference appreciative of his visit:

1. That we hereby express the heartfelt satisfaction which it gives us to welcome among us, for the first time, our beloved and revered brother, Rev. George Bowen.

2. That we assure him that we have appreciated more fully than we can express in words, the service which he has rendered us and the honor which he has bestowed upon us, by casting in his lot among us, bringing with him a ripe experience in missionary work, and a rare reputation as a Christian minister and a devout believer.

3. That we express the hope that our dear brother Bowen may be permitted to meet with us again, even though separated by Conference boundary lines, inasmuch as we feel that his godly counsel, instructive teaching and deep spiritual experience must ever prove a source of comfort and profit to us at our Conference sessions.

To his sisters, from Poona, May 12, 1876:

I had fever (in March). Sister Miles came out for me one evening and insisted on my going with her. I stayed at her house, enjoying her kind nursing about ten days. Brother Fox, in charge of the work here, went to Karachi at my request, and I came here to carry on the work. I have been here three weeks and expect to return on the 15th. This is the hot season when the gentry get away to the hills. In the middle of the day, the external air is hot as an oven, and people shut up their houses to keep the air out. The nights are pleasant. I have been very well since I came up here. I am living in Bro. Fox's nice little house, though I take my meals with the people. They are all very kind. Six European soldiers have sought the Lord since I came up, and are rejoicing in Him. Dr. Fraser was very ill when I came up and has gone to Bombay for a change.

I do not think you can have any idea of the way we Methodists are spoken of in India. Scarcely any of the upper class have joined us, nor do they even come near us. The few such who have joined need a great deal of grace not to get separated from us, they are brought so much into collision with people that detest us. No stone is left unturned to hinder people from coming near us. The papers lose no opportunity of running us down. It is simply because we seek to be lights in the world, holding forth the word of life, telling what Christ is to us and commending Him to others. All this has been greatly blessed to us. It enables us to have a single eye to the Master. It is to me a matter of constant thankfulness that God has given me a place among this people. Did you see Rev. Mr. Thoburn, of our work in Calcutta? He left two months ago for America. I gave him your address. He is a man of power and at the same time is much loved by all who know him. He is coming out again in a few months. The Bissells have also gone home, and you may possibly have seen them before this. I got acquainted lately with a sculptor, a Mr. Acton, said by some to be the greatest sculptor of the day, a man of real genius. He was the guest of a Mr. Meakin, who had also two native princes as his guests. Mr. M. is a Wesleyan. One of these princes is a Christian by conviction, though never baptized. I had the opportunity of giving them my testimony. Mr. A. professed to take no interest in religion, but came and heard me preach and stayed to the after-meeting. I know not if he received any impression, as I left Bombay immediately afterward, and he has since returned to Europe.

To his sisters, Aug. 29, 1876:

If you have an opportunity I recommend you to read the *Memoirs of Samuel Hebich,* German missionary in India. When I came to India he was very much talked about. He seemed to have great power of impressing himself upon others. He had great strength of will and it was for the most part consecrated to Christ, wholly perhaps as far as he knew.... My health is as good as ever it was, e. g., I preached three times last Sunday, the evening service lasting two hours—twice in English, once in Marathi. But it is a little too much perhaps. Twice a day is very comfortable. When I was a young man I had the idea that I should die young and that what I did I must do quickly.

Brother Taylor has some financial difficulties. He supports himself and family by his books. Returning to America he must get six or seven missionaries and send them out to India. He has to pay their passage himself. A fire in London burnt up many of his books. A heavy duty in New York has enhanced their cost. He wrote lately saying that he expected to be detained some time longer in America on these accounts. But we have written telling him that we will relieve him of these burdens, which is but right as they were incurred on our account. By we, I mean Bombay, Madras and Calcutta. I do not feel the need of men from America much. The Lord raises up in this country excellent men.

My thoughts seem much lately upon the importance of being able to see Christ in one another. "I in them." If the Spirit is in them, then Christ is in them, for God is One. In every way He seeks to lure us to find Him in our brethren. Matt. 25, "I was much," etc. This is perhaps the final victory of faith.

I have not yet received Dr. Ellinwood's book. As I am not now Secretary of the Bombay Tract and Book Society, it is not expedient to send anything to the care of the Sunday School Union, London. I dare say this will reach me, though.

I thank the Lord for all the kindness shown you by Frank. May he himself see the hand of the Lord in it, and above all may he take God's best gift, eternal life in Christ. Surely he must see that life is but a whirlpool of vanities, until a man has an understanding with Him Who is at the helm, and Who has the happiness of every creature in His own hand.

Mr. A. H. L. Fraser, son of our Dr. Fraser, born about the close of the year I came to India, now a member of the Civil Service in India, had a month's leave lately and spent it among us in Bombay and Poona preaching. He is an excellent preacher of the Gospel in its simplicity, and great numbers came to him. He was a Plymouth Brother, I believe, but seems to be heartily in sympathy with us and our work. He wrote the article on "Fellowship" in the last *Guardian,* Sept. 1.

To his sisters, Feb. 5, 1877:

Bishop Andrews left last week for Europe. He will reach America in the autumn. I gave him Kate's address. He is a dear man. We were all remarkably drawn to him. A man of genuine humility, thinks everybody is in advance of him. He has great power as a preacher. Miss Sparks and Miss Pultz from the North India Conference Mission returned by the same steamer. I also gave Miss Sparks Kate's address. You will like her much.

Your last brings news of Frank's new appointment. I am very glad and hope it will be sanctioned at Washington. I am so glad to hear that he is better. And I am glad he is to be stationary in New York. The Lord's hand is in all this. All his life he has been very unsure as to prayer. May the time soon come when he will recognize the value of prayer, and ask and receive that without which all temporal blessings will only tend to his condemnation.

There were two steamers approaching each other from different directions in the Red Sea, one was commanded by my friend Captain Hanscom. He ported his helm according to the rules of the admirality. They would have passed each other safely, but the other Captain did not do so. He did not understand Captain Hanscom's maneuver, but thought he wanted to get near him so as to speak. He discovered his error too late, and ported his helm but the steamers came into collision, and the steamer whose Captain had made a mistake went down with her Captain and others. The difficulty was that there was not an understanding between the two Captains. This may illustrate the necessity of having an understanding with God. God's way is very different from the sinner's, and it is not God that will turn. Just now it is supremely important that the sinner should come to an understanding with God, find out what God means and get into harmony with Him. I have written the illustration for Frank. "Come now, let us reason together, saith the Lord."

To his sisters, March 26, 1877:

> I hope to hear soon that your affairs are straightening out again, in some way. I am sorry you have lost by your kindness in lending money, but I do not think you will lose by it in the end. He that giveth to the poor lendeth to the Lord. There is no lack to them that fear Him, if they have faith. I am very well. My only trials are in connection with the work of the Lord. It is a stupendous work, heaving up a true and pure church out of the accumulated filth and corruption of this land, but "He will not fail nor be discouraged." I was thinking lately that Moses spent forty of the best years of his life without even making a convert of his own wife, as appears by Ex. 4:24-26.

To Harriet, April, 1877:

> I am so thankful that you can stay staunchly as you do on God. Blessed are all they that put their trust in Him. He does not exempt those whom He loves from very keen suffering. He does not show His love by letting us choose our own trials. Out of 1,000 possible trials, if we pick out one and say, "Spare me this: I will suffer any of the 999 gladly, but this I utterly deprecate," that one abhorred trial will be the very one appointed to us, for the reason that it will be a trial (test) the others would not be. This at least has been my experience. But when the dreaded trial came it was found to be most bearable. It is the glory of the Lord that He knows how to sustain the faith of His people at the very time His providence is raining arrows upon them. Not all are counted worthy to suffer these

things. The faith of many is such a bruised reed, such a sickly plant, that it has to be fostered with kindly providences for a season. Count it all joy when you fall into divers temptations knowing that the trial of your faith worketh patience. Patience! Is that all? Patience is more than all. In patience is the secret of invincible peace, joy and power.

Your story about the $5 and the washer-woman, reminds me that in 1849 I was without the means of paying the dhobi (washer-man). I remembered that a friend had charged me if ever I were in need to apply to him. I was tempted to do so, I felt so keenly the distress of owing anything. But I resisted the temptation, and abode by my principle never to ask any man for help. In due time, the deliverance came. A still more unpleasant thing happened to me, some years after that, when I owed the postman two annas (6c) on a letter insufficiently stamped, and when he came four or five days in succession, and every day I had to make the same acknowledgment to him. But I noticed that he took it most good-humoredly, not complaining a bit. Afterwards I received money from some quarter and paid him. And I have been in worse straits than this. Nobody knew of it at the time. When I was a little boy I often dreamt that I was falling from a great height; but always came down gently and softly without any bones broken; and at length I carried into my dreams this conviction of a gentle descent and when I found myself falling was not a bit afraid. So it is in our trials. Experience worketh patience, and patience hope, and a hope that maketh not ashamed.

How gladly would I help you, if I had the means or could by industry obtain them, and had an arm 10,000 miles long. But I cannot doubt that long before your letter reached me, you were delivered from the severest pressure of your trial. Oh, how I wish that Frank would recognize the hand of God in his afflictions, and take note, that that hand was pierced for him and by him. God prospered him for a couple of years and enabled him to help you which he did most generously, but still without recognizing the kind hand that placed him in a position to do this. God saw his unsubdued self-trust, and let him lose that position, and experience how unable we are, even with good prospects, to make our way. He feels very keenly no doubt the humiliation and bitterness of this trial, and feels it the more because you are concerned. Perhaps our prayers have had to do with this very trial. It was needful that Frank should be taken in just such a net, like a bull, and find out how absolutely dependent on God he is, that he may at length come to his right mind, and give glory to the Almighty and the All-living and receive life eternal.

May 1st I left this for Karachi. The voyage is by steamer 500 miles. I went as a deck passenger, but could not have been treated better than I was. A cabin was placed at my disposal, and all showed me great kindness. Brother Fox, who was before in Poona, is in charge of the work at Karachi. I spent ten days there, visiting Kotree, 100 miles by train. I have an old friend at Karachi, a Mrs. Russell, eighty-five years of age, still very hearty, and who came out several times to hear me preach. I got back here on the 17th.

I had a visit from a Hindu gentleman the other day. He had belonged to the Lingæt caste; had spent large sums of money in trying to get right with God; had learned from a Kubeerpunthi to worship the one God; had been recommended to read the Bible; had got it and read it through; was a thorough believer in Christ; but what seemed to have made the most impression was that Christ was to come again in glory. He was daily waiting for Christ. Was sure He would come this very year, in fact, on Sunday, December 2nd. He seemed to be familiar with many portions of Scripture, and so far as I know, had not learned from missionaries.

To his sister, Aug. 9, 1877:

I should be very glad if I could meet all your necessities. But it does not seem to be the Lord's will. I enclose an order for $50. This is *Guardian* money over and above my own wants. I have arranged with the printer of the *Bombay Guardian* to pay me Rs. 50 a month. I suppose I will be able generally to spare the half of this, but the Lord knows.... I hope you will be seeing Brother Taylor again before long. He hopes to leave for India in Oct. Is very much urged to visit Peru and Chile and inaugurate a work there, which would delay him a year if he did. Our 2nd Annual Conference is to be held Nov. 15th, at Calcutta. I expect to visit Calcutta on that occasion for the first time.... This season has been rather trying. There was never so much sickness, or so great mortality in Bombay as this year. Yet I have been kept in excellent health. I was never thinner than I am. Usually the rains cool the atmosphere, but this year the thermometer reached 87 or 88 degrees every day, and this for four months.

To his sisters, Oct. 22, 1877:

Before I left America I gave myself into the hands of God to suffer all that He might appoint, to be dealt with in any way that should please Him, stipulating only for one thing, that I might always have unwavering faith in His love. Well, I have never lacked this faith and have been most kindly treated, and have had a great deal of respect from Christians, and much love, but the great desire of my heart has been constantly baffled, and all beside this is like the small dust of the balance. For thirty years God has employed extraordinary means to strip me of my confidence, without success. I speak of things as they appear. For all I know, there may be many others passing through similar experiences. Isaiah 64:4-5.

Association with the Methodist Church in India

To his sisters, Dec. 29-31, 1877:

Brother Osborne is a man full of holy enthusiasm, and burning to have Christians know and enjoy the fullness of their privileges in Christ. He is already a great blessing to us. And he is not unlike Brother Taylor. I resigned the Presidency Eldership in his favor and I shall have less call now to track about. You will have seen the notice of my visit to Calcutta. I cannot sleep in the train, and when it comes to a journey of 1,500 miles, this is rather serious. Yet strange to say, I was quite fresh when I arrived in Calcutta at 6 a.m. Thursday, Nov. 15, and spent the day in conference. Nothing could exceed the kindness shown in Calcutta. I stopped with some warm-hearted Christians, Brother and Sister Mayers. I was told that they wished me to be President of the Conference but I declined and Brother Thoburn was chosen. Calcutta is so very different from Bombay and certainly exceeded my expectations. But I do not know that the Gospel has made much more progress there than here. Perhaps it has. There is less prejudice there and less of orthodox Hinduism.... Dear Harriet, give up the struggle to make your heart a worthy object of contemplation. Since Dec. 4, 1845 I have no good news but Christ, and I live with Him as the branch in the vine. When thus united to Christ in momentary and everlasting repentance, we are what God would have us to be.

I am very much obliged to Kate for copying Dr. Metcalf's letters. I have not yet had time to read them, but my eye falls upon this sentence on the first page, and I am much struck with it: "Your great difficulty lies in an intense and constant self-contemplation." You see the Lord told you this a quarter of a century ago. Not that you have not learned the lesson: you have learned it; but you have still perhaps some tendency of the kind to get rid of, and you know how, by living with Jesus. All sin in my opinion is in separation; and all separation is sin. That is, separation from life, from Christ. The law of the spirit of life in Christ Jesus hath made me free from the law of self—of sin and death.... I do not speak to you of my sorrows. I am often deeply saddened—all in connection with the Lord's work, or rather because of His not working. Psa. 119: 126. The Lord knows all about it—He bottles our tears. Has a lackey waiting for me and one for you. I have had experiences of late that call to my mind John 6:66-67 and 2 Tim. 1:15. I allude to native brethren. One misguided man has printed letter after letter, defaming me, and trying to turn away the native brethren from us, with a certain measure of success. I have not replied a word, leave all with my Lord. 2 Cor. 12:15. Do not trouble yourselves about these things. All will come right.

In 1878 Bowen began to use one of the primitive typewriters of the day and the rather crude product of these machines displaces his fine copper plate handwriting.

To his sisters, March 16, 1878:

> I look eagerly to see if there is any word of a change in Frank. Hope deferred maketh the heart sick. I see that Mr. Müller of Bristol says that he has been praying since 1844 for the conversion of some person. God has so far answered our prayers for Frank as to keep him alive all these years. When we remember how often his life has been threatened during these years, we cannot but see the hand of God in this. It is very painful to me to think of your constantly recurring pecuniary trials. When we pray for another we must be prepared to let the Lord use us in any way that may be demanded, for the fulfillment of our prayers, whether actively or passively. The Lord does not willingly afflict or grieve His children and I am constrained to believe that what you are suffering is a part of God's providential work to influence Frank.
>
> With reference to some remarks of Harriet's about the misery that is in the world I wish to say a word or two. There are certain views of God's sovereignty that greatly wrong God by imputing to Him the responsibility of existing things. God repudiates this responsibility. It is not His will that men should suffer, but He cannot dissociate suffering from sin, because this would involve the abnegation of His own perfections. There is love enough showered down upon this world to satisfy all creatures; but sin has blinded men so that they cannot see it and receive it. When God created free agents He (so to speak) bound Himself to let men sin until by experience of the ruin wrought by it, they should ask for deliverance. The suffering in the world is God's protest against sin, and a means whereby God is seeking to persuade men to turn and trust in Him. Many are misled by a wrong conception of the divine omnipotence. Cannot God do all things? He can do all things that are the proper subjects of power. He cannot do anything that would be a violation of His engagements with men, His declared principles of administration. In one sense He can put forth His power in the heart of every man so as to crush the man's inclinations; but in another He cannot, because it would be a contravention of His own decrees, a revocation of His own gifts. Christ knocks at the door of the sinner declaring His desire to enter, but if the man is unwilling to admit Him there is no admittance. If God could enter whether we willed or nilled, His goodness would compel Him to enter the hearts of all sinners. How often would I (says Christ) but ye would not. Faith opens the door for God to come in; unbelief bars the door against omnipotence and the

sinner can get no benefit from the fact that a God of infinite benignity is on the throne. He chooses to be without God and that becomes his punishment.

You will rejoice with me in the beautiful gift of this typewriter received from kind Christian friends. I find it a wonderful help. Writing is no longer a burden but a pleasure. I write with this machine faster than I could with a pen. My nerves are sensible of a great relief. How kind of our heavenly Father to provide me with this labor-lightener. Yes, our Mr. Osborne is your friend Miss White's friend, and he asks me to send her through you his kindest regards. We value him greatly.

With regard to the trip to Calcutta, we all traveled third class, and traveled most comfortably. They have not separate compartments for Europeans. Not that I object to travel with natives, but it is not pleasant to be packed in with fifty of them in one carriage. I mention for Kate's enlightenment that in the Berean lessons we in India follow the American churches at the distance of three months. Brother Shaw promises to send me a likeness of myself. It was taken at Calcutta in a group with Thorburn and Hard. I am told it is very good. When I get it I will send it to you.

You object to a certain view of regeneration. To say that a man once made the child of God cannot ever be anything else is the same as saying that a man who once believes will always believe. It is our faith that makes us children of God (John 1:12), and faith keeps us in that relation. But we are not saved by a faith once exercised; it must be a faith continually exercised. God has nowhere pledged Himself to see that a believer's faith shall never cease. What He does is to provide the highest motives and stimulants and warnings to induce us continually to look unto Jesus. We are made partakers of Christ if we hold fast the beginning of our confidence firm unto the end, i. e., if we keep confiding, trusting, "lest I should be a castaway." I have not known what it is to have a doubt of my ultimate salvation, because since 1845, it is the instinct of my being to look to Christ moment by moment for the grace I need moment by moment. I every moment repudiate all my past Christian experience as a ground of confidence, and look to the Savior for grace to do His present will. Some seem to understand by faith in Christ, a belief that God excuses our failures for the sake of Christ's righteousness. Others consider that faith in the Savior means the momentary appropriation of His power to be and do what God would have us to be and do. This last is in my opinion the true conception. His blood propitiates for sins that are past and brings us into that relation to Christ that we have His power to keep us from sinning. The great lesson that the Church needs to learn is the availability of Christ for the every moment's work of the believer.

Kate mentions this text: "No man can come unto me except the Father who hath sent me draw him." This is the meaning: that which draws you to me is the operation of God. It seemed to the Jews that Christ was drawing them away from the Father. But on the contrary God was in Christ reconciling the world unto Himself. He draws, not drags. The Lord will open Frank's eyes whenever Frank will recognize his need of something higher than himself. God has long been dealing with him as He dealt with the prodigal son. The prodigal son consented to learn the lessons of God's providence. My hope is that God will not cease to afflict Frank till the latter has learnt this lesson. Your share in these afflictions is distressing to me; but it is intended to keep alive the spirit of prayer in his behalf. If you fully consent to God's method you will yet have the joy of winning your brother. And that joy will more than compensate you for all you have suffered, and in the process perhaps your own spiritual life will have become much brighter.

To his sisters, June 21, 1878:

By the typewriter I am enabled to write a great deal more than I could before, without feeling it in the least. I cannot be too grateful to God for having supplied me with this wonderful help. Mr. Bruce of the American Mission has one of them, and I was surprised to hear him say that he only used one finger in manipulating it. My facility with the piano is a great help to me, enabling me to write very rapidly without fatigue. I am glad you are content with my photograph. I came across the other day a letter from Nat in which he informed me of Pa's death and urged upon me the necessity of an immediate return to America for the sake of the family left destitute. Then four months afterwards I was brought to death's door by sickness and assured by the doctors that I could not live in this country. I had to fight these two battles the first year. Are you proving the unsearchable riches of Christ's love? The spirit of all grace be with you.

To his sisters, Sept. 13, 1878:

You will see by the *Guardian* that there is no end to the fight we have to wage here against infidelity and corrupt Christianity. Like Jeremiah, there is nothing in the world more distasteful to me than disputation. But God has made me a man of contentions to all the world. Yet His help is so vouchsafed that I am scarce conscious of any burden. My days pass on in sweet content. We have had an unusually heavy monsoon this year, over 100 inches of rain so far. It is hoped that there will be a good

Association with the Methodist Church in India

harvest. In the south of India where the famine raged last year, thousands of the rural natives are giving in their admission to Christianity.

My health is very good. I do not know that it was ever better. I am having of late a sweet consciousness of the love (1 John 4) over and above the faith of it which I have ordinarily, and which I long ago consented to be satisfied with.

To his sisters, Dec. 23, 1878:

My visit to Madras only occupied twelve days, but in order to go I had to do more work than usual for some days before leaving. I enjoyed greatly the visit to Madras especially in meeting so many dear brethren and sisters in the Lord. We were all much drawn to Bishop Bowman, a man of much power, mental and spiritual, and most genial and amiable. If you ever have an opportunity of meeting him I am sure you will like him. I wish your lot were cast among Methodists. You would be so much happier, I think. The Methodists I know are the happiest people I have ever known. The joy of the Lord is their strength. . . .

I was preaching yesterday on the words "He is the Rock," and found it good to dwell upon the fact that the discoveries made at one time of the loving-kindness of God, are good for all time. For instance, there was a period when our hearts ran over with a sense of all that Christ was to us, not because of anything peculiarly favorable in our circumstances, but simply because the Holy Spirit enabled us to do justice to some revealed truth. But our God is unchanging. And what He was then He is now, save that He may be grieved with us for not recognizing the fact. It betrays a sad want of faith to allow the sense of His goodness to be dimmed because the way in which we are led is a trying one. Whom the Lord loveth He chasteneth. This was one of the first lessons taught us. He doeth all things well. The trial of our faith is more precious than of gold that perisheth. To chafe against His providences, to allow ourselves to be inwardly vexed because the Lord carries out His own plans instead of ours, is nothing less than rebellion. We must acquiesce in His leading, however strange it may appear to you. Think it not strange, says Peter.

To his sisters, Feb. 24, 1879:

I find that I continually need to be learning over again the mystery of "God is love." It is our tendency to let the door get shut which the Lord opens to us. Our own natural ideas of God shut it, and the love of God shed abroad in our hearts by the Holy Spirit opens it. We are so prone to think of God as simply one that is kindly disposed towards

His creatures, generous, condescending, but on the whole not much exercised in feeling for us, as one who can very well get along without us, tranquilly and placidly benevolent. But the feeling which a mother has for her sucking child, that which a bridegroom has for his bride, is very different from this. It is absorbing and constraining. God is love, which means a world more than loving. Why not love Him with all the heart, soul, mind and strength. Nothing less than this will satisfy Him, and if nothing less than this will satisfy Him, it is evident that it must be an extraordinary love that He has for us. I have always found that nothing pleases God more than faith in this impassioned love of His. Not to be made perfect in love, John speaks of as a very culpable thing. I do not know how you will like the reminiscences I am publishing in the *Guardian* since the beginning of this year. People here like them very much and encourage me to go on with them. I hope that you and Kate will not object to them. It was impressed on me that something of this kind would be useful and that it was due to the Savior to show what He had saved me from.

To his sisters, Aug. 1, 1879:

God can do nothing unless the sinner is willing to submit. To imagine that God compels sinners to submit by the exercise of His sovereign power, is a calumny on God, as it conveys the idea that God is a being Who cannot get people to love Him unless He forces them. God can only offer men His love and the Spirit of God Who witnesses to this love is the Spirit of truth, and reaches the heart by means of the word declared by the lips or embodied in the life. It is always saddening to me to hear of Frank's leaving you, for it seems to me that God brings him near to you, expressly that he may see the truth exemplified in you. I can hardly wonder, however, at the failure of this evidence when I have so much proof at hand of the failure of my own preaching and living to convince men of their need of Christ. . . . Pray much for me in connection with the native work. I am sorely tried. Our best native Christians have to go where they can get employment, and thus they are scattered over the country. Good is done in this way, but it interferes very much with the raising up of an effective witnessing church in Bombay.

To his sisters, Nov. 29, 1879:

Mrs. Amanda Smith, the colored lady, has been holding meetings here the last fortnight, and has been greatly used of the Lord, both as regards Christians and others. Many educated natives have been to hear her and have been much impressed. She has had uncommon revelations of the love and power of Christ and it is this that enables her to speak without self-consciousness, with great effectiveness. Her heart is full of love and she seems to be specially drawn towards the natives. We have never had meetings so crowded.

Dec. 1. I have never seen anybody more manifestly called of God to preach the Gospel than Amanda Smith. Last night, Sunday, more than a dozen came forward as seekers of salvation, and most of them appeared to find peace in believing.

You say, dear Harriet, "is it not God Who inspires the first earnest desire for a will conformed to His?" Certainly. No man can call Jesus Lord without the Holy Ghost. He is the author of experimental religion from the Alpha to the Omega. But the question between us is by what agency does the Spirit of God ordinarily work? It is by that of converted persons, made to realize the danger of others, conscious of Christ's love, and earnestly desirous that others should participate with them. In at least nine cases out of ten, that which awakens a sense of sinfulness and danger is the sight of somebody else deeply sensible of that about which we have been insensible.

No man is saved by waiting for salvation, nor can we get our friends saved by waiting for them to be saved. If we offer the prayer of faith may we not expect the salvation of those we are interested in? The faith which shrinks from direct efforts for their salvation, is not the faith that offers prevailing prayer. . . . You say that I am becoming Methodistic in doctrine, and lean to the human will. No people hold more profoundly than the Methodists the absolute dependence of man on the Holy Spirit for the power to do anything pleasing to God; but they do not believe that the operations of the Spirit imply passivity on our part. They believe in spiritual agency as well as in spiritual influence. . . . The reason why I like the Methodists so much is that they realize so deeply the responsibility to bring the truth before those whom they wish to influence. In the other Churches evangelization is too much done by proxy. . . . I am studying Hindustani with a moonshi and hope some day to be able to preach in it.

Learning a new language at the age of sixty-three!
To his sisters, Jan. 24, 1880:

I am studying Hindustani with the hope of preaching in it, and when I have got that I may take up another language. Besides the Marathi, I have not learnt any Indian language well. Since I wrote you last I have been away to Allahabad to attend our annual conference. It is a railway trip of about 800 miles. How much our work owes to the railway. You will see from the list of appointments in the *Guardian* how very extended our work is over all India. It would have been, humanly speaking, impossible to organize such a work apart from the facilities afforded by the railway lines. Four or five of us went together and came back together and this made it very pleasant. I am still unable to sleep in the train, and as we are out two nights in going to Allahabad, you will think that I reached the end of the journey completely knocked up. On the contrary, reaching there at sunrise I spent the whole day in meetings and was as fresh as though I had had my usual rest.

You will see that they elected me president of the Conference. A bishop only comes to India once in two years, and during the alternate years we elect our own president. I dreaded the burden and did my best to escape it but without success. You know the presiding officer is responsible for the appointments and I shrunk from that responsibility. I enjoyed exceedingly the week I spent at Allahabad. I find my greatest happiness (leaving out private communion with the Lord) in seeing the grace of God in others. I told them there in one of the love feasts that when I was a young man I visited many cities to become acquainted with the monuments, statues, pictures, etc. But now, when I come to a strange place, what interests me and endears the place to me is the Lord's people there.

I do not remember when I wrote to you last, or whether I have spoken to you of Mrs. Amanda Smith, the colored lady who is visiting India, very much through Mr. Osborne's persuasion. Her work is wonderfully used of the Lord both as regards Christians and others. We have never had anybody here whom people so crowded to hear. I suppose you never heard her. She is a person of unusually deep experience and produces the impression upon those who know her best of one who is filled with the Spirit. Her faith is remarkable. She gives herself very heartily to prayer, and seems to speak as the Spirit gives her utterance. She is a regular negress and has many of the ways of that class, speaking generally with unexceptionable diction, but without any pretension, and she is so natural that she disarms criticism.

To his sisters, Feb. 21, 1880:

A little boy and girl are looking on while I write this, wondering at the process. There are many children in the row of buildings where I live and they are fond of running into my place. I am very fond of children but have not much time to spare for them. You want to know about myself. Well, I live in a house 10ft. wide and about 25ft. deep, one of twenty similar ones, inhabited mostly by Europeans and East Indians in humble circumstances. I get up at five o'clock in the morning and spend an hour in prayer. I then wash my face and hands, it being too cold to bathe. I then read the Bible in Hindustani for an hour. I then make some pastoral calls till nine or half past nine, when I breakfast. Three or four mornings in the week, I breakfast at the Row's and I am often there to tea. Once a week, I breakfast with the Firths, friends living opposite to me; once a week with Major Oldham or Brother Manock Jee Mody (living with the Major) and once a week with Mr. and Mrs. Grieve, missionaries of the Free Church. These are my regular breakfast engagements which of course are liable to be broken in upon. At these places I conduct family worship generally. I get home to work soon after ten and seldom leave home till four o'clock or after. I get about six hours every day for the *Guardian* and for reading and correspondence, minus the time given to visitors. I dine at home about three o'clock, getting my bread early every morning from the baker and also getting at the door whatever I want to eat with it. Mrs. Townsend, an old lady, sister of Mrs. Baker, a good Christian sister, sends occasionally for my clothing that needs any mending, and puts it in repair. At four I bathe, and then make a pastoral call or two and go to the Esplanade to preach in Marathi. I generally go by train or by tram, it being two or three miles from my house. After that tea, and then some meeting. Five nights in the week we have church meetings in English or vernacular. I get home at nine when I can, and have an hour or so for reading and then to bed.

At our open-air meetings the first thing is to get an audience. Some native brother joins me and we begin to sing or I begin to read a tract. People do not like to stop until they see something of a crowd, so that it is sometimes difficult to get an audience, but generally we get one in the course of half an hour, sometimes in a few minutes.

I have spoken of things that are of daily occurrence, but there are many other things that enter into my life that are not daily. I get fifty rupees from Mr. Vishnupunt for editing the *Guardian,* he taking all the pecuniary responsibility. Now as to my expenses I am getting very extravagant. I pay Rs. 10 a month for my house rent; Rs. 6 to my moonshi (Hindustani teacher); Rs.1-4-0 to my dhobi (washer-man); Rs. 1-10 to my baker; plaintains, etc., 1; tram, etc., Rs. 4-1; send Sister Row Rs. 10 a month. She opposes this but they are dependent on the church and I see no reason why they should be at charges on my account. Wearing apparel averages I suppose Rs. 2 a month or possibly 2-8-0. I subscribe to certain charities and have applications from the poor which generally make away with the remainder of the money. . . . I was weighed about a year ago and my weight was 92 lbs., a good weight for a jockey. Perhaps I should have been one.

To his sisters, April 3, 1880:

You will see by the *Guardian* that we have had our annual camp-meeting again this year. I returned on Wednesday last, having left on the previous Friday (Good Friday). Nothing could have been more delightful. It was like apples of gold in pictures of silver. The apples of gold being the spiritual refreshment and the pictures of silver, the charming rural accessories. Here we fulfilled the apostolical command, "If any among you be merry let him sing Psalms"; but the praying was not confined to the afflicted. The place is eighty miles from Bombay, on the top of the Bhore Ghaut (mountain) where the high table land begins which gradually inclines to the Bay of Bengal. There is a miniature forest, a gem of picturesqueness, grand old trees, enormous creepers, almost rivaling the trees in bulk, utterly baffling to your imagination as you try to guess how they grow in such anacondane windings, going sometimes forty or fifty feet in an oblique direction or even a horizontal one in mid air. Except in the area where our camp was there was a great deal of underwood, shutting us in most effectually from the outer world. Close to our gathering place there was, however, a little Hindu temple and every evening we would hear the bell go to wake the god.

The Lord blest us much. Mrs. Amanda Smith added much to the interests of the meeting. She is always in the Spirit, with a heart attuned to the work of the Spirit, and intent on getting others blessed. There was a Miss Anstey there who has a large orphanage of 400 or 500 children under her care in the south of India, who refused to apply to Government for any of the money that was being divided among the orphanages, wishing in all things to walk by faith. She afterwards received without application a considerable sum from Government. But the most interesting account of her narrative related to her own healing by faith after she had been kept in England two or three years by sickness that the doctors could not remove. Her return to this country depended on her restoration and at length she was able to reach a perfect conviction that it was the will of the Lord she should be healed and looking to Him in unwavering faith she received what she looked for instantly; and at once made her arrangements to return to India.

The water at Lanoli did not agree with me and on my return to Bombay I got a severe attack of colic. For twenty hours the pain was excruciating. I had calculated on the two days from Wednesday noon to Friday, to bring up the arrears of the *Guardian*. However, though I saw the whole of Thursday go by without being able to do anything, I did not allow myself to feel in the least worried, knowing by past experience that the Lord always sends help in time, and knows a great deal better than I do how much time I want for anything. And all came out right.

To his sisters, May 21, 1880:

My life is not at all eventful. If I were very much used of the Lord in bringing sinners to Himself, or in saving Christians from falling into the snare of the devil, I would have more to relate. My principal business is to learn of Christ and to make known what I learn. You think you get all this in the *Guardian,* and wish me to talk about that small fraction of myself which may be treated apart from this. I don't wish to be always preaching to you, but I would like the privilege of writing about these things in which I am chiefly interested. My happiness, my peace, my serenity depend upon the things of the Spirit, the things which I have learned of Christ; and my great desire concerning all whom I love is that they should get hold of the same truths that have been so rich in blessing to me. . . . Christians are either looking for the gradual extension of Christ's kingdom in the world or for the second advent of Christ to put down all His enemies by an exhibition of His power. I differ from almost all in believing that we are placed under responsibility to bring the New Jerusalem down out of Heaven from God by putting on the garments of salvation so that the bride shall be adorned for her Husband. When the bride is ready for the Bridegroom, the latter will not be long in appearing in His glory. In the three first chapters of Revelation we have a key to much that is contained in the closing chapters. The things that are predicated of the church and Christ are, in the letters to the seven churches, predicated of the believer and Christ.

To his sisters, July 2, 1880:

Dear Harriet, with reference to what you say about people being repelled from Christianity by the doctrine of eternal punishment, I have not found that the qualifying account of the Bible teaching given by such men as Farrar has had the effect of drawing these persons to the Bible. They do not like the way in which it is put by our Lord and the apostles, however you may tone down those statements. I am sure that our Lord designedly chose the most emphatic and alarming expressions that language admits of, in order to carry as far as possible the impression of the formidable nature of the sufferings of the lost. Any impression that anyone may form of those sufferings is necessarily inadequate. There is a great deal of pain in this world of which no man can form a conception unless he has had experience of it. I believe the sufferings of the unredeemed will be natural, springing directly out of the facts of the case. Hell is the state of a soul enlightened as to its sin, conscious of inability to depart from sin, conscious that sin is the greatest of all curses, and cognizant of the blessedness of those who were willing to be guided by God, compassed about by all manner of pleasant things which he regards as rightfully his but which were designed to win him to God. The effect of the manifestation of God in the last day will just be to pour fullness of light upon the souls of men. That light will be beneficent to believers, agonizingly painful to the wicked.

I once talked with a man who told me how, under the preaching of some revivalist he had been brought under such convictions of sin that one day as he stood before a great forge in a blacksmith's shop he became keenly conscious that if he were thrown into that flame it would not add anything to the suffering he was experiencing. "My word shall judge them at the last day." Alas, for those who refuse to be now judged by it. God is a being of infinite benignity and love and our highest conceptions of the matter fall short of the reality. This very thing, the indisputable goodness of God, will constitute an element in the suffering of the lost. The judgment in Matt. 25 is of those nations among whom Christ's Gospel has been proclaimed and Christ's little ones have dwelt. What the law says, it says to those that are under the law, and what the Gospel says, it says to those who are under the Gospel. God uses language that is best fitted to impress us, just as, in addressing the Jews of old regarding the things of the Messianic times He used the language with which they were familiar, and apart from which they could have only formed most erroneous ideas of the matter. I am habitually looking for an event that is probably not far off, and which is spoken of in the New Testament as the coming of the Son of Man and also as the manifestation of the Sons of God, but which will differ very materially from the second advent as conceived by many in these days.

To his sisters, Sept. 10, 1880:

You may have seen notices of the Theosophical party, as they call themselves, who came from New York to Bombay two years ago to save the simple-minded natives of this country from the sophistries of the missionaries and show them that there was nothing better than their old Vedic religion. A good many natives ran after them as is always the case when anything new turns up. They have now fallen out, and many of the natives have lost all confidence in them. . . .

I have been looking this morning, (the 11th) at the passage, "the Spirit of God maketh intercession for us." We may be diffident about the reception of our own petitions, but ought not to have the slightest doubt that the mind of the Spirit prevails with God, for the Spirit is God. The

Spirit of God in the believer identifies Himself with the believer; the very fact that He has taken up His abode in us is a guarantee that He makes our interests His own. We may be diffident about our utterances, but God knows how to distinguish the will of the Spirit. We have then the strongest ground of confidence that we shall be heard when we pray in the Spirit, and this we may always do. Really, all the fullness of the Godhead is in the Spirit, and having Him we have all things that pertain to life and godliness, including victory over temptation, sinful habits, etc. "Helpeth our infirmities"; that is, supplements our deficiencies. That which we cannot of ourselves express, the Spirit knows how to express. These groanings are connected with the groanings of universal nature mentioned in the preceding verses, longings for the manifestation of the sons of God. It is a wonder to me that this text about the manifestation of the sons of God as the great thing to be looked forward to by the church, should have received so little attention, compared with the passages that speak of the advent of the Son of Man. That manifestation will be this: "I am glorified in them."

In October he had a serious illness of inflammation of the bowels which served to reveal to him the host of loving friends he had in Bombay. On Oct. 29 he wrote after recovering, against the expectation of his doctors, "It is a perfect marvel to me how I should have the affection of so many. It is God's own love that comes to me by all these channels."

To his sisters and Frank, Jan. 1, 1881:

> Some person or persons unknown entered my house on Christmas day with false keys. I do not know that they took away anything. They left behind them a bundle of new clothes, perhaps by mistake. Or perhaps it was intended as a calumnious satire on my clothes just as though they were not good enough. . . . What changes the revolving years witness. But One changeth never. Our views of Him brighten. I never had a sweeter sense of the Lord's presence than since the beginning of this year. The riches of Christ in the Word are indeed unsearchable. The Lord has perhaps some years more of waiting and watching for me. I am saving up some money which I hope to send you before long. Not much.

To his sisters, Feb. 15, 1881:

> Pray much for me that I may reach the measure of the stature of a perfect man in Christ. I wish to reach that state of devotion to Christ that I shall think all grace bestowed upon my brother or sister a sufficient answer to my own prayer for grace. In the natural ambitiousness of my

nature I have often prayed to the Lord to make me the holiest and most useful of men by whatsoever process; and the Lord has showed me again and again that He answers these prayers by giving special endowments to others and raising up men of surpassing usefulness without my part in the matter ever appearing. And surely I have the best reason to be content. And content I will be. Some years ago I told the Lord that I was content to be everlastingly insignificant. What a bother it would be to a kind parent to have his several children each clamoring to be first in the father's regard. But when each comes to rejoice in the honor accruing to his brother, as his own, then everything is righted.

His sisters think some of his letters too didactic and frankly tell him of his defects and he as frankly replies about his own weaknesses and theirs and especially Frank's. Frank is a constant care to the sisters and is off on all sorts of ventures which fail, always, in his opinion, not because of his weakness but because of ill luck. George continues to send what money he can and has any remuneration from the publication of his books in America and Scotland sent to Harriet.

To his sisters, May 13, 1881:

We had a delightful and most profitable time at our camp-meetings last month. The power of the Lord was present to heal in the best sense. Some that were greatly blest there have carried the revival spirit to distant places. I have spoken to you about our present preacher-in-charge here, Mr. Jacobs. In some respects he is one of the greatest anomalies I have seen. A most uncompromising and devoted man, fully determined to do what he believes to be right no matter whose convictions may differ from his, but rather disposed to exaggerate the importance of particular modes of manifesting piety, not always, as it seems to me, those upon which the New Testament lays most stress. When borne as he believes by the Spirit, he seems to take a grim joy in riding rough-shod over people's sensitiveness. One thing I am very glad of, he takes a great interest in the native work, going out to street-preaching, with an interpreter. He sometimes keeps us at the evening meeting till ten o'clock, and sometimes prays for half an hour at a stretch. Yet he is a man of no mean ability, and could easily shine as a preacher if he would. Sister Jacobs is an admirable woman but thinks there is nobody in the world like her husband, and her only idea of unity seems to be that all should agree with him. I have been spending a great deal of time in prayer that there may be no collision, and no unfaithfulness on my part. My prayer for us all is that the Spirit of Christ may reign in us.

To his sisters, Nov. 23, 1881:

> I think I love you as much as when I took leave of you. I suppose that there ought to be this one result of the perpetuated celibacy of us four that we should cherish for one another an unabated love. . . . I was three weeks away from Bombay, at Ahmednagar and at Bangalore. I went to Bangalore without the slightest idea that I should be chosen President of the Conference, and fully determined not to be, if it were proposed. There were strong and special reasons why I did not wish to have any responsibility for the appointments. But I was obliged to accept of the position and immediately concluded that God would give me all the help I needed. There were some things of a painful character, especially the necessity of telling Bro. Jacobs all that I had against his ministry.
>
> I stayed with an excellent Wesleyan missionary and his wife, Mr. and Mrs. Symonds, and received from them the greatest kindness. It is a constant wonder to me when I go anywhere how much kindness I receive from everybody. I enjoyed greatly the visit to Ahmednagar. . . . When I went away last month, I left my key with Aunty Miles (as we call her) and when I returned I found to my dismay that all things had been set to rights. It seemed to me confusion worse confounded. But I am now after days getting to know where things are. . . . We shall be losing in a few days Major Oldham of whom I have often spoken, one of the noblest Christian men I have ever known. He took his equally excellent wife home last April, returning three months after to fulfill his time with Government, and is now leaving for good. No man has done more for the poor.

To his sisters, Feb. 22, 1882:

> Guiteau seems to have persuaded himself that he was under the guidance of Deity when he assassinated the president. This is just another proof of the utterly distorted views concerning God that men have. Sinful and selfish men first dwarf and deform their own conscience and then make God to be the reflection of this. How very unsatisfactory is human justice. Let him continue in this state of mind and when executed he will consider himself a martyr and there will not have been anything of the true nature of punishment. For you do not really begin to punish a man until you make him condemn himself. I must today write something on this subject.
>
> You will have seen from the *Guardian* that we had Mr. and Mrs. Joseph Cook with us last month. We enjoyed the visit very much. There is something very genial, frank and manly about Mr. Cook. I spent some hours with him the day he arrived. He is very outspoken,

and gave offense to some by his plain way of putting things. We have not seen many indications of fruit resulting from his lectures among the natives, but good was done, I think, among the Europeans. The class of Europeans that most needed to hear him did not condescend to leave their dinner-tables to come and hear him. . . .

Two or three years ago you may remember that I spoke to you of a case of discipline in the carrying out of which I was pretty intimate. One who used to buy all the new books and lend them to me, was found to be culpably careless in the matter of debt, and I myself formulated the charges against him on which he was tried. For two nights we were up to 12 or 1 o'clock. He and his advocate were most bitter and denounced me in very strong language. Finally, seeing how the case was likely to go, he resigned his connection with the church. Well, this proud-spirited and obstinate man has been completely changed. Misfortune helped no doubt to open his eyes. He stood up in one of our meetings and humbly apologized to those whom he had injured, acknowledged the justice of the course pursued with regard to him, and asked for the prayers of the brethren that he might have the help of God and be enabled to show by his life the sincerity of his repentance. He afterwards came to me and expressed his great regret for the way in which he had treated me. I must confess that I was at first slow to believe in the genuineness of the change, but I was compelled to believe it at last.

To his sisters, April 19, 1882:

Though there are things that I regret in the Salvation Army I am persuaded that the church must be more aggressive than it is. There must be demonstrations that will force the subject of religion upon the community. If processions and music will help, let them be used. We want a jubilant Christianity.

To his sisters, August 18, 1882:

We are greatly interested in the proposed expedition to India of the Salvation Army. I am praying much that they may come in the fullness of the blessing of God. I cannot but hope that they are coming in the Name of the Lord, though I cannot well understand how they will get an entrance among the people. But the Lord can open a door that no man can shut. . . . Great changes are probably impending in the Levant. What prophecy calls the times of the Gentiles have about run out. The day of the Lord draws on apace. The word of Christ will judge us in that day. How important that we should judge ourselves by it, and let it reign in us, expelling all that is not conformable! Then shall we anticipate and be prepared for the revelations of that day. The way to know Christ is to follow Him, to live Him. Thousands of Christians are stultifying themselves by seeking to advance in the knowledge of Christ, while they do not let Christ live in them, clinging to their own life.

The Lord reveals Himself gloriously to me, quite indescribably, and satisfies me that He is not unmindful of my prayers and calculations, and every hour brings near the consummation of this present unnatural condition of things which may be compared to the infant in the mother's womb with germinant power for which there is no sphere visible. Let us trust God till the day dawn.

I have been asked to attend the Decennial Conference of Missionaries at Calcutta and submit a paper on the work of the Spirit, or something of that kind. Unless our own Conference is put off from November to December I shall not be able to attend the other.

To his sisters, Jan. 19, 1883:

I am a good deal amused at the effect my drum beating has had upon you. I fear you think me a much more respectable person than I am. Why for the last two years I have not worn shirts—except sometimes on Sunday. While I am on this subject I will tell you about what I wore in Calcutta. I took with me a black frock-coat, wearing on the journey a coat that I have worn about the house for two years, and which even *I* would not have thought of wearing in public. Before reaching Calcutta I told the Lord I was willing to be last of all the 460 gathering together for the Decennial Conference. The first night, going out of the house of my kind host, Mr. Cooke, I managed in some unaccountable way to fall; I held up my head to save my face and came with great force with my chin against the ground. I had on my best coat and before I could get it off it was covered with blood and quite spoiled. So I had to make all my public appearances in that despised coat. All the missionaries and missionary ladies were got up in a most proper way. But I concluded that it was the Lord's will and that He had some object to accomplish by it, so I accepted the situation with the best grace in the world. It is true the kind friends I was staying with got me a new coat and put it in my room, but I was ashamed to put it on till the day I was leaving. And to make you happy I will say that since I returned to Bombay I have got me a coat that the most dignified clergyman might wear, paying Rs. 8 for it.

But about that fall? Well, it hurt my jaw somewhat, so that I could not eat solid food for some days and am still conscious of a little soreness. I suppose when the Lord promises His angels to keep us from falling, He means that no real harm shall come to us. I enjoyed my visit to Calcutta very much, meeting with many warm-hearted friends, some of whom I had never seen, but that had read the *Meditations* or the *Guardian*. People insist upon putting me among the old men. Before the Decennial Conference broke up, three addresses were given by the old men: one, Mr. Bennett, had been in Burmah fifty-three years, another Mr. Newton in India forty-eight, and George Bowen thirty-five.

Our Bishop Foster was greatly tried with the South India Conference because we would not see the necessity of drawing upon the missionary treasury at New York for money with which to carry on our native work. He spoke out his mind with great freedom and plainness and so did some others. . . .

I managed to sleep a little in the train returning. During my three weeks' absence I seldom slept three hours a night. I got a severe cold in Calcutta. You express surprise at my getting cold in this country. I never was in such a country for colds. I am seldom without one. They are not so dangerous as in America, but are far from pleasant. You remember dear Pa used to be troubled with phlegm. It is just so with me.

I must tell you of some curious observations on my sleep made by others. Years ago I was told by others that I made alarming noises in my sleep by some peculiarity of breathing. Mr. McGrew of Calcutta told me that he counted some twenty respirations of Mr. Shaw while I breathed once; he counted seventy ticks of the clock between my respirations. According to this my sleep would seem to be a sort of suspended animation, and the gasping noise would be that made by the returning breath. I would seem to have no business to be alive.

Mr. and Mrs. Tucker (Salvation Army) were at the same house with me in Calcutta. They are thoroughly devoted Christians. When he was occupying a high position in the Punjab, she used to have meetings with soldiers. She told me she used to read and prize the *Bombay Guardian*.

This is the last of Bowen's home letters which has been preserved, unless a very poorly typewritten letter, inadequately dated, addressed to Kate may have been later. In this letter he referred to his correspondence with Mr. Rankin:

He has sent me a number of books which I shall be noticing in the *Guardian*, among them two lives of Emerson. What a mercy that I was delivered from the influence of that man. What was good in him he got from Christ without acknowledging it. There is such a thing as stealing character. Emerson would have been shocked at the idea of taking the goods of another man. Yet he stole what was best and clothed himself in it as his own, making light of Christ in comparison with Emerson. His Christ was 1,800 years away from him. And God was a cloud. I am weary of these intellectual humbugs.

As he indicates, he attended the Second Decennial All India Missionary Conference held in Calcutta, Dec. 28, 1882 to Jan. 3, 1883. Of the 475 members, one had been at work over fifty years—the Rev. C. Bennett of the American Baptist Mission in Rangoon, three over forty years, and seven over thirty years, Bowen being one of these. His name appears in the list of the representatives of the American Methodist Episcopal Church. The Chairman of the Conference was General the Honorable Sir Henry Ramsay, K.C.S.I., C.B., Commissioner of Kumaon. The Lieutenant-Governor of Bengal, the Honorable A. Rivers Thompson, C.S.I., presided at the public missionary meeting. The Church of England was fully represented by missionaries of the Church Missionary Society and the Church of England Zenana Mission but the Bishop of Calcutta wrote that he could not participate because "important principles are involved which my conscience will not allow me to compromise."

Bowen's paper on "The Promotion of Spiritual Life and Enthusiasm in the Churches of India" is presented in the Report of the Conference (pp. 85-90). "This," Bowen says, "is really the vital question concerning all Christian churches throughout the world. We shall solve the problems relating to the Christians of India most effectually, when we have solved them for the Christians of Europe and America." He proceeds to name some of the things which "lie in the way of the full development of life and enthusiasm among Christians generally": 1. "The tendency to regard the measure of spiritual life which we find in the church, as practically the measure of the attainable." 2. Crucifixion of the flesh is needful but difficult. 3. The influence of the world. 4. "In the nature of things, the measure of piety among native Christians will bear some proportion to that which obtains among the missionary body. We may shrink from admitting this; may call to mind missionaries of life and enthusiasm whose converts are still weighted down with the evil customs of their old nature. But there is often a good deal of Christian experience that does not verify itself to the consciences of the native Christians. It may have cost the missionary great sacrifices to leave his own kin and country to become a preacher in a foreign land, but this is not always obvious to the Christians under his care; what impresses them chiefly, perhaps, is the superior style of his living to theirs. It is not easy for them to see the evidences of self-denial where they perceive so much more of this world's goods than falls to their own lot." 5. The lives of Europeans on the mission field. 6. The too great dependence of the churches upon the missionaries.

Then he proceeds to plead for enthusiasm founded on God's Word, for love which begets enthusiasm, for missionary example in imitation of the model of Paul, for faith in the power of the Spirit to impart fullness of life. "With regard to the uncultured heathen," he says, "we are apt to think that much time must elapse and much instruction be given, before we can hope to see him reach a conspicuous measure of Christian devotion and fruitfulness. It is a grand thing if we can get him saved from adultery and lying and abusive speech and other prominent sins, but we may not hope to get him for some time to realize his need of deliverance from more subtle sins. A great assault is made upon our faith, to hinder us from believing that he may attain those fruits of the Spirit which are thought to belong to a more advanced phase of the Christian life. Now while culture is a thing of time and opportunity, there does not appear any sufficient reason for limiting the power of the Holy Spirit to confer fullness of life. At all events, we should not yield this point until it has been demonstrated, that the more 'abundant life' promised is not for those who have lately come out from heathenism. God forbid that our want of faith should be the hindrance.

"The Epistles to the Colossians, Philippians and Ephesians are addressed to those who had not long escaped from the darkness of heathenism; yet these Epistles abound with evidence of Paul's earnest desire that they should know the utmost of God's power to redeem, and exhibit a standard that would be startling at the present day to many even advanced Christians. Paul would not listen to the suggestion that so naturally might have presented itself, that much time must elapse before the converts could rise above the lowest rounds in the ladder of grace. He believed in the mighty power of the Spirit of God and sought to inspire believers with his own conceptions of the matter."

He closed with an appeal for an evangelistic church and a tribute to the constancy of Indian Christians in the Mutiny: "The churches of India must be evangelistic, must themselves engage in Mission work to the unevangelized, far or near, if they would experience the fullness of the Spirit's operations. Enthusiasm in this line of things will grow by what it feeds on. . . . We would not think it just to our native brethren to conclude this paper, without bearing a cordial testimony to the grace of God bestowed upon them. In the days that tried men's souls, twenty-five years ago, many of them exhibited the heroism of true faith, cheerfully laying down their lives for the cause of Christ, and as a body, they signally and triumphantly belied the vaticinations of those who had predicted that in such a crisis they would recreant to their faith. It is in the piping times of peace and immunity from peril that (like the rest of us) they are more likely to lose sight of the great incentives to whole-hearted devotion, and stand most in need of earnest exhortation and thorough-going examples."

Bowen made two other contributions to the Conference. He does not appear to have volunteered any part in the discussions but Dr. J. Murray Mitchell called him out to give an account of the Bombay Tract and Book Society when the Conference was discussing "the Distribution of Vernacular Literature," and in the closing meeting he was chosen to make one of the three farewell addresses by senior members of the Conference, the others being Mr. Bennett of Rangoon and then Dr. Murray Mitchell, who read some original verses and added two sonnets on missionary work in India written in 1846 and 1882. Bowen's remarks were the briefest:

> In the parable of the wheat and tares, the owner of the field said, "Let both grow together until the harvest." At present we are rapidly approaching the harvest time: events are rapidly maturing; formerly centuries were required for bringing about results: now it is far otherwise. We should remember that the ministries of nature which developed the wheat developed the tares: even so the wonderful inventions and facilities of this age belong to those opposed to Christianity. Agnosticism, spiritualism and other forms of error can use these to enable them to triumph. Let us therefore not rely so much upon these things, not even upon the expanded heaven of science, but upon our great Leader. The sun, we are told, is 800,000,000 miles in diameter: if a hundred worlds like ours were placed upon it they would make but a feeble, black line; how ample the expanse! And yet rays of light are sent down not only to this earth but to everyone's feet. Even so the Sun of Righteousness sends His rays to you, to each of us: great promises, invitations and gracious declarations pour forth from Him a mighty volume of love and light, to you.
>
> Lay hold of this thought, that the whole of the omnipotence of the Lord Jesus Christ is given to each one of us. Christ sits at the right hand of the Majesty on high; the Holy Spirit dwells within your heart. "No man can call Jesus Lord without the Holy Spirit." Let this spiritual omnipotence come into your heart to cleanse and fill and use it. Christ said, "Have I been so long time with you, and dost thou not know me, Philip?" The Spirit often says, "Have I been so long with you, and have ye not known me?" Are we not often looking for the consciousness of the Spirit, instead of realizing the fact that the Spirit is present with us? Let us recognize His presence and seek for mightier manifestations.
>
> I am glad and thankful for the privilege of attending this Conference. When it was proposed to us in Bombay, in my short-sightedness I said, "No, we already possess all the information we need." But the past week has been a time of blessing and refreshing, and I have been glad to look upon the faces of so many earnest workers for Christ, our common Master.

Bowen returned from the Conference to Bombay and spent the remaining five years in his work of writing and preaching and unceasing pastoral ministry to all types of folk— Indian, Eurasian, European, American, rich and poor, high and low, good and evil—"the wheat and the tares," as he would have said. All of his associates are now gone. There are, however, a few reminiscences of those who worked with him in his Methodist affiliation. I have a few of Bishop Taylor's brief notes to Bowen, like field communications from a commander-in-chief, but they tell nothing new of Bowen. Bishop J. M. Thoburn knew him well and honored him and was honored by Bowen. In an undated letter to Kate, Bowen writes:

> During the last month we have had our South India Conference, and while the meetings were full of blessing and spiritual power, I was employed from about 5 a.m. to 11 p.m. I thank God that He allowed me to see the formation of this Conference, by which all the work that Brother Taylor initiated is consolidated and made one. We were delighted with Bishop Andrews, a man of a very sweet spirit and at the same time of much spiritual and mental power. Brother Thoburn is one of the most effective preachers I ever heard. A man of culture and refinement, of a most earnest spirit, very eloquent, he takes his audience captive at once and maintains his hold of them to the end. Many sought the Lord under his preaching.

"In his later days," Bishop Thoburn wrote me, "Mr. Bowen wrote very long letters and I never kept any of them." In the *Christian Advocate* of February 23, 1888, after Bowen's death, Thoburn wrote an article in which he said of him:

> In going to live among the people Mr. Bowen adopted no disguise. He continued to wear his European clothing and he retained his European habits, and in this he no doubt acted wisely. In China a foreigner sometimes smoothes his way by adopting the Chinese costume, but in India, where the people are familiar with the sight of Europeans, nothing whatever is gained by such a change. He hired a room, put a little plain furniture into it and lived on a most frugal fare. He earned his livelihood by teaching a few private pupils but kept his expenses within less than $200 a year. He was in no sense an ascetic and when invited out, as he often was, he always ate cheerfully whatever was set before him. His tastes were simple and in his own little home his fare was simplicity itself. On one occasion he entertained the members of the Bombay Missionary conference at breakfast and when the meal was served it consisted of bananas and bread. He was too transparently honest and consistent to assume a style of life even for the once, above that which he daily maintained. Friends often tried to add to his comfort but always in vain. On one occasion when he was absent some unknown ladies invaded his room and refitted it throughout, putting in a new and almost luxurious bed, and other articles corresponding with it. The next day all the new articles were quietly distributed among the poor and the room resumed its old-time appearance.

Association with the Methodist Church in India

It might have been expected that the course pursued by Mr. Bowen, so noble, so unselfish, would have won the admiration and approval of everyone but such was by no means the case. The European community of Bombay felt itself humiliated, if not disgraced, by the erratic missionary and for some time the local papers indulged freely in gibes and jokes, as rude as they were stupid, at the expense of a man of whom the world of Bombay was not worthy. Nor did the natives appreciate his course as intelligently as he had anticipated. He was among them but he was not of them. When I first met him he had been pursuing this mode of life for seventeen years and in reply to my questions he spoke with the utmost freedom of his experiment. "I have discovered," he said, "that the gulf which separates the people of this country is not a social one at all; it is simply the great impassable gulf which separates between the religion of Christ and the unbelieving world." But he did not regret the course which he had adopted and never wavered in pursuing it. He conquered foes; prejudices gradually melted away in the presence of his serene and Christlike life. The natives as the years passed by learned to respect and love him, and in his later years he was venerated as a saint. He has often been spoken of as the "White Saint of India" and has, perhaps, more nearly won a right to that title than any other Indian missionary of the century.[6]

When Bishop Taylor began his work in Bombay, Mr. Bowen cooperated heartily with him, and as the work advanced and began to assume an organized form he was led to see his duty to cast in his lot with the new people, and soon after he formally united with the Methodist Episcopal Church. This step was made easier by the fact that he had adopted theological views which were substantially the same as those held by the Methodists, but this fact alone would not have induced him to take so important a step had it not been for his conviction that he could thereby help forward the great work which he had at heart more effectually than in any other way. He came among us as a lowly saint, humbly clad, and like his Master, "without form or comeliness," but he brought with him the power of a Name and an influence which gold could not have bought, and which the world could not have bestowed.

When Bishop Andrews organized the South India Conference, Mr. Bowen was made presiding Elder of the Bombay District, and on two different occasions he was elected President of the Conference. He

---

6 Cf. Lawrence's *Modern Missions in the East,* ch., "The Home and Rest of the Missionary," pp. 206-209, for a discussion of the ascetic and celibate ideal in missions, with special mention of Bowen. There is a mention of Bowen's asceticism in Murdoch's *Indian Missionary Manual.* Bowen himself, however, disavowed any sympathy with asceticism. He contended only for frugality and simplicity.

would have been elected to this position on every occasion when a Bishop was absent but for his peremptory refusal to serve.

All India will pause to pay a tribute of respect and love to the memory of George Bowen. All India is the debtor. He was a peerless saint among Christians, a royal prince among missionaries. One had to see him and know him in his simplicity, but yet in his strength, in order to understand what our Savior meant when He said that we must become as little children. He had done his work; he has fulfilled his mission; he has finished his course; he has won his crown.

Mrs. L. D. Osborn, for many years later principal of the Union Missionary Training Institute in Brooklyn, was with her husband among the very useful Methodist missionaries who knew Bowen in Bombay. She writes:

> Once while he was at Conference, friends wishing to add to his comfort—for all his friends had noticed he would not make provision for his own comfort—put a new mattress on his bed. Some weeks after it was learned he had taken it to a poor, sick widow. He possessed great musical talent and it was thought he would greatly enjoy an organ, so one was presented to him. But soon it was ascertained he had donated it to a chapel where one was needed. The only gift I know of his keeping was a typewriter, as later in life he had found it difficult to do all the writing required in his position as editor.
>
> While I was in Bombay in '78 and '79, Mr. Bowen breakfasted every Thursday morning in the home where I was staying, that of Col. G. W. Oldham. He always conducted family prayers on these occasions and his comments on the Scripture portion read were worthy of being put in print.
>
> His lack of thoughtfulness for his own comfort was apparent in all little things; for instance, he would never select an easy chair for himself on entering a room.
>
> He always had an intense desire to be an evangelist, felt that work with the pen was not as effective as with the voice; yet it was by his writings God used him most.
>
> When Mr. Osborn and I were married, Nov. 22, 1879, he performed the ceremony and presented me with a little card that had a value beyond all other gifts. On it was a sere leaf, and within the words, "Dead in trespasses and sin"; followed by a fresh leaf with the words "Quickened together with him." And lastly, "Walk worthy of the vocation wherewith you are called."
>
> His was a life of varied usefulness. One hour he might be found in the hut of the poorest native, the next at Government House called by the

Governor to consult with him regarding methods of dealing with natives.

By the natives it was said of him, "There is a man that is like Jesus Christ."

Another of his associates, a much younger man, was the Rev. Albert H. Baker. He writes:

> He was one of the most approachable men I ever knew, and hence, though I believed him to be one of the greatest, spiritually and intellectually, I had ever met, I did not stand in awe of him as of some other great men I happened to know about the same time. I felt he was just as great as the greatest of them, but somehow he was different....
>
> When I met Brother Bowen his great genius and talent were lost sight of. He was *Brother* Bowen. In years he was old enough to have been father of some of us, but to everyone of us he was brother, an elder loving brother, in whom we could confide and from whom we were sure to receive invaluable counsel and help. He made himself one with us and in doing it he did not seem to have to make an effort, he never seemed more natural than with a young man or company of young men. I have in mind an annual Conference gathering, but with any company of young people he seemed a young person among the young. He was witty, but never frivolous. He was learned, but never pedantic. He was brim full of information on all subjects upon which any of us thought, and his knowledge was at our command, but he never thrust it upon us. His accomplishments were many and of a very high order. What a delight it was to listen to his playing on the piano, especially if it was an impromptu production of his own. How careful we had to be that no word of approbation escaped our lips, and to keep him unconscious of the fact of our presence. Those were occasions to be coveted and never to be forgotten when once enjoyed. He was a saint. He belonged to Christ. He did not have to tell you this; you knew if you knew him. He lived his religion as naturally as a lamp burns and scatters its rays. I never was with him for any length of time without feeling that I must be better. I thank God I ever knew him.

Recollections of Bowen's work as a Methodist were published by the Rev. C. P. Hard (father of William Hard, the journalist) who appears in a photograph with Thoburn and Bowen, when the three were the presiding elders of the three districts of the Methodist Church in India, in the *Ocean Grove Record* in 1878 and in the *Wesleyan Methodist Recorder* of Bombay, May, 1888. Mr. Hard wrote me on March 17, 1904:

As Secretary of the Conference of which Brother Bowen was at times President in the absence of a Bishop, and as Presiding Elder with him when the Districts of Dr. Thoburn and Brother Bowen and mine covered 250 millions of people, and entertaining him in our home in Allahabad as well as having him in our Bombay home each week on his day off, at night, tender memories cluster around his name. After his anniversary sermon at Conference one year, Bishop Andrews said to me, "Brother Hard, in the light of that sermon I am a poor Christian." So high was the standard of a meek and holy life held up by the man that while lying for his burial in Bombay, Parsis and Hindus, weeping, spoke of him to me with deep affection.

Some of the extracts from Mr. Hard's scrap books may well conclude these recollections:

The Bombay Church has congregations in the south, north and center of the city; and in home, halls and in the streets proclaims the Gospel in scores of meetings weekly to the people in English, Tamil, Marathi, Gujerati and Hindustani. They are a royal people, "the children of a King," a worthy mother church to Methodism in South India. They breathe the spirit of their leader, George Bowen, who says: "Loving the Lord Jesus Christ, we shall regard our being as for the purposes indicated in the exemplar of His own life. We shall love that world for which He died, and willingly spend and be spent, that we may help them to know the love of God in Christ." Thus many of them testify to the enjoyment of perfect love, as Brother Bowen has said to them: "We believe that God does hear the prayer and grant the desires of those who hunger and thirst after righteousness, and we are sure that when these have received the baptism of the Spirit which they sought, it is almost impossible for them to keep silence with regard to this blessing, and it would generally be culpable for them to do so. If we have been brought into conscious union with the Lord in a remarkable degree, love to others will constrain us to let them know what the Lord is willing to do for them. Where this is done intelligently people will see that the object is not at all to exhibit oneself; it is rather like the joyful Eureka of one of a company of thirsty wanderers who has found a spring of excellent water, and communicates the tidings."

Rev. C. P. Hard writes in *The Christian Advocate,* New York, August 7, 1879: "A high authority says, 'Give and it shall be given unto you.' This finds an illustration in Bombay just now. When Rev. William Taylor had gone from Bombay, where he began operations in 1871, to Calcutta, where after an opening success he needed a church building,

Association with the Methodist Church in India

Rev. George Bowen, the talented and saintly pastor of the M. E. Church in Bombay and for thirty years editor of the *Bombay Guardian,* had given to our infant church in Bombay five thousand dollars, of which a bank had notified him as being left for him by a friend who had taken steamer for England. The noble Bombay Church, though having halls for places of worship, postponed its own comfort, and heroically sent the five thousand dollars across the continent, and soon our first church edifice in South India was erected in the capital of the empire. The McAllister will has just left $5,000 for our Mission in Bombay."

January 1883, Rev. C. P. Hard, in editing a supplement to the India Methodist *Watchman,* Bombay, says that "George Bowen read the majority report of the Committee on Missions which was unanimously adopted by the South India Conference:

"In reviewing the native Work of the Conference during the past year, we are highly gratified with the general revival of interest and activity in this Native Work all over the Conference. While we are fully aware that the principles of Christianity thoroughly imparted to the mass of the Natives in India must elevate the social life, purify the homes from whatever corruption may exist therein, either material or moral, and bring into the homes the marks of self-reliance and cultivation, yet we would deprecate converts making these outward changes faster then their pecuniary abilities will allow, thus involving themselves in debt and prejudicing the cause by an outward appearance unaccompanied by any radical change of heart."

In his *Bombay Guardian,* Editor George Bowen said in 1884: "The Calcutta Methodist Missionary Society was organized a few years ago for the purpose of carrying on missionary work among the people. Its appropriations are on the grant-in-aid principle. In this connection we would remind our readers that while the M. E. Church of Bombay, in addition to the entire burden of the English work, spares what it can for the native work, this latter work needs to be supplemented from other sources. It might easily take on proportions much greater than the English work itself; there is an almost unlimited scope for its expansion. But even at the present there are needs that go beyond the ability of English and native church to meet, and the friends of missions generally are hereby reminded of it. The writer of this is connected with this work and has never taken a pice from the Church or from any Society since 1848, or asked any man for aught for himself. Much more faith is involved in the course of the Rev. Mr. Hard, his colleague, who has a family and who goes forward in the work, as far as we know, without any guarantee from any quarter, except the word of the Master which indeed is adequate, but perhaps does not approve this notice, written without Mr. H's knowledge. After all, this is perhaps what is chiefly wanted in the Lord's work, a more exclusive and unquestioning dependence on Him. The laborer is worthy of his hire and the Master will see that he gets it."

In the *Illinois Methodist Journal* Rev. C. P. Hard writes: "While crying to God for a manifestation of His power among the heathen, the Rev. George Bowen, the revered and now ascended, had expectation at times that miracles would attend his words, to convince the hearers. Indeed we are told that his exclamation of horror, at the duplicity of a false witness in testimony meeting in the early days of the Taylor introduction of testimony, and his prayer, 'Lord, close his lips,' were followed by the immediate answer, as demonstrated by the fact that the profligate was dumb in hospital quite a time; 'some weeks,' says William Taylor in his *Four Years' Campaign in India,* page 146."

The question has been raised as to whether Bowen changed his theological views in transferring from the Congregational to the Methodist Church. Some have held that he remained a Calvinist and joined the Methodists simply because of their evangelistic earnestness. This was the view of his old friend, Dr. Wallace Atterbury. Others regarded his change of position as involving also a surrender of his Calvinistic theology and an acceptance of Arminianism. The truth probably was that he was neither a Calvinist nor an Arminian but both, according to the New Testament. He believed in the Sovereignty of God and he believed in the freedom and responsibility of man. He believed in an atonement made in Christ adequate to the sins of the whole world and he believed in the liberty of man to accept or reject this atonement. But his belief in human freedom and responsibility was associated with his recognition that we love God because He first loved us, that it is God Who works in us and that our choice of God is but our response to God's choice of us. He wrote in the *Guardian* of June 5, 1880, "The doctrine of the entire dependence of the sinner or the Christian upon the grace of Christ for all right action, is held as strongly among the Methodists as among any other bodies. And many Methodists would doubtless be surprised to learn how strongly the doctrine of human responsibility is held among Calvinist bodies." (cf. two editorials, "Responsibility, Human and Divine," *Bombay Guardian,* May 22, June 5, 1880).

His letter of March 16, 1878, to his sisters already quoted stated the convictions which are spread over the pages of the *Guardian* across the years.

There has been frequent mention in the letters of Bowen which have been quoted of the Rev. Narayan Sheshadri, a convert of the Scotch Mission in

Association with the Methodist Church in India

Bombay. He was a man of great ability and of rich and striking personality. He visited America in 1873 and was one of the notable figures at the great meeting of the Evangelical Alliance, in New York City, one of the most important Christian Councils ever held. He was deeply influenced by Bowen and on Dec. 16, 1876, wrote to Bowen's sisters from Jalna in the Nizam's Dominions, telling them of his debt:

> Your dear brother's encouragement in Bombay during the last few years has been beyond his expectations. As I told you when in New York, he and I were privileged to declare the glad tidings of salvation in Bombay for many years. The visible fruit of his or my ministrations was very little indeed, but it is otherwise now. I believe of late, the pleasure of the Lord has been prospering in his hands.
>
> Though I am away from him this side, nearly five hundred miles and at Indapur, our oldest Rural Mission, some two hundred miles, yet while going backwards and forwards, I take a run to Bombay, have a short season of prayer with him and see a few friends and then return to my stations, either Jalna or Indapur. In this way I think I see him once or twice every quarter and I assure you I invariably return from his place greatly refreshed and strengthened. It is a pity that in these days I cannot have his company as often as I used to have when residing in Bombay.

17. Bowen as a Writer

George Bowen was a tireless preacher. Day in and day out for forty years he preached on the streets, by the seaside, at fairs and festivals, in rooms and chapels and churches. It is evident that he was not a great preacher as the world judges. He simply talked colloquially and often without preparation, drawing from the inspiration and necessity of the occasion and from the inexhaustible stores of his own knowledge and reflection. His greatest preaching by far, reaching in its influence to the end of the world, was by his writing.

As already reported, he was consumed in his youth by the ambition to be a great author. He wrote constantly and at the time of his conversion, as we have seen, was engaged on what was to be a masterpiece which he called *Agathon,* and in which Christ, in Whom at the time he did not believe, was to appear as a leading personality. Of all these early productions—essays, dramas, novels—only single copies of *Oluph,* the Scandinavian tragedy, and *A Pupil of Raphael,* the Italian novel, remain.

His first writings, after beginning his work in India, appear to have been the report of his "Sea-side Discussions," the debates that he carried on alone or in association with others like the Rev. Narayan Sheshadri, one of the most notable of the early converts, or fellow missionaries.

In 1854 he issued his *Life of Mohammed.* A copy of the third edition is dated "Bombay, Printed at L. M. D'Souza's Press, 1856." The title page does not bear the name of the author. In writing of Mohammed, Bowen, of course, had no original sources to draw upon but he used the books available as mentioned in his "Preface": Bush's *Life of Mohammed,* Washington Irving's *Life of Mohammed,* Religious Tract Society's *Life of Mohammed,* Sale's *Koran and Preliminary Treatise,* Gibbon's *Roman Empire.*

The little book was a frankly and unequivocally adverse judgment both of Mohammedanism and of Mohammed. It concludes:

> Controlled under British authority in the east, and watched by all Europe in the west, Islam is like the lion, brought from the Arabian desert, in the keeper's den; or like the eagle, from the rocky mountains of Petraea—his plumage faded, his wing broken, pining in his cage. All the powers now active in the world forbid the hope, or the fear, that scenes like those of former centuries should be repeated; and, if they are not repeated, the history of Mohammedanism points out its end, not less clearly than it has shown its beginning. The discoveries of science are against it. The inventions of art are against it. The improvements

in government are against it. The whole progress of nations is against it. Above all, the truth of the Christian religion is against it. The spelling-book, the magnet, the telescope, the printing-press, the Bible—now freely circulated in the languages of the east—are all against it. These weapons cut deeper than the sword; reach further than the cannon; and whatever errors we may make in calculating "time and season," here are elements of power which neither the religion nor the empire of Mohammed can finally resist.

It is difficult to make a fair comparison of Mohammed with Jesus Christ.

Even if religious reverence towards "the Son of God" did not restrain us, how could we compare the licentious polygamist, the robber, the fiery warrior, the inexorable bigot, with the benevolent and majestic "Son of Man"?

The contrast in some of its stronger features is obvious enough. Jesus lived and died in Judaea: Mohammed had traveled and mingled with men of various nations, and of conflicting religions. Mohammed was a leader of Arabian plunderers: Jesus went about doing good. Mohammed became a warrior at the head of armies: Jesus was "the Prince of peace." Mohammed was a man of unbounded sensuality: Jesus was "holy, harmless, undefiled, separate from sinners." Mohammed was ambitious: Jesus was "meek and lowly in heart." Mohammed rested his claims on secret revelations: Jesus did "the works which none other man did," healing the sick, and raising the dead. Mohammed called his followers to blood and conquest: Jesus summoned His disciples to repentance, humility, and love. Mohammed escaped from his enemies by flight: Jesus, by a miracle, in open day. Mohammed taught a religion which contradicts itself: Jesus was always the same. Mohammed was a destroyer: Jesus is The Savior.

Bowen points out in one of his letters, that the little book does not appear to have brought upon him any increase of opposition from the Mohammedans in Bombay, in spite of its positive anti-Mohammedanism.

Bowen's best pamphlets were reprints of articles in the *Bombay Guardian* in a series entitled "Friendly Words to Educated Natives." They appeared in the *Guardian* in 1882. They were issued in tract form by the Bombay Tract and Book Society in 1883. This was the Society with which Bowen was connected for many years. Indeed, in a sense, he was the Society. His account of it as given by him to the Decennial Missionary Conference in Calcutta in '82-'83 was as follows:

> When I arrived in the country thirty-five years ago, the Rev. R. W. Hume, father of the Mr. Hume, present in the Conference, was Secretary

of the T. and B. Society, and by his vigorous and wise management gave it an impulse that has been felt ever since. I was subsequently for eighteen years Secretary of the Society. The Society is very much indebted to the Rev. Baba Padmanji for the many valuable works in the vernacular supplied by him. The operations of the Society, though they cannot be compared with those of the Madras Tract and Book Society, have nevertheless been considerable. The principal vernaculars are the Marathi and the Gujarati, in the last of which the Gujarat Tract Society is a valuable agency.

The Lord's servants are sometimes tempted to despond when they think of the myriads of religious tracts circulated, each one of which might, by the blessing of God, be saving to some reader, yet altogether resulting in so few conversions. A single drop of rain is a very wonderful thing in itself, yet the multitude of such that make up the rain-fall of a district is simply inconceivable; if, however, a harvest is secured, we think it a matter of thankfulness. It is a mistake to suppose that the mere dissemination of religious tracts or portions of tracts will of itself secure the conversion of the nations. The work of Missions, the preaching of the Gospel, Biblical instruction, the elevation of the church, the work of Bible Societies and Tract Societies, these and other Christian agencies must advance pari passu, hand in hand, and the progress of the one will depend upon that of the others. That the wide dissemination of religious tracts may be fruitful of good, it is necessary not only that the number of readers be increased, but that the susceptibility to Christian truth must become more general. This implies diminished interest in erroneous systems, the weakening of prejudice, etc.

The titles of the twelve tracts in the series of "Friendly Words" were:

What is it to be a Christian?	Mission of Christ.
What is Saving Faith?	Miracles of Christ.
Must we be Baptized?	Christ's Unworldliness.
Light Brings Responsibility.	The Faultlessness of Christ.
Why did Jesus Die?	The Gospels.
The Law of Progress.	Results of Preaching.

Several years before this series appeared Bowen issued in 1875 a single tract entitled "Some Friendly Words," addressed "To Hindus, Mohammedans, Parsis, Nominal Christians, and all who have not peace with God." This was his beginning:

> You have been sometimes told that certainty in religion, if attainable at all, is only reached after a very thorough examination of the different systems of religion. You know that a great deal has been said against

Christianity, and many works have been written on the evidences; much time and careful thought will be necessary in order to feel that you have mastered this subject. But that is only one religion; and there are some religions that profess to have so vast a collection of sacred books that a lifetime would be needed to become well acquainted with them. If one were guaranteed an existence like that of the Antediluvians, if several centuries of life were secured to one, then he might hope to get a sufficient acquaintance with the various religions of earth to justify him in deciding which was worthy of his attention. Only there would still be the possibility that new religions might spring up before he had mastered the old; nor could he be sure that there was not in some quarter of the globe an unknown religion more worthy of his attention that all the rest. Further, there is this difficulty, that men in general have no taste for prolonged, earnest investigation. Again, the reflection arises that Divine providence would not have placed anything that was really necessary to the salvation of men, so far beyond the reach of common men. There is the strongest presumption that the truth upon which the abiding happiness of men generally shall depend, will be presented in a way easily laid hold of by dying sinners. I may die before another sun rises to bless the world; the salvation that I need is something immediately available.

Now the Gospel of Christ differs from all other systems by professing to be immediately realizable. The apostles went forth into all the world; they preached to Jews and Gentiles, Greeks and Barbarians; and we find in the Acts of the Apostles that men in the very hearing of the Gospel, got assurance of its being from God, at once availed themselves of it, and immediately stood forth as witnesses of its genuineness and preciousness.

This is the grand distinction of the Gospel, that it announces a gift of God to every man; a free gift of God to every sinful man who will receive it, a free gift of eternal life to every believer. The wages of sin is death; but the gift of God is eternal life through Jesus Christ our Lord. A man is in the bazaar making purchases; one man offers him his wares at one price, another at another; but when a person appears with a gift and presses upon his acceptance what more than meets all his demands, the various vendors may stand aside. The Gospel means glad tidings; it is the announcement of happiness unbought; eternal life: deliverance from sin and the curse of sin; offered to all alike. The reflection at once arises: This is a reality or a fiction; the gift is what it professes to be, or it is a shadow that will leave me just as poor when I have clutched it as I was before; I prove it then by taking it. In this respect it meets the demands of my nature; I may die before nightfall, I want a salvation that can be had before nightfall.

Among the pamphlets issued by the Tract Society from Bowen's pen, taken from the *Guardian*, where they appeared in series were "The Abiding Miracles of Prophecy," 1874; "Friendly Words to Romanists," 1876; "What is the Religion That Man Needs?" 1880; "Is Christianity of God? Did Christ Rise Again?" 1881.

The question of Bowen's return to his early views on the subject of infant baptism is clearly answered by Bowen's tract in 1878: "We fully believe, without the slightest question or hesitation that Infant Baptism is of God, and that it is a most blessed institution when the parents maintain their plighted faith towards God."

Bowen's best known writings, however, which carried his name all over the world were the three volumes entitled *Daily Meditations, The Amens of Christ* and *Love Revealed.* All of these were made up of his devotional articles in the *Guardian* and that rich quarry would yield half a dozen more volumes like them. The first to appear was *Daily Meditations.* Readers of the *Guardian* urged the collection of the Bible reflections which were appearing weekly and Bowen gathered them into a book which was published in Bombay[7] and a copy was brought to the attention of his seminary class-mate, the Rev. J. W. Dulles, who after a brief service under the American Board in Ceylon had returned on account of ill health to the United States and was Secretary of the Presbyterian Publication Committee in Philadelphia. Mr. Mornay Williams told me that his father, W. R. Williams, who, like his son, was a man of remarkable genius, once told him that he had urged Robert Carter, the publisher, to take the book and that when he declined, he and Dr. Atterbury had taken it to Dr. Dulles. The Presbyterian Committee published the book in 1869 with the following preface by Dr. Dulles:

> Greatly though the church of this day, and all its activities, lacks deep heart experience of religion, yet there are many who hunger and thirst after righteousness, who desire a fuller work of the Spirit in their souls. Conscious of poverty of soul, they long for manna from Heaven. To such this volume will prove a grateful gift. . . . The reader will here find deep, precious and suggestive thoughts made vivid by a glowing imagination and striking inferences. If desiring a higher Christian life, and willing to meditate and pray, he will be edified by the fruits of a proposed study of God's Word and of a rich experience of the workings of the Spirit. His faith will be strengthened by contact with the Author's faith, and his zeal be kindled by his passionate jealousy for the glory of God.

---

7 In his diary of Jan. 6, 1867, Bowen wrote: "I sent the Governor (Sir Bartle Frere) a copy of *Daily Meditations.* He says (Dec. 19) 'Accept my warm thanks for the copy of *Daily Meditations* and for this very kind note which came with it. I shall keep and value both as memorials of one for whom I have long felt esteem.'"

Of the work, one eminent New York pastor[8] says, "It is a book of rare merit, marked by deep piety, insight into the Scriptures, original genius and ever-compromising directness. I know of no book of its class, equal to it."

The author, the Rev. George Bowen, formerly of New York, has been for eighteen years a missionary in India. He issued a Volume of Meditations at Bombay, where there is a considerable English community. This volume was brought to the notice of the Committee by the Rev. William Wallace Atterbury, and by him, at the request of the Committee, revised, new papers by Mr. Bowen being inserted in the place of some that seemed of less merit.... Let the reader, as he reads, pause to meditate and ask the blessing of the Spirit upon the truth.—J. W. D.

The British edition of *Daily Meditations* appeared in 1873, issued by David Douglas of Edinburgh, with an introduction by Dr. William Hanna, son-in-law of Dr. Thomas Chalmers. In his introduction Dr. Hanna quotes from Bowen's account of his conversion and adds some comments of his own and of others:

All who have known him in Bombay concur in the same loving admiration of one who, for twenty-five years, has exhibited a kind and degree of self-sacrificing devotion to which there is perhaps no existing parallel in the whole wide field of missionary labor. In the published *Memorials of Robert Brown, Esq.,* late of Bombay, the writer states that:

"Among the many friends he so easily attached to himself through life, none held a higher place in his estimation than the devoted missionary referred to in the following letter. As he still lives and labors in Bombay, we forbear to indulge in well-merited eulogium, simply remarking that Mr. Bowen is an American missionary who has literally given up all for Christ. His labors among the heathen are abundant, and they are emphatically labors of love, unrequited and unacknowledged by any earthly Society, since he prefers to give his services without fee or reward; living upon a few rupees a month, and thereby removing one argument from the mouth of the heathen, who are slow to allow the disinterestedness of their religious teachers.

"We had Bowen dining with us last night, and I only wish some reporter had been behind the scene to take a note of his 'droppings.'... Oh, I wish you had been with us! You would have been elevated when listening to Bowen discoursing on these wondrous themes. A meek, lowly, despised man, but, oh how happy! Living in that miserable hut in the bazaar, holding converse with his God. Hunter is greatly enamored of him, the more so because he is very musical. Last night, before going away, he played an accompaniment on the piano to Hunter's violoncello—'Weep not for sorrow.' You need not be surprised if you

---

8 Rev. William R. Williams, D. D. And in this judgment the Rev. Thomas H. Skinner, D. D., than whom no one is more competent to judge of a spiritual work, concurs.

hear of both of us taking up our quarters with Bowen in the Bazaar at Rs. 10 a month." pp. 268-9.

One who knew Mr. Bowen long and intimately at Bombay, on being asked about him, writes:

"If expressions of the deepest reverence, admiration, and affection were all that is required, I should not be found wanting; for, taking him all in all, I have always thought him the most delightful and remarkable Christian man I ever met. He was at one time an infidel. Afterwards he gave up friends, country, fortune (his father was a rich man), and consecrated himself and his whole life to the service of Christ among the heathen. You know how he has labored for so many years, night and day, in Bombay; how he preaches every day to the native population; and you also can tell how great has been his influence for good on the Europeans there. For many years he actually lived in the native bazaar, and among that sadly degraded population, until asked to become Secretary to the Religious Tract Society, at whose depot he now resides, managing the affairs without fee or reward, in addition to his other labors.

"Probably it has added to his weight in the consideration of the English section of the community, that he is a most accomplished and highly intellectual man, having traveled much in Europe at one time; knowing French, German, Spanish, Italian, and I don't know how many other European languages, in addition to Hindustani and Marathi. Many years ago he used to try and enlighten my dear brother in the mysteries of astronomy; and his musical powers are quite remarkable. It is seldom anyone has an opportunity of testing them; but on meeting him one evening quietly, after hearing him play a long and difficult piece of music, I asked for a repetition of part, when I was surprised to find that the whole had been impromptu improvised as he went along.

"Perhaps one should add that, in spite of Mr. Bowen's abundant labors, little visible fruit has been the result. His standard is scrupulously high and rigid. Other missionaries have frequently baptized natives instructed and impressed by his teaching. I asked him once if he did not often feel discouraged. 'Thank God,' he said, 'I can truly say I have never experienced such a feeling. This thought, "In Thy favor is life," swallows up all others. It is enough for me.' I believe eternity alone will reveal the amount of his unconscious influence, and reveal the bearing his noble, self-sacrificing life has had on the hearts of others."

It is by keeping it in mind that such has been Mr. Bowen's life that the reader will be prepared to appreciate some passages in the following volume, the key-note of which might otherwise fall upon his ear as if struck too high.

Among his other labors Mr. Bowen has for many years acted as sole editor and conductor of the *Bombay Guardian,* a journal well known to all interested in the religious condition of our possessions in the East. One feature of that journal has been the appearance in it weekly, and for years, from the pen of the editor, of a series of "Hints and Comments" for daily reading. So many of these as covered a year were re-printed some years ago and published in a separate volume at Bombay. The Presbyterian Publication Committee of Philadelphia republished this volume in America in 1865, and a second edition of it has appeared there. The present volume consists of a selection from the one issued at Bombay and Philadelphia, and from the "Daily Hints and Comments" in the *Bombay Guardian* for the year 1858.

Books of this description are already numerous; but the habit they are meant to foster—that of quiet, secluded, meditative thought—is one that in times of keen ecclesiastical excitement and bustling religious activities, we cannot do too much to cultivate, whilst among such books we shall scarcely find another which exhibits the same freshness and vividness of idea, the same fervor of faith, the same intensity of devotion. Marks of genius and of a faculty of expression which, if cultivated, might have won for the author distinction in the world of letters, are to be found on almost every page. I may be permitted to add, that I count it a great privilege to introduce in this country a book so fitted to attract and to benefit, and to be associated even in this indirect way with so faithful and self-denying yet withal so gifted and heroic a servant of our Lord and Savior Jesus Christ.

As indicated by Dr. Hanna the British edition is quite different from the American in its contents.

It was sometime before these two editions had paid for themselves. As soon as they had done so, the publishers began to make remittances to Bowen's sisters, in accordance with his request.

So useful did *Daily Meditations* become that Col. Oldham urged the publication of a series entitled *The Amens of Christ* from the *Guardian* of 1868 and 1869. Douglas issued this in 1879 and Dr. Daniel Steele of Boston, editor of *Zion's Herald,* who had been deeply impressed by *Daily Meditations* urged upon McDonald, a Boston publisher, that he should issue an American edition (1886). Dr. Steele wrote me, Feb. 13, 1903:

> McDonald said that he would do so if I would write the introduction. Wishing some little biographical data I wrote to Bowen. His reply is the first letter, a copy of which is enclosed. More fully explaining my purpose in a second letter I received the second enclosed reply. These

replies are chiefly valuable for their revelation of the modesty of the man and the indication of the sources from which the materials of his biography may be drawn.

Bowen's two letters to Dr. Steele were as follows:

My Sister (Miss Harriet Bowen, Fordham, New York) sent me the other day a letter to Dr. Dulles in which you kindly intimated your wish to prepare a biography of myself. I have much reason to be thankful that the Lord has disposed one whom I so highly esteem as yourself so favorably toward me. Anything prepared by you would command the attention of a considerable portion of the Christian public in America. But my name is known to few in America, as I have never corresponded with any paper in America since I came to India. There is nothing in my life of any significance apart from the goodness and longsuffering of the Lord vouchsafed to me. As a missionary my life has been singularly sterile, and on this account it is a trial to me to have the attention of people directed to me.

I write especially to inform you that I have published in the *Bombay Guardian,* some years ago, extending through five volumes of that publication, "Reminiscences" containing all the information which you were asking for, giving detailed accounts of the Lord's dealings with me in bringing me into His marvelous light. As Henry W. Rankin, an unseen friend of mine, living at Northfield, Mass., at Mr. Moody's Seminary, has all these volumes, and has expressed to me a desire that the "Reminiscences" should appear in book form, I wrote him that when I have once published anything in the *Guardian,* I commit it to providence and take no steps myself to reproduce it in another form, having learned that all such steps are infructuous. The *Daily Meditations, Love Revealed,* and *The Amens of Christ,* were all first published in the *Guardian,* and reproduced independently of my action, though not without my consent. I have no objection to the reproduction of the "Reminiscences," or an abridgement of them, though I would not recommend anyone to take the necessary risk connected therewith. If you think the Lord would have you give your valuable time to the preparation of an account of the Lord's dealings with me, you might send this note to Mr. Rankin who I think would gladly cooperate, by placing the volumes at your disposal, or otherwise (March 17, 1885).

Many thanks for your very kind letter of May 10th apprizing me of my mistake regarding your purpose. I now understand the matter. I think it is one year since Bro. McDonald wrote asking leave to print the *Amens,* and I supposed that on second thought he had concluded not to.

I suppose you have seen Dr. Hanna's introduction to *Daily Meditations,* Eng. Edition. Barring the eulogy, it was very kind of him to engineer it before the public. And now the Lord raises up for me a friend in America whose endorsement is equally desirable. I am most thankful to Him for your friendly offices. I truly trust that the Lord may fully restore to you your vigor of brain which you say has been impaired by nervous prostration, and that you may go from strength to strength. "Unto him that hath shall be given and he shall have abundance."

I think very highly of Mrs. Booth's meetings. She seems to me more single-eyed than the General, but the Lord knoweth His own. They, the S. Army, have not the success in India that we hoped, and they sometimes seem to set the Salvation Army above Christ. We Methodists gave them a most cordial greeting when they came and worked with them while we could. But their course has lost them a measure of our sympathy.

I have daily impressed upon me that the 17th of John indicates the way in which Missions are to be made fruitful. To get near the heathen, we must get near to God (June 28, 1885).

Dr. Steele's introduction is an adequate account of Bowen's book. It is quoted here because it has been out of print for many years:

It occurred to two distinguished writers, at about the same time, to group these important Scriptures together (i. e., the "Verily," sayings of Jesus) and make them the themes of devout meditations. These are George Bowen and Andrew Jukes. To which of them belongs the credit of the original conception is unknown to the writer. It is quite probable that it was original with both. But here all resemblance ceases. Jukes, with a kind of Swedenborgian insight, sees in every word a fanciful type. Bowen, with a penetration guided by strong common sense, sees in every word a practical truth. Jukes leans constantly towards millenarianism, with the Jewish notion of the Messiah's kingdom; while Bowen takes the Pauline view of the reign of Christ on earth, the gathering together of the spiritual Israel under the dispensation of the Holy Spirit.

I count it a rare privilege to introduce on this continent a book so inspiring, because itself is, in no mean sense, inspired of the Divine Spirit; a book which will attract and edify thousands of thoughtful souls blessed with lofty spiritual aspirations. Jesus might have pronounced on the Mount an eighth beatitude: Blessed are they who break the bread of life to those who hunger after righteousness, and blessed are the servitors who bring the tray laden with loaves.

All the books of Rev. George Bowen are strongly marked with his individuality. They are all meditations on the Holy Scriptures, exhibiting the same high literary finish; the same glowing love to God and men; the same freshness and striking aptness of illustration; the same vividness of conception; the same breadth of view, with power to discover the subtle, interior connections of thought in Scriptural exegesis; the same ability to illuminate a text as if an electric light had been suddenly hung in its very center; the same scathing rebuke of a merely formal type of Christianity; the same revelation of the sunlit heights of assurance and cloudless communion with the Father and the Son, through the Holy Comforter; summits on which the author himself is manifestly dwelling; and the same high estimate of the transcendent privileges of the believer under the Pentecostal dispensation, deliverance from inbred sin and that perfection of love which casts out all tormenting fear, and places an artesian well in the heart and makes the Magnificat of the Virgin ever warble from the fire-touched lips.

In reviewing the many influences which have become factors in molding my own Christian character, I wish in this public manner to record my sense of indebtedness to this good man whose pen, guided by the Holy Spirit, has, for nearly a quarter of a century, under the sultry skies of India, been as a chisel in the hand of a skillful sculptor, conforming me to the image of the Son of God. More than a score of years ago I secured and read with great spiritual profit Bowen's *Daily Meditations*—three hundred and sixty-five passages of God's Word, beautifully opened and applied with the unction of the Spirit to the heart of the reader. Some years afterwards I obtained another devotional and expository volume by the same author, *Love Revealed,* which suggested to me a title for my own first literary venture, *Love Enthroned.*

Love Revealed is a series of profound and devout reflections on five chapters of St. John's Gospel, beginning with the thirteenth and ending with the seventeenth, which section of the fourth Gospel one of the Christian Fathers has aptly styled "The Heart of Jesus."

Our author is a modern John who has so long reclined on the bosom of Jesus that he has become qualified beyond any other writer of this century to be the interpreter of His heart. Both of these books are published by the Presbyterian Board of Publication, in Philadelphia. This will account for their limited circulation among other denominations, especially among the Methodists, to whom they are peculiarly adapted, bating a slight savor of predestinarianism in the *Daily Meditations,* and some faint, lingering reminiscences in *Love Revealed.* The reason for the disappearance of these traces of this doctrine in this more recently written book, *The Amens of Christ,* will appear as the reader advances in this Introduction.

Already you are inquiring, Who is George Bowen? How could so eminent a Christian writer be so unknown to so many American readers? The answer to this question is found in the fact that he was never a correspondent of any periodical in this Western World. We have neither the data nor the space for the detailed biography, such as might be compiled from a series of "Reminiscences" written by himself and extending through five volumes of the *Bombay Guardian*. Another American admirer, who, like the writer, is "an unseen friend," has begged the privilege of introducing this autobiography to the American public.

It is sufficient for our present purpose to say that Mr. Bowen is an American citizen who some forty years ago offered himself to the Presbyterian (!) Board as a missionary to India. Reaching Bombay, his appointed field, he entered with all earnestness upon his life-work. He soon discovered that the Hindus were strongly prepossessed by the idea of self-sacrifice as the chief characteristic of religion, and were correspondingly prejudiced against religious teachers who received stated salaries for their services, and whose style of living, instead of evincing painful self-denial, was not much below the plane of other foreigners who resided in India for worldly and selfish ends. No sooner did he discover this barricade which stood between him, as God's water-carrier, and the thirsty and dying millions about him, than, with his own hands, he tore it down by cutting himself off from his base of supplies, the missionary treasury in America. He adopted the Pauline principle of self-support in order that "the Gospel might not be hindered." He cut down his expense to the bare necessaries of life in the Orient. He resolved that his only wife should be India, and his only offspring should be dusky Hindus begotten by the Spirit.

Paul took the needle and made tents. Bowen took the pen and made books; first in the form of expository editorials in the *Bombay Guardian*, which have been subsequently gathered into book form for enlightening other lands and future ages. The motive which impelled him to his course is very clearly described in the "Verily" expounded on page 69, in which he argues that the disciple of Christ should announce the Gospel to the world accompanied by all the proofs which naturally pertain to it, especially by a holy and self-denying life:

"Perhaps if we were more careful to give men such evidence as would be furnished by a more apostolic simplicity of life, self-denial, and unworldliness, by faith in God for all that we ourselves need, by a more perfect conformity to Christ, by more mutual love, by the power of its spirit put forth in our own characters, God might bear testimony from Heaven by such displays of His power as are best fitted to impress the minds of unconverted men."

In this attempt to condescend to men of low estate, and to become all things to all men that he may save some, Mr. Bowen has jealously guarded Christianity from all association in the minds of the Hindus with the vile mendicant teachers of their own religion. He does not, like Major Tucker, the head of the Salvation Army in India, put on the dress of a fakir and go barefoot with a gourd-shell from house to house begging food, in order to gain converts to Christ. Paganism, in the opinion of our author, is to be leveled up to Christianity, and not Christianity leveled down to paganism. He does not believe in what the India Salvation Army boasts of, "being saved from shoes."

Mr. Bowen is far removed from any self-complacency because of his self-denying life; and equally far is he from all feeling of censoriousness towards other missionaries to whom it is not given to be celibates for the sake of the kingdom of God and to step out upon the platform of self-support.

The first effect of his attempt to approach the pagans in Bombay, as nearly as possible on their own level, was met by violent opposition. Satan, who saw the vantage ground which the missionary was taking for his Master's cause, raised tumults when he attempted open-air preaching, and gave him a chance to sympathize with Paul: "Once was I stoned." But none of these things moved the apostle to India. Long since has persecution ceased. The power of a godly life, in manifest self-abnegation for the salvation of others, has conquered. The Hindus now call this self-sacrificing preacher "the white saint."

His order of intellect fits him to instruct and stimulate believers aspiring after a perfect conformity to Christ, rather than to sway the unsaved multitudes by melting entreaties or by irresistible appeals to their religious fears. For this reason he regards his missionary life as "singularly sterile." In writing this depreciatingly in regard to his public labors, Mr. Bowen forgets that St. Paul, in Eph. 4:12, sums up the work of the minister of Christ without mentioning the conversion of sinners, so intent was he on "the perfecting of the saints."

In the autumn of 1871, a tall man, with a patriarchal flowing beard, appeared in the streets of Bombay, preaching the Gospel on a self-supporting basis. He was endowed with the evangelistic gift, and was attended by the power of the Spirit in an extraordinary degree. This man was William Taylor, now Bishop of Africa. Mr. Bowen saw that he was a man after his own heart, a true yoke-fellow, with whom he desired to be yoked for drawing the Gospel plow through the fallow fields of India. William Taylor's work, at first non-denominational, was at length organized into a Conference of the Methodist Episcopal Church, and George Bowen became a member and a presiding elder. William Taylor once said to me, "I found that grand man and Pauline minister of Christ still wrestling with the inherited doctrine of unconditional election of some to eternal life, while others were either reprobated to eternal death, or passed by and left without that special call of the Spirit necessary to regeneration. I had several talks with him, and succeeded in taking every kink of Calvinism out of him." This accounts for its absence from his later writings.

There are, in the life and spirit of George Bowen, striking points of similarity to Archbishop Leighton. Both were sanctified from their earliest years; both while as yet boys heard and obeyed the divine call to the ministry of the Gospel; both evinced the same spirit of self-denial to enable them to draw others to Christ; both remained unmarried for the sake of the kingdom of Heaven; both resigned their salaries when convinced that they were obstructions of their own growth in holiness, and of their highest usefulness as soul-savers; for the same reason both changed their church relations midway in their ministry; both went from a Presbyterian to an Episcopal form of church government; both were noted for their unselfish liberality in bestowing upon others the gifts of money which providentially came into their hands; both lived in the Holy Scriptures, and left behind them for the edification of the future church most precious meditations on portions of the Word of God. To both of them do the exquisite lines of Cowper apply:

> "When one, that holds communion with the skies,
> Has filled his urn where these pure waters rise,
> And once more mingles with us meaner things,
> 'Tis e'en as if an angel shook his wings:
> Immortal fragrance fills the circuit wide
> That tells us whence his treasures are supplied."

We know of no books which are better models of expository preaching than these books of Mr. Bowen. This style of preaching is becoming more and more necessary to the spiritual life of the church, as the modern press is deluging our center-tables with its floods of tempting secular literature illustrated by the brilliancy of the engraver's art and sparkling with the wit and wisdom of the most charming writers. The Word of God, crowded out of our homes, should find more ample space in our pulpits, if we would have the church of the future filled with vigorous, stalwart, vertebrate members. Such must be developed by digesting the strong meat of the Holy Scriptures. One objection to expository preaching is the erroneous notion entertained by many preachers, that this style of address is necessarily dry and unattractive to the people. This would be the case if it consisted of a formal and grammatical exegesis after the fashion of our modern commentators. This is not the style advocated by us, and exemplified by Mr. Bowen. He, by his example, teaches us how to use what Sir William Hamilton aptly styles the "Representative Faculty," or Imagination, the power the mind has of realizing the distant scene and vividly picturing the attendant circumstances and divining the motives of its actors. The dramatic sensibility of human nature is not to be surrendered to Satan as his own by prescriptive usurpation. It is a creation of God and should be consecrated to His holy service.

The preacher should dramatize the Bible, not with costumes and curtains and the vulgar machinery of the stage addressing the eye, but in graphic word pictures addressing the mind. In this art of seizing the golden thread of unity which runs through an entire book of the Scriptures and of unrolling its successive scenes in one panorama, the Scotch and the English pulpit excel, as will be seen by an examination of the historical sermons of that foreign importation into New York, Dr. William M. Taylor, one of the best modern representatives of this style of preaching.

We cannot close this Introduction without a suggestion to editors and writers for our weekly periodicals. This class of literary toilers complain that their labors are forgotten with the paper which is old the day after its date, and fit for the attic or for fire-kindlings. But here is a writer for the weekly press whose work, instead of sinking in the gulf of oblivion, is rising steadily in the esteem of the best judges. The secret is, he has hung all his periodical contributions on the staple of God's Word. It was good old Bengel who said that if a man desired immortality on earth, the surest way of attaining it would be to connect his name with the Word of God, which abideth forever.

Dr. Steele refers to the volume entitled *Love Revealed* which appeared in America before *The Amens of Christ* but was published by Douglas later, in 1887. In the Edinburgh edition of *Love Revealed,* Douglas quotes the *Daily Review* comment on *The Amens*:

> Mr. Bowen is already favorably known as the author of one of the very best books issued under the often repeated title of *Daily Meditations.* . . . Fresh thoughts, pious aspirations, sage reflections and pithy, practical suggestions are to be found in almost every page.

Love Revealed consisted of meditations in the *Guardian* on the parting words of Jesus to His disciples in chapters 13-17 of the Gospel according to John. It was issued by the Presbyterian Publication Committee with the special satisfaction and delight of Dr. Dulles.

These three books were the great devotional books of the Church two generations ago. Saintly souls all over the English speaking world were nourished on them. One generation ago Douglas issued a new and uniform edition of them. There are even now no books of the deeper life which surpass them. If the Christian Church ever outgrows them it will be evidence of a fading away of the faith of the church in the supernatural Gospel of the New Testament and of the reality of the life of God in Christ in the soul of man.

That Bowen's books still live, in hidden places at least, is indicated by a communication from a Scotch minister who wrote over the signature of "Pathstruie" in the *Record* of the United Free Church, now the Church of Scotland, in July, 1925:

> Among devotional writers of the end of last century few have held such an honorable place as George Bowen. Whether there be many who still read his *Daily Meditations* it is difficult to say, but I must confess my indebtedness to him. From Smellie and Fosdick and others I come back in the quiet moments to Bowen. His *Daily Meditations* is one of the few books which in thirty or forty years one has had to get re-bound. Bowen, with Whyte on the Shorter Catechism and A. B. Davidson on Hebrews, has "attained to the first three" in one poor library.
>
> At a northern manse I remember being introduced to a worthy minister of our Church who had lost the use of his limbs and was wheeled about in a Bath chair, and being told that the only other book besides the Bible he chose to occupy himself with was Bowen's *Meditations*. It was not a bad choice, for where can you find clearer insight, a more incisive touch, more trenchant and vigorous grasp, a surer sense of sincerity, and more worthy expression? You feel as you read Bowen that you are in touch with a writer who himself is committed to follow Jesus all the way. And apart from the devotional hour, when you happen to find that he has touched on a text which you have chosen, you often find that he strikes more fire out of a flinty text than all the commentators.
>
> The short biographical notice in Dr. Hanna's preface does much to draw the reader's attention to the Meditations. Bowen was a converted infidel, a man of varied and outstanding gifts, and a missionary living in voluntary poverty in the bazaar of Bombay. But one would like to know more about him. He wrote other books besides the Meditations, which indeed were gathered from the pages of the *Bombay Guardian*. There are at least two other works—*The Amens of Christ* and *Love Revealed*. I have just finished reading the latter, which is a devotional commentary on John 13-17. If there is a commentary with deeper insight and more enthralling and compelling power, it is unknown to me.
>
> In the absence of fuller information about Bowen, lovers of him may welcome the following notes which an Edinburgh lady who had been acquainted with him in Bombay wrote at my urgent request:

"I was having my first meal, after arriving in Bombay, with a goodly company of missionaries, at the hospitable board of Dr. Mackichan, then the Principal of Wilson College, when a stranger was ushered into the dining-room—a tall, gaunt figure, with hollow cheeks and straggling gray hair. His clothes were threadbare and shabby, and yet he carried himself with ease and grace as a gentlemen. My host invited him to share our meal, and he sat down at the table. My first impression had been that he was a poor European who had probably come to get some help, but I soon learned that our guest was no other than the saintly George Bowen, a man of powerful intellect and deep spirituality.

"I often met him during the years I was in Bombay. He was on a committee, which met in a house adjoining the one where I lived, for the revision of the Marathi Bible; and we invited him to have a meal with us on the evenings the committee met. He did not dine in the evening as most Europeans do in India, but liked to have tea with us, and it was a high privilege to listen to his conversation. He did not talk much, but his words had a genuine ring of truth, and were always memorable, for he was a great soul. . . ."

On the subject of apparent unfruitfulness, readers who possess Bowen's *Love Revealed* will find, on pages 154-156, an illuminating paragraph revealing his well of consolation.

The core of this passage in *Love Revealed,* which is a comment on John 15:5, is in the words: "He that is sincerely bent on bringing forth much fruit to Christ will rest with satisfaction in this conception alone, namely, that the favor of God is fruit. Am I doing that which has the approbation of the almighty Disposer of all? If I am then I am bringing forth the best possible fruit. It will appear in His own good time, though it be a thousand years hence. One man insists on seeing his fruit, and God gives way to him and lets him have what he seeks; he sees his work prospering in his hands, but, unhappily, it does not endure; there is in the end the bitterness of disappointment. Another asks but one thing—that he may please to the uttermost Him Who has called him to be His servant. He is willing to wait in apparent sterility until God shall give the increase; he knows that God is the author of all true fruit, and has the absolute control of all resources, and can accomplish by the wave of His hand the renovation of the world, and accordingly he puts his seed into the hand of God, sure that, in the best of times, he will see the best of harvests. Let us abide in Christ, bury ourselves in Him, be found in Him. 'Except a corn of wheat fall into the ground and die, it abideth alone; but if it die, it bringeth forth much fruit.'"

Bowen's great literary work, of which these books are only a partial expression, was in his production for more than thirty years of the weekly issues of the *Bombay Guardian*, only once temporarily discontinued and never interrupted by vacation or furlough. Of this achievement and its unfolding of Bowen's thought and mind it will be necessary now to speak more adequately.

Bowen's thought was set forth week by week in his paper. Twenty-three volumes of it are preserved. It is manifestly impossible to summarize such a mass of material or to give an account of his opinions volume by volume. All that can be done is to pick out several volumes representative of each decade (1866, 1867, 1869, 1872, 1879, 1880, 1881, 1887), especially volumes covering his more critical years and indicate the themes with which he dealt and the nature of his opinions.

His fundamental concern, of course, was the matter of the relations of God and man in Christ. His training in Union Theological Seminary was in the type of Calvinism taught in the New School Presbyterian churches which, from the division of Old and New School in 1837 to their Reunion in 1871, had done their foreign missionary work through the American Board. He seems always to have had his own version of Calvinism and after he joined the Methodists he clearly had his own version of Arminianism. On the one hand he defends the view "All of God, not of man." Once in Christ, he holds, always in Christ. The soul's utter dependence is on God. There is such a thing as depravity. He holds that true Calvinism does not teach preterition. He writes both Calvinistically and Arminianly:

> While it is thus true that a sinner is saved by his own act of faith, his own submission, his own reception of Christ, he will have a very inadequate basis of faith if he does not discover that God has been from the very first moving in the matter of his conversion, arranging for it in the atonement of Christ, sending His Gospel to him, controlling providences with reference to it, and influencing his mind in the entire process by which he was brought to receive Christ. . . . God seeks the salvation of all, offers eternal life to all, is rich in mercy to all, is not willing that any should perish, and if any perish it is because of their unwillingness to receive, not because of God's unwillingness to bestow. There is salvation for all, otherwise it could not be offered. And what we read about election, predestination and the like, is not, we may be sure, intended in the least degree to invalidate, or weaken the force of what is said about the mercy offered to all.
>
> Election is not intended to inspire me with a feeling of complacency in the thought that I have something which is denied to others; election does not involve reprobation; but it is simply intended to assure me of the fact that the interest which God takes in me He has always taken in me; to recognize in His character, His love, His eternal purpose the ground of my confidence and the argument for everlasting gratitude.

Later he writes, quoting the Westminster Confession of Faith: (May 25, '72, p. 99f)

> From these extracts the reader can see that we have rightly stated the doctrine of election as held in Calvinistic churches. Some are saved because they were eternally elected; the rest perish for ever because they were not elected, because there is no salvation for them and never was any. . . .
>
> That there is a doctrine of election in the Bible we have freely admitted. We have taken up the passages chiefly relied upon by Calvinists, and have shown that their object is not to close but to open a door; to assure the Gentile converts that the Gospel was always designed for them. . . .
>
> If the sinner is to be drawn to the cross by the exhibition of divine love, and if he cannot possibly know himself to be elect until he has believed, will the doctrine that God has from eternity foreordained the great body of mankind to condemnation, help him to understand that mighty love by which alone the enmity of his heart can be overcome? Will it not naturally tend greatly to enhance the difficulty in the way of his being drawn? If you say that he is to be drawn by a sovereign power, irresistible, that alters the matter; but then this solution creates a thousand difficulties where it removes one. It makes almost all the invitations and entreaties of the Gospel meaningless. As ambassadors of God we beseech you, be ye reconciled to God; but if you are elect you are certain to be, and if not elect you are certain not to be. Love proves a failure, and sovereign power comes in to do the thing.

He believes in full grace and no reprobation. It is man's choice which determines. Human responsibility is real. All men can believe. There must be human cooperation in establishing the Kingdom of God. He holds both to God's sovereignty and to man's freedom. Wesleyanism is true (Dec. 17, 1887, p. 806). He likes the warmth of Methodist fellowship meetings though he disapproves of Methodist boasting. He approves Dr. R. W. Dale's neo-Calvinism (Nov. 17, 1883, p. 723). God's will is to be done, not borne. He is both Calvinist and Arminian (June 5, 1880, p. 158). He combines the two in the opening note of the paper for 1883 (Jan. 6, 1883, p. 1). "Theophila," probably his sister, whose letters he quoted, finds them both in the Bible (Aug. 28, 1887, p. 338). "God's sovereignty, man's free will . . . these two truths in the Scripture run side by side. It may be difficult to reconcile them logically but there they are, and our conscience bows to both. This determination to analyze, to separate what God has joined, has led to the greater part of the errors of the church."

And in the same issue Bowen writes on "Free Will" (p. 339):

> Without free will there could have been no loving service of God or man, no moral worth. There would indeed have been no sin, but very much for the reason that the dead cannot commit sin. God is love: His glory and His happiness are therein; and it is not strange that He desired to have loving subjects capable of loving Him and serving Him in filial affection, and capable of interpreting His love to one another, rather than have millions of intelligent machines compelled to carry out His will. The commandments are all addressed to voluntary beings; the promises furnish motives that only free agents can appreciate; the penalties are designed to influence such only. God does not create the character of men but allows every man to take part in the formation of his own character, while carefully showing him the tendencies and results of all his moral acts. The object of God's government of this world is to show men the evil of choosing what God has not chosen for them, and to provide a system of redemption for those who make this discovery and wish henceforth to be wedded to God's will.

In truth, he holds neither Calvinism nor Arminianism but simple Christianity: "Many people have the idea that a broad gulf separates Calvinism and Methodism. . . . His (D. L. Moody's) teachings are not distinctively Calvinistic or Methodist but simply Scriptural" (Dec. 6, 1879).

His spirit and thought are inclusive, not separatist. He advocates Christian unity (Mar 1, 1879, p. 4): "Our charter of the future (or rather of what Christ would have the present to be) is found in the closing words of Christ's great prayer in behalf of His people, that they may be one in the Father and in Himself as He was one with the Father, seeking their glory in this unity, and not in denominational superiority." He defends Moody's sponsorship of Drummond. He is not interested in denominationalisms. And yet he recognizes their validity and usefulness. Real Christian union is not necessarily doctrinal. He desires the cosmopolitan school of Christ (March 13, 1880): "Other teachers seek to enlighten a particular class, a limited portion at the most, a nation or an age, but here is one who offers to be the teacher of all generations of mankind, and promises to be with His pupils to the ends of the earth."

He was always interested in prophecy and at times allowed himself to indulge in what later he regarded as vagaries. As years went on he seems to have become increasingly careful and restrained in the matter. His interpretations from the beginning indeed were fundamentally ethical and spiritual, but there were queer notions. He wrote much about the symbolism of the Book of Revelation, but neither as a Futurist nor as a Literalist. He thought the world was growing both better and worse. He dealt with sanity and good sense with all predictions of the world's end and with the truth of Christ's Second Coming. The Second Coming, he thought, would not accord with our presuppositions and schedules (Jan. 7, 1879):

> We have abundantly read the writings of those who advocate and of those who reject the premillennial theory and if we allow that the 1,000 years of Ch. 20 (Rev.) are to be understood literally, we cannot deny that there is much that is plausible in what is advanced by the premillenarians. We believe that there is important truth on both sides and that the principal difficulty in the way of seeing alike disappears when we understand the 1,000 years to indicate a really brief period. We are told in 2 Peter 3 that a thousand years are with the Lord as one day and one day as a thousand years. It is a mistake to suppose that all the prophecies of the Apocalypse are consecutively fulfilled. The prophet follows one line of thought down through the history of the church till he reaches its full development, and then goes back and follows out another line of thought, another aspect of truth.

He disbelieved in any physical rapture in the air (Oct. 15, 1877). He regarded the Millennium as a figurative period and the Papacy as Anti-Christ and the Man of Sin. The Resurrection of Christ he deemed not a stone only but the Keystone in the arch of history. He was not interested in the return of the Jews to Palestine (Dec. 22, 1883, p.802):

> We do not see at the present time any indication of the speedy return of the Jews to Palestine, and we do not believe that they would be any better off in that misgoverned country than they now are. So long as they are not in Christ, it matters little where they are. In Him, all things would become new, and freedom to serve Him would give them a holy land anywhere.

From the beginning of his Christian life two of his greatest interests were miracles and prayer, and he treats of these constantly in his articles. Prayer is a reasonable reality. It is not to be measured by quantity. If we pray for others we must do our part toward answering our prayers. We are to expect answers. Even what we call "unanswered" prayer is efficacious. He writes with great good sense about praying for power instead of bringing forth the fruit of the Spirit. And he held that there was no warrant for praying for the outpouring of the Holy Spirit. In his own life, prayer was as natural as breathing.

Some of his most interesting articles set forth his original and accurate views of conscience. Nowadays many people regard conscience as infallible and authoritative. Whereas with many of these very people conscience is nothing but the faculty by which they persuade themselves that whatever they want to do is right. St. Paul admits that he did many wrong things conscientiously. And our Lord forewarned His disciples that those who killed them would do so conscientiously, thinking that they were serving God by committing murder. There have always been and there are many today who fall under Izaak Walton's description of certain folk who mistook their desires for their conscience and complained of being persecuted because they were not allowed to persecute others. Bowen's mind was as clear as day on this matter. Sincerity in his view was no sufficient certificate of rectitude. In the paper of March 3, 1883, he writes:

> But what is sincerity? It is akin to candor and is without partiality, and welcomes light. A man has strong convictions for the reason that he does not test them and shrinks from everything that would show them to be wrong. It is in this way that superstition retains its hold of men from generation to generation. A belief in ghosts is handed down from father to son, and retains its hold just so long as men refuse to let the light in upon it, just so long as they refuse to test it. The great progress in civilization, in modern times, is due to the adoption of another spirit altogether, the willingness to test everything. There are men today who speak apologetically of heathen nations because of their supposed sincerity, who owe all their own intellectual enlargement and illumination to the fact that they dismissed from their minds this pseudo-sincerity and determined to hold nothing for which they could not find good reasons. A man's devotion to his own convictions is in the inverse ratio to his love of truth. The Pharisees thought they were doing God service when they put the apostles to death. How came they to think so? Simply by shutting the door of their mind against light, and by making an idol of their own opinion and their own will. Let us hear no more of this pretended sincerity; let us at least call it by its own name, obstinacy, self-will. The Scriptures call the Jews a stiff-necked people because of their devotion to their own will, their unwillingness to submit their notions to the test of truth.

Again and again he recurs to these ideas (March 21, 1868, March 23, 1872, Apr. 19, 1879, July 9, 1881). On Aug. 23, 1879 he writes on "Errors Regarding Conscience":

> It is not really the conscience that determines what is right or what is wrong.... We often hear it said that it is wrong for a man not to obey his conscience. But what is it that conscience demands? It demands that we should do what is right but it does not tell us what is right; for

that information we depend on our judgment and understanding and especially on our faith towards God. . . . It is the misguided consciences of men that constitute the greatest barrier to the progress of Christianity.

In his diary of Sept. 25, 1848, he writes: "I must have nothing to do with conscience as a master. Christ must be my only Master. It is a grievous sin against Christ when I go about anything merely because conscience dictates. I must be scrupulous to guard against this." The Bible is a far better guide than conscience, in Bowen's view. To him it was God's unquestionable word, the final court, "the infallible rule of faith and practice." Its evidence was internal both to itself and to ourselves. Our views both of the Bible and of Church history, he taught, were dependent on ourselves (Apr. 23, 1887). Our study of the Bible and our use of it should depend not so much on the quotation of verses as on the discernment of principles (Jan. 22, 1887). He speaks of "the necessity of such graduated revelations as we find in the Old Testament" (Aug. 18, 1883). As to whether inspiration involves inerrancy, his views appear to have varied. On April 28, 1883 he wrote:

> There is world-wide distinction between the proposition "the Bible is the Word of God" and "the Word of God is in the Bible." If the latter only is the expression of the truth then it is for every man to make a Bible for himself. The Sadducee, the Socinian, the Ritualist, the Brahmist, will each for himself determine what things in the Bible are of God and what are not. We deny that there can be any real revelation upon this principle. On the supposition that God really wished to give men a revelation, we should have thought it of the highest importance that it should be unmixed. What if the body of English law were to be treated simply as containing and not as constituting the legislation of the country? What author is there who would be willing to have his works published with such a proviso?
>
> His ideas are in the book, but the book does not consist of his ideas. Imagine a preface to our Bible in which the divine Author would say: "Dear people, I have done my best to give you a revelation of my will and character, and am sorry that the wretched human writers have insisted upon introducing their own ideas. Those who are not well acquainted with me (and who is, among men?) will have a good deal of difficulty in distinguishing what I have given from that which these audacious writers have written out of their own hearts. I would have been glad to employ amanuenses upon whom I could safely rely, but I have not succeeded in finding any such. So you must just do the best you can to find out what is true in the Bible and what is not." Thank God, this is not the sort of revelation that we have. God knows how to fill men with His

own very Spirit, and cause them to say just what He would have them to. Yes, even against their will, as in the case of Balaam. Jesus says, "The Scriptures cannot be broken, and not a jot or tittle can fail."

A great deal of Scripture was given specially for the advantage of those to whom it was first addressed, and aimed to produce temporary effects, and must be looked at with reference to the times when it was uttered, the people for whom it was given, and the like. The kind of instruction needed by the Israelites just emerging from Egypt, must not be ascertained by the consideration of what is demanded in this century. The records are none the less valuable to us because they enable us to see the process by which God for so many thousand years has been engaged in uplifting man. The principle that the Word of God is contained in the Bible and may be there sought for, more or less successfully, throws a vagueness and uncertainty over the whole of Scripture. What makes a strong and effective Christian is the thoroughness of his conviction that the Word of God is everywhere present in the Bible, and that he can trust his soul to any promises that he finds there adapted to his position. Otherwise, a man would be like one that beateth the air. The enemy would laugh him to scorn.

Earlier on Aug. 9, 1879, he wrote: "The original writers and subsequent copyists of the sacred text are not deprived of their freedom or of their fallibility. . . . Biblical criticism is the last thing they fear; they demand, however, that it should be thorough and impartial." And on June 14, 1879, he writes, "The sacred writers were so far guided and the presentation of the text was so far secured, that no errors were allowed to occur except such as were insignificant or such as could easily be corrected from the Bible itself. . . . They who insist upon these inaccuracies as evidence that the Bible is uninspired and unreliable may be compared to a man who, standing before some noble tree whose branches extend a hospitable shade and are at the same time laden with excellent fruit, fancy they demonstrate that it is not the work of the Creator, because the stem does not spring from the ground with the straightness or smoothness of a column, because there appears in the trunk a hole into which you can insert your fist and there bulges out a huge knot. Such a man would only show by such criticisms that he had very peculiar ideas as to what should be the characteristics of a work of God."

But he writes on July 30, 1881, in connection with the Robertson Smith case in Scotland:

> Nobody claims inspiration for anything but the original texts of the Bible. . . . The divine authority is constantly claimed for the Word, for what was spoken or written. In fact we could not have a reliable

revelation upon any other scheme. Imagine that the code of law to which a nation is subject were to be dealt with on the understanding that the authority did not reside in the words themselves? The letter of the law is accepted as the truest statement of what was in the mind of the lawgiver.

But if only the original texts were inspired what becomes of our present Bible? The Westminster Confession doctrine differs from Bowen. It holds our own Bible to be inspired as well as the original. He identifies Luke and Silas and thinks that Paul erred in the matter of his vow. He holds the Bible to be the only standard, not the Confession of Faith. But the supreme relationship is that of Christ and the Bible (Sept. 24. 1887, p. 614).

His interest in theology was to the end of life. Christ had come that men might have life. Salvation was from sin and death to righteousness and life. His constant concern was for "sanctification" and he was ever discussing its New Testament meaning and what the privilege of the Gospel is in the matter of the preservation of the believer from sin. The Christian was called to live in Christ, and to live a life of Christ. He was to be a witness by deed as well as by word. He anticipated the ideas and the very phrases of "Keswick" and of the "Oxford Groups." (Aug. 7, 1880, Aug. 28, 1880, Jan. 27, 1883, Feb. 8, 1883; Oct. 1, 1881 as to "guidance"; Oct. 22, 1881; Nov. 5, 1881, as to religion and health). Consecration he held to be essential to power. We are to do what we ask God for, and yet it is God Who does all. As to "spiritual victory" and "all for God" and many phrases easily misused, Bowen's sound sense is unfailing (May 11, 1872; Feb. 26, 1887). He appeals for more apostolic singularity of life and in his description of "The Salt of the Earth" all unconsciously reveals his own personal religious life and character (Jan. 15, 1887). It was no monastic withdrawal of the recluse that men saw in him but love walking daily the streets of Bombay and revealing Christ Who went about doing good. The one missionary sine qua non, he held, is love (Aug. 13, 1887). He wrote once on "What is the religion that man needs," but his life was a better statement even than his words. He deprecated "wishing without willing" and he acted as he taught. He set convenience and public opinion over against Christ (Apr. 24, 1880), (May 1, 1880) and made the choice which he urged upon others.

Of necessity Bowen wrote constantly of missionary principles and policies and practices and of the basis of missions. This basis he found in the nature and fruitage of the Gospel, the uniqueness of Christ, the universal need of salvation, the love of God, the sole atonement through Christ and the loving purpose of God in His Kingdom. It is interesting to note his sympathetic consideration of the question of a future probation for those who have not heard the Gospel in this life as that question emerged in the "Andover Controversy" in 1880-86. His first comments on "the larger hope" were very cautious but his early and his final statements were alike positive. No one will be condemned for not believing what he has never heard (Oct. 19, 1872). Men who have not heard the Gospel will be judged by their attitude toward the light they have (Oct. 1, 1881). But there will not be any future probation:

> *March 24, 1883.* Probation means testing. God is testing men with regard to their willingness to be saved and guided by Him. Are men not well tested in this world? Is it easy to conceive of any better adapted in that respect? They who undergo a university examination and fail, may complain that the examination has been too severe. The more severe it is the better it is as a means of ascertaining their scholastic attainments. They may complain that the standard was too high; they may think that Government has too high a standard of proficiency, and might well be satisfied with less. But Government knows what it wants. And the Almighty knows what He wants. It is for Him to prescribe the standard of citizenship in the kingdom of Heaven. There were once some very exalted beings that kept not their first estate. God has accordingly made this world as a preliminary arena for ascertaining the character of those who are candidates for the heavenly kingdom, and it is impossible for anyone to prove that it is not well suited to the purpose.
>
> It must be borne in mind that the object of probation is to find out the weak places. A Bacon might be well pleased to be placed in circumstances where his magnificent qualities should be demonstrated, and his moral weakness remain unbetrayed. That would not be a probation at all. If there is the slightest reason to fear that one link of a long chain on which the destinies of some costly argosy are to be dependent, is weak, the test must be applied to that link. It will amount to nothing to test all the other links and spare that. God wants to have an army in Heaven upon every member of which He can confidently rely in the most momentous crisis, and whom He may unhesitatingly commission to carry out any work; persons redeemed from all iniquity and confirmed in all goodness. How admirably then is this world fitted for such probation as will secure this result. We are daily and hourly coming into relations and into scenes that are fitted to discover our weaknesses. If there is the slightest vestige of impatience, the least remainder of cupidity, or an iota of selfishness it will surely be exposed.
>
> While we perhaps are fretting because we cannot find a sphere grand enough for the exhibition of our vaunted perfections, the Judge of all takes note of our continual failure with regard to matters overlooked by us. We are photographing ourselves every day in the scenes of every day. The true judgment is here and now; the final judgment will simply

submit to the eyes of all the things previously determined concerning us. Nations as well as individuals are being thoroughly tested. The Gospel is conveyed to a nation, set forth in their own language; the perfections of the true God are therein exhibited; their sins are faithfully declared to them; and salvation is offered to them as a thing realizable here and to be consummated hereafter. If they are at all willing to give up falsehood and sin, if they are even willing to examine sincerely as to what is true, what false, what is sin, what is redemption, they will not reject the Gospel. But they do reject it; they prefer to it the grossest forms of idolatry, and the most debasing servitude of sin. That is, those of them who have the opportunity of knowing it, do this, and they may be considered the representatives of the nation, and it becomes demonstrated that the nation desires not the knowledge of the true God, desires not the salvation of the Gospel.

We can conceive of a world where things will be made favorable to the sinner, simply because the probation will not be so perfect. But who will say that this is what is wanted? On the same principle we should ask for a police more lenient to criminals. The idea of another probation will tend to make sinners even more careless than they are, and the present life will come to be regarded simply as a time for self-indulgence and entertainment. There is no book in the world more directly fatal to the supposition of a future probation than the Bible. Now is the day of salvation, now is the accepted time.

The important question for us is not the method of God's dealing with the ignorant but His judgment on us who know and do not. He did not at one time regard a belief in a future probation as a disqualification for missionary service, though, he held, there was no Scripture warrant for it.

In addition to the series of devotional articles republished in his three books, Bowen published scores of other series which might well have been reissued, in addition to long series of comments on the International Sunday School lessons and to "Notes from an Interleaved Bible." Some of these series were: "Fruits of the Spirit," "What is Truth?" "Reason in Faith," "Thoughts on Revelation," "The Coming Kingdom," "Homilies for the Times," "The Kingdom of Heaven," "Conformity to the World," "Is Christianity of God?" "Potent Words," "Keep Yourselves from Idols" (in which some of the idols were "intellect," "charity," "righteousness," "children"), "Visions of God," "Anti-Christ," "Christian Perfection," "Occasional Thoughts," "Prophetic Subjects," "The Hebrew Bible," "The Resurrection of Christ," "Behold, the Man, an Invitation to the Truth-Seekers of All Nations," "The Millennium," "Titles of Christians," "Apocalyptic Sketches," "Friendly Words to Educated Natives," "Whatsoever Things Are True," etc.

Bowen dealt constantly in the *Guardian* with political and social issues. He watched the whole moving life of the world, which he surveyed in his weekly news summaries and in his quotations from the papers and magazines of India, America, Great Britain and the Continent. He advocated disarmament and peace. He opposed Bradlaugh's exclusion from Parliament but also any special legislation on his behalf. He criticized the proceedings of the Thirty-Ninth American Congress, especially in its policy toward the Southern States. He had clear views on taxation. And he argued for a protective tariff against the position of John Bright. He believed in and defended capital punishment. He supported the conception of Scriptural communism but regarded the theory of secularistic economic communism as fallacious. He saw what was and what was not the value and function of laws in relation to the improvement of men and conditions. He commented on American politics with great shrewdness and good sense. He never returned to the United States but he never lost his patriotism, and he spoke out in strong defense of the American Constitution.

In the main, of course, his social and political articles deal with India and with British rule in India. He analyzed the causes of the Indian Mutiny and showed the folly of the accusation that it was due to missionary influence or to the Christian activity and interest of any British officials. He approved of British conquest of Afghanistan but set forth the folly of great war expenditures when multitudes were dying of famine. But he is equally concerned over "Famines and the Banyans." He deals fearlessly with great evils—the opium traffic, lotteries, child marriage, taxation, the land system, liquor licenses, prostitution and especially the provision of brothels for soldiers. He opposed government subsidy of idolatry and its tolerance of temple immorality. He disapproved of some of the methods of the Salvation Army but he disapproved far more and with caustic comment of some of the ways of British society and of Sir Lepel Griffin and his attitude toward the Salvationists.

He dealt with pauperism in Bombay, its causes and remedy. Again and again he returns to the attack upon caste as irrational, uneconomic and unsocial. He is strenuous in his defense of India's economic rights and of a true Indian Nationalism. Like many missionaries and British administrators he was opposed to the government type of education. In this he was seventy years in advance of Sir George Sanderson. Often he was called into counsel by the Government and his advice sought on questions of public policy. He was a member of Sir Bartle Frere's Commission on the liquor traffic and local option but withdrew, in disagreement with the dilatory course of the Commission, and presented his own separate report, of which he writes in the *Guardian* of Sep. 1. 1883:

> We referred last week to a minute or memorandum forwarded by the writer to Sir Bartle Frere when he was Governor of Bombay, regarding

the modifications desirable in the Abkari Act. The writer confined himself to recommendations which there was some reasonable hope that the Government might act upon; specially pointing out that to bring about a gradual diminution of the consumption of intoxicants, it was necessary that there should be a gradually rising scale of duty, tending to enhance the cost to the consumer, care being taken to guard against illicit production. The scale of enhancement should be so graduated that the actual amount of revenue should not be increased, and the Government should be prepared even to see the revenue decrease from year to year.

In 1866 he had high praise for Sir Bartle Frere, but in 1879 he condemned him severely for what Bowen regarded as the folly of his policy in dealing with Cetewayo and the Zulus in South Africa. It was interesting to find in a man who lived so wholly and habitually in another world such a competent student and acute critic as Bowen was of the world that now is and all its affairs. He comments with shrewd foresight on the development of labor organization in the Knights of Labor. He thinks that suicide is too easily blamed on insanity. His sense of personal moral responsibility was too strong for easy views. He writes a stinging editorial on "Orissa and Epsom," contrasting the famine destitution of Orissa with Epsom's gambling extravagance. He deals wisely and sympathetically with the beginnings of Indian nationalism and sets up over all narrow and separatist nationalisms the larger Christian conception of international interdependence (Dec. 3 and 10, 1881).

The paper contained frequent reviews of books. Sometimes these reviews were the leading editorials but always they bore the clear impress of Bowen's thought. Never were they perfunctory or superficial. Sometimes they were caustic, as in the case of Browning's *The Ring and the Book,* and always in the case of books defending Romanism and Ritualism. Often they were unexpectedly tolerant and sympathetic as with Drummond's *Natural Law in the Spiritual World.* A very partial list of his reviews must suffice to show the width of his reading: Spence Hardy, *The Legends and Theories of Buddhists*; De Pressense, *The Religions Before Christ*; Seeley, *Ecce Homo*; Caird, *The Philosophy of Religion;* Ram Chundra Bose, *Hinduism and the Hindu People*; *Memorials of Frances Ridley Havergal*; Bryan, *The Retention of Candahar*; *Life and Letters of James Hinton*; *Memorials of Peter Thomson*; Hamley, *Voltaire*; Joseph Parker, *Ingersoll Answered*; Fyfe, *The Atonement*; *Log Cabin to White House*; Conran, *Memoir of Col. Wheeler*; Kirk, *The Age of Man*; *Memorials of James Henderson*; Smith, *Life of Duff*; *Correspondence of Carlyle and Emerson*; Mahan, *Introduction to the Critical History of Philosophy*; Conway, *Emerson at Home and Abroad*; Robson, *The Bible: Its Revelation, Inspiration and Evidence*; Meurin, *The Basis of Christian Fellowship;* *Memorials of the*

Rev. John Pouree; *The Life and Correspondence of Mr. Thomas Slingsby Duncombe, M. P.* (The "Dear Tommy, do come and make us gay" with his poor, sad story); Kalisch, *Historical and Critical Commentary on the Old Testament*; Brown, *The Divine Glory of Christ*; Macpherson, *The Resurrection of Jesus Christ*; Pearse, *Life and Labors of the Rev. E. E. Boardman*; Major Seton Churchill, *Forbidden Fruit for Young Men*; Griffin, *Memories of the Past*; Murray Mitchell, *Christianity and Ancient Paganism*; Clark, *The Principles and Teaching of the Arya Samaj*. And hundreds more. Outside of the Gospel he thinks there is no better book about Christ than Horace Bushnell's *The Character of Jesus Forbidding His Possible Classification With Men.* He closes a review of Hastie's *Hindu Idolatry and English Enlightenment* in the issue of Jan. 27, 1883 with these words:

> We would like this better if it did not insist so much on the contrast between Hinduism and Western enlightenment. We have a very poor opinion of humanity in general, and think that Christians have no reason to use language that may to others savor of boasting. Let us remember the rock from which we were hewn, our Druidic fathers, and address our Hindu friends as fellow-sinners, asking them to accept a salvation that had its origin in Asia, and has been very imperfectly embraced in Europe.

The paper is the self-revelation of the editor. It revealed his optimism, his distrust of the very introspection of which his early journals were so full, his constant concern for the poor and his ceaseless struggle to abate and relieve and remove the causes of poverty. "Every man," he wrote, "is bound to do for the amelioration of this world all that he, plus God, could do." He shows always his clear, sure moral sense. He was a lover of persons and his loyalty to friends like Major Oldham and Bishop Thoborn is constantly appearing. He is the constant advocate of simplicity of life and of closeness to the people but he never wore native dress or sought to imitate Indian modes of life. He set forth his views with unflinching force but he deprecated the pugnacity of some fellow missionaries. He seems never to have repeated his early attempt at a miracle but to the very end he deplored the want of miraculous attestation of the Gospel (Sept. 3, 1887, p. 563).

But the supreme revelation of the paper was Bowen's single-minded, single-hearted devotion to Christ. Christ was all in all. "Christ will make you," he would say (Mar. 22, 1879). "Oh, that all who name the Name of Christ would reach the experience embodied in these words: For to me to live is Christ. This is my conception of life: not a mere breathing, sentient existence in the atmosphere of this world, but having Christ as an atmosphere in Whom we breathe and through Whom we see all things."

"We are free," he wrote, "to say that the words of 1 Cor. 2:9-10 have been continuously fulfilled in our experience and always through the truth" (May 17, 1879). If anyone were to think of him as a fanatic or devotee it would suffice to direct him to the sanity of Bowen's mind as to spiritual guidance (Apr. 5, 1879, p. 62), as to "perfectionism" (Apr. 12, 1879, p. 74; May 31, 1879, p. 159), as to the limits of prayer (Apr. 5, 1879, p. 65). He had the good sense of knowing the boundaries of his knowledge (Dec. 13, 1879, p. 497).

Throughout Bowen's entire editorship, the *Guardian* is full of the evidence of his culture, the wide range of his knowledge and interest and of his intellectual power. He has a thorough knowledge of Greek, seen in his defense of Mark 16:9-20 (Sept. 3, 1887). He compares with careful knowledge the Greek and Indian types of architecture. He discusses building domes on square or circular drums. He anticipated Pasteur in his "heterogeny." He treats of the future of comic journalism and of the effect on war of the invention of new and deadlier guns. He criticizes the Athenaeum's critique of Browning's *The Ring and the Book.* He blasts Bryon and his poetry. He holds the language of Jesus to have been Aramaic. He takes note of the introduction of rubber-tired engines and of the use of oil to produce steam. He has interesting notions about gravitation and about the rotation of crops. He deals with the problems of cotton, agriculture and industry in the states recently in the Southern Confederacy in America. He opposes child labor in the mills.

He is deeply and intelligently interested in Indian art. He welcomes the progress of communications in India, especially the shortening of the mail time between Calcutta and Bombay from nine to four days in 1868. Astronomy was always a great interest to him and he writes of eclipses, comets, and the qualities of sun and moonlight. He loves to dwell on the perfection of Christ's character and the coordination of geniality and outspokenness. He does not believe in asceticism and takes a very liberal view as to Sunday travel and as to amusements and relaxations allowable in the Y.M.C.A. in Bombay. He has remarkable knowledge of the Bible manuscripts and he shows a discriminating critical judgment in his comments on the Revised Version when it appeared in 1885.

In *Zion's Herald*, Boston, Feb. 22, 1882, the Rev. C. P. Hard writes:

> It seems wonderful that thirty years of editorial labor for the *Bombay Guardian* have not caused weariness to the pen of Rev. George Bowen, the President of the South India Conference of the Methodist Episcopal Church at its recent session in Bangalore. In hot months or monsoon the vigor of the editorials never decline. As some look into the papers for the weekly market prices, so do many missionary workers of each denomination, and many laymen watch for the weekly editorials, the wise and kind criticisms of the *Guardian*, for a conscientious standard

of judgment concerning passing events or permanent institutions and customs.

In a late number, in his notes on the International Sunday School lessons, we see a definition of idolatry which is very different from the imagination of many among us that it is simply a mistake in the simplicity of an untutored mind: "Idolatry is man's device to shield himself from contact with the living God. The religious instinct in man does not allow him to shake off all reference to the authority of God; hence the resort to idolatry, which allows men to appear to themselves religious at the same time that it enables them to follow their own inclinations. The frightful representations of God found among the heathen do not prove their ignorance of God, but their unwillingness to have to do with the living and true God."

In the din of the discussion as to Revision some may like to hear what an accomplished scholar in India has to say about the new Greek text of the New Testament. Mr. Bowen states his view that "in very much that is being written with regard to the Revised Version of the New Testament, the most important point is overlooked, viz., How far is the Greek text, of which it professed to be a version, the genuine text of the sacred writers? The translation may be more or less felicitous, and is likely on the whole to convey the meaning of the original; but if a mistake has been made in determining what Greek text to follow, the book will be to that extent misleading, withholding from us what God gave, or giving what was not from Him. When the Sinaitic Codex was published by Tischendorf, we ventured to express the opinion that it was not safe to allow the testimony of the great body of manuscripts to be set aside by that of two or three uncial manuscripts, supposed to be of higher antiquity, but still separated by several centuries from the time of the Apostles. It seems to us a long time since the inventing of printing, but the interval is not much greater than that which elapsed between the writing of the Gospels and the age in which these ancient codices are supposed to have been written.

"Since the appearance of the New Revision, we have reiterated these cautions, and we are glad to see that persons much more competent than ourselves are writing in a similar strain. The theory of Messrs. Westcott and Hort leads them to reject the last twelve verses of Mark. But every reader who will consider the matter, must perceive that it is in the highest degree improbable that Mark would terminate his Gospel with such a verse as this: "And they went out and fled from the tomb; for trembling and astonishment had come upon them; and they said nothing to anyone, for they were afraid." The passage is found in the Peshito, and in all the old versions. Irenaeus, who lived two centuries before the date of the oldest of the codices, refers to the 19th verse of the 16th chapter of Mark, as being at the close of Mark's Gospel in his day. His testimony is really the testimony of the church of the second century to that effect. It is constantly found in the most ancient lectionaries. This evidence is set aside because the MSS. of the lectionaries are comparatively modern. The question is, When were these lectionaries, or selections of passages for Sunday reading in the churches, adopted? The same ones seem to be in universal use, and their institution must have been of high antiquity. The fact is, that a prejudice was entertained against the concluding portion of Mark's Gospel because it was supposed not to be in harmony with the other accounts of our Lord's resurrection. Mark writes very briefly and his narrative does not aim to be complete. There are lacunae, or gaps, to be filled up from the other evangelists. Not noticing this, some supposed that he was stating things as consecutive which were not really so."

He deals carefully with the case of Henry Ward Beecher and with thoroughy competent criticism of Macaulay on Mediaeval Romanism. He was a terribly dangerous controversialist, as for example, in his treatment of the theory that Abraham was a mythical character (*Guardian,* May 2, 1869, p. 67, 74) and his discussion of "the Ape-produced Man" (Jan. 11, 1879). He has a good sense of humor, too, both in his editorial notes and comments and in his news selections from Western papers. One can see him chuckling over the story which he prints in the *Guardian* of Jan. 21, 1888, regarding John L. Sullivan's account of the interview with Edward VII, then Prince of Wales, sought by the Prince and not by John L. "He is a nice, sensible fellow," Sullivan reported, "with splendid manners, and taking into consideration all he has had to fight against in the way of family, a splendid, good, all-round man. He is the sort of man you like to meet anywhere, and at any time, and introduce your family to."

And on Nov. 27, 1869 he prints a stanza of a poem, sparing his readers the rest:

> Major General Sir Herbert Edwardes
>   Claims somewhat from my poor muse,
> And had I the gift of some now dead bards
>   The claim I dare not refuse;
> But as it is, I must try to do my best,
>   Nor shirk from the noble theme;
> The traits of his life, they warm my cold breast,
>   And give me a pure esteem.

His wide knowledge and his humor were in frequent evidence in his dealing with undecided or debatable issues or with issues on which he thought unsound contentions were advanced. He dealt with competent criticism with Colenso and his Old Testament views and his arithmetic, with Canon Taylor and his representations regarding Mohammedanism and Christian Missions, with Spencers's *Data of Ethics*, with adulations of the Renaissance in which he saw "truth sacrificed to sentimentality, Christ to the Virgin, the divine oracles to tradition" (August 4, 1883), with the *Pioneer's* contempt for Exeter Hall, with Darwin's theories, with the relations of religion and science, with matter and spirit, with the significance of sleep in the matter of the relations of the mind to the brain, with Tyndall, with the nature and power of motives. His general good sense appears in his opening editorial note on Jan. 2, 1869:

> Instead of asking, "What shall this coming year bring to me?" let us individually ask, "What shall I bring to it?" Instead of asking, "What changes are likely to take place in the world?" let a man enquire, "What changes may reasonably be looked for in me? What changes for the better can I accomplish, in myself and around me?"
>
> God has brought you to the threshold of a new year. It is a terra incognita to you. But He that has brought you here, knows what is beyond; and the best thing for you to do is to look up to Him, as the child that cannot see afar off looks up to its father's face. It is He that has brought you here; He has an object in it. He made the world and He made you; the world is His and you are His; you have no right to be or to do in this world of His, anything but what pleases Him. You have certain powers; how are you to use them? It is for Him to say. Have you instructions? Is His Word with you? Is it in your heart? Does it rule you? Surely it is in studying His instructions that we shall get the best insight into the future. We are as it were His operatives, sent forth into this field of His, this year 1869, to do His work; we are His messengers, sent forth with His missives to mankind. If we have the Word of God in our hands and in our hearts, then we have in an important sense the making of this coming year in our hands. As the stream that descends from some mountain in a broad, parched, barren plain, fertilizes it and makes it a region of verdure, a place for cattle to browse and for birds to sing, so they who have the Word of life in their hearts, vanquishing the evil of their nature and energizing them for the work which Christ has assigned them, are empowered to change the aspect of society, and make the moral wilderness blossom as the rose.
>
> But before we can be sent, we must be drawn. Have we been drawn to Christ? Has the attraction of the cross separated us from the world and made us one with Christ? "I have chosen you out of the world." "They are not of the world even as I am not of the world." No man is fitted to go into this year 1869 and enter into its privileges and its tasks,

unless he has first been separated from the world unto Christ, and then commissioned by Him to go forward and do His will. No truth is more clearly written in God's Word than this, and it is a truth that may well make many pause on the threshold.

The late Professor Bowman of Glasgow, whose return to Scotland was a great loss to Princeton University and whose death is a loss to the world of scholarship and especially of philosophy, once declared that we ought to be more preoccupied with God than with things, even wholly preoccupied with God and not at all with things. This was George Bowen's preoccupation. "No man," he wrote, "can possibly see anything aright until he sees in it the revelation of the mind of God" (Mar. 15, 1879). To him, as to Browning, the knowledge of God in Christ was the solution of all things. He held God to be the most knowable of beings. He anticipates Borchert's argument in *The Original Jesus* with regard to the personality of Jesus as unique and uninvented by the Evangelists, on the ground not that they could not have invented it but that if they had been bent on invention they would never have constructed this figure. It was Christ Who produced the New Testament, not the New Testament which produced Christ. Christ was more than Christianity.

The Incarnation was wholly reasonable. It was *mystery* to be sure but, as he writes, Mar. 1, 1879: "When, on the whole, the thing affirmed is quite as reasonable as any other alternative that I can conceive of, I consider that it is an abuse of language to call that thing a mystery.... People suppose that certain doctrines are mysterious because they have been generally spoken of in this way; which doctrines if tried by the test that we have proposed, would cease to be so spoken of: that is, they would be found less attended with difficulty than any alternative doctrines that might be proposed." And Christ's humanity and deity are equally real to him. The atonement is fundamental but all illustrations of it he regards as defective and inadequate. The "blood of Christ" is simply Christ. Regeneration and belief he thinks are simultaneous but our faith is essential to the Holy Spirit's work. If men dislike the atonement they do not have to accept it. They can enjoy the full consequence of their sins here and hereafter.

A whole volume on the non-Christian religions, especially the religions of India, and the relation of Christianity and of Christian missionaries to these religions could be compiled from Bowen's articles in the *Guardian*. He knew the Indian religions thoroughly, Hinduism and Buddhism in books and in their popular forms, Mohammedanism including the Koran, the faith of the Parsis with whom he had frequent discussions, the Reform Movements and importations like Madame Blavatsky's theosophy. He writes of the Brahmic salvation, the Hindu mythology, tree and serpent worship, the Vedic religion, the Vedanta and idolatry, Chaitanya, Tukaram, the pilgrimages and the cholera horrors especially of Hardwar, of the Brahmin priesthood. He deals uncompromisingly with the evils of caste and child marriage and the prohibition of widow-remarriage and the real idolatry of Hinduism, of Ganpati and the rest, and the intolerance of Hinduism which made conversion to Christianity a civil death. As against Max Muller he held that Hinduism was idolatry and that its idolatry was not mere symbolism but real and degrading. He maintained that we know nothing authentic and trustworthy of Buddha, and Mohammed he believed to be an impostor but (May 7, 1878) "his system had more of truth in it than the polytheism prevailing in Mecca in his day, and so this word Impostor does not cover all the facts in the case."

He had no zeal to save the honor of Hinduism by complementing it with Christianity, but no one followed more closely than Bowen the development of the Reform Movements in Hinduism especially of the Brahmo Somaj and the career of Keshub Chundra Sen. He traced all the good in this movement to the influence of Christianity and was never deceived as to its real character and the unlikelihood of any enduring effect, at least in the direction of the strengthening of the Christian church. The deep pervasive power of Christianity in modifying Hinduism he clearly discerned. But he did not believe in the view that the non-Christian religions were so essentially kindred to Christianity that the aim of missions should be to effect any religious merger or easy equalitarian truce. He long anticipated and rejected Mr. Gandhi's notion that every man should remain "in his own religion." In the *Guardian* of Mar. 27, 1869, he writes: "In various particulars the Parsi and the Hindu religions seem to conflict each other; so that if one be true, the other cannot be; unless we suppose that God abhors in one religion what He inculcates in another." And on Dec. 21, 1872:

> All over the world we find this disposition to receive as divine, the religion professed and practiced by one's parents. But is this an inviolable law? If it had been, no religion would ever have been propagated from one people to another, from one land to another. In fact no one would ever have attempted such a thing. An inviolable law speaks for itself, and the futility of attempting to go against it, is soon evident. Yet we find that religions have been propagated from land to land. Our contemporary says that Christianity is the religion of Europe. Well, it is so nominally. But how came it to be the religion of Europe? Was it always that? When the command to preach the Gospel among all nations was given by Christ to His disciples, Palestine was surrounded on every side by countries in which very opposite systems of religion prevailed. There is no greater contrariety between Christianity and Hinduism, than there was between Christianity and the religions of Greece, Rome, Egypt, Assyria, Persia, Carthage, Spain, Germany, Gaul, Scandinavia and Britain. In all these lands it was death to teach anything opposed to the existing religions,

as was abundantly made manifest when the preachers of the Gospel in all these countries were compelled to seal their faith with their blood. Christianity was planted in all these countries in the face of the mighty obstacles referred to by the *Hindu Reformer*, made its way from heart to heart by the force of conviction, and at length supplanted all mere hereditary religions existing in those countries. Evidently then, this is not an inviolable law, this supposed necessity of following the faith of our parents.

We ask in the second place, is it a divine law, an ordinance of God that man is under obligation to observe? Hindus profess to think so. They say that the greatest sin of all, is to leave one's ancestral religion. If they are right, we are brought to the conclusion that God gave divine wisdom to the first ancestors of a people, to be handed down from generation to generation, and that every one of the forty generations that may have passed away, has been thoroughly faithful to its trust. But the sacred books of the Hindus contain descriptions of the earth and of the heavenly bodies and of natural operations that are completely at variance with the facts of the case; and educated Hindus recognize the falsity of these descriptions. If God has decreed that all men are under a sacred obligation to follow the religion of their forefathers, then three things are demonstrated, viz., 1st, all religions are from God; 2nd, no religion can possibly propagate itself outside of the lines of descent; 3rd, no religion can possibly be altered in the course of transmission. But these three points are all disproved by manifest facts, patent to everybody.

He wholly rejected the modern view, also set forth by Mr. Gandhi, that all religions are essentially one. To Bowen, Jesus was not in the same category with Nanak or Krishna (Mar. 27, 1869, p. 26). The Bible was not one of many revelations (Mar. 14, 1868, p. 10). Christianity is not one of many religions. Religions are man's, but Christianity is God's (Jan. 18, 1887, p. 386). He thought Principal Miller showed too much deference to non-Christian faiths (Apr. 24, 1880, p. 4). But his own attitude was not harsh or unsympathetic.

In the issue of Jan. 8, 1881 (p. 526) he wrote: "Every true missionary must have a feeling of genuine love, not merely for the Brahmanists but for all the Hindus, but it would be a great mistake to think that love is expressed by ignoring or making light of whatever is contrary to the truth. The servant of the Lord is unfaithful to Christ and to those whom he addresses when he encourages them in the belief that Christ is simply one of the spiritual guides of men instead of being the Way, the Truth, the Life. These Oxford Missionaries say, 'We have not merely to learn. We *think* that we have also something to teach.' We should think so. Why else should they come out as missionaries?"

And he was full of love for India and the Indians and of praise for the fine qualities of Indian character. On Dec. 24, 1887 (p. 820) he said: "There is very much that is pleasing and attractive in the Native (he was accustomed to write the word with a capital) character, if we can speak of such a thing where there is such a variety of races, tribes and castes: and we would much rather hear them commended than hear them disparaged as they so often are by men who have enough faults of their own to answer for."

The *Bombay Guardian* was of course primarily a missionary paper. It was established to set forth the conception of Christianity held by the evangelical missions of Bombay, as against the aggressive anti-Protestant Romanism and European Ritualism of the time. It was the organ of the missionary community also for the discussion of missionary methods and problems. The correspondence columns were in constant use and Bowen used his editorial opportunity to set forth his own convictions. He argued for simplicity, directness, reality, courage, persistence and faith. He welcomed the Salvation Army but later severely criticized its methods and its results.

He believed in self-support both for missionaries and for native churches from the outset and would have retained Taylor's "locally supported missions." He did not harshly condemn those who followed a different course but never regretted his own course as to salary and mode of life. "Christians need to be conformed to the instruction of the Master, and when they are we shall see the tardy measure of our progress wonderfully accelerated" (Feb. 1, 1879). But he deprecated asceticism and, though very poor, he had no Manichean ideas of poverty or as to amusements. As to native self-support, he wrote (Jan. 4, 1879), "It is most desirable that native pastors should be supported by their own people. . . . The very worst thing we can do for the native church is to relieve it of those burdens that would naturally come upon it. The habit of dependence has been fostered to a lamentable extent."

Unpaid personal witness, such as Dr. Nevius advocated in China, Bowen regarded as the best method of evangelism and nationalization. He believed in the naturalization of the church and he deprecated its foreignization just as he himself retained his own natural dress and character and disapproved of missionaries appearing as fakirs. He did not want converts to be separated from their own homes and natural relationships and condemned the harshness and intolerance of caste which cast them out. He would have no caste in the church. He favored missionary celibacy although there was one time in Bombay when he would have married if family difficulties had not arisen.

He believed in direct evangelism and was all his life a vernacular preacher. He advocated and practiced street preaching (Apr. 21, 1866). He published "Apothegms on Preaching" (March 6, 1869) and "Hints to those who seek to set forth the Gospel in Gospel Hall, Picket Road," Apr. 21, 1883:

We do not think that we will do the people who assemble to hear us, any good by attacking their peculiar views, and endeavoring to carve our way to their hearts by argument. We cannot do this without allowing them to reply, and turning the place into an arena of controversy. But it is well, it is important to know what is in their minds, and shape our presentation of truth in such a way as to bear upon their preconceived ideas. When we make them acquainted with the demands of God, and with the character of God, we are really laying the axe at the root of those ideas. When we tell them that sin is to be estimated by the greatness, holiness and justice of the Lord of lords and King of kings, we are really showing them the erroneousness of many of their favorite notions.

Apr. 28, 1883:

When we speak of Bro. Taylor, the readers of the *Bombay Guardian* know to whom we refer. He used to say, and strongly to insist upon it, that when we preached to those whose religious ideas were quite different from ours, we should at the outset make mention of those things about which we and they were in accord. We should seek some common ground where we could shake hands with them, so to speak. For it is evident that they are our listeners only so long as they choose to be. In justice to them, it is needful so to proceed. Such a common ground and meeting-place was furnished to Paul in Athens by the altar "to the Unknown God" which he found there. Men who have been in the habit from childhood of connecting obligation with a particular class of tenets, naturally take alarm when they hear their convictions opposed, and conclude that the speaker is an enemy, trying to weaken the force of religious obligation.

Illustrations of the same principle appear in the ministry of Christ, Who often found Himself in the presence of those who believed that eternal life was to be obtained by keeping the commands of God. Without directly seeking to overthrow this idea He undertook to make them better acquainted with the law of God as demanding the entire affections and ruling the whole being.

The principal object of the Sermon on the Mount is to show that God's righteousness, the righteousness demanded by Him, is something immeasurably beyond the righteousness of the Pharisees. He takes up the laws of God one by one and shows that they refer ultimately to the state of the heart. It is a small thing comparatively that a man refrain from murder, adultery, perjury, and from assaulting others; the mental states that lead to these sins are sinful. The command, "Thou shalt not kill," really means, "Thou shalt love thy neighbor as thyself." Even the

Lord's Prayer in that discourse, is for the purpose of showing the vanity of imagining that your long and studied prayers make you acceptable to God. The Lord's Prayer does not take more than a minute to repeat and it contains a statement regarding the worshiper that is most important; he is a man who freely and cheerfully forgives the greatest injuries done to him by others. He is a man who, coming with his gift into the temple, knows that God will not accept it from him while he is on bad terms with some neighbor; so, leaving it there before the altar, he seeks out the man with whom he has had the disagreement and comes to terms with him; he then returns to offer the gift, unacceptable otherwise. The people whom our Lord was addressing believed in good works; so, instead of railing against good works as a ground of acceptance, Jesus simply proceeds to show what really are the good works required by God.

He defended Samuel Hebich for his outspoken conversation about Christ wherever he might be, after the fashion of Uncle Johnnie Vassar.

Though himself always an evangelist, he never opposed mission schools. And he supported the policy of Government grant-in-aid and the acceptance of such grants provided they did not hamper in any way the definite evangelizing character of the schools. He advocated required Bible teaching in mission schools and thought that the facts about the different religions should be taught in government schools. He believed that it was the business of school and hospital as well as of pastor and preacher to make known the Gospel by word as well as by deed and to seek to win patient and pupil to Christian discipleship. He disagreed with Duff's and Macaulay's policy of substituting English for the vernacular and he was critical of William Miller's missionary philosophy in giving schools precedence as a missionary method and of Miss Carpenter's unsuccessful effort to establish training schools for girl teachers, excluding the Bible.

He favored camp meetings and women speaking in church, holding that Paul was to be interpreted as sanctioning this. He thought Paul's missionary methods to be equally valid today. He was not in favor of mass movements, but that is not to say that he would disapprove of the "mass-movements" of today. Brahmin and outcaste alike should be converted individually and won to Christ out of a sense of personal sin and need of the Savior. There should be no hasty baptisms or baptism in advance of admission to communion. Polygamists might temporarily be baptized. There should be revivals. Men must be convinced. The Gospel should be preached for a verdict. The Holy Spirit and the natural laws of the human mind were both realities. With almost no visible fruitage from his own preaching he still preached through forty years in daily expectation of immediate results.

He had no misgiving as to the ultimate result. Alexander Duff's grand hopes had not been fulfilled but the final triumph was more certain than time. The ruins of Bujapur showed that there might be retrogression and decay. Apparent successes might fade away, but the promises of God would not fail. The Savior would see of the travail of His soul and be satisfied. Every knee would bow and every tongue confess that Jesus Christ is Lord to the glory of God the Father.

In 1870 Bowen published an article entitled, "The Problem in Missions." This was repeated in full in 1888, after his death, the editor who succeeded him evidently regarding it as a just expression of Bowen's basic conceptions. As such it should be preserved here:

> We believe that the tendency of matters, for a number of years past, has been to bring the feeling more and more home to the hearts of missionaries, that the existing system, if system it can be called, is paralyzing not only to the native churches but to the mission body itself; and in many quarters there has been a grappling with the evil and the introduction of measures calculated to diminish it. There are we believe one or two churches that support their own pastors; there are a number of others who have begun to contribute a portion of this support. But the very difficulty that is found in making even a distant approach to a rectification of the evil, only shows how formidable it is, and how deep-rooted is the idea that Missionary Societies exist and gather funds not merely for the support of missionaries and for the prosecution of their evangelistic work, but for the support of the churches planted by them. Suppose for a moment this latter idea to be correct, and it follows that missionaries, after their first success, must demit their proper functions, and become to a large extent financial agents of their Societies, enchained to the churches whose interests they are to look after and whose needs they are to supply; the sphere of the Missionary Society will become more limited from day to day; their income may annually increase, and yet the proportion available for foreign mission work rapidly diminish; so that it shall become necessary for new Societies to be formed for proper mission work.
>
> Serious as is this aspect of the evil, there is another even more to be deprecated. Missions are suicidal that gather converts only to teach them dependence. Everything depends upon the standard of piety in the Native churches. If these churches have no vitality of their own, if they know so little of union to Christ that they cannot stand alone without the aid of foreign Christians, there is really no testimony for Christ in

the land, the Gospel is deprived of its power to advance by the inability to refer to the witnesses whom it has regenerated. And if the Christians of this country are allowed from the outset to entertain the idea that it is not incompatible with their profession of faith in Christ to rely on Missionary Societies for all expenses connected with their churches, the education of their children, etc., it will be found exceeding difficult to disabuse them of their opinion afterwards. They will say, "If this thing is not according to the Gospel, now, why were we allowed to think that it was before?"

It is not, however, true that the work of the missionary terminates with the introduction of converts into the church, and that he is absolutely free to turn from these to the heathen. He must care for their growth in grace and in the knowledge of the Lord Jesus Christ. But this is a mighty work; who is sufficient for it? If he give all his time and strength to the work of raising up a body of noble witnesses for Christ, will he be giving too much? But what, then, becomes of the out-lying work, the evangelization of the masses? Well, the difficulty is not so utterly irreconcilable as it appears. In order to understand this matter we must come back to first principles. There is one great truth of primitive Christianity which if we leave out of our account, the missionary work is a mere jumble of contradictions and absurdities. "Tarry ye in Jerusalem until ye be endued with power from on high," said Christ, to His disciples, to His apostles. Everything that His personal ministry could give, had been given them; yet they were powerless and incompetent, and might not take a step until Christ's gift from on high, the Holy Spirit, had descended to energize them and made them meet for their work. Then, when they went in the Spirit, the Spirit bore witness to them and made their word effectual in the hearts of converts. Under the powerful teaching of the Spirit of God, the rapid advances were made by those who joined the people of Christ. So we find the apostles traveling about the world, gathering churches, not renouncing the care of them, laboring assiduously for them, and yet not hindered from pursuing their evangelistic work.

We believe that all our difficulties head up in this, and find their solution here. Given the Missionary Societies, ample funds, wise direction, providential openings, cultivated missionaries, men as well furnished as the apostles themselves were on the day when Christ ascended on high, we believe that still the measure of success will be little more than shall suffice to keep faith in missions from dying out in the church. We need a baptism of the Spirit; we need to depend on the Spirit, to honor the Spirit, to do all in the Spirit. As matters now are, how much glorification of men, even when the results are anything but imposing! What account is made of our plans, methods, arrangements, systems! What a trusting there is in the wisdom of the age, in its inventions and facilitations and marvelous appliances, its arts and its literature, in the ascendancy of Protestant powers, in education, etc., etc.!

Must we go back as little children, to the beginning, to the days before Pentecost? Will the Lord have us to learn that we know very little of the Spirit, and need to wait upon Him until endued with power from on high? It is difficult to see how we can learn this lesson; it comes so much more natural to us to try some new method, to patch and mend the existing mechanism, and hope, that by mere stress of time tares will turn to wheat. Nevertheless, if this be the thing we have to learn, the Lord will know how to reveal it unto us. To some all this may seem mere truism and a blinking of the practical difficulty. But if the Gospel itself may be allowed to exhibit its own laws of propagation in the Acts of the Apostles, it is hardly loyal to shut our eyes to the way in which the gates of the kingdom of Heaven were opened to Jews and Gentiles.

This is the dispensation of the Spirit; and it is only as we honor Him and are guided by Him, and only as our plans and processes are from Him, that we may expect to see the kingdom of God extended through our agency. If consciously or unconsciously, there is a deferring to the spirit of the age, a desire to justify ourselves and our work in the eyes of the world, a shrinking from reproach, a hankering for reputation, a disposition to compromise our high calling by conciliating the peculiar temper of the times, then we can hardly expect that there will be any signal manifestation of the Spirit's presence in the midst of us.

The grand desideratum in India is a body of consecrated native Christians; men and women that know Christ and have the witness in themselves, and have taken up their cross to follow Him, and in whom is unmistakably manifest the power of the Holy Spirit; evangelists because they are Christians; powerfully rebuking the covetousness and worldliness of their countrymen; manifesting so undeniably a spirit of disinterestedness, a readiness to forego the things that are generally coveted among men, that the heathen shall be driven to the conclusion that they have really found in Christ what abundantly compensates them for the loss of all else. In other words we want a body of martyrs.

The word martyr means witness; one who testifies to that which he professes; the truth being not merely on his lips but in his life. He professes to follow Christ; if death stands in the way he will encounter death; if a prison, servitude, scourging are in the way, he will meet these unflinchingly; if disgrace, rejection from his class, poverty, a low estate, discomfort, toil, whatever comes between him and Christ he will not allow it to turn him back, but will prove himself a martyr, a witness to the truth, in other words, a true Christian. The martyr spirit is the spirit of Christianity. There was an age when Christians coveted what they called the honors of martyrdom; there is reason to look with some suspicion upon the eagerness shown by many of them; there was an attraction in the conspicuousness of the suffering; the thought of suffering before the eyes of a multitude, and exhibiting one's superiority to pain, is one that appeals to the imagination of the natural mind, and in so far fails to verify to us the influence of the Spirit of God. But the true martyr spirit is that which quietly and humbly takes up the particular burden which providence has placed at our feet, unflinchingly encounters whatever comes between us and a full confession of Christ.

There is something of far greater urgency than that all our converts should be turned into accomplished preachers and that is, that they give unequivocal and undeniable evidence to their fellow-countrymen that they have not been influenced by any worldly object in going over to the ranks of Christ's followers. Many of them have given what we regard as excellent evidence of the purity of their motives; they have made sacrifices that we can appreciate; but what is evidence to us is not to those whom they have forsaken; as a matter of fact it is found exceedingly difficult to persuade them that the converts were not influenced by the desire for the favor and friendship of Europeans, increased salary, improved status, a better worldly prospect for themselves and family. When we search the Gospels, we fail not to find that Christ attaches the very highest importance to this kind of testimony, and carefully guarded His disciples against everything which would in any way obscure it. They were to commend themselves to every man's conscience in the sight of God, as the sons and daughters of the Lord God Almighty, having their affections set on things above, not minding earthly things, walking by faith and not by sight.

Now if we find reason to assent to this proposition that the grand need in Indian Missions is a body of native converts, evidencing their faith in Christ by lives of unmistakable consecration, we are immediately met by this question: Do they from whom native Christians have received their knowledge of the Gospel, present in this unchallengeable way the evidence of entire consecration? Do their lives incontrovertibly declare that they count all that men commonly covet loss that they may win Christ? The stream will not rise higher than its source; the disciple is not above his master; it is hardly in the nature of things that the faith of Hindu converts should be more manifest than that of their teachers; and if a more self-evidencing consecration is demanded in the former, it cannot reasonably be looked for until it has found an unerring exhibition in the lives of European missionaries.[9]

The European missionary believes that he has given good evidence of a self-denying spirit in coming to this country. He has made sacrifices from which he would have naturally shrunk. But, as we have frequently had occasion to point out, the sacrifices are not of a kind that demonstrate themselves to the convictions of the people of this country. Self is not visibly crucified. Appeals to native Christians, to consecrate themselves more heartily and take up their cross more manifestly, are often met and frustrated by the secret conviction on their part that the self-abnegation demanded is not exhibited by the missionary.

We conclude that what is wanted is a common blessing, to be sought in common by missionaries and native Christians, with penitential sorrow, humiliation, confession, fasting and persevering prayer. All must stand on the same level, and humble themselves beneath the mighty hand of God. And there must be a willingness that the Spirit of God Whose powerful descent we implore must work in us in the way that seems best to Him, setting aside our own predilections, tastes, habitudes, and making us at whatever cost, a peculiar people, witnesses for Christ, in the true sense of the word, a body of martyrs.

---

[9] In replying once in the *Guardian* to a letter from a "Skeptic," who pointed out the inconsistency of Christians as one of his difficulties, Bowen wrote: "Our correspondent has given a good deal of attention to the failings and inconsistencies of Christians. We cannot guarantee that he will be without the opportunity of making such observations; but his time might be better bestowed. A great many barnacles attach themselves to the bottom of a noble vessel that comes steaming into our harbor, but this does not prove that she has not a valuable cargo on board. We do not judge of an army by the sutlers and hangers on. The parable of the sower, and that of the wheat and tares show that many have to do with Christianity who are not in Christ."

Appendix to Chapter 17
Select Comments and Choice Sayings
From the Writings of
The Late Rev. George Bowen
(from *The Indian Witness*, Sept. 1, 8, 15, 22, 29, 1899)

I. The Person and Work of Christ (*Indian Witness*, Sept. 1, 8, 15, 1899).

   1. Reasons for His humiliation.

Thus poor did He become, wherefore? For your sakes. That His example might take hold upon your consciences, and lead you to follow in this path of renunciation. He teaches you, like Him, to lay aside glory, honor, and power, wealth and comfort. But what glory have you, the very dregs of creation to renounce? The thing is this. In departing from God you have made for yourself a world of delusion, and constituted yourselves Lord of that world. You have put yourselves in the place of God, as the law-giver of yourselves; you have put your honor in the place of God's, and desired to have the whole creation enraptured with yourself, rather than God; yet were urgent to have all things declare your glory rather than His. Renounce then, oh renounce then this usurped dignity, and the wealth that you have chosen to call yours! Follow the example of Christ, and become poor. This is needful in order that subsequently, through His poverty, you may be made rich. You must be changed into His image at the foot of the ladder, and then shall you ascend it with Him, even the very ladder by whose multitudinous steps He came from His sublime throne to earth.

   2. How He reconciles and saves.

By His death He reconciles the Godhead to us. By His Gospel He reconciles us to God. He redeems us from all iniquities, finally, by His Spirit and sanctifying Word. This result is accomplished by inspiring enmity between our souls and our iniquities. We discover these to be so many folds of an anaconda about our soul. We are made to hate them with a perfect hatred; also to know our own impotence; then to know our strength in Him; then to burst these successive chains, and walk emancipated in spirit. In general, we may understand that there is no actual deliverance from any sin until the odiousness of that sin has been seen. The odiousness of it is often first seen when we come into actual conflict with it: but most seen when we contemplate the opposite perfection in the lovely character of Christ.

3. His sufferings and death a complete satisfaction.

The sufferings and death of the Lord Jesus Christ, our willing substitute, were such a satisfaction for sin, such a reparation to the law of God, that it has become every way consistent with divine justice, wisdom and truth to accord mercy to sinners, and bless them without any restriction other than that which their own unwillingness and unbelief interpose. There is a fountain opened for sin and uncleanness; and whosoever will, may take of the water of life freely, "The well is deep, and thou hast nothing to draw with," said the Samaritan woman to Christ. One might be embarrassed at a well or fountain to know how to avail himself of the waters; but if he saw another draw water and drink, he could profit by his example. On the cross, we see Christ dying, the just for the unjust, and perhaps many wonder how the unjust are to profit thereby, until we see the thief on the cross put out his hand and drink of that fountain, and obtain life forever more. Then our difficulty is removed; we see that we have just to believe, and be cleansed from all our iniquities.

4. His blood has power with God and man.

We may plead the merits of this blood as an indemnification for all our sins, so that we may ask and receive from the same all-willing hand that blesses the angels. And the blood has not only the power to conciliate God; it has power over hearts. Not only in the way of inspiring us with faith in God's forgiving grace, but also with hatred of the sins that caused the death of Christ.

5. His death more than reparative.

Christ has much more than repaired the ruin wrought by Adam, in the case of all those who avail themselves of the salvation wrought out by Him. Instead of the one throne where death sat and swayed the destinies of man, there are now myriads, millions of thrones, on each of which a believer is to sit and give the universe a visible demonstration of what Christ can bestow upon the soul that comes to Him.

6. He is an uttermost Savior.

The reason is assigned, and it is unanswerable: "He ever liveth to make intercession for them." He lives for ever, clothed with all the power derived from His propitiatory death and animated by the same heart of love that led Him to die; He lives in the very place where we most need Him; He is there perpetually in our behalf. He was not more truly on the earth for us than He is in Heaven for us, and we may confidently expect to be saved unto the uttermost.

7. He is an unchangeable Savior.

Amidst the mutations of character, the fluctuations of time, and the vicissitudes of events, the soul longs for something that does not and that cannot change, to which it may attach itself and thus find compensation for all the mutabilities of which it is compelled to have experience in this world. There needs, of course, something else besides immutability in order to constitute an object worthy of our earnest attention and heartfelt confidence. We cannot desire immutability where there is anything less than perfection. But where the highest possible excellence resides, there unchangeableness becomes a thing greatly to be desired. Above all when we stand in a certain relation to this incomparable object; when the perfections of this unchangeable One are made available for us; when His power supplements our weakness, His wisdom our ignorance; when He in all this plenitude of perfection is our own particular treasury whence we may draw everlasting supplies—then, oh, then, let change approach Him not, but stand respectfully beyond the circle drawn by His divine nature.

8. He is the sinner's Substitute.

That we might not fall into the hands of the living God, Christ was delivered into the hands of sinful men. He stood before an earthly tribunal where injustice sat in state, in order that we might escape the dread tribunal where infinite justice sits. He was delivered up by sinful men to sinful men. Yet He was delivered up by a righteous God, with His own glad consent, to all the sufferings that man could inflict. He that was delivered up was the only sinless being that ever walked this earth; was divine as well as human; His sinlessness as a man made Him a meet sacrifice for the sins of men; His divine nature gave infinite value to His sufferings, so that it became right in view of them to offer all men deliverance from all the woe that they are obnoxious to, by sin.

9. He is infinitely precious.

Christ is precious to me, because I believe that the beauty and attractiveness of all admirable things owe their charms to Him, and yield their charm to Him. They crossed my path, that they might speak to me of Him. My enthusiasm staggered like a drunken man in the pathway of this world, and only knew its vocation when it discovered Him. When He cometh, the new Jerusalem cometh, the paradise of God cometh; the river of the water of life; saints; angels; the new heaven; the new earth; all beauty, all splendor, all sanctity; the fruition of all right desires, the realization of all lovely dreams; love; in a word, all that is precious cometh; nor will it ever after be possible for me to conceive of a good not found in the region irradiated by His smile.

10. How He subdues iniquities.

He subdues our iniquities, then, by making us despair of ever subduing them ourselves; by pointing out to us some trophies of His power, some incorrigible Peters, some wrathful Pauls, who have been emancipated by His act; by convincing us of His willingness to take our foes in hand; by giving us a conception of His marvelous love shown to sinners, in the surrender of His only-begotten; by giving us through faith, a heavenly experience of that love. We feast upon it, and our enemies are not. They are gone without a battle.

11. He is an ever-living Intercessor.

Christ lives today, tomorrow, and every day, making intercession for you; this means, by interpretation, that Christ lives to perfect you day by day in wisdom, knowledge of the Word, spiritual power, patience, self-denial, love, faith, humility, beneficence, purity and submission.

12. He lives to bless us.

The death of Christ was one exhibition of the love of Christ; He lives that He may, for ever and for ever, give us newer, still newer, still newer expressions of His unfailing goodness. Being reconciled, there is no longer anything to hinder the forth-flowing of the divine beneficence toward us. God is love; and we belong to the number of those whose whole business in life, in everlasting life, is to be making advances in the experience of God's love. But there will be ever something special in the manner by which we have become reconciled, to make us singularly dear to God and to Christ. He hath graven our names upon the palms of His hands. He was pierced for us. We were chosen in such a furnace of afflictions as had never been kindled by Babylonian kings. He can never look upon us without the thought of what He suffered to bring us nigh unto God.

13. He is a true Shepherd.

A shepherd and his flock constitute a unity; the one is not found without the other. The interests of the flock are those of the shepherd. Their wisdom is in him. They take no thought for the morrow; he taketh it. They are not anxious about nourishment or protection; he watches for their welfare. He knows them; knows their need, their ignorance, their wandering; and they know him; know his faithfulness and his all-sufficiency.

14. He is the Bread of life.

If we would have a lively illustration of the meaning of these words, "I am the bread of life," we should give our attention to the few barley loaves that were taken from the basket of that lad, multiplied and distributed to the apostles which kept multiplying as they kept breaking and distributing to the multitude; which kept on multiplying as the multitude kept breaking and handing it every man to his neighbor; which abundantly met the wants of five thousand men, besides women and children, and which have met the wants of the whole world had it been there; which was so much greater for all its communications that it required twelve baskets to hold it, after the banquet was over.

15. Where He may be found.

We cross sea and land to visit the holy places. We exult to look upon the wretched city that bears the name of the place where Christ was condemned to death. We say, this stream He crossed, this mountain He stood upon, this valley He traversed, this shore He visited, in this town He was born, in this place He was brought up. Romanists, Greeks, Armenians who know of no other holy places, jostle us and outstrip us. But the question, "Where is Christ to be found now?" is far more important than the question, where He once was. "The world seeth Me no more, and thinketh of Me in the past, but ye see Me. The hour cometh when ye shall neither in this mountain, nor yet at Jerusalem, worship the Father; but when true worshippers shall worship the Father in spirit and in truth." The little companies that come together in upper chambers and by-places in the Name of Christ, remembering His promises, seeking His presence, cherishing His spirit, honoring His Word—in these little companies Christ is to be found.

16. His example stimulative.

"Be not weary in well doing." This is said to the well-doers—to one even who is no novice in well-doing; but has been sometimes engaged in deeds of beneficence. You have begun well; you have gone on well; but persevere. It may be that your kindness is not appreciated; that your self-denial for the sake of others is even ridiculed; that your motives are misrepresented; and that the more you love, the less you are loved. But your well-doing is not well-doing, if it be gone about chiefly for the sake of man's appreciation. He doeth well whose labors of love are amply rewarded by the smile of God. There was a time when you were not weary in seeking your own ease, pleasure, or advantage. Should you labor longer or more cheerfully for that solitary sinner than for a world of unhappy ones around you?

17. His power to save demonstrated.

Men were challenging Christ to come down from the cross and prove Himself a Savior; but He remained on the cross and proved Himself a

Savior by taking the very thief that was crucified with Him to glory. The word which was despised and rejected by the distinguished men around the cross, was taken to heart by his poor malefactor, and found to be life, eternal life. Here we see what is the exceeding greatness of His power to usward. Nailed to the cross, His mere word proves a ladder of glory by which His companion on Calvary may ascend to the highest and brightest regions of blessedness.

18. The advantage of His spiritual presence.

Christ in His visible presence could only be with one company; let them be separated, and someone would have Him not. His disciples were scattered all over the land, in towns, villages, hamlets, on the sea, on land, on mountains, in plains, in the field, in the house. But every believer needed that Christ should be with him always; how else could he have fullness of joy? Here was a grand difficulty, and how it should be surmounted the disciples could not at that time see. On the day of Pentecost all became plain. Christ was no longer visible; He was at the right hand of the Father; but His friendship, His faithfulness, His grace, His power all were theirs, just as they had been, and far more fully. The divine power and wisdom and love of the Father, these were all theirs, and all were available at all times, in all places, through the mere Name of their Christ.

II. Affliction (*Indian Witness*, Sept. 29, 1899)

1. Often more fully reveals God.

Men go down into deep wells that they may see a star, a mere star; let us not shrink from any position to which the angels of divine providence may beckon us, and from which we are likely to behold more gloriously the revelation of the countenance of God.

2. Enables us to understand God.

What would this world be without calamity! Men talk about the mystery of present things. The mystery would be infinitely greater, if there was no affliction. We should be utterly at a loss to know what to make of the character of God, if unmingled prosperity were the lot of man. This world would then resemble a Hindu heaven; and it would be necessary to suppose Hindu gods presiding over it, in order to get rid of the monstrous anomaly of impenitent sinners occupying the seats of the blessed.

3. Is an effective teacher.

When Jonah came up from the depths of ocean he showed that he had learned the statutes of God. One could not go too deep to get such knowledge as he obtained. Nothing now could hinder him from going to Nineveh. It is just the same as though he had brought up from the deep an army of twelve legions of the most formidable troops. The Word of God, grasped by faith, was all this to him and more. He still, however, needed further affliction; for there were some statutes not yet learned. He was to descend into a further vale of humiliation. Even the profoundest affliction does not, perhaps, teach us everything; a mistake we sometimes make. But why should we compel God to use harsh measures with us? Why not sit at the feet of Jesus and learn quietly what we need to learn?

4. Believers are not exempt from.

The Bible does not mock the anguish-bitten soul by telling it that the Christian cannot experience unhappiness or disappointment; or by telling it that it has no business to be wretched. The followers of the righteous Jesus are told distinctly that there are afflictions for them; and that these afflictions are many. So in drawing up an inventory of what belongs to them they may put down many afflictions. These are a part of their property.

5. Is never unassuageable.

Your affliction is very great; but there is a corresponding greatness in your Comforter. I that died on Calvary, that have all power in Heaven and in earth, Who am from everlasting to everlasting, I am He that comforteth you. I looked upon your sorrow long before you came into existence, and on every page of My Word that I caused to be written I introduced some word of comfort with reference to you. Turn over the leaves of Scripture and see how much I have been occupied about you in days of yore. With all wisdom and kindness I sought out such expressions as were calculated to dissipate your grief. In due time I became incarnate, and every loving thing that I did, I commanded that the news of it should be conveyed to you. I showed My pierced hands and feet to My disciples, and instructed them to tell the Gospel of My grace to you. I have comforted thousands, and tens of thousands, whose misery was quite as invincible as thine. Shall I at last fail with thee? Must I experience a new humiliation? Must it be at length proclaimed that thou hast lost something of superior value to what I can bestow, of greater worth than Myself?

6. Sources from which it springs.

The afflictions of the righteous are those that he encounters in the attempt to walk righteously. Some come upon him from his unsubmissive nature struggling against the new principle that seeks to control it. Many from the wickedness of men, who do their utmost that he may not continue in a path that they abhor. Many from the lukewarmness and want of sympathy of his brethren. Some from the suggestion of the adversary, seeking to undermine his faith. Others again from the strange procedure of God, very different from what he had erringly anticipated. He thought that God would never let him be cast into a pit or sold to Ishmaelites. He thought that God would move with the speed of lightning to his rescue. He thought that God would call to him out of the clouds, "I have heard thy prayer." Some afflictions come upon him from wounded affections. Some from the disappearance of loved ones. Happy for us if we are able to feel in all our afflictions that they are the afflictions of the righteous. Not brought upon us by our own folly—by the neglect of divine guidance—by the contravention of providence.

Sermon Outlines

By the late Rev. George Bowen (*Indian Witness*, Sept. 1, 1899)

Mr. Bowen was accustomed to make brief outlines of his sermons and addresses on the backs of used envelopes, newspapers, wrappers, and scraps of paper of all sorts. Many of these outlines reveal the true homiletic instinct, but few probably would meet the rigorous requirements of one of our modern professors of homiletics. They furnish a very meager idea of the feast of helpful practical Biblical truth set before his audiences. But we nevertheless regard them as particularly valuable for their rich suggestiveness. Mr. Bowen never used a reference Bible; he preferred to make his own references, and he sought to strengthen memory by refusing crutches of every kind. With this object he never wrote down chapter and verse of texts in his outline. The effort to recall these when about to deliver the sermon, fixed them permanently in the mind.

1. The Trial of Faith.

Text: "The trial of your faith, being much more precious than of gold that perisheth," etc. 1 Peter 1:7.

Faith may be genuine or counterfeit. How much depends upon it: your own salvation, that of others, all the good possible to you in eternity. Key of Heaven's treasury.

Many imitations. Satan endeavors to pass off a false article.

Trials not only reveal but develop faith.

Faith is tried by riches, by privations, by humiliation, by duties, by disappointments, by temptations, by depression, by backsliding of others, by uncongenial associations. "All these things are against me." Tried daily.

True faith is victorious. Let God be true; let God reign, guide, allot.
Faith sees love in everything. The most important of all victories. Illustrations: Cecil's child; Jeremiah in the dungeon.

Praise, and honor and glory.

2. The sin of not doing good (*Indian Witness*, Sept.8, 1899)

Text: "To him that knoweth to do good and doeth it not, to him it is sin" (James 4:17).

The connection—knowledge of the law, v. 11. The implication is that we were created to do good. We were created to be happy. The two identical in such a sense that if we live to do good out highest interests will be secured.

That we were created to do good appears from the character of God, from our constitution, from our powers, from the constitution of society. Men dependent on each other.

The Christian is one who has recognized this vocation; repented of past unprofitableness. "Peculiar people zealous of good works." "Sent him to bless you in turning everyone of you away from his iniquities." Lights in the world. Vine and branches. None of us liveth unto himself. "We are His workmanship, created in Christ Jesus unto good works."

The two great commandments bind us to do all possible good.

Means of knowing how to do good: Our own necessities— whatsoever ye would that men should do to you, do ye even so to them; what pleases others. Scriptures show us their need. The means of grace all so many means of learning to relieve.

To "grow in grace" is to grow in aptitude for doing good. Biographies, reports, show what can be done. How to read these? How does the artisan read works on his art? Christ our great example. The cross our great treasury of motive. Practice will teach.

What is Salvation? Salvation from what? From that state of mind which is indifferent to others. The promises place us in communication with God's helpfulness.

"To do good." We are always doing good. Let us do what we do in the best way, with amiability, patience, good nature, cheerfulness, and fidelity to the truth; with prayer and without discouragement, not expecting reward of men. Illus.: self-consuming.

"Doeth it not." This is a very intelligent age. Every new invention popularized. So in the church. We hear of the power of united prayer, of fervent prayer, of tracts, of Scripture passages, of what is done in London. Conceptions of possible good arise in the mind. What becomes of them? Your thoughts of this kind would perhaps fill a volume. Great responsibility. Some pride themselves on these speculations. How such thoughts are to be treated? They may be from the Spirit. Carefully examine. "Peace I leave with you." (A much longer outline than the average).

3. Casting Down Imaginations (*Indian Witness*, Sept. 15, 1899)

Text: "Casting down imaginations, and every high thing that exalteth itself against the knowledge of God, and bringing into captivity every thought to the obedience of Christ" (2 Cor. 10:5).

Men imagine—No God, all is God, no Bible, no sin, no hell, no mediator, no Heaven. They imagine ways of worshipping God, means of getting forgiveness, themselves good.

These imaginings are against the knowledge of God.

The Gospel casts down the highest thoughts of the mind as statues. A great trial this for man. It gives the true knowledge; restores God to His throne. Christ must reign in the heart. The Gospel has done this in thousands of minds. Nothing else could do it. Imaginations thousands of years old are cast down. The Gospel the power of God. It shows the man his danger; his need of inward change, the blessedness of such a change.

Man's sin and danger according to resistance made. Illus: a rebellious city. Holy War. Estimate a man's sin by what he resists. Receive the king and serve under his banners.

4. The Ever Happy Man (*Indian Witness*, Sept. 29, 1899)

Text: "Happy is the man that feareth always" (Prov. 28:14).

a. *Not All Fear Is Good*—Much wrong fear in man. "The fearful and unbelieving." "Fear hath torment." Men generally without true fear.

b. *The True Fear* is the fear of displeasing the true God; the fear of sin and temptation; the fear of our own impulses, the fear of judgment and divine wrath.

c. *Reasons Why Men Do Not Fear*—They have wrong ideas of God, of themselves, of sin, of delay of God's judgment, of the number of sinners, of their own strength, of their own righteousness, of traditions.

d. *Reasons Why Men Should Fear*—The force of sinful habits is great; the best have fallen; the heart is deceitful; there are no promises to the unfearing; much at stake.

e. *How Fear Conduces to Happiness*—By leading to repentance, vigilance, Scriptures, self-examination, cutting off right hand, prayer, confidence in Christ, guidance of the Spirit.

The Cross begets true fear, destroys false.

18. Bowen's Correspondence with Henry W. Rankin

It was in 1884 that Mr. Rankin's correspondence with Bowen began. He had been a subscriber for the *Guardian* for some years, his file of the paper beginning with Jan., 1879. In Feb., 1884, he sent Bowen some books and subscribed in his behalf for the *Independent.* In acknowledging his letters and thanking him, Bowen wrote on May 1, 1884:

> I missed the *Independent* when it stopped coming, and was glad when it made its appearance again. There is much in the *Independent* for which I do not care, and wonder why it should be admitted there; and there is other matter of which I do not approve, yet am glad to see because it lets me know the current of thought in certain spheres. . . .
>
> It is not for me to say if Socinians are ever saved. As many as are the children of God are led by the S. of G., and the Spirit glorifies Christ, and leads the Socinian and Romanist out of his own views into the true light.

A few other letters to Mr. Rankin have been preserved.
To Mr. Rankin, Oct. 16, 1884:

> I beg of you, dear Brother, seek by faith to appropriate the utmost that God can give you, and let Christ have the comfort of seeing one fully conformed to His image.

To Mr. Rankin, Feb. 11, 1885:

> I deeply feel that what you want is not that God should take up some new attitude toward you, or do anything, or be anything but what He is, but that you, should recognize Him as revealed at the cross. What makes Heaven to be Heaven is that the truth which you fail to see, is there seen by all. . . .
>
> Remember Lot's wife. There is not the slightest use in giving your thoughts to the past. You are by the direction of providence in a certain sphere, in certain relations to others, and God would have you live in the present, live with Him in the present, love Him in those with whom you come in contact. We are to keep ourselves from idols—idols in the imagination, idols in memory. An idol is that which diverts the heart from its legitimate object. After my conversion, I found that my faith in Christ could not be developed while I was giving my thoughts and reverence to a certain shrine in memory, and for Christ's sake I dismissed it, leaving God to care for the departed one, and have never

found it good to occupy myself with past things. I have on my hands the great task of redeeming the present. God's will is interpreted to me by the circumstances in which I find myself. The great necessity is that I should daily know Christ better and so be made like to Him, but in order to know Him I must subordinate my mental exercises to the Word, and live therein, and beware of day-dreams. I make all allowance for the state of your health, but to be looking to Christ is no greater strain upon the mind than to be occupied with earthly things. In fact, nothing is so renovating, new-creating as faith. Faith is not an effort, but cessation from effort—letting that be true which is true. It is much easier walking on rock than on water, as Peter found.

Love to Christ is the magic wand that turns all to gold, so that we no longer single out this or that object of admiration, but learn to find beauty and excellence in the commonest objects, and joy in the commandments. And how do we get this love for Christ? Not by efforts, struggles, self-reproaches, tears, fastings, etc., but by just seeking to know Christ's love to the unworthy. The one thing needed is to know our unworthiness, and found our hopes not upon our greatness, but upon our badness; not upon ignoring our malady, but upon knowing it, so as to turn to the right physician. I never have striven to love Christ, since He showed me this, but only to know His love, as the one medicine needed. He that is faithful in that which is least is faithful also in much. Lazarus at the gate of Dives was pleasing God all the time, and needed not to envy Spurgeon his gift of utterance. Let us do heartily what our hand findeth to do, if it be sweeping the street or shoveling the snow or sawing wood, or teaching stupid boys, or suffering pain. Let God's will be our fruit, our paradise.

The best use we can make of our past sins is to turn from them to Christ. Anything that diverts our attention from Christ does us harm. This and that sin may appear very odious to us, and are so truly, but with God the most odious sin is that of not accepting His offer of love. . . .

There is not the slightest use in trying to correct anything amiss in our mental habits by direct efforts. We get the victory by faith, i. e., by ceasing to combat them and making them over to Christ. Do not even be impatient with these evils. Nothing so discomfits Satan as when you praise the Lord. 2 Chron. 20:22.

To Mr. Rankin, June 15, 1886:

I have received from time to time papers and books from you. You have been so kind as to send to me your copy of *The Pupil of Raphael*. It cost you no little trouble to get it, and I will take care to return it to you shortly. I am reading it, but have no desire that anybody else should read it. Not a single incident or a single character remained in memory. There are portions of it that I regret exceedingly, showing the effect of Balzac's writings. I am very glad that the Lord so completely snuffed the book out. Above all am I grateful that He has saved me from myself.

I live in hope that you will send me word some day that you are believing these words of God that offer eternal life to whomsoever, and banish that sense of condemnation and all vain thirsting. Whatever your nature really demands for its highest development is in that word "eternal life." I wish that you would make up your mind that nothing more is ever to come to you from God than has come to you, and give your attention to what has come to you and is ignored by you. It was a blessed hour for me when I lost my faith in the future, and began to interrogate the present.

I think I see a prisoner in a cell. On a table a letter has been lying many days which he fancies for somebody else and not for him. It authorizes him to claim the right of egress and to go out of his yard and to go to a comfortable dwelling provided for him. But, he says, it is not for me; if it were for me it would not leave me here. He is there because he has not faith.

Why should you make light of all that God has done to inspire you with faith? You do this when you fail to recognize what God offers you. The lying spirit of unbelief will say to you, This does not suit your case. Let not the spirit continue in his post of doorkeeper of your heart. How glad should I be to hear that you have decided to let God be true, though every man a liar.

All happiness is in the recognition of Him Who sits upon the throne, Whose nature and Whose Name is Love, Who gives Himself and is Himself Love Almighty to every atom, and is excluded only by man's unbelieving heart. God has never done anything for me, or will do, that He is not offering to every creature, for He offers Himself and He is Love. You have only to let God be true, let Him be Himself, and you will find yourself in paradise. The New Jerusalem comes down from God out of Heaven when men discover this. But it is hid from them by the great concern that they have for self. Do not allow your heart to cheat you out of the blessings contained in this truth. Let go the Future; interrogate the Present. What I mean is, Find God in the present.

To Mr. Rankin, Dec. 9, 1887:

Many thanks for all the papers and books kindly sent me from time to time. The memoir of Bro. Lawrence I read years ago. What does it show? That the "blessed life" is not an attainment, but the reception of a gift, the same gift that is offered by the Gospel to every creature. How is it that some are seeking year after year and not finding? Because of their preconceived ideas? If any man will be wise, let him become a fool, that he may be wise. Many a man has idols and he insists that these idols shall help him in coming to a true knowledge of Christ. Some of these idols are made to look like Christ, and are therefore tolerated; but are nevertheless idols. Some people have a great admiration of the Emperor Marcus Aurelius and his writings. So far as there is truth in these writings, it originated with Christ, and having been refashioned is given forth as the man's own. But what about the 50,000 Christian men, women, and children, the salt of the earth, the best of all Rome's populations, murdered by order of the Emperor, and their property given to the informers, thus bribed to denounce them, all without disturbing the philosophic complacency of this man? I say that one who gives his enthusiasm to Marcus Aurelius, need not wonder if he is hindered from finding Christ as Lawrence found Him.

You speak with great admiration of Emerson and of the great benefit derived from his teachings. I say of him what I said of Aurelius. In Christ are given unto us all things that pertain to life and godliness. What is true and valuable in Christ's teaching may in some measure be found in Emerson's books, but with Emerson's stamp upon them; they do not lead to Christ, but to Emerson. He passes them off as intuitional, thus glorifying man, the very thing that Christ is most against. Man must be in the dust, and man's wisdom, before we can profit by Christ. What has Emerson done for you? Has he taught you the blessed art of finding all in Christ? Has he shown you the kingdom which is righteousness, peace and joy in the Holy Ghost?

You give me your experience in the words of Job: Oh, that I knew where I might find Him, etc. You have intense desires, but no satisfaction. Your picture of yourself is unmistakably sad. One thing you need, and Emerson has not helped you to get it. Lawrence says, "All consists in one hearty renunciation of everything which we are sensible does not lead to God," and that includes abandonment of our ideas and of other people's ideas, and coming to Christ as a little child to learn the A. B. C. of religion. The Gospel is the glad tidings of a gift, and that gift received in the heart will do its own divine work, of purifying the heart. The pollution and depravity of the heart are no barriers to the reception of the gift by faith. So please do not talk any more of God's whipping the old Adam out of you. Give up all you know of adoration, for this has not brought you into God's marvelous light. Come to Christ with nothing but teachableness. And praise God for realities before you arise from your knees, whatever your heart may say.

You will have seen in the *Guardian* that on the 4th of Sept. I had a fall and fractured my thigh, and am lame for life. I have not walked in the street since then and have not got back to my own room. One that rejoiced in his independence has been made very dependent on others. I thank God that I have not been tempted to fret. I find Christ all-sufficient here as elsewhere.

My letter is short, but long enough to show you the secret of a happy life, if you are willing to find it.

On January 15, 1888, Mr. Rankin wrote a long letter in reply, acknowledging the immeasurable help which he had received from Bowen and setting forth his more favorable view of Emerson and his influence. Bowen died, however, before this letter reached him and it came back to its author.

No more discerning and philosophical estimate of Bowen has ever appeared than is found in Mr. Rankin's letters to me and these letters may well be set forth here, in part at least, in connection with the letters from Bowen to Mr. Rankin just quoted. It may be doubted whether any other person either in Europe or America or India had read as thoroughly and as critically all that Bowen had written both in the *Guardian* and in his books.

From Mr. Rankin, May 24, 1902:

> In my own case, and in one or two minor matters, Mr. Bowen did not quite understand my attitude, as in my view of Emerson, to whose writings I am peculiarly indebted, though never committed to him in the manner Mr. Bowen seemed to think. My letters to him were largely intended to provoke some editorial comment on the questions proposed, and the books I sent him were to provoke reviews in the *Guardian* so that many others might share with me in the benefits of his answers. In this purpose I was successful, besides being privileged to receive his more direct and personal response. In the letters you will find his most characteristic views effectively expressed in his exquisite chirography.

From Mr. Rankin, Dec. 21, 1902:

> Bowen's immense range of intellectual interests and reading gave an unusual value to the selections that his paper reprinted and his own discussions in many directions. He had been deeply influenced by Balzac and among these selections is an extraordinary account of the last days of that writer. I don't think Bowen was infallible but I never knew any writer out of the Bible more just, more liberal, more

comprehensive, more profound, more rational or more experimental. His knowledge of the Christian religion, in its three-fold combination of a philosophical, historical and experimental point of view, was in my poor judgment never surpassed by any writer in the whole range of Christian literature.

From Mr. Rankin, Dec. 23. 1902:

George Bowen belongs in the very first rank of great missionaries, while possessing like the members of his class, an individuality that was unique. There are several features of his career that render its record exceptionally pertinent to our own time. His special experience as a missionary is at several points highly instructive in its bearing upon the method of the enterprise at large. He went out under the direction of a Board of Missions, but soon cut loose, and for many years tested the merits and possibilities and limitations of independent work. He returned to take a place in the organized activity of a denomination. His conduct, method, reasons and results are peculiarly worthy of study by all managers of the enterprise; for the personal quality of the man was such as to make his experience a better test of methods than that of most other men.

This personal quality of the man was very exceptional even among missionaries, although more nearly approached and duplicated among them than in any other order of men. His personal experience in the external conditions and accidents of life was large, but much smaller than that of many others. His personal experience of the fundamental factors and possibilities of the inner life comprehended the entire scale of these factors as fully, perhaps, as that of any man who ever lived. It would be difficult to name any man more entirely self-centered in his earlier years, or more entirely God-centered in his subsequent life than was George Bowen. He began with one towering ambition of a kind that appeals to great numbers of educated and gifted youth. He began with the utmost confidence in his own goodness and wisdom and powers. He had a consuming passion for his own glory, that effectually closed his mind to truth, while he conceived himself to be wholly bent on truth; and although superciliously self-righteous he exhibited great infirmities, and was led into a course marked by no little triviality and some sensuality.

We live not only in an age of Missions, but of infidelity covert and avowed, more prevalent, and more completely organized, more popular and more destructive of Christian teaching and ideals, than the world has ever known. George Bowen passed through every leading phase of infidelity, between his 14th and his 28th years of age—the most intelligent kind of infidelity, fostered and stimulated and supported by an immense range of reading, intense and continuous thinking, and, for his years, large opportunities of observation and association among men. The fundamental premises of all infidelity were perfectly familiar to his mind; and all the oral traits that accompany this direction of thought made up his character. He was well acquainted with the history of thought, and the historic positions of philosophy. There is no aspect of skepticism in the world today which, in all essential respects, he had not known and shared and overcome when he became a Christian. But even before his conversion he was led to see the utter insufficiency to reason as well as to life of all excepting the most refined forms of infidelity.

The circumstances that brought about his radical change in thought and character were such as befall many others, though not always with a similar happy issue. Looking back upon them in consecutive review their indications of a supernatural ordering appear unusually marked. And the entire mental experience through which he passed between two extremes of darkness and light is such as must possess an extraordinary value for all educated minds disposed to serious inquiry regarding the things that signify most for life; whether bent on practical applications or merely on scientific research. This latter interest is also one that is more pronounced today than ever in the past.

The United States has passed its majority, and reached its imperial epoch of international pre-eminence and ambition, wealth, art, luxury, dilettantism, material splendor, and all the strongest appeals to the pomp and pleasure of life. Never before did the glamour of the world so powerfully appeal to all well conditioned youth in the United States. The accomplished man of the world supplies a fascinating ideal to many such.

George Bowen was emphatically such a man. He was rich, polished, accomplished, read, traveled, experienced, proud, gifted, and aspiring to the glory of this world. He was well enjoyed among his associates, possessing a charm of manner and culture and social advantages, when all those things, which were gain to him, he counted loss for Christ. Yet having done this he was not required to lose by disuse his natural advantages and cultivated powers; but placed where all these could be employed to infinitely greater profit than they ever would have been in his originally chosen course. He had believed with David Strauss that "human nature alone is equal to all its exigencies" and that "where miracles begin there history ends"—the popular creed of our day. He was led to see that the largest wealth of natural endowment and acquirement was utterly insufficient either to meet the exigencies of this life, or to satisfy the insatiable demands of the human heart; and that if this wealth were all a man could possess, then the greater it was, the more intensely accentuated was his essential poverty.

He was also led to see that even though common nature and common history be regarded as a revelation of God, yet if this were all the revelation God had made, then are we no better off, but rather worse off, than if there were no God to be revealed. For a God who can do all this and will not do something more to meet the necessities of human kind, may show His power and intellect, but shows no character worthy of worship, confidence or love; and wholly fails to provide for our deepest needs.

We live in an age that regards Christianity as merely the highest natural development of the ethnic religions, all of them parts, of which this is the sublimated whole. It is an age in which universities are endowed with chairs of comparative religion held by scholars who study religion as a "closet naturalist" studies outward nature, without any immediate and vital contact with or direct experience of any one of the faiths on which they speculate. George Bowen lived in precisely such vital contact with as wide a range of ethnic cults as any city in the world presents; and he studied these doctrines and practices with such a rare experience of Christianity as supplied him beyond most men with adequate criteria for his views. He understood as few men ever did or could on the philosophical, historical and experimental plane, the essential antagonism of Christianity to every pagan and Mohammedan religion, as well as the points of partial agreement.

The conclusions he reached were those of an expert in the very best sense of the word; and they entirely agreed with the Biblical presentation of this subject. He regarded every other religion as a departure from, not an approach to the standard faith, which last alone, in its most Scriptural form, without addition or subtraction, met every human need, in so far as it is accepted on its own prescribed condition. And this religion alone carried its own adequate credentials of a source strictly supernatural, and was communicated by a method characteristically miraculous.

George Bowen reigned for forty years in the city of Bombay, scarcely leaving the neighborhood of that city. But his personal character and the influence of his writings covered all India, and have somewhat passed beyond the confines of that land. He has been a powerful quickener of thought in many a strong and noble mind—Cuyler, Drummond, Joseph Cook, and doubtless many in Great Britain and this country. No man ever showed more plainly the powerfully molding effect of Christian faith on thought and literary style than did George Bowen. The chasm is wide and deep between his writings before and after his conversion.

His few published volumes as religious classics are unsurpassed in the literature of Christianity, since the New Testament canon was made up.

For effective simplicity of style, felicity and wealth of illustration, range of intellectual interest, discrimination of essentials and incidentals in the religious life, proportion of emphasis, sublimity of ideals; for correlation with religion of other matters, conduct, science, art, history, politics, commerce, and common life; for interpretation of Scripture, for knowledge of the human heart, for philosophical grasp upon the principal factors—God, nature, man, and for evidence of a most comprehensive experience in the writer—I doubt if any other books can be found more excellent than these.

The multitude of religious publications now in vogue are to the books of George Bowen as moonlight to sunlight and water to wine. It is only an affliction and calamity to the Christian church that every popular preacher who comes along should supplant with his diluted pages the Lachrimae Christi of George Bowen's books. Here are the pearls and rubies and diamonds of literature swept into a corner out of sight and mind, to make way for the imitation gems and inferior values of this shallow tawdry and pretentious ore. There is not one religious writer living today of popular recognition whose pages I have ever scanned who does not seem to me poor and pale and thin besides George Bowen, Brother Lawrence, Luther, Tauler, Eckhart, Boehme, Joseph Alleine, Bunyan, Fénelon and Augustine.

And why will our writers waste the real strength which they often have, and spread themselves so thin, by the incontinent and perpetual outpour of their books? Why not better wait before they print till they can put more weight into their words? The daily and weekly journals must be written, and an editor must always write—for 'tis his nature and his business, too. But when it comes to making up a book why not more choice and more quintessence of the good—and not this deluge of the commonplace?

In reply to a question as to any evidence of Henry Drummond's knowledge of Bowen, Mr. Rankin wrote Jan. 1, 1903:

As to Drummond, during his first visit to Northfield in 1887 we were both staying for several weeks together, except short absences, at Mr. D. L. Moody's house. We had rooms opposite, and met at all hours of the day. We talked over favorite themes and men, and these included Emerson and Bowen. I came to think that Bowen was much better known in Scotland than in this country, not only through the handsome edition of his three books, but through many personal reports of his Scotch friends who had known him in India. Drummond had read at least one of the books, I forget which, probably the *Meditations,* which has a good introduction by Hanna and he spoke as if Bowen had strongly impressed him. I do not recall allusions to Bowen in Drummond's writings, yet possibly you may find some. But when *Natural Law* appeared it was reviewed by Bowen with considerable favor, if I remember rightly. Subsequent allusions to Drummond in the editorials of the *Guardian* are partly based upon my communications with Bowen, in which I defended Drummond from current misrepresentation.

On Bowen's death Mr. Rankin wrote to the surviving sister Harriet, March 1, 1888:

> It is eight years since I began to become acquainted with him in his writings, and to rate him among the very highest interpreters of truth and life who have ever lived. He was one of those whose intrinsic greatness is far greater than that of many whose greatness is more apparent to the world. But I also think that the influence he leaves behind him is likely from this time to become much more extended than that he exerted during his life among us. I was pleased last summer to find from a daughter of Andrew Bonar that your brother's name was a household word in her father's family, and that his books are read and loved by many in Scotland. I had the pleasure of telling Henry Drummond what I knew about him, and to find that he also had become already much interested in Mr. Bowen by reading his books. Mr. Bowen has been extremely kind to me in replying to my occasional letters, whenever I have written, and sending me always good and strengthening words. I cannot help feeling better acquainted with him than I do with most of the friends whom I have most often seen. I felt also that he was my friend, and a friend of the rarest value. I think I have known no other man since my own father's death years ago, with whom I should have felt so free to open my whole heart.

18. Closing Testimony

On Sept. 4, 1887, in getting out of a tram-car, Bowen fell, "through his own carelessness," he said in the *Guardian* of Oct. 15, and for some weeks was unable to walk except with crutches. The neck of the right thigh bone sustained a fracture and the injury was likely to be permanent. He had some help in producing the next issues of the paper but he went on with his work and before long was able to lay aside his crutches and get on with a cane.

The last number of the *Guardian* for the year 1887 contained an editorial entitled "1887, 1888" in which he compared the outlook for 1888 with the world conditions in 1588, 1688 and 1788 and drew from the comparison great hope for the future. The closing paragraph was:

> But there is much to bid us look hopefully upon the coming year. In the Established Church and out of it, in England, in America, on the Continent, in many lands, those who are led of the Spirit of God have a better understanding of what Christ is to them, have a higher conception of their privileges in Christ, have a union, than have perhaps ever before been seen on so large a scale. The great work of opening up relations with out-of-the-way nations and tribes has been carried well forward this last year. We cannot begin to mention all the matters of cheer that present themselves. But it is well to look appreciatively upon all the developments of this time. Is it not the time of the harvest when good and bad are growing together?

Among the editorial notes in the first issue of 1888 was the following with regard to a full-page laudatory article in the London *Christian* of Dec. 23, 1887:

> In a few days the writer of this will have completed forty years in India, and if our contemporary had referred to his missionary work as a failure, we should have had nothing to say in reply. But we are surprised and chagrined to see in the last received *Christian* an announcement that the next number will contain a portrait and sketch of this very individual. His life has been remarkable for many blessings and consolations. The less said about the rest, the better.

The issue of Jan. 28, 1888, contained an advertisement of the Woman's Medical Missionary training School of Bombay in which "Biblical instruction will be regularly given by Rev. George Bowen and others." And the next issue,

Feb. 4, reported the twelfth annual session of the South India Conference of the Methodist Church held at Poona on Jan. 26. Bowen was present and, in the absence of a bishop, was elected President. He took active part, preaching on Sunday morning, and baptized a little child. On the adjournment of the Conference, he took the midnight train back to Bombay, but his work was done, and on the following Sunday, Feb. 4, 1888, at the age of seventy-two, he finished his earthly course and entered into rest.

Dr. J. E. Robinson, who had long been associated with him and who succeeded him shortly in the conduct of the *Guardian,* wrote in the leading editorial of the paper on Feb. 11 the account of the end, under the title "A Prince and a Great Man Fallen":

> The pen that for more than thirty years enriched the pages of the *Bombay Guardian* has for ever been laid aside! The busy brain that week by week devised such liberal things and so unfailingly spread rich feasts for a host of appreciative readers not only in India but in other lands has ceased to be occupied with things terrestrial! Before the *Guardian* of the 11th February reached its readers it had become known to most of them that in the early hours of the previous Lord's day, February 5th, the venerable and saintly George Bowen rested from his labors and ceased at once to work and to live. Alone on the top of his Pisgah, with "no man save Jesus only" to catch his last whisper, to witness his exodus, in the early dawn of the quiet Sabbath morning, he left his body to this pleasant country's earth, for which he so devotedly loved and labored, and the good and faithful soldier surrendered
>
>> "His pure spirit unto his Captain, Christ,
>> Under Whose banner he had fought so long."
>
> The blow has fallen upon his numerous friends of many races and various creeds in this city and in other parts, and more especially upon those whose great privilege it was to have been more closely associated with him in Christian work, with crushing suddenness. No intimation of his illness having reached the public, the news of his death proved a great shock to the whole Christian community. Stunned by this great overshadowing bereavement which has befallen us, our stricken hearts cry out "My father, my father, the chariot of Israel and the horsemen thereof."
>
> On Wednesday, January 25th, Mr. Bowen left Bombay for Poona to attend the South India Annual Conference of the Methodist Episcopal Church, of which he was a revered member. He appeared to be in (for him) excellent health, though troubled with a cold, during his few days' stay in Poona. His brethren greatly rejoiced to find him so

Closing Testimony

encouragingly recovered from his lameness, he being able to move about with considerable ease without his cane, which for some weeks had been substituted for crutches. Elected to the presidency of the Conference, he entered upon its varied duties and responsibilities.

On Sunday morning he preached one of his rare sermons on "Union with Christ" and the consequent obligations and blessedness of believers, speaking also in Marathi to the midday mass-meeting of school children and enjoying the further services of the day. The Conference adjourned Tuesday morning, the 31st, and that night, in company with several ministers, he left Poona for Bombay by the 11 o'clock train.

Wednesday night Mr. Bowen participated in the farewell meeting to Dr. Stone, the departing pastor of the Grant Road M. E. Church, with whom he had been sojourning for several weeks, and presided at the sacramental service. Before retiring to rest he was taken with a severe chill, which seriously affected his feeble frame. He spent a restless night and found himself very weak the next day. Medicine prescribed by his physician afforded him helpful relief, insomuch that he expressed his surprise at the benefit apparently derived. He had very little sleep on Thursday night, and on Friday it was resolved to take him to Dr. Armstrong's private hospital, to which arrangement he cheerfully consented. All that skill and loving care could do for him was done. Ordinarily prone to chafe under special attention, he quietly and gracefully submitted to the gentle ministries of those to whom it was a precious privilege to minister unto him.

Friday night, though he slept but little, was an easy one. On Saturday he told the writer that, whereas Wednesday and Thursday nights seemed as long as months, Friday night was not at all tedious. Doubtless he slept more through its silent hours than he supposed. All through Saturday he expressed himself as being much easier and in every way better. To the writer was given the sad but unspeakably sweet privilege of having the last friendly conversation and of engaging in prayer with him about 7 o'clock on Saturday evening. He then spoke hopefully of being able to write at least one article for the *Guardian* of the 11th February, expressing his thanks for the assurance given him that the paper would be cared for in his sickness. We freely talked together for a short space concerning the kingdom of God in our own souls and in the world, and at his own request prayer was offered. Then the parting words were spoken, neither for once supposing that we had parted never again to meet, until, by the mercy of God, we meet in the Father's many-mansioned house to go no more out for ever.

During the night he was visited by his kind physician, and the night nurse looked in on him at frequent intervals. At 6 on Sunday morning the nurse took him refreshment, but, while making no complaint of weakness, he excused himself from partaking. At 7 o'clock the day nurse on entering the room was startled by his appearance and on drawing near concluded he was dead. The doctor was immediately summoned and found that it was even so. In the short interval, and most probably while lightly sleeping, the weary wheels of life stood still, and "he was not, for God took him." The earthen vessel which for years past had seemed ready at any moment to crumble to pieces yielded to the final pressure and suffered the imprisoned spirit to escape to its immortal home—the palace of the angels and of God. While pneumonia was the proximate cause of death, it was evident to all that the real cause was the collapse of the frail wasted organism which for years had barely maintained existence, and which during the past year had been additionally so enfeebled by the fall which he sustained. The candle had burned to its very socket.

He was buried the next day in the Sewree cemetery. "His death," wrote one of his closest and earliest friends, Dr. W. W. Atterbury, whom Bowen was constantly mentioning in his home letters, "produced a deep impression through Western India. Seldom if ever had there been so large a gathering in Bombay, on such an occasion, as at his funeral." The church was filled with hundreds standing and the whole city mourned the loss of its saint. The *Indian Witness* of Feb. 11, 1888, remarked: "The funeral of the Rev. George Bowen was one of the largest ever seen in Bombay. High English officials mingled their tears with the natives' around the good man's dust."

A movement was at once begun to erect a large hall in Bombay for Christian uses as a monument to Bowen and in due time was carried successfully through. But his true memorial was the life whose memories were deathless. For weeks after his death the *Guardian* printed letters from all types of men expressing their gratitude and devotion, which more than justified the closing words of Dr. Robinson's account of Bowen in the *Guardian* of Feb. 11:

> George Bowen belonged to all denominations that honored Christ. To him people of all churches, of the various grades of society, of every walk in life, turned as to a true friend and counselor, and as an example of all that is good and beautiful in a Christian life. How he was loved and reverenced by Methodists is well known; but in this city, where he has gone in and out among his fellows these forty years—in this land where his name has ever been as ointment poured forth—there are thousands who are not Methodists who love and revere his name, and who will affectionately cherish his memory as long as life endures.

> Knowing how accessible he ever was, how quick and sensitive and responsive were his sympathies, everybody, irrespective of race or creed, felt that he had a prescriptive right to go to him in any time of trouble or distress. And so for these many years he has been at the service of every man, woman or child needing his counsel or his help, his sympathies or his prayers. The more destitute and degraded and feeble the one who appealed to him the more glad was he to wholly give himself to that one in love and prayerful sympathy. If since apostolic days there has lived a man on earth who unselfishly and disinterestedly sought the good of his fellows in Christlike willingness to spend and be spent for them, and who stood ever ready to lay down his life for the brethren, that man, we hesitate not to say, was George Bowen.

A tribute of overflowing affection from Dennis Osborne, for whom Bowen had a great regard and who was one of the most eloquent preachers in the Methodist Church in India and one of the most eloquent advocates of missions on his visits to America, appeared in *The Indian Witness* of Feb. 18, 1888:

> For nearly half a century that life has been to infidels and unbelievers an evidence of the truth of the religion he professed which could not be gainsaid. To Brahmin and Parsi, to Jew and Moslem, the life of George Bowen has been an open book, every line of which has portrayed godliness and truth—an embodied illustration of the letter press of God's book. And multitudes who believed not in the Bible, believed in George Bowen, and not a few were led from wondering admiration of this remarkable product of grace to devout adoration of the Gracious Giver. . . . Christlike character, endowed with mental gifts of the rarest kind, enriched with eminent scholarship and culture, strengthened by vigorous and constant study, and beautified by uncommon affability and geniality of manner, it was nevertheless his likeness to his Master that magnetized his life and made it the attracting power that it was. Christ lived in that life and shone from it at every point. . . . His genuine and intense repugnance to self-esteem in any form. . . . Genuinely pained and annoyed he was at any laudatory allusion to himself. . . . That Gibraltar of moral integrity for near half a century, unswayed by sound or strife, unmoved and unmovable, a fragile frame, a lowly form, a feeble voice, one of the world's weak things—but a wall of adamant, by tongue, by pen and by life against the inroads of evil, however sparkling or specious.

During his lifetime and ever since his death Bowen's name has been a synonym for pure devotion to Christ. From the multitude of testimonies of those who knew him or who only knew of him only a few can be selected:

From the Rev. L. B. Tedford, for thirty years a missionary in the Western India Mission of the American Presbyterian Church:

> Shall I ever forget the scene of this lowly servant of the most High God standing on the steps of the old monument just in front of the Bombay Tract and Book Society? Standing in the cool of the evening with some other friends preaching to the crowds lingering around. Would that a picture of him in his mean attire, his long hair and little skull cap, could be produced representing him on his usual round of visits to the destitute and unfortunate of the great heathen city. Can my wife and I ever forget his most gentle manner and real Christian interest shown in his timely call upon us new missionaries in a Bombay hotel? . . . It is difficult to state the whole truth concerning him—not to fail to represent him as a natural man on the one side, an unnatural on the other, shunning to picture him as a Hindu holy man and unduly flattering his virtues.

From the General Minutes of the South India Conference of the M. E. Church, January, 1889, p. 114:

> As a missionary his career was altogether unique. While we admired the spirit that animated him in adopting the style of living which he clung to and had the profoundest confidence in the purity and sincerity of his motives, few regarded his course as wise. . . . He himself says, "My passion is for winning souls but it does not please the Lord to use me in that way." . . . His spirit was nobly catholic, while at the same time he manifested a rigidly intolerant attitude toward flagrant errorists of every school.

From the Rev. J. G. Potter of the Baptist Mission in India:

> An educated Mohammedan called on me at Agra and stated that he had years ago lost faith in the Koran, and been led to believe that if any religious book was true it was the Bible. Yet the teaching of Christ as represented by the Sermon on the Mount seemed to set before us an impossible standard of living. He decided therefore to see for himself if any Christians lived up to it. Hearing of George Bowen of Bombay he called upon him at his house in the bazaar and found him making tea for himself. He was asked to be seated and offered a cup of tea. When prepared he said he was sorry it was not to his taste, wishing to test George Bowen's patience. A second was prepared of which he still said it was not as he liked it, so a third was prepared and handed to him. He thus felt satisfied that George Bowen had the grace of patience to a marked degree, and came up to the Christian standard. In course

of conversation Mr. Bowen told him of his own conversion which had largely been due to the influence of the lady to whom he was engaged but who died before they were married. He then showed this Mohammedan visitor the Bible that she had left him. Thinking that such a Bible must be greatly valued by George Bowen he decided to test him as to his temper and when the old well worn book was placed before him on his knees he pushed it aside saying it was very dusty. Then he said the old man without a murmur dusted his soiled garments and picked up the book which had been so rudely pushed aside and his Mohammedan visitor marveled at such an exhibition of Christian patience and went away convinced that at least one man lived up to the teaching of the Sermon on the Mount.

From Rittonji Nowroji, a converted Parsi, of the Church Missionary Society:

I never lived in Bombay for any length of time, but used to visit it twice a year for the Church Missionary Conference, when I had the pleasure of meeting him there. The missionaries of Bombay had arranged to meet and welcome him for breakfast at their houses, and Tuesday morning it was the turn of the C. M. S. Secretary to expect him for breakfast. He was always asked to conduct the family prayers. He used to read a portion of Scriptures, making a few passing comments and leading prayers. His prayers were earnest and solemn, addressed to the Great Hearer and Answerer of prayers as if he was accustomed to approach Him at all times. At breakfast table he spoke but little but whenever he spoke it was evident that he spoke of such matters as were precious to his soul, and edifying to his hearers.

His dress was of the simplest and cheapest kind. Friends would send him new clothes by post, but whatever was showy and costly he would pass it on to others who were in need, keeping for his own use whatever was simple and cheap.

During the day he was busy in editing the *Bombay Guardian,* free of charge, accepting only two copies, the proceeds of which he used to spend for his simple midday meal which consisted of a small but an ordinary loaf and a plantain.

In appearance he was thin, and somewhat sad, but he had only to open his mouth to convince his hearers that his heart was full of peace, and temper full of cheerfulness. Whenever he was tired and wearied out by reading and writing his only recreation was to spend a few minutes at a baby organ playing and singing with great delight. Once a missionary asked him to mention in his well-circulated paper that he needed a large organ for his newly built church. His reply was remarkable: "What do you want a large and expensive organ for when one small like mine would be sufficient to fill the church with its sweet tone?" Mr. Bowen preached daily in the evenings. He was listened to with attention and respect. The passers-by saluted him, and once the writer of these few lines witnessed that the Governor of Bombay, passing by the road, had his carriage stopped, with uplifted hat, to salute the man of God.

I met a Parsi Victoria driver who was converted and baptized by Mr. Bowen. The man was exposed to persecution by his people which had a depressing effect on his mind. But as we passed along he pointed out the various corners of the road where Mr. Bowen used to take his stand and preach the Gospel to attentive hearers. With tears in his eyes he recalled the happy scene when the man of God spoke so lovingly of the great mercy shown by God in the Salvation prepared by the Lord Jesus Christ. "Alas!" said he, "I am not the same man that I was when Mr. Bowen was alive. His words were full of comfort. He would turn my sorrow into joy, and if he were here on earth I would have been a strong and a rejoicing Christian." I told him that our Redeemer ever liveth—and He is the same yesterday, today and for ever—and can sympathize and cheer and help us as no man can ever do. The natives of Bombay of all castes and creeds held Mr. Bowen in great respect and admiration, calling him a great Sadhu, or a Saint.

Once he was seriously ill when friends took him to their home on Malabar Hill to nurse and look after him as if he were a member of their family. Three or four eminent medical men visited him daily, morning and evening. They did their best out of love for him and for the Master Whom he loved and served so well. At last they thought that a visit to his native country, America, would be beneficial. As soon as this recommendation reached the ears of a wealthy Parsi gentleman he sent him a check for 3000 Rupees, begging of him to take a voyage, first class, to America and back. But he told his medical friends that India was his home and country and that he would live and die for its inhabitants. When he left his bed he wrote and thanked the Parsi friend for his generosity, offering to return his money. The gentleman begged of him not to return the money but to keep it with him for any future use. The money remained for years in some bank, increasing with compound interest. Some years afterwards he was asked by the Calcutta Methodist Mission if he would bring their need before the Christian public through the *Bombay Guardian* as they were in debt to the amount of about ten thousand Rupees. Mr. Bowen remembered the money that was in the bank, amounting with interest to the sum needed by the brethren. He once more wrote to the generous donor whether he would like to have it back, and when told that he was welcome to use it in any way he liked, Mr. Bowen sent the whole amount to Calcutta, relieving the anxiety of the brethren with one stroke of his pen.

Mr. Bowen took much interest in the prosperity of the Tract and Book Society, acting as its Honorary Secretary for years. His room was a small corner of the Depot and his only bed its hard and uncomfortable bench! He had selected and employed an elderly Christian clerk who helped him in the work. His pay was one hundred Rupees. He acted as Treasurer also, and once having three or four thousand rupees in his hand, the clerk in a moment of temptation used the money in trading in leather, sending it to England, fully intending to refund the same as soon as the ship laden with the leather reached England. To his great sorrow and disappointment the ship and the cargo went down to the bottom of the sea. The man pleaded guilty and tried various fruitless efforts to refund the lost amount but was pardoned by the Committee of the Tract Society. They proposed that another responsible clerk should be employed. But Mr. Bowen proposed that as he had some time to spare he would himself act in that capacity and save the funds of the Society. For years he quietly and patiently worked, which kept him busy in addition to his other duties which were neither few nor easy. After making up the loss by his unpaid services he retired when it was known that he had thus paid up for the fault of the erring clerk.

From the Minutes on Bowen of the Bombay Missionary Conference, reported in the *Guardian* of April 7, 1888:

> The most striking trait of his character was the catholicity of spirit which enabled him without wavering in his adherence to principles and methods of work which he deemed most in accordance with the Word and Spirit of the Gospel, and the needs of the time, to cooperate heartily with Christians of every name, and to sympathize with every form of effort which had as its aim the glory of the Redeemer.

From the *Encyclopedia of Missions:*

> Living a life of habitual self-abnegation, he was singularly free from asceticism and although uncompromising in his views of Christian principle he was welcomed in the houses of high and low. It was by his personal ministry that he became known, at first despised and ridiculed and then esteemed among the people of India. He acquired wide influence by the eminent ability and spirituality of his writings. . . . His death produced a deep sensation in Bombay and Western India.

Those most competent to form a judgment concur in the estimate that he exhibited a degree of self-sacrificing devotion to which there is perhaps no existing parallel in the whole field of missionary labor.

From the Rev. Henry Haigh, in a lecture delivered in the Central Hall, Manchester, England:

Let me tell you of a man I knew in India—George Bowen by name. He was a classical scholar of distinction, and was at home in four of the principal languages of Europe. For years he reveled in poetry and philosophy, in romance and controversy, in all those languages. He was, besides, a fine musician; could compose as well as perform. In his early manhood Bowen was a philosophic skeptic and a rank pessimist. At last, however, there came to him a great experience, which made him feel the need and ultimately see the truth of immortality. From that point he was led on, until one night he sat down and wrote these words: "If there is One above all Who notices the desires of men, I wish He would take note of this fact, that if it pleases Him to make known His will concerning me I should think it my highest privilege to do that will wherever it might be and whatever it might involve." It was a cry out of the darkness, and not long after that Jesus Christ became to George Bowen the peace and enthusiasm of his being.

There soon grew up in him a new sense of obligation to humanity. He was led to leave wealth for poverty, to turn from the society of the cultured and friendly that he might care of the needs of the ignorant and prejudiced, to renounce a luxurious home for a mud-walled hut. He went to India, and for forty years, without one single change, he dwelt among the people of that land. Persecution, epidemic, and fierce enervating heat would not drive him away from the crowded streets of Bombay. For forty years the thin, frail man spent himself in varied and unwearied self-denial, among a people who were persistently unresponsive and many a time violently hostile. During that time he would accept no alleviation of his self-imposed hardships, and would permit himself to receive no human honor. He was consumed with a passion for bettering the people amongst whom he lived, and he laid down his life on their behalf. That is the enthusiasm for humanity which the foreign mission enterprise in a hundred cases proves to have been developed among those who have embraced Christianity.

From the Rev. Theodore L. Cuyler, D. D.:

I never put my eye on that unique and heroic George Bowen, or ever had a line of correspondence with him. His volume of *Daily Meditations* is the most fresh and spiritually fertilizing book of that kind that has appeared in my time; its keen insight of God's Word and of human hearts was worthy of old Matthew Henry.

Alexander Duff—whose magnificent missionary address was the high-water mark of all the eloquence I ever heard—and George Bowen were widely different men. But it was worth planting Christian Missions in India if it were only to produce two such superb successors of the apostles . . . the record of a life "hid with Christ in God" but not to be hid from the loving admiration of God's people the world over.

From Bishop Edward G. Andrews, D. D.:

He was a Saint, pure, spiritual, self-sacrificing, full of simple victorious faith, and full of the missionary spirit of his Lord. His book of *Daily Readings* is one of the choicest of the devotional works of my library, and I never take it into my hand but what it brings to remembrance what I saw in his life, and emphasizes with unusual power the particular utterances of the successive days. I think that his general characteristics would be rather those of the mystic, than of the executive and administrative servant of the Lord Jesus Christ. He lived continually in communication with his Lord.

From the Rev. J. Sumner Stone, M. D., an article entitled "The White Yogi" in *Forward,* Dec. 23, 1889:

Two young men just landed from America on "India's coral strand" started out to see the curiosities and celebrities of a great city on the shore of the Indian Ocean. There were monuments, temples, and palaces by the score; there were princes and princelings, governors and generals and nabobs. But this morning we were hunting a prince, but not among palaces. So we picked our way through the crowded native district till we came to a broad street called Grant Road, and stopped in front of a low, one-storied building divided into narrow apartments, two rooms deep. This was the office of the *Bombay Guardian* and the home of its editor and proprietor—one of the celebrities of India. Americans and English called him George Bowen; natives called him the "White Yogi," or white saint. To our timid knock the door opened and—I started. It was December, 1880, yet we seemed to be in the presence of a Huguenot, Geneva Calvinist, or Scotch Covenanter of the sixteenth century. The figure that greeted us might have been John Calvin or John Knox. Spare body, thin face, gray beard, narrow, high forehead, surmounted by rimless skull cap, thus the "White Yogi" stood framed in the door, bidding the strangers to enter.

How shall I picture to you that room? It was small, its furniture was of the plainest type and limited. The editorial table was a chaos of books, copy, manuscripts, and periodicals. Among the books, placed without order in the bookcases, I noticed a loaf of bread next to a dictionary, and a few bananas sharing a shelf with some works on theology and sociology. I realized that I was in the presence of a remarkable man, in the sanctum of one of the leading writers of the Indian empire, one of the most distinguished representatives of Christianity in the eastern world. At once there flashed into my mind the words of Jesus concerning John the Baptist: "What went ye out into the wilderness to see? A man clothed in soft raiment? behold, they that wear soft clothing are in kings' houses. But what went ye out for to see? A prophet? yes, I say unto you, and more than a prophet."

George Bowen was a scholarly man; he was by birth and training a gentleman. He was widely read, widely traveled, a thoroughly trained man. When he wrote golden words flowed from his pen; gems of thought fell from his lips when he spoke. He had the brain of a philosopher, the soul of a poet, and the genius of a musician. I wish I could convey to you the impression produced by the strangely-gifted man when he sat down at the organ to let his fingers "wander idly over the noisy keys." He lived in poverty, yet he was rich—he had all that the millionaire possesses—sufficient. He lived among the poorest of the people, was a comrade of the coolie, yet he was sought by the cultured and the noble. . . .

Once a distinguished gentleman said to George Bowen: "I will come and have breakfast with you."

"Come and welcome," replied the White Yogi.

When the noble guest arrived he was received into the little editorial sanctum and seated amid the confusion of books and papers before described. There were no signs of breakfast. At last, when his appetite was beginning to call rather loudly for substantials, Mr. Bowen remarked: "We would better break our fast." He then set out a soap box, placed on it a loaf of bread, a bunch of bananas, a pitcher of water, two knives, and two glasses, and invited his guest to draw up and share his meal. There were no apologies. This was his daily fare. He counted it no discourtesy to share his ordinary meal with any man who might be his guest, be he bishop or beggar. . . .

The White Yogi differed from other saints of church and heathen history in many respects. He was not sour or sanctimonious. He was not austere or critical. He never complained of other people's style of living. He went, like Jesus, gladly to the feasts and festivals of rich and poor alike. In palace and hut George Bowen was always a welcome guest, ready by any means in his power to contribute to the joys of young and old.

He was not a monk in dress or manner. He was a brother among men of all degrees. He was an indefatigable worker, a student, a writer, a preacher, a missionary, a minister of Christ.

Nothing went on in the world—social, religious, or political—that escaped his notice. For nearly thirty years his journal spoke forth truths, commendations, admonitions, denunciations, that men of all creeds and ranks in India gave heed to. His editorial sanctum could be an Olivet or a Sinai.

This remarkable man finished his fortieth year of work in India without a furlough or vacation. One evening, shortly after this fortieth anniversary, he was induced by two Christian ladies, medical missionaries, to come to their home for a day or two, on the ground that he was not well and needed a little home nursing. It seemed strange for him, but he yielded and allowed himself to be cared for by them, as if they were his daughters. Several times during the night these ministering spirits looked into his room. About six in the morning he opened his eyes and saw one of the sisters, and smilingly greeted her with a cheery "Good morning!" At seven, when she came again, he was gone. The worn shell was lying on the cot like an abandoned chrysalis.

Dr. Stone has supplemented his account of "The White Yogi" in the following letter:

It was my good fortune to meet the Rev. George Bowen late in December, 1880, in Bombay, India. Landing that day from America I improved the opportunity to get acquainted with one with whose fame I was familiar. As he welcomed me to his humble home in a remote part of Bombay, he had the appearance of some long departed saint. Huss, Calvin or Knox, with thin face crowned by skull cap, emaciated frame, a reincarnation seemed to be greeting me with gentle voice in kindly welcome. He had the appearance of a recluse devoted to study and good works. I was fascinated by the man. He was living in extreme poverty, in two small rooms devoid of any luxuries. Yet if contentment implied riches, George Bowen was a multi-millionaire. No wonder he was named the "White Yogi." He was like one of the hermits of the early centuries without one of their vices. He was fastidious in dress, a perfect gentleman of culture in his devotion to high thinking, clean living and delight in human friendships. From the Government House on Malabar hill to the home of the humblest cottages he was prized as a friend. English, Americans, Eurasians, Hindus, Parsis, Moslems, all classes and conditions looked upon him as a saint. Yet he seemed utterly unconscious of sainthood.

His latch string was always out to callers, no matter whom. The scholar, the writer, the recluse never showed signs of annoyance when a visitor knocked at his door. It may be that only a box was available for a seat, yet with unaffected courtesy it was proffered, even to the high ecclesiastic, a Bishop delegated by Her Majesty Queen Victoria, when by her special orders he called to convey her respects. I, a young missionary, was received with the same courtesy as was the Queen's Chaplain. We both were served with a cup of tea brewed by Mr. Bowen. The great churchman related with delight how Mr. Bowen took a loaf of bread from behind some books on a library shelf, sliced and buttered the bread, then, when tea was ready, invited his distinguished guest to lunch with him. There was no display of affectation, but the utmost simplicity on the part of George Bowen in the hospitality extended. The chaplain of Her Majesty the Queen Empress of Great Britain and India, was entertained as would be an humble Eurasian or a poor missionary. Mr. Bowen's conversation was always adapted to the mental equipment of his guest. The great churchman spoke with delight of the feast of reason and flow of soul that made his hour with the saint and scholar memorable. . . .

It was my good fortune to be appointed in charge of the Methodist churches in Bombay and thus for a period of four years I became the pastor of Mr. Bowen. He was in my home when he passed away. On a day in February, 1888, we laid his wasted body under the grass and flowers. February is the month of roses in India. A group of his friends sang the old hymns of hope as we lowered the frail tenement of clay into the grave. In addition to his remarkable mental and spiritual gifts, George Bowen was a musician of unusual talent. His visits to our parsonage, where he dined with us once a week, will ever be remembered as musical treats. Sitting alone at the organ his improvisations reminded us of the Lost Chord as his fingers wandered over the keys evoking music strange and beautiful.

It has been my privilege to meet many distinguished men, but never one to compare with George Bowen, the White Yogi of Bombay, India. Gentle, humble, beloved by all, he was a ten talent servant of his Master Christ. He lived, served, passed to his reward an Imago Christi.

Another of those who knew Bowen in Bombay was Mrs. W. W. Bruere, who wrote under date of January 6, 1937:

I knew Bro. Bowen only a little over a year, as he died the first part of my second year in India.

A few things concerning him stand out in my memory very vividly.

The first few days after I arrived in Bombay with H. C. Stuntz and family Bro. Prautch took me to call upon Bro. Bowen. He lived alone in a little cabin-like house, as I remember, in the vicinity of Grant Road Church. We talked for a short time and then when we were ready to go, he arose and closed the door, and we knelt with him in prayer. As I remember he prayed for the new missionary and for the work that was being done by the missionaries in India.

He performed our marriage ceremony at a Mission House. Afterward he sat down and played on my organ, which I had taken with me to India, from Boston, Mass. He played so beautifully that I asked him what he played. He replied, "I don't know. I improvised it." Once when I was very ill he prayed for me and claimed, "The gifts of God are without repentance." He was greatly beloved, very humble, sincere, deeply religious.

Very popular—received daily invitations to dine at the home of Anglo-Indians and missionaries. He was our Dist. Supt.—so humble that when my husband, the Rev. W. W. Bruere, asked him to give him directions or orders about the work in Bombay he replied, "I prefer to take orders from you."

My husband was not on salary when we married, as he had gone as a volunteer to India at the call of Bishop William Taylor from Pennington, N. J., Seminary. Therefore he had no spare change—neither had I as I went out to India in a Faith Mission.

Unknown to me, my husband got up his courage and borrowed a small sum from Mr. Bowen for a short, inexpensive third class wedding trip to a nearby hill station.

Rev. George Bowen was of medium height, very thin, clothing hung loosely, wore a thin long gray beard, had beautiful blue eyes, always wore a black silk skull cap, never a sun helmet, worked early and late, walked long distances, always first to visit the sick, always ready to help the poor native who came to him.

As a listener or preaching, he was usually at the services held on the Sabbath, in three languages: English, Marathi and Tamil.

He had no cook, was very frugal, eating a banana only for breakfast while writing at his desk.

He literally lived the life of Jesus, preaching in the churches or on the streets and at a central square each evening at five o'clock.

Bishop William Taylor first instituted street preaching in Bombay (?). Crowds followed him from place to place, to hear the same talk, the blessed Gospel, which they never before heard in like manner. Among the converts were heads of families from among the educated English-speaking Hindus, Parsis and Anglo-Indians, the latter members of the Church of England. Some of these became stalwart members of the Methodist Episcopal Churches, the Church of England and Scottish Churches. These new converts were deeply attached to Rev. George Bowen. Great numbers of Hindus who never did outwardly become Christians reverenced him as a saint, a holy man.

In church while listening to a sermon, he had a habit of stroking his beard. I've often watched him in church doing this.

A funny thing was that he had an imitator in the person of a lowly Parsi Christian.

Mrs. Frances Hazen Gates, still living in 1937, remembers the impression which Bowen made upon her:

> I wonder if I am not the only person living who knew and loved George Bowen! My recollection of him goes back to 1857 when I was a girl of five years.
>
> Father and Mother were very fond of Mr. Bowen, and he frequently came to our house (we were living in Bombay) for a Sunday dinner.
>
> I think, probably, he was the homeliest man I have ever seen—plain of countenance, and thin, to ungainliness. But I think we who knew him realized his inward beauty. The children would rush to the door when we knew Mr. Bowen was coming and each would try to grasp at least a finger. I think perhaps I was his favorite, as he seemed to like to talk with me.
>
> I presume you have mentioned his early life as a non-Christian, parading as a fop the streets of New York City.
>
> At one time my mother hearing that Mr. Bowen had no bed, but lay on his desk, busied herself with another missionary lady and arranged a comfortable cot with all appurtenances. This was left in his room during his absence at one time. Some little time later Mr. Bowen said to mother, "Do you know of any poor woman who needs a bed? I found one in my room the other day, and I cannot sleep on it when I think some one else needs it."
>
> Some years later he visited us at Ahmednagar. Mother asked him, "Did you sleep well, last night?" His answer was truthfully characteristic, "To tell the truth, Mrs. Hazen, I did not sleep very well. I am so accustomed to sleeping on my office table that the soft bed kept me awake."
>
> My most vivid and delightful recollections of Mr. Bowen are when I was eleven and over. He used to come to the Annual Mission meeting held in Ahmednagar. In all social occasions he was the "life of the party." His jokes and funny doings kept every one laughing.
>
> At a picnic one time he called to Dr. Bissell, "I dare you to climb that tree"—(a very high tree with no low branches). He threw off his coat and rushed forward, as though he could easily climb it.

Closing Testimony

The Governor of Bombay and other officials thought highly of Mr. Bowen. Quaint as he was he mingled freely with cultured society. They recognized in him superior intelligence. An English lady told me once of being at Government House for a great reception. She saw an ungainly man, poorly dressed (not in evening dress) come in. The Governor excused himself to the group and went forward to eagerly meet the newcomer. My friend had thought him the Goanese cook, and was much surprised at the Governor's cordiality. She was later introduced to the "ungainly man" and had a chance to converse with him. She said to me, "What a wonderful man that Mr. Bowen is—he is a *genius*." Uncouth as he appeared, he never forgot his early life, and when in society, was refined in his manner.

The Indians loved him—as did the Europeans who knew him.

As a girl, Mr. Bowen wrote quite regularly to me and never was a letter ended without some beautiful thought in the way of advice. How I regret the necessity that came—owing to my coming to America—of having to dispose of those wonderful, helpful words. But I always remembered one of the last he wrote before I left. He was sorry to have me leave India. He felt there was a great work for me to do there and wrote something in this way: "Education does not always mean going to college. A man with a pencil and books can get a fine education."

I never saw Mr. Bowen "out of patience," or riled by anything.

I feel as though I had made a very feeble effort to give any kind of impression of a man who was truly a "man of God."

I never heard any criticism from any one as to his sincerity and matchless character. Every one who knew him loved him.

The late Bishop Oldham of the Methodist Episcopal Church, one of the saintliest men of the last generation, wrote:

Regarding George Bowen. The first time I met him was under rather remarkable circumstances. I was a young surveyor in the service of the British Government. He was located in Bombay in a humble tenement in one of the bazaars where who-so-ever would could approach and converse with him. But to return to my first meeting him. 'Twas on this wise:

I was on my way to Bombay from a town in the Western ghats, waiting for a train to Bombay. Presently a train rolls in with one of its carriages filled with English and Eurasian young people. I learned they were going home from a camp meeting held up in the hills. When the train rolled out the young people began to sing; but after a few minutes the voices became lower and finally ceased entirely. I had recently been converted and was very much alive to religious phenomena of any kind. The stopping of the singing was accompanied by a subdued thrill of feeling and I turned to my nearest neighbor to enquire "What ails the company?" The man silently pointed to the middle of the carriage where George Bowen was seated with his eyes closed and a rapt look on his face. "That's George Bowen and he is praying."

I recall this saying of his. We were talking of an Anglo-Indian missionary who was complaining of his scant salary. Bowen, who knew the man and the situation, quietly said, "A man can always double his income by halving his desires."

From Lieut. Col. G. W. Oldham, for many years in India in the Royal Engineers, and father of the Rev. J. H. Oldham of the International Missionary Council:

It was in the year 1870 that I first made the acquaintance of George Bowen of Bombay. My wife and I began then to attend an evening meeting for the study of the Word and prayers, at the house of the Rev. J. S. Robertson, Secretary of the Church Missionary Society. This weekly meeting was, at this time, almost the only center of social religious intercourse in Bombay. On the second or third occasion, as we were driving to the Mission House through the cocoanut groves in Girgaum in the moonlight, we passed two figures on the railway bridge walking quickly as if late. I remarked to my wife that I thought they were going to the meeting. Should we not offer them a seat in the carriage? She looked at the spare figure of Mr. Bowen, clad in white trousers and well worn alpaca coat, and hesitated. However, we picked up the strangers and found we had entertained an angel, whose friendship we afterwards prized among our greatest privileges.

I have always thought of George Bowen as man who had got 100 miles start in the Christian race, and no one seemed able to catch him up. He was then living at the Depot of the Religious Tract and Book Society, of which he was the unpaid agent. He lived in a small apartment adjoining the bookshop, without any comforts. His room was open to the road—hot and dusty. Many a passing beggar stopped to ask for alms which were bestowed if any pice were available. He preached two or three times a week in Marathi from his doorstep. In the sale room he received his visitors high and low of every name and nation. He was brother to every man, and especially welcomed all who were members of the household of faith. His ordinary fare consisted of bread and plantains, but he frequently breakfasted or had his evening meal with friends, at whose houses he was always a welcome guest.

I remember his telling me how he had been troubled with small ants getting into the bread place on his shelf. Those who have lived in India know how difficult it is to expel these intruders from a loaf of bread. Mr. Bowen prayed about it, and was presented with a tin box which delivered him from his enemies.

When the revival under William Taylor resulted in the formation of a Methodist Episcopal Church in Bombay, Mr. Bowen gave up the work he had so long carried on for the Tract Society, and helped as a minister to build up the Methodist Episcopal Church, which started on the lines of a self-supporting church and Mission. Mr. Bowen had long maintained that if the Indian Church was ever to become self-supporting it must have set before it the example of a church, with a spirit of self-sacrifice, whose pastors would be content to live on salaries such as Indian Christians could afford as members to give. I have heard it said that he never spent more than Rupees 20 a month on himself. When he removed to live in a room in Moos Buildings, Grant Road, he continued the same simple mode of life. He came to breakfast with us once a week. If he arrived a little before the time when we assembled, he would open the piano and improvise sweet harmonies, or recall the music of his early days. Although his life was that of an ascetic, he made no profession of asceticism. He protested against any such idea. There was a story current that one of the Cowley fathers visited him and inquired as to his rules of diet. He replied that he ate what was set before him, asking no questions.

On one occasion when he was absent from Bombay a friend got the key of his room from the neighbor with whom it was left. We had his room thoroughly cleaned, and his scanty wardrobe renewed. The next time we met at breakfast, Mr. Bowen who had a real vein of humor, and suspected our complicity, complained that during his absence thieves had broken into his house.

The heading of one of his articles in the *Bombay Guardian,* in the hottest week of the year, was "Mangos." It began somewhat in this way. "Circumstances being favorable (meaning if he got one) we eat one mango every hot season." Then followed one of those deeply spiritual articles which like the four streams that went out from the Garden of Eden issued week after week from his pen to refresh weary souls throughout India and in the regions beyond.

The late Dr. Hanna of Edinburgh, who wrote the short account of George Bowen which prefaced the edition of *Daily Meditations* published by Douglas, Edinburgh, told me that when staying in Liverpool at the house of a former Bombay merchant, his host, in bidding him good night put into his hand a copy of the American edition of the *Meditations* and asked him to let him know his opinion of the book. Dr. Hanna sat up late, reading page after page, and next morning he said to his host, "I want to know something of the life of the author, because the book is written from a higher standpoint in Christian experience than almost any book I have ever read." This led Dr. Hanna to make further enquiries as to George Bowen's life and to give the result in the preface. Mr. Bowen was no great preacher, but his life was a sermon after the pattern of the Sermon on the Mount, and it was consistent to the end, which was peace. I left India in 1881 but returned for a few weeks in December, 1887. He was crippled then with a broken thigh-bone but the same humble, loving, saintly man.

I thank God on every remembrance of him because of his likeness to his Master.

George Bowen's conversion from unbelief to faith was a spiritual movement to which every part of his nature gave consent, and the life which followed was the harmonious expression of his whole being thus raised to a higher plane by the revelation of God in Christ. That reality which is referred to in this sketch as the leading characteristic of all his religious life, was the result of this transformation. All he did in the service of the Savior Who had revealed Himself to him was done with the calmness, the resolution, the rationalness of one who found in the atmosphere of a consecrated Christian life his soul's true element. This was the secret of the joy and beauty of his self-sacrifice. There is a kind of self-denial which is ever conscious of itself. But his was true and beautiful in proportion as it was free from this selfish taint. It was attractive because it was so unconscious....

To those of us who were intimately associated with the departed missionary leader, the sense of loss has day by day grown deeper. Christian work with which he was associated and Christian assemblies which he was wont to frequent, have seemed almost less Christian by reason of the absence of one who gave the high tone of his own spirit to everything with which he was identified. As we contemplate the end of his conversation we are not strangers to the danger of resting satisfied with a vicarious devotion. It was inspiring and strengthening to know that one lived and worked so nobly in the midst of us.

But perhaps the most striking and adequate appreciation of Bowen was from a purely secular source, representing not the missionary community but the British civil and military viewpoint. It was the tribute of the *Times of India,* Feb. 11, 1888, the leading English paper then in Western India:

> The death of Rev. George Bowen, the tidings of which passed rapidly through our city on the 5th instant, has deprived this community of one of its oldest and most widely honored members. The sorrow awakened

by his unexpected removal is not confined to any one section of the Christian Church, or to any one class of the community. One who has for forty years occupied a unique place as a missionary among us has passed away, and the sense of loss is intensified by the feeling, present doubtless to the minds of all who knew him, that the place of George Bowen will always remain empty. His was a work and a personality sui generis, and, in the ordinary acceptation of the word, he can have no successor. The removal of George Bowen marks the close of an epoch in the history of our community. Those who were acquainted with the select spirits who engaged in the first beginnings of Christian enterprise in this part of India will recognize in his departure the passing away of the last link that bound the present to that memorable past, and many Anglo-Indians living in retirement in the homeland will feel that the only remaining living tie between them and the city of their former habitation has now been broken. Nearly thirteen years ago one of the great leaders—John Wilson—fell, and now another, different in the bent of his mind and in the methods of his life, but of similar purpose and similar wide-reaching influence, has followed.

An outline of Mr. Bowen's life has already appeared in our columns; in the present sketch we shall attempt only a brief estimate of the character and influence of the man. George Bowen was a man of rare individuality. In any community this individuality would have asserted itself, but in a community like ours, in which the conditions of society so manifestly tend to the leveling down of all men to the same tone of thinking and action, a man who could stand alone, who could mold his life according to his own high convictions of responsibility, and who felt bound by no artificial standards, could not but stand forth as a conspicuous personality. Hence it was that many a visitor passing through our city, intent upon noting not merely the outward features of our life in Western India but also the moral forces which are at work among us, sought out before all things the humble dwelling of this saintly man, that they might be brought in contact with something of the inward movements that are silently molding the life of the community.

Mr. Bowen was known to most as a missionary who chose, for the furtherance of the cause to which he had devoted himself, a style of life marked by extreme self-sacrifice and privation; by many he was regarded as a kind of Christian faqir. But this latter conception of him must appear to those who knew him best as singularly misleading and incomplete. In his own autobiographical sketches he has himself set forth the reasons which impelled him to select this particular mode of life and to desire to be independent of any foreign support. He aimed at divesting himself of everything that might stand as a barrier between him and the people of the land, and that might prevent them from discerning the true disinterestedness of Christian effort. He chose the example of St. Paul as his model, and working, not with trained hands as did the apostle, but with his versatile and cultured mind, he became chargeable to none. This naturally called forth a mode of life of the simplest and most self-denying kind lived among the dwellings of the humble.

From his humble dwelling he issued every morning on missions of love to those needing Christian guidance and consolation and on visits to his Christian friends and fellow-workers. He might be seen returning with quick step when the sun was already well up, and during the hotter hours of the day he would be found busy at his desk engaged in study and correspondence, in receiving visits from inquirers whom he instructed, or in the editorial duties connected with the *Bombay Guardian*. Again, as evening drew near, he sallied forth to the places where he was wont to preach in the open air to the passing crowds. On many an evening he might have been seen standing on the steps at the base of the great lamp in front of the Money School proclaiming his message to the large congregation of passers-by that usually gathered around him. In the later evening he would be found conducting religious services in the church with which he was connected, or taking part in the important work of Bible translation or revision, or visiting the homes of his most intimate friends, into which his presence seemed always to bring something of the higher atmosphere in which he lived and worked.

It might be thought that such a life would gradually have tended to narrowness and exclusiveness, and this may have been the impression formed by casual observers who saw only the outside of his life and knew nothing of the man. But George Bowen's self-denial sprung from a genuine love of men, and this love, in combination with the high culture of his early life, preserve him from that narrowing of sympathy which occasionally accompanies some forms of intense religiousness.

Mr. Bowen in his early life had enjoyed the best opportunities which wealthy and cultured surrounding could supply. The story of his early life, his dark time of skepticism, and his remarkable transition from darkness to light has already been told in our columns. The change in his life was so marked, so distinct in his own consciousness, that we need not wonder that it was followed by a life of corresponding intensity and decision. St. Paul, whom he chose as his apostolic model, passed through a great crisis followed by a life the most pronounced that the church has ever furnished, and so was it, in his own measure, with this devoted missionary who sought humbly to follow in his footsteps. He, too, retained throughout his new life all his breadth of culture, and no circumstances or surrounding, however humble, could dwarf the moral and spiritual dignity of the man; on the contrary, they only served to render it more conspicuous. In his most humble dwelling he could entertain the humblest and make him feel welcome; but in the same dwelling the highest had no consciousness of the exceptional surroundings and no feeling of condescension in the presence of one who received them with true gentlemanly courtesy and dignity.

The same breadth of nature was conspicuous in his relations with men and with churches. During the later years of his life he was specially associated with the Methodist Episcopal Church of America; and yet he seemed to be the exclusive property of no one denomination, and to have the power of sympathizing with every method of Christian activity that was directed to the same high aim to which his life was consecrated. His views of missionary methods were characterized by a breadth that is not too common, and to those who knew him best there will always remain the memory of one who was ever self-denying, yet ever genial, intensely devoted to his own work, yet ever ready to sympathize with the work of others. This geniality found frequent expression in the families which knew him best, in the wider social circle, and in the company of his fellow-workers. It explains the quiet humor which brightened the pages of his *Guardian,* and our readers must often have noted it in the extracts which we frequently brought into our pages, dealing with men and with things.

Within the brief compass of an article we can only touch upon the literary side of Mr. Bowen's activity. The *Bombay Guardian,* which for many years was conducted under his sole editorship, supplied a constant field for the exercise of his literary gifts. His expositions of Scripture were marked by a rare insight and keenness of perception akin to genius, and some of these collected into works of devotion, notably his *Daily Meditations,* have attained a wide circulation in this country, in Great Britain, and in America. His keen observation was directed also to other subjects, and in questions of government and policy his judgment was often fearlessly given.

His republican sympathies could never blind his vision to the reality of the blessings of the mild despotism by which monarchy rules in India, and our Government has often received the support of his independent and fearless pen in matters in which superficial criticism has sometimes misled thinkers of less penetration and weaker judgment. Nor was he slow to condemn the actions of those in power when he felt them to be unworthy of the representatives of a great Christian nation. The natives of India will miss his advocacy of their just rights, and the Government of Bombay ought to feel the loss of a conscientious critic of its policy and an unbiased supporter of all that is just and righteous in its administration. Such writers and such editors are a strength to the public press of any country, and we believe that Mr. Bowen's example and influence as an editor have borne good fruit.

Mr. Bowen's whole life was a testimony to the disinterestedness of his aims; but special instances of it were of frequent occurrence. One of these, which is strikingly characteristic of the man, may be mentioned. A wealthy gentleman of this city, who had been greatly impressed by Mr. Bowen's life and who knew also the independence of his character, was desirous of expressing in some tangible form his admiration for the man. He knew that he could not offer him any pecuniary gift, but as he left the country he placed a large sum of money at his credit in one of the banks with instructions that, after he had sailed, Mr. Bowen should be apprized of his possession. Soon after an appeal came from Calcutta for aid in the erection of a church, and the whole of this large amount, thus secretly gifted to the missionary, was immediately contributed by him to meet the urgent need of his Christian brethren in Calcutta. And throughout his life of privation, although he had little consciousness of his own needs, he was ever mindful of the wants of others, and contributed to the help of Christian and other benevolent schemes on a scale which few were able to understand and fewer still were able to follow.

The life of such a man could not fail to make a deep impression on all earnest minds in this community. We have no doubt that many of our native fellow-citizens have felt its influence, and some of them have not been slow to acknowledge it. We know of many amongst our own countrymen who owe all that is best in their lives to their contact with him and of others who were made better through their reverence for his character; and no one enjoyed the love and confidence of the Native Christian community more truly than the missionary who so thoroughly identified himself with all their interests. It is a mark of true greatness to be able thus to attract such a diversity of men and minds. The poor and the rich, the uneducated and the cultured, alike found a point of attachment in the character of the man. There can be little doubt where that point lay.

Reality and self-forgetting sympathy were the most marked features of his character, and these are the qualities which most inspire confidence and affection. His was a nature incapable of affectation and free from all self-consciousness. He was self-denying, not because he was conscious of the esteem and admiration which self-denial wins, but because this was the form in which his life found its most natural expression. He was humble, not because humility is beautiful and attractive, but because he had learned to be meek and lowly in heart. Hence the power and influence of his devotional writings, so different from much that is written on similar subjects; hence the manly vigor of his thought when it entered the most sacred regions of the soul and touched the highest themes.

We have dwelt upon these features of the life of this man of faith. Through forty years that life has been among us, from its very character mingling little with the busy currents of public movements that have been flowing onwards, guided by other aims and other plans; and yet we cannot but feel poorer that a life so rich in noble purpose and lofty aim has passed away from among us. Gladly and ungrudgingly, therefore, do we offer this tribute of honor to the memory of one who neither loved nor sought it while he lived.

To this estimate of the *Times of India,* Mr. Rankin's judgment may be added. From Mr. Rankin, Dec. 23, 1902:

There was never such a paper as the *Guardian* under Bowen's hand. No great interest was unrepresented in that journal. Its political influence was strong, and of the very best kind in India. Its selections and discussions showed the extraordinary range and quality of the editor's mind, while everything was viewed in the light of the highest criteria, and with such a threefold knowledge of Christianity—philosophical, historical and experimental—as in its combination never was surpassed, so I believe.

The kind of personal contact with representatives of all religions which was possessed by Bowen made him an expert, if there ever was one, in comparative religion. His conclusions are shared by every great missionary scholar who ever lived in India, China or elsewhere—Duff, Carey, Kellogg, Legge, Williams, Martin, McCartee and all the rest. And these conclusions are set at naught by the confident exponents of our modern thought, who have nothing but a superficial acquaintance—however great their erudition—with the Bible, or the pagans, or even their own souls. But they are preparing the way for a general apostasy from the faith once delivered to the saints—*me judice.* Bowen, like Schwartz, was also an example of the political value of the missionary. He held the confidence of all parties except parties to wrong. He was known to understand intimately the sentiments of the natives. He also was *persona grata* with the best foreign families and officials.

The political value of the missionary may often be summed up in his common function of *interpreter,* but interpreter raised to the nth power, such as that mentioned in Elihu's address to Job. Think of Livingstone interpreting England to Africa and Africa to England! What if all interpreters were like him! Robert Morison, Gutzlaff and Medhurst interpreting England to China and China to England; Bridgman, Parker,

Williams, Martin, McCartee interpreting China to America and America to China—interpreting each at its truest and best to the other, holding in themselves and promoting between countries confidence, conciliation and some measure of fraternity, not only as indispensable linguists, but always as confidential and trusted advisers in the most important matters, without whose agency nothing could issue but misunderstanding and strife.

The missionary is often the real and principal agent of negotiations, while another man bears the title; and often he molds the impression made, he supplies a great part of the facts and the wisdom called for in each exigency; not only this, but he often initiates measures of the utmost importance, which without him would not be considered. He supplies the intelligence by which the political parties find possible a rapprochement; and above all he exemplifies that good faith with all parties concerned, on which alone treaties, conferences, conventions ever can stand. He is without duplicity while he shows the best diplomacy, and he combines the utmost loyalty to his own government with an ardent purpose to promote the welfare of the people among whom he lives. He interprets man to man, country to country and Heaven to earth, while he shows that whether in earth or Heaven the justification of any moral being or party is contingent on the observance of good faith, without which moral, social and political alienation must ensue. Thus he proves that his theology is in accordance with the nature of things and the whole order of the moral universe. . . .

But Bowen's political value was not only thus in his direct and personal offices, his personal advice being often sought, but also through his periodical, which both summed up all important news and contained the most weighty discussion of public measures, international relations, and those between the British Government and all classes of the India natives. Bowen was not less a missionary for this political work, but all the more one. He believed with John Milton that "there are no politics like those which the Scriptures teach," and he taught and exemplified in India the politics of the Hebrew prophets and also of St. Paul. The missionary is the heart of all the best things in our outward state, no less than the means of the largest inward good. He not only preaches the Gospel, but teaches men to observe all things that Christ has commanded. And he teaches not only by precept; he exemplifies these teachings in the common affairs and common relations of life.

From Mr. Rankin, Dec. 30, 1902:

> In the entire history of missions no man can be named who exemplifies a more perfect combination of character and culture than George Bowen; or who more completely reproduces under modern conditions of life

and thought that are highly pronounced, the apostolic experience of truth and ideal of life. Some particular aspects of Christian experience appear in larger relief in some other persons; but no one has shown an experience more symmetrical and complete. Perhaps as nearly parallel an instance as exists is that of Catherine Adorna, Saint of Genoa, than whom the Church of Rome can show no Christian character more lofty, evangelical, symmetrical and sane. But in George Bowen may be found all that is best in her experience, and in that of Augustine, Bernard, Tauler, Luther, Boehme, Hermann, Fénelon, Bunyan, Alleine, Jonathan Edwards, Brainerd and J. B. Taylor.

Bowen was not only converted to Christ from pronounced infidelity, and an intensely world life, but as well as any modern ever did, he understood the whole meaning of Pentecost. Of all that is said best in J. C. Shairp's *Culture and Religion* Bowen supplies a luminous example, as also of all that is best in the books of Law and Murray and Meyer, while his own books on the Christian life are religious classics of first quality, unsurpassed in many ways in the literature of Christianity. The lesson of his life is peculiarly pertinent, if not uniquely so, to this very hour of history and thought.

George Bowen's method of life and work was not an absolute method. There is nothing in the Scriptures which makes it prescriptive and while the spirit of his life is the right spirit for all workers for Christ and for man, experience did not demonstrate that his methods were the only methods or the most effective methods. They were probably much more effective than Bowen himself believed. He referred with some despondency at times to the apparent fruitlessness of his work, but at his funeral, Mr. Hume, speaking of the great indirect influence he wielded over the natives of Bombay, mentioned "cases which had come under his own observation of heathen who had been brought to Christ through the holy life of him who for forty years had been before the people as a living example of the saving, keeping, sanctifying power of Christ as no other man had been."

Those who deny the absoluteness of Bowen's method are in a position of real peril, however. We may easily turn back from such self-sacrifice to a spiritual easiness and self-indulgence which are fatal to the highest power. It may be feared sometimes that over-reaction from the ascetic ideals of earlier days will carry us too far. Those who say, "We will not fast with the outward fast," easily forget that fast of the heart which is the gate of God. Those who would "use this world without abusing it" find the road, though the right road, very slippery. After all, it is better to err on the side of robust sacrifice, of completeness of self-denial, and to give up all literally, rather than under the plea of moderation to cover over a love of the world, or of pleasure, or of ease which is the death of holiness and of the might of God in a man.

Bowen was no narrow-minded ascetic recluse. "It is too common in these days," says Dr. Mackichan of the United Free Church of Scotland, in a little sketch of Mr. Bowen, "to look upon every form of high devotedness as the offspring of a certain one-sidedness, verging on fanaticism, the result of excess or defect in some emotion or faculty in minds otherwise rational and well furnished. We have little doubt that the popular conception of George Bowen's life amongst those who had but slight contact with it was not very different from this. The study of this sketch of the life which it enfolds will show how far such conceptions fall short of the realities of the Christian life. It exhibits the development of a mind singularly free from the enthusiasm of mere emotion, broad enough to be able to assimilate the best elements of the culture of other times and other lands, and strong enough to retain its own originality in the midst of all the influences which crowded in upon it."

An outstanding characteristic of Bowen was his reality. The *Times* editorial emphasized this. All who knew Bowen felt it. Dr. Mackichan refers to it: "George Bowen's conversion from unbelief to faith was a spiritual movement to which every part of his nature gave consent, and the life which followed was the harmonious expression of his whole being thus raised to a higher plane by the revelation of God in Christ. That reality which is referred to in this sketch as the leading characteristic of all his religious life, was the result of this transformation. All he did in the service of the Savior Who had revealed Himself to him was done with the calmness, the resolution, the rationalism of one who found in the atmosphere of a consecrated Christian life his soul's true element. . . . And this reality was the secret of the joy and beauty of his self-sacrifice. There is a kind of self-denial which is ever conscious of itself. But his was true and beautiful in proportion as it was free from this selfish taint."

No faintest shadow of uncandor, of hypocrisy, of professionalism, darkened George Bowen's life. He was what he appeared. He appeared what he was. And he tried to be and appear what he ought. A bad man may claim to possess the virtue of reality because he is really bad. But Bowen believed that the only reality of life is the right adjustment of itself to God and goodness and he strove thereto. And men were influenced by him through his reality. The missionary finds sincere men among Mohammedans, Hindus and Buddhists, not men who are living up to all the light they have, but men who honestly believe what they profess and in human measure live by it. The same thing in the missionary will not convince them that he is right and themselves wrong. His type of reality must be larger and fuller. He must be sincere and honest and true but the truth which he represents must be the complete truth, the divine element, and his reality must mean the adjustment and coordination of his life to that.

Bowen's spiritual fervor and devotion did not blind the accuracy of his intellectual judgments. There is a pious goodness, which desiring to speak evil of no man, is derelict in its testimony to the truth and defective in its defense of righteousness. Bowen was the soul of charity but he was the servant of the truth and he did not sacrifice truth to amiability. "I am convinced," he wrote to Mr. Rankin, "that Chundra Sen was more intent on his own glory, throughout, than on that of Christ. He honored the Christ of his own conception, the Christ that was plastic in his hands, to be molded as the Hindu national pride demanded. There was no unconditional surrender to Christ at any time. The Christ that he favored was one that would give greatness to Chunder Sen." This was Bowen's spirit in the study of comparative religion. He was not deceived. He saw the truth clearly, unobscured by the immoral tolerance of a false liberalism, and the truth he saw he spoke. Because he was good, he was not "gullible," to use Vivakanda's adjective in expressing his judgment of the American people. All religious expressions were not the same to Bowen. Some of them rested as he had told his pundit at the beginning on a foundation of untruth. There are false religious elements as there are true and they are not to be mixed indiscriminately.

As with all great religious leaders, so with George Bowen, his doctrine grew out of his experience. "You will have seen," he writes to Mr. Rankin, "that I wrote something about the Trinity. The Bible does not undertake to explain it to us. What it most positively teaches us is the Trinity of God, and what is said about the manifestation of God in Christ is never treated as though it conflicted with that in any way. We get at the right conception of these things not so much by intellectual effort, as experimentally. As we grow up into Christ, we apprehend Christ. There should never be a shadow of doubt in the mind (there never has been in mine) that in honoring Christ we honor the Father."

On the same subject, he writes later, "I have no trouble or confusion as that you speak of in regard to the persons of the Godhead. I conceive of God as absolutely one, yet have no difficulty in apprehending God in Christ and God the Spirit in me. Without this trifold manifestation I have never known God. There is more approach to a mystery in the distinguishing between the Christ of God and His brethren fully redeemed, in whom too is all the fullness of the Godhead. John fell at the feet of one of these. But I suppose there will be practically no difficulty. He is always the Savior and they are always the saved. John 17 and Ephesians 3, etc., show that we must get where Christ was when about to ascend. The more fully we are conformed to Him, the better we shall understand all things."

Bushnell solved the mystery of the Trinity in the same way and in the end we shall find that what theology is unlivable will be difficult of permanent propagation in mission fields. Religious value is not the right criterion of truth, but the truth whose religious value is not known and evidenced in our own life we shall find it hard to communicate to others.

His deep Christian experience, his attempt to make his Christian life real and his shrewd knowledge of the heart, led Bowen to anticipate by many years that form of Christian teaching represented in many contemporary movements for the deepening of the spiritual life. As Bowen put it in his *Daily Meditations* (for December 30th): "You believe in Christ and not in yourself; in His goodness, not in yours; in His power and wisdom, not your own; in His word, not in yours; in His work, not in yours; in His sufferings, not in yours; in His prayers, not in yours. When a man believes his vessel to be on the point of going to pieces, and is hailed by another that is seaworthy, you will quickly find him removing all his goods from the first to the other one. His faith finds unequivocal utterance in his conduct. And he that believes in Jesus Christ makes haste to get everything that he values transferred to Him." And he wrote in 1880 in a personal letter: "The best use we can make of our past sins is to turn from them to Christ. Anything that diverts our attention from Christ does us harm. This and that sin may appear very odious to us, and are so truly, but with God the most odious sin is that of not accepting His offer of love. . . . There is not the slightest use in trying to correct anything amiss in our mental habits by direct efforts. We get the victory by faith, i. e., by ceasing to combat them and making them over to Christ. Do not even be impatient with these evils. Nothing so discomfits Satan as when you praise the Lord (2 Chron. 10:20)."

It is an intensely interesting thing to see in church history how the teaching of Christian men regarding the higher spiritual life repeats itself from age to age and how the heresies of the earlier days arise recurrently, and especially in both matters in connection with Christian missions.

The wisest and most practical attempts of today to feed the hungry human soul, Bowen anticipated. Human hearts crave the sense of assurance, the secret of peace, the way of a larger life, something more than the conventional teaching gives, or the conventional standard requires. What Bowen said is just what those who attempt to meet these higher spiritual demands must always say: "I live in hope," as, we have seen, he wrote to Mr. Rankin, "that you will send me word some day that you are believing these words of God that offer eternal life to whomsoever, and banish that sense of condemnation and all vain thirsting. Whatever your nature really demands for its highest development is in that word 'eternal life.' I wish that you would make up your mind that nothing more is ever to come from God than has come to you, and give your attention to what has come to you and is ignored by you. It was a blessed hour for me when I lost faith in the future, and began to interrogate the present.

"I think I see a prisoner in a cell. On a table a letter has been lying many days which he fancies for somebody else and not for him. It authorizes him to claim the right of egress and to go out of his jail and to go to a comfortable dwelling provided for him. But, he says, it is not for me; if it were for me, it would not leave me here. He is there because he has not faith. Why should you make light of all that God has done to inspire you with faith? You do this when you fail to recognize what God offers you. The lying spirit of unbelief will say to you: 'This does not suit your case. Let not the spirit continue in his post of doorkeeper of your heart.' How glad should I be to hear that you have decided to let God be true, though every man a liar. All happiness is in the recognition of Him Who sits upon the throne, Whose nature and Whose Name is Love, Who gives Himself and is Himself Love Almighty to every atom, and is excluded only by man's unbelieving heart. God has never done anything for me, or will do, that He is not offering to every creature, for He offers Himself and He is Love. You have only to let God be true, let Him be Himself, and you will find yourself in paradise. The New Jerusalem comes down from God out of Heaven when men discover this. But it is hid from them by the great concern that they have for self. Do not allow your heart to cheat you out of the blessings contained in this truth...."

Again he writes: "I deeply feel that what you want is not that God should take up some new attitude towards you or do anything, or be anything but what He is, but that you should recognize Him as revealed at the Cross. What makes heaven to be heaven is that the truth that you failed to see is there seen by all." Bowen counseled thus out of his own experience. "As you would wish your own word to be honored," he wrote (August 11, 1885), "honor God's. Salvation is in that very thing. I was just on the border of despair in 1845, till on the 4th of December I saw that all I had been seeking in myself, I had in Christ. I had been tormenting myself by looking hourly to my own heart for the dawn of a brighter day, looking (if you please) for Christ in my heart rather than for Christ in the Word, and I found life, joy, and peace when I let go my own heart and looked to Christ alone, as the Israelites looked to the brazen serpent." The path he urged upon others he had trod himself and he knew whither it led.

One supreme test George Bowen met. Little children loved him and felt that in him they had a friend without dissimulation or suggestion of distrust. Can a man ask more than that? When he died, says Motley of the great William, in *The Rise of the Dutch Republic,* "the little children cried in the streets."

Men fall fast out of memory and George Bowen would not have lifted a finger to prolong his fame. But he is a man whom we cannot afford to forget. In reviving his story, one is conscious of the danger to which Dr. Mackichan referred just after Bowen's death:

> To those of us who were intimately associated with the departed missionary leader, the sense of loss has day by day grown deeper. Christian work with which he was associated and Christian assemblies which he was wont to frequent, have seemed almost less Christian by reason of the absence of one who gave the high tone of his own spirit to everything with which he was identified. As we contemplate the end of his conversation we are not strangers to the danger of resting satisfied with a vicarious devotion. It was inspiring and strengthening to know that one lived and worked so nobly in the midst of us. But to admire and describe this life is the least part of that which it requires of us. In every department of Christian service the same spirit of reality and consecration is needed, and if this brief record of his life shall in any measure help to keep alive the memory of this man of God, and lead those who have a part in the same work to become partakers of his higher faith, it will be contributing to the accomplishment of no unimportant part of the work for which George Bowen lived and labored and died.

It is easy for us to be content with looking at such sacrifice and total devotion in a Christian missionary of a past generation. But there was no standard of duty or ideal of character before George Bowen that is not before us. If he utterly denied himself and wholly sought to live unto God in all things, it was in response to no call that does not also sound in our hearts and summon us to the same task of the world's evangelization and to the same life of Christlike candor and reality. In the quiet of our souls can we not hear the Voice saying to us, "And you, why do not you, too, follow Me, as he followed whom men called 'The Lamb of India'?"

Index

Aikman, Dr. Robert, 7, 139, 143, 147, 180
Anderson, Rufus, 150, 163, 178, 225, 233, 236, 292, 294, 299, 300, 302 f, 351
Andrews, E. G., 373, 398 f, 402, 481
Arminian or Calvinist? 122, 358, 404, 423 ff, 481
Atterbury, John G., 13, 109, 125, 153, 271
Atterbury, W. W., 6, 13 ff, 16, 116, 271, 391, 396 f, 475
Aurelius, Marcus, 464

Baker, Albert H., 387
Ballantine, H. W., 286, 290, 318, 338
Barrows, Mrs. S. J., 6, 323 ff
Bible, 405
Bombay Guardian, 5 f, 8, 10, 16, 19, 21, 28, 30, 33, 90, 113, 117, 145, 163, 168, 246, 271, 289, 303, 331, 332, 334, 338, 340 ff, 344 f, 347, 366, 369, 376, 392, 400 ff, 404, 407 f, 413 f, 417, 421, 423, 436, 443, 445, 472, 477, 479, 481, 489, 493
Booth, Mrs. William, 415
Bowman, A. A., 440
Bowman, Bishop, 380
Bruere, Mrs. W. W., 485
Bulkley, Edwin A, 7, 141

Carlyle, 64 f, 291, 314, 435
Cassidy of Poona, 279, 284
Colenso, Bishop Jon William 439
Conscience, 18, 71, 74, 103, 109, 110, 120, 130, 168, 171, 201, 213, 220 f, 230, 241, 250, 279, 295, 342, 344, 391, 395, 424, 426 f, 429, 449, 451
Cook, Joseph, 391, 468
Cuyler, Theodore L., 7, 468, 480

Dale, R. W., 425
Dashiell, Alfred H., 7, 141
Dayspring, 189, 192
Dean, Mrs. S. C., 7, 333
Decennial Missionary Conference, 393, 395, 407
Doremus, T. C., 343
Drummond, Henry, 425, 434, 468 ff
Dulles, J. W., 145, 410, 414, 420
Dyer, Alfred S., 344 ff

Eastman, O., 157
Emerson, 86, 314, 394, 434, 464 f, 470
Evangelist, New York, 186, 302, 371

Fairbank, Rev. Edward, 283
Field, Henry M., 371
Ford, Joshua E., 121, 157 f, 237
Fraser, A. H. L., (son of Dr. Fraser) 330, 373
Fraser, Dr., 246, 270, 283, 340, 349, 372
Frere, Sir Bartle, 330, 410, 433 f
"Future Probation," 430 ff

Gandhi, 441 f
Gates, Mrs. F. H., 486
Gillespie, John, 15 ff
Gray, Robert, 141
Greenwood, Mrs. W. G., 7, 328, 331
Griffin, Sir Lepel, 433

Haigh, Henry, 480
Hanna, William, 411, 413, 415, 421, 470, 489 f
Hanscom, Captain, 7, 353 f, 360, 373
Hard, Rev. C. P, 7, 401 ff, 404, 436
Harding, Charles, 326, 349 f, 359
Hebich, Samuel, 372, 445
Hume, Rev. E. S., 6, 19, 32, 89, 187, 192, 239 f, 246, 270, 283, 290, 296, 335, 407

Independent, The, 461
Indian Mutiny, 315, 433
Irving, Edward, 194, 262, 286

Jacobs, 390 f
Jukes, Andrew, 415

Kelvin, Lord, 152
Ker, C. B., 355
Keshub Chundra Sen 362, 441, 499
Kirby, Colonel, 354, 358
Kittredge, George A., 335

Larkins, 276, 341
Lawrence, Brother, 463 f, 469
Lawrence, Henry, 319 f
Lawrence, "Modern Missions in the East," 399
Leeds, S. P., 7, 141, 143

Mackichan, Principal, 298, 335 f, 422, 498, 502
Maroncelli, 30
Morris, Emma, 92, 103
Martineau, Harriet, 314
Maynard, J. Douglas, 344, 347 f
Miller, William, 442, 445

Mitchell, J. Murray, 7, 289, 340, 396, 435
Molesworth, 324
Moody, D. L., 7, 371, 411, 425, 469
Munger, Mrs. 300, 308, 349

Nesbit, 306
Oldham, Col. G. W., 6, 385, 391, 400, 413, 435, 488
Oldham, Bishop W. F., 487
Oluph, 5, 21 ff, 24 f, 37, 406
Osborn, Mrs. L. D., 7, 400
Osborne, Dennis, 7, 377, 379, 384, 475

Park, Miss A. M., 7, 337
"Pathstruie," 421
Phillips, Philip, 371
Potter, J. G., 7, 476
"Problem in Missions, The," 446
Pupil of Raphael, 7, 90 f, 406, 462

Rankin, H. W., 7 f, 15, 91, 368, 394, 414, 461 ff, 465 f, 469 f, 495, 497, 499, 501
Rittonji Nowroji, 477
Robinson, Dr. Edward, 117, 146 f, 158
Robinson, Bishop, J. E., 5 f, 207, 344, 472, 474

Salvation Army, 392, 394, 415, 418, 432, 443
Sanderson, Sir George, 433
Sheshadri Narayan, 231, 245, 272, 275, 286, 312, 319, 404, 406
Skinner, Rev. Dr. T. H., 113 f, 142 f, 158 f, 163, 281, 411
Smith, Amanda, 382 f, 385
Smith, Robertson, 429
Stearns, 325, 354, 358, 360
Steele, Daniel, 343, 413 ff, 420
Stevenson, Dr., 176, 289, 340
Stone, J. Sumner, 7, 473, 481, 483
Strong, Stephen C., 172
Stuntz, H. C., 344, 484
Sullivan, John L., 438

Taylor, Bishop William, 7, 246, 343, 358 f, 361 ff, 364 ff, 367 f, 370, 372, 376 f, 398 f, 402, 404, 418, 420, 439, 443 f, 485, 489
Tedford, L. B., 7, 475
Thoburn, J. M., 6 f, 343, 361, 367, 372, 377, 398, 401 f
Thomson J. J., 152
Times of India, 490, 495
Tripe, Colonel, 357

Victoria, Queen, 369, 484

Wales, Prince of, 369 f, 438
Walton, Izaak, 427
White, Henry, 117, 145
Williams, Mornay, 15, 410
Williams, W. R., 15, 410 f
Williams, Mrs. W. R., 7, 15
Wilson, John, 202, 491
Wood, Mr. and Mrs., 145, 165, 186

A Note from the Publisher

The annals of the Church are replete with the names of missionary saints: Francis of Assisi, David Brainerd, David Livingstone, Mary Slessor, Adoniram Judson, Hudson Taylor, Mother Teresa—the list is virtually unending. With Edwin and Lillian Harvey as my parents, it is not surprising that I grew up, as it were, on these saints. They were my heroes and heroines—my standards of devotion, my blueprints of sacrifice.

But it was not until I was in my early teens that I heard about George Bowen of Bombay. While browsing in a secondhand bookstore in Belfast, Northern Ireland, my father struck up a conversation with the owner who mentioned the author, George Bowen. "If you ever come across one of his books," he told my dad, "grab it. It's a prize." Some years later, my father remembered this advice when he visited a skid row mission in Chicago. After preaching to the men, he was browsing in their library and stumbled across *Love Revealed* by Bowen—devotional meditations on the upper room chapters of St. John's Gospel. Borrowing it from the mission, he took his treasure back home to England, read it to his family and fellow mission workers, digested it from cover to cover, reprinted it, and mailed several copies to the mission in Chicago.

This, then, is how George Bowen entered my life and our publishing. But it was not until after my dad's death that my mother obtained the unabridged biography of George Bowen. I remember my husband reading it to her day by day as she sat in her recliner, by then well into her nineties and diagnosed with dementia. It was probably the last book we read to her, bar the Bible, of course.

As the years have passed and an increasing number of our readers have been blessed by *Love Revealed*, it has been our intention to make Bowen's remarkable life-story accessible to them. At first, we attempted to abridge it but that attempt never materialized. And yet although this biography is very lengthy and written in Victorian English, it is a gripping and inspiring portrayal of the "White Saint" as Bowen came to be called. His intellect was mind-boggling in its scope and depth as anyone reading his books soon discovers, and his sacrificial life-style was virtually unparalleled in the history of missions. Christ and Christ alone was his passion, his consuming love, and his inseparable Friend.

While proofing the manuscript several times during the past months, I have become increasingly aware that George Bowen was entering the inner sanctums of my heart. In fact, I found it almost impossible to describe my emotions as I closed the book for the fourth time several days ago. What was there about this man, I ask myself, that has moved me so deeply? His rare combination of genius and spirituality? His faithfulness to his missionary call whatever the cost? His humility and sacrifice? All this, admittedly, has greatly influenced me, but it is something more that makes me, even now, want to fall down and worship my Redeemer. It is, in fact, nothing more or less than George Bowen's obsession, and I use that word deliberately, with Jesus Christ! This humble and eccentric missionary has made me fall in love afresh with my Lord and Savior. And that is recommendation enough, is it not?

Trudy Harvey Tait
trudytait@gmail.com
October, 2021

Writings of George Bowen available from Harvey Christian Publishers:
Love Revealed — www.harveycp.com
Daily Meditations — email harveycpbooks@gmail.com for a digital file.
The Amens of Christ — email as above for a digital file.

www.ingramcontent.com/pod-product-compliance
Lightning Source LLC
Chambersburg PA
CBHW032012230426
43671CB00005B/62